VIETNAM
FRONT PAGES

VIETNAM FRONT PAGES

Edited by Hal Drake

BONANZA BOOKS
New York

This 1987 edition is published by Bonanza Books, distributed by Crown Publishers, Inc.,
225 Park Avenue South, New York, New York 10003, by arrangement with Hugh Lauter
Levin Associates, Inc. and *Pacific Stars and Stripes*.

Printed and Bound in the United States of America

Library of Congress Cataloging-in-Publication Data

Vietnam front pages.

   Reprint. Originally published: New York : Hugh Lauter
Levin Associates, 1986.
   1. Vietnamese Conflict, 1961–1975.   I. Drake, Hal.
DS557.7.V5624   1987   959.704′2   87-20843
ISBN 0-517-65354-0
h g f e d c b a

FOREWORD

This is a first-shot to last-hurrah history of the Indochina War, told in the headlines of the American newspaper closest to the scene—*Pacific Stars and Stripes.*

This was the Thirty Years War of the 20th century, and during much of the gunfire and gavel-pounding, *"Stripes"* was uniquely involved. It certainly had the most involved and interested readership—the advisers, riflemen, fighter pilots, and helicopter door gunners fighting the war. That blue-bordered newspaper, flown daily from Tokyo and distributed free, told not only of daily life in the armed forces but of happenings back home, which seemed like another planet when compared with violent and unreal Vietnam.

On the front page of the first edition, October 3, 1945, a headline told of an impending clash between French troops and Viet Minh rebels, the roots of a war a just-born American generation would sadly come to know.

When the last assault engulfed Dien Bien Phu and banished the French, a headline as dark as a mourning band spanned page one. As a country was divided by a protocol in Geneva, there were again a few exact and telling words over a comprehensive news story.

How many American newspapers reported the first three Americans killed in Vietnam, slain by a terrorist bomb in 1959? In *Pacific Stars and Stripes,* it was a dark headline and a top story. It had to be.

As American involvement on the side of Saigon expanded, so did the follow-the-troops coverage of *Pacific Stars and Stripes.* There were correspondents at the edge or in the thick of every major action. One of them, Specialist 4.C. Paul Savanuck, was killed.

The headlines marched along—inscriptions on the scroll of history. Yet assembling a retrospective account of the "Longest War" through headlines was, in a word, difficult, for there was never any war like it. World War II, while terrible and costly, was a war of unified purpose and defined goals: the seizure of Rome, Berlin, and Tokyo, the destruction of unanimously despised enemies.

When Lyndon B. Johnson dispatched the first of many thousands into Vietnam, he said their purpose was "to prevent the success of aggression," that is, to fight a contained war in which an enemy would be discouraged rather than defeated. That made it a war fought out of fire bases and helicopter pads, often over the same ground that had been bloodied and boottracked before. This was a war of constant grief and drama but no significant movement and finality. History—or at least headlines—frequently seemed to repeat themselves.

In World War II, so easily told in the headlines of the London-to-Paris *Stars and Stripes,* there was no event to compete with what was happening in Tunis or on Guadalcanal. Not so in the six-edition newspaper of later days. Editors in Tokyo were internationalists, and war dispatches often had to be judged beside what Charles DeGaulle or Neil Armstrong were doing. A moonwalk could easily wedge the Mekong Delta out of print. How many Air Force and Navy jets were snared in anti-aircraft fire around the Thanh Hoa Bridge? Its destruction was certainly major news—but on that day, it had to bow beneath the balcony headline that told of the reversion of Okinawa from American to Japanese control. On other days, the war sat in the back row as negotiators in Paris argued over the shape of a conference table or as massive antiwar marches assembled at the Washington Monument.

Yet there was probably no newspaper in the world other than *Pacific Stars and Stripes* that had a better grasp of the war as it approached, as it raged, and as it waned and died. We were the closest and the most sensitively involved. It was our story.

Hal Drake
Senior Staff Writer
Pacific Stars and Stripes

STARS AND *Pacific* STRIPES

PUBLISHED DAILY IN TOKYO   FOR U.S. FORCES   IN JAPAN AND KOREA

VOLUME 1, NUMBER 1   DISTRIBUTION: FREE   WEDNESDAY, OCTOBER 3, 1945

ANNAMESE GIRD FOR BATTLE IN INDO-CHINA

Casualties Mount as Rebellion Continues; Java Is New Hot Spot

SAIGON (ANS-AP)—As rebellious Indo-China natives appeared Tuesday to be gathering on the outskirts of Saigon for a concerted attack on 1,000 French reinforcements who were to land Wednesday, late totalling of casualties for last week's sporadic fighting rose to 319 dead and 234 wounded, of whom at least 100 were French civilians.

Th Annamese are reported to have a force of 20,000 men, of whom three-fourths are said to be armed. Meanwhile, an unestimated number of armed natives are said to be massing in the southern sector.

The Associated Press reported that the British Control Commission of the Saigon Control had ordered active participation of Japanese troops in an effort to quell the Annamese.

Chinese Ask Questions

In Chungking it was reported that the Chinese foreign office had instructed the embassy in Washington to ask the Siamese minister to the United States for an explanation of the recent clashes in Bangkok between the Chinese and Siamese.

The Chinese asked what steps were being taken to prevent a recurrnce and what compensation was being arranged for the victims. The influential newspaper, Takungpao, Demanded that Siam be completely disarmed and put under Allied control. It urged punishment for all Siamese war criminals, pro-Japanese and fascist perpetrators of
(Continued on Page 4)

'MAGIC CARPET' TO TAKE VETS HOME

2,000,000 Pacific Troops Due Boat Ride

(By Combined Press Service)

A Naval "magic carpet" that will take home 2,000,000 Pacific servicemen within the next 12 months began operating Tuesday when the aircraft carrier, Ticonderoga, left Honolulu carrying 2,500 service personnel.

Code name for the operation is "magic carpet," the Navy announced. Barring unforseen changes in the Japanese occupation plan, it will be using 40 escort carriers and 200 attack transports by the end of the year.

Some 400,000 men from the Pacific are to reach Stateside ports within the next three months, the army revealed. Tentative plans will send 75,000 home in October; 141,000 in November, and 180,000 in December.

Planes were due for an increasing role. A Tokyo announcements said U.S. troops in China within about 10 days will start flying to Shanghai to board ships. Two hundred fifty planes will shuttle men to the No. 1 Chinese ports from Chungking, Liuchow, Chengtau and Chinking.

The over-all demobilization picture was clarified in statistics released
(Continued on Page 4)

London Train Wreck —Kills 28; Injures 94

LONDON (ANS)—Twenty-eight persons were killed and 94 injured when the Scottish Express locomotive and six front coaches of the London-bound flyer plunged over an embankment 20 miles from London Monday night as it neared the end of a 45-mile journey from Perth Scotland.

The train ground itself into a heap of steel 30 feet high after hitting an open switch.

Home-Bound Yanks Set Speed Record in B-29s

Sacramento, Calif. (ANS)—Completing a 2,400 mile hop from Hawaii 25 minutes ahead of schedule, 14 B-29s of the global 20th Air Force landed at Mather field this morning They brought home the first of a large group of Superfortress airmen set for demobilization.

The Weather

Japan north of Tokyo—Cloudy with drizzles Wednesday, cloudy with rain Thursday; little change in temperatures.

Japan south of Tokyo—Cloudy with showers Wednesday, cloudy and colder Thursday.

Korea—Rain Wednesday, cloudy and colder Thursday.

Truman Looks In

WASHINGTON—President Truman paid an unprecedented visit to the opening session of the Supreme Court and saw his first nominee to a high bench, Harold H. Burton of Ohio, sworn in as an associate justice. Court attaches said the visit was the first made by a president in the 125-year history of the high tribunal.

FRESH FOODSTUFFS ARRIVING SOON

Thirty Days' Supply Due in at Yokohama

YOKOHAMA—Hungry GIs in Japan soon will polish their biscuspids on fresh pork chops and potatoes. An 8th Army source said that a refrigerator ship, hauling fresh foodstuffs and steaming north from Okinawa, was due in Yokohama shortly.

The ship is jam-packed with meat, stuffs. It is carrying a 30 days' stuffs. It is carrying a 30 days' shpply of fresh food for all units drawing rations from the St Army, which occupies the Tokyo area and Northern Honshu. There is everything aboard except fresh eggs, which will be shipped up at a later case.

The refrigerator ship will anchor off Yokohama and barges will bring the foodstuff ashore. When the refrigerator ship's supplies run low, other boats carrying food from the States and from Manila will replenish its larder. This will make it unnecessary to erect extensive reefer facilities at the Quartermaster depots.

To further appease the GI palate, Army agencies are looking for facilities for making icecream. PX supplies are expected to arrive in the near future. And Army officials predict that life in Japan soon will be even more cushy than it was in Manila.

Current plans call for the Army to feed its men without drawing upon Japanese produced foodstuffs, since the civilian food shortage here would become even more critical.

Diet staples now are canned B-rations. But an Army official states that chow in Japan soon will be equivalent to GI meals in the States.

Six Corregidor Vets Given Purple Hearts To Go With Freedom

TOKYO (INS)—General MacArthur has announced the award of the Purple Heart for wounds received three and a half years ago on Corregidor to the following recently liberated war prisoners:

Pvts. Estil J. Cohorn, Covington, Ky.; Leland Crumett, Vale, Ore; George W. Middleton, Wichita, Kan; Willie Templin, Coleman, Tex.; Joeseph Viterna, Lackawanna, N.Y.; and Franklin L. Wiggs, Augusta, Ark.

'Democracy' Heard In Chinese Confabs

CHUNGKING, (AP)—A program designed to erase the difference between the Chinese communists and Kuomintang has emerged from current conferences, it was announced Tuesday. Final decision hinges on whether the communists yield their demand for virtual autonomy. Danger of failure still is prevalent but prospects are brighter.

The program includes formation of a political council of all parties; peaceful reconstruction; recognition of the equal status of different political parties; punishment of traitors; disbanding of puppets; democratization of politics; nationalization of armies; release of political prisoners and abolition of laws at variance with freedoms enjoyed by other democratic countries.

Korean Occupation Ousting Japanese

SEOUL (AP)—Latest reports in Korea indicate that American occupation of this peninsula is progressing smoothly.

Following early criticism that American forces were relying too heavily on Japanese officials in establishing a temporary control for the liberated country, indications now are that the policy of weeding out all Japanese is being strictly adhered to, with a steady increase in number of Koreans in the government.

Japanese Air Force Demobolized by GHQ

TOKYO (UP)—General MacArthur's headquarters announced yesterday the complete demobilization of the Imperial Japanese general air force.

All Japanese matters pertaining to the air are now handled by the U.S. Army aeronautical headquarters.

308th At Seoul

FIFTH AIR FORCE, Korea—Headquarters of the 308th Bomb Wing of the Fifth Air Force, air arm occupying Korea, has been established at Keijo University in Seoul, capital city of Korea.

Halsey Ready to Bow Out

Honolulu (AP)—Admiral Halsey has announced that he has asked to be retired. I am an old man, he said. "Let the young fellows take over."

ANOTHER FIRST FOR THE FIRST

YOU ARE NOW ENTERING TOKYO
Courtesy of 1st CAVALRY DIVISION
The First Team
FIRST IN MANILA   FIRST IN TOKYO

The First Cavalry Division rang up another record and is telling the world about it. First in Manila, the First Cav has been selected as honor guards of Tokyo.

Pacific Stars & Stripes Photo

World Government For Atomic Power Control Recommended By Roberts

(By Combined Press Services)

WASHINGTON—With the U.S. and the world awaiting a message this week from President Truman baring his recommendations for control of the atomic bomb, former Supreme Court Justice Owen D. Roberts and 38 other prominent Americans recommended establishment of a world government to control the atomic bombs.

"Let us be done with Big Threes, Big Fours and Big Fives," said the group in a direct appeal to the President. "Let us have the Big One."

A world government, the recommendation stated, would prevent battles over atomic power.

Meanwhile, the President has conferred with Prime Minister Mackenzie King of Canada. It was understood the two leaders discussed problems of atomic power, since Canada is one of the countries now sharing the secret.

The President characterized the conversation as "interesting and important" and said they were satisfactory.

House Says "Keep Secret"

The House appropriations subcommittee, meanwhile, recommended to President Truman Tuesday that the secret of atomic energy be kept by the United States pending a study of its development by a commission of scientists.

One scientist, Larry Crosby head of the Crosby Research Foundation, said that a defense technique had been devised against the atomic bomb, so simple that bombs can be detonated without knowing their exact location. No details were announced, but Crosby said the
(Continued on Page 4)

Allies To Relinquish Large Portion of Italy

WASHINGTON (AP)—All of Italy with the exception of small areas on the Yugoslav border will be turned back to Italian control late this fall, the Allied commission announced today.

At the same time, the political section commission abolished the political advice being given Italians by the British and American embassies. The commission's report disclosed that Italian naval, air and land forces gave the Allied forces heavy support as co-belligerents with the Army in combat against the Germans as early as March, 1944.

Red Light Off

TOKYO—Military Police have placed more than a hundred houses of prostitution off-limits to soldiers and sailors by order of Brig. Gen Hugh Hoffman, Provost Marshal of Tokyo. The action by the MPs was taken on Monday and Tuesday after a medical survey showed that most of the women had at least one venereal disease. In one area, almost 100% of the women were contaminated.

In another order by the Provost Marshal of Tokyo, most Military Police, with the exception of those guarding prisoners, money and occupied buildings, were prohibited from carrying sidearms.

DEGAULLISTS WIN IN LOCAL VOTING

National Victory Seen At Oct. 21 Elections

PARIS (ANS)—Nearly complete results of the run-off balloting for local French government offices apparently assured victory for the DeGaulle policies in the national elections October 21.

Returns covering nearly 2,400 of the 3,028 councillors general to administer French departments give the DeGaulle Socialists and affiliate groups 844 seats. Leon Blum's Radical Socialists followed with 693 the Rightist parties won 530 seats Communists, 321.

Passenger Sky Giant Reaches Calcutta In Globe Hopping Trip

CALCUTTA, (ANS)—Five minutes ahead of schedule the globe encircling Globester, giant C-54, arrived in Calcutta yesterday and then hopped off for Dullang, China.

Nineteen passengers picked up in Cairo increased the passenger list to 28, all air corps crewmen bound for China and India. The C-54, which left Washington Friday afternoon and is expected back late tomorrow, picked up two hours lost in rain and fog over the Azores in the Atlantic crossing, and passed into the "hot" phase of its flight.

The trip from Tripoli to Cairo measuring 1,097 miles was made in five hours and 13 minutes.

World News Coverage Now On Daily GI Menu

This is the first issue of Pacific Stars and Stripes, the daily newspaper for U.S. occupational forces in Japan and Korea.

In addition to its coverage of events and activities among members of the armed services in the occupational zones of Japan and Korea, Pacific Stars and Stripes will furnish a complete relay of news from the United states and other parts of the world. Facilities being used, are those of Army News Service, Associated Press, United Press and International News Service.

The newspaper is published in Tokyo by the Information and Educa-

---

Christmas at Home Possible for 60s

By Cpl. PETER GRODSKY
Pacific Sta and Stripes Staff Writer

YOKOHAMA—Enlisted men with as low as 60 points have a fair chance of being home for Christmas, Col. L. B. Shaw, the Eighth Army's G-1 executive officer, predicted yesterday, emphasizing that only a shortage of shipping facilities will prevent completion of that goal.

"There's not an empty bunk on any sort of vessel or plane bound for the States which is not being used to return men for discharge," Colonel Shaw declared.

The Eighth Army expects to have shipping available to send back 34,000 officers and enlisted men during October, and 38,000 during November.

Thousands of enlisted men became eligible for discharge on October 1, when the War Department lowered the score to 70 points. Additional thousands will become eligible November 1, when points drop to 60.

However, having points in the 60s and 70s does not mean that on October 2 or November 2 all men within those groups will board Stateside-bound vessels. Men will be called from their units as soon as shipping is available, with the highest-point men getting first call.

Once a man is called out of his outfit, he knows that shipping is available for him and that he won't be in the replacement depot for more than an average of 48 hours.

He will be "processed" at the depot, meaning that his personal records—pay, allotment, clothing, service record, etc.—are brought up to date.

"Processing" will not delay a man's departure, said Colonel Shaw. He told of an instance where a Navy ship radioed it would have room for 112 men, but could stop for just a few hours. The men were hastily summoned to the depot, processed and on their way home the same day.

"Though the replacements depot in Yokohama has just been set up and can handle about 50 men a day, by October 15 it will be able to accommodate 10,000 men. As the need grows, the depot will be expanded.

There have been instances—and there are probably cases now—the colonel asserted, where high point men are in Japan, while lower point men are on their way home. He explained that these men who should have been on their way earlier are now being given priority on discharge.

Those men haven't left yet due to the fact that they or their records were probably in transit when the lower point men were sent back to the States. "It's strictly a transitional problem and is being rectified," Colonel Shaw declared.

Army headquarters is keeping a close tab on units to assure their prompt compliance with demobilization, officials reported.

No C. O. can hold any enlisted man eligible for discharge—with very few enumerated exceptions—until a replacement comes. The C. O. has no alternative but to let the man go home. He may keep an officer for 30 days beyond the time he becomes eligible.

Any man who feels he is being retained unjustly may report it to his local Inspector General's office and expect to receive satisfaction. The War Department regulations on the duties of the C. O. with regard to discharge are very clear, experts agree.

UNION CLAIMS AUTO MAKERS STIR STRIKES

R. J. Thomas Charges Companies Not Ready For Reconversion

CHICAGO (ANS)—R. J Thomas, international president of the United Automobile Workers, CIO. Tuesday charged automobile manufacturers with being "on strike," and declared they were seeking to provoke labor troubles now because they were not ready for reconversion.

"The automotive industry, and not the union, is on strike," Thomas said at a meeting of 150 UAW regional representatives. "Cutting of wages and provoking of grievances are aimed at getting unions to strike at this time."

Thomas said the Ford Company's dismissal of workers because of a strike at Kelsey Hayes Company, manufacturers of Ford wheels, was unjustified.

"Kelsey Hayes Company was not the only source of supply for wheels of the Ford Motor Company, "He said. "No firm as large as Ford has only one source of supply. If we settled the Kelsey Hayes strike tonight, Ford still would not open tomorrow."

Nation's Strike Idle Cut As Workers Return

CHICAGO (ANS)—Strike idleness throughout the country fell to approximately 352,000 Tuesday, in the first major reduction in more than a week.

The total was whittled down as 38 000 white collar workers of Westinghouse Electric Company, who struck September 18 in demand for bonus or incentive pay plans, voted to return to work. This strike had spread to 14 plants in Pennsylvania, Ohio, New Jersey, Massachusetts, Maryland and New York.

Leo F. Bollens, president of the Federation of Westinghouse Salaried Unions, said members had voted to go back pending outcome of negotiations.

8 MILLION IDLE BY NEXT SPRING

Jobs, Demobilization Fail to Keep Pace

WASHINGTON (ANS)—Reconversion Director John W. Snyder said Tuesday there might be 8,000,000 unemployed by next spring with "high unemployment" persisting through 1946.

He made this prediction in a 46-page report to the President and Congress.

Snyder's forecast was based on the contention that jobgiving will be unable to keep pace with a prospective million-a-month demobilization.

He said 6,700,000 men would be released from the Army and 3,-000,000 from the Navy by next July.

But he was "firmly optimistic" about the future, provided the nation works as a team. He asserted:

1. Prompt peaceful settlement, of labor-management differences is a reconversion must.

2. Congress should act promptly on those four points in the presidents program calling for full employment, transitional tax adjustments, broadening and raising unemployment compensation and raising minimum wages.

The tax steps recommended were repeal of the three per cent normal tax on individuals, repeal of excess profits tax effective Jan. 1, 1946, and setting a definite date for reducing excises.

3. The executive branch "must and will be as vigorous in its policies and programs to solve peacetime problems as it was in solving wartime problems."

"Cooperation and teamwork among management and labor; business and farmer; federal, state, and local governments, is indispensable if there is to be rapid expansion of peacetime production, jobs for all those willing and able to work and stable markets for business.

Pointing to prospects of about 8,000,000 unemployed by spring. Snyder said the country must face the fact that substantial unemployment lies ahead.

"That in itself will not stamp reconversion successful or unsuccessful. It takes time for industry to turn around to stop work on munitions and retool for work on peacetime products," he said.

Argentine Government Frees Revolutionists

BUENOS AIRES (ANS)—Tension appeared to be relaxng in Argentina Tuesday as hundreds of hundreds of persons detained last week under a state of siege proclaimed by the military government.

Gen. Arturo Rawson, who led the abortive revolt by the Cordoba garrison which helped precipitate the state of siege, had been flown to Buenos Aires for questioning by Vice President Juan Peron.

ODs by Oct. 10, Army Promises

TOKYO—The U.S. Army soon will take action against the brrs and chills of the Japanese climate. A GHQ spokesman retorted Tuesday that men will be issued winter OD uniforms by Oct. 10.

Men stationed in northern Japan and in the mountainous areas where the cold becomes most bitter will be first on the priority list for the issue. In the meantime, to make sure that there are branches and shirts and jackets for everyone, the Army is maintaining a continuous shipment of cold weather garments to Japan.

Tokyo to Have Face Washed

TOKYO (INS)—Nettled by caustic comments of Allied correspondents, the Japanese have proclaimed a cleanup drive during which every effort will be made to brighten the face of Tokyo. Face-lifting began Monday, will extend through the 10th.

Shakeup in Japanese Cabinet Rumored In Capitol This Week

TOKYO (INS)—Tokyo buzzed today with undercurrent rumors of an impending major shakeup in the Japanese cabinet under premiership of Prince Naruhiko Higashikuni.

While Nippon public newspapers called for retirement of Japanese war leaders from political, economic and other fields to "make way for men of ability to assume leadership in the new Japan," observers said that the feeling in high places among the Japanese was "not to stick our necks" for fear that they would land on MacArthur's war criminal list when their names are checked against wartime records.

However, they also pointed out that if potential leaders all crawl into shells for fear of allied actions occupation forces will face a tough time administering the country without Japanese heads to lead their own country along democratic lines as outlined by the allies.

The main upheaval expected by many high ranking Japanese will come after Oct. 15 when complete disargament of all Japanese services is scheduled to be completed.

One of the most serious hurdles facing Higashikuni appears to be the intense popular dislike of some men mentioned for cabinet posts despite their asserted non-affiliation with wartime machines.

Urges Carefulness

NEWTON, Mass. (UP)—To remind motorists that the end of gasoline rationing does not mean the start of a new era of speed, the Newton Police Department has posted signs reading "Motorists be careful. Remember—death is permanent."

Raw Rubber Hits U.S. From Pacific

SAN FRANCISCO (ANS)—The Goodyear Tire and Rubber company Tuesday announced receipt of the nation's first shipment of rubber from the Pacific since Pearl Harbor.

Forty-two tons of crude produced under the noses of Japanese in the Philippines were landed in San Francisco by the steamer Thomas Nelson.

---

tion Detachment, GHQ AFPAC. Editorial offices are on the third floor of the Nippon Times plant, circulation and business offices on the fourth floor of Radio Tokyo.

Free distribution by truck, train and plane will be made to members of the U.S. armed services in all parts of Japan and Korea. Units are invited to appoint news correspondents for Pacific Stars and Stripes. Individual contributions of news items, feature stories and pictures will be welcomed. All correspondence should be signed, and should be addressed to Pacific Stars and Stripes, Tokyo, APO 500.

The newspaper is published in Tokyo by the Information and Educa-

STARS PACIFIC AND STRIPES

UNOFFICIAL PUBLICATION OF UNITED STATES FORCES, FAR EAST

Vol. 10, No. 127 | Entered as third-class matter in the Tokyo Central Postoffice | **TOKYO-YOKOHAMA EDITION** | AP, UP, INS | **Saturday, May 8, 1954**

Dien Bien Phu Falls Before Human Avalanche

Troop Use Unsuitable Now: Dulles

WASHINGTON, May 8 (AP)—U.S. Secretary of State John Foster Dulles said today the free world can block Communist conquest of Southeast Asia but that "this may involve serious commitments by us all."

Dulles said flatly that in Indochina present conditions "do not provide a suitable basis" for the U.S. "to participate with its armed forces."

At the same time, he solemnly warned in a nation-wide television-radio address that the U.S. "would be gravely concerned" if any Indochina armistice agreed to by France "would provide a road to a Communist takeover and further aggression."

Need for Action

"If this occurs," he said, "or if hostilities continue, then the need will be even more urgent to create the condition for united action in defense of the area."

His speech, changed at the last minute to take the Dien Bien Phu defeat into account, paid high tribute to the anti-Communist defenders for the "staggering losses" inflicted on the enemy.

Dulles frankly acknowledged that "difficulties have been encountered" in his drive to line up the U.S. and nine other free government in a "united front" to stem the Red advance in Southeast Asia.

Progress Made

But, he added:

"Under all the circumstances, I believe that good progress is being made. I feel (Continued on Page 16, Col. 2)

Anti-Communist Plan Developed

WASHINGTON, May 8 (AP)—Secretary of State John Foster Dulles has developed a two-stage program for organizing an anti-Communist coalition in Southeast Asia and hopes it will produce a provisional arrangement in a matter of weeks.

Dulles is due to hold a series of diplomatic discussions here shortly for the first stage of negotiations. Officials said today it seems certain to begin with a multi-nation military staff conference.

The military conference, and possibly additional diplomatic talks, would be designed to produce a provisional security arrangement to stand until later second-stage talks eventually resulted in a formal security treaty.

A minimum of five and a maximum of 10 or a dozen countries could be represented in the first conferences. Authorities said the British have agreed to cooperate, and they termed this a forward step.

JAMES MCGOVERN | WALLACE A. BUFORD
AP Radiophoto

Two Yanks Dead in Indochina Supply Run as C-119 Explodes

SAIGON, Indochina, May 8 (AP)—A C-119 Flying Boxcar blew up yesterday on a supply drop mission to Dien Bien Phu, killing its two American civilian pilots and the French crew chief.

One of the Americans, James B. McGovern 32, Elizabeth, N.J., was one of the most famous and intrepid airline pilots in the Far East. The Chinese Communists had held him captive for five months in 1950 after he crash-landed in Red territory.

The other American killed was Wallace Abbott Buford,

28, Ogden, Utah, who narrowly escaped death 10 days ago when his plane was riddled by AA-fire, which wounded the American pilot with him.

An official French Command announcement said the cause of the explosion was not known but unofficial observers thought possibly it had been hit by Vietminh antiaircraft.

McGovern and Buford were Civil Air Transport pilots working under contract to the French Air Force. The American civilians are paid $35 a flying hour above their regular airline pay.

Senate Blocks T-H Revision

WASHINGTON, May 8 (AP)—The Senate today voted to send President Eisenhower's Taft-Hartley revision bill back to the Labor Committee, in effect killing it for this year.

The roll call vote was 50-42. Southern and Northern Demo-

crats, disregarding an appeal by Senate Republican leaders, voted together, but for entirely different reasons, to recommit the bill.

Northern Democrats said the measure failed to go to the heart of "inequities" in the law.

Silent Radio Signals End; French Refuse to Surrender

See Geneva Story Page 16, Indochina Story Page 2

By Jean Barre

HANOI, Indochina, May 8 (UP)—Dien Bien Phu fell today in an Asian debacle that sealed with blood one of the most glorious and disastrous chapters in the annals of French arms.

A Communist Vietminh human avalanche at last claimed the blood of an heroic French Union garrison that had beat them off for eight weeks.

One after another, pitifully outnumbered French Union outposts toppled in a night and morning of terrible hand-to-hand fighting.

The last words heard from the dying fortress were from the bastion's gallant commander, Brig. Gen. Christian de Castries:

"After 20 hours of fighting without respite, including hand-to-hand fighting, the enemy has infiltrated the whole center. We lack ammunition.

"Our resistance is going to be overwhelmed. The Vietminh are now within a few meters from the radio transmitter where I am speaking. I have

Ike Praises 'Symbolic' Resistance

WASHINGTON, May 8 (UP)—President Eisenhower said today the "heroism" of the "gallant garrison at Dien Bien Phu . . . will forever stand as a symbol of the free world's determination to resist" Communist aggression.

He sent similar messages to French President Rene Coty and Bao Dai, Vietnam chief of state. He said the "heroic resistance" of the French and native Indochinese forces "to the evil forces of Communist aggression has given inspiration to all who support the cause of human freedom."

Joins Congressmen

Eisenhower joined such congressional spokesmen as House Speaker Joseph W. Martin Jr. (R-Mass.) and Senate Republican Leader William F. Knowland (R-Cal.) in hoping that the fall of the free fortress in Indochina will cause a stiffening of resistance against the Reds.

In his message to Bao Dai, Mr. Eisenhower pledged that "we of the free world are determined to remain faithful to the causes for which they have so nobly fought."

Knowland said the fall of Dien Bien Phu is a "setback" to the free world.

HANOI, Indochina, May 8 (INS)—The only clue to what happened to Dien Bien Phu's commander Brig. Gen. Christian de Castries and his troops was one of his last orders to turn its guns on himself and the rebels if they succeeded in reaching his post.

given orders to carry out maximum destruction.

"We will not surrender."

Static, Silence

Then came sputtering static and finally silence, as the end was written in blood. At 10 p.m. yesterday (JST) the French Supreme Commander General Henri E. Navarre messaged Paris that the central bastion had been seized.

Defenders of "France's Almo" fell powerless at last to halt the human sea attacks.

Headquarters here said de Castries' headquarters at the nerve center of the shrunken defense perimeter was penetrated at mid-morning yesterday. Shortly after, all organized resistance ceased in the central bastion.

But at 6 p.m. (JST) a few groups of the defeated garrison still were reported holding out, divided and hopeless but determined not to surrender. (Continued on Page 16 Col. 1)

Hull Gets Close Look At Malaya's Red Battle

KUALA LUMPUR, Malaya, May 8 (AP)—The U. N. Far East Commander, General John E. Hull, yesterday had a close look at Malaya's battle against Communist guerillas.

Hull, who arrived from Singapore in an RAF plane, spent the morning talking with police and military chiefs. Hull was shown confidential maps, and operations being carried out against the rebels were explained to him in detail at Army headquarters.

BANQUET BANTER — Former president Harry S. Truman takes time out to enjoy himself at last night's $100-a-plate Jefferson-Jackson dinner. Following his speech, Truman leans over to talk to a friend (center), laughs at something a speaker said and (right) turns to listen. (See Lewis Box Page 16) (AP Radiophoto)

STARS Pacific AND STRIPES

UNOFFICIAL PUBLICATION OF UNITED STATES FORCES, FAR EAST

Vol. 10, No. 151 — Entered as third-class matter in the Tokyo Central Postoffice — **TOKYO-YOKOHAMA EDITION** — UP, INS, AP — **Tuesday, June 1, 1954**

Ike Hits Red Hunts 'For Glory'

NEW YORK, June 1 (INS) — President Dwight D. Eisenhower struck out today at "demagogues thirsty for personal power and public notice" and warned that those who set Americans to quarreling over communism are playing into the hands of the Reds.

The chief executive, as is his custom, did not mention any names in an address at a Columbia University bi-centennial dinner at the Waldorf-Astoria Hotel.

Opposition to Reds

Mr. Eisenhower declared in his soberly worded speech there is no other purpose in which Americans are so completely united in their opposition to communism, but added:

"Is there any other subject that seems at this moment to be the cause of so much division among us as does the matter of defending our freedoms from Communist subversion?"

Such a division, the President said, is just what the Communists want as they pursue their policy of "divide and conquer" against the free world.

Familiar Theme

The President's theme was a familiar one—that we must not destroy our basic freedoms while struggling against the menace of Communist subversion—but his language was sterner than usual.

He said Americans must apply "more knowledge and intellect and less prejudice and emotion" to the problems of Red subversion, and not permit anyone to inspire quarrels which lead "good citizens bitterly to oppose other good citizens."

One paragraph of the half-hour prepared speech was (Continued on Page 16 Col. 1)

Turkish Minister Arrives in U.S.

NEW YORK, June 1 (AP)—Prime Minister Adnan Menderes of Turkey arrived today for a week's visit and discussion with President Eisenhower and other top officials in Washington.

The prime minister arrived at Idlewild Airport aboard U.S. Admiral William Fechteler's private plane. He was to remain in New York overnight and leave by plane tomorrow for the capital where he is expected to stay until June 4.

Queen Flies to London To Resume Royal Duties

LONDON, June 1 (AP)—Queen Elizabeth II flew back to London last night from her country home at Balmoral, Scotland, where she had been resting since returning from her world tour.

She left immediately for Buckingham Palace to resume her round of state duties and visits.

U.S. May Train Vietnamese

VUKOVICH (R) WINS AS BRYAN STARTS LAST LAP

AP Radiophoto

Vukovich Wins 2nd Straight '500'

By Jerry Liska

INDIANAPOLIS, Ind. June 1 (AP)—Bill Vukovich, poker-faced throttle demon from Fresno, Cal., zoomed to a record-breaking triumph today in becoming the third man in history to win the grueling Indianapolis Speedway 500-mile race two successive years.

As the huge, sprawling crowd of an estimated 175,000 held its breath while black clouds threatened to deluge the finish, Vukovich became a Speedway immortal with Wilbur Shaw

and Mauri Rose.

Shaw won two straight 500's

INDIANAPOLIS, Ind., June 1 (UP)—Final standings in the 500-mile race:

1) B. Vukovich	6) F. Agabashian
2) J. Bryan	7) D. Freeland
3) J. McGrath	8) Russo-Hoyt
4) T. Ruttman	9) L. Crockett
5) M. Nazaruk	10) C. Niday

Average speed of winner 130.840 MPH, new record. (Old record 128.922 MPH, Ruttman, 1952).

in 1939 and 1940 and Rose in 1947 and 1948. Vukovich,

buried in the seventh row at the start of the four-hour grind, moved into first place at the 230-mile mark and then battled it out with Jimmy Bryan, Phoenix, Ariz., and favored Jack McGrath, South Pasadena, Cal., the rest of the way.

Vukovich gunned his grey Fuel Injection Special 500 miles at 130.840 miles an hour to finish exactly one lap ahead of runner-up Bryan. Third went to McGrath, who was the pole car driver after a (Continued on Page 15, Col. 4)

President Leads Rites

By The Associated Press

For the first time in four years Americans honored their war dead in Memorial Day observances today (U.S. time) with their servicemen everywhere at peace.

At Arlington National Cemetery President Eisenhower laid a wreath at the Tomb of the Unknown Soldier, then stood with hat over heart while taps echoed over the surrounding hills.

From the tomb the President and Mrs. Eisenhower walked to the amphitheater nearby for memorial ceremonies in which Secretary of the Navy Charles S. Thomas was the principal speaker.

Plea For Unity

Thomas' main theme was a plea for national unity, without which he said, "We can lose victory before the final battle is fought." As a nation united, the secretary said, America "need fear no foreign foe or agnostic creed."

The nation's lawmakers took the day off, too. Both the Senate and House were in recess, and the Army-McCarthy televised dispute will not resume until tomorrow.

The weather, in most states, was fair.

OUSTED — Chief Minister Abdul Kasem Faziul Huq and all his East Pakistan cabinet ministers were dismissed as Pakistan's governor general declared a state of emergency in the bitter differences between the divided sections of the country. (See story Page 2) (AP Radiophoto)

18 Die in Plane Crash On Brazil Mountain

RIO DE JANEIRO, Brazil, June 1 (AP)—Eighteen persons, all Brazilians, were killed today when a National Airline plane crashed and burned 60 miles from Belo Horizonte, Brazil, Meridional News Agency reported.

The wreckage was found on a mountain near Itabira.

Anderson, Taylor Exit

TOKYO, June 1 (INS) — Eighth Army Commander General Maxwell D. Taylor arrived in Tokyo this morning from Korea, en route home on leave to the U.S. Taylor will leave Japan this afternoon.

Compiled From Wire Services

SEOUL, June 1—Two of the highest ranking American military leaders in Korea left here today for the U.S.—one permanently and the other temporarily.

Lt. Gen. Samuel E. Anderson relinquished his command of the Fifth Air Force to Lt. Gen. Roger M. Ramey in ceremonies prior to his departure for Tokyo, where he will spend several days.

General Maxwell D. Taylor, Eighth Army commander, left for Japan, from where he will go to Washington for about three weeks to confer with Pentagon officials and spend (Continued on Page 6 Col. 1)

TOKYO, June 1 (S&S)—U.S. Ambassador to Japan John M. Allison left here for the U.S. at 9 a.m. today by plane. His return to Washington precedes a world tour by Japan's Prime Minister Shigeru Yoshida. Allison is accompanied by Japanese Financial Minister Gengo Suzuki.

'Thousands' Said Needed As Cadre

GENEVA, Switzerland, June 1 — Authoritative sources said today thousands of U.S. Army officers and noncommissioned officers will assume training of native troops in Viet Nam under a new plan reported nearing completion.

The sources said the French government finally consented to permit the U.S. to take over the task of whipping together the Vietnamese Army and save it from the internal collapse with which it is said to be threatened, INS reported.

In Hanoi, Indochina, Maj. Gen. John W. O'Daniel was reported to have reached an agreement with the Vietnamese high command to train five Indochinese combat divisions before the end of the year.

2 Training Centers

According to the report, Viet Nam has agreed to place two training centers at the disposal of "Iron Mike" O'Daniel and to allow American officers train the new troops, UP said.

So far, the French government has been bitterly opposed to all proposals that the U.S. help train native troops in Viet Nam, Laos and Cambodia.

The INS report from Geneva said the training program will have two main objectives:

1) To develop the Vietnamese Army into an effective force to guard those parts of Viet Nam which may remain free under the partition arrangement now taking form at the Geneva Conference.

2) To build the native Army into an efficient fighting force to carry on the war with the Communist-led Vietminh rebels in case no armistice agreement is concluded at Geneva.

4 Red Divisions Nearing Hanoi

Compiled From Wire Services

HANOI, Indochina, June 1—French authorities announced today the bulk of four Communist divisions marching on the Red River Delta from Dien Bien Phu had advanced to within 42 miles of Hanoi.

French intelligence reports said heavy artillery and supply convoys of Molotov trucks arrived at the big Red town of Phutho, just northwest of the Delta's western point.

Below Phutho, the Red River Valley broadens out into the

HANOI, Indochina, June 1 (UP)—The Vietminh have refused to allow the release of 27 members of the French medical unit captured at Dien Bien Phu, it was reported last night.

vital triangle of rich rice fields and plantations.

The whole of the four divisions was expected to be concentrated in the Phutho region within 10 days.

(Continued on Page 16, Col. 5)

FRENCH, REDS SIGN INDOCHINA TRUCE

STAR**S** AND **S**TRIPES
PACIFIC
UNOFFICIAL PUBLICATION OF UNITED STATES FORCES, FAR EAST
TOKYO-YOKOHAMA EDITION

Vol. 10, No. 201 — Entered as third-class matter in the Tokyo Central Postoffice — Wednesday, July 21, 1954

'U.S. Won't Defend Line'

Wilson Says Only Signatories Committed

Compiled From Wire Services

WASHINGTON, July 21 —U.S. Defense Secretary Charles E. Wilson said today that the defense of the prospective truce line in Indochina would be up to "the people who reached the agreement in Geneva."

Wilson said at a news conference he is sure the U.S. will not commit itself to the defense of the line "in any unilateral action." He added, however, that this country might undertake a commitment as part of "an alliance."

Wilson, meeting reporters for the first time here since May 4, said a truce in Indochina may be the "best answer at the moment." He added he "would think" that any truce line agreed upon would be one that would be militarily defensible. He said "It isn't anything I enthuse too much about."

Common Ideas

In replying to questions about the current visit here of Field Marshal Lord Alexander, British defense minister, Wilson said that the U.S. and Britain are "getting closer to accepting each other's ideas about guided missiles and new weapons."

He said the two nations already have arrangements to cooperate in the field of research and development and that talks now underway should make those arrangements more workable.

New AFFE Staff Chief Due

ZAMA, Japan, July 21 (AFFE)—Maj. Gen. Albert Pierson, newly designated AFFE chief of staff, is scheduled to arrive in Yokohama today aboard the transport General Buckner.

He will be met at the port by Maj. Gen. C. H. Chorpening, AFFE G-4.

Pierson comes to his AFFE assignment from duty as director of the Joint Airborne Troop Board and senior Army member of the Joint Air Transportation Board and Joint Tactical Air Support Board at Ft. Bragg, N.C.

In World War II, Pierson was assistant division commander of the 11th Abn. Div. which fought in the South (Continued on Page 7, Col. 1)

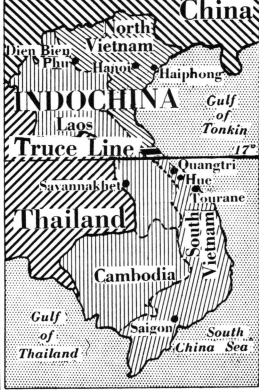

S&S Map

U.S. Heat Kills 22 More

By United Press

A lethal heat wave kept its burning grip on the nation's mid-section today, claiming at least 22 lives and threatening farmers with disaster.

The heat wave, the worst in years, has caused at least 249 deaths since it spread across the nation last week. It killed 224 during last week's scorchers and 22 more died following a brief weekend respite.

The U.S. Weather Bureau said the temperature would shoot again into the 100s today in Oklahoma, Kansas, Nebraska, and southeast South Dakota.

High temperatures yesterday included 109 at Kansas City, Mo., 105 at St. Louis, Mo., 108 at Ponca City, Okla., and 107 at Presidio, Tex., and Omaha, Neb.

Academy to Open at Lowry Field

WASHINGTON, July 21 (AP) — The Air Force announced today that Lowry Field at Denver, Colo., will be the temporary location of the new Air Academy.

Air Force Secretary Harold Talbott made the announcement in a statement which said the grounds and buildings in the northeast portion of the existing air base will be rehabilitated to provide facilities for the new school.

The first class of the Air Academy, numbering 300 cadets, will begin their training at the temporary location next July. The school will remain at Lowry until the permanent buildings on the site near Colorado Springs are ready for occupancy in July 1957.

Communists to Get Northern Vietnam, 12 Million People

See Indochina stories Pages 2, 16

GENEVA, Switzerland, July 21 (UP) — France and her Communist enemies signed a historic ceasefire agreement today all but ringing down the curtain on eight years of Indochina bloodshed.

The ceasefire agreements were signed at 10 a.m. (JST) by General Henri Delteil on behalf of General Paul Ely, French commander-in-chief in Indochina, and Ta Quang Buu, Vietminh vice minister for defense as representative of Communist Generalissimo Vo Nguyen Giap.

The signing took place in a conference room of the Palace of Nations. The top delegates to the Geneva Conference were not present at the ceremony.

In signing, France accepted the partitioning of war-torn Vietnam, the surrender of its rich, teeming north and the turning over of more than 12 million of its inhabitants to Red rule.

The French termed it "peace with honor," but it set the seal on one of the West's worst defeats yet at the hands of Communist aggression.

The agreements provided only for ceasefires in Vietnam and Laos.

The Cambodian document was held up by last minute hitches over details.

The delegation chiefs of France, Soviet Russia, Vietminh and Cambodia huddled in emergency session at the British delegation villa until

Union Guns Fall Silent

HANOI, Indochina, July 21 (UP)—French batteries throughout the Red River Delta subsided into silence today and planes idled on airfields as Hanoi waited in suffocating heat for the long war to end.

From one corner of the delta defense pocket at Sontay east to the marshes and rice fields around Haiphong on the China Sea hardly a shot was fired.

A flight over the delta showed no French Union activity.

Vietnamese Exhausted

The Vietnamese, exhausted spiritually and physically by 7½ years of bitter war, displayed neither terror nor joy at the prospect of Communist masters after a ceasefire is concluded at Geneva. Fatalistically, they waited and hoped there would be no purge, at least not a big one.

In the few administrative offices of Hanoi still staffed by the French, civil servants already talked of their next assignments — Madagascar? Dakar?

They felt Indochina already belonged to the past.

Some Fighting

Monday, there was still some fighting.

French columns pushing north and west from here to relieve Red pressure on Hanoi made little contact with the enemy. South of Kesat, east of here on the Hanoi-Haiphong road, a Vietnamese battalion was attacked by Communist troops and suffered "appreciable" losses.

Present estimates say 50,000 to 100,000 citizens of Hanoi's 400,000 would leave after a cease fire. Thirty thousand have already left in a "spontaneous" exodus.

GENEVA, Switzerland, July 21 (UP)—Switchboard operators at the Palace of Nations said that one of the night's most persistent callers was a Zurich map manufacturer who kept telephoning long distance for an exact description of the Indochina ceasefire line "so I can put my new maps on sale in the morning."

after 9:30 a.m. JST and reached agreement in principle.

Finally, it was agreed to defer the Cambodian signing until later today.

This will be followed by a final plenary session of the conference at 11:00 p.m. JST.

The historic agreements signed today provided for:

1) Ceasefires in Vietnam and (Continued on Page 16, Col. 3)

Danish Passenger Ship Afire, Radios SOS

GREAT YARMOUTH, Britain, July 21 (AP)—The 3,968-ton Danish passenger ship Kronprinsesse Ingrid radioed last night that she is afire 40 miles east of this English port.

Several trawlers immediately altered course to speed to her position and one, the Cockerel, reported she was almost alongside and that the fire appeared to be getting under control.

A later message from the Cockerel said the Danish ship appeared to be in no immediate danger.

2 AMERICANS KILLED BY SAIGON TERRORIST

PACIFIC STARS STRIPES

AN AUTHORIZED PUBLICATION OF THE ARMED FORCES FAR EAST

FIVE-STAR FINAL 5¢ DAILY 15¢ SATURDAY

Vol. 15, No. 190   Friday, July 10, 1959

SAIGON, Viet Nam (AP)—A communist terrorist slipped into an American military billet 20 miles north of here Wednesday night during a movie and exploded a bomb, killing two U.S. military advisers, himself and three South Vietnamese.

Another American officer was wounded, and two others escaped injury.

The wounded American was flown to Clark AB at Manila for treatment. A communique from the Republic of Viet Nam government and the U.S. embassy said his condition was not serious.

Following the bomb attack, other members of the terrorist band opened fire from outside the billet with small arms and automatic weapons, the communique said.

Vietnamese Army guards returned the fire, "forcing the terrorists to flee to the nearby river from which direction they had come," the communique reported.

The South Vietnamese killed were two Army guards and an attendant who tried to prevent the terrorist from exploding his bomb. Another terrorist who had slipped into the building with the bomber escaped before the charge went off.

In Washington, the Army identified the American casualties as:

Killed—Maj. Dale R. Buis, whose wife, Virginia Lee, lives in Imperial Beach, Cal., and M/Sgt. Chester M. Ovnand, whose wife, Mildred, lives in Copperas Cove, Tex.

Wounded—Capt. Howard B. Boston, whose wife, Ardys Allene, lives in Blairsburg, Iowa.

THE ATTACK OCCURRED at the South Viet Nam Army's training center at Bienhoa. The five U.S. officers were members of the U.S. Military Assistance Advisory Gp. stationed in South Viet Nam to train President Ngo Dinh Diem's anti-communist forces in the use of American weapons.

President Diem, now touring Central Viet Nam, was informed (Continued on Back Page, Col. 4)

Herter Says Pact Possible

WASHINGTON (AP)—Secretary of State Christian A. Herter said Thursday there may be some possibility of allied agreement with Russia over the future of Berlin.

At his first news conference since taking office, he stressed, however, he is not optimistic about the outcome of Big Four foreign ministers' talks due to resume in Geneva Monday.

He reiterated that President Eisenhower would shun any summit meeting with Russia's Premier Nikita Khrushchev unless progress was made at a lower level on easing East-West problems.

BUT UNDER questioning, he declined to say just how much progress would be adequate for Mr. Eisenhower to attend a summit parley.

In a 40-minute meeting with newsmen, he said he believed the Soviets are genuinely trying to reach agreement with the U.S., Britain and France on German issues.

Thus far, he said, the Soviets have avoided using the Geneva talks mainly as a propaganda forum. The talks ended three (Continued on Back Page, Col. 1)

Korean Floods, Slides Kill 42

SEOUL (S&S)—At least 42 persons have been killed by floods and landslides in the Republic of Korea this week, National Police reported.

The Central Weather Bureau predicted more heavy rains.

Four thousand persons have been left homeless and thousands of acres of valuable crop land has been flooded.

RESCUE WORKERS are keeping a close watch along the Han River, which threatens to overflow near Seoul.

Kozlov Inspects Steel Plant

RUSSIA'S FROL KOZLOV dons a small white cap before putting on a "hard hat" to enter the United States Steel plant at Gary, Ind., Wednesday. The Soviet first deputy will spend three days in and around Chicago. He arrived in the Windy City from a visit to Michigan. (UPI Radiophoto)

Russian's Sales Tour Runs Out of Steam

CHICAGO (AP) — The current Soviet traveling salesman's tour in the United States appeared Thursday to be running out of steam and enthusiasm.

As he did elsewhere, first Deputy Premier Frol R. Kozlov got along famously in Chicago with some of the capitalists.

But the proletariat — the people the communists invariably call the "toiling masses" — continued to greet his presence with a tremendous surge of apathy.

A COUNT of noses Wednesday night at the Drake Hotel disclosed that there were exactly 49 persons waiting to see the departure for dinner of the man who some say may succeed Premier Nikita S. Khrushchev.

Some were there only because a police line impeded their progress.

THIS IS beginning to make the Russian propagandists on the tour appear a bit desperate. Time is running out and the toiling proletariat has yet to make its appearance to cheer—or even look at—the representative of a movement sworn to "liberate" them.

If a Soviet documentary film (Continued on Back Page, Col. 5)

Rickover To Bare Data

WASHINGTON (AP)—Vice Adm. Hyman G. Rickover, Navy atomic expert, reluctantly agreed under congressional fire Thursday to name retired officers who visited him and tried to influence his programs.

But in a stubborn debate with Rep. F. Edward Hebert (D-La.), chairman of an investigating subcommittee, Adm. Rickover won an agreement that he would submit the names in confidence and they would not be made public unless an inquiry into any impropriety became necessary.

The admiral, who told the subcommittee he never would win any popularity contests with (Continued on Back Page, Col. 1)

U.S. Citizens Protected After Raid

SAIGON (UPI)—Special precautions were taken Thursday to protect American residents in the Republic of Viet Nam after two Americans were killed and a third injured in a communist terrorist raid Wednesday night.

American officials reported that the Vietnamese had increased police guards on buildings housing American government offices and at residences of official Americans.

Close watch also was ordered on all American vehicles at all times and security check on all packages brought into the American Embassy was tightened.

Embassy officials said the Wednesday night attack was considered an isolated incident.

Japan Weather

Saturday Forecast
By Tokyo Weather Central

	H	L
Tokyo—Partly cloudy with showers	87	74
Chitose—Cloudy with showers	76	66
Misawa—Cloudy with rain	79	67
Niigata—Cloudy with showers	83	72
Nagoya—Partly cloudy	88	74
Miho—Cloudy with showers	86	74
Fukuoka—Mostly sunny	90	77

Viet Cong Ambush, Kill American

SAIGON (AP)—Clyde
F. Summers, a 45-year-old
American civilian con-
struction engineer, died
here early Sunday of
wounds he suffered in a
communist Viet Cong am-
bush Saturday.

Summers was identified as
construction superintendent
of the E. V. Lane Corp. of Palo
Alto, Cal., which has a contract with the U.S. aid mission
here to build a new runway at
Saigon's Tan Son Nhut Airport.

Summers' Vietnamese wife, the
former Phan Thi Bong, is expecting a child. The couple, who
had met in Karachi, were living
in Saigon.

U.S. sources said Summers and
his Vietnamese driver were mo-

*Vietnam Needs Equipment,
Not U.S. Troops: Harriman—P. 3*

toring along a road in a light
truck with Vietnamese license
plates about 12 miles northeast of
Saigon at the time of the ambush.
The driver, who was wounded but
survived, said an unarmed man
in military uniform had stepped
onto the road to stop the truck,
but Summers ordered his driver
to keep going. Four or five armed
men reportedly jumped from con-
(Continued on Back Page, Col. 3)

JFK, CLAY AGREE ON BERLIN POLICY

PACIFIC

STAR AND STRIPES

AN AUTHORIZED PUBLICATION OF THE
U.S. ARMED FORCES IN THE FAR EAST

SATURDAY 10c DAILY

Vol. 18, No. 7 FIVE-STAR EDITION Monday, January 8, 1962

BERLIN AT A GLANCE

President Kennedy and General Lucius D. Clay (ret.) confer, report agreement on
how to handle Berlin
crisis.

American MPs delay Soviet
Army bus 75 minutes at
Berlin wall. P. 16

Berlin still dangerous, Secretary of State Rusk says.
P. 16

WASHINGTON (AP)
—President Kennedy con-
ferred Sunday with Gen-
eral Lucius D. Clay on
conditions in Berlin and
Germany and reported
they agreed fully on how
to handle possible crises
effectively.

The Chief Executive talked
for an hour with his personal
representative to Berlin.

While Clay and Secretary of
State Dean Rusk insisted Saturday that there are no policy differences between them over Berlin, there was little doubt that
Clay still believed the U.S. commander in the city should have
greater authority to handle unexpected emergencies.

Again Sunday, after the Clay-
Kennedy session, the word was
(Continued on Back Page, Col. 4)

West Irian Ultimatum

Leave or We'll Invade,
Sukarno Tells Dutch

BONTHAIN, South Celebes (AP)—President Sukarno, in
an ultimatum to the Netherlands Sunday, said that unless
the Dutch hand over administration of West Irian (West
New Guinea), Indonesia will invade.

Sukarno said at a rally:

"The Dutch used bloodshed to drive the Spaniards from
Holland. We will use bloodshed to drive them off our soil.

**"We don't mind if our action will arouse the world.
We don't care about international opinion."**

Sukarno's threatening speech, his toughest to date, came
in the wake of military moves in East Indonesia. Troop reinforcements are arriving in South Celebes, according to the

(Continued on Back Page, Col. 1)

AMBASSADOR JONES

U.S. Envoy
Under Fire

THE HAGUE, Netherlands (AP)
—The Netherlands government is
expected to ask the United States
government for an explanation of
U.S. Ambassador Howard P. Jones'
behavior in shouting "merdeka"
(freedom) when accompanying Indonesian President Sukarno to the
South Celebes, informed government sources said here Sunday.

The Foreign Ministry refrained
from comment on Sukarno's
weekend tour of South Celebes.
High officials privately however
expressed indignation at "the
(Continued on Back Page, Col. 3)

Reserves Not Ready, Arends Says

WASHINGTON (UPI)—A top Republican said Monday the United
States does not have a "fully effective reserve force in a complete
state of readiness" and called for
an exhaustive study of the military
reserve program.

Rep. Leslie Arends of Illinois,
Republican whip, said he was
determined to have an inquiry
made by the House Armed Services Committee of which he is
ranking minority member. He
said it was apparent there are
weaknesses in the reserve program.

He blamed military administrative procedures. But he also said
Congress may be at fault and said
"it is imperative remedial action
be taken at the earliest possible
date."

Weather
FORECAST

Tuesday:
Cloudy with rain; High 44, Low 33
Wednesday:
Partly cloudy to fair; High 50, Low
35
Sunday's Temperatures:
High 49, Low 28
(USAF Weather Central, Fuchu AS)

Shirp, Shirp!
Robins on a Bender

SAN FRANCISCO (AP) — The
ravenous robins have struck
again.

Thousands of hungry robins
descended en masse on pyra-
cantha bushes at various homes
last weekend and stripped them
of their winter-ripened red berries—with startling results in
nearby Los Altos.

It seems that the berries
around Los Altos, in addition to
their attraction as food, have a
formidable alcoholic content.

An estimated 12,000 robins
swarmed in Los Altos yards
Saturday, gorged on the berries
and many of them got drunk,
falling off rooftops, staggering
drunkenly in the streets and
otherwise conducting themselves
in a most disorderly manner.

An Oakland visitation didn't
seem to be attended by the
alcoholic side effects reported
in Los Altos. But many birds
were so filled with berries they
could barely fly.

Nehru Loses Temper at Rally

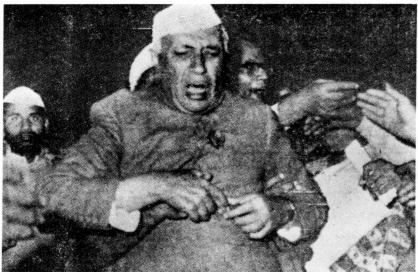

ANGRY—Prime Minister Jawaharlal
Nehru of India struggles against the restraining arms of security guards as he attempts to enter a yelling crowd in Patna,
India, in a personal attempt to restore
order at a Congress Party session. When
he was stopped, he angrily shook his fists
at the guards and then stalked out of the
meeting. Nehru was unable to give his
scheduled speech. (AP Radiophoto)

Battle Off New Guinea

DUTCH NAVY SINKS INDONESIA INVADERS

Space Balloon Fizzles

CAPE CANAVERAL, Fla. (AP)—A huge space balloon broke apart hundreds of miles above the Atlantic Ocean Monday as it was inflating to the size of a 13-story building.

The breakup of the big ball—dubbed "Big Shot"—showered several pieces of aluminum coated plastic into the ocean about 600 miles southeast of the Cape. The pieces, illuminated brilliantly by the rays of the rising sun, provided a spectacular show for observers.

The 500-pound bundle of plastic sheeting was folded neatly in a canister in the nose of a Thor rocket which blasted off at 6:06 a.m. in an experiment aimed at testing techniques for launching an advanced Echo communications satellite.

Newsmen at the Cape saw the beginning of the inflation process as the sun reflected off the gleaming surface. The balloon at first appeared as a solitary star drifting slowly upward in the dark, clear sky.

Suddenly, several other bright objects appeared to surround it. The fragments climbed upward for approximately the intended maximum altitude of 950 miles before starting a quick descent, leaving wavy vapor trails in their wake.

"Big Shot" was to have inflated (Continued on Back Page, Col. 3)

PACIFIC STARS STRIPES

AN AUTHORIZED PUBLICATION OF THE ARMED FORCES FAR EAST

FIVE-STAR EDITION   10¢ DAILY   15¢ SATURDAY

Vol. 18, No. 15   Tuesday, January 16, 1962

U.S. Must Take Risks In S.E. Asia: Kennedy

WASHINGTON (AP)—President Kennedy said Monday the United States is taking obvious chances in attempting to build independent nations in Southeast Asia and all over the world. But he contended the risks are a necessary alternative to conflict.

Kennedy also told a news conference that U.S. Ambassador Llewellyn Thompson would continue his talks with Soviet Foreign Minister Andrei Gromyko on a possible basis for solution of the Berlin crisis.

He said the potential success or failure of the discussion may be discerned after "a reasonable period" but refused to make any forecast. Neither would he set any limit on what he considers (Continued on Back Page, Col. 1)

President Kennedy at his news conference Monday in Washington.
(AP Radiophoto)

HOLLANDIA, Dutch New Guinea (UPI) — Dutch naval units sank one and possibly two small Indonesian ships Monday in the first outbreak of violence in the dispute over Dutch New Guinea.

Two Indonesian motor torpedo boats, which the Dutch said appeared to be heading an invasion fleet, were spotted on radar screens by Dutch fighter bombers off southern Dutch New Guinea.

"We flashed a warning to those ships that they were in Dutch territorial waters," said naval spokesman Capt. R. M. Elbers. "When they refused to alter course we had no choice but to open fire.

"We sank one motor torpedo boat and left the other ablaze in a sinking position. A third vessel of the same type fled."

The government information office said a number of survivors were picked up from the Indonesian boats but a spokesman refused to give the exact figure.

The office said, however, that the number indicated the boats carried "twice the normal crew," leading authorities to believe they had frustrated an invasion attempt.

They said that following the battle what appeared to be a fleet of small Indonesian craft was forced to flee.

Elbers said the Indonesian ships appeared to be the spearhead of a potential invasion fleet. President

JAKARTA, Indonesia (UPI)— Indonesia accused the Dutch Tuesday of an unprovoked attack on Indonesian vessels in the open sea and President Sukarno called an emergency session of his special operational command for the "liberation" of Dutch-held West New Guinea.

Sukarno of Indonesia, who claims Dutch New Guinea (West Irian) as Indonesian territory, has repeatedly threatened to invade if the territory is not handed over to Indonesia.

"Our radar had spotted a large number of ships," Elbers said. "The total number of men carried by them could presum— (Continued on Back Page, Col. 1)

Indonesians, Dutch Clash In Jungles

BIAK, Dutch New Guinea (AP)—A Dutch official said Monday that small bands of Indonesians have attempted to infiltrate West New Guinea and that some had been killed in skirmishes with Dutch patrols.

Hendrick Assink, district officer of Biak, estimated the total number at "perhaps a couple of hundred." He said their purpose is "to try to make the Papuans restless." The groups "have been a total loss as they have not been supported with supplies," he added.

"They cannot live in the jungle so they come to villages and the people tell us right away."

This island off the northern coast of the main island is the largest center of Dutch military installations.

Weather

Helpless 14 Hours In Her Wrecked Car

DALLAS (AP) — Mrs. Rosie Johnson Pool, 24, lay badly injured in the wreckage of her car 14 hours before help came. She was in fair condition, Monday.

During her ordeal she was soaked by rain in temperatures in the 40s.

"I thought I was going to die," police quoted Mrs. Pool.

Her car plunged off a 40-foot embankment at 9:15 p.m. Saturday and under a bridge and was difficult to see from the street.

Not until 11 a.m. Sunday did

help come after an unidentified truck driver crossing the bridge happened to spot the crumpled car below and spotted Mrs. Pool waving her hand.

She suffered compound fractures of both legs in addition to chest, head and internal injuries.

Though not pinned in the wrecked car, Mrs. Pool was unable to crawl for help because of her injuries. She told investigating officers she screamed until her voice gave out, but could not attract attention.

PICK U.S. VIET CHIEF

PACIFIC
STAR AND STRIPES

AN AUTHORIZED PUBLICATION OF THE
U.S. ARMED FORCES IN THE FAR EAST

SATURDAY 10c DAILY

Vol. 18, No. 39 **FIVE-STAR EDITION** Friday, February 9, 1962

Full General To Head Units

Kennedy Holiday on Ice

Mrs. Robert F. Kennedy and a Japanese girl hold hands as they glide across the ice Friday during their visit to Tokyo's Korakuen Ice Palace. Atty. Gen. Kennedy is on the left.

(S&S Photo by Masaichi Sumiyoshi)

WASHINGTON (AP) — The United States Thursday created a new command to be headed by a four-star general for conducting the greatly expanded U.S. effort to help the Republic of Vietnam beat off the communist threat.

A Defense Department spokesman said the move stresses that "we intend to win" the struggle.

The new command will direct activities of U.S. aircraft and other units which have been flowing into South Vietnam over the past few months.

The Pentagon spokesman stressed that "we are not in combat." He said U.S. efforts are limited to supporting and strengthening the pro-Western South Vietnamese with additional equipment, training and advice.

President Lt. Kennedy Thursday nominated Lt. Gen. Paul D. Harkins, now deputy Army commander in the Pacific, to head the new command. The nomination, carrying a promotion to full general, was sent to the Senate.

The new command will provide a framework for directing any U.S. combat forces if a decision ultimately is made to use them in South Vietnam.

The action follows new expressions of determination by Kennedy to preserve the anti-communist Republic of Vietnam government.

It also follows two recent visits

(Continued on Back Page, Col. 1)

USA Photo
GENERAL PAUL HARKINS

British OK Christmas Isle A-Test

A-Shot in Nevada: P. 5

WASHINGTON (AP)—The United States and Britain agreed Thursday on U.S. use of Britain's Christmas Island in the mid-Pacific and British use of the U.S. Nevada underground site for atomic testing. At the same time, both governments called for an East-West foreign ministers' meeting on disarmament.

The proposal for a foreign ministers' meeting was made by President Kennedy and Prime Minister Harold Macmillan to Soviet Premier Nikita S. Khrushchev.

A joint U.S.-British statement said that foreign ministers of the three powers should meet in advance of the proposed 18-nation disarmament conference which will open at Geneva March 14, and

(Continued on Back Page, Col. 2)

JFK Acts On Censors

WASHINGTON (UPI) — President Kennedy invoked his power of executive privilege Thursday to prevent a Senate subcommittee from obtaining the names of individuals who censored specific Defense and State Department speeches. His claim was upheld by the chairman of the Senate group.

The President's instructions that the historic doctrine be used in the investigation of alleged military "muzzling" were read

(Continued on Back Page, Col. 2)

Paris Police Battle Red Mobs; 8 Killed

PARIS (AP)—Police and mobs of communist demonstrators fought fierce battles in the historic Place de la Bastille for three hours Thursday night while plastic bombs set off by right-wing terrorists blew up in scattered sections of Paris. At least eight persons were killed in the riots and 140 policemen injured.

The deeply worried French government appealed urgently for a restoration of order.

One bomb shattered the Paris office of the Soviet news agency Tass.

More than 200 persons, including policemen, were reported injured

in the club-swinging, stone-hurling clashes that erupted after communists, joined by other leftists and students, rallied in defiance of a government ban against public demonstrations.

The French government ap-

(Continued on Back Page, Col. 4)

Tour Defended, P. 3

TOKYO (S&S)—Atty. Gen. Robert F. Kennedy's program to meet the Japanese people was on the ice Friday—but the reception he and his wife received from a cheering crowd of Japanese couldn't have been warmer.

Kennedy and his wife, Ethel, apparently not tired by their two-day whirlwind tour of Japan's Kansai area, started out shortly after dawn Friday by joining skaters at Tokyo's big Korakuen Ice Palace.

The couple was greeted by the cheers of more than 400 youthful employes of the Ricoh Camera Co. as they put on ice skates and gracefully skated onto the rink.

The attorney general left the skating rink 20 minutes later and

(Continued on Back Page, Col. 1)

Weather

FORECAST

Saturday: Cloudy; High 47, Low 35
Sunday: Partly Cloudy; High 49, Low 30
Thursday's Temperatures: High 56, Low 38

(USAF Weather Central, Fuchu AS)

Weather 'Moon' Up

WASHINGTON (UPI) — The United States hurled into orbit Thursday a new weather satellite which will help forecast conditions for Marine Lt. Col. John Glenn's scheduled space flight Wednesday.

The Tiros IV's television cameras and infra-red sensors, alternating as the satellite passes through daylight and darkness, were sending back cloud-cover pictures "of excellent quality" from 450 to 525 miles up.

This most advanced of Ameri-

ca's experimental weather-watching devices was launched from Cape Canaveral, Fla., by a three-stage Thor-Delta rocket. It completed its first orbit in about 100 minutes.

The satellite's speed was ranging between 16,700 and 17,000 miles an hour. The weather satellite is expected to perform a variety of duties.

Dr. Morris Tepper of the National Aeronautics and Space Ad-

(Continued on Back Page, Col. 3)

No Combat Role in Vietnam: Harkins

Related Stories: P. 2
HONOLULU (AP) — Lt. Gen. Paul D. Harkins strongly emphasizes that the creation of his new command in the Republic of Vietnam does not prophesy the use of U.S. combat troops against the communists.

"There is no change in U.S. policy," he said.

The role of the U.S. military in South Vietnam will continue to be training and support of native troops against the communist Viet Cong guerrillas, he said.

Harkins underscored Pentagon statements that the U.S. troops in South Vietnam were "not combat," but advisory. The men do have orders to defend themselves if attacked, he said, but not to attack.

Harkins, deputy U.S. Army commander in the Pacific, was named

(Continued on Back Page, Col. 1)

BAR RED SQUEEZE ON AIR CORRIDOR

PACIFIC
STAR AND STRIPES

AN AUTHORIZED PUBLICATION OF THE
U.S. ARMED FORCES IN THE FAR EAST

SATURDAY 10c DAILY

Vol. 18, No. 40   **FIVE-STAR EDITION**   Saturday, February 10, 1962

WEST BERLIN (AP) —The three Western Allies balked what they called illegal attempts by the Soviets to reserve temporarily two of the air corridors to Berlin for Soviet military planes, an Allied spokesman disclosed Friday.

The spokesman said that the Soviets served notice that on Thursday and Friday mornings they would require the corridors for Russian military planes up to certain altitudes.

The Allies resisted this demand, saying that the Soviet planes would have to abide by four-power rules.

The Allies told the Soviets that "reserving of blocks of altitude" in the corridors is illegal and announced their planes would fly as usual.

All the normal commercial flights between Berlin and Frankfurt, Hanover and Hamburg were made as usual. The Allies also sent extra military transports through the corridors as a further demonstration of their rights.

There were no incidents and the pilots of Allied planes sighted no

(Continued on Back Page, Col. 5)

Police Wade Into Rioters

With a clubbed demonstrator on the pavement behind them, police charge a group of rioters in Paris. The riot grew out of a mass communist gathering called to protest the Secret Army Organization's terrorism. **(AP Radiophoto)**

Paris Workers Stage Strike In Protest of Police 'Brutality'

PARIS (AP) —A one-hour strike, protesting police methods in a riot in which eight persons were killed and hundreds injured, stalled much of Paris business and industry Friday.

Workers were called out by communist, socialist and Roman Catholic unions after Thursday night's bloody clashes in which demonstrators were killed and injured in protesting government failure to suppress terrorism by the right-wing Secret Army.

Communists accused police of "unbelievable savagery" in the three hours of street fighting.

Friday's strike was the first of a series of demonstrations that are expected.

City and suburban buses halted, and the Paris subway and suburban train service was affected.

There were these other developments:

1) In Algiers, Moslem and Eur-

(Continued on Back Page, Col. 2)

German Mine Toll Increases to 287

SAARBRUECKEN, West Germany (AP) — Three more coal miners died in hospitals, bringing the total death toll in the mine disaster here Wednesday to 287.

About ten miners are still missing.

Kennedys End Visit To Japan

Related Story: P. 6

TOKYO (S&S) — Energetic Atty. Gen. Robert F. Kennedy wound up his 6-day "rice roots" tour of Japan Saturday morning and flew to Hong Kong for a rest before going to Indonesia, the next stop on his worldwide tour.

Kennedy and his wife, Ethel, were to make a one-hour stopover in Taipei en route to Hong Kong. They will arrive in Jakarta Monday.

At Tokyo International Airport Saturday morning, the attorney general told a cheering gathering that he and his wife "will always have lasting memories of our warm welcome to Japan."

The crowd of about 100 applauded when Kennedy called Japan "one of the greatest countries in the world."

"The Japanese people are aware of the burdens, welcome burdens, of democratic living," he said. "I leave this country with a feeling of great optimism for its future."

Mrs. Kennedy made a brief farewell speech in Japanese after shaking hands with several Japanese school girls at the entrance to the airport.

There was no sign of leftist demonstrators who had occasionally created disturbances during the Kennedys 6-day tour.

The crowd packing the upper

(Continued on Back Page, Col. 4)

Weather

FORECAST

Sunday: Partly cloudy; High 52, Low 30.
Monday: Fair; High 51, Low 25.
Firday's Temperatures: High 59, Low 30.
(USAF Weather Central, Fuchu AS)

REFUSED—Col. Andrei I. Solovyev, Soviet commandant in East Berlin, attempted to enter the American sector Friday in defiance of a U.S. ban. He was turned back. Story, Page 24. **(AP Radiophoto)**

Seize $1.5 Million in Fake Bills

NEW YORK (UPI)—The Secret Service seized a near record $1.5 million plus in counterfeit $10 bills Thursday night, but still does not know the whereabouts of the plates being used to flood the eastern U.S. with bogus money.

Agents got no help from Joseph Anthony Maggio, arrested after a patiently planned raid on his Brooklyn apartment house. Albert E. Whitaker, special agent in charge of the Secret Service's New York office, said Maggio, 35, would not make a statement.

Maggio, identified as a utility company employe, was arraigned Friday before a U.S. commissioner on a charge of possessing counterfeit money. He was returned to jail when he could not post $100,000 bond.

It was one of the biggest hauls

(Continued on Back Page, Col. 1)

For Defense in Vietnam

U.S. TO RETURN FIRE IF FIRED ON: KENNEDY

PACIFIC
STARS AND STRIPES

AN AUTHORIZED PUBLICATION OF THE
U.S. ARMED FORCES IN THE FAR EAST

SATURDAY   10c DAILY

Vol. 18, No. 45 **FIVE-STAR EDITION**   Thursday, February 15, 1962

PRESIDENT KENNEDY

AP Radiophoto

WASHINGTON (AP) —President Kennedy said Wednesday that American soldiers in the Republic of South Vietnam have been ordered to fire back if fired on. But he said they are not combat soldiers in the usual sense.

Kennedy, speaking at a news conference, thus confirmed lower level reports that U.S. military men in the Red-pressed Southeast Asian country have been told to defend themselves.

The main purpose of the assignment of a reported 4,000 or more American armed services personnel to Vietnam is to help train and give technical assistance to Vietnamese who are fighting the communist attackers.

Kennedy acknowledged Wednesday that what he termed the war in Vietnam has grown over the past two years.

The President took issue, however, with Republican charges that he has failed to inform the American people about the extent of U.S. involvement in South Vietnam.

"I think we are being as frank as we can be" within security limits, he said.

He appealed to headquarters of
(Continued on Back Page, Col. 1)

French Troops Battle Moslem Mobs in Oran

ALGIERS (AP)—French troops fought thousands of screaming Moslems in the western Algeria city of Oran Wednesday while the government's secret police clashed with European terrorists in several areas in Algiers.

French headquarters for Algeria said one French officer was killed, one wounded and four French soldiers wounded in Oran by shotgun-firing and hatchet-wielding Moslems.

At least nine Moslems were reported killed and eight wounded when French infantry opened fire on Moslem crowds, spurred to battle by screaming, veiled women.

The clash was sparked by 44 bomb explosions in Moslem areas, blamed on the European terrorist Secret Army Organization. Authorities were unable to determine the number of victims as no police or rescue units entered the Moslem quarter.

As dusk fell on Oran, thousands of armor-backed French troops sealed off Moslem areas on the outskirts of the city. Army sources in Oran said sporadic gunfire continued late into the evening.

Unofficial sources in Oran said the blue-shelled missile over-
(Continued on Back Page, Col. 1)

R. Kennedy Parries Quiz in Indonesia

JAKARTA, Indonesia (UPI)—An Indonesian demonstrator threw a duck egg at Atty. Gen. Robert F. Kennedy Wednesday, and Indonesian students threw hard questions at him about American history.

The duck egg missed Kennedy, but he fielded the questions of the students with skill, answering them with some of the frankest talk ever heard from a high official discussing his own country.

The egg-throwing incident occurred as Kennedy was entering the auditorium of the University of Indonesia's law school.

The blue-shelled missile over-
(Continued on Back Page, Col. 5)

Water Breaks Dike, Sweeps Idaho Town

CHICAGO (UPI)—The northern Rocky Mountain area's worst floods in memory smashed through new dikes Wednesday, but the watery onslaught which left 6,000 persons homeless in six states appeared to be easing.

A wall of Portneuf River water 5½ feet high punched through the three-tiered sandbag dike protecting Pocatello, Ida., razing three houses and flooding a park with depths of five feet.

Almost immediately afterward, the Portneuf began falling at Pocatello, leaving 1,000 persons homeless and one residential district awash under six feet of water.

Two huge sheets of water closing in on Blackfoot, Ida., "simply disappeared" into the ground, according to a civil defense official.

Elsewhere in a flood belt which extended into Southern California:

1) Airborne dynamiters broke up two ice jams and saved Greybull, Wyo., from flooding after the town's 2,300 residents had fled.

2) The Big Horn River fell three feet at Worland and Tensleep, Wyo., but the little town of Manderson, Wyo., was still cov-
(Continued on Back Page, Col. 3)

New Orbit Attempt Readied

CAPE CANAVERAL, Fla. (AP) —The United States is going to try again Thursday to rocket John H. Glenn Jr. around the earth.

The National Aeronautics and Space Administration (NASA) announced late Wednesday it was going ahead with plans for the space shot sometime after 7:30 a.m. EST (9:30 p.m. JST).

Sources said the weather in the recovery areas may get worse after Thursday.

The weather source said the condition was somewhat improved late Wednesday afternoon in the one-orbit recovery area of the Atlantic, where rough seas caused Wednesday's postponement.

Indonesian soldiers seize the youth who threw a duck egg at Atty. Gen. Robert F. | Kennedy as he was entering an auditorium in Jakarta.   (UPI Radiophoto)

Weather
FORECAST
Friday: Fair; High 49, Low 22.
Saturday: Fair to partly cloudy; High 51, Low 24.
Wednesday's Temperatures: High 42, Low 22.
(USAF Weather Central, Fuchu AS)

U.S. Set for Any Threat: McNamara

CHICAGO (AP)—Defense Secretary Robert S. McNamara Saturday spelled out in bald terms a wide spectrum of military moves the United States would use to cope with communist war of different kinds in different places.

The possibilities he posed ranged from a "single massive attack" in nuclear retaliation to operations by a few men in the twilight zone of war against guerrilla snipers.

In between, he sketched such things as strikes at enemy bases and use of U.S. forces, with threat of further attacks, to halt war.

McNamara put his views into a major speech prepared for an American Bar Assn. dinner here.

McNamara said, "Nuclear and nonnuclear power complement each other, in our own military forces and within the NATO Alliance, just as together they complement the nonmilitary instruments of our policy.

"Either without the other is, overall, not fully effective.

(Continued on Back Page, Col. 4)

McNAMARA

74 DIE AS STORM BATTERS EUROPE

PACIFIC STAR AND STRIPES

AN AUTHORIZED PUBLICATION OF THE U.S. ARMED FORCES IN THE FAR EAST

SATURDAY 10c DAILY

Vol. 18, No. 48   FIVE-STAR EDITION   Sunday, February 18, 1962

LONDON (UPI) — A screaming winter storm, one of Europe's worst in living memory, cut an 800-mile swath of death and destruction through the northern part of the continent and east beyond the Iron Curtain Saturday.

Worst hit was West Germany's low-lying North Sea coast, where flood tides whipped up by furious winds left at least 56 persons dead, untold numbers injured and 40,000 homeless.

Throughout Europe, snowstorms, icy roads, floods, avalanches and sledge-hammer winds claimed at least 74 lives by an unofficial count. There were 11 deaths in Britain, three in Denmark, two in France, and one each in East Germany and Sweden.

Disaster operations headquarters in Hamburg, on Germany's Elbe River, said it was Germany's worst storm in 100 years.

Chancellor Konrad Adenauer kept up with rescue operations by telephone from Bonn as the West German Armed Forces poured 11,000 men into disaster areas.

Railroad and air traffic throughout much of northern Europe slowed to a crawl or was halted. Snow blanketed Sweden and Denmark, and two persons were killed in a snowslide on Devil's Peak in the French Alps near Grenoble.

The storm moved across the Iron Curtain into East Germany,

(Continued on Back Page, Col. 2)

Officials Doubt Viet War To Flare Into 2d 'Korea'

WASHINGTON (UPI) — High administration officials said Saturday that the war in the Republic of Vietnam is being fought under a "counter-guerrilla strategy" in which the U.S. combat troops should play no part.

In the wake of Republican National Committee charges that President Kennedy has been "less than candid" about the U.S. role in Vietnam, officials are attempting to

Villagers Organize Defense: P. 5

more fully explain both the nature of the Vietnam war and the extent of U.S. involvement in it.

Administration sources made these points:

1) There is little possibility of another "Korean War" in Vietnam. It is believed neither the north Vietnamese nor the communist Chinese are prepared to launch any mass attack with conventional armies.

2) The United States has done less to organize and direct South Vietnamese operations than many

(Continued on Back Page, Col. 5)

S&S Man in Patrol

By M/SGT. AL CHANG
S&S Staff Photographer

TRUNGLAP, Vietnam—A patrol in the guerrilla-ridden Republic of Vietnam is a tense experience. Especially when you encounter the enemy, and capture him, as we did in a recent patrol near the Ranger school here at Trunglap.

We caught only one Viet Cong prisoner. But, the excitement—and danger—was the

CHANG

same as if we had uncovered a large communist unit.

This one Viet Cong guerrilla was busy sending radio signals about our ranger patrol when our Rangers pounced on him.

He was a scrawny, high-cheek-boned individual, small, but dangerous.

And, he tried to escape when one of his guards left his guard position temporarily to seek his relief man.

But he didn't get far. As he ran for it, one of the tough, well-

(Continued on Back Page, Col. 1)

Pictures, Pages 12-13

Liz Taylor Reportedly Stricken

ROME (UPI)—An Italian Red Cross ambulance attendant said he took actress Elizabeth Taylor, who was unconscious, from her villa Saturday night to a Rome hospital, the Italian news agency ANSA reported.

Paolo Renzini told the agency he was called to the villa and found Miss Taylor unconscious in her bedroom. He said he drove her to a hospital.

No immediate confirmation was available from Miss Taylor's secretary.

Renzini was quoted as having said he thought Miss Taylor was in a rather grave condition.

A crowd of photographers gathered outside the hospital after an ambulance was sent from there to Miss Taylor's villa and returned with a patient.

ANSA said that "According to unconfirmed reports, Elizabeth Taylor may have suffered a hemorrhage of the throat although on the ambulance log was written the word 'paralysis'."

The hospital denied that Miss Taylor was registered there.

Weather

Monday: Fair to partly cloudy; High 48, Low 27.

Tuesday: Fair to partly cloudy; High 50, Low 25.

Saturday's Temperatures: High 48, Low 24.

(USAF Weather Central, Fuchu AS)

Congo Detains Girl In Colonel's Death

LEOPOLDVILLE, Congo (AP)—A Congolese court Saturday committed Elizabeth Thring to prison in connection with the murder of U.S. Army Lt. Col. Hulen Dorris Stogner, assistant military attache of the American Embassy in Leopoldville.

An official communique said Miss Thring is now held in the women's wing of Leopoldville's Makala Prison.

She has engaged a lawyer, the

statement said.

The communique gave no indication that a formal charge has been issued against the blonde 21-year-old American, who said she was alone with Stogner in his house at the time of the murder.

An embassy spokesman and Congolese officials refused to elaborate on the official statement prepared by the Congolese Security Branch.

(Continued on Back Page, Col. 2)

Smashed buildings and debris-littered streets in Hamburg, Germany, show the damage caused by one of Europe's worst storms of the century. (AP Radiophoto)

Space Flight Could Fail, Glenn Warns

WASHINGTON (UPI)

—Astronaut John H. Glenn warned Congress Tuesday that some future U.S. space flights will fail, possibly with loss of life. He urged the lawmakers not to lose faith in the space program.

"We don't envision every flight coming back as successfully as the three so far," Glenn told a jampacked hearing before the House Space Committee.

"There will be failures. There will be sacrifices.

"I hope we will all continue to have the same confidence in the program that we have now, de-

Other Space News, Pictures, Page 3

spite the fact there will be times when we are not riding such a crest of happiness and successes as we are right now."

Glenn, complimented by a committee member for his "down to earth" space talk to a joint meeting of Congress Monday, also told the space group America's multi-billion-dollar space exploration work would be more than worth what it costs whether or not Russia was in the space field.

In what appeared to be an indirect answer to the doubts of some lawmakers about President Kennedy's announced plan to put

(Continued on Back Page, Col. 5)

Reserves Rush to Algiers

PARIS (UPI) — President Charles de Gaulle's government ordered army troops and tanks to move in force into Algiers and Oran Tuesday to end anarchy and mass terrorism which threaten to block an Algerian peace.

The troops, drawn from units held in reserve outside both cities, sped into downtown areas and patrolled streets 10 abreast in some spots in an effort to curb attacks.

But scattered incidents of terrorism continued to take a toll of dead and wounded, even as De Gaulle and his Algerian Affairs Committee met in Paris to consider further measures to restore order.

In eight separate attacks in Algiers before noon, three Arabs were shot to death and four were wounded by European terrorists.

Five Europeans were wounded. In Oran, an Arab was shot dead near the city hall.

European terrorists raided a sporting goods store in Oran and seized 12 hunting rifles, 8 automatic

(Continued on Back Page Col. 1)

Ear Infection Delays Engler

TOKYO (S&S) — Maj. Gen. Jean E. Engler, commanding general, U.S. Army Japan, was to arrive here from Taiwan Wednesday afternoon, winding up a two-week tour of Army units in the Far East.

Doctors delayed Engler's departure from Taipei Wednesday af-

(Continued on Back Page Col. 1)

PALACE BOMBERS KILLED 3, HURT 20

PACIFIC
STAR AND STRIPES

AN AUTHORIZED PUBLICATION OF THE
U.S. ARMED FORCES IN THE FAR EAST

昭和三十四年一月二十二日週間発売特別郵便物認可第175号 (その)

SATURDAY   10c DAILY

(昭和4月22日第3種郵便物認可)

Vol. 18, No. 58   FIVE-STAR EDITION   Wednesday, February 28, 1962

Aftermath of Rebel Attack

Troops and tanks move into position at the gate of the burning Presidential Palace in Saigon after the building was bombed and strafed.   (AP Radiophoto)

SAIGON (UPI)

—Three persons were killed and about 20 wounded in Tuesday's air attack on the Republic of Vietnam Presidential Palace, the Vietnam press said Wednesday. The two pilots accused in the strafing-bombing raid were in custody.

The press quoted Vu Tien Huan, prefect of Saigon, as saying 10 of the casualties occurred among the "civil population."

Among the injured was Madame Ngo Dinh Nu, sister-in-law of President Ngo Dinh Diem. One of her maids was among the dead.

Huan said about 10 persons were wounded defending the palace. Diem himself was unhurt.

The two rebellious Republic of Vietnam pilots who executed the attack in American-made AD-6 fighter-bombers were in custody Tuesday. Vietnamese troops captured Sub-Lt. Pham Phu Quoc when his disabled plane crash-landed in the Khanh Hoi River

(Continued on Back Page Col. 1)

JFK Calls Bombing 'Vicious'

WASHINGTON (AP) — President Kennedy Tuesday described the bombing of Republic of Vietnam President Ngo Dinh Diem's palace as a "destructive and vicious act."

Kennedy made the statement in a brief cable to Diem expressing relief that the Vietnam leader had escaped unscathed the attack by two South Vietnamese planes.

Meanwhile, the United States was expected to give a strong reaffirmation of support for Diem in

(Continued on Back Page, Col. 2)

For Overseas Service
Army Approves 5-Year Tours

S&S Washington Bureau

WASHINGTON—Voluntary extensions of overseas tours to a maximum of 60 months are possible for many Army men now serving overseas.

A new Army message (DA-590811) authorizes this five-year tour in line with earlier instructions which offered any individual then overseas the opportunity of voluntarily serving more than 48 months on his current tour.

The mandatory six-month extension of last October applied to those who have previously extended to 48 months, making their entire tour 54 months.

When the phase-back of involuntary extensions began the Army directed that each individual be given a chance to state a preference in order to firmly establish a new rotation date.

Those wishing to take advantage of the 60-month tour must request such extensions in 6-month increments no later than Dec. 7.

In no case may the tour exceed 60 months, the Army said.

In the future, commanders are authorized to approve, or forward, as appropriate, requests for extensions in increments of six months only.

The requests may be submitted as early as desired, but no later than eight months before established rotation dates.

An exception to the eight-month rule is made in the case of persons whose rotation dates have been re-established to fall during next July, August and September.

Weather

Thursday: Fair; high 48, low 26.
Friday: Partly cloudy; high 50, low 28.
Tuesday's Temperatures:
          High 46, low 30.
(USAF Weather Central, Fuchu AS)

Discoverer Lofted Into Polar Orbit

VANDENBERG AFB, Cal. (UPI)—A Discoverer satellite was shot into polar orbit Tuesday from this Pacific missile base in a continuing quest for more knowledge to add to America's space program.

Discoverer No. 38 carried an instrument package containing undisclosed experiments which was to be ejected in one to four days by a radio signal from the ground.

Air Force planes, towing nets, and surface ships will attempt to recover the capsule off Hawaii.

Plan 'Ready' Units

WASHINGTON (AP) —The Defense Department has ordered the Armed Services to set up special pools of reservists who could be called to fill understrength reserve or National Guard units in any future Cold War mobilization.

It said the Army, Navy, Air Force and Marines will "pre-select the fillers for its organized reserve units, carefully screen those individuals to insure that they are in fact available" and notify them that they have been listed for priority call to active duty.

A Pentagon spokesman said (Continued on Back Page, Col. 1)

Join in Missions

Report U.S. Pilots Train Viets on Combat Flights

PACIFIC
STAR AND STRIPES

AN AUTHORIZED PUBLICATION OF THE U.S. ARMED FORCES IN THE FAR EAST

昭和三十四年一月二十二日第三種郵便物認可新聞紙 175 号 (日刊)

SATURDAY   10c DAILY

(昭和34年4月22日第3種郵便物認可)

Vol. 18, No. 68   FIVE-STAR EDITION   Saturday, March 10, 1962

WASHINGTON (UPI) —An authorized U.S. source disclosed Friday that U.S. military personnel are flying on bombing and strafing missions in Vietnam in a training capacity.

A formal State Department statement issued at about the same time skirted the question, however. It merely said U.S. Air Force pilots are working with the Vietnamese, the objective being the training of their pilots and other Air Force personnel.

It said nothing about combat missions.

But the source said U.S. military personnel have flown on some combat missions against communist guerrillas in the Republic of Vietnam. He stressed to reporters that they did not do such missions "alone" but accompanied Vietnamese pilots in order to train them.

He declined to answer questions on whether Americans or Vietnamese are in command of the aircraft on such missions.

President Kennedy told a news conference Feb. 14 that the role of U.S. military personnel working with the Republic of Vietnam's armed forces was logistics and training.

"We have not sent combat troops there, though the training missions that we have there have been instructed if they are fired upon to . . . .fire back to protect themselves," he said.

The State Department statement was issued by Acting Press Officer Joseph W. Reap in answer to questions as to whether Americans (Continued on Back Page, Col. 4)

Ex-Junta Leader Spared

SEOUL (AP) — An appeals tribunal of the Republic of Korea revolutionary court Saturday reduced a lower court's death sentence against former junta chairman Lt. Gen. Do Young Chang to life imprisonment.

The death sentence against Chang's secretary, Col. Hoi Yung Lee, also was reduced to a life term.

The 38-year-old former army chief of staff was accused of sending military policemen in an unsuccessful attempt to block the entry of coup forces into the capital on the morning of the coup, May 16, 1961.

Chang also was accused of obstructing enactment of an extraordinary law by the junta council last June which forced him to give up the post of Army chief of staff.

AF Crash Kills 12 in France

ALENCON, France (AP) — Wreckage of a C-130 U.S. Air Force transport plane, missing with 12 men aboard since Thursday, was found Friday in heavy forest land near here.

French gendarmes who went to the area after a forest guard reported finding a wing of the aircraft said there were no survivors.

The big plane was reported missing while on a routine training mission over western France.

Student Punches U.S. Nazi Chief

San Diego State College student Ed Cherry (left) squares himself for more action after punching American Nazi Party leader George Lincoln Rockwell (right). Cherry, of Jewish descent, became angered when Rockwell made derogatory remarks about Jewish Americans during a speech at the school. Cherry was restrained by students and an associate of Rockwell and there was no more violence.   (AP Radiophoto)

SAN DIEGO, Cal. (UPI) — American Nazi Party leader George Lincoln Rockwell was hit with a right to the jaw Thursday after he made derogatory remarks about Jewish Americans during an address to a group of students at San Diego State College.

Ed D. Cherry, 22, a physical education major, climbed to the stage in an attempt to debate (Continued on Back Page, Col. 5)

10 Terrorists Slain In Oran Gun Battle

ALGIERS (UPI) — Soldiers and riot police fought a fierce gunbattle Friday with Moslem terrorists in a warehouse in the port city of Oran.

At least 10 Moslems were killed.

The incident brought the day's toll of bloodshed in Algeria's

EVIAN, France (UPI)—French-Algerian peace talks continue to make good progress and there is a good chance of achieving a cease-fire agreement by March 15, informed sources said.

cities to 28 killed and 25 wounded.

The shooting in Oran was sparked by a Moslem slaying of a young European. European youths surged into the streets bent on reprisal.

Meanwhile, artillery fire subsided around the fortified posts on the Tunisian frontier.

Fisher Denies Split With Liz

ROME (AP)—Eddie Fisher was quoted Friday night as scoffing at a U.S. newspaper story that he and actress Elizabeth Taylor are splitting up.

"Absolutely ridiculous," said a family spokesman after talking with the 33-year-old singer. "Eddie said he wouldn't dignify the story by saying anything about it."

Miss Taylor is here starring in "Cleopatra." The newspaper reporting the split said the 30-year-old actress had fallen "madly in love" with British actor Richard Burton.

Navy to Rate Officers' Wives

WASHINGTON (AP)—The Navy is going to appraise the wives of its officers for social graces and diplomacy in a new "fitness report" form.

So far as is known, this is the first time any of the military services has put down in printed form the question of how a wife—as well as her husband-officer—measures up.

In an announcement on issuance of the new form to replace the present one used by senior officers in judging the qualifications of their juniors, the Navy said that:

An officer "may comment on the officer-wife team as to their suitability and desirability as representatives of their country and the Navy."

The fitness report presents the question this way:

"Considering the requirements for social and diplomatic con- (Continued on Back Page, Col. 4)

ALGERIAN CEASE-FIRE!

Referendum to Decide Future Ties

PACIFIC STARS AND STRIPES

AN AUTHORIZED PUBLICATION OF THE
U.S. ARMED FORCES IN THE FAR EAST

SATURDAY   10c DAILY

Vol. 18, No. 77   FIVE-STAR EDITION   Monday, March 19, 1962

Tie Blast To Lost Airliner

Reporter Joins Search: P. 6

TOKYO (S&S)—Fears that a missing military charter plane with 107 persons aboard may have exploded in flight early Friday increased as the massive round-the-clock sea and air search entered its fourth day Monday.

Some 50 Air Force, Navy and Coast Guard planes and eight Seventh Fleet ships Monday resumed their "maximum effort visual search" of a 50,000-mile swath of the Pacific west of Guam where the Flying Tiger Airline Super Constellation vanished Friday.

U.S. Naval authorities on Guam said Sunday night that "more

(Continued on Back Page, Col. 2)

Explosion Injures 29

SPOKANE, Wash. (UPI) — At least 29 persons were injured when a gas explosion followed by fire ripped through half a city block in north Spokane Saturday night.

One of four stores demolished, a pizza parlor, was open for business when the explosion occurred and Police Inspector Robert Piper said it was not known whether anyone had been trapped in the blazing rubble.

None of those hospitalized were reported critical. Some two hours after the blast, law officers were poking through the demolished buildings.

Piper said the explosion was believed to have occurred in the one-story North Monroe Furniture Exchange Co. The blast knocked out windows as far away as a mile.

One policeman told of tearing away rubble to reach an injured woman, badly cut in the explosion.

(Continued on Back Page, Col. 3)

Urges Strike End

HONOLULU (AP)—Gov. William F. Quinn of Hawaii has telegraphed an appeal to President Kennedy to order an end to the West Coast shipping strike "to avert serious short range and dire long-range difficulties" in Hawaii. He said essential food supplies and other items were at low inventory in Hawaii.

Charming Envoy

VISITS UDAIPUR—Mrs. Jacqueline Kennedy waves a greeting to crowds of Indians who came to meet her upon her arrival for a visit in Udaipur, India. Bystanders with her were unidentified. Story, Page 5.   (AP Radiophoto)

NCO Shot to Death

TOKYO (S&S)—An Air Force sergeant stationed at Johnson AS near Tokyo died Sunday from a gunshot wound allegedly inflicted by his 15-year-old daughter.

An Air Force spokesman said S/Sgt. Edgar E. Wilson, 38, of Det. 1, 2127th Communications Sq., died at 2:20 p.m. Sunday after having been shot at his Johnson AS home with a 16-gauge double-barreled shotgun reportedly held by his daughter, Beverly.

The spokesman said Wilson was hit in the chest by a shot fired from one of the barrels of the shotgun.

Wilson was reportedly shot at 1:35 p.m. Sunday as he entered his bedroom.

The spokesman said the Office of Special Investigation, the Air Police and Japanese police are investigating and no further details are immediately available.

Wilson's wife, Jessie Lee, is being treated at Tachikawa U.S. Air Force Hospital for shock. Beverly was taken to the Johnson

(Continued on Back Page, Col. 4)

Algiers Ripped by Grenades

ALGIERS (UPI)—A series of explosions accompanied by the rattle of small arms fire shook Algiers Sunday night in the wake of the French-rebel cease-fire announcement.

First reports indicated the explosions were caused by localized attacks by French Algeria extremists.

At about the same time soldiers exchanged shots in Oran with thousands of Europeans milling in the streets of the European section.

The explosions and shooting came about 8:30 p.m., a little more than two hours after the cease-fire was announced over the state-run radio and television network.

Earlier, the extremist Secret Army Organization (OAS) issued a communique announcing crea-

(Continued on Back Page, Col. 5)

Compiled From Wire Services

EVIAN-LES-BAINS, France—France and the Algerian rebel regime Sunday signed a cease-fire effective at noon Monday.

In Paris, President Charles de Gaulle told France of the cease-fire in a broadcast speech and called on the people to give it their unqualified approval.

The way was now open, he said, for an independent Algeria which could march on the road of civilization, closely linked with France.

De Gaulle said it was French national interest which had commanded her to let the Algerians govern themselves.

He asked the European population of the country—1 million among 9 million Moslems—to stay on and

Related Stories: P. 3, 5

co-operate with the new Algerian state.

French Algerian Affairs Minister Louis Joxe said the cease-fire and related documents were signed by rebel Vice Premier Belkacem Krim and by Joxe and his fellow ministers at the peace conference, Public Works Minister Robert Buron and Sahara Minister Jean de Broglie.

Terms of the agreement as disclosed in an official French government summary include:

All armed combat both inside Algeria and on its frontiers is to cease. Prisoners of war will be released within 30 days. An amnesty will be proclaimed. All armed forces will stay out of politics. Emergency measures gradually will be abrogated.

Algeria remains under French

(Continued on Back Page, Col. 4)

Copter Assault Hits Viet Cong Bastion

(Following is an eyewitness report of the first major military operation backed by U.S. Army helicopters in the rugged mountains of central Vietnam. Associated Press correspondent Roy Essoyan and Pacific Stars and Stripes photographer Al Chang were among newsmen who accompanied the mission.)

By ROY ESSOYAN

TOURANE, Vietnam (AP)—Daredevil U.S. Army helicopter pilots flew nearly 1,000 Vietnamese troops into action this weekend in a hazardous two-day military operation that wiped out a communist Viet Cong battalion headquarters and trapped one and possibly two Viet Cong guerrilla companies.

It was one of the biggest military operations supported by American helicopters in Vietnam so far and the first such operation against communist guerrillas in the rugged mountains of central Vietnam. Earlier operations have been centered in the flatlands of the southern delta area.

The communist force, estimated at up to two battalions totaling 1,000 men, broke and ran at first contact. Some of them have melted into the jungle before the helicopters roared down on them.

"It looks like most of them escaped but we estimated one Viet Cong company is trapped and possibly another," said Maj. James Robertson of Saint Petersburg Beach, Fla., adviser to the 5th Regt. of the 2d Inf. Div. based here.

Casualties were light on both sides and included no Americans, according to the first day's reports. Two Viet Cong soldiers and 14 suspects were captured Saturday night.

The outcome of the operation

(Continued on Back Page, Col. 1)

Tracking Up The Kitchen

CORPUS CHRISTI, Tex. (UPI)—A passenger train rounded a curve near here and roared into a house.

The Missouri-Pacific passenger train swept around the bend just as house movers crossed the track. The train struck the house in the kitchen area.

Housemover Juan Gutierrez of Robstown was fined $22.50 for unlawfully permitting an overwidth load to be moved on a public roadway.

About $1,500 damage was caused to the house and $800 damage to the train engine.

Weather

FORECAST

Tuesday:
Partly cloudy, becoming cloudy; High 50, Low 32

Wednesday:
Cloudy, becoming fair; High 52, Low 35

Sunday's Temperatures:
High 54, Low 30

(USAF Weather Central, Fuchu AS)

S&S Camera Covers Jungle Raid, Pages 12, 13

PACIFIC
STAR AND STRIPES

AN AUTHORIZED PUBLICATION OF THE
U.S. ARMED FORCES IN THE FAR EAST

SATURDAY   10c DAILY

Vol. 18, No. 80   FIVE-STAR EDITION   Thursday, March 22, 1962

ON THE MOVE—Republic of Vietnam troops spring into action from a U.S. Army helicopter in mountainous jungle country in the central part of the embattled nation. They were among some 1,000 troops flown into the Viet Cong guerrilla stronghold last weekend by 12 U.S. copters. The rebels were driven back, but managed to escape a trap which would have encircled the main body of about 1,000 troops. (S&S Photo by Army M/Sgt. Al Chang)

* * * *

Won't Give Up Disarmament Talks: JFK

WASHINGTON (AP)—President Kennedy said Wednesday he does not propose to abandon the Geneva disarmament talks now under way, even though there seem to be some very basic differences between the United States and the Soviet Union on inspection of nuclear tests.

"I think the talks should go on," he said. "I am not prepared to abandon it and it would be a mistake for us to feel that there, the prospects are finished."

* * * *

The President also said in his press conference:

1) "I have received this morning Chairman Khrushchev's reply to my letter of March 7 on outer space co-operation. I am gratified that this reply indicates that there are a number of areas of common interest. The next step clearly is for the United States representative on the U.N. Outer Space Committee, Ambassador Francis Plimpton, to meet in New York with the Soviet representative to make arrangements for an early discussion of the specific ideas of the Soviet Union and the United States."

2) The United States will take the proper action at the proper time in recognizing the new Algerian government once it is formed.

3) The President made a long and spirited defense of the United Nations after a speech by Sen. Henry M. Jackson (D-Wash.), who had declared Tuesday that the (Continued on Back Page, Col. 2)

Deadlock On Issues In Geneva

GENEVA (UPI)—The United States and Russia were reported Wednesday night to have reached complete deadlock on major cold war issues with the Soviet Union continuing to pursue a "collision course" on Berlin.

A series of big power meetings over the past 10 days and one week's session of the General Disarmament Conference have failed to cast the slightest ray of hope on the proceedings. It was understood no progress on the perilous issues threatening nuclear war is anticipated before the Russian, British and (Continued on Back Page, Col. 2)

Weather

FORECAST
Friday: Fair: High 63. Low 35
Saturday: Fair: High 65. Low 34
Wednesday's Temperatures: High 49, Low 38
(USAF Weather Central, Fuchu AS)

McNamara Sees Long War In Vietnam, Mum on Troops

HONOLULU (AP)—Secretary of Defense Robert S. McNamara said Wednesday that the war in Vietnam is likely to last a long time.

But he declined to say whether the U.S. would commit combat troops into the communist-threatened area if the situation worsens.

Interviewed at planeside as he arrived for the fourth in a series of monthly strategy conferences on the Southeast Asian nation, McNamara told newsmen that the United States would continue sending military advisers and aid to the Republic of Vietnam "as it's necessary."

The defense secretary and the eight Pentagon officials who accompanied him on his flight from Washington began an all-day conference with diplomats and military leaders from the Vietnam area.

The meeting was being held at the Pearl Harbor headquarters of Admiral Harry Felt, commander-in-chief, U.S. Forces Pacific. Felt accompanied McNamara from Washington.

After the meeting, McNamara was scheduled to fly to San Francisco for a Friday meeting with (Continued on Back Page, Col. 5)

Say Callups to Start Getting Out Aug. 25

WASHINGTON (AP) — The Defense Department reportedly has set Aug. 25 as the date to start releasing more than 155,000 reservists and national guardsmen called into uniform last fall at the height of the Berlin crisis.

Informed sources said the aim would be to have all, or virtually all, the reservists and guardsmen back home by about Sept. 25.

This would be just short of the one-year limit Congress authorized for their active service tour.

Sources emphasized that the plan still is tentative.

Release much earlier than this is considered unlikely, largely because of the continuing communist threats in Berlin and the Republic of Vietnam.

Earlier, General George H. Decker, Army chief of staff, made public a stern letter to his top commanders in the United States, saying the U.S. is "in a very real sense at war" and that "prompt and effective steps" must be taken to make reservists understand why they must remain on active duty now.

Planes Spot New Debris

CLARK AB, P.I. (S&S)—Two sightings of debris raised hopes Thursday in the seven-day search for a missing airliner with 107 persons aboard.

Naval authorities on Guam said a destroyer escort was dispatched Wednesday night to recover a 3-foot tank, a green cloth and an unidentified 20-foot object sighted by one of 53 search aircraft during the largest aerial search of the six-day hunt.

From the Philippines the destroyer escort Brister was speeding to a point 500 miles east of Manila where other unidentified debris was spotted from the air.

Rain, Snow, Wind Sting U.S.

By United Press International

Spring is here, the calendar said Wednesday, but much of the nation's weather had the bitter sting of winter.

On the first full day of spring, flooding rains poured down on the Middle West, ice jams piled up in northern rivers, snow slowed city traffic, and tornadic winds hit parts of the South.

The temperature was below freezing from northern New York and New England to northern Illinois, Kansas, and most of the Rockies.

In the South, a windstorm unroofed houses and tore down power lines at Canton, Ga. Winds which may have been a tornado caused damage in the Birmingham-Anniston, Ala., area.

At Hindsville, Ark., Tuesday night, a funnel cloud chewed a path a block wide and three miles long, causing an estimated $100,000 damage.

Mrs. Raymond Villines, 23, of Ponca, a town 20 miles west of Hindsville, was hurled 150 feet through the air by what the Weather Bureau said was a strong wind, not a tornado. She suffered cuts, bruises and a possible broken leg. Her home and two barns were destroyed.

There was little spring in the air at Chicago, where slushy snow, driven by 30 mile-an-hour winds, piled up an inch thick. North of the city, families near suburban Libertyville abandoned homes close to the rising Des Plaines River.

Elsewhere in the Middle West, an ice jam pushed flood waters into low-lying areas south of West Des Moines, Iowa, and dynamiters tried to break up ice packs near Grand Rapids, Mich., and Racine, Wis.

The Burlington Line railroad tracks were washed out north of Clarksville, Mo., after a drenching 2.37 inches of rain fell on Vandalia, Ill., in 24 hours.

In the West, the arrival of spring meant snow across much of Utah and light snow, plus gale warnings for Oregon.

Copter-Borne Viets Kill 40 Rebels

SAIGON (AP)—Units of the Republic of Vietnam's 42d Regt. supported by U.S. Army helicopters mounted a three-pronged attack on a communist mountain stronghold last weekend, killing about 40 Viet Cong in the first two days of fighting.

The operation was reported here Monday by Jack Foisie, special correspondent for the San Francisco Chronicle, who accompanied the mission.

No details were available from any military source. The attack was described as the largest yet conducted in that area.

The attack began Saturday in a remote, mountainous section of central Vietnam about 270 miles north of Saigon. Twelve U.S. Army helicopters of the Eighth Light Helicopter Co. based at the coastal town of Qui Nhon carried (Continued on Back Page, Col. 3)

NASSER BACKERS REVOLT IN SYRIA

PACIFIC STAR AND STRIPES

AN AUTHORIZED PUBLICATION OF THE U.S. ARMED FORCES IN THE FAR EAST

Vol. 18, No. 92   FIVE-STAR EDITION

SATURDAY   10c DAILY

Tuesday, April 3, 1962

DAMASCUS, Syria (UPI) — Syria was gripped in a pro-Nasser revolt Monday, only five days after an army coup d'etat ousted the civilian government of President Nazem Kudsi.

Army officers in northern Syria early Monday declared their loyalty to United Arab Republic President Gamal Abdel Nasser and called for a restoration of Syria's merger with Egypt, which was dissolved six months ago.

The rebels appeared to be gaining strength and were believed to have the support of the major northern Syrian population centers of Aleppo, Lattakia, Homs, Hama and Deirezzor.

Damascus Radio, speaking for the army command, countered with its own promise of friendship toward Egypt. It offered a plebiscite to decide whether or not Syria should unite with "the liberated Arab countries and especially Egypt" on a sound basis that would avoid the "mistakes of the past."

Damascus-based army units surrounded the capital Monday morning leaving helmeted police, armed with rifles and machineguns, to maintain order in the city.

By order of the army command, meetings of more than five persons were banned and an 8 p.m. to 5 a.m. curfew was imposed. All borders, harbors and airports were closed.

The revolt of the pro-Nasser offi- (Continued on Back Page, Col. 5)

Midwest Flood Cuts a 2-State Link

A bystander observes the broken interstate highway bridge which was washed out by flood waters of the Big Sioux River near North Sioux City, S.D. The bridge, which is on the borders of South Dakota and Iowa, washed out on the Dakota side first, and then a section on the opposite bank collapsed. (UPI Radiophoto)

By United Press International

Weekend snow and rain brought floods Monday in 10 states from South Dakota to the Atlantic Coast.

The flooding Big Sioux River swept away an interstate highway bridge at Sioux City, Iowa. High water broke through a dam at Middletown, Conn., flooding buildings of a mining company.

High water washed out a Delaware and Hudson Railroad track between Gamesfort and Fort Edward, N.Y., causing derailment of 10 freight cars and a caboose.

Caledonia, Minn., reported 9 inches of snow. Waukon, Iowa, had 8 inches. Western Pennsylvania had up to 4 inches of snow Sunday and sections of Indiana and Ohio measured 3 inches. Rochester, N.Y., received 2 inches of snow in six hours Sunday night.

There was snow reported as far south as Tennessee and as far north as Maine. Seven inches of (Continued on Back Page, Col. 5)

Liz and Eddie to Get Divorce

Earlier Story, Page 3

NEW YORK (AP)—An attorney for Elizabeth Taylor and Eddie Fisher said Monday night they have agreed to separate and seek a divorce.

A spokesman for the attorney, Louis Nizer, made the formal announcement of the break-up after weeks of rumors that the marriage was going on the rocks while romance blossomed between the beautiful actress and her British co-star, Richard Burton.

The statement said:

"Elizabeth and Eddie Fisher announce that they have mutually agreed to part. Divorce proceedings will be instituted soon."

The spokesman said the statement had been approved by Miss Taylor, in Rome, by telephone, and by Fisher, who is in New York.

The announcement came after Fisher had been visited at the Hotel Pierre over the weekend by an agent for Miss Taylor, who bore a message from the actress to her husband.

Earlier Monday, Fisher had conferred with his accountant and Michael Todd Jr., son of Miss Taylor's third husband.

The formal statement was handed to reporters in the 23d floor offices of Nizer's law firm by a member of the firm.

He did not disclose further details of the couple's plans.

Segregationist Warned By Church Asks Hearing

Related Pictures, Page 5

NEW ORLEANS (AP)—A militant segregationist who claims she was threatened with excommunication from the Roman Catholic Church sought an interview Monday with Archbishop Joseph Francis Rummel.

Mrs. B. J. Gaillot, president of Save Our Nation, Inc., said she wants to discuss segregation with the archbishop.

"If I'm wrong, I'll get down on my knees and ask for mercy and forgiveness," Mrs. Gaillot said.

(United Press International reports the Roman Catholic archdiocese of New Orleans confirmed (Continued on Back Page, Col. 1)

Shapley Will Retire June 30

WASHINGTON (AP)-Lt. Gen. Alan Shapley, commander, Fleet Marine Force, Pacific, will retire June 30.

President Kennedy has named Maj. Gen. Carson A. Roberts, commanding general of Aircraft Fleet Marine Force in the Pacific, to succeed Shapley. Kennedy also nominated Roberts for promotion to lieutenant general.

At the same time, the President also promoted two Army major generals to three-star rank and gave them new assignments.

Maj. Gen. Charles H. Bonesteel, (Continued on Back Page, Col. 5)

Weather

Wednesday:
Generally cloudy; high 55, low 40.
Thursday:
Fair; high 53, low 33.
Monday's Temperatures:
High 66, low 34.
(USAF Weather Central Fu for AS)

FELL 75 FEET —AND SHE'S OK

RESCUED—After falling 75 feet and spending 11 hours on a rocky ledge near Niagara Falls, April Hubbard, 3, daughter of Mr. and Mrs. Harry Hubbard, of Niagara Falls, Ont., reaches the top of the river bank in a mine basket with her rescuer, Russell Sanderson. April tumbled over the bank while playing with friends, landing in a bush. Her playmates were too young to give searching police accurate information on her whereabouts. Apparently suffering only scratches and bruises, she was sent to a hospital for observation. (AP Photo)

Biggest Operation
VIET DIVISION OPENS DRIVE

PACIFIC STARS AND STRIPES

AN AUTHORIZED PUBLICATION OF THE ARMED FORCES FAR EAST

FIVE-STAR EDITION

10¢ DAILY
15¢ SATURDAY

Vol. 18, No. 93   Wednesday, April 4, 1962

OAS Kills 10 In Hospital

ALGIERS (UPI) — European gunmen of the outlawed Secret Army Organization (OAS) invaded a Moslem hospital here early Tuesday, machine gunned patients in their beds and wrecked part of the building with a bomb.

Early reports said 10 Moslems were killed and 8 wounded, most of them seriously.

There was no immediate indication whether the terrorists were after certain Moslems in the hospital. But it appeared to be the latest move in the continuing OAS campaign to provoke the Moslems to a point where they would launch mass onslaughts against the European sections of Algiers and Oran.

This would compel the French Army to intervene and thus break the cease-fire agreement.

The attack on the Beaufrasier Moslem Hospital in the Algiers suburb of Bouzareah was carried out at 6:35 a.m. by a commando unit of about 15 gunmen. Some eyewitnesses said the OAS attackers wore stolen uniforms of the Republican Security Guards (CRS).

About 100 patients were in the hospital at the time—mostly tuberculosis or lung cancer sufferers.

The gunmen, who drove up in (Continued on Back Page, Col. 3)

Lemnitzer Faces Busy Schedule

TOKYO (S&S)—General L. L. Lemnitzer, chairman of the Joint Chiefs of Staff, was to arrive in Japan Wednesday afternoon for three days of visits with top U.S. and Japanese military and government officials.

Lemnitzer was to fly to Tachikawa AB from the Republic of Korea where he was to be met by Lt. Gen. Jacob E. Smart, commander of U.S. Forces Japan and Fifth Air Force.

The four-star general is on a tour of military installations in the Pacific and Asia that has taken him to the Philippines, Thailand, the Republic of Vietnam, Taiwan, Okinawa and the ROK. He leaves Japan Friday (Continued on Back Page, Col. 5)

(Beverly Deepe, a free-lance correspondent, accompanied the largest drive yet mounted by the government against communist rebels. She telephoned the first report of the operation to the AP bureau in Saigon.)

By BEVERLY DEEPE

CAO LANH, Republic of Vietnam (AP)—Some 8,000 Vietnamese troops — the largest force ever thrown against communist guerrillas in the Republic of Vietnam — combed a 10-square-mile section of the upper Mekong River delta Tuesday.

Two AD-6 American-built fighter planes strafed and killed about 40 fleeing rebels.

By the end of the day, ground forces had made no contact with the communists, but reportedly were in an encirclement position and prepared to move in on a large force. An L-19 light observation plane was patrolling the area.

The operation was under direct command of Col. Huynh Van Cao, Seventh Inf. Div. commander, who has established a command post here. With him are nine U.S. military advisers, including Col. Frank B. Clay Jr., senior adviser for the Seventh Div. Clay is the son of General Lucius D. Clay, presidential adviser for Berlin.

The ground force, almost a full division, was supported by Republic of Vietnam Navy units operating on the river and by an air cover of fighters. Site of the operation, which was still in progress, is about 30 miles south of the Cambodian frontier in Kien Phong Province.

The government threw most of the Seventh Div. into the operation, and reportedly was opposed by elements of a Viet Cong battalion scattered over the province. (Continued on Back Page, Col. 1)

Schools Told To Integrate

NEW ORLEANS (AP) — One week after the Catholic Church ordered its schools desegregated, a federal judge Tuesday threw open to Negroes the first six grades of all New Orleans public schools.

U.S. District Judge J. Skelly Wright made his order effective at the beginning of school next fall, same as the order of March 27 by Archbishop Joseph Francis Rummel applying to all Catholic elementary and secondary schools, grades 1 through 12.

In speeding total desegregation in New Orleans public schools, Judge Wright threw out Louisiana's Pupil Placement Law under which only 12 Negro children now attend six scattered schools.

JFK May Hit It Rich at 45

WASHINGTON (UPI) — When President Kennedy turns 45 on May 29, he may get direct possession of perhaps $4 million to $5 million of the fortune formerly held in trust for him.

It was understood Tuesday that this would represent half of the trust funds set up for him in 1926, 1936 and 1949 by his father, Joseph P. Kennedy.

Equal sums were provided for each of the President's two brothers and four sisters.

President Kennedy received direct ownership of one-fourth of the principal of his trust funds when he reached 40. He is reported to be eligible for a second one-fourth when he becomes 45.

The age levels are reported to be conditions prescribed by the elder Kennedy for the trust funds he started for his children in 1926. He added to the sums later.

Shortly before assuming office in January, 1961, Kennedy removed his personal fortune from the field of speculative investment for the duration of his White House service. He disposed of all stock holdings and reinvested in government bonds—federal, state and municipal.

At the time he entered office—and presumably at present—Kennedy derived about $100,000 a year after taxes from the trust funds.

On the basis of authoritative information this represented a gross income of $500,000 a year (Continued on Back Page, Col. 4)

Weather

Thursday:	Fair to partly cloudy; High 57, Low 32
Friday:	Fair to partly cloudy; High 60, Low 38
Tuesday's Temperatures:	High 62, Low 57

(USAF Weather Central, Fuchu AS)

Maris Hits 1st Homer

It's homer No. 1 in game No. 1 for Roger Maris.

Maris, who set an all-time record of 61 home runs last year, blasted his first homer of the 1962 season in the opening game Tuesday, a three-run clout in the fifth inning as New York edged the Baltimore Orioles 7-6 at Yankee Stadium.

Maris did not hit his first homer last year until the Yanks' 11th game on April 26.

Mickey Mantle and Bill Skowron also homered for world champion New York.

Other scores and details, Page 19.

How U.S. Soldiers Died

Too Wounded to Walk, 2 Are Slain by Guerrillas

DA NANG, Republic of Vietnam (AP)—Communist guerrillas killed two captured U.S. Army sergeants because they were too badly wounded to walk any farther, the survivors of a jungle ambush reported Wednesday. The Americans' arms had been bound behind them.

Vietnamese patrols and air forces were still searching the jungle area 45 miles east of the Laos frontier for two other American army sergeants who were captured in the attack on a bivouac Sunday.

The U.S. Army identified the slain soldiers as Staff Sgt. Wayne E. Marchand of Plattsmouth, Neb., and SP5 James Gabriel of Honolulu.

The two missing men are SFC Francis Quinn of Niagara Falls, N.Y., and Sgt. George E. Groom of Stewartsville, Mo.

All four soldiers were members of an Army Special Forces unit which specializes in anti-guerrilla warfare and were engaged in training a village self-defense group.

Survivors told U.S. authorities the two slain Americans were seriously wounded in the attack by Viet

(Continued on Back Page, Col. 1)

PACIFIC STAR AND STRIPES

AN AUTHORIZED PUBLICATION OF THE U.S. ARMED FORCES IN THE FAR EAST

SATURDAY 10c DAILY

Vol. 18, No. 100   FIVE-STAR EDITION   Wednesday, April 11, 1962

E. Berlin Boy Leaps To West

WEST BERLIN (AP)—A 9-year-old German boy jumped from the roof of a five-story building in

WEST BERLIN (UPI)—A 9-year-old East Berlin boy who jumped into West Berlin from a border rooftop will be sent back home to his parents, western authorities said Tuesday.

The boy said he had quarreled with his parents and wanted to run away from home.

the communist sector to safety in West Berlin Tuesday.

Landing in a safety net, he was taken to a hospital where he was found to be suffering

Airlift Wife To Hospital

Picture, Page 6

TACHIKAWA AB, Japan (S&S)—The wife of a U.S. navyman was reported slightly improved Wednesday at the Air Force Hospital here after being airlifted from southern Japan where she began hemorrhaging internally.

Mrs. Nobue Cantwell, 32, wife of Boatswain's Mate/1C Leo D. Cantwell, 27, of Indianapolis, Ind., was flown here Tuesday aboard a C-130 Hercules turboprop cargo plane of the 815th Troop Carrier Sq., 315th Air Div. from Itazuke AB, Japan.

After News of Oscar Victory

Italian actress Sophia Loren embraces her husband, Carlo Ponti, in Rome Tuesday, after learning she had won an Oscar for the best performance by an actress in 1961. She won the award for her role in "Two Women." (AP Radiophoto)

SANTA MONICA, Cal. (UPI)—Sophia Loren, whose fear of losing kept her from appearing at the scene of her greatest triumph, Tuesday was acclaimed by Hollywood as the best actress of 1961.

Sharing her victory was Vienna-born Maximilian Schell who won the best actor Oscar at Monday night's 34th annual Academy Award presentations at Santa Monica Civic Auditorium, making it a double win for foreign stars.

"West Side Story," voted the best picture of the year, almost swept the boards, winning 10 of its 11 Oscar nominations.

Miss Loren, an international glamor girl, won the award for her sexless role of a tattered mother in war-torn Europe in "Two Women."

Earlier Monday the actress, in Rome for a new film, said, "I guess I didn't go to Hollywood because I am scared." On hearing of her victory she said, "I'm so happy I just can't believe my ears. It's just wonderful, wonderful, wonderful."

Schell won his award playing

U.S., U.K. In Joint Plea For A-Ban

WASHINGTON (UPI) — The United States and Britain made an 11th-hour appeal to Russia Tuesday to agree to a safeguard nuclear test ban. Otherwise, they said, the United States will have no alternative but to resume atmospheric tests.

The joint plea was issued simultaneously by the White House and read before the House of Commons by British Prime Minister Harold Macmillan. It was designed to court world opinion for the Western stand if Russia remains adamant on the issue.

"There is still time to reach agreement," the statement said. "We continue to hope the Soviet government may reconsider their position and express their readiness to accept the principle of international verification."

The United States is making arrangements to resume atmospheric shots in the Pacific later this month to check out newly developed weapons and match reported gains made by the Soviets in their recent massive test series.

Officials said other expressions of urgency similar to

Fly to Cuba for Ransom Talks

HAVANA (UPI) — Four Cuban exiles representing the families of 1,179 captured Cuban invaders arrived Tuesday to bargain with Premier Fidel Castro on his $62-million ransom demand for the prisoners' freedom.

* * *

50,000 Imprisoned

WASHINGTON (UPI) — Cuba is holding an estimated 25,000 to 50,000 political prisoners in overcrowded jails, U.S. officials reported Tuesday.

The figure on political prisoners —aside from those taken in the abortive invasion—came from intelligence estimates.

The delegation, which flew here from Miami, has been authorized to offer $28 million in "goods and products" to meet Castro's stiff ransom demand.

The Cuban premier is seeking cash for the release of the men sentenced last Saturday to 30 years at hard labor in an unprecedented four-day mass trial.

The three men and a woman making the trip expressed confidence their mission would be successful and expected to meet personally with the Cuban dictator.

Castro, who has asked individual ransoms of $25,000 to $500,000 for members of the Pig's Bay inva-

sion force, authorized the group to fly to Havana.

The group, representing the "Cuban Families Committee for the Liberation of Prisoners of War," left aboard a Pan American plane.

Meanwhile, the Kennedy Administration appeared Monday night to be adopting a policy of remaining officially aloof but not opposing private negotiations on Castro's prisoner ransom offer.

This word was given to newsmen by officials after a series of high-level policy meetings—which included President Kennedy — on Castro's offer to free 1,179 invasion prisoners for $62 million.

Weather

Thursday: Partly cloudy; high 68, low 52.

Friday: Partly cloudy; high 70, low 55.

Tuesday's temperatures:
High 71, Low 53.

(USAF Weather Central, Fuchu AS)

READY TO GO

Technicians at Cape Canaveral, Fla., make final adjustments on Ranger 4 before mounting it on an Atlas-Agena B booster rocket which will be launched toward the moon Monday.
(UPI Photo)

U.S. Set to Launch TV Moon Rocket

CAPE CANAVERAL, Fla. (AP) —All systems were reported ready Sunday for an attempt to launch the Ranger 4 spacecraft toward the moon Monday.

Project scientists reported minor problems had cropped up earlier in the Atlas-Agena B booster and in the payload but had been corrected.

The huge rocket is scheduled to blast off late Monday afternoon to start the 730-pound gold and silver spacecraft on a 60-hour journey to the moon, 229,541 miles away.

The launching is the first of three space shots scheduled here this week by the National Aeronautics and Space Administration.

Wednesday, the Saturn super booster is to have its second test firing, to be followed Thursday by the once-postponed effort to orbit an international satellite developed by the United States and Great Britain. The maiden test of the Centaur high-energy space vehicle, postponed a fifth time

Saturday, also may squeeze into the schedule.

If all goes right, Ranger 4 will approach the moon early Thursday morning and begin snapping television pictures of the surface from an altitude of 2,400 miles down to 15 miles. A picture is to be relayed to a tracking station at Goldstone, Cal., every 10 seconds for a period of 40 minutes.

Then an 89.3-pound sphere is to eject from the spacecraft and is to be slowed by a braking rocket so it will impact on the moon at about 80 miles an hour. Instruments in the

(Continued on Back Page, Col. 3)

Weather

FORECAST
Tokyo Area

Tuesday: Partly cloudy. High 75; Low 49
Wednesday: Partly cloudy. High 76; Low 50
Sunday's Temperatures: High 72; Low 47

(USAF Weather Central, Fuchu AS)

Record Airlift Held

Viet Rebels Fire On U.S. Copters

PACIFIC STARS STRIPES

AN AUTHORIZED PUBLICATION OF THE ARMED FORCES FAR EAST

FIVE-STAR EDITION   10¢ DAILY
                      15¢ SATURDAY

Vol. 18, No. 112   Monday, April 23, 1962

U.S. to Test Live Polaris

WASHINGTON (UPI)—U.S. plans call for a submarine-launched Polaris missile with a live nuclear warhead to be tested in the atomic series in the Pacific, it was learned Sunday.

It was also learned that a new type antisubmarine weapon with an atomic warhead will be given a live test in an under-ocean shot.

The nuclear tests are scheduled to start in a few days.

The Polaris warhead and the antisubmarine weapon would be the first missile-carried nuclear weapons tested by the U.S.

The Navy has two new antisubmarine weapons—ASROC and SUBROC—and it was not established which would be fired.

ASROC, for antisubmarine rocket, is carried aboard destroyers. SUBROC, submarine rocket, is to be carried by submarines for launching against other submarines.

The Polaris missile has a range of 1,200 miles. In the Pacific tests, the range may be greatly shortened, adding to the height the missile will reach when its warhead explodes.

The target area is reported centered around U.S.-owned Johnston Island, about 800 miles south of Honolulu, and British-owned Christmas Island, about 1,300 miles south of Honolulu.

AN HUU, Vietnam (AP) — Two full companies of U.S. military helicopters — the largest helicopter force yet used in the Republic of Vietnam — spent Easter Sunday shuttling Vietnamese troops to a major mopping up operation in the Mekong River Delta.

In all, 29 copters were used.

It was the first such mission carried out by the U.S. Marine copter company in Vietnam since it arrived last weekend. It also was the heaviest use of combined copter movement and air support against communist guerrillas so far.

After leaving the staging area here, the big H21 troop carriers skimmed to their targets along the canals at 90 miles an hour only a few feet from the ground.

As they touched down near the hamlet of Ap My Qui to unload their troops, bursts of enemy fire came from the banks of an adjacent canal, raising spurts of dust near the idling machines. The Viet Cong also fired on them as they passed over the junction of two canals.

However not a copter was hit. They were on the ground in the various landing zones less than three minutes. American gunners returned the communist fire when—

(Continued on Back Page, Col. 2)

*   *   *

Say Cambodia Reds Killed 54 in Vietnam

SAIGON (UPI)—The government confirmed reports Sunday that 54 Vietnamese were massacred and 29 wounded Saturday by a group of Cambodian communists in a raid on a border hamlet in Long Xuyen Province, some 106 miles southwest of here.

Press reports said 100 Cambodian communists, known as Issarak Khmers, crossed the border and attacked the hamlet of Vinh Lac in the province's Tinh Bien district at around 8 p.m. Saturday.

The reports said the Cambodians also burned 60 houses.

Observers noted the raid may have been an attempt by the communists to stir up trouble between Republic of Vietnam's citizens of

pure Vietnamese stock and those of Cambodian origin.

Large numbers of Vietnamese citizens of Cambodian stock live in the southern provinces of Long Xuyen, Kien Giang, Ba Xuyen, and Vinh Binh.

(A highly informed source told AP Sunday that Vietnam is creating a kind of demilitarized zone along its border with Cambodia, in which all persons suspected of be-

(Continued on Back Page, Col. 3)

Bucs' 10th Win Ties Record

Bill Mazeroski tripled home an eighth-inning run Sunday that gave the unbeaten Pittsburgh Pirates their 10th consecutive victory, a 4-3 skim over the New York Mets that tied the modern major league record for most consecutive triumphs at the start of a season.

The defeat was the ninth straight for the still winless Mets—a string that tied the major league record for futility at the start of a season.

Details, page 11.

U.S. Seeks Kennedy-Nikita Phone Link

GENEVA (UPI) — The United States proposes to add another to the list of "hot" telephones that all chiefs of state in this nuclear age keep on their desks for instant contact with their military commanders.

This additional "hot" phone would make it possible, for instance, for President Kennedy

to telephone Soviet Premier Nikita S. Khrushchev on a moment's notice.

The idea of a top priority telephone line linking the White House in Washington to the Kremlin in Moscow is contained in the detailed U.S. disarmament plan just presented to the Geneva disarmament conference.

American leaders have been concerned for some time that too little is being done to prevent the risk of war by accident, miscalculation, surprise or a breakdown in communications.

The American plan now presented in detail calls for reduction of the risk of war by advance notification of military movements and

maneuvers; by establishment of observation posts at major ports, railway centers and motor highways, river crossings and air bases to report on massing and movement of military forces; and the exchange of military missions between states or groups of states for improving communications

(Continued on Back Page, Col. 1)

SMALL PROTEST

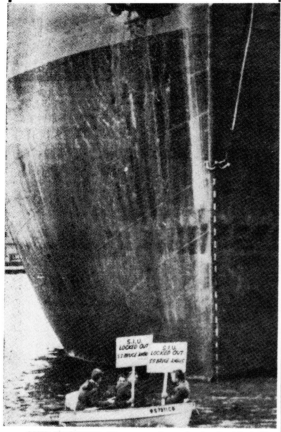

SHIP PROTEST—Four men in a rowboat picket the Canadian grain carrier R. Bruce Argus docked at Milwaukee. The men carried signs to indicate they represented the Seafarers International Union. The picketing stemmed from a jurisdictional dispute between the SIU and the Canadian Maritime Union. (AP Photo)

PACIFIC
STARS AND STRIPES

AN AUTHORIZED PUBLICATION OF
U.S. ARMED FORCES IN THE FAR EAST

5c SATURDAY   10c DAILY

Vol. 18, No. 126   FIVE-STAR EDITION   Monday, May 7, 1962

REPORT FALL OF NAM THA

´VIENTIANE, Laos (UPI)—Pro-communist forces crushed 5,000 troops of the Royal Laotian Army between two assault columns Sunday, and drove them from the embattled city of Nam Tha, reliable sources reported.

American military sources confirmed the beleaguered Nam Tha garrison was hit with a "major attack" early Sunday.

They said all 12 U.S. military advisers had been forced to evacuate by helicopter.

The northern Laotian city of Muong Sing fell to rebel troops a few days ago, in an operation which the Royal Government charged was carried out in part by communist Chinese troops.

Laotian leaders, now touring Asia's pro-Western countries in search of moral and material support, charged in Saigon Saturday that communist Chinese troops are active in Northern Laos.

The military advisers said an estimated four enemy battalions dealt the garrison a stunning blow along its lightly defended northwest perimeter at dawn Sunday.

Other forces of unknown strength swarmed down from their trenches in the hills to the southeast and east at the same time.

The advisers said the Royalist troops "put up a good fight."

The sudden smash into Nam Tha again revived speculation that the Royal Laotian Army high command may have been right in its frequent claims that Laos is now under invasion from Red China.

Observers have long known that the town was only lightly screened by local military in the north—
(Continued on Back Page, Col. 2)

Connally to Face Yarborough in Texas Runoff

DALLAS (UPI) — John B. Connally, former secretary of the Navy, and New Frontiersman Don Yarborough will meet in a June 2 runoff Democratic primary election for governor of Texas.

The winner in the runoff is virtually certain to be the next governor.

Robert Johnson, manager of the Texas Election Bureau, said after the 2 p.m. tabulation of returns that Connally had 357,749 votes to Yarborough's 268,475 in Saturday's bitterly fought primary. Nearly a million and a half votes were cast.

Gov. Price Daniel, 52, ran third in the race. It meant he failed in a bid for a fourth term. Edwin A. Walker, 52, a former major general and a member of the John Birch Society, finished last among the six Democratic candidates, with 119,013 votes.

The other candidates were Atty. Gen. Will Wilson, and Marshall (Continued on Back Page, Col. 5)

They Made It

YARBOROUGH   CONNALLY

They Didn't

DANIEL   WALKER

Won't Quit Fight, Says Walker

DALLAS (UPI)—Edwin A. Walker, former major general, who finished last among six Democratic candidates for governor of Texas, vowed Sunday to continue his fight against communism.

"We've had a lot of support," Walker said, "and I will continue the fight."

Walker, a member of the John Birch Society, was relieved of his command of the 24th Inf. Div. in Germany after accusations that he taught his troops Birch Society doctrine. He resigned from the Army.

"I find a lot of enthusiasm for the cause," Walker said, "but, of course, there was only so much time to educate the people."

Walker, 52, got 119,013 votes of the nearly 1.5 million cast.

A-Warhead Polaris Launched, Fired

WASHINGTON (UPI)—The United States launched and fired a nuclear warhead Sunday from a Polaris submarine in the Pacific.

The Atomic Energy Commission and the Defense Department, in a joint announcement, said the test using a Polaris missile was conducted in the Christmas Island range. It was the fifth of the new series of U.S. atmospheric nuclear tests.

The announcement said the warhead was set off at about 7:45 p.m. The size of the detonation was not given.

(The test apparently was a successful experiment with the entire system—from launching deep in the ocean to the firing point perhaps many miles away, AP reported.)

Sunday's shot was the first missile-carried nuclear explosion to be conducted by the United States.

It has been reported previously that the Polaris warhead has a destructive force equal to 500,000 tons of TNT.

The missile in its current version has a range of 1,200 miles. But presumably the rocket used in Sunday's shot was sent to a higher altitude, rather than down-range as it would be used in battle.

In addition to the Polaris experiment, the United States is expected to try out an underwater atomic warhead. The Navy (Continued on Back Page, Col. 4)

Weather
FORECAST

Tuesday: Cloudy; High 64, Low 53
Wednesday: Cloudy with rain; High 62, Low 54
Sunday's Temperatures:
High 76, Low 48
(USAF Weather Central, Fuchu AS)

Truce Violated, U.S. Charges

WASHINGTON (AP)—The State Department charged Sunday that the new heavy communist assault on the government bastion of Nam Tha in Laos violates the year-old cease-fire which has provided an uneasy peace in the Southeast Asian kingdom.

A spokesman said the United States will do everything possible to "restore the cease-fire."

In administration quarters here initial reaction to the apparently imminent loss of the town was regarded as simply an (Continued on Back Page, Col. 5)

Rookie Hurls No-Hitter

Rookie lefthander Bo Belinsky, almost released in the spring for complaining about his salary, pitched the first American League no-hitter in four seasons Saturday night as his Los Angeles Angels beat the Baltimore Orioles 2-0 in Los Angeles. Belinsky struck out nine, walked four and twice had runners on third base in scoring his fourth victory against no defeats.

Details, sports section.

57 Viet Cong Killed in Mop-Up

SAIGON (AP)—Fifty-seven communist guerrillas reportedly were killed Sunday in a large government mopping up operation in the Mekong River delta supported by U.S. Marine Corps helicopters.

According to a first account from an informed source, no government losses were reported.

Units of the Vietnamese Civil Guard were airlifted into the attack zone near the town of Tra Keo about 70 miles southwest of Saigon early Sunday morning. Government troops reportedly caught a Viet Cong concentration completely off guard, and overran the communists quickly.

Captured communist equipment reportedly included five rifles, five carbines and eleven pounds of TNT.

The airlift was provided by H-34 troop-carrying helicopters flown and serviced by the Marine Corps' 362d Helicopter Co. stationed at Soc Trang in the delta.

The site of operation is in Vinh Binh Province, on a finger of land largely covered by mangrove swamps and heavily infiltrated by the Viet Cong.

Elsewhere about 1,000 Viet Cong attacked a land development center 90 miles west of Saigon Friday night and killed 13 civilians, Vietnam Press reported Sunday. The semi-official government (Continued on Back Page, Col. 1)

Air, Ground Forces

4,000-MAN BUILDUP ORDERED IN THAILAND

PACIFIC
STAR AND STRIPES

AN AUTHORIZED PUBLICATION OF
THE ARMED FORCES FAR EAST

10¢ DAILY
15¢ WITH SUPPLEMENTS

Vol. 18, No. 135   **JAPAN EDITION**   Wednesday, May 16, 1962

Given Thailand Commands

U.S. COMMANDERS—Army General Paul D. Harkins (left) has been named to take operational command of a new U.S. Military Assistance Command, Thailand, in addition to similar duties in the Republic of Vietnam. Lt. Gen. James L. Richardson, deputy commander of U.S. Army Pacific, has been given command of all combat units in Thailand. The assignments were announced Tuesday by Admiral Harry D. Felt, commander-in-chief, U.S. Forces Pacific. (USA Photo, left; S&S Photo, right)

President Kennedy orders Army, Air Force and Marine Corps units into Thailand to defend it against a communist thrust. Tactical air units of the Marine Corps and Air Force were to land momentarily.

General Paul D. Harkins is given operational command of U.S. military units in Thailand. Lt. Gen. James L. Richardson Jr. will command combat units in the task force.

The United States and Russia agree on the need for a cease-fire in Laos. Laotian factions delay on resuming negotiations.

The U.S. is reported asking its SEATO Allies to put military forces in the area.

Royal Laotian troops continue to flee into Thailand.

Stories on Pages 1, 5 and 24

Compiled From Wire Services

WASHINGTON — President Kennedy Tuesday ordered air and ground forces into Thailand to guard that Southeast Asian nation against a communist thrust.

The buildup of Army, Air Force and Marine Corps units will add some 4,000 men to the 1,000 American troops already in Thailand, the Defense Department said.

President Kennedy's announcement made plain that U.S. forces will fight if the communists in neighboring Laos cross the Thai border.

Marine Corps and Air Force jet attack planes were due to land in Thailand momentarily as the first units of the buildup.

A contingent of 1,800 marines aboard a Seventh Fleet carrier was to go ashore at dawn Thursday Thailand time (7 a.m. Thursday, Japan time).

Army units will move in in the near future to bolster a battle group already in Thailand.

"These forces are to help insure the territorial integrity of this peaceful country," the President said.

The Defense Department said the marines probably would be landed at the Bangkok naval base by helicopters from the Valley Forge, a carrier converted to a helicopter and troop-carrying ship.

The Valley Forge draws too much water to move into the docking area.

In a follow up to the President's announcement, Defense Secretary Robert S. McNamara said the U.S. military force in Thailand would be given a new over-all command and strengthened to about 5,000 men.

These forces are involved:

1) The 1,000 men of the 1st Battle Group, 27th Inf., 25th Div., from Fort Shafter, Hawaii, which has been in Thailand for nearly a month and is now moving up to the Laotian border.

2) About 1,200 Army men from the Pacific area to be moved in the near future. This will include approximately 1,000 more troops from Hawaii.

3) The 1,800-man marine contingent now poised to land.

4) A Seventh Fleet Marine attack squadron and elements of a 13th Air Force tactical fighter squadron. First units of these were to fly in momentarily and the rest at about the same time the marines are to land, Admiral Harry D. Felt, commander of U.S. Pacific Forces, disclosed in Honolulu. They are from Pacific bases.

General Paul D. Harkins, now commander of the 6,000-man advisory force in the Republic of Vietnam, will be given the job of heading U.S. forces in both Thailand and Vietnam.

A spokesman said Lt. Gen. James L. Richardson Jr., deputy commander of U.S. Army forces in the Pacific, has

(Continued on Back Page, Col. 1)

Reorganization Set For 41st Air Div.

FUCHU AS, Japan (5th AF)—The 41st Air Div. will be reorganized June 1 and its headquarters moved July 1 from Johnson AS to Yokota AB to increase the air defense capabilities of the U.S. Air Force in Japan.

Announcement of the move was made Wednesday by Lt. Gen. Jacob E. Smart, commander, U.S. Forces Japan and Fifth Air Force.

He said Brig. Gen. Thomas R. Ford, 41st Air Div. commander since June 1, 1961, will take command of the Kanto Base Command at Tachikawa AB June 11.

Smart named Col. Leo Hawel Jr., who commands the 3d Bombardment Wing at Yokota AB, as new division commander.

Movement of the headquarters to Yokota has been directed in order to place the operational headquarters as close as possible to its six operational squadrons, Smart explained.

The reorganization, he said, will remove the 8th Tac. Fighter Wing at Itazuke AB on Japan's southernmost island of Kyushu from the air division and place it directly under Hq., Fifth Air Force.

The senior Air Force commander in each of the Air Force defense sectors in Japan will then report directly to Smart.

(Continued on Back Page, Col. 5)

Weather

TOKYO AREA FORECAST

Thursday: Partly cloudy; high 76, low 54.
Friday: Partly cloudy; high 78, low 58.
Tuesday's Temperatures: High 73, low 52.

(USAF Weather Central, Fuchu AS)

Paratroops Dropped In Irian

HOLLANDIA, New Guinea (AP)—Indonesian paratroopers landed near Fakfak, in West New Guinea (West Irian), in a dawn raid Tuesday in an apparent effort to relieve beleaguered comrades, already trapped by Dutch forces.

The exact number of paratroopers was not immediately known but the Dutch say they have counted at least 40 and there could be a total of 80.

Four Dakota C-47 airplanes, supported by two Mitchell B-25 bombers, participated in the mission which it is believed took off from the Indonesian-held Ceram Island, about 120 miles to the southwest.

Dutch forces immediately seal-

(Continued on Back Page, Col. 1)

MARINES IN THAILAND

Unit Lands, Prepares to Move Inland

PACIFIC

STAR AND STRIPES

AN AUTHORIZED PUBLICATION OF
THE ARMED FORCES FAR EAST

10¢ DAILY
15¢ WITH SUPPLEMENTS

Vol. 18, No. 136   JAPAN EDITION   Thursday, May 17, 1962

BANGKOK (UPI) — United States marines, armed and ready for battle, began landing here Thursday by assault ships and helicopters to bolster Thailand's defense against communist aggression.

The first contingent of 485 marines landed shortly before 6 a.m. local time (8 a.m. JST) by helicopter at Don Muang Airport on the outskirts of the Thai capital.

About an hour and one-half later the first troops began landing at Klong Toey, main port of Bangkok, from the troop transport Navarpro.

The group landing by helicopter was made up of marines from various units of the 3d Bn., 9th Marine Regt., 3d Marine Div., based on Okinawa.

The 9th Regt. is classified as a "reinforced" regiment. This, according to Marine Corps sources, means that it has heavy 8-inch howitzers and Honest John rockets.

The first group landed was to begin organizing motorized and airlift convoys for moving the marines to positions closer to the border of neighboring Laos, where communist rebel forces launched a series of attacks that resulted in President Kennedy's decision to send American combat forces to this Southeast Asian country.

Communist China has reacted violently to the American decision to send troops to Thailand, warning through its official newspaper — the Peiping People's Daily — that "The Chinese people cannot remain indifferent."

American officials indicated that the troops of the Marine battalion landing team and other American ground forces would be deployed in a horseshoe-shaped area with a 500-mile front on the Mekong River bordering Laos.

Already in Thailand was a 1,000-man U.S. Army battle group from the 27th Inf. Regt., 25th Inf. Div., from Hawaii.

It is to be reinforced by troops from the parent division and by a unit from Okinawa. Marine airplanes also will be brought in. When all units have landed, U.S. forces in Thailand will number about 5,000. American officials indicated that the chief anchor points for the U.S. forces would be the

(Continued on Back Page, Col. 2)

Russ Readying Tests: Nikita

VARNA, Bulgaria (AP) — Soviet Premier Nikita S. Khrushchev said Wednesday the Soviet Union is preparing a new series of nuclear tests in answer to recent American shots in the atmosphere.

The Soviet leader made the statement to Western correspondents covering his state visit to Bulgaria.

Asked whether he had said earlier in the day that the Soviet Union would renew its atom blasts, Khrushchev replied: "Yes I said it. We are forced to renew our tests because, despite our appeals, the Americans did not refrain from renewing theirs."

Khrushchev spoke with Western newsmen after attacking them during a speech at a public meeting in Varna's main square. "They say one thing and write another,"

(Continued on Back Page, Col. 5)

S.E. Asia Situation

First group of 1,800-man Marine force begins landing in Thailand on heels of arrival of Air Force jet fighters and transports.

Officials in Washington say they expect Australia, New Zealand and perhaps other Pacific allies to send some military forces to Thailand.

Communist China warns it "cannot remain indifferent" to U.S. action in Southeast Asia. Izvestia blames U.S. for new tension.

Laotian rebels say they will not surrender Nam Tha.

Details on pages 1, 5 and 24

Nominate 2 Backed By Ike

WASHINGTON (AP) — Two men endorsed by former President Dwight D. Eisenhower won Republican gubernatorial nominations by heavy margins in Nebraska and Pennsylvania and Gov.

HARTFORD, Conn. (UPI) — Sen. Prescott Bush, 67, (R-Conn.) announced Wednesday he would not seek re-election and Rep. Horace Seely-Brown (R-Conn.) announced his candidacy for the Senate.

J. Millard Tawes won Democratic renomination in Maryland by a surprisingly large margin.

The Eisenhower-backed winners in Tuesday's primary elections were Rep. William Scranton in Pennsylvania and former Secretary of the Interior Fred Seaton in Nebraska.

Tawes handed Baltimore contractor George Mahoney his

(Continued on Back Page, Col. 2)

Chofu Work Under Way

TACHIKAWA AB, Japan (OI) — Ground was broken Thursday during ancient Shinto purification rites for the 900-unit family housing area at Chofu that will replace housing at Tokyo's Washington Heights.

Attending were Col. Lloyd W. Brauer, vice commander of the Kanto Base Command, top officials from the Japanese Ministry of Construction, and representatives from U.S. commands in the Kanto Plain.

The first phase of the construction, 240 family housing

(Continued on Back Page, Col. 5)

4 Die Fighting B-47 Flames

UP IN FLAMES — Black clouds of smoke billow from a burning Air Force B-47 bomber which exploded as it was being prepared for a flight at Whiteman AFB, Mo. Four firemen died fighting the blaze. Story, Page 24. (AP Radiophoto)

Identify U.S. Units Aiding Thais

WASHINGTON (AP) — The Air Force is sending reconnaissance, transport and tanker planes into Thailand from Okinawa and Japan.

A Defense Department spokesman disclosed this in identifying the various Army, Marine, Navy and Air Force elements taking part in the 5,000-man U.S. operation to defend Thailand's border.

The main Air Force unit is the 510th Tactical Fighter Sq., flying F-100 fighter bombers, from Clark AB in the Philippines.

The RF-101 reconnaissance planes are the 15th Tactical Recon Sq. from Okinawa and the 45th Tactical Recon Sq. from Japan.

Also moving in from Japan are big C-130 and C-124 transport planes and KB-50 tankers, along with communications and air rescue detachments.

(Stars and Stripes Washington Bureau said the C-130 and C-124 transports are from the 315th Air Division and the KB-50 tankers are from the 421st Aerial Refueling Sq., both based in Japan.)

The Air Force's Mobile Strike

(Continued on Back Page, Col. 1)

Weather

TOKYO AREA FORECAST

Friday: Cloudy with occasional light rain; high 65, low 54
Saturday: Cloudy becoming partly cloudy; high 70, low 55
Wednesday's Temperature: high 62, low 54
(USAF Weather Central, Fuchu AB)

Thailand Buildup Pushed

Compiled From Wire Services

BANGKOK—An additional 500 American soldiers and marines began landing Saturday at Karat Airfield, about 130 miles northeast of Bangkok, to bolster the 2,800 U.S. combat troops already in Thailand, according to high-ranking military sources here.

The sources said an advance party of 185 members of the Hawaii-based 1st Battle Group, 27th Inf. Regt. 25th Div., arrived here aboard two U.S. Military Transport C-135 jets Saturday.

They will be joined momentarily by about 300 others of the same unit.

Most of the 500 American troops being flown here aboard five U.S. Air Force transports are combat specialists and combat troops of the 27th Inf., 25th Div., which already has 1,000 men deployed near Karat. The new group also includes a small number of marines.

They join about 1,000 compatriots who have been in Thailand almost a month participating in after the (Continued on Back Page, Col. 4)

Peiping Sounds Warning

TOKYO (UPI) — Communist China Saturday declared she "can absolutely not tolerate . . . any new military bridgeheads" by the United States in areas bordering on the China mainland.

In one of her strongest warnings in years, Red China said if war comes in Southeast Asia the United States "will suffer a worse defeat than it did in Korea."

"We must serve a fresh warning to the Kennedy government that it shall be held fully responsible for all grave consequences arising from its policy of playing with fire," the official Peiping People's Daily said in an editorial.

The editorial was broadcast in (Continued on Back Page, Col. 2)

Thousands Visit U.S. Bases in F.E.

TOKYO (S&S)—American servicemen in the Far East Saturday — Armed Forces Day—opened their bases to thousands of Asian neighbors in a "Partners for Peace" program to show how they work in defense of peace throughout the year.

At some bases in Japan the celebration was held over to Sunday, a day of rest for many Japanese, to give more of them an opportunity to take a close look at static displays of aircraft and Americans at work and to join in athletic contests.

The 13th annual Armed Forces

Day was also observed on Okinawa, in the Republic of Korea, on Guam, in the Philippines and on Taiwan. But, in the face of increased tension in Southeast Asia, Americans stayed alert.

Thousands of Japanese were welcomed at Camp Zama, Hq., U.S. Army Japan and Fifth Air Force bases at Itazuke and Misawa.

Sailors at U.S. Fleet Activities, Yokosuka and Sasebo, on Kyushu, and marines at Iwakuni MCAF on southern Honshu (Continued on Page 6, Col. 1)

Hurled at U.S. Billet

3 SOLDIERS HURT BY SAIGON BOMB

PACIFIC STAR AND STRIPES

AN AUTHORIZED PUBLICATION OF THE ARMED FORCES FAR EAST

10¢ DAILY
15¢ WITH SUPPLEMENTS

Vol. 18, No. 139   JAPAN EDITION   Sunday, May 20, 1962

Bishop's Car Injures 20 at Church Parade

NEW YORK (AP)—A bishop's car went out of control during a children's religious parade in New York Saturday and plowed into a crowd, injuring some 20 persons, mostly children. At least two of the children were reported in critical condition at one of two hospitals where the injured were taken.

Police said Auxiliary Bishop Joseph P. Denning of the Brooklyn Roman Catholic Diocese, who was to administer the sacrament of confirmation to which the children were marching, was the driver of the car.

Bishop Denning, 55, had just alighted from his car, police said, when it started to roll ahead. He jumped back inside and put his foot on what he thought was the brake. Instead his foot struck the accelerator.

The car sped into the crowd watching the parade and witnesses said two children were dragged half a block before the auto could be stopped.

Many of the injured children were members of a drum and bugle corps which had been marching in the processional to St. Rita's. They had stepped aside to join those watching the remainder of the parade.

After going to the police station for brief questioning, Bishop Denning returned to St. Rita's Catholic Church in Astoria and administered the sacrament of confirmation.

During the services, he asked (Continued on Back Page, Col. 1)

Scott in 'Orbit'

ASTRONAUT'S BOUNCE—Astronaut Lt. Cdr. M. Scott Carpenter bounces high in the air as he exercises on a trampoline at Cape Canaveral, Fla., during training for his orbital flight, which has been postponed again, until Thursday. Story on Page 24.   (AP Radiophoto)

SAIGON (AP)—Three American servicemen and eight Vietnamese were injured Saturday night by a homemade bomb thrown onto a crowded sidewalk in front of the United States military billet near downtown Saigon.

It was the second bombing incident in the city in three days and touched off widespread fears that this capital of the Republic of Vietnam is in for a campaign of violence. Two Germans were injured slightly Thursday night when a bomb was thrown into a sidewalk cafe.

The bombs in both Thursday's and Saturday's incidents were said to be of the same type, crude homemade devices fashioned from pipes.

None of the 11 persons hit by fragments Saturday was believed to have been injured seriously. The three Americans were rushed to a dispensary for treatment. Injured among the Vietnamese on the crowded sidewalk in front of a nearby theater were five children and three adults.

(UPI said all three Americans (Continued on Back Page, Col. 3)

GOP Blocks Progress, JFK Says

NEW YORK (AP) — A frankly partisan President Kennedy, accepting a "birthday salute" at Madison Square Garden Saturday night, accused the Republican Party of trying to stop his program at virtually every turn.

Telling a huge Democratic rally that his program is "a policy of constructive action" on every front, Kennedy added: "Our opponents prefer to be against everything."

In his prepared speech, he accused the Republicans of being "against every new program, against every appropriation, against every attempt to help the individual citizen find a better life for himself and his family."

To the cheers of Democrats who had paid up to $1,000 a head to attend the celebration—a birthday which actually will occur May 29—Kennedy said:

"We stand for a world community of free and independent nations—and we have broken (Continued on Back Page, Col. 2)

Weather

TOKYO AREA FORECAST

Monday: Cloudy with rain: High 67, Low 58
Tuesday: Cloudy to partly cloudy; High 70, Low 58
Saturday's Temperatures: High 67, Low 55

4 U.S. Officers Wounded in Vietnam

SAIGON (UPI)—Four U.S. Army officers were wounded Wednesday and one U.S. helicopter damaged in a fiercely fought battle against communist guerrillas about 75 miles southwest of here, a U.S. military spokesman reported.

An informed source told newsmen that among those wounded was Lt. Col. Frank B. Clay, son of retired General Lucius D. Clay and senior adviser to the Vietnamese 7th Div., which planned and carried out the operation.

Clay was not seriously wounded and was released by medics after preliminary treatment, the source said.

Others wounded were:

Lt. Col. H. C. Blazzard, wounded (Continued on Back Page, Col. 1)

U.S. TO TAKE IN H'KONG REFUGEES

PACIFIC
STAR AND STRIPES
AN AUTHORIZED PUBLICATION OF THE ARMED FORCES FAR EAST
10¢ DAILY
15¢ WITH SUPPLEMENTS

Vol. 18, No. 143   JAPAN EDITION   Thursday, May 24, 1962

WASHINGTON (UPI)—President Kennedy said Wednesday the United States plans to take in several thousand Chinese refugees from Hong Kong who are already on waiting lists.

This was the first concrete step by the United States to aid thousands of hungry mainland Chinese who have been seeking to enter the British crown colony but have been turned back because Hong Kong already is overcrowded.

Kennedy's statements were made at a news conference. He was asked whether there was any possibility of the United States providing surplus grain to communist China. He replied that the communist regime had given no indication of interest in or desire for such help and that the U.S. government would want some idea about the need for such help before considering it.

Kennedy indicated the U.S. action would be taken under parole provisions similar to those under which Hungarian refugees were admitted to this country on an emergency basis in 1956.

The president said the United States would continue, as it has in the past, to provide surplus U.S. food to Hong Kong.

The United States has been providing food for about half a million refugees in Hong Kong, he said, and several thousand refugees have been cleared by consular officials for admission to the United States.

(Justice Department officials said admission of refugees from (Continued on Back Page, Col. 2)

Jet Breaks Up in Storm; 45 Dead

National guardsmen and rescue squads remove the bodies of victims from the main part of the fuselage of a Continental Airlines Boeing 707 jet which crashed Tuesday night about 20 miles southwest of Centerville, Iowa. Forty-five passengers died in the crash. The plane was en route from Chicago to Kansas City. (AP Radiophoto)

List of Dead—Page 5

UNIONVILLE, Mo. (AP)—A Continental Airlines jet came apart in storm-laced skies Tuesday night, possibly under hammering of fierce winds, and fell to earth in pieces. All 45 persons aboard lost their lives.

A young Japanese-born engineer survived the crash and seven agonizing hours in the wreckage, but died in a hospital about 70 minutes after he was rescued early Wednesday when the full scope of the tragedy became known.

Authorities said there was a possibility the $5.5 million plane was literally torn to pieces by tornadic winds.

The chance that it had collided with a small plane also was being (Continued on Back Page, Col. 4)

Say Reds Stemming Refugees

Pictures, Pages 12, 13

HONG KONG (AP)—Unconfirmed reports from Hong Kong's frontier said Red China border guards began late Wednesday to curb the flow of refugees into Hong Kong.

The reports from border area residents said communist guards first shouted orders that groups waiting to cross should return to their home villages and then fired warning shots at those who still attempted to cross.

(UPI reported more than 6,000 refugees were deported from Hong Kong Tuesday.)

Orbit 'Go' Weighed

CAPE CANAVERAL, Fla. (UPI)—Launch crews Wednesday successfully completed the first phase of the split countdown for Navy Lt. Cdr. M. Scott Carpenter's scheduled orbital flight Thursday and officials said the "go" or "no go" decision would be made Wednesday evening.

If scientists decide to proceed, the countdown will be resumed at 11:30 p.m. EST Wednesday (1:30 p.m. JST Thursday).

A spokesman indicated that everything checked out perfect in the space vehicle in the first (Continued on Back Page, Col. 4)

2 Red Guards Shot In Berlin Wall Duel

BERLIN (AP)—West Berlin police Wednesday shot two East German border guards who were firing on a 15-year-old boy refugee, a police spokesman said.

The spokesman said one border guard was hit and fell from a wall. The second staggered away with his tunic open. Both were carried off in an ambulance.

The East border guards shot first, police said, firing several hundred rounds from submachine guns.

Their target was a youth swimming the 30-yard wide Landwehr Canal, which forms the inter-sector border in the Tiergarten section of downtown Berlin.

The youth reached the West bank, with severe bullet wounds. He was rushed to a hospital for an emergency operation.

Police said the young refugee had bullet wounds in a lung, thigh and arm.

It was not clear from the Western side whether the Eastern border guards had been killed or wounded.

Two vopos, as the East guards are nicknamed, were standing on a wall, firing bursts from their (Continued on Back Page, Col. 3)

Weather

TOKYO AREA FORECAST

Friday: Fair to partly cloudy; High 78, Low 58.

Saturday: Partly cloudy; High 80, Low 58.

Wednesday's Temperatures: High 70, Low 62.

(USAF Weather Central, Fuchu AS)

3-MAN RULE FOR LAOS

SITUATION AT A GLANCE

Laos' three rival princes sign an agreement setting up a troika-type leadership for their coalition government.

U.S. indicates it will now resume financial aid to Laos.

A State Department spokesman says there are no present plans to pull U.S. troops out of Thailand.

Premier Khrushchev cables President Kennedy that the settlement shows East-West differences can be resolved peacefully.

* * *

PLAINE DES JARRES (UPI)—Laos' three rival princes Tuesday signed an agreement setting up a troika-type leadership that gives each faction, including the pro-communist rebels, veto power over important decisions.

The agreement establishing coalition rule for this jungle kingdom was aimed at ending the nearly two years of civil war that has threatened to spread through Southeast Asia.

But it provided that the neutralist premier-designate, Prince Souvanna Phouma, must have unanimous consent of the pro-Western and pro-communist factions for any major policy move.

"The three princes are in accord that the three important departments of national defense, interior, and foreign affairs will be given to personalities belonging to the party of Prince Souvanna Phouma," the agreement said.

"All decisions related to these three departments must be sanctioned by a unanimous accord of the three chiefs of the factions."

Thus Laos will be governed by the three-headed leadership first proposed by Soviet Premier Nikita Khrushchev to replace the one-man secretary-general's post in the United Nations. It was turned down there as unworkable.

Souvanna will head the government as premier and defense minister, with pro-Western General Phoumi Nosavan and pro-communist rebel Prince Souphanouvong as his deputy premiers. Prince Boun Oum has no office in the coalition.

The agreement divides 19 cabinet posts in the new government among the three factions.

Neutralists will have 11, and the two opposite factions will have four each.

The four cabinet posts that went to the pro-communist Pathet Lao gave them control of the economy, public works and information.

The right wing got control of education and cultural affairs in addition to finance and Phoumi's

(Continued on Back Page, Col. 2)

PACIFIC
STAR AND STRIPES

AN AUTHORIZED PUBLICATION OF THE ARMED FORCES FAR EAST

昭和五十四年一月二十二日第三種郵便物認可紙 175号（日刊）

10¢ DAILY
15¢ WITH SUPPLEMENTS

Vol. 18, No. 163   JAPAN EDITION   Wednesday, June 13, 1962

3 Dig Out of Alcatraz; May Have Fled on Raft

SAN FRANCISCO (AP)—Three Alcatraz convicts vanished Tuesday from the island rock prison after long, secret months of chipping with spoons through their concrete cell walls.

Their escape from three separate cells through air vents into a pipe tunnel apparently was covered for hours without detection by life-like plaster-headed dummies they left in their beds.

Prison officials express belief they used a driftwood raft to flee the island in what may turn out to be the first successful break in the 28-year history of the federal government's toughest prison.

Alcatraz sits like a battleship in San Francisco Bay 1¼ miles north of the city.

A widespread hunt for the three convicts included a military police search of Angel Island, a timbered state park 1¾ miles north of the bleak rock prison.

Eleven previous escape attempts all ended in failure since Alcatraz became a federal prison in 1934. Thirty-five men made the escape tries. Two made the attempt twice.

Tuesday's fugitives were identified as:

Frank Lee Morris, 36, under 14-year sentence for the 1955 burglary of a Slidell, Ala., bank carried out after Morris had escaped from the Louisiana State Prison at Angola. He was serving a 10-year term there for armed robbery.

John W. Anglin, 34, under 15-year sentence for the January, 1958, robbery of the Bank of Columbia, Ala.

Clarence Anglin, 28, John's brother, under 10-year sentence for the Columbia robbery.

Olin D. Blackwell, Alcatraz

(Continued on Back Page, Col. 2)

JFK Cites Red Peril To F.E.

WASHINGTON (UPI)—President Kennedy told Congress Tuesday that free Far Eastern nations are threatened by communist forces known to include 200 combat divisions, more than 4,000 jet aircraft and sizeable naval forces.

In an annual report to the lawmakers on the mutual security program, the President said these communist forces "are being steadily improved through training and modernization."

The report said that in the face of this threat the independent nations of the Far East have increased their self-financed defense efforts by 15 per cent.

The United States, in turn, programmed a total of $782.2 million in military assistance for the area's nations in 1961. The biggest share of this—$260.3 million—went to the Republic of Korea.

In sending the report to Congress, the President said that it "marks the end of one decade in our aid programs and the

(Continued on Back Page, Col. 2)

4th Russian Ship Spying on A-Tests

WASHINGTON (AP)—Russia has sent a fourth ship bristling with scientific instruments to spy on U.S. nuclear tests in the Pacific.

This addition to the Russian "snooper" patrol was disclosed Tuesday as the United States prepared for a second try at firing a nuclear device at a high altitude over Johnston Island.

Informed sources indicated the shot—biggest of the U.S. test series—is likely late this week. The Federal Aviation Agency said Monday the shot more than 500 miles over the test area is expected to instantly blot out all high frequency radio communications—including Loran and other navigational aids—in the Pacific. Some of the disruption will last 32 hours or longer, the FAA said. Some civilian aircraft will be grounded indefinitely because of the communications knockout.

The presence of three Russian instrument ships within 10 to 15 miles of the Pacific test area was announced by the Defense Department 18 days ago. It said they were "obviously on a large-

(Continued on Back Page, Col. 5)

Weather

Tokyo Area Forecast

Thursday: Cloudy; High 74, Low 63
Friday: Mostly cloudy; High 80, Low 66
Tuesday's Temperatures: High 74, Low 63
(USAF Weather Central, Fuchu AS)

Rooney Broke; Owes Half Million

HOLLYWOOD (AP) — Actor Mickey Rooney Tuesday filed petitions of voluntary bankruptcy in federal court here.

Rooney listed debts of $484,914 and assets of $500 worth of household goods and clothes.

His biggest debt, he said, is $168,000 due on a personal loan from Fryman Enterprises, Beverly Hills. The U.S. Internal Revenue Bureau demands $106,686 in income taxes and the State of California $9,826 in state income taxes.

Horses and women both contributed to his financial difficul-

(Continued on Back Page, Col. 5)

U.S. Soldier Defected: Korea Reds

TOKYO (UPI) — An American soldier, who deserted his post near the Demilitarized Zone in Korea almost two weeks ago, has defected to communist north Korea, Pyongyang Radio said in a broadcast monitored here Tuesday.

The soldier is PFC Larry A. Abshier, 18, whose home address was listed in his records as the Illinois Soldiers and Sailors Home. His mother, Mrs. George O. Abshier, lives at Garfield Heights, Ohio, records indicate.

It was not known whether the soldier actually had defected. U.S. military authorities in Seoul indicated earlier that there was a "good possibility" he was hiding

(Continued on Back Page, Col. 1)

This is a general view of Alcatraz island and the federal prison. Some 250 of the nation's most dangerous convicts are housed in the buff-colored cell blocks on the 12-acre island.   (UPI Photo)

House Passes Aid Bill

WASHINGTON (AP)—The House of Representatives passed Tuesday and sent to President Kennedy a $4.672 billion foreign aid program that preserves the President's discretionary authority to give limited aid to communist countries.

The roll call vote was 221 to 162.

The compromise measure, previously passed by the Senate, includes $600 million for the Alliance for Progress this year.

The President had requested $800 million for each of the three fiscal years through 1966.

The authorizing legislation, which must be backed up by the later (Continued on Back Page, Col. 3)

'Crucial' 60-90 Days

MAJOR RED PUSH SEEN IN VIETNAM

PACIFIC
STAR AND STRIPES

AN AUTHORIZED PUBLICATION OF THE ARMED FORCES FAR EAST

昭和三十四年一月二十二日国鉄東京特別承認新聞紙第175号

10¢ DAILY
15¢ WITH SUPPLEMENTS

(昭和34年4月22日第3種郵便認可)

Vol. 18, No. 205   JAPAN EDITION   Wednesday, July 25, 1962

HONOLULU (UPI)—A Defense Department spokesman says the next 60 to 90 days will be the most critical in the struggle against Viet Cong guerrilla forces in the Republic of Vietnam.

The statement came as Defense Secretary Robert S. McNamara concluded a day-long conference on Southeast Asia with advisers and flew back to Washington Tuesday. McNamara was optimistic over measures taken by this country to strengthen Vietnamese military forces.

The spokesman — a member of McNamara's official party — said the Viet Cong forces may make a

WASHINGTON (AP)—Defense Secretary Robert S. McNamara returned from another series of conferences with military leaders in Honolulu Tuesday, "very much encouraged" over the anticommunist struggle in Vietnam but he said he felt it would take years to resolve the situation.

major effort in the next two or three months to seize a portion of southern Vietnam and then press for a negotiated settlement based on the recent Laos neutrality treaty.

The spokesman denied the validity of reports from Saigon that sizable numbers of Pathet Lao troops had crossed the border into Vietnam. He said those reports were at variance with everything discussed at Monday's conference.

McNamara told the conference: "Our military assistance to Vietnam is paying off. The Vietnamese are beginning to hit the Viet Cong insurgents where it hurts the most —in winning the people to the side of the government."

Assistant Defense Secretary for (Continued on Back Page, Col. 1)

No. 19 Joins the Chief's Crew

JOINS THE FOLD—Navy CWO Francis L. Beardsley holds the latest addition to his family, Joseph John, 2 weeks old. The baby brings the family to 21 members. Beardsley, a widower with 10 children, and Mrs. Helen North, a widow with 8 children, were married last September. Gathered around the couple's first baby in their Carmel, Cal., home are (from left, seated) Joan, 1; Beardsley, holding Joseph; Mrs. Beardsley; Teresa, 1, Phillip, 4; Germaine, 4; Gerald, 3, and Joan, 5. Standing are Rosemarie, 12; Colleen 11; Charles, 15 and Gregory, 14. The cake in foreground welcomes Mrs. Beardsley and Joseph home from the hospital.   (AP Photo)

127-MPH Typhoon Aimed at Shikoku

TOKYO (S&S)—Typhoon Louise, her center winds howling at 127 miles an hour, was expected to lash across Shikoku, one of Japan's main islands, late Thursday.

Forecasters at Air Force Weather Central, Fuchu AS, Japan, predicted the island, 400 miles southeast of Tokyo, would be battered by the big storm as it swirled north across the Pacific.

Weathermen said it was too early Wednesday to determine what effect the typhoon would have on weather in the Tokyo area.

Louise was reported 690 miles south-southeast of Tokyo at 9 a.m. Wednesday. The typhoon was (Continued on Back Page, Col. 3)

Telstar Sends Shot Of Berlin Wall

WEST BERLIN (AP)—A live television view of the Red Berlin wall was successfully transmitted to the United States via Telstar Tuesday.

It was the first Telstar transmission from this city, 110 miles behind the Iron Curtain.

The program was sent from Heinrich-Heine-Strasse, in the American sector, where there is a crossing point for West Germans to enter East Berlin.

Viet Reds Capture 2 NCOs; 1 Escapes

SAIGON (UPI)—Communist guerrillas Monday ambushed a hunting party made up of two American military advisers and two Vietnamese militiamen about 100 miles northeast of Saigon, a U.S. military spokesman reported Tuesday.

One of the advisers, M/Sgt.

Carl E. Brown, escaped, the spokesman said. The other American, also a sergeant but not identified, was kidnaped along with one of the Vietnamese, he said.

The spokesman said an "all-out" search by Vietnamese ground troops and aircraft has been under way since late Monday but so far has failed to turn up any trace of the missing men.

The spokesman could furnish no other details, but Vietnamese military sources said the hunting party was ambushed shortly before dusk while riding in a jeep along a jungle road about three miles southwest of a Vietnamese militia training camp near the coastal town of Phan Thiet.

The sources said Brown, of (Continued on Back Page, Col. 2)

Diver Saved From Ocean Trap

YOKOSUKA, Japan (CNFJ)—An American diver was rescued by the Navy Tuesday, after spending two hours trapped in 60 feet of water off South Koshiba, Japan, about five miles north of here.

The diver, Jack M. Philpott of Honolulu, a Department of the Army civilian, became trapped

when the buoy mooring-chain he was checking suddenly shifted, pinning his arm and leg. Philpott is diver foreman of the Operations Div., U.S. Army Transportation Agency, Japan, at North Pier, Yokohama.

The Navy sent a 30-ton floating crane, diving boat and divers from

the Ship Repair Facility here.

Philpott was freed after two Navy divers attached the crane hook to the chain and lifted it free.

Participating in the rescue were Boatswain's Mate/1C James R. Taylor, Indiahoma, Okla., of Ship Repair Facility and Chief Boiler (Continued on Back Page, Col. 3)

Weather

Tokyo Area Forecast
Thursday: Partly cloudy becoming cloudy with showers; High 89, Low 74
Friday: Fair to partly cloudy; High 91, Low 76
Tuesday's Temperatures: High 89, Low 76
(USAF Weather Central, Fuchu AS)

JAPAN EDITION

PACIFIC

STAR STRIPES

10c DAILY
15c WITH SUPPLEMENTS

昭和三十四年一月二十五日國鉄東京局特別扱承認新聞紙第175号（日刊）

（昭和34年4月22日第3種郵便物認可）

Vol. 18, No. 246

AN AUTHORIZED PUBLICATION OF THE U.S. ARMED FORCES IN THE FAR EAST

Tuesday, Sept. 4, 1962

U.S. Aid Airlifted To Iran

WASHINGTON (AP)—The State Department says that over $500,000 in relief measures has been taken to earthquake-stricken Iran.

An airlift was organized to carry 10,000 blankets, 1,000 tents and a 100-bed hospital unit from U.S. Forces in West Germany to Tehran, State Department Press Officer Joseph Reap said.

The relief supplies, aboard 12 planes, are expected to arrive within 48 hours.

In addition, two rescue helicopters are to be flown in.

Direct financial aid also has been provided the Iranian government, Reap said. U.S. Ambassador Julius C. Holmes provided $10,000 in federal funds and the U.S. Agency for International Development also provided $10,000.

The American Red Cross has (Continued on Back Page, Col. 3)

* * *

Fearful Quake Toll Still Rising

TEHRAN, Iran (UPI)—A shocked and bewildered Iran, stricken by the worst earthquake in its 2,500-year recorded history, mobilized all its forces Monday for relief.

Premier Assadollah Alam, who openly wept at the devastation during a tour of the battered northwestern area, told newsmen he estimated the toll of dead and seriously injured at "well above 20,000." This "frightful" figure may rise, he said.

A spokesman for the premier said, "Many more than 10,000 have died, maybe 20,000, maybe more."

Throughout the quake area, thousands of peasants searched for loved ones. Others sat stunned amid piles of mud-brick rubble.

Officials said medical teams were working frantically to prevent an outbreak of disease.

Thousands of troops and civilian (Continued on Back Page, Col. 4)

U.S. Ready to Do More In Vietnam, Taylor Says

General Maxwell D. Taylor, accompanied by U.S. Ambassador to Japan Edwin O. Reischauer (rear) arrives at the American Embassy in Tokyo. Marine embassy guards form an honor guard. Another picture, Page 6. (S&S Photo)

By FOREST KIMLER
S&S Staff Writer

TOKYO—The United States is prepared to do more in the Republic of Vietnam if necessary and does not plan to pull its troops out of Thailand in the near future, General Maxwell D. Taylor declared Monday.

Taylor, special military adviser to President Kennedy, flew into Yokota AB, Japan, Monday from Honolulu on the first leg of a "self-orientation" tour of Asia before becoming chairman of the Joint Chiefs of Staff Oct. 1.

He told newsmen in a planeside press conference that his visit had no particular significance as to added military emphasis in the Far East.

During his last trip to the Far East in October he visited the Republic of Vietnam.

"I think our progress in Vietnam is encouraging," he declared, "and I don't think our efforts there should be criticized.

"That doesn't mean the end is in sight and I am going to talk to the people on the ground here.

"One thing is certain — our whole government is watching the (Continued on Back Page, Col. 2)

'Reds to Help Wall Victims'

GENEVA, Switzerland (AP)—The All-Swiss International Red Cross Committee said Monday East German authorities have pledged first aid to the victims of the Wall, provided there is no interference from the Western side. The committee announced that this was the result of recent discussions by its delegate, H. G. Beckh, with the president of the East German Red Cross.

110 Viet Cong Slain In Major Battle

SAIGON (UPI)—More than 110 communist guerrillas were killed Sunday in a major battle south of here as Republic of Vietnam forces leaped from U.S. helicopters and nearly destroyed a crack battalion of Viet Cong regulars, informed American military sources said Monday.

The sources said communist casualties were climbing as reports flowed in from government units still returning from the field.

Confirming earlier reports of the government press agency and adding details, the sources said the battle involved some 2,000 government troops, including the crack Ranger companies.

They said blocking forces of civil guards and self-defense corps —militiamen—were used to trap the guerrillas.

The battle was kicked off early Sunday as 10 U.S. Army helicopters airlifted the Rangers and civil guards in waves into two strike zones on the eastern edge of the Plain of Reeds, some 30 miles south of Saigon.

In one strike zone, the communists fled across the flooded rice paddies and man-high reeds after light contact. In the second target in the Ben Tranh Province, the Rangers and civil guards surrounded the communist 514th Bn. in the village of Hung Thanh My where they had gone to celebrate the (Continued on Back Page, Col. 1)

Russians Defy U.S. In Berlin

WEST BERLIN (UPI) — The Russians defied Western Allied instructions Monday and sent three more armored cars past Checkpoint Charlie into the American Zone.

But an Allied spokesman said no more Red convoys will be allowed through as soon as a 'deadline' given to the Soviets expires.

The exact time when the deadline runs out was not disclosed. But it was understood to be either Tuesday or Wednesday.

After that Soviet convoys will be barred from crossing Checkpoint Charlie at the Friedrichstrasse crossing point, the spokesman said.

Some 250 West Berliners, ap- (Continued on Back Page, Col. 1)

MAY BE AIMED AT MOON

Mariner's 'Ears' Wander

PASADENA, Cal. (AP)—The antenna of the Venus-aimed spacecraft Mariner 2 may be locked electronically on the moon instead of the earth, delaying plans for a course adjustment.

Scientists added, however, that the problem can be solved and is not a threat to success of the mission. The delay was called for greater assurance of success.

The delicate and critical course change, designed to bring the flying laboratory within 10,000 miles of the planet Venus, had been scheduled for Monday. Without correction Mariner would miss by more than 200,000 miles and fail to achieve certain goals.

An announcement from the vehicle's designer, the Jet Propulsion Laboratory, said a delay of at least 24 hours is necessary to determine whether the antenna—supposed to beam signals back to earth—is trained on earth or moon.

The yard-wide antenna was swung out Sunday on command from a timer aboard the 447- pound craft. Laboratory scientists afterward announced that it had achieved "earth acquisition" — meaning it was locked electronically on the earth. The next step was to be a signal, from earth, ordering a small rocket motor to blast for a few seconds, adjusting the course. Then the scientists found the antenna may be aimed at the moon.

The announcement said it is not detrimental to the long range success of the mission (Continued on Back Page, Col. 2)

Weather

Tokyo Area Forecast

Wednesday: Partly cloudy, showers; High 83, Low 74
Thursday: Partly cloudy; High 85, Low 75
Monday's Temperatures: High 84, Low 74
(USAF Weather Central, Fuchu AB)

Yanks Win It All 1-0 on Terry's Gem

SAN FRANCISCO (AP)—The New York Yankees won their 20th world championship Tuesday—the hard way in the finale of a seven-game Series that will go down in the books as one of the most exciting ever. The Bronx Bombers beat the San Francisco Giants 1-0 behind the 4-hit pitching of Ralph Terry.

The only run scored on a double play in the fifth inning.

The Giants put runners on second and third with two out in the ninth on a bunt single by Matty

Other Pictures, details, pages 19, 20, 21 and 24.

Alou and a double by Willie Mays but Willie McCovey lined to Bobby Richardson on Terry's second pitch to end the game.

It was the second straight world championship for the American League perennials and they did it in the showdown, seventh game and 13th day of the weather-plagued Series, winning four games to three.

It was the second victory for the 26-year-old Terry in the competition. He had won the fifth game 5-3 after losing a 2-0

(Continued on Page 20, Col. 1)

VIET REDS DOWN 2 U.S. PLANES

PACIFIC STARS AND STRIPES

AN AUTHORIZED PUBLICATION OF THE ARMED FORCES IN THE FAR EAST

JAPAN EDITION

昭和三十四年一月二十二日国鉄東局特別扱承認新聞紙第175号（日刊）
（昭和34年4月22日第3種郵便物認可）

Vol. 18, No. 289   **Wednesday, Oct. 17, 1962**

10¢ DAILY
15¢ WITH SUPPLEMENTS

Compiled From Wire Services

SAIGON—Viet Cong communists have shot down two U.S. aircraft in the Republic of Vietnam's highlands, killing three Americans.

A big U.S. Army H-21 helicopter was also destroyed—deliberately—because a mechanical failure forced it down in communist-controlled territory.

The first crash was Monday afternoon. An L-28 spotter plane was downed by communist groundfire north of Ban Me Thuot, killing the three Americans aboard.

A U.S. Air Force T-28 fighter plane flying over the wreckage Tuesday morning was also downed by the communists but the American pilot survived after riding his crippled plane down.

Guerrillas opened up on the hovering U.S. spotter plane with automatic weapons late Monday during a daring government raid on communist positions in mountainous jungle 10 mile north of Ban Me Thuot.

The first announcement of the L-28 crash said the cause had not immediately been determined.

In Washington, the Defense Department identified those killed in the crash of the L-28 as Air Force Capt. Herbert W. Booth, the pilot, whose wife is Nancy J. Booth of Sarasota, Fla.; Army Capt. Terry D. Cordell, whose wife is Mrs. Susan M. Cordell of Sanford, Fla., and Air Force T/Sgt. Richard L. Fox, whose wife is Mary J. Fox

(Continued on Back Page, Col. 1)

* * *

New U.S. Role in Vietnam

By MALCOLM W. BROWNE

SAIGON (AP)—U.S. servicemen, who in the past have served purely as support for the Republic of Vietnam's war against communist guerrillas, are moving closer to active combat roles.

The old directive—not to shoot at the Viet Cong until the Viet Cong shoot first—apparently is no longer rigorously applied.

While there has been no official change in top policy, it has become clear in recent weeks that American servicemen may now fire the first shots, provided they feel they must protect themselves.

U.S. Marine Corps and Army helicopter gunners often open fire as they move toward objectives, to "sanitize" areas of possible snipers.

The new turbine-powered HU-1A, with fixed, forward-firing

(Continued on Back Page, Col. 4)

New York Yankee pitcher Ralph Terry is carried off the field on the shoulders of his teammates and fans after he held the San Francisco Giants to four hits to give the Yankees the World Series. The Yankees downed the Giants 1-0 at Candlestick Park in San Francisco. (AP Radiophoto)

U.S. Indicts 2 Congressmen

Compiled From Wire Services

BALTIMORE—Two Democratic congressmen, Thomas F. Johnson of Maryland and Frank W. Boykin of Alabama, have been indicted on charges of receiving money for interceding in behalf of an accused mail fraud operator.

A special federal grand jury which has been sitting since last December returned the indictments Tuesday. They charge a conspiracy in behalf of J. Kenneth Edlin, 63, of Miami and Baltimore.

The indictments involved almost $25,000 in alleged payments and

at least $3.25 million in real estate transactions.

Atty. Gen. Robert F. Kennedy said the two congressmen were charged with conspiring to accept the money and to participate in the real estate deal in exchange for attempting to influence the Justice Department to dismiss an indictment against Edlin, a Maryland savings and loan association figure.

Boykin, whose name had been linked with the Maryland savings and loan scandal previously, was defeated this summer in Alabama's Democratic primary.

Edlin and Miami attorney William L. Robinson, 37, an associate, also were named as defendants in the eight-count indictment.

Kennedy said the conspiracy count listed 36 separate or joint telephone, mail or personal contacts made by the congressmen with the Justice Department in behalf of Edlin between March and November, 1961.

The first count of the indictment charged the four defendants with conspiring from April, 1960, to December, 1961, to defraud the United States by trying to obstruct the impartial

(Continued on Back Page, Col. 2)

JFK, Gromyko Meeting Set

WASHINGTON (UPI)—President Kennedy and Soviet Foreign Minister Andrei A. Gromyko will meet Thursday, the White House announced.

No official reason was given for the meeting, which comes amid growing U.S. concern about a possible new and serious East-West flare-up over Berlin.

But there was some speculation in official quarters here that Gromyko might use the occasion to arrange for an American visit by Soviet Premier Nikita S. Khrushchev.

Weather

Tokyo Area Forecast

Thursday: Partly Cloudy; High 68, Low 52

Friday: Cloudy; High 70, Low 58

Tuesday's Temperatures: High 67

(USAF Weather Central, Fuchu AS)

Blast Wrecks Indiana Plant—10 Die

TERRE HAUTE, Ind. (AP) — An explosion ripped the Wabash River plant of the Home Packing Co. here Wednesday morning, killing at least 10 workers and injuring 55, four of them seriously.

One hundred rescue workers, wearing gas masks, dug into a mountain of rubble, hunting for victims.

Ten bodies were recovered by late Wednesday and at least five more were believed buried under tons of brick.

About 1,200 day workers had just reported for duty when the blast demolished a third of the two-story meat packing plant about 7:30 a.m.

The plant had been closed for the Christmas holidays. Some firemen thought a gas leak may have caused the blast, but a fire department official said, "I just don't know. No one smelled anything—it just went whoomp."

Ammonia fumes gushed from broken refrigeration lines after the explosion.

Among the dead was Donald W. Scott, a salesman and brother of the firm's president, Robert Scott.

George Obenchain, secretary-treasurer, estimated damage to the plant at close to $2 million.

(Continued on Back Page Col. 1)

PACIFIC STAR AND STRIPES

AN AUTHORIZED PUBLICATION OF THE U.S. ARMED FORCES IN THE FAR EAST

10c DAILY
15c WITH SUPPLEMENTS

Vol. 19, No. 3   FIVE-STAR EDITION

昭和三十四年一月二十二日国鉄局別扱承認新聞紙第175号（日刊）
（昭和34年4月22日第3種郵便物認可）

Friday, January 4, 1963

BIG VIET BATTLE; 3 AMERICANS DIE

SAIGON (UPI)—A U.S. Army captain and two sergeants were killed Wednesday during a furious battle in which communist gunners shot down five American helicopters in the Plain of Reeds south of Saigon.

Their deaths raised to 30 the number of Americans killed in action since the United States began aiding the Republic of Vietnam in its war with communist rebels.

The Army captain was hit while serving as an adviser to a Vietnamese Army battalion taking

Vietnam's Deadly Waiting Game—Page 5

part in an assault. He was hit in the chest and neck by a burst of automatic weapons fire while helping lead the attack.

He was flown back to the airfield here by helicopters but died while undergoing emergency treatment.

"He was one of the best we had," said one comrade of the unidentified captain. "Like most battalion advisers he was out front trying to help move them on when he got it."

(Continued on Back Page Col. 1)

Philadelphia's Worst Fire

Smoke continues to rise from a fire described as the worst in Philadelphia's history. It destroyed a 9-story factory building, at least 25 homes and 3 other buildings and caused the evacuation of 2,000 persons in 29-degree weather. The 12-alarm fire in north Philadelphia started in the factory building (center) and spread to a row of houses. For a time it threatened a 9-square block area near Temple University but firemen controlled it after more than three hours. No serious injuries were reported. (AP Radiophoto)

Guns Reply To Tshombe

LEOPOLDVILLE, The Congo (UPI)—The United Nations Command, in the face of the heaviest fighting thus far in the current action, pushed an advance assault force across the Lufira River Wednesday in its drive on reported Katangese strongholds at Jadotville and Kolwezi.

A United Nations spokesman (Continued on Back Page, Col. 1)

Weather

Tokyo Area Forecast
Friday: Fair; High 50, Low 23.
Saturday: Fair; High 47, Low 28.
Wednesday's Temperatures: High 48, Low 23.
(USAF Weather Central, Fuchu AS)

Cancer Kills Jack Carson

ENCINO, Cal. (UPI)—Comedian Jack Carson, 52, died at his home Wednesday of cancer.

The heavy-set comedian was stricken with the disease two months ago and failed to respond to treatment. The malignancy was in his liver.

Norstad Gives NATO Reins to Lemnitzer

PARIS (UPI)—General L. L. Lemnitzer took over as supreme commander of NATO forces in Europe Wednesday with a pledge to carry on the Alliance's collective defense "for the preservation of peace and security."

Lemnitzer, 63, assumed his new post in impressive change of command ceremonies from

General Lauris Norstad, 55-year-old U.S. Air Force officer who is retiring to civilian life after six crisis-filled years as chief of the North Atlantic Treaty Organization. He has had 36 years of service in the American armed forces.

Norstad said at the change-over at Allied Headquarters

just outside Paris that Western strength at present provides "confidence and hope" for the future.

Lemnitzer, former chairman of the U.S. Joint Chiefs of Staff, said he would seek to justify the "confidence and trust" placed in him by the 15 NATO member nations. He will com-

mand more than 1 million Allied fighting men.

Norstad later took off by plane for Lisbon and Ottawa for short farewell visits to Portugal and Canada, both members of the Atlantic Alliance, on his way home to Washington and retirement.

(Continued on Back Page, Col. 2)

Telstar Fixed in Space Feat—TV on Again

Compiled From Wire Services

NEW YORK—Two multi-million dollar communications satellites, long silent because of malfunctions, spoke up Friday and performed their duties as though nothing had happened.

Telstar, speechless since last November because of excessive space radiation, was "tricked" into life, enabling scientists to resume live transatlantic television broadcasts.

Relay, which never beeped a sound after its launching last Dec. 13 because of a power drain, suddenly came to life

and relayed television test patterns between Andover, Me., and Pleumeur-Bodou, France.

In Washington, National Aeronautics and Space Administration officials said Relay's three-week journey through space apparently allowed its solar cells to build up to normal energy output.

Viewers on both sides of the Atlantic said the reception of images from both satellites was very clear.

Telstar's radiation sickness was overcome by a kind of electronic aspirin.

Engineers of the Bell Telephone Lab-

oratories diagnosed the trouble and found a way to restore normal operation.

In essence, one transistor in Telstar's command decoder was running an electrical fever, refusing to act on command.

The remedy was a trick code which cut off the electrical fever, not unlike an aspirin.

For 11 minutes Friday, Telstar transmitted a television description of its ailments and remedy from a panel of engineers in New York and then French and British stations transmitted back

their congratulations via the satellite.

"The pictures seem as good as ever," said A. H. Mumford, of the British Post Office. "It is a wonderful achievement, in some respects almost more wonderful than the original launching."

W. C. Hittinger, of Bell Telephone Laboratories, said Telstar had encountered radiation in the Van Allen Belt 100 times greater than anticipated. This caused an ionization in one transistor, particularly in the decoder which receives and acts on commands from the

(Continued on Back Page, Col. 2)

PACIFIC
STARS AND STRIPES

AN AUTHORIZED PUBLICATION OF THE ARMED FORCES FAR EAST

10¢ DAILY
15¢ WITH SUPPLEMENTS

Vol. 19, No. 5   **FIVE-STAR EDITION**   Sunday, January 6, 1963

Terror in Katanga

Belgian miner Albert Verbrugghe gets out of his car screaming and bleeding from face wounds after United Nations troops machine-gunned it near Jadotville, Katanga, Friday. His wife and a friend riding in the car were killed. The car was riddled as Verbrugghe attempted to speed past U.N. troops advancing on Jadotville, an important mining center. (UPI Radiophoto)

U.S. FORCES CAPTURE 17 VIET REDS

TAN HIEP, Vietnam (AP) — A makeshift outfit of about 60 Americans discarded their military advisory role for four hours here Friday to trap communist guerrillas fleeing from the bloody battleground at Ap Bac.

The Americans were ordered into action at 10 a.m. Friday by Col. John Paul Vann, chief American adviser to Vietnam's 7th division. They took 17 communist prisoners before disbanding their hastily assembled force in early afternoon and returning to their advisory duties.

Vann, of El Paso, Tex., said he ordered all available Americans into action to protect an American major at a post in the path of escaping guerrillas near the Mekong River.

Guerrillas had killed 65 government troops in the Ap Bac battle four miles to the north Wednesday.

Vietnamese civil guard reinforcements were expected in the area to block the escape route but as guerrillas started slipping through the rice fields four hours later, they had not arrived, and the major was alone.

Vann said later, "I'm not

(Continued on Back Page, Col. 4)

Report Clay Paid Ransom

DES MOINES, Iowa (AP) — General Lucius D. Clay (ret.) borrowed $1.9 million on his own signature to help meet a $2.9 million ransom asked by Premier Fidel Castro for release of Cuban prisoners, the Minneapolis Tribune and Des Moines Register said Friday

The newspapers said in a copyrighted story from their Washington bureau that Clay now is asking officials of the nation's top corporations to help him repay the loan.

Atty. Gen. Robert F. Kennedy raised the other $1 million in a telephone call to an anonymous friend.

Castro demanded the $2.9 million at the last moment, in addition to $53 million worth of food and medical supplies for the release of 1,113 prisoners of the Bay of Pigs invasion.

Clay, head of an advisory committee assisting the families of the Cuban prisoners and president of the Continental Can Corp., set about trying to raise the $2.9 million as soon as Castro's terms were received.

(Continued on Back Page, Col. 1)

JFK Attends Rites for Kerr

OKLAHOMA CITY (UPI) — President Kennedy attended the funeral of U.S. Sen. Robert S. Kerr of Oklahoma Friday.

A crowd estimated at 10,000 came to pay their last respects to the man who was one of the most powerful men in the U.S. Senate.

After the funeral, Kennedy flew back to Palm Beach, Fla.

Weather

Tokyo Area Forecast

Sunday: Fair; High 46, Low 22.
Monday: Fair; High 45, Low 20.
Friday's Temperatures: High 46, Low 19.
(USAF Weather Central, Fuchu AS)

Fire Strikes Ocean Liner

LONDON (UPI)—The Pacific & Orient Lines liner Canberra was reported proceeding under her own power to Malta Friday night after an early morning fire in her engine room.

The liner's crew put out the fire. No one was injured when the more than 2,000 passengers were called from their beds to lifeboat stations, the line's spokesman in London said.

The liner Strathaven was standing by the Canberra, which was expected to berth in Malta Saturday night.

U.S. Opposes Congo Truce; U.N. Troops Halt Advance

Compiled From Wire Services

WASHINGTON — The United States reportedly is trying to convince Britain, Belgium and the United Nations that it would not make sense to stop action by U.N. forces in Katanga now that Katanga President Moise Tshombe and his forces are on the run.

The reports of these diplomatic communications came Friday following reports charging that the United Nations had violated an understanding with the Belgians whereby U.N. troops would not enter

Jadotville, the important mining center in Katanga.

Jadotville was taken Thursday by U.N. Indian troops led by Brigadier Reginald Naronha.

The report of the diplomatic maneuvers followed a U.S. statement urging Tshombe to give up his secessionist ambitions and cooperate with the United Nations in Congo reunification.

"We expect Mr. Tshombe to end promptly the Katanga secession," a U.S. government statement said.

U.S. State Department sources stress that it would be

illogical, both politically and militarily, to restrain the United Nations from going ahead and wiping out secessionist ambitions.

Tshombe is believed to be in his last remaining stronghold of Kolwezi, 180 miles northwest of Elisabethville.

Officials in Washington said Tshombe is still threatening to use the scorched earth policy and poisoned arrows to support his secessionist ambitions and has made no attempt to communicate either directly or in-

(Continued on Back Page, Col. 5)

VC HIT SAIGON

Reds Invade Embassy, Air Base

PACIFIC

STARS STRIPES

AN AUTHORIZED PUBLICATION OF THE
U.S. ARMED FORCES IN THE FAR EAST

10¢

Vol. 24, No. 31   FIVE-STAR EDITION   Thursday, Feb. 1, 1963

SAIGON (UPI)—Viet Cong forces launched heavy attacks against Saigon Wednesday. Guerrillas fought their way into the U.S. Embassy and occupied five floors of it for several hours.

Other Reds invaded Saigon's Tan Son Nhut airport and battled American and Vietnamese troops and tanks.

American military policemen fought around the gleaming, new embassy for more than four hours. Helicopters dropped troops onto a roof-top pad to help rout the Communist suicide squad.

Radio reports from the embassy reported at 9:15 a.m. that it was secure and said 19 Viet Cong had been killed inside.

American casualties were reported as eight dead with an unknown number wounded.

Another 21 U.S. military police were killed while defending the military billets.

A U.S. spokesman said Ambassador Ellsworth Bunker was not in the embassy when it was attacked.

"There were no senior officials in there," the spokesman said.

The Communists bombed at least four American military hotels in Saigon and struck Independence Palace, the office of President Nguyen Van Thieu, with rockets and mortars in a pre-dawn raid. There was fighting in the streets near the palace.

The headquarters of the South Vietnamese military also came under ground attack.

The attacks were the most audacious of the new Communist offensive which erupted in eight cities Tuesday.

The attacks in Saigon began shortly before midnight. One of the American billets was reported still under heavy attack at mid-morning.

The Communist force fought defenders on three sides of Tan Son Nhut and then battled their way inside the barbed wire.

The military police made several assaults against the Embassy but the Viet Cong threw grenades and drove them back.

Saigon Radio also was attacked. A U.S. tank that came to rescue it was knocked out. But at mid-morning it broadcast a curfew announcement by Vice President Nguyen Cao Ky.

Viet Cong terrorists stole an American jeep with a .50-caliber machine gun mounted on the

(Continued on Back Page, Col. 4)

A South Vietnamese soldier fires from behind an improvised barricade during street fighting in Da Nang. A dead guerrilla lies in right background. At left is a fleeing man, and more furniture used by soldiers as barricades.   (AP Radiophoto)

Blast Kills 9, Hurts 20 Near Pittsburgh

Compiled From AP and UPI

PITTSBURGH — A bone-jarring explosion ripped through a business district in suburban Ingram Tuesday, killing at least nine persons and injuring 20 others.

The explosion leveled two buildings where utility workers were searching for a gas leak. Five of the dead were members of a 15-man gas company crew boring test holes in the street.

"There's nothing there," said one of the first newsmen on the scene. "I can't even tell what was there."

The explosion threw debris in all directions and shattered windows of homes and stores blocks away. Bits of clothing hung grotesquely from phone lines as a shroud of smoke drifted over the area.

A gas company spokesman said the 15-man crew was working on a four-inch low-pressure main. He said the gas was turned off at the curb bordering the buildings.

"At this time we have no idea what caused the explosion," the spokesman said.

Bulldozers and highlifts were used to clear away the rubble. Four of the bodies were taken from the smouldering debris.

"It sounded just like a bomb," said Mrs. Samuel Simpson, who lives just across a railroad track from the blast scene. She said she was walking into her kitchen when the explosion took place.

"I looked out and saw people and debris everywhere. It blew one of the workers clear across the tracks."

Gas and electric power were shut off over a wide area of the community, which has a population of about 6,000. A grade school about two blocks from the blast scene was evacuated.

Runaway In 1st Gear

LONDON (UPI) — Gareth Reeves ran away from home Monday.

But before slipping out of the house he left a note saying, "I'm leaving . . . and taking the car with me . . ."

Now his parents are not only wondering where he and the car have gone, but how he learned to drive. Gareth is 12.

PACIFIC STAR AND STRIPES

AN AUTHORIZED PUBLICATION OF THE
U.S. ARMED FORCES IN THE FAR EAST

10¢ DAILY
15¢ WITH SUPPLEMENTS

Vol. 19, No. 145   FIVE-STAR EDITION   昭和三十四年一月二十二日国鉄東京局特別扱承認新聞紙第175号（日刊）
（昭和34年4月22日第3種郵便物認可）   Sunday, May 26, 1963

'5 Russ Died in Space'

NEW YORK (AP) — High congressional and space authorities have reported evidence of manned Russian space shot failures, with perhaps as many as five or more cosmonaut fatalities, the New York Journal-American said Friday.

The reports came after a federal space agency official told a congressional subcommittee there have been Soviet failures, but refused to divulge any information on abortive manned Russian space efforts.

George L. Simpson Jr., an assistant administrator of the National Aeronautics and Space Administration, indicated he would be willing to testify more fully in a closed session.

Official secrecy was maintained at NASA, at the Department of Defense and the Central Intelligence Agency.

(Continued on Back Page, Col. 1)

House Unit Slashes Military Building Funds

WASHINGTON (UPI)—The House Armed Services Committee—reflecting the mood of an economy-minded Congress — cut nearly $243 million Friday from Pentagon requests for military construction projects at home and abroad.

The committee approved a $1.66 billion measure authorizing buildings, hospital and other facilities at military bases.

Large chunks of the funds, still needing congressional approval, would go to installations throughout the Far East, including some in the Republic of Korea, Okinawa, Japan, the Philippines and the islands of Midway, Guam and Wake.

Included in the measure were 10,000 new homes which Defense Secretary Robert S. McNamara said were needed to house some service-men now living in "shocking" quarters. Those homes will cost $181.51 million.

The Defense Department sent to the committee—headed by Rep. Carl Vinson (D-Ga.) — requests totaling $1.87 billion. The committee whacked about 13 per cent from that figure. The vote was unanimous.

Defense agencies had their re-

(Continued on Back Page, Col. 3)

Pouncing on a Viet Red

A communist Viet Cong soldier is captured during a helicopter raid in Bac Lieu Province, Republic of Vietnam, and searched by SP5 Albert L. Apel of the 114th Air Mobile Co. before being loaded aboard a helicopter for a quick flight to a rehabilitation center. Twelve communists were captured in this raid. Related Story, Page 4. (S&S Photo by SP6 Henry C. T. Chang)

Injunction Sought Against Wallace

WASHINGTON (UPI) — The Justice Department asked the U.S. District Court in Birmingham, Ala., Friday to issue an injunction preventing Gov. George Wallace from interfering with the enrollment of Negroes at the University of Alabama.

Atty. Gen. Robert F. Kennedy said the complaint was filed to get an immediate court test of Wallace's announced position of "legal resistance and legal defiance" of Federal Court orders admitting two Negroes to the University June 10.

Wallace has said he personally will bar enrollment of Negroes Vivian J. Malone and David M. McGlathery to the University.

The complaint was filed in the same court where Judge H. Hobart Grooms on May 21 ordered Miss Malone and McGlathery admitted to the University under a 1955 court order.

Judge Seybourn H. Lynne set a hearing for June 3, to show cause why the order should not be issued.

Shortly after Grooms ordered the two Negroes admitted, Wallace publicly stated he would be present to bar the entrance of any Negro attempting to enroll in the University. He said this would test his "constitutional standing" as Governor and as "direct representative" of the people of Alabama.

Judge Lynne ordered Wallace to appear before him June 3 in Birmingham to show cause why the preliminary injunction should not be issued.

"This action is brought by the United States in its sovereign capacity to safeguard the due administration of justice in its courts and the integrity of its judicial process," said the complaint filed by Atty. Gen. Kennedy.

The Justice Department, answering the constitutional challenge from Wallace, had told the Supreme Court Thursday the Federal Government has an obligation to preserve order and safeguard individual rights if there is a breakdown of local authority.

The statement was made in the Federal Government's answer to a motion filed with the Supreme Court by Wallace challenging President Kennedy's decision to station troops in Alabama during the Birmingham racial crisis.

Wallace's suit asked the court to declare unconstitutional a section of law which Kennedy used

(Continued on Back Page, Col. 1)

Inside Today

The Mercury space program is nearing a close, with the Gemini program just around the corner. So what happens to America's seven original astronauts? See Page 2.

• • •

Mutual respect may replace suspicion between the U.S. and Canada now that the Canadians have a new prime minister. Walter Lippmann. Page 8.

• • •

What to do about telephone calls to a teenage boy—at all hours of the night—is a problem brought to Abby on Page 17.

Kennedy 'Steels' the Show From Ike

NEW YORK (UPI)—President Kennedy got a star-spangled birthday salute from some of his wealthier fans and he topped off the fun by gently kidding his Republican predecessor and the steel industry.

The President, who will be 46 on Wednesday, was given a birthday party by some 600 rooters who paid $1,000 apiece to the Democratic Party to attend what a Kennedy aide insisted was a "non-partisan" affair Thursday night.

For putting up their money, members of the New York President's Club were visited at their tables by Kennedy during dinner. They also saw an all-star show that $600,000 couldn't buy, and heard their guest of honor at his jocular best. A hundred club members had donated $1,000 each to Kennedy's political cause.

The dinner and show at the Waldorf-Astoria capped a one-day visit to Manhattan. Kennedy re-turned to Washington Friday morning. He was to be honored and entertained again Friday night at the annual White House Press Dinner.

Before joining his well-wishers, Kennedy stopped at the Waldorf Towers apartment of 88-year-old Herbert Hoover for a 10-minute courtesy call on the former Republican president. Another former GOP president, Dwight D. Eisenhower, also was in the hotel but Kennedy did not see him.

Instead, Kennedy told his audience that Eisenhower was nearby receiving from the steel industry

(Continued on Back Page, Col. 1)

Weather

Tokyo Area Forecast
Sunday: Cloudy with rain; High 72, Low 60
Monday: Cloudy; High 75, Low 57
Friday's Temperatures: High 74, Low 55
(USAF Weather Central, Fuchu AS)

NEGROES ENROLLED
Wallace Makes Stand, Then Bows

National Guard Brig. Gen. Henry Graham informs Alabama Gov. George Wallace (left photo) that the state guard was under federal control and must enforce the admittance of two Negro students to the University of Alabama as the two meet at the door of Foster Auditorium at the University. At right, University Dean of Admissions Herbert Mate confers with Vivian Malone and James Hood after Wallace was forced to allow the Negroes to enter and sign up for their courses during the next school term. (AP Radiophotos)

PACIFIC
STARS AND STRIPES

AN AUTHORIZED PUBLICATION OF
THE ARMED FORCES FAR EAST

10¢ DAILY
15¢ WITH SUPPLEMENTS

Vol. 19, No. 163   **FIVE-STAR EDITION**   Thursday, June 13, 1963

A Fiery Suicide In Saigon Protest

SAIGON (AP) An aging Buddhist monk surrounded by 300 fellow monks calmly put a match to his gasoline-drenched yellow robes in a main intersection here Tuesday and burned to death before thousands of watching Vietnamese.

The victim, the Rev. Quang Duc, more than 70 years old, was protesting what he called government persecution of Buddhists. Banners carried by nuns and monks encircling him read "a

Buddhist priest burns himself for five requests."

The grisly demonstration was the latest in a wave of incidents between Buddhists and Saigon government authorities. The Buddhists demand guarantees of religious freedom and social justice. The government denies it has discriminated against any religion.

(United Press International reported President Ngo Dinh Diem later charged in a nationwide radio broadcast that the demonstration was staged by "a number of people (who) got intoxicated (Continued on Back Page, Col. 1)

(Continued on Back Page, Col. 1)

Inside Today

Association with Hitler's Nazi Germany cast Wagner's music into the shadow for years. Now his works are making a comeback. Page 16.

*   *   *

The money is still in the pot waiting to be taken. To see how close you came to winning Coinprize A-7, read Page 14.

Caracas Reds Hit U.S. Site

CARACAS, Venezuela (UPI)— Pro-Castro terrorists carrying Tommy guns attacked and burned the U.S.-owned Goodyear Tire and Rubber Co. warehouse Tuesday. There were no casualties but damage was estimated at about $500,000.

Police said at least four men were involved in the attack and said some of them, identified by a warehouse night watchman, were members of the Venezuelan Communist Party. They used two stolen cars for the raid.

Tuesday's attack came less than 24 hours after Deputy
(Continued on Back Page, Col 2)

(Continued on Back Page, Col 2)

TUSCALOOSA, Ala. (AP)—The segregation barrier raised by Gov. George C. Wallace at the University of Alabama fell without a shot Tuesday.

Two Negro students were enrolled under the protection of Alabama National Guardsmen called to the national colors by President Kennedy.

The fiery segregationist governor of Alabama, who had made his promised threshold stand by barring the students Tuesday morning, made no effort to resist the might invoked by the federal government after the student turndown.

He climbed into a car and rode away after commenting that it was a "bitter pill" for Alabama guardsmen to have to enforce desegregation.

Beaten in Tuesday's quickly developing events, he nevertheless proclaimed:

"We are winning this fight because we are awakening the people of the nation to the trend toward military dictatorship...we must have no violence today or any day."

A few minutes after he made this statement at Foster Hall, where he made his doorway stand Tuesday morning, the two Negroes quietly walked in with federal officials and marshals, paid their fees and registered.

Thus a last citadel of U.S. segregation fell. Alabama had been the only state in the union without at least token integration of some public educational facilities.

With green-clad National Guardsmen standing on the alert at Foster Hall, the registration of the Negroes came almost as an anticlimax.

Vivian Juanita Malone, 20, who is bent on studying
(Continued on Back Page, Col. 1)

(Continued on Back Page, Col. 1)

JFK Commends Alabama Student Body

WASHINGTON (AP) — President Kennedy said Tuesday night of the entry of Negroes to the University of Alabama under troop escort that he hopes "every American will stop and examine his conscience" about this and other incidents.

Kennedy said there is in American cities "a rising tide of discontent that threatens the public safety."

Kennedy addressed the nation by radio and television on a chain of events that wound up with the admission of two Negroes to the University of Alabama at Tuscaloosa under troop escort.

Kennedy had commanded Alabama Gov. George C. Wallace to cease what the President called "unlawful obstructions" to admission of Vivian Malone and James Hood.

At the University of Alabama, the President said, the fact that two qualified Negroes were enrolled was due in large measure to the attitude of other students.

Kennedy first outlined the day's developments in Tuscaloosa, noting that Alabama National

to force registration of two qualified Alabama residents "who happened to have been born Negro."

He praised the conduct of the students at the university.

He said students of any color ought to be able to select their college without having to be backed up with federal troops.

Consumers should be able to get service in places like hotels
(Continued on Back Page, Col. 1)

(Continued on Back Page, Col. 1)

Guardsmen were necessary to force registration of two qualified Alabama residents "who happened to have been born Negro."

Weather

Tokyo Area Forecast

Thursday: Cloudy with rain: High 72. Low 65
Friday: Cloudy with rain: High 70. Low 63
Tuesday's Temperatures: High 74. Low 66
(USAF Weather Central Fuchu AS)

U.S. TROOPS SEEN OUT OF VIET BY '65

PACIFIC STARS AND STRIPES

AN AUTHORIZED PUBLICATION OF THE ARMED FORCES IN THE FAR EAST

FIVE-STAR EDITION

昭和三十四年一月二十二日国鉄東局特別扱承認新聞紙第175号（日刊）
（昭和34年4月21日第3種郵便物認可）

10¢ DAILY
15¢ WITH SUPPLEMENTS

Vol. 19, No. 276   Friday, Oct. 4, 1963

President Kennedy gets a firsthand report on the situation in the Republic of Vietnam from General Maxwell D. Taylor (left), chairman of the Joint Chiefs of Staff, and Defense Secretary Robert McNamara. (AP Photo)

Koufax, L.A. Top N.Y. 5-2

Compiled From AP and UPI

NEW YORK—Lefthander Sandy Koufax set a World Series strikeout record Wednesday as he pitched the Los Angeles Dodgers to a 5-2 victory over the New York Yankees in the first game of the fall classic.

Catcher John Roseboro powered the Dodgers to the win with a three-run homer into the right field stands

off New York starter Whitey Ford capping a four-run outburst in the second inning. Bill Skowron, a former Yankee, drove in the other runs with two singles.

Koufax, 25-5 during the regular season, struck out 15 Yankees, one more than Carl Erskine of the Brooklyn Dodgers did against the Yankees, 10 years ago to the day.

Roseboro set another Series record with a total of 18 putouts on strikeouts and fouls to smash the mark held by Mickey Cochrane of the Detroit Tigers and Roy Campanella of the old Brooklyn Dodgers.

The Yanks, who managed to get only 6 hits off Koufax, scored all their runs in the eighth inning on a homer by Tom Tresh.

The crowd of 69,000 at Yankee Stadium also saw the team strikeout mark set. The total of 25 strikeouts for the two teams bettered the old mark of 22 established by the St. Louis Cardinals and the St. Louis Browns in 1944.

SANDY KOUFAX

WASHINGTON (UPI) — The White House said Wednesday night after hearing a report from a two-man inspection team that the U.S. military effort in the Republic of Vietnam should be completed by the end of 1965.

The White House said the situation in the Southeast Asian country was "deeply serious."

The statement came after President Kennedy met for nearly an hour with the full Security Council to hear a detailed report on the Vietnamese situation from Defense Secretary Robert S. McNamara and General Maxwell D. Taylor, chairman of the Joint Chiefs of Staff.

McNamara and Taylor returned to the U.S. early in the day after an on-site survey.

Highlights of the White House statement:

1—The U.S. government will continue to support the people and government of south Vietnam in their battle against the aggression of the communist Viet Cong.

2—McNamara and Taylor conceded that improvements could be made in the current military program but they thought progress had been made recently.

(Continued on Back Page, Col. 2)

JFK Signs Military Pay Bill

WASHINGTON (AP) — President Kennedy signed Wednesday, with "great pleasure," a bill granting an average 14.4 per cent pay increase to most of the 2.7 million men and women in the U.S. armed forces.

In a cabinet room ceremony, Kennedy used more than a dozen fountain pens to sign the measure, which will cost the government $1.2 billion a year. It is the biggest military pay boost in history.

Kennedy said that, while he is impressed with new and powerful weapons, he is mindful
(Continued on Back Page, Col. 1)

1931 GANG KILLINGS

Valachi Fingers Genovese

WASHINGTON (AP)—Joseph Valachi Wednesday linked Vito Genovese—the man he says now runs a U.S. criminal syndicate from a prison cell—to the 1931 violent deaths of two gangland bosses.

Tracing the history of the syndicate known as La Cosa Nostra,

Valachi did not name Genovese as the actual killer, but told the Senate investigations subcommittee:

1) The shooting of Guiseppi Massaria, alias Joe the Boss, in a Coney Island (N.Y.) restaurant in April 1931 was set up by "Charles Lucky," Vito Genovese

and Ciro Terranova."

2) Salvatore Maranzano, gunned down the following September, had been in a meeting that day with Genovese and Charles Lucky.

Massaria and Maranzano at the time were leaders of rival
(Continued on Back Page, Col. 2)

Weather

Tokyo Area Forecast
Friday: Cloudy; High 68, Low 58
Saturday: Partly Cloudy; High 70, Low 56
Wednesday's Temperatures: High 75, Low 47
(USAF Weather Central, Fuchu AS)

FIERY MONK SUICIDE

★ ★ ★ ★ ★ ★ ★ ★ ★ ★ ★ ★ ★ ★ ★ ★ ★ ★ ★ ★

Viet Police Beat 3 U.S. Newsmen

Rusk Protests Beatings

WASHINGTON (UPI) —Secretary of State Dean Rusk said Saturday that the United States will press the Republic of Vietnam government for an explanation of the beating Saturday of three American newsmen by secret police in Saigon.

In addition, Senate Democratic leader Mike Mansfield of Montana denounced mistreatment of the three and said the Vietnam government should apologize and pay damages.

The newsmen were badly beaten by the secret police of President Ngo Dinh Diem while covering the latest human torch suicide of a Buddhist monk. They are David Halberstam of the New York Times and two National Broadcasting Co. representatives, Don Sharkey and Grant Wolfkill.

Rusk reported that U.S. Ambassador Henry Cabot Lodge has protested the incident to the Vietnam government "in the most serious terms."

"The treatment of news correspondents," Rusk said, "is a matter that the United States has pressed with the authorities of Vietnam for many months. Unfortunately, repeated assurance given to American officials (Continued on Back Page, Col. 1)

PACIFIC

STAR STRIPES

AN AUTHORIZED PUBLICATION OF THE ARMED FORCES IN THE FAR EAST

FIVE-STAR EDITION

昭和三十四年一月二十二日国鉄東局特別扱承認新聞紙第175号（日刊）
（昭和34年4月21日第3種郵便物認可）

10¢ DAILY
15¢ WITH SUPPLEMENTS

Vol. 19, No. 279   Monday, Oct. 7, 1963

A young Buddhist monk burns himself to death in Saigon's central market. It was the sixth protest suicide in the Republic of Vietnam in the last four months and the second in public by a monk. (AP Radiophoto)

Weather

Tokyo Area Forecast
Monday: Partly cloudy; High 70, Low 58
Tuesday: Partly cloudy; High 69, Low 56
Saturday's Temperatures: High 74, Low 57
(USAF Weather Central, Fuchu AS)

SAIGON (AP) — A young Buddhist monk burned himself to death before hundreds of stunned spectators in Saigon Saturday.

The fiery suicide set off a rapid-fire chain of events.

It brought another confrontation between the U.S. government and the authoritarian regime of President Ngo Dinh Diem.

It also raised the specter of more protest suicides and anti-government demonstrations.

Three American newsmen covering the suicide outside Saigon's teeming central market were beaten by plainclothes Vietnamese police.

And Henry Cabot Lodge, the new U.S. ambassador here, promptly protested to the Vietnamese government.

Lodge said he "objected strongly to the way American citizens had been treated." His protest stated this was "not a proper way to treat men who are doing their duty and who had a perfect right to be there."

The suicide monk was identified in a Buddhist leaflet as Thich Quang Huong. He was the sixth Buddhist to burn himself alive in protest against Diem's regime in the last four months.

His suicide brought troops and riot police rushing to the scene. Tanks and armored cars were posted at downtown intersections (Continued on Back Page, Col. 1)

Overseas Pay Cut 'Unfair'

TOKYO (UPI) — American servicemen in Japan greeted with groans, gloom and bitterness the news that their special foreign duty pay has been eliminated.

And they got plenty of sympathy from buddies elsewhere in the Far East who won't be affected by the measure.

Of 15 career enlisted men polled from all services in Japan Saturday, 12 said the measure was unfair. Three said it would create hardships for them and their families. All asked that their names not be used.

Several said the measure caught them by surprise. Some said they went out and bought refrigerators, television sets — even cars — on buy-now pay-later plans in anticipation of pay raises they would receive under the general military pay increase voted by Congress earlier this week.

But, they noted, the order eliminating their foreign duty pay, issued Friday by Defense Secretary Robert McNamara, will all but cancel out new raises.

"We got a raise on one hand only to have it taken away on the other," one Air Force sergeant said.

The sergeant said he received a $20-a-month pay raise, which is taxable, under the increase, but now will lose his $16-a-month foreign duty pay, which is not taxable. The result would be about a dollar increase over his old pay, he said.

"That just about eliminates any (Continued on Back Page, Col. 1)

Drysdale Blanks Yanks 1-0; N.Y. Needs 4 the Hard Way

Details, Page 19

LOS ANGELES (AP) — Don Drysdale stopped the New York Yankees on 3 hits Saturday and the Los Angeles Dodgers, capitalizing on their only break, beat the American League champions for the third straight time in the World Series 1-0.

The Dodgers can clinch the championship by winning the fourth game Sunday. Their ace, first game winner Sandy Koufax, is scheduled to pitch against Yankee ace Whitey Ford.

Los Angeles scored the third game's only run in the first inning on a walk, a wild pitch after two were out, and Tommy Davis' single that caromed off the glove of Yankee second baseman Bobby Richardson.

Drysdale, a 19-game winner this year after winning 25 last year

when he was awarded the Cy Young Trophy as top pitcher in the majors, had been saved for the Dodgers' home opener so that the lefthanders, Koufax and Johnny Podres, could pitch at Yankee Stadium.

He came through with a strong game all the way, striking out nine men and walking only one.

Bouton, a sturdy young man who graduated from the Yankee bullpen in May, had trouble with his control. But he deserved a better fate. The Dodgers got only four hits off him in his seven-inning string and all four were singles.

Shoup Impressed

By S/SGT. VERNON HAMILTON
S&S Staff Writer

TOKYO (S&S) — Marine Corps Commandant General David M. Shoup said Saturday that most Leathernecks stationed in the Far East today have better housing, recreation, and mess facilities than when he last visited Asia in (Continued on Back Page, Col. 2)

Nazi Newlyweds Catch Heil

LONDON (AP) — The leader of Britain's neo-Nazi movement took a French bride Saturday and set off on his honeymoon in a shower of eggs, stink bombs and mud clods.

The wedding of Colin Jordan, 40, and Francoise Dior, 31, niece of the late fashion king Christian Dior, was solemnized in a

civil ceremony at the Coventry register office.

Disorder broke out when Jordan and Francoise emerged and greeted an angry crowd of 500 with Nazi salutes. A police cordon of 30 protected the newlyweds from booing and cheering spectators and escorted them to a waiting taxi. They appear-

ed to have escaped any direct hits from the missiles hurled in their direction.

One of the followers of Jordan's movement who yelled "sieg heil" as his leader emerged from the register office was less lucky. A piece of turf thrown from across the (Continued on Back Page, Col. 3)

'VIET VICTORY NEAR'
1,000 to Leave Soon—Harkins

By S/SGT. STEVE STIBBENS
S&S Staff Writer

SAIGON—The top two U.S. military leaders in Vietnam say that "victory, in the sense it would apply to this kind of war" is just months away and the reduction of American advisers can begin at any time now.

General Paul D. Harkins, over-all commander of the 15,000 American troops in this country, told Pacific Stars and Stripes that "about 1,000 troops will be gone from Vietnam by the end of this year" and will not be replaced.

Harkins' personnel chief said detailed reduction plans have been drawn up and approval from the Pacific commander-in-chief in Hawaii is expected "within a few days."

Defense Secretary Robert S. McNamara said earlier this month in Washington that it might be possible soon to start cutting U.S. military strength here.

It is expected that the bulk of the first strength cut will come from the approximate 60 per cent which makes up the rear echelon administrative and logistics element.

In separate interviews, both Harkins, who is commanding general, U.S. Forces Military Assistance Command, and Maj. Gen. Charles J. Timmes, chief of the U.S. Military Assistance Advisory Group, painted a highly optimistic picture of the military effort here.

Timmes, who commands all U.S. field advisers in Vietnam, explained that "our job here was to train an army for the Government of Vietnam."

"I feel that we have completed that part," he said. **"The Vietnamese armed forces are as professional as you can get. Sure, they worry about political and religious disputes but, just like the American soldier,** (Continued on Page 5, Col. 2)

GEN. PAUL D. HARKINS

MAJ. GEN. C. J. TIMMES

PACIFIC STARS STRIPES

AN AUTHORIZED PUBLICATION OF THE ARMED FORCES IN THE FAR EAST

FIVE-STAR EDITION

昭和三十四年一月二十二日国鉄東京特別扱承認新聞紙第175号（日刊）
（昭和34年4月21日第3種郵便物認可）

10¢ DAILY
15¢ WITH
SUPPLEMENTS

Vol. 19, No. 304   Friday, Nov. 1, 1963

American, Russian Nabbed in Spy Plot

John W. Butenko, 38, ducks his head to avoid having his picture taken as he is escorted by FBI agents to jail in Newark, N. J., after being arrested on charges of passing classified information to the Russian U.N. delegation.   (UPI Photo)

NEWARK, N.J. (AP)—The FBI Tuesday night arrested an American electronics engineer and a chauffeur for a Russian trading agency on spy conspiracy charges.

Two Russian diplomats also were detained but later were released because they had diplomatic immunity. A third Soviet diplomat was named in charges filed (Continued on Back Page, Col. 4)

3 Aides Seized In Vietnam Battle

SAIGON (AP) — Communist guerrillas smashed a Republic of Vietnam task force after disrupting its radio communications Tuesday, and probably captured al' three U.S. Army advisers with the 120-man Saigon outfit.

The three Americans, listed as missing and believed captured, were two officers and an enlisted medic. Stragglers returning from the rout said both officers had been wounded early in the fight —one in the head and the other in the leg.

The Army identified the three as Capt. Humbert R. Versace, Baltimore; 1st Lt. James M. Rowe, McAllen, Tex.; and Sgt. Daniel L. Pitzer, Spring Lake, N.C.

A second government force of about 200 men, operating only a few thousand yards from the main fight, learned of the disaster too late to help. U.S. authorities said communist radio jammers had knocked out both the main channel and the alternate channel on all local military radios.

The operation cost the Vietnamese special forces an estimated 20 killed, 30 wounded and 12 missing and presumed captured. Heavy weapons losses included a 60-millimeter mortar. Viet Cong losses were unknown.

Late in the day, the U.S. casualty list rose to four, when the U.S. Air Force pilot of a light spotting plane was hit by an enemy machinegun. The pilot flew back to base, however, and was evacuated to Saigon.

The fight was in the same general area 140 miles southwest of (Continued on Back Page, Col. 2)

Tycoon in the Broom Closet

NEW YORK (UPI)—A janitor at a New York City high school made $53,000 last year—more than any other public official in the United States, with the exception of the President and Vice President, it was disclosed Tuesday.

The high-salaried city employe is D. Paul Bishop, 66, supervisor of a 15-member janitorial staff at Bushwick High School in Brooklyn.

Eugene E. Hult, superintendent of design, construction and physical plans for New York City, said it was reported last week that Bishop made $43,695

from a Board of Education allowance. But these figures were based on an old contract. A check of the new contract disclosed the higher sum.

The high price of cleaning the city's schools has been under investigation by a special (Continued on Back Page, Col. 3)

Weather

Tokyo Area Forecast
Friday: Fair; High 70, Low 45
Saturday: Partly Cloudy; High 68, Low 47
Wednesday's Temperatures: High 71, Low 51
(USAF Weather Central, Fuchu AS)

DIEM TOPPLED
Military Forces Rule Saigon

PACIFIC
STARS AND STRIPES
AN AUTHORIZED PUBLICATION OF THE ARMED FORCES FAR EAST
10¢ DAILY
15¢ WITH SUPPLEMENTS

Vol. 19, No. 306   FIVE-STAR EDITION   Sunday, Nov. 3, 1963

By AL KRAMER
S&S Staff Writer

TOKYO—A military revolt toppled the government of President Ngo Dinh Diem Saturday after bitter fighting in the streets of the Republic of Vietnam's capital city.

In a direct telephone call to Saigon, a U.S. military spokesman told *Pacific Stars and Stripes* the Diem government had surrendered to the

Other Stories, pictures, Pages 6, 19 and 24.

rebel forces after artillery and mortar fire demolished the presidential palace.

The spokesman said there were no American casualties in the fighting, but the toll among Vietnamese troops was believed high.

The Vietnamese government was being run Saturday morning by a council of generals who led the revolt, the spokesman said.

He said the council had named former Vice President Nguyen Ngoc Tho to head a new government under the title of prime minister.

Rebel forces were in control of the city Saturday morning, the spokesman said.

But he added that scattered gunfire was still heard

(Continued on Back Page, Col. 1)

ICE SHOW BLAST KILLS 68 IN U.S.

INDIANAPOLIS (AP) — An explosion and masses of roaring flame blew out a 60-foot section of seats in the Indiana State Fairgrounds Coliseum Thursday night, three minutes before the scheduled end of an opening-night performance of Holiday on Ice.

Stunned Indianapolis officials, many of them among the 4,000 spectators, reported a

Story and Pictures, Pages 12-13.

death toll of 68, with 39 persons gravely injured.

City and state fire officials agreed the explosion evidently was from gas of an undetermined type.

The blast lifted a section of 128 box seats and dumped them on a stretch of 240 bleacher seats just below.

Bodies were thrown high in the air and fell on the ice amid the skaters. The stars of the show were waiting in the wings to skate out for the finale. It was a glittering production, representing the Mardi Gras, and the band was playing Dixieland jazz.

The band kept on playing and

(Continued on Back Page, Col. 4)

Inside Today

Maj. Gen. Duong Van Minh, a former presidential adviser, reportedly headed the military revolt in the Republic of Vietnam Friday which has overthrown the government.
(AP Radiophoto)

U.S. Protection For Americans

WASHINGTON (AP) — The United States Friday ordered military forces to move toward the Republic of Vietnam area to protect American lives if necessary.

A Pentagon announcement emphasized that this is purely a precautionary measure for protection of Americans, and does not represent any participation by U.S. forces in the situation in South Vietnam.

The announcement by Arthur Sylvester, assistant secretary of defense for public affairs, said:

"As a precautionary measure and with approval of the President, Secretary of Defense McNamara has directed the movement of U.S. military forces toward the area of South Vietnam.

"The order went out through the Joint Chiefs of Staff to Admiral H. D. Felt, commander in chief, Pacific, to take the necessary action."

"This order has been given should it be necessary to protect American lives in South Vietnam.

(Continued on Back Page, Col. 4)

Not Involved in Coup, U.S. Declares

Compiled From AP and UPI

WASHINGTON — The United States Friday emphatically declared it had nothing to do with the military coup in the Republic of Vietnam.

Richard I. Phillips, State Department press officer, said:

"I can categorically state that the United States government was not in any way involved in this coup attempt."

Other officials said all U.S. aid to Vietnam was being held up pending the outcome of developments.

President Kennedy met in urgent conference with top military and diplomatic advisers to evaluate the coup. The 10 a.m. (EST) session followed at least seven hours of close watch on the developing situation.

Kennedy had been roused at 3 a.m. with first reports and had received a full briefing at 6 a.m.

Secretary of State Dean Rusk had been on the job since well before dawn, and high-command offices in the Pentagon were manned.

Pierre Salinger, White House press secretary, said those called to meet with Kennedy included Rusk, Defense Secretary Robert S. McNamara, Chairman of the Joint Chiefs of Staff General Maxwell Taylor, Under Secretary of State Averell Harriman, Assistant Secretary of State for Far Eastern Affairs Roger Hilsman and McGeorge

Bundy, Kennedy's special assistant for national security affairs.

While his name was not on the

(Continued on Page 6, Col. 5)

Weather

Tokyo Area Forecast

Sunday: Partly Cloudy; High 68, Low 50.
Monday: Cloudy; High 62, Low 53.
Friday's Temperatures: High 62, Low 52.
(USAF Weather Central, Fuchu AS)

DIEM, NHU DEAD— FIGHTING IS OVER

★ ★ ★ ★ ★ ★ ★ ★ ★ ★ ★ ★ ★ ★ ★ ★ ★ ★ ★ ★

Saigon—A Happy Mob Scene

PACIFIC
STARS AND STRIPES

AN AUTHORIZED PUBLICATION OF
THE ARMED FORCES FAR EAST

10¢ DAILY
15¢ WITH SUPPLEMENTS

Vol. 19, No. 307   FIVE-STAR EDITION   Monday, Nov. 4, 1963

Compiled From AP and UPI Dispatches

SAIGON—The nine-year regime of Republic of Vietnam President Ngo Dinh Diem and his strongman brother Ngo Dinh Nhu ended with their deaths Saturday.

The end came for the controversial pair after an 18-hour military revolt spearheaded by Vietnamese Marines.

The revolt began Friday and toppled the government Saturday after bitter fighting in the streets of the capital city.

An air of "calm and normalcy" had settled over Saigon Sunday, a U.S. military spokesman reported. "There is nothing particularly unusual

Pictures, Pages 12-13.

this (Sunday) morning," he said. "Things are fast returning to normal."

How Diem and his brother met their end remained uncertain— but there was little doubt about their deaths.

(Continued on Back Page, Col. 2)

A crowd jeers a statue being carried through the streets of Saigon following the military coup. The statue was demolished because of its resemblance to Madame Nhu, the President's sister-in-law.   (AP Radiophoto)

Vietnam At Glance

Republic of Vietnam President Ngo Dinh Diem and his brother-in-law Ngo Dinh Nhu are dead. Military controls Saigon. Page 1.

* * *

The United States prepares to recognize the new government. Page 1.

* * *

Elements of the 3d Marine Div. head for Southeast Asia. Page 6.

* * *

Madame Nhu calls the death of her husband and Diem a "dirty crime and nothing less than murder." Page 3.

* * *

Overjoyed Saigon crowds celebrate the successful coup. Page 1.

U.S. Set To Give OK

WASHINGTON (AP)- The United States is preparing to recognize the new Republic of Vietnam regime early next week probably Monday following the formation of a mixed military-civilian government.

U.S. officials disclosed this Saturday after President Kennedy canceled plans to attend an Air Force Academy-Army football game in Chicago to confer with top military and State Department (Continued on Back Page, Col. 1)

SAIGON (AP) — Tens of thousands of Vietnamese danced and paraded through littered streets in Saigon Saturday in a rowdy and exuberant celebration of the overthrow of the authoritarian government of Ngo Dinh Diem.

There was little doubt the coup was a popular one. But in some sections of the city celebrants got out of hand, pillaging pro-government newspaper, smashing pro-government stores and tearing down government statues and posters.

For the first few hours victorious revolutionary troops stood by, not interfering. But by noon they started moving in to protect property and to restore order.

Weather

Tokyo Area Forecast

Monday: Partly Cloudy; High 60, Low 49

Tuesday: Fair; High 63, Low 47

Saturday's Temperatures; High 63, Low 44

(USAF Weather Central, Fuchu AS)

"We did not want to interfere at first," a Vietnamese colonel told the Associated Press. "The people have looked too long on the Army as its enemy. We want to re-establish the fact that we are all friends now."

Students paraded through the streets with banners proclaiming "Down with Diem, down with Nhu," a reference to Diem's brother and once powerful adviser.

They stormed into the National Assembly building (Continued on Back Page, Col. 5)

MILITARY SPENDING REQUEST SLASHED

PACIFIC
STARS AND STRIPES

AN AUTHORIZED PUBLICATION OF
THE ARMED FORCES FAR EAST

10¢ DAILY
15¢ WITH SUPPLEMENTS

Vol. 20, No. 19   **FIVE-STAR EDITION**   Monday, Jan. 20, 1964

WASHINGTON (UPI) — President Johnson's new defense budget will slash Air Force manpower and sharply reduce purchases of weapons and equipment for all services, it was learned Saturday.

For the fiscal year starting July 1, Johnson will ask Congress to appropriate $2 billion less for military procurement than the $15.7 billion provided for the current year.

The new military blueprint, which goes to Congress Tuesday, will cut Air Force personnel by more than 16,500 as that service continues to curtail bomber fleets and air bases.

The Navy, on the other hand, will gain close to 8,000 men in an expanding Polaris submarine force and to keep up aircraft carrier fleets that once faced cuts but now seem safe for the next few years.

Army manpower will increase slightly—about 2,500—for continued testing of new air assault units. But the longer range prospect is for a troop cutback. Increases for the air assault experiments, begun this year, have been officially described as temporary.

A highlight for servicemen in the new budget will be a request for a pay raise amounting to $172 million, a cost of living increase on top of the $1.2 billion increase voted last year.

With a net reduction of 6,100 uniformed personnel, the scheduled manpower strengths for the start of the new fiscal year July 1 and for the end June 30, 1965, respectively, will be:

Army: 971,527 and 973,999.

Navy: 669,992 and 677,896.

Marine Corps: 190,000 and 190,060.

Air Force: 855,302 and
(Continued on Back Page, Col. 1)

Johnson To Urge Tax Cut

WASHINGTON (UPI) — President Johnson will tell Congress Monday that the U.S. economy soared to a record $600 billion level late in 1963. He will call for quick approval of the proposed $11.1 billion tax cut to bring greater prosperity this year.

White House sources said Saturday that Johnson also will picture Senate passage of the House-approved tax reduction as the key to avoiding recession and spurring growth.

The sources, giving an advance peek at the President's economic message, said the Chief Executive would disclose that the gross national product (GNP) has climbed by a record $100 billion during the past three years. He also was expected to announce:

The GNP figure—total of all
(Continued on Back Page, Col. 2)

U.S. crew members of a H-21 combat helicopter lift a wounded gunner from his aircraft to a stretcher after landing at Thanh Phu in the Mekong Delta, Republic of Vietnam. Six Americans have died in the battle. **(AP Radiophoto)**

Kennedy Spends Day at the DMZ

ALONG THE DMZ IN KOREA (UPI)—Atty. Gen. Robert F. Kennedy stood on the Korean truce line Sunday and looked through a field telescope at north Korean communist fortifications 2½ miles away.

Kennedy, who spent Saturday night with American troops about three miles behind the demilitarized zone, went in the morning to the front to visit observation post "Mazie," manned by the 1st Recon. Sq. of the 9th Cavalry, 1st Cav. Div.

The outpost is located on a hill which overlooks the DMZ, separating communist north Ko-

Kennedy Visits Tokyo's Waseda University, Page 6

rea from the Republic of Korea, where American and ROK troops are on guard in the 10-year-old armistice.

The attorney general ate breakfast in the squadron's mess hall and then attended Roman Catholic mass.

He arrived at outpost "Mazie"
(Continued on Back Page, Col. 3)

TOLL RISES TO 6

2 More U.S. Fliers Killed in Viet Battle

SAIGON (UPI) — Two more U.S. Army helicopter men and a British Royal Air Force wing commander were killed Saturday when their HU-1-B helicopter crashed during a battle with Vietnamese communists 65 miles southwest of Saigon.

The helicopter went down in the sea after a strafing run on the communist stronghold at Thanh Phu Island. Vietnamese government troops backed up by air support were in the sec-

ond day of an offensive against communists there.

Loss of the two helicopter men raised to six the number of Americans to lose their lives in the Thanh Phu battle. A seventh U.S. helicopter crewman was killed in a separate action Friday.

The battle was still continuing Sunday, but the Vietnamese communists were demonstrating an ability to break off contact when they wished. Hopes of trapping

large numbers of them have not yet been realized.

Losses in American lives and equipment have been high.

During the two-day assault, the helicopters have run into intense fire from automatic weapons, including the newly introduced .50-caliber heavy antiaircraft machine guns.

A Vietnamese Army observer also was lost on the helicopter which went down Saturday.

Saturday's crash occurred while the helicopter along with several other "Hueys" were protecting unarmed helicopters which were unloading assault troops on the coast near the southernmost tip of Thanh Phu Island.

Vietnamese Air Force fighters and bombers had strafed the landing zone for a half hour before the heliborne assault began to wipe out Viet Cong
(Continued on Page 5, Col. 4)

Weather

Tokyo Area Forecast

Monday: Partly cloudy, High 46, Low 33

Tuesday: Cloudy; High 51, Low 39

Saturday's Temperatures: High 45, Low 40

(USAF Weather Central, Fuchu AS)

PARIS AND PEKING ESTABLISH TIES

PACIFIC
STARS AND STRIPES

AN AUTHORIZED PUBLICATION OF
THE ARMED FORCES FAR EAST

10¢ DAILY
15¢ WITH SUPPLEMENTS

Vol. 20, No. 28   FIVE-STAR EDITION   Wednesday, Jan. 29, 1964

PARIS (UPI)—France and communist China announced jointly Monday they have established diplomatic relations and will name ambassadors to each others' capitals within three months.

Establishment of diplomatic relations was announced in a two-paragraph communique released in Paris and Peking.

It said:

"The government of the French Republic and the government of the People's Republic of China have decided by common agreement to establish diplomatic relations.

"For this purpose they have agreed to name ambassadors within a period of three months."

Recognition of Red China by French President Charles de Gaulle was given despite sharp protests by the United States and other allies of France.

Diplomats here expected it would touch off a chain reaction of recognition of the Peking regime by other countries particularly many French-speaking (Continued on Back Page, Col. 3)

'SITUATION REMAINS GRAVE'

Viet Cong Gaining, McNamara Says

WASHINGTON (UPI)—Defense Secretary Robert S. McNamara reported to Congress Monday that the anti-communist cause in the war in the Republic of Vietnam has deteriorated since the overthrow of the Diem government in November. The communists have made "considerable progress," he said.

The Pentagon chief said the United States must continue to maintain powerful military forces and demonstrate willingness to risk their use despite improved world prospects for peace.

Appearing before the House Armed Services Committee, he said the Russian-Chinese dispute has gone beyond ideology to involve vital Soviet-Chinese interests. But he said this may only increase U.S. difficulties around the world.

McNamara's statements were contained in a 171-page "posture" statement submitted to the committee in support of President Johnson's military spending requests for the new fiscal year beginning July 1. Johnson wants $51.2 billion, compared with $52.3 billion in the current 12 months.

Referring to South Vietnam, McNamara said "the situation there remains grave. . .I must report that they (the communists) have made considerable progress since the coup." (Continued on Back Page, Col. 5)

Stock Tax Hit By Japan

TOKYO (AP)—Japan appealed to the United States Monday to remove restrictions which might impede Japanese liberalization of trade and aid to the underdeveloped nations of Asia.

This keynote was sounded at the opening session of the third U.S.-Japan Committee on Trade and Economic Affairs. It was repeated later by Prime Minister Hayato Ikeda who said that "United States economic policy affects our capacity for economic cooperation."

The conference, which has brought Secretary of State Dean Rusk, Commerce Secretary Luther Hodges, Labor Secretary W. Willard Wirtz and three other top officials to Japan, got under way in an atmosphere of uncertainty created by the French recognition of Red China.

The economic subjects being examined during the meeting may have to be revised in the months that follow in the light of the French move.

The specific restrictions mentioned by Japan during an exchange with President Johnson's top economic adviser, Walter Heller, Wirtz and Interior Under Secretary James K. Carr, centered on the U.S. interest equalization tax, quotas on Japanese exports and (Continued on Page 6, Col. 1)

AP Radiophoto

LOUIS BARBE, COSA NOSTRA FRAUD TRIAL WITNESS, WRITHES IN PAIN AFTER A BOMB EXPLODED IN HIS CAR.

Gang Trial Bombing

CHICAGO (AP) A bomb planted in a parked automobile critically injured a star state witness in a Cosa Nostra fraud trial Monday as he left the Chicago Criminal Courts Building.

Investigators said the bomb was attached to the ignition system of Louis Barbe's car, parked across the street from the courthouse, during the few minutes he was appearing for arraignment before Judge Alexander Napoli.

As Barbe, 32, tried to start the engine the bomb exploded, virtually destroying the automobile and blowing 200 window panes from a factory nearby.

Bleeding from his face and (Continued on Back Page, Col. 3)

Sen. Smith in Race

WASHINGTON (UPI) — Sen. Margaret Chase Smith announced Monday she will run for the presidency to repudiate the argument that a woman should not seek the nation's highest office.

The 66-year old Maine Republican became the first female candidate for the U.S. presidency representing a major party.

She told the Women's National Press Club that she found the arguments against her candidacy "far more compelling" than those arguments raised as (Continued on Page 5, Col. 4)

NEW VIET COUP

General Khanh Seizes Control; 4 Top Junta Members Arrested

PACIFIC STAR STRIPES

AN AUTHORIZED PUBLICATION OF THE ARMED FORCES IN THE FAR EAST

FIVE-STAR EDITION

10¢ DAILY
15¢ WITH
SUPPLEMENTS

昭和三十四年一月二十二日国鉄東局特別扱承認新聞紙第175号（日刊）
（昭和34年4月21日第3種郵便物認可）

Vol. 20, No. 30   Friday, Jan. 31, 1964

19-Ton Satellite Orbited by U.S.

Compiled From AP and UPI

CAPE KENNEDY, Fla. — A Saturn I super rocket propelled the world's heaviest satellite into orbit Wednesday and presumably vaulted the United States over Russia in the race for space rocket supremacy. Forerunner of rockets which will boost American astronauts to the moon, the 164-foot, 562-ton rocket flooded its launching pad with a rush of flame and sent a thunderous shock wave rolling across Cape Kennedy as it blasted off on its first full-scale test flight.

Slightly more than 10 minutes later, the Saturn I—its second stage live for the first time—orbited a mammoth 84-foot-long satellite weighing 37,700 pounds nearly three times heavier than the Russian heavyweight champions of space.

More powerful than six rail-(Continued on Back Page, Col. 4)

Downed Jet, Russ Admit

By The Associated Press

The Soviet Union confirmed Wednesday that one of its fighter planes had downed an American jet trainer over East Germany, killing all three officers aboard.

The United States immediately protested the "shooting down" of the plane, accusing Russia of an "inexcusably brutal act of violence."

The protest was made to the minister-counsellor of the Soviet Embassy in Washington, Georgi M. Kornienko, who refused to accept it.

The disclosure of the fate of the trainer plane came in a Soviet protest note released in Moscow accusing the United States of a provocative flight designed to increase tensions.

The Soviet note said the plane appeared over communist East Germany and ignored warning shots fired in the Weimar area and the conventional signals from (Continued on Page 5, Col. 1)

Alan Ladd Dies at 50

Compiled From AP and UPI

PALM SPRINGS, Cal. — Alan Ladd, the dead-pan actor who could serve as an ideal example of the all-American success story, was found dead Wednesday in his resort home here, police said.

Ladd, 50, who gained stardom as the killer in "This Gun for Hire" and later starred as "Shane," was found by his butler. Ladd lay on the bed dressed in pajamas, police said.

Death apparently was from na-(Continued on Back Page, Col. 2)

SAIGON (UPI)—Dissident members of the ruling military junta seized control of the capital in a bloodless pre-dawn coup Thursday, U.S. military sources said.

Tanks surrounded junta headquarters and the residence of junta chairman Maj. Gen. Duong Van Minh.

Reliable reports said Maj. Gen. Nguyen Khanh, First Army Corp commander, seized control of the government and arrested four top-ranking junta members.

Paratroopers took up key positions in the capital in support of the lightning coup.

The junta members reported arrested were Maj. Gen. Tran Van Don, commander-in-chief; Maj. Gen. Le Van Kim, chief of staff of the general staff; Maj. Gen. Mai Huu Xuan, chief of the national police; and Maj. Gen. Ton That Dinh, interior minister.

The status of former junta chairman Minh was unclear, although it was reported he may be under house detention.

Khanh told some Americans here he staged the coup to save the Republic of Vietnam from being forced into Laos-style neutrality, reliable informants said.

Khanh implied to the Americans that the four arrested junta members had been plotting with alleged French government agents here to push the country into a neutralist position.

(French President Charles de Gaulle has suggested the reunification of North and South Vietnam, free of outside intervention, along neutralist lines.)

Khanh indicated that the alleged neutralist plot was to coincide with De Gaulle's recognition of communist China and hinged upon the French proposal for a neutralist solution to this nation's war against communist Viet Cong guerrillas.

Khanh also arrested Lt. Col. Nguyen Lan, a former French Army intelligence officer of Vietnamese extraction. He reportedly entered the country clandestinely a few days ago.

The coup, in the first hours, had been bloodless. Not a single shot was heard in or around the capital.

Khanh was, according to reli-(Continued on Back Page, Col. 1)

GEN. DUONG VAN MINH
...surrounded by tanks.

GEN. TON THAT DINH
...arrested by coup leaders.

GEN. NGUYEN KHANH
...leader of the coup.

F-102 Squadron at Itazuke Will Return to U.S. by July

TOKYO (UPI) — The U.S. Air Force announced Thursday it will withdraw more combat airplanes from Japan.

The Air Force announced that a squadron of F-102 jet fighter planes will return to the United States from Japan by July 1. An Air Force spokesman said 20 F-102s will be pulled out of Japan.

This was the second reduction in American airpower announced in Japan in the past month.

Maj. Gen. Charles M. McCorkle, acting commander of the Fifth U.S. Air Force and U.S. military forces in Japan, said the 68th Fighter-Interceptor Sq. will be returned to the United States.

The squadron now is stationed at Itazuke AB on Kyushu, southernmost of the Japanese islands.

The U.S. announced its first Air Forces withdrawal from Japan Dec. 31.

At that time, the U.S. Air Force said it would pull about 3,500 American air men and some 2,000 members of their families out of Japan during 1964.

About 78 fighter, bomber and troop transport planes would leave Japan under the announced December withdrawal.

About 46,000 U.S. military men and some 54,000 dependents are stationed in Japan under the U.S.-Japan mutual defense agreement.
(Continued on Back Page, Col. 4)

Weather

Tokyo Area Forecast

Friday: Cloudy with Rain; High 58, Low 26.
Saturday: Partly Cloudy; High 55, Low 30
Wednesday's Temperatures: High 48, Low 33

Vacation Special Derails, 51 Hurt

ALLENDALE, S.C. (UPI)—Eighteen cars of the Seaboard Air Line Railway's Silver Meteor with 400 passengers aboard derailed near here Saturday night, seriously injuring 51 persons.

Scores of other passengers received minor injuries.

The train was bound for New York with vacationers returning from Florida.

Hundreds of curious spectators milled about and hampered rescuers at the accident scene, about 7 miles north of this South Carolina-Georgia border town.

Four South Carolina hospitals were pressed into service to administer first aid and admit the most seriously injured.

Fairfax Police said an estimated 1,000 persons gathered around the derailment and hampered the more than 10 ambulances moving in and out of the area.

PACIFIC STARS AND STRIPES

AN AUTHORIZED PUBLICATION OF THE ARMED FORCES IN THE FAR EAST

FIVE-STAR EDITION

昭和三十四年一月二十二日国鉄東局特別扱承認新聞紙第175号（日刊）
（昭和34年4月21日第3種郵便物認可）

10¢ DAILY
15¢ WITH SUPPLEMENTS

Vol. 20, No. 153   Tuesday, June 2, 1964

Rusk and Lodge Arrive in Hawaii

HONOLULU (UPI)—Secretary of State Dean Rusk arrived here Sunday for a top-level conference of U.S. civilian and military policy makers directed by President Johnson to review the critical situation in Southeast Asia. Rusk, accompanied by U.S. Ambassador to the Republic of Vietnam Henry Cabot Lodge, flew in from Saigon, where he had met briefly with U.S. officials and Vietnamese leaders.

The conference, scheduled to get under way Monday morning, will include, in addition to Rusk and Lodge, Defense Secretary Robert McNamara; Central Intelligence Agency Director John A. McCone; General Maxwell D. Taylor, chairman of the Joint Chiefs of Staff; Admiral Harry D. Felt, commander in chief of U.S. Pacific Forces; and other military and diplomatic officials from Washington and Southeast Asia.

"The meeting has not yet begun," Rusk said at a brief planeside news conference, "so I'll say little about it. We will discuss further recommendations that might be made to President Johnson."

Lodge said, "I think this meeting is going to do a lot of good." He said the situation in South Vietnam "isn't hopeless. We've got cards on our side and a lot of strong,

(Continued on Back Page, Col. 1)

Traffic Deaths Soar

CHICAGO (UPI)—The holiday weekend traffic toll soared above the 300 mark Sunday, heading toward a possible record for a three-day Memorial Day period.

However, a spokesman for the National Safety Council, which estimated that from 410 to 490 persons would die in traffic accidents during the 78-hour period, said, "it still looks like it will be at the low end of our estimate, maybe even a little below it."

The record of 371 traffic deaths for a three-day Memorial Day weekend was set in 1958.

A United Press International count at 5:30 p.m. EDT (6:30 a.m. Monday JST) showed 336 persons killed in traffic accidents and 103 persons killed in other accidents since the holiday started at 6 p.m. Thursday.

The breakdown:

Traffic	336
Drownings	36
Planes	2
Miscellaneous	65
Total	439

Secretary of State Dean Rusk (left) and Ambassador Henry Cabot Lodge are greeted by Admiral Harry D. Felt (right) in Honolulu. (AP Radiophoto)

PASSENGERS BEATEN

N.Y. Teens Riot, Rip Up 'D' Train

NEW YORK (AP)—Twenty or more teen-agers rioted on a subway train in Brooklyn early Sunday, police said.

They beat up and robbed passengers, wrecked three cars of the train, then surged into the street and smashed store windows and broke into a beauty parlor.

Fourteen patrolmen and four detectives rounded up 12 of the youths. Police said 8 to 15 got away.

They said the situation nearly erupted into a riot when angry residents surged from their homes and had to be held back by officers.

Three of the passengers were taken to hospitals for treatment, along with one of the arrested youths who suffered a leg cut when he kicked out a train window.

Detective Raymond Sheerin said the youths apparently boarded the independent line "D" train in Coney Island after a night of drinking.

"Most of them were half stoned," he said. "They started acting up in the train and just went haywire."

He said they smashed windows and practically every light bulb in the first three cars, and also

(Continued on Back Page, Col. 5)

Shots Fired At Bella's Guards

ALGIERS (UPI)—Shots were fired Sunday at security men guarding President Ahmed Ben Bella's Algiers residence and his official headquarters across the street, sources c'   the presidency reported.

Police did not say whether there were any casualties. Other reports spoke earlier of automatic weapon fire being heard in the area.

Police armed with submachine guns set up roadblocks and for two hours prevented any vehicles from passing in front of the two buildings. The roadblocks were later removed but several police trucks remained in the area.

Ben Bella, who recently returned from a visit to Moscow,

(Continued on Back Page, Col. 4)

Near Miss for LBJ at 70 MPH

JOHNSON CITY, Tex. (AP)—President Johnson, at the wheel of his white automobile, narrowly avoided running over a broken bottle Sunday while he was driving to church at 70 m.p.h.

The President was leading a four-car caravan through a light drizzle. The Secret Service car second behind him hit the bottle and tore a large hole in a front tire.

The driver stopped the car without incident while the rest of the motorcade drove on.

The President and Mrs. Johnson and their 20-year-old daughter, Lynda Bird, drove from the LBJ Ranch near here to Fredericksburg, 20 miles to the west, to attend morning services at the Edison Street Methodist Church.

Johnson, once accused of speeding on the winding highways of this Texas hill country, carefully observed the 70 m.p.h. speed limit on the drive to Fredericksburg.

The bottle the Secret Service car hit was sitting upright on the road, with its neck broken off. Agents believe it was dropped from a passing car and said they doubted it was placed there deliberately.

Weather

Tokyo Area Forecast

Tuesday: Partly Cloudy; High 76, Low 62

Wednesday: Partly Cloudy, showers; High 75, Low 63

Sunday's Temperatures: High 75, Low 60

(USAF Weather Central, Fuchu AB)

JOHNSON DENIES PLAN TO EXTEND VIETNAM WAR

WASHINGTON (AP)—President Johnson said Tuesday at a surprise news conference that he knows of no plans to extend the war in the Republic of Vietnam to north Vietnam.

Johnson, who gave newsmen some basic guide lines governing U.S. policy in Southeast Asia, was critical of Rep. Melvin Laird (R-Wis.), who told the House the Administration was planning to extend the fighting into north Vietnam.

"Mr. Laird is not yet speaking for the Administration," Johnson said. "I know of no plans that have been made to that effect."

This touched off a prompt retort from Laird who said that in making that statement Johnson "deliberately misled the American people."

Laird had said over the weekend that the Administration has been preparing plans for several months "to move into north Vietnam" but he stopped short of saying whether the preparations will be carried out.

(Laird, chairman of the 1964 Republican Platform Committee, took the House floor to read accounts of Johnson's news conference, UPI reported.

("This is just simply not the case," Laird told the House. "We have plans and we should not tell the enemy that we have no plans.

("The President, I believe, deliberately misled the American people."

(Laird said his information came to him from Secretary of State Dean Rusk, and that he had used no classified information received through House Defense Appropriations Subcommittee hearings.)

Laird said Monday that current talks in Honolulu on U.S. policy in Southeast Asia will be unproductive unless the Administration discards what he called ineffectual "false premises" of
(Continued on Back Page, Col. 3)

Pierre Salinger relaxes with a cup of coffee while awaiting California primary returns. (AP Radiophoto)

PACIFIC STARS AND STRIPES

AN AUTHORIZED PUBLICATION OF THE ARMED FORCES IN THE FAR EAST

FIVE-STAR EDITION

10¢ DAILY
15¢ WITH SUPPLEMENTS

昭和三十四年一月二十二日国鉄東局特別級承認新聞紙第175号 （日刊）
（昭和34年4月21日第3種郵便物認可）

Vol. 20, No. 155   Thursday, June 4, 1964

Poisoned Spears Kill 100 Troops

LEOPOLDVILLE, Congo (UPI)—Communist-led rebels wiped out a National Congolese Army company of 100 men with poisoned arrows and spears in an ambush in Kivu Province, according to reports reaching here Tuesday.

The report of the ambush in Rizizi Village, south of the Kivu capital of Bukavu, came as the Congo army regrouped troops that retreated to Bukavu in the face of rebel victories. Two companies took up defensive positions 10 miles south of the capital.

The Congolese government Monday proclaimed a state of emergency in Kivu. Reliable sources said the situation there was deteriorating badly.

The situation in Bukavu was "serous but not grave," diplomatic sources said.

However, U.N. civilian personnel have been evacuated to Goma, which has an airport, or to the neighboring Rwanda.

The Swedish Protestant mission headquarters also evacuat-
(Continued on Back Page, Col. 5)

THE '64 QUESTION

Barry Takes Early Lead

SAN FRANCISCO (UPI) — Sen. Barry Goldwater took an early lead over New York Gov. Nelson Rockefeller Tuesday night in California's presidential primary. With 11 percent of the vote counted, Goldwater had 126,123 votes to Rockefeller's 105,923, National Broadcasting Co. said.

Compiled From AP and UPI
SAN FRANCISCO—Nearly 5 million Californians went to the polls Tuesday in a presidential primary election highlighted by the hot fight between Gov. Nelson Rockefeller of New York and Sen. Barry Goldwater of Arizona.

Both the candidates wound up their campaigns Monday by exchanging charges in back-

*   *   *

to-back rallies at Los Angeles Airport.

When Goldwater arrived he was greeted by cheers from his supporters. Some of them stayed on to give Bronx cheers to Rockefeller, who was finishing a tour of the state and trying to talk to his own backers.

Police kept on the alert to prevent trouble, and Rockefeller joked about his chance to talk to Goldwater fans, who were booing him.

Rockefeller gave the hardest hitting speech of the day-long tour and he explained why:

"I am delighted so many of Sen. Goldwater's followers are here. It's the first time I've had a chance to talk to you."

At this the Goldwater supporters started booing and walking away, but Rockefeller shouted:

"Don't go away until I talk to you. Goldwater has taken an impulsive and irresponsible stand on the use of nuclear weapons."

A chorus of boos from the Goldwater group drowned out the rest of his remarks, and then his own supporters, numbering about one half of the crowd of 1,000, started chanting, "We want
(Continued on Back Page, Col. 4)

'Sorry, Gov. Brown But You Can't Vote'

SAN FRANCISCO (AP)—Gov. Edmund G. Brown tried to vote Tuesday and was turned down.

"I'm sorry, but you can't vote, governor," said the precinct officer, George Patterson.

He noted that Brown had registered as an absentee voter. The governor explained that he hadn't filed the absentee ballot, and that it was on his desk in Sacramento.

Brown arranged to have a messenger deliver it to him here.

The election code provides that if one receives an absentee ballot, then decides to vote in person, he must first turn over the unused absentee ballot to the precinct inspector.

20,000 Ligtas Troops Await D-Day Signal

Related stories by S&S reporters on Pages 6-7
By JOSEPH SCHNEIDER
S&S S.E. Asia Bureau Chief

MINDORO ISLAND, P.I. — A mighty armada of warships carrying a 20,000-man striking force is nearing this Philippine island for a D-Day landing Thursday in Southeast Asia Treaty Organization exercise Ligtas.

The combat troops taking part in the giant training operation are supported by some 300 planes and 75 ships.

Taking part in the exercise

are military units from the U.S., Britain, France, Australia, New Zealand, Thailand, Pakistan and the Philippines.

Special forces units of the U.S.
(Continued on Page 6, Col. 4)

Weather

Tokyo Area Forecast

Thursday: Cloudy; High 70, Low 60
Friday: Partly cloudy; High 70, Low 60
Tuesday's Temperatures: High 78, Low 68

(USAF Weather Central, Fuchu AS)

Off Coast of North Vietnam

3 PT BOATS ATTACK AMERICAN WARSHIP

PACIFIC
STARS AND STRIPES
AN AUTHORIZED PUBLICATION OF
THE ARMED FORCES FAR EAST

10¢ DAILY
15¢ WITH SUPPLEMENTS

Vol. 20, No. 216   **FIVE-STAR EDITION**   Tuesday, August 4, 1964

AP Radiophoto
ADMIRAL U.S. GRANT SHARP DISCUSSES PT-BOAT ATTACK WITH NEWSMEN IN HONOLULU.

PEARL HARBOR, Hawaii (AP)—The Navy destroyer Maddox was attacked with torpedoes and gunfire Sunday by three unidentified PT boats in the Gulf of Tonkin off north Vietnam, the Office of the Commander-in-Chief of Pacific Forces announced Sunday.

The announcement said the destroyer was not damaged and there were no injuries to personnel in the "unprovoked attack."

The PT boats were damaged and driven off by gunfire from four aircraft from the carrier Ticonderoga. The attack from the PT boats was answered by the Maddox, the announcement said.

In New York, Secretary of State Dean Rusk said the torpedo boats which attacked the Maddox were north Vietnamese.

"The other side got a sting out of this," Rusk told a reporter. **"If they do it again, they'll get another sting."**

He identified "the other side" as "the north Vietnamese."

In Washington, President Johnson called in high-level diplomats and military advisers, presumably to discuss the attack.

The White House made no announcement on results of the conference, held in the executive mansion.

Among those reportedly in attendance were Under Secretary of State George W. Ball, Deputy Secretary of Defense Cyrus R. Vance, and General Earle G. Wheeler, chairman of the Joint Chiefs of Staff.

Earlier, a White House spokesman had said the President had been advised of the early-morning incident but there would be no comment at present.

The coast of north Vietnam is to the north and west of the Gulf of Tonkin, and communist China is to the north and east. China's Hainan Island is to the east.

A Navy spokesman in Washington said one of the attacking boats was badly damaged by U.S. planes firing Zuni rockets and 20mm machine guns. It was lying in the water "not moving," the (Continued on Page 2, Col. 2)

AP Radiophoto
MISS UNIVERSE

Miss Greece Wins; Turkey Walks Out

MIAMI BEACH (UPI)—Miss Greece, a tall, flashing-eyed brunette from Athens, was named the new Miss Universe Saturday night and Miss Turkey immediately walked out in an apparent political protest.

The winner, 20-year-old Kiriaki Tsopei, said, "I'm thrilled —I just can't believe it" in Greek, then tried to recite a speech she had memorized in English.

Standing in a shimmering blue evening gown before a nationwide television audience, she faltered, stopped and stammered "I'm sorry."

The runners-up, in order, were Miss England, Brenda Flacker of London; Miss Israel, Ronit Rinat of Haifa; Miss Sweden, Siv Marta Aberg of Gavle, and Miss Free China, Lana Yi Yu of Taipei.

Immediately after the nine judges, noting Miss Greece's "noble features and very dignified profile," named her the 1964 Miss Universe, Miss Turkey walked off the stage.

Miss Turkey, Inci Duran, was not among the semifinalists and was apparently staging a protest because her country and Greece (Continued on Page 2, Col. 4)

'ATTACK CALLS FOR NEW LOOK'

Dirksen Raps Posture in F.E.

WASHINGTON (AP) — Republicans pointed to Sunday's attack on a U.S. destroyer off north Vietnam as support for their assertions that the Johnson Administration is not handling things well in that troubled part of the world.

Sen. Everett M. Dirksen of Illinois, the Republican Senate leader and a frequent critic of U.S. policy in south Vietnam, said the PT boat attack on the Maddox calls for "a new hard look" at the U.S. position in that area:

Both Republicans and Democrats applauded the U.S. Navy's prompt and apparently effective return fire against the unidentified PT boat. But among those commenting there was no demand for retaliatory offensive action against north Vietnam.

There was no indication of whether a protest would be lodged against the apparent violation of the freedom of the high seas.

Sen. Richard B. Russell (D-Ga.), chairman of the Senate Armed Services Committee, said approvingly that the incident shows (Continued on Page 2, Col. 1)

Weather

Tokyo Area Forecast
Tuesday: Partly cloudy; Min. Mid 70, Max. Near 90.
Wednesday: Fair; Min. Mid 70, Max. Near 90.
Sunday's Temperatures: Min. 77, Max. 92
(USAF Weather Central, Fuchu AB)

DESTROY ATTACKERS, LBJ ORDERS NAVY

WASHINGTON (AP)—President Johnson has ordered U.S. naval forces in the Tonkin Gulf area off Vietnam to destroy any force that attacks them.

The President also ordered the Navy to strengthen the size of its patrol forces there.

Johnson summoned reporters to his office Monday to tell them of the orders, which, he said, were issued Sunday after the U.S. destroyer Maddox was attacked by three north Vietnamese patrol torpedo boats.

Johnson said the commanders of combat aircraft and destroyers in the area where Sunday's attack occurred — in international waters—have been told "to attack any force which attacks them in international water and to attack them not only with the objective of driving off the attack force but of destroying them."

With emphasis in his tone, the President said that these orders "will be carried out."

As commander-in-chief, Johnson issued a series of instructions to the Navy:

1) To continue the patrols in the Gulf of Tonkin off the coast of north Vietnam.

2) To double the force by adding an additional destroyer to the one already on patrol.

3) To provide a combat air patrol over the destroyers.

4) To issue the orders to drive off and destroy any force which attacks the U.S. force.

The Seventh fleet, in the western Pacific, has an ample force of destroyers from which to assign an additional ship to the patrol. Normally, the fleet operates with no fewer than 30 destroyers.

The air cover which the President ordered will come from a carrier operating in the general area off the coast of Vietnam.

Customarily, carriers do not move into the comparatively confined waters of the gulf, bounded
(Continued on Back Page, Col. 1)

PACIFIC STAR AND STRIPES

AN AUTHORIZED PUBLICATION OF THE ARMED FORCES FAR EAST

10¢ DAILY
15¢ WITH SUPPLEMENTS

Vol. 20, No. 217   FIVE-STAR EDITION   Wednesday, August 5, 1964

Heavy Seas Break Freighter in Two

The Liberian iron ore freighter Pella is battered by the sea after heavy waves broke the ship in two when it ran aground near the German island of Amrun in the North Sea during a storm. (UPI Radiophoto)

U.S. to Make Protest to N. Vietnam

WASHINGTON (AP)—The United States is making a formal protest to the communist north Vietnam government for an allegedly unprovoked attack on the U.S. Navy destroyer Maddox in international waters, the State Department said Monday.

The attack is viewed as a serious incident, State Department Press Officer Robert J. McCloskey said.

McCloskey said the means of delivering the American protest and the channel to be used is still under consideration.

However, authoritative sources said the three-nation International Control Commission, composed of India, Poland and Canada, will be the means of conveying the protest to Hanoi.

This is the first direct diplomatic protest the United States has made to north Vietnam. Generally the north Vietnamese are believed acting on the instigation of communist China.

McCloskey said the attack by three north Vietnamese torpedo boats Sunday was unprovoked.

"Anytime or anywhere that American ships are attacked for unprovoked reasons, that, in our opinion, is a serious incident," he said.

While declining to speculate on the motivations for the attack, McCloskey said it "is consistent with continued aggressive actions against South Vietnam."

At the Pentagon, officials said U.S. destroyers on Tonkin Gulf patrol are understood to have reported no previous attempt at actual interception by communist torpedo boats, although it was known they operate out of ports on the gulf.

A chronological report issued by the U.S. Navy said the Maddox opened fire with her five-inch battery after three warning shots failed to slow the attackers.

Two of the boats closed to 5,000 yards, the account said, and each fired one torpedo. The Maddox took evasive action and the missiles passed alongside,
(Continued on Back Page, Col. 1)

S&S Photo
PAUL H. NITZE

U.S. Ships To Continue Gulf Patrol

By AL KRAMER
S&S Staff Writer

TOKYO—Navy Secretary Paul H. Nitze said here Monday that U.S. Navy ships will continue to sail the international waters where the destroyer Maddox was attacked Sunday by north Vietnamese PT boats.

Nitze said U.S. Navy ships have been operating, as "a regular practice over a period of years," in the Gulf of Tonkin
(Continued on Page 6, Col. 3)

Military Pay Bill Passed, Would Be Effective Sept. 1

WASHINGTON (UPI)—Congress voted a $207 million pay raise Monday for two-thirds of the members of the Armed Forces and indicated it would increase the pay of the rest next year.

The Senate passed bill, effective Sept. 1, was approved by the House without a word of debate and was rushed to the White House for President Johnson's signature. It covers about 1.8 million members of the armed forces but does not apply to lower ranking enlisted men with less than two years of service.

Efforts to include draftees and other enlisted men still serving their two-year obligation were defeated earlier in the House for fear the entire bill would become bogged down in the rush for adjournment before the Democratic National Convention.

Rep. L. Mendel Rivers (D-S.C.) will become chairman of the House Armed Services Committee next year if the Democrats retain control of Congress, said he would introduce legislation next year to raise military pay again. "But something is better than nothing," Rivers said.

(AP said the bill would provide these increases:

(1 A 2.5 per cent increase for all officers and enlisted men
(Continued on Back Page, Col. 1)

U.S. PLANES KO 5 N. VIET BASES

PACIFIC
STARS AND STRIPES

AN AUTHORIZED PUBLICATION OF
THE ARMED FORCES FAR EAST

10¢ DAILY
15¢ WITH SUPPLEMENTS

Vol. 20, No. 219   FIVE-STAR EDITION   Friday, August 7, 1964

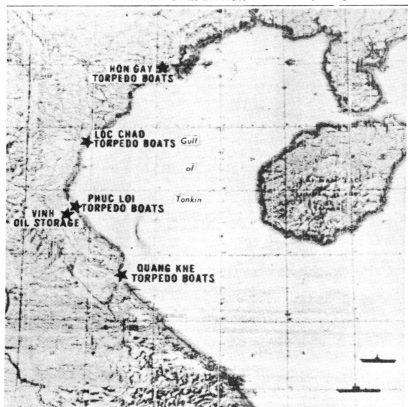

This is a portion of the map Defense Secretary Robert S. McNamara used to point where U.S. Navy bombers attacked north Vietnamese bases. (AP Radiophoto)

WASHINGTON (UPI) – U.S. Navy planes striking back at communist attackers Wednesday damaged or destroyed approximately 25 Red patrol boats at four bases in north Vietnam.

Two American planes were shot down by antiaircraft fire from ground batteries. Their pilots were presumed lost. One other plane was damaged slightly.

Besides knocking out a large portion of north Vietnam's patrol boat fleet, the U.S. planes from the carriers Ticonderoga and Constellation blew up an oil depot and other base facilities.

The low-level air attacks were carried out over a period of about five hours, from noon to 5 p.m. Vietnam time (1 p.m. to 6 p.m. JST).

(North Vietnam claimed to have shot down five U.S. aircraft, damaged three, and captured one American pilot during the attacks, the New China News Agency said in a broadcast monitored in Tokyo.)

The U.S. action, the first against north Viet-
(Continued on Back Page, Col. 1)

7th Fleet Massing In Vietnam Area

By LARRY ASHMAN
S&S Staff Writer

TOKYO—Battle elements of the U.S. Seventh Fleet were steaming at full speed Thursday for the Vietnam area amid reports of a major U.S. show of force off the coast of communist north Vietnam.

Vice Adm. Roy L. Johnson, Seventh Fleet commander, left the U.S. naval base at Yokosuka, Japan, Thursday aboard his flagship, the light cruiser Oklahoma City.

A fleet spokesman confirmed reports that the aircraft carriers Kearsarge and Valley Forge left Yokosuka Wednesday presumably for the Vietnam area. An undisclosed number of destroyers also have been ordered out of Yokosuka.

He also confirmed reports that the Seventh Fleet—more than 125 ships, 650 aircraft and some 64,000 sailors and marines—had been put on alert to
(Continued on Page 7, Col. 1)

LBJ Calls Attacks Deliberate, Willful

SYRACUSE, N.Y. (UPI) — President Johnson Wednesday denounced north Vietnamese hostility against U.S. naval vessels as "deliberate, willful, and systematic aggression" which the United States could not permit to go unchallenged.

In a speech at ceremonies dedicating the Samuel I. Newhouse Communications Center at Syracuse University, the Chief Executive said while the U.S. offered no threat whatever to any peaceful power, there could be "no peace by aggression and no immunity from reply."

Shortly before going on the speakers platform at the university, Johnson received a telephone report from Defense Secretary Robert S. McNamara

who had new figures on the U.S. air sorties against the north Vietnamese installations early Wednesday.

Johnson described the north Vietnamese attacks of Sunday and Tuesday against American destroyers as "deliberate . . . unprovoked."

"The attacks have been answered," he said.

The President told his audience that no one could be detached about the flareup of hostilities in Southeast Asia.

"Aggression—deliberate, willful and systematic aggression —

has unmasked its face to the world," he said. "The world remembers — the world must never forget — that aggression unchallenged is aggression unleashed."

This, the President added, was why the U.S. had to answer aggression with action.

Explaining that the U.S. acted only after "long provocation" he said the government of north Vietnam was now willfully and systematically violating agreements of 1954 and 1962 when the north Vietnamese approved the
(Continued on Back Page, Col. 1)

Bulletin

TOKYO (UPI) — Communist China said Thursday that "aggression against (communist north) Vietnam means aggression against China," and added that "the Chinese people will not sit idly by without lending a helping hand."

(map labels: HON GAY TORPEDO BOATS; LOC CHAO TORPEDO BOATS; PHUC LOI TORPEDO BOATS; VINH OIL STORAGE; QUANG KHE TORPEDO BOATS; Gulf of Tonkin)

PACIFIC

STARS AND STRIPES

AN AUTHORIZED PUBLICATION OF THE ARMED FORCES IN THE FAR EAST

FIVE-STAR EDITION

昭和三十四年一月二十二日国鉄東局特別扱承認新聞紙第175号（日刊）
（昭和34年4月21日第3種郵便物認可）

10¢ DAILY

15¢ WITH
SUPPLEMENTS

Vol. 20, No. 226   Friday, August 14, 1964

HELICOPTERS FLY TOWARD A MASSIVE ATTACK ON THE VIET CONG.

UPI Radiophoto

2,000-3,000 Viet Cong

96 COPTERS HIT REDS

Helicopters swoop down on a communist stronghold in the jungle, 30 miles northwest of Saigon.

AP Radiophoto

XA BA HAO, Republic of Vietnam (AP)—One of the largest helicopter assaults of the Republic of Vietnam's war was hurled into jungles near here Wednesday where intelligence reports had indicated between 2,000 and 3,000 Viet Cong had massed for a strike.

Ninety-six helicopters, both Vietnamese and U.S. Army were thrown into attack, carrying close to 1,000 Vietnamese troops.

But minutes after the assault began, a young U.S. Army first lieutenant slumped dead at the controls of his attack helicopter, a .50-cal. armor-piercing machinegun bullet through his heart. The slug came right through the windshield as the helicopter was making
(Continued on Back Page, Col. 2)

Ian Fleming Dies at 56

CANTERBURY, England (AP) —Ian Fleming, 56, the novelist who found his way to a mint of royalties by sending James Bond through a labyrinth of intrigue, died Wednesday of a heart attack.

Stricken Tuesday night, the author, ex-journalist and World War II intelligence agent succumbed in the Kent and Canterbury Hospital here.

With him went his creation, secret agent James Bond —
(Continued on Back Page, Col. 1)

Goldwater Wins Ike's Full Support

HERSHEY, Pa. (AP)—Republican presidential candidate Barry Goldwater won former President Dwight Eisenhower's full support Wednesday after promising to follow the Eisenhower foreign policy line and renouncing extremism on either the left or right.

Eisenhower read to a news conference concluding a party summit meeting a statement in which he said that Goldwater had made it clear that if elected he would follow the basic policies of the Eisenhower administration.

Goldwater himself said, in response to questions at the joint news conference, that a statement of his position which he read to a closed meeting of 36 party leaders had been drafted after he had consulted with Eisenhower in Gettysburg recently.

In his statement to the meeting, Goldwater said he would not accept the support of extremists of either the left or the right. He pledged full im-
(Continued on Back Page, Col. 3)

LBJ Signs Pay Bill

WASHINGTON (UPI) - President Johnson signed into law Wednesday a $207 million pay raise for servicemen. He said it gives America's "uniformed citizens a fuller measure of the respect they have earned."

Johnson said the pay bill, which will go into effect Sept. 1, reflects "our historic trust of our professional military men."

The President is expected to follow up Wednesday's action later in the week by signing a civilian pay bill.

LBJ REPLACES B-57S DESTROYED BY REDS

PACIFIC STAR AND STRIPES

AN AUTHORIZED PUBLICATION OF
THE ARMED FORCES FAR EAST

昭和三十四年一月二十二日国鉄東局特別扱承認新聞第175号（日刊）

10¢ DAILY
15¢ WITH SUPPLEMENTS
(昭和34年4月21日第3種郵便物認可)

Vol. 20, No. 307   **FIVE-STAR EDITION**   Tuesday, Nov. 3, 1964

WASHINGTON (AP)—President Johnson sought means Sunday to tighten defenses against mortar attacks such as raked a U.S. air base in South Vietnam Saturday, and he immediately replaced the jet bombers destroyed in that strike.

The attack on Bien Hoa airfield near Saigon killed four Americans and destroyed five B-57 twin-engine jet bombers.

The President's moves were announced by the White House after a 75-minute Sunday afternoon meeting between Johnson and top aides including Secretary of State Dean Rusk, Defense Secretary Robert S. McNamara, international security affairs adviser McGeorge Bundy, Under Secretary of State George W. Ball and William P. Bundy, assistant secretary of state for Far Eastern affairs.

The Administration tended to regard the affair as serious because of the loss of life and planes, but not as a major development in the war against the communist insurgents. It was seen as an episode of a type difficult to prevent in such a war where the enemy has many opportunities for such hit-and-run surprise attacks.

Presidential Press Secretary George Reedy issued this statement after Johnson was briefed by his advisers:

"The President met with the secretaries of state and defense

(Continued on Page 2, Col. 1)

General Praises Force

SAIGON (AP) — General William C. Westmoreland, commander of U.S. forces in South Vietnam, said Sunday he had no criticism of either the Vietnamese or American forces at Bien Hoa Air Base which was hit by Viet Cong mortars Sunday morning.

"U.S. personnel acquitted themselves in a magnificent fashion," he told new men.

At the same time, Westmoreland said security precautions at all bases "were constantly under review."

He said a great deal of time and effort had been put into security at Bien Hoa "but evidently it was not sufficient."

U.S. Ambassador Maxwell D. Taylor and Westmoreland flew to the base Sunday morning as did former premier Maj. Gen. Nguyen Khanh and Air Force Commander Brig. Gen. Nguyen Cao Ky.

U.S. combat planes throughout Vietnam were being parked in
(Continued on Page 2, Col. 8)

AP Radiophoto

WEAPONS ARE REMOVED FROM USAF BOMBERS DESTROYED IN VIET CONG MORTAR ATTACK ON BIEN HOA AIR BASE.

Halloween 'Treat' Is Ant Poison

COMMACK, N.Y. (AP)—A mother accused of handing out pellets of ant poison to Halloween pranksters was ordered committed to a state hospital Sunday for psychiatric examination.

District Court Judge Victor J. Orgera ordered the test for Mrs. Helen Pfeil, 47, mother of two teen-age sons and a married daughter.

Mrs. Pfeil was charged with endangering the health of a minor after a parent recognized
(Continued on Page 2, Col. 5)

Weather

Tokyo Area Forecast

Tuesday: Partly Cloudy; Min. Mid 40's, Max. Near 60
Wednesday: Fair; Min. Near 40. Max. Near 60
Sunday's Temperatures: Min. 58. Max. 69
(USAF Weather Central, Fuchu AS)

Candidates Set Last Stops On Bumpy Campaign Trail

WASHINGTON (AP) — One of the roughest presidential campaigns in modern history neared its end Sunday with the usual last-gap flurries—and with the shadow of Vietnam hovering over it.

On Tuesday (Wednesday Japan time) more than 70 million voters answer the critical question that has always worried, sometimes excited and often bored the United States for two hectic months:

Should Lyndon B. Johnson be kept on as president for the next four years, or should the job be given his Republican challenger, Sen. Barry Goldwater?

As far as the four principals were concerned, Sunday was an unusually quiet day politically.

For Johnson it meant church—and a conference with Secretary of State Dean Rusk and Secretary of Defense Robert S. McNamara over a communist attack on the Bien Hoa AB in Vietnam.

Both candidates have used Vietnam as an issue.

"We will not be worn down," Johnson has said. "We will not be driven out. We will not be provoked into rashness."

"If I am elected I intend to come to grips with this vital question," Goldwater has said. ". . . It becomes more apparent every day that this Administration is drifting—that it has no policy worthy of the name."

For Goldwater, Sunday meant a day at home in Phoenix, Ariz. Monday, he will return to California with a final bid for its 40 electoral votes.

For Rep. William E. Miller, the Republican vice presidential candidate, this also was a day off, here in Washington.

Only Sen. Hubert H. Humphrey, the Democratic vice presidential candidate, was flailing away at
(Continued on Page 2, Col. 4)

PACIFIC STARS AND STRIPES

AN AUTHORIZED PUBLICATION OF THE ARMED FORCES IN THE FAR EAST

FIVE-STAR EDITION

昭和三十四年一月二十二日国鉄東局特別扱承認新聞紙第175号（日刊）
（昭和34年4月21日第3種郵便物認可）

10¢ DAILY
15¢ WITH SUPPLEMENTS

Vol. 20, No. 329   Wednesday, Nov. 25, 1964

TAYLOR'S VIEW:
Vietnam Victory 'Much in Doubt'

SAIGON (AP)—U.S. Ambassador Maxwell D. Taylor says that victory over the communists in South Vietnam "is very much in doubt."

He said aerial assaults against north Vietnam and Laos supply routes and bases could contribute to a victory over the communists.

In an interview with Life magazine, released by the U.S. Embassy Monday, Taylor said "military action outside the

WASHINGTON (AP) — Sen. Wayne Morse (D-Ore.) said Monday that if Ambassador Maxwell D. Taylor recommends an expansion of the South Vietnam fighting into north Vietnam and Laos "he should be summarily fired."

Morse added that any others in the State Department or the Pentagon who might be associated in any possible recommendation of what he called "international outlawry" should be fired along with Taylor.

country just as pure military action inside the country will not win in itself."

During the same interview with top members of the U.S. mission here, General William C. Westmoreland, commander U.S. forces in Vietnam, said "it is absolutely inconceivable to me that the Viet Cong could ever militarily defeat the armed forces of South Vietnam."

Deputy Ambassador U. Alexis Johnson, echoing the view that the Viet Cong has no hope of military victory, said the communist strategy at present "is designed toward bringing about a negotiation between some government in Saigon and their political arm which is the National Liberation Front. . . ."

The interview was released as Taylor prepared to fly to the United States Wednesday for top-level policy review on the Vietnam situation. One of the questions to be discussed is whether strikes at Viet Cong supply lines and bases (Continued on Back Page, Col. 1)

FIREFIGHTERS WADE THROUGH FOAM AS THEY EXTINGUISH FLAMES OF TWA AIRLINER THAT CRASHED IN ROME.

AP Radiophoto

7 Tunnel Out of Prison

WALLA WALLA, Wash. (AP)—Seven convicts, including three convicted murderers, crawled to freedom through a tunnel Sunday night from their maximum security cell block at the Washington State Penitentiary.

Washington and Oregon state police set up roadblocks for the seven, all veterans of previous jailbreaks.

Andrew and Cora Jeppe, both (Continued on Back Page, Col. 1)

44 Killed as Jet Crashes on Takeoff

ROME (UPI)—A Trans-World Airlines jet with 73 persons aboard faltered on takeoff Monday, swerved into a steamroller and exploded in flames with the rumbling sound of a volcano.

In New York, TWA announced that 44 persons were killed. Some of the survivors were in critical condition. Among the dead was Bishop Edward Celestin Daly of Des Moines, Iowa.

The pilot, Capt. Vernon Lowell of Old Westbury, N.Y., sensing something wrong, tried to halt the big Boeing 707 as it was taking off from Rome's Fiumicino airport.

It skidded 1,500 feet, leaving streaks of burning rubber on the runway, and hit the bulldozer on another runway under construction. Apparently the right wing tanks exploded.

The plane was TWA Flight 800-22. It originated in Kansas City and made stops in Chicago, New York, Paris and Milan. It was taking off for Athens and Cairo when disaster struck.

It was carrying 30 passengers and a double crew of 17—10 regular crewmen and seven who were to take another plane from Cairo to Bombay—and 26 airline employes on the flight to Athens. Among the 26 were six French hostesses going to Athens to pick up another flight.

All regular crew members survived.

Some of the survivors said they were saved by the quick thinking of a stewardess who began opening emergency doors as the pilot was trying to brake the plane.

The survivors scrambled to safety through the emergency doors. A number of the crewmen survived, apparently because the cockpit in a 707 is far ahead of the swept-back wings, and they escaped the full fury of the flames.

Among the survivors at San Camillo Hospital were Lowell, (Continued on Back Page, Col. 1)

Quints Born in France

PARIS (AP)—Quintuplets which doctors said are the first on record for Europe were born Monday to the 27-year-old wife of a postman. The babies—three boys and two girls—were reported in good condition and the mother in excellent health.

It was in a modern private clinic in the industrial suburb of Asnieres that the babies started coming at 2:10 p.m. (Continued on Back Page, Col. 2)

Stanleyville Battle Expected in 2 Days

LEOPOLDVILLE, Congo (AP)—A final drive by mercenary-led government troops is expected against the rebel capital of Stanleyville within 48 hours.

This was indicated Monday by military and diplomatic sources as preparations got under way to provide medical supplies and food to foreigners held in the rebel zone.

A motorized column spearheaded by South African Maj. Michael Hoare was reported in Lubutu, about 125 miles from Stanleyville. There is a good road between these cities and normally the distance can be traveled in less than four hours.

The government force has encountered no important opposition. Several ambushes have harried its flank, however.

(UPI reported Congolese Pre-(Continued on Back Page, Col. 5)

Might Have Saved JFK, Jackie Thought

WASHINGTON (AP)—In the anguished aftermath of the assassination, President Kennedy's

The Warren Commission's report on the Kennedy assassination goes on sale Nov. 28 at all *Pacific Stars and Stripes* bookstores.

The price for the hard-cover summary is $1.50.

You can also get a copy by asking your Stripes newsboy or by calling your local Stripes district office.

young widow was deeply troubled for a time by a thought that she might have saved him.

It occurred to her that if she had happened to be looking at her husband when the assassin opened fire in Dallas Nov. 22, she might have been able to pull him down out of the path of the fatal bullet. He was hit twice, the second bullet taking his life.

Evidently sh_ finally reached the conclusion that this might-have-been could not really have happened, because in telling the Warren Commission about it she employed the past tense "I used to think."

Mrs. Kennedy gave her testi-(Continued on Back Page, Col. 2)

Weather

Tokyo Area Forecast

Wednesday: Fair; Min. Mid 30s, Max. Mid 50s
Thursday: Partly cloudy; Min. Near 30, Max. Mid 50s
Monday's Temperatures: Min. 33, Max. 57
(USAF Weather Central, Fuchu AS)

FBI Nabs 'Sniper' Near SAC Base

DAYTON, Ohio (UPI)—The FBI Saturday charged Gilbert H. Hagerman, 68, with waging a one-man sniper war against some of the Strategic Air Command's (SAC) biggest jet bombers, apparently because they disturbed the cattle on his farm, seven miles northeast of Wright-Patterson AFB.

The FBI said a sniper on the ground used a high-powered rifle to score hits on five flying planes, including two giant B-52 bombers, whose total value was more than $26 million. The bullets did no serious damage. No interior pressurization loss was noticed.

The FBI in its announcement gave no motive for the attacks.

An agent said Hagerman apparently opened fire on the planes as they went in for landings because livestock were disturbed. His wife said they "had some milk cows" on their farm, which is operated by a couple. There also were reports that the Hagermans were bothered by poor television reception when the planes flew by.

The FBI said three rifles were confiscated at the Hagerman home.

Hagerman was described as the engineer who was in charge of production of the Norden bomb sight at the Robbins and Myers plant here during World War II. Hagerman is wealthy and has a "violent temper," a close friend said. He is director of manufacturing at the plant.

An Air Force spokesman this week, revealing that shots had been fired at the planes, declined to say if they carried nuclear weapons. He said, however, that a direct hit by rifle fire on a nuclear weapon would not cause an explosion.

Apparently the persons aboard the planes did not realize the craft had been hit by gunfire. The FBI said the bullet holes were discovered in the routine inspection given each plane after its landing.

Hagerman has lived on the farm for 24 years.

The FBI flew the three rifles con-
(Continued on Back Page, Col. 2)

PACIFIC
STAR AND STRIPES

AN AUTHORIZED PUBLICATION OF
THE ARMED FORCES FAR EAST

昭和三十四年一月二十二日第三種郵便物認可第175号（日刊）

10¢ DAILY
15¢ WITH SUPPLEMENTS

(昭和34年4月21日第3種郵便物認可)

Vol. 20, No. 341   FIVE-STAR EDITION   Monday, Dec. 7, 1964

AP Radiophoto
PRESIDENT JOHNSON BESTOWS MEDAL OF HONOR UPON CAPT. ROGER DONLON.

Army Captain Gets Medal of Honor

WASHINGTON (AP)—President Johnson Saturday presented the Medal of Honor to Capt. Roger H. C. Donlon, the first man to win America's highest honor for action in South Vietnam.

Donlon stood ramrod straight as the President lauded his bravery and while Secretary of Defense Robert S. McNamara read the citation. The ceremony took place at the White House.

Johnson said he hoped Donlon's heroism "will help inspire others to step forward and say 'yes' when their country calls."

The ceremony should remind all Americans, he said, of this country's commitment "to the struggle between peace and war . . . freedom and tyranny."

He said the country needs the best talents and minds, both in military and civil service. He cited McNamara, who gave up the presidency of the Ford Motor Co. to join the Cabinet, as an example of those willing to make sacrifices to serve in a civilian post.

Johnson said during the presentation:

"The Vietnamese are seeking triumph over communism manifested by insurgency, terrorism and aggression. Because we recognize the justice of their cause and its importance to all free men, we provide them with support and assistance.

"Let any who suggest we cannot honor our commitment in Vietnam find new strength and resolution in the actions of this brave man and his comrades in arms far away.

"To you, Capt. Donlon, may I personally express the gratitude and respect of all your fellow countrymen. The example you have set shall not be lost.

"As we pray for peace in the world—as we maintain the strength that supports our resolve to uphold freedom and the cause of justice around the world—we shall be always grateful for the inspiration you have given us in these times."

Donlon, 30, was commanding
(Continued on Back Page, Col. 1)

$1 Million in Wampum

KANAB, Utah (AP)—An attorney who has been helping Indians with their legal problems almost from the time he left law school says he will receive $1 million from one grateful tribe.

The tribal council of the Hopi tribe in northeast Arizona voted the sum this week for John S. Boyden of Salt Lake City who helped win an important land case after 26 years of work.

The council said $778,009 was for legal fees and $220,000 was in appreciation for "taking the case when no one else would."

The case involved a dispute with the nearby Navajo Indians over more than 2 1/2 million acres of resource-rich land.

Under a lower court decision
(Continued on Back Page, Col. 2)

FBI TRIED A PAYOFF —SHERIFF

PHILADELPHIA, Miss. (AP)—Sheriff Lawrence Rainey, one of 21 men charged in the slaying of three civil rights workers, said Saturday that FBI agents had offered him money for information about the killings. Roy K. Moore, FBI agent-in-charge at Jackson, immediately called the charge ridiculous.

Rainey returned to his duties as sheriff after arraignment Friday on federal conspiracy charges. He said two FBI agents who picked him up at his office told him during an automobile ride to Meridian:

"If you will come on and tell us what you know, we will take care of you and pay all your debts and you will leave here with more money than you'll ever make."

The sheriff told newsmen the agents also promised that he would be given immunity from prosecution if he cooperated.

Told by newsmen of Rainey's charge, Moore said, "He can say whatever he wants. I wouldn't dignify that by a comment. Let's just say 'No comment' on such a statement as that."

It was not known yet whether any of the men swept up in the FBI net would be charged with murder.

Murder is not a federal crime
(Continued on Back Page, Col. 4)

Turk Jets 'Buzz' Pontiff

ROME (UPI) — Four Turkish jet fighters flying close to Pope Paul's plane Saturday caused a commotion among his entourage and were warned off by the Italian pilot.

Cameraman Vittorio Dellavalle, who traveled on the plane, said the honor escort of four super-sabre fighters with red devils painted on the fuselage, flew close to the jetliner for nearly half an hour after it entered Turkish air space on its flight from Bombay to Rome.

"They were obviously playing," Dellavalle said, "but they came alarmingly close and passengers, including the papal suite, were scared."

The fighters on either side of the jetliner almost touched its wings. The other two fighters flew extremely close to the first two.

At one point, the tip of one fighter's wing passed first above and then under the wing of the papal plane.

Pope Paul himself was in his special compartment at the time and his reaction to the buzzing was not known.

The fighters continued their aerobatics for about half an hour and stopped only after the Italian pilot warned them several times to be careful. They dropped behind and were later replaced over
(Continued on Back Page, Col. 4)

Weather

Tokyo Area Forecast
Monday: Cloudy; Min. Near 40. Max. Mid 50's
Tuesday: Cloudy with showers; Min. Mid 30's, Max. Near 50
Saturday's Temperatures: Min. 36. Max. 44
(USAF Weather Central, Fuchu AB)

LBJ, Wife Hospitalized With Colds

PACIFIC
STAR AND STRIPES

AN AUTHORIZED PUBLICATION OF
THE ARMED FORCES FAR EAST

10¢ DAILY
15¢ WITH SUPPLEMENTS

Vol. 21, No. 24   FIVE-STAR EDITION   Monday, Jan. 25, 1965

Buddhist Protests Grow

VIETS SACK U.S. LIBRARY

SAIGON (UPI)—A mob of 3,000 young Buddhists stormed the United States Information Service (USIS) library in the old imperial capital of Hue Saturday night and burned more than 5,000 books.

The U.S. vice consul in Hue, Anthony Lake, was stoned by the mob when he tried to enter the library to put out the fires. He was not hurt.

U.S. authorities placed Hue off limits to American soldiers stationed in and around the city.

The mob appeared to be led by a core of about 100 young agitators. They first demonstrated and shouted slogans at a billet occupied by American servicemen and at the U.S. Consulate.

Their leaders then turned them toward the library building.

Until then the demonstrations had been peaceful.

Suddenly, rocks were thrown, smashing ground floor windows of the library. The mob surged forward and into the building.

USIS branch director William
(Continued on Back Page, Col. 5)

Mrs. Lyndon Johnson and daughter Lynda (background) leave their auto at Bethesda Naval Hospital where the President is confined with a severe cold. Mrs. Johnson was hospitalized later, also for a cold.   (AP Radiophoto)

WASHINGTON (UPI)—President Johnson and his wife Lady Bird were hospitalized Saturday with severe colds.

Johnson, taken to Bethesda Naval Hospital by ambulance in the pre-dawn hours, also was suffering from a throat infection which impaired his breathing. But his doctors reported later that he was "greatly improved." His illness was diagnosed as tracheitis, an inflammation of the upper windpipe.

Mrs. Johnson was admitted to the hospital about 12 hours later for treatment of a severe head cold described as "an upper respiratory infection."

The President demonstrated that he was responding to treatment when he allowed a small group of newsmen to interview him at his bedside.

"I wouldn't hesitate at all to put my britches on and go back to the office if anything had to be done," he declared in a hoarse voice. "I think we'll be all right in a day or two."

He talked to the reporters while occasionally leaning over a steaming vaporizer.

Mrs. Johnson was hospitalized
(Continued on Back Page, Col. 1)

Churchill Sinking

LONDON (AP) — Sir Winston Churchill's physician, Lord Moran, reported that the deterioration of his patient was "more marked" Saturday night.

Lord Moran spent 43 minutes with the 90-year-old Churchill before issuing his 19th medical bulletin.

It said: "The deterioration in Sir Winston's condition is more marked. There will be another bulletin tomorrow morning."

Sir Winston, Britain's wartime
(Continued on Back Page, Col. 3)

AF School Probe Widens, 29 Quit

WASHINGTON (UPI)—At least 100 Air Force Academy cadets, including 30 football players, may have cheated on examinations, Air Force Secretary Eugene M. Zuckert revealed Saturday. The incident rivaled the 1951 "cribbing" scandal at West Point involving 38 Army gridders.

Twenty-nine cadets at the Colorado Springs, Colo., service academy already have resigned in the cheating probe.

Zuckert said he would take final action on "all resignations or dismissals after review by a board of officers in my office."

The secretary said the probe "so far indicates the existence of a well-organized group of 10 or 12 cadets who were stealing examination papers and offering them for sale."

He added that an "overwhelming majority of the 2,700 cadets" studying to be Air Force officers "are not involved."

But, Zuckert said, "It appears that more than 100 members of the cadet wing may be involved, of whom about 30 may be members of the football squad."

The scandal at West Point 14 years ago saw 90 cadets dropped from the school, including 38 football players. Among them was quarterback Bob Blaik, son of the now-retired head coach, Col. Earl Blaik. West Point basketball and baseball players also were named in the "cribbing" scandal.

Air Force Academy officials said the names of the resigned cadets will not be made public and refused to say whether the
(Continued on Back Page, Col. 1)

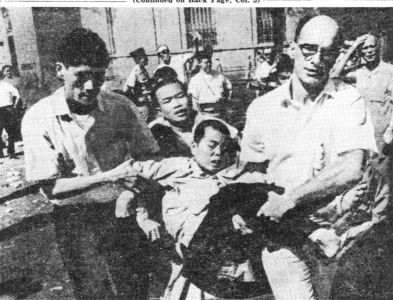

An unidentified American and a Vietnamese man carry an injured Buddhist monk from the scene of demonstrations in front of the U.S. Embassy in Saigon.   (AP Radiophoto)

Weather

Tokyo Area Forecast
Monday: Fair; Min. Near 30, Max. Near 50
Tuesday: Fair; Min. Mid 20s, Max. Near 50
Saturday's Temperatures: Min. 29, Max. 55
(USAF Weather Central, Fuchu AS)

8 AMERICANS KILLED, 62 HURT IN VIETNAM

PACIFIC
STAR AND STRIPES

AN AUTHORIZED PUBLICATION OF
THE ARMED FORCES FAR EAST

10¢ DAILY
15¢ WITH SUPPLEMENTS

Vol. 21, No. 38   FIVE-STAR EDITION   Monday, Feb. 8, 1965

SAIGON (AP)—Eight Americans were killed and at least 62 injured Saturday night when Viet Cong forces launched coordinated attacks on two big U.S. compounds at Pleiku, 240 miles north of Saigon.

At least seven parked aircraft were destroyed.

U.S. officials said the heaviest of the two attacks, backed up by mortar fire, was on a Pleiku Airport detachment at Camp Holloway.

Seven Americans were killed at Camp Holloway and 48 wounded, 15 of them critically.

One U.S. Army Caribou transport plane and six helicopters were destroyed. Three other planes and 11 helicopters were damaged. (UPI said 17 helicopters and 3 transport planes were destroyed.)

The Viet Cong apparently followed up the mortar barrage on the airport detachment with an infantry attack.

It was not immediately known whether they penetrated the airport compound.

A coordinated attack was mounted at the same time against the U.S. advisory detachment at Second Army Corps headquarters in the town of Pleiku.

One American was killed and 14 wounded at the Army corps headquarters.

The attack on the headquarters involved a heavy barrage of 57mm recoilless rifle fire and rifle grenades fired at short range.

A U.S. spokesman also reported that the Viet Cong launched a mortar attack on oil storage tanks in Tuy Hoa, a coastal city 240 miles northeast of Saigon, and destroyed a large quantity of fuel. However, no American casualties were reported.

Pleiku is a sprawling town of about 100,000 in the center of a vast prairie. The main American detachment just outside the town commands an open view of several miles in almost all directions.

Despite this, the Viet Cong apparently got within striking distance of the camp without tipping their hand.

Nearly 1,000 Americans are stationed at the two big detachments. The largest is the headquarters compound for American advisers serving with the Second Corps and its dependent units.
(Continued on Back Page, Col. 4)

Russian Premier Alexei N. Kosygin (left) talks with north Vietnamese President Ho Chi Minh (center) and Premier Pham | Van Dong at reception in Hanoi celebrating Kosygin's arrival for a four-day visit.
(AP Radiophoto)

Kosygin Vows to Back Hanoi

MOSCOW (AP)—Premier Alexei Kosygin expressed strong Soviet support Saturday for unification of Vietnam under the communist regime in Hanoi. He attacked the American role in South Vietnam.

Speaking on his arrival in Hanoi at the head of a delegation that is expected to extend military aid to north Vietnam, Kosygin called his visit "an important political action."

He hinted at an intention of trying to detach north Vietnam from its close adherence to Peking in the Soviet-Chinese dispute. Cooperation between the Soviet Union and north Vietnam is getting stronger and is "a worthy contribution to unity of the socialist camp," Kosygin said.

The Soviet premier flew into Hanoi from Peking, where he held talks Friday night with Premier Chou En-lai. The brief official announcements on the **(Continued on Back Page, Col. 4)**

86 Killed as Chilean Plane Plows Into Andes Peak

SANTIAGO, Chile (AP)—Eighty-six persons were killed Saturday when a Chilean passenger plane crashed and burned near the top of a 13,000-foot Andean mountain, a rescue patrol reported.

First reports from the crash area said there were no survivors among the 79 passengers and seven crew members.

The report was radioed to Santiago by the first rescue patrol to reach the spot, after a horseback and foot climb of several hours over rugged mountain terrain.

The plane, a DC-6 of the Chilean National Airline, crashed and burned near the summit of La Corona Mountain, in an area known as Los Valdes, deep in the heart of the Andes range and some 50 miles east of Santiago.

(An airlines spokesman said many of the passengers were members of the soccer team from the Antonio Varas Sports Club in Santiago en route to Montevideo for a match, UPI reported.)

Twenty-eight foreigners — including an American woman, 12 Argentines, three Italians, two Germans, two Brazilians, two Uruguayans, two Peruvians, two Bolivians, one Czech and one Russian—were aboard, the spokesman said.

The American woman's name was not reported.

The wreckage was spread over a wide area, approximately 1,200 feet below the mountain top, the patrol said.

This is Latin America's second worst plane disaster. A Brazilian airliner crashed in Lima, Peru, Nov. 27, 1962, killing 97 persons. The previous worst air tragedy in Chile was in 1960, when 24 persons were killed.

The plane was en route to Montevideo, Uruguay—via Buenos Aires. The flight originated in Santiago.

The craft crashed about five minutes after takeoff.

There is no indication yet of what caused the tragedy. The crash area — among towering Andean peaks, is normally a zone of severe air turbulence. This, plus the rugged, rocky nature of the terrain prevented helicopters **(Continued on Back Page, Col. 1)**

LBJ Urges King See Atty. Gen.

WASHINGTON (AP) — The White House Saturday asked the Rev. Dr. Martin Luther King to meet with Atty. Gen. Nicholas Katzenbach on the Alabama racial situation.

King left Selma, Ala. Saturday after spending five days in jail. He was going to Washington, where he had hoped to confer with President Johnson.

(Press Secretary George E. Reedy said the present suggestion was for King to confer with Katzenbach and other top Justice

Department officials "who are engaged in considering legislation on this matter," UPI reported.

(Reedy said this would not block a meeting between King and the President.)

Reedy said King had not yet responded to the White House's suggestion.

King said he wanted to talk with the President about getting new right-to-vote legislation.

Meanwhile, the battle for racial equality in Alabama shifted back for the moment to the state capi-

tal in Montgomery, where King first achieved fame a decade ago.

From Washington, King plans to fly to Montgomery to spearhead a Negro voter registration march Tuesday through the downtown streets of the onetime confederate capital. King once led a boycott in Montgomery of segregated city buses.

In Selma, the voter registration campaign paused for the weekend. King's associates said street marches would start again next **(Continued on Back Page. Col. 3)**

Weather

Tokyo Area Forecast
Monday: Partly Cloudy; Min. Near 30, Max. Near 50
Tuesday: Cloudy w/Rain; Min. Mid 30s, Max. Mid 40s
Saturday's Temperatures: Min. 32, Max. 36
(USAF Weather Central, Fuchu AS)

U.S., VIET PLANES STRIKE NORTH AGAIN

PACIFIC
STAR AND STRIPES

AN AUTHORIZED PUBLICATION OF
THE ARMED FORCES FAR EAST

10¢ DAILY
15¢ WITH SUPPLEMENTS

Vol. 21, No. 40   FIVE-STAR EDITION   Wednesday, Feb. 10, 1965

American children leave the American Community School in Saigon for the last time Monday, carrying their books and personal belongings. American dependents in Vietnam are being evacuated. Story, Page 4. (AP Radiophoto)

DA NANG, South Vietnam (AP)—American and Vietnamese fighter bombers struck communist north Vietnam Monday for the second consecutive day.

Vietnamese Air Force Commander Brig. Gen. Nguyen Cao Ky said the raid by his A-1E Skyraiders and U.S. Air Force F-100s was highly successful.

Ky, who personally led the 24-plane Vietnamese flight, was grazed on the left arm by shrapnel.

He said his flight destroyed major portions of three north Vietnamese military camps and left them burning.

Ky identified the villages in the Vinh Linh area as Liem Cong Tay, That Le and Song Song. The three towns are near the frontier and along a route leading toward the border.

Ky said four U.S. F-100s
(Continued on Back Page, Col. 3)

* * *

Johnson Warns Reds

WASHINGTON (UPI) — President Johnson followed up two military strikes against north Vietnamese targets Monday with a verbal warning to the communist world that it should not miscalculate U.S. determination to preserve freedom.

He did so after meeting with the National Security Council for the

WASHINGTON (UPI) — The White House said Monday President Johnson still hopes to exchange visits this year with the new Soviet leaders despite the flare-up of military action in Vietnam.

third time in as many days to deal with the suddenly explosive Southeast Asian crisis. The purpose of Monday's session was to hear Presidential Asst. McGeorge Bundy report on his survey trip to South Vietnam.

Monday's second aerial strike against north Vietnamese targets also was discussed at the meeting, although no details of the raid were made public here. The Pentagon, however, said that Navy planes returned to the scene of
(Continued on Back Page, Col. 4)

Airliner Plunges Into Sea Off N.Y. With 84 Aboard

NEW YORK (UPI)—An Eastern Airlines DC-7 airliner with 84 persons aboard crashed in the Atlantic Ocean Monday night, minutes after taking off from Kennedy International Airport.

The plane plunged into the water about 15 miles from the airport.

(Two hours later there was no trace of survivors, despite a huge air-sea rescue mission, AP reported.)

A massive search for the propeller-driven, four-engine plane was launched by the Coast Guard and police with boats, planes and helicopters.

The plane was Eastern's Flight 663, which originated in Boston and was slated to go as far south as Atlanta with stops in New York, Richmond, Va., Charlotte, N.C. and Greenville, S.C.

A spokesman for the Federal Aviation Agency said the plane had cleared Kennedy Airport here at 6:22 p.m. EST and headed out over the Atlantic.

He said a preliminary check showed the plane had made a "generally normal" departure from the airport and then mysteriously was lost on radar.

The FAA spokesman said no reports of any difficulties aboard the plane had been received by the control tower at the airport or any of the FAA ground radio stations.

The Coast Guard said its station at Short Beach, on Long Island's south shore, had observed an "explosion" offshore about the time the plane crashed.

The FAA spokesman said the plane had been instructed by ra-
(Continued on Back Page, Col. 4)

House Bows, Backs LBJ on UAR Food

WASHINGTON (AP) — The House of Representatives, bowing to an appeal from President Johnson, voted Monday to give him a free hand to continue or curb surplus food shipments to the United Arab Republic.

It declined to bind its members of a Senate-House conference committee to stick to the position taken originally by the House Jan. 26.

At that time, by vote of 204 to 177, the House added to a $1.6 billion emergency farm appropriation bill a ban against completing a three-year agreement with the
(Continued on Back Page, Col. 1)

Navy Pilot's Luck May Have Run Out

WILKES-BARRE, Pa. (AP)— Almost a year ago a snowbank saved the life of Navy Lt. Edward A. Dickson, 26, of Wyoming, Pa., the pilot who ejected from a bomber shot down at sea Sunday in bombing attacks against north Vietnam.

Dickson ejected from his crippled airplane over the Sierras in California at an altitude of 1,000 feet. Officials at Oakland Naval Hospital reported at the time that Dickson's parachute failed to open when he ejected, but that he landed in a 40-foot snowbank.
(Continued on Back Page, Col. 3)

Weather

Tokyo Area Forecast

Wednesday: Cloudy with showers; Min. Mid 30s, Max. Mid 40s
Thursday: Fair; Min. Mid 30s, Max. Near 50
Monday's Temperatures: Min. 40, Max. 55
(USAF Weather Central, Fuchu AS)

VIET REDS BLOW UP U.S. ARMY BARRACKS

★ ★ ★ ★ ★ ★ ★ ★ ★ ★ ★ ★ ★ ★ ★ ★

Johnson Meets With Top Advisers

WASHINGTON (AP)— President Johnson held a lengthy, emergency meeting with the National Security Council Wednesday, but there was no indication of any imminent action in the Vietnamese situation.

The White House displayed no signs of anxiety as a result of communist blasting of an American enlisted men's hotel at Qui Nhon, or a severe defeat that cost the lives of perhaps 300 South Vietnamese troops.

Johnson walked out into the front yard of the White House and strolled around after the Security Council session, showing no signs of tension.

Nevertheless, developments in Vietnam were grave enough to warrant the almost 2-hour meeting of the National Security Council, and word afterward from George Reedy, presidential press secretary, that "the situation is receiving the closest attention."

But, from then on, Reedy fended **(Continued on Back Page, Col. 1)**

PACIFIC **STARS AND STRIPES**

AN AUTHORIZED PUBLICATION OF THE ARMED FORCES IN THE FAR EAST

FIVE-STAR EDITION

昭和三十四年一月二十二日国鉄東京局特別扱承認新聞紙第175号（日刊）
（昭和34年4月21日第3種郵便物認可）

Vol. 21, No. 42

10¢ DAILY
15¢ WITH
SUPPLEMENTS

Friday, Feb. 12, 1965

'Embassy Must Be Protected'

WASHINGTON (UPI) — President Johnson Wednesday condemned as "wholly inadequate" Soviet police protection given the U.S. Embassy during an anti-American demonstration Tuesday.

In a statement issued by the White House, Johnson insisted that the Soviet government provide better safeguards in the future.

"Expressions of regret and compensation are no substitute for adequate protection," the statement said.

Johnson made a particular point that Soviet officials had been given prior notification of the demonstration which protested the U.S. retaliatory raid against north Vietnam.

The statement declared:

"The President takes a most serious view of the fact that police protection furnished the American Embassy in Moscow was wholly inadequate despite prior notification to the Soviet government of an impending demonstration.

"The United States Government must insist that its diplomatic establishments and personnel be given the protection which is required by international law and custom which is necessary for the conduct of diplomatic relations between states."

President Johnson waves at newsmen during a short stroll around the White House grounds after he met with the National Security Council Wednesday to discuss the Viet Cong bombing of a U.S. Army billet. (UPI Radiophoto)

SAIGON (UPI)—Communist Viet Cong terrorists blew up a U.S. Army barracks housing at least 40 Americans Wednesday night and rescue workers searched for the dead and wounded. At least 26 Americans were unaccounted for.

High explosives ripped apart the four-story building in Qui Nhon, 275 miles northeast of Saigon, at 8 p.m.

Rescue workers reported Thursday morning that voices of six Americans were heard coming from under the charred, smoldering wreckage.

The spokesman said shortly after dawn that the bodies of two American dead had been removed from the wreckage and 12 other wounded Americans were rescued.

(In Washington the Defense Department said one U.S. serviceman is known dead and an estimated 25 are missing in the bombing, AP reported.)

It was the second major communist attack against U.S. forces in South Vietnam since Sunday.

Rescue workers had to dig slowly through the twisted maze

More Vietnam news, Page 5.

of wreckage to prevent the rubble from collapsing and crushing trapped survivors.

The American spokesman said the blast cut four-story building to one-story.

It was not immediately clear how rescue workers determined that the shouts for help came from six men unless the men were able to identify themselves by name.

The barracks housed 57 American military men, but some of **(Continued on Back Page, Col. 1)**

Viets Take Beating

SAIGON (UPI) — Communist Viet Cong guerrillas have dealt the government its worst military setback in the Vietnamese civil war, smashing the equivalent of two government battalions in fighting Monday, U.S. military officials said Wednesday.

Government losses in the battles, excluding wounded, were believed to have exceeded 300 dead, captured or missing.

Meanwhile, an American military spokesman said a U.S. Army helicopter crewman was killed and another three wounded over Phuoc Long province Wednesday. They were aboard an armed helicopter downed over a communist-held village.

Other helicopters in the area evacuated the crew, the spokesman said.

The series of coordinated com- **(Continued on Back Page, Col. 5)**

LBJ Orders Curbs On Dollar Flow

WASHINGTON (AP)—President Johnson ordered sweeping measures Wednesday to "bring an end to our balance-of-payments deficit," including a penalty tax on overseas loans as well as investments.

He also asked a voluntary mobilization of private banking and industry to restrain spending and lending abroad.

In a special message, Johnson asked Congress to slash the duty-free exemption on foreign purchases brought home by returning American tourists from $100 wholesale value to $50 retail value—in effect, a reduction to less than one-third of the present limit.

The President said the recent abrupt widening of the payments deficit need not alarm Americans or foreign holders of dollars, since the 1964 deficit of $3 billion reflected continued year-to-year improvement.

Johnson proposed exemption from the interest equalization tax of new securities issued or guaranteed by Japan up to $100 million each year.

The limited exemption would **(Continued on Back Page, Col. 2)**

Weather

Tokyo Area Forecast

Friday: Fair; Min. Near 30. Max. Near 50
Saturday: Cloudy with rain; Min. Mid 30s. Max. Mid 40s.
Wednesday's Temperatures: Min. 35. Max. 57
(USAF Weather Central, Fuchu AS)

3 Rescued From Barracks Debris

QUI NHON, Vietnam (AP) — Rescue workers Thursday pulled three living American soldiers from the rubble of a barracks destroyed here by Viet Cong terrorists Wednesday night.

Rescue workers also said they had definitely heard voices of two other Americans in the wreckage and possibly the voice of a third.

One trapped serviceman, who was sheltered in a small cave-like space, said "get me a chisel and hammer and I will dig my own way out." In the late afternoon a hole was opened to him, chisel, hammer and cigarets were passed through and he began digging from the inside.

It was believed he would be out soon.

One of the three American survivors was dragged out through a tunnel dug in the debris. A Korean doctor had amputated his leg in order to free him.

The doctor, one of a Korean medical team stationed here, crawled into a tunnel dug through the concrete debris.

The doctor, Capt. Un Sup Kim, stayed with the American in the tunnel from about 3 a.m. Thursday morning until the man was pulled out Thursday afternoon.

Faint cries from the trapped man were heard at 2:30 a.m., about six hours after huge Viet Cong bombs crumpled the four story enlisted men's barracks.

Nothing has been heard from 20 other Americans still buried in the 30-foot-high pile of rubble.
(Continued on Back Page, Col. 3)

150 PLANES HIT 2 N. VIET BASES

PACIFIC STARS AND STRIPES

AN AUTHORIZED PUBLICATION OF THE ARMED FORCES IN THE FAR EAST

FIVE-STAR EDITION

10¢ DAILY
15¢ WITH SUPPLEMENTS

昭和三十四年一月二十二日国鉄東京局特別扱承認新聞紙第175号（日刊）
(昭和34年4月21日第3種郵便物認可)

Vol. 21, No. 43   Saturday, Feb. 13, 1965

SAIGON (AP)—Striking from land and sea, about 150 U.S. and South Vietnamese warplanes smashed at targets in north Vietnam Thursday in reprisal for Viet Red attacks capped by the blasting of a U.S. billet in Qui Nhon.

Three carrier-based U.S. Navy planes and one pilot were lost as a result of the action, otherwise described by an American spokesman as highly successful. The lost pilot later was reported captured by communist north Vietnamese.

The bombing and rocket raids were launched while rescue workers still combed debris of the four-story U.S. enlisted men's billet in Qui Nhon for the living and dead of a terrorist bombing Wednesday night believed to have killed 22 Americans.

It was the third and heaviest reprisal since Sunday against north Vietnam, which trains and supplies the Red guerrillas.

The attacks were made through low, broken clouds.

Targets were officially described as barracks areas at Chan Hoa and Chap Le. They were left wreathed in columns of smoke.

Chan Hoa is 50 miles north of the border and about four miles northwest of Dong Hoi, a coastal point struck by Navy planes Sunday. Chap Le is 8.5 miles north of the border.

More than 100 Navy jets from the carriers Hancock, Ranger and
(Continued on Back Page, Col. 1)

Woman Trapped In Tub

ROCHESTER, N.Y. (UPI) — An elderly woman was found alive Wednesday night after being trapped for 15 days in a bathtub with only her face above water.

Authorities said Mrs. Maude Rathbun, 75, apparently became paralyzed from a fall when she slipped getting into the tub. She was listed in critical condition Thursday at Highland Hospital.

Police said Mrs. Rathbun slipped while getting into the tub Jan. 26 or 27. She could barely move one arm and was capable of making only weak sounds, they said.

A neighbor became suspicious, police said, when he failed to see the woman for some time and noted that a light burning in the house had gone out two days before. The light which burned out was in the bathroom.

Police, acting on the neighbor's
(Continued on Back Page, Col. 2)

RESCUERS WORK TO REACH VICTIMS TRAPPED UNDER RUBBLE OF QUI NHON HOTEL.

Copters Halt Red Junk Force Attack

QUI NHON, Vietnam (UPI) — Viet Cong guerrillas in 50 armed junks atempted an amphibious assault on the port town of Qui Nhon Thursday morning following their demolition of an American barracks with about 50 men inside Wednesday night.

They were driven back by armed American helicopters which attacked as communist guerrillas tried to swarm ashore less than 200 yards from the destroyed barracks.

Col. Theodore Mataxis, commanding American forces here, said the Viet Cong tried to use a human shield of 400 Vietnamese civilians to get onto the beach.

He said his helicopters hovered overhead while artillerymen fired rounds across the path of the junks in an effort to stop them.

The artillery fire failed to halt the advance and the helicopters then attacked, driving the junks back across the bay to a mangrove swamp.

(The AP reported that about 100 Viet Cong who assaulted the city in junks were still fighting Thursday night from a spit of land across the harbor from the city Thursday. U.S. helicopters were striking the position hard.)

In the meantime the once bustling city of 50,000 took on the aspects of a war center in the wake of the bombing and the attempted assault.

American soldiers were manning rooftops with machine-gun emplacements in the downtown area.

Trucks raced about dropping coils of barbwire, which were thrown up into hasty barricades by American and Vietnamese soldiers. Trucks mounted with machineguns were posted in main streets.

Weather

Tokyo Area Forecast
Saturday: Partly cloudy; Min. Mid 20s, Max. Near 50
Sunday: Cloudy with rain; Min. Mid 30s, Max. Mid 40s
Thursday's Temperatures: Min. 38, Max. 42
(USAF Weather Central, Fuchu AS)

American-Piloted U.S. Jets In Viet Combat for 1st Time

PACIFIC
STAR AND STRIPES

AN AUTHORIZED PUBLICATION OF
THE ARMED FORCES FAR EAST

10¢ DAILY
15¢ WITH SUPPLEMENTS

Vol. 21, No. 56   FIVE-STAR EDITION   Friday, Feb. 26, 1965

PFC Arnold Edward Anderson Jr., 19, of Hamilton, Ohio, is all smiles at 1st Cav. Div. headquarters near Seoul, Korea, after being told his mother, whom he had not seen for 18 years, had been located. His brother, Larry, is in the Marines and stationed on Okinawa. (AP Radiophoto)

Situation at a Glance

U.N. Secretary-General U Thant calls for East-West talks on Vietnam "that would enable the U.S. to withdraw gracefully . . ."

France agrees to cooperate with the USSR in pressing for an international conference to negotiate a Vietnam settlement.

U.S. reaffirms its policy to take "continuous action" in the Vietnam war in ways that would be "appropriate, fitting and measured."

The White House says there are no "meaningful proposals" before the U.S. government for a negotiated settlement of the Vietnam crisis.

Communist Chinese and U.S. negotiators meet in Warsaw for the first time since the U.S. bombed north Vietnam. Observers say it is virtually certain that the Chinese repeated their threat to intervene in the Republic of Vietnam if the U.S. continues to strike against north Vietnam.

Democrats in Congress advocate a strong U.S. stand in Vietnam.

Mme. Nhu, former first lady of Vietnam, charges that the U.S. is ready to make a face-saving deal over the fate of her country.

Former Vietnam strongman Lt. Gen. Nguyen Khanh returns to Saigon to hand over his powers to Maj. Gen. Tran Van Minh.

*   *   *

SAIGON (UPI)—The United States disclosed Wednesday that U.S. jets piloted by Americans have gone into combat action inside the Republic of Vietnam for the first time to give "maximum assistance" to the Vietnamese in the war against the communists.

A U.S. spokesman said twin-jet B-57 bombers first went into action last week against communist Viet Cong forces in Phouc Tuy Province, about 40 miles southeast of Saigon.

The B-57s and American F-100 jet aircraft from two jet bomber bases in South Vietnam blasted the communists anew Wednesday to help rescue Vietnamese troops trapped by a Viet Cong offensive 240 miles north of Saigon.

U.S. jet aircraft had previously been used in a series of retaliatory air strikes against communist north Vietnam. But inside South Vietnam, U.S. jets had been limited to reconnaissance (Continued on Back Page, Col. 3)

Mother Telephones 'Lost' Son

HAMILTON, Ohio (UPI)—"He said, 'Mother I love you,' and those words meant everything in the world to me," Mrs. Betty Greer said after speaking to her son, PFC Arnold Edward Anderson Jr., whom she had not seen for nearly 18 years.

The 10-minute telephone hookup to Seoul, Korea, Sunday night was the first contact she has had (Continued on Back Page, Col. 4)

Silent Screen Star Marries Blind Veteran as Act of Mercy

LOS ANGELES (AP) — Silent screen star May MacLaren was married Tuesday to a crippled, blind World War I veteran in what she termed "a marriage of mercy."

Miss MacLaren, 65, said one-time lion tamer Robert S. Coleman, also 65, "is an interesting man and companionable," and, she said, "he tells me he loves me dearly."

But for her, she said, "This is a marriage of mercy. I know it means a great deal to him to feel he has someone who wishes to be with him always."

Miss MacLaren, who played the queen opposite Douglas Fairbanks Sr. in the silent version of "The Three Musketeers," lives in the Los Angeles home she bought in 1917 at the height of her screen career.

She said she met Coleman three years ago when a friend told her of a blind veteran who had been beaten and robbed in his hotel room, was hospitalized and had no place to go when he left the hospital.

"I brought him home and he has been at my house ever since," she said.

Last year, she said, Coleman's right leg was amputated above the knee.

SKYSCRAPER DRAMA

Dad Hangs On to Son's Life

CHICAGO (AP)—A pipefitter working on the 32d floor of the Civic Center, under construction in downtown Chicago, fell into a shaft Tuesday night, but was grabbed by his father who was working two floors below.

The man, James Davis Jr., 25, was taken to a hospital suffering a fractured wrist and cuts. He was reported in good condition.

Davis fell into the shaft when a guard rail he was leaning against broke, witnesses said.

His father, James Davis Sr., 48, heard the noise and looked up from the 30th floor in time to see his son tumble into the shaft. He grabbed his son's wrist as the younger Davis fell past the 30th floor.

Weather

Tokyo Area Forecast
Friday: Fair; Min. Near 20, Max. Near 50
Saturday: Partly Cloudy; Min. Mid 20s, Max Near 50
Wednesday's Temperatures: Min. 23, Max. 42
(USAF Weather Central, Fuchu AS)

160 U.S., VIET PLANES RIP BASES IN NORTH

PACIFIC STAR AND STRIPES

AN AUTHORIZED PUBLICATION OF THE ARMED FORCES FAR EAST

10¢ DAILY
15¢ WITH SUPPLEMENTS

Vol. 21, No. 62   FIVE-STAR EDITION   Thursday, March 4, 1965

LBJ Asks Congress to OK Massive Urban Aid Plan

WASHINGTON (AP) — President Johnson asked Congress Tuesday to create a cabinet-level department of housing affairs, proposed federal grants to help cities build basic community facilities and asked federal funds to pay part of the rent of needy persons.

Johnson, in a special message, said he wants to begin now a far-reaching program to help urban areas solve their many problems.

He told Congress the programs he proposed will require sound, long-range development programs by urban areas as a condition of federal assistance.

He requested $100 million for the fiscal year beginning July 1 for building new basic community facilities. Communities would have to match the grants.

Johnson said these grants would be contingent upon comprehensive, area-wide planning for future growth, and would be made only for projects consistent with such planning.

Johnson described his proposal for what he calls rent supplement as the "most crucial new instrument in our effort to improve the American city."

"Up to now government programs for low and moderate income families have concentrated on either direct financing of construction; or on making below-the-market-rate loans to private builders," he wrote. "We now propose to add to these programs through direct payment a portion of the rent of needy individuals and families."

"These homes themselves will be built by private builders, with Federal Housing Administration insurance, and where necessary, mortgage purchases by the Federal National Mortgage Assn. The major federal assistance will be the rent supplement payment
(Continued on Back Page, Col. 1)

National Aeronautics and Space Administration photographers film smoke rising from the scene of the explosion of an Atlas-Centaur rocket at Cape Kennedy, Fla., Tuesday. (AP Radiophoto)

SAIGON (UPI)—United States and Republic of Vietnam jet fighters and bombers penetrated into communist north Vietnam Tuesday and blasted two key targets.

A U.S. Air Force spokesman described the 160-plane strike as "the biggest ever" against that country.

It was the first time that the powerful U.S. B-57 Canberra jet bombers have been used against north Vietnam.

The previous punitive strikes against the north were limited to Skyraiders, plus the smaller U.S. fighter-bombers.

The spokesman said at least three of the raiding planes were downed by antiaircraft fire from communist positions.

The planes crossed the military demarcation line shortly after 3 p.m. and blasted a key naval base at Quang Khe and supply depots at Xom Bang.

An American military spokesman said both targets were between 70 and 80 per cent destroyed.

U.S. Air Force F-100, F-105 and B-57 Canberra planes flew the raids along with Vietnamese Air Force A-1E Skyraiders.

"We had several losses but I won't go into that because operations are still going on," Lt. Col. Harold L. Price of Orlando, Fla., said. Price is U.S. Air Force operations director for the Sai-
(Continued on Back Page, Col. 2)

RED CHINA
NORTH VIETNAM
HANOI
LAOS
XOM BANG
THAILAND
CAMBODIA
REPUBLIC OF VIETNAM
SAIGON

Stars and Stripes Map

Raid Is Warning To Reds, U.S. Says

WASHINGTON (UPI)—Top U.S. officials said Tuesday that the new air raids on north Vietnam were intended as a clear military message to the communists that continued aggression in the south will not be tolerated.

They said the action did not signify any change in U.S. policy —merely a continued reply to north Vietnamese involvement in the Republic of Vietnam war.

The White House, the Pentagon and congressional leaders rejected any suggestion that the strike by more than 160 U.S. and Republic of Vietnam planes constituted an unprovoked extension of the anti-communist war.

They cited the U.S. policy which has been stated time and again: To take "continuing actions ... made necessary by the continuing aggression of others."

In Saigon, U.S. Ambassador Maxwell D. Taylor put it this way:

"These air actions are joint actions by the Vietnamese Air Force and our own for the purpose of replying to the continuous aggressive acts across the 17th Parallel coming from the north."

Presidential Press Secretary George E. Reedy traced U.S. policy back to the congressional resolution of last August authorizing the President to take whatever steps necessary to resist aggression.

The Soviet Union denounced the attacks as "piracy."

Secretary of State Dean Rusk and Soviet Ambassador Anatoly F. Dobrynin traded official views on the Vietnam situation Tuesday in what the Russian envoy termed a "business-like" discussion, AP reported.

(Rusk called the Kremlin representative to the State Department for the talk of more than an hour which also covered a number of other subjects.)

President Johnson talked to Rusk and Defense Secretary Robert S. McNamara Tuesday and
(Continued on Back Page, Col. 1)

10-Story Atlas-Centaur Explodes on Pad

CAPE KENNEDY, Fla. (AP)—A 10-story tall Atlas-Centaur space rocket exploded on its launch pad Tuesday as it was about to blast off in an attempt to send a model of the Surveyor spacecraft toward a make-believe moon.

The big rocket had struggled only inches off the concrete and steel pad when it erupted into a massive fireball which sent flames and a huge cloud of black smoke hundreds of feet into the air.

Flaming fragments and blazing propellant from the shattered $9 million rocket sprayed several hundred yards in all directions. The firing crew was protected inside a reinforced concrete blockhouse several hundred feet from the pad.

The flight control center said there were no injuries to personnel.

The launching was to have been an important rehearsal for gently landing a "live" Surveyor spacecraft on the moon next autumn to determine if the surface is strong enough to support astronaut expeditions.

The Atlas-Centaur was to have propelled the dummy spacecraft toward an empty spot in the sky 248,000 miles away where the moon will be next fall.

The flight would have provided
(Continued on Back Page, Col. 5)

PACIFIC STARS & STRIPES

AN AUTHORIZED PUBLICATION OF THE ARMED FORCES IN THE FAR EAST

FIVE-STAR EDITION

昭和三十四年一月二十二日国鉄局特別承認新聞紙第175号 (日刊)
(昭和34年4月21日第3種郵便物認可)

10¢ DAILY
15¢ WITH
SUPPLEMENTS

Vol. 21, No. 66   Monday, March 8, 1965

3,500 Marines Ordered to Viet

WASHINGTON (UPI) — The Defense Department announced Saturday that 3,500 marines are being sent to the Republic of Vietnam to protect Da Nang AB.

A spokesman said two battalions of marines will take over the job of insuring the security of the air base complex. Terming it a "limited action," the Defense Department said the marines were ordered in after consultations with the Republic of Vietnam government, which requested the action.

The troops will "relieve government of South Vietnam forces now engaged in security duties for action" against the Viet Cong, the Defense Department announcement said.

The Defense Department did not disclose when the marines would land.

The marines apparently will be drawn from units in the Pacific area.

The addition of the 3,500 marines in Vietnam brings American military strength in the area to approximately 27,000.

"The limited mission of the marines will be to relieve government of South Vietnam forces now engaged in security duties for action in the pacification program and in the offensive roles against communist guerrilla forces," the announcement said.

Dockers Go Back To Work

GALVESTON, Tex. (AP) —West Gulf Coast district longshoremen started returning to their jobs Saturday after voting overwhelmingly to accept a new contract.

Most piers in Galveston idled since Jan. 11 were busy by mid-afternoon and all other ports from Brownsville, Tex., to Lake Charles, La., were expected to be back in full operation by Monday morning.

Ralph A. Massey, district International Longshoremen's Assn. (ILA) president, said returns from the some 7,000 dock workers in the district were "98 to 99 per cent in favor of accepting the contract."

In Washington, President Johnson was described as very pleased that the strike had been settled.

Voting by the membership started early Saturday in the Galveston-Houston area of Texas where more than half of the long-
(Continued on Back Page, Col. 1)

Ex-Boxer Scores TKO at 80

NEWARK, N.J. (AP) — A vigorous 80-year-old man fought a robber Saturday and managed to floor the man with a punch and wound him with a gun.

Police followed a blood trail and arrested a suspect.

The hero of the day was William Brown, who says he was a boxer more than 50 years ago. He suffered only a neck abrasion.

Brown told police a man wearing a kerchief over his face entered his office at the Perfect Dice Co.

"I belted him," Brown said.

Then he ran to a safe, grabbed a revolver and shot at the man. Two shots were high but one hit in the jaw.

KILAUEA VOLCANO ON HAWAII ISLAND SENDS UP FIERY FOUNTAINS OF LAVA.

AP Radiophoto

Exercise Points Up Gun Gap

CAMP PENDLETON, Cal. (AP)—Twenty thousand U.S. marines landed on the southern California coast Friday and moved inland in an exercise that top officers said showed several weaknesses in U.S. equipment.

The marines stormed ashore under simulated battle conditions.

But General W.M. Greene Jr., Marine Corps commandant, said Exercise Silver Lance, involving 58 ships and 65,000 men, showed a need for faster assault ships, missiles to clear the skies of low-flying planes and helicopters and new craft such as hydrofoils, which could land and move well inland before stopping to unload troops.

At a news conference after the first waves of marines landed at this training ground south of Los Angeles, Greene acknowledged that what he called a "gun gap" exists in amphibious operations.

The landing was made spectacular by explosive charges buried on the beach and detonated to simulate impact of shells from ships offshore, but in actual combat, Greene said, inshore fire-support of amphibious attacks leaves much to be desired.

Greene said steps are being taken to bring back the rocket-firing ship of World War II and said cruisers with 8-inch guns may be retained in service, instead of being mothballed, to augment fire-support.

50-FOOT LAVA FOUNTAIN

Hawaii Volcano in 2d Spectacular Blast

HILO, Hawaii (AP)—Tempestuous Kilauea Volcano on the island of Hawaii erupted again Saturday, spewing a fountain of molten lava 50 feet high inside its huge crater.

The activity broke out about 100 feet from where the volcano erupted 24 hours earlier, creating a river of lava that flowed into trees outside the crater at one point.

Volcano observatory scientists said there was an increase in tremors Saturday — indicating that lava was moving down in the volcano's plumbing.

They said violent activity may break out at any time along the Puna fault line running eastward from Kilauea to the sea.

They said their instruments indicate a steady river of lava is being forced from the main dome under Kilauea into the fault, which could erupt to the surface at any place along the fault line.

The new eruption was not unexpected but came after lava fountains had tapered off.

Kilauea belched forth with a lacy 1,000-foot curtain of fire Friday and put on a spectacular show for more than nine hours. Then the activity began sputtering out.

Red-hot lava still continued Saturday to flow into the wastelands of the Puna fault zone on the east cape of Hawaii Island.

RUSS TAKES 'WALK' FROM ORBITING SHIP

PACIFIC STARS AND STRIPES

KOREA EDITION

AN AUTHORIZED PUBLICATION OF THE
U.S. ARMED FORCES IN THE FAR EAST

10¢ DAILY

15¢ WITH
SUPPLEMENTS

Vol. 21 No. 78   Saturday, March 20, 1965

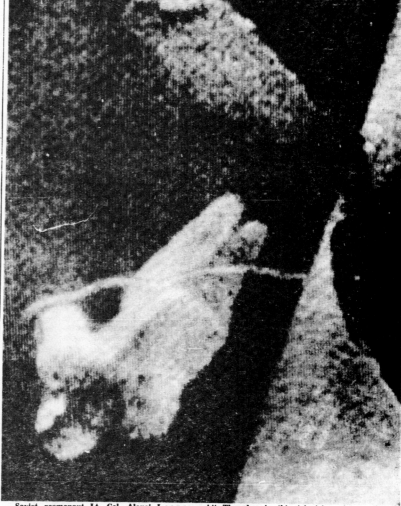

Soviet cosmonaut Lt. Col. Alexei Leonov bit Thursday in this television picture viewed floats free from his Voskhod-2 spacecraft in or- in Moscow.   (AP Radiophoto)

Wallace Asks U.S. Officers to Shield Marchers

MONTGOMERY, Ala. (AP)—Alabama Gov. George C. Wallace called on President Johnson Thursday to provide a "sufficient number" of federal officers to help protect civil rights marchers on their Sunday trek from Selma to Montgomery.

The governor told the Alabama Legislature that U.S. help will be necessary to guarantee the "safety and well-being" of the civil rights marchers, as well as other residents of the state.

(President Johnson in Washington advised Wallace that he will federalize the Alabama National Guard to protect the march if Wallace is "unable or unwilling" to call out the guard to do the job, UPI reported).

Wallace spoke to a joint assembly of the Alabama House and Senate in the wake of a U.S. District Court order permitting Negroes to march from Selma to the state capitol and requiring the state to protect tnem.

The governor promised to obey the court order as long as it remains in effect. His attorneys

---

More racial news, Page 6.

---

earlier in the day had asked the federal court to stay enforcement of its order, pending an appeal to the U.S. 5th Circuit Court of Appeals.

Wallace said the cost in manpower and money would be an unfair burden for the state to bear alone.

(Continued on Back Page, Col. 2)

U.S.-Thai Units Begin Push on Foe

By JOSEPH SCHNEIDER
S&S S.E. Asia Bureau Chief

SOUTHERN THAILAND—Nearly 3,000 U.S. and Thai marines hit the beaches in this remote part of Southeast Asia Saturday and immediately launched a thrust inland to destroy a mythical aggressor force.

Preceding the landing in Exercise Jungle Drum III, clouds of smoke and sand erupted from the beaches as explosives were set off to simulate a naval and aerial bombardment of the area.

U.S. and Thai troops came across the beaches in four waves. The first rode through the surf in amphibious armored personnel carriers (LVT) and three successive waves rode ashore in the

(Continued on Page 7, Col. 4)

MOSCOW (AP) — A Soviet rocket hurled two cosmonauts into man's highest orbit Thursday and one of them spent 10 minutes outside the space ship.

Tass News Agency said he was "in condition of outer space" for 20 minutes including 10 minutes outside the ship. This indicated he spent 10 minutes in an airless chamber attached to the pressurized main cabin before going outside.

There were indications that the new space venture was intended as another step toward a trip to the moon by experimenting with the techniques needed to join space ships together.

Tass, the Soviet news agency, said Lt. Col. Alexei Leonov, 30, co-pilot of the space ship called Voskhod-2, went 16 feet from the space capsule. He appeared to be attached to the ship by a lifeline.

Soviet television stations showed a film of Leonov floating outside the space ship, with the curve of the earth and the blackness of space visible in the background.

Tass said Leonov spent about 20 minutes inspecting the surface of the ship, taking pictures with his camera, and conducting visual observations of the earth and outer space.

Leonov wore what was described as a special "autonomous life-support suit." On television, the helmet was heavy. What appeared to be oxygen containers were strapped to his back.

The 30-year-old cosmonaut did somersaults in space and floated in a loose, relaxed manner in the weightlessness.

Tass said the venture into space —the first time man has trusted himself outside the protective

(Continued on Back Page, Col. 3)

LBJ Off to Texas

WASHINGTON (UPI) — President Johnson will fly to his Texas ranch Thursday night for the weekend and will hold a news conference there at 5 p.m. Saturday.

---

20 Pupils Killed in Bombing of Red Cave

DA NANG, Republic of Vietnam (UPI)—An estimated 20 to 30 South Vietnamese school children were killed near here this week when their Viet Cong schoolmaster herded them into a cave that collapsed during an air attack.

A spokesman for the Vietnamese army said the children were crushed or suffocated when the ceiling of the cave collapsed from the concussion of bombs aimed at Viet Cong terrorists who had been using the schoolhouse as a military post.

The incident occurred in the village of Man Quang Tuesday afternoon. Man Quang, located only seven miles from this vital port city, had been listed as a town free of Viet Cong influence.

But when a Vietnamese Air Force observation plane flew over the village making a landing approach to Da Nang Air Base, it was fired upon by 12 armed men in the schoolyard.

The plane circled back, spotted the red-blue-gold flag of the Viet Cong flying from the school flag

(Continued on Back Page, Col. 1)

EMBASSY HIT

★ ★ ★ ★ ★ ★ ★ ★ ★ ★ ★ ★ ★ ★ ★ ★

Saigon Building Ripped by Bomb; Americans Among Heavy Casualties

PACIFIC
STAR AND STRIPES

AN AUTHORIZED PUBLICATION OF
THE ARMED FORCES FAR EAST

10¢ DAILY
15¢ WITH SUPPLEMENTS

Vol. 21, No. 89   FIVE-STAR EDITION   Wednesday, March 31, 1965

Wallace To Meet Marchers

MONTGOMERY, Ala. (AP)—Gov. George C. Wallace of Alabama agreed Monday to meet with a group of civil rights leaders.

His decision was announced amid growing criticism of a proposed nationwide boycott of Alabama products as a part of the civil rights campaign.

Wallace's office said he would meet at 9:30 a.m. Tuesday with a committee of civil rights leaders.

Negro leaders said then they wanted to petition the governor to help remove barriers to voting, including the $1.50 per year poll tax. They also said they would protest "police brutality."

Meanwhile, State Atty. Gen. Richmond Flowers said he hoped to have enough evidence to seek first-degree murder indictments next month in the night-rider slaying of Mrs. Viola Liuzzo of Detroit, a participant in last (Continued on Back Page, Col. 4)

New Jolts In Chile

SANTIAGO, Chile (UPI)—New tremors shook north central Chile Monday in the wake of Sunday's huge quake which killed at least 247 persons.

Seismologists said the new earth movements were customary aftershocks. There were no immediate reports of new casualties or damage.

The government moved swiftly to provide aid and relief to the

Quake disaster scenes, Pages 12-13.

zone shattered Sunday by Chile's worst earthquake since 1960.

Police said at least 214 dwellers of El Cobre Village were buried alive by tons of slime when a copper mine dam burst. There were 33 counted deaths in other cities.

Police said the dam rupture at (Continued on Back Page, Col. 3)

Deputy Ambassador U. Alexis Johnson was inside the American Embassy in Saigon Tuesday when a blast tore through the building. He was cut by flying debris but was not seriously hurt. Contacted inside the embassy shortly after the blast he was asked if he was all right. He said, "Yes, but we have been hit. We will need some medical assistance."

SAIGON (AP)—A huge bomb exploded at the U.S. Embassy here Tuesday an hour before noon and it was believed there were heavy casualties.

At least 20 Vietnamese were killed. Many others were badly wounded.

(At least one American was killed, UPI said.)

Deputy U.S. Ambassador U. Alexis Johnson was inside the building and was cut by flying glass. Ambassador Maxwell D. Taylor is currently in Washington.

The blast was heard throughout the city.

(The explosion rocked all of downtown Saigon and some buildings are belived to have collapsed as far as two blocks away from the embassy, UPI reported.)

Several hundred embassy officials and employes work in the five-story concrete building.

The street outside the embassy was a bloody mess of broken bodies.

At least seven Americans were carried, badly wounded, from the building.

At least seven vehicles in the street outside were smashed and burning.

The bomb appeared to have been placed in a vehicle in the street. This was the apparent cause of the number of Vietnamese wounded by the blast.

The U.S. consulate on the ground floor of the building was wrecked.

It was a scene of chaos. Seven ambulances arrived within five minutes of the explosion.

Bloody footprints were left by the injured but there was no immediate estimate of the number of Americans wounded or killed. It was believed that at least a score were casualties.

Three Americans were seen being carried and bleeding heavily.

(Continued on Back Page, Col. 2)

★ ★ ★ ★ ★

Navy Jets Attack Red Radar Base

SAIGON (AP) — U.S. Navy planes from the aircraft carrier Coral Sea Monday bombed radar installations on Bach Long Island.

It was the second American raid on Bach Long, deep in the Tonkin Gulf, and the northernmost target since American and Republic of Vietnam planes began hitting north Vietnam Feb. 7. The Bach Long radar station was first hit last Friday, in the 12th attack on north Vietnam. The island is about 140 miles southeast of Hanoi, 100 miles south of the Chinese mainland and 80 miles west of Hainan, a big Chinese island that is a base for MIG interceptors.

Forty-two Navy fighter-bombers took part in the raid. The attack cost the Navy one Skyhawk jet fighter shot down by enemy ground fire.

The pilot reportedly was rescued from the sea uninjured.

The raid was led by Cdr. Henry P. Glindeman of Coeur D'Alene, Idaho, skipper of Airwing 15 on the Coral Sea.

Glindeman, who flew directly to Saigon following the raid, said the primary objective had been substantially damaged. He said he could see smoke rising and many secondary fires in the target area.

He said the raid was carried out to finish the work started last week in which a half-acre radar installation reportedly was only moderately damaged.

Glindeman's team also attacked a communications center and Army troops Sunday took 30 prisoners, including 13 they described as hard-core Viet Cong, in an operation in Quang Nam Province, (Continued on Back Page, Col. 1)

Ready for Viet Talks

JOHNSON PROPOSES $1 BIL. S.E. ASIA AID

PACIFIC
STAR AND STRIPES

AN AUTHORIZED PUBLICATION OF
THE ARMED FORCES FAR EAST

昭和二十四年一月二十二日國鐵局特別(山泉蛛新聞紙第176号)

10¢ DAILY
15¢ WITH SUPPLEMENTS
(最和 54 年 4 月 21 日第 3 種郵便物認可)

Vol. 21, No. 98   **FIVE-STAR EDITION**   Friday, April 9, 1965

A Prayer for Peace

Chaplain (Lt.) John F. Walker leads U.S. marines at Da Nang AB, Republic of Vietnam, in a prayer for peace. Religious services are frequently held outdoors. (UPI)

Text of President's speech, Page 16.

BALTIMORE, Md. (UPI)—President Johnson said Wednesday that the United States is ready for "unconditional discussions" to bring peace to the Republic of Vietnam as a first step toward a $1 billion aid program to develop Southeast Asia.

In an address at Johns Hopkins University which was broadcast to the world, Johnson said that any such peace "demands an independent South Vietnam—securely guaranteed and able to shape its own relationships to all others—free from outside interference—tied to no alliance—a military base for no other country."

Until then, he added, the United States will not be defeated, not grow tired, and will not withdraw, "either openly or under the cloak of a meaningless agreement."

But he held out the promise of a bright future for Southeast Asia if there is peace.

He said he would ask Congress to join in a $1 billion American investment in this development program, and expressed hope that the Soviet Union would assist. He also said, "We would hope that north Vietnam will take its place in the common effort just as soon as peaceful co-operation is possible."

As for the prospects of peace, he said he hoped it would come swiftly—"but that is in the hands of others besides ourselves."

He then declared in a major statement on the U.S.
(Continued on Back Page, Col. 4)

U.S. Aide Faces Death, VC Warns

TOKYO (AP)—The communist Viet Cong warned Wednesday that a high-ranking American civilian captured in Saigon two months ago will be shot if Republic of Vietnam authorities execute one of its men.

The warning was announced by the "South Vietnam National Liberation Front" in a communique issued Wednesday and carried by Hanoi Radio in a broadcast heard here.

"If the U.S. and its henchmen execute Nguyen Van Thai, the front will immediately give the order to execute G. Hertz (Gustav Hertz of Leesburg, Va.), a member of the USOM (U.S. Operation Mission) in South Vietnam who is guilty of spying activities and many bloody crimes against the South Vietnamese people," the front said.

The front said Nguyen Van
(Continued on Back Page, Col. 3)

That's The Limit!

REDDING, Cal. (AP)—For seven days the Siskiyou County Sheriff's office has been investigating the theft of five valuable paintings from the 75,000-acre Hearst estate.

Wednesday deputies made a vital discovery. The building from which the paintings were stolen is 300 feet inside Shasta County. Promptly, Siskiyou County Sheriff A. B. Cottar turned the investigation over to Shasta County Sheriff John Balma.

Weather

Tokyo Area Forecast

Friday: Cloudy with rain; Min. Mid 40s, Max. Near 50
Saturday: Fair; Min. Near 40, Max. Near 60
Wednesday's Temperatures: Min. 31, Max. 60
(USAF Weather Central, Fuchu AB)

PACIFIC STARS AND STRIPES

AN AUTHORIZED PUBLICATION OF THE ARMED FORCES IN THE FAR EAST

FIVE-STAR EDITION

昭和三十四年一月二十二日国鉄東京局特別扱承認新聞紙第175号（日刊）
（昭和34年4月21日第3種郵便物認可）

10¢ DAILY
15¢ WITH
SUPPLEMENTS

Vol. 21, No. 147   Friday, May 28, 1965

RUSSIAN MISSILE SITES GOING UP IN NORTH: RUSK

Senate Passes Vote Bill

WASHINGTON (AP) — Amid echoes of a bitter southern assault, the Senate Wednesday passed President Johnson's voting rights bill and sent it to the House.

After a 25-day debate, Johnson's top-priority measure won Senate passage on a 77-19 roll call vote.

If the Senate version is approved by the House and signed into law by the President, state literacy tests would be barred and a federal voter registration system would be set up in much of the South.

The bill also calls for a court challenge of state pool taxes.

Under its terms:

1. Literacy tests would be ruled out and federal registration authorized in any state or county with a 20 per cent nonwhite population which used a literacy test or similar device in enrolling voters for last year's election and had registration or voter *(Continued on Back Page, Col. 1)*

Grew Dies; Ex-Envoy To Japan

MANCHESTER, Mass. (AP)— Joseph Clark Grew, 84, who was U.S. ambassador to Japan in the period preceding Pearl Harbor, died Tuesday at his home.

Grew was in Japan for nine years marked by Japanese violation of treaties and aggression.

An American "White Book" issued by the State Department in 1943 revealed that Grew had cabled on Jan. 27, 1941, that the Japanese had plans for a "surprise attack" on Pearl Harbor.

When the attack came on Dec. 7, Grew was stunned but not surprised.

Grew would have celebrated *(Continued on Back Page, Col. 1)*

The destroyer Craig stands guard duty astern of the attack aircraft carrier Midway off Vietnam as a Skyhawk jet glides in for a landing. The aircraft had just returned from a strike on military installations in north Vietnam.
(USN Photo by PH2 Karl S. Hedberg)

WASHINGTON (UPI)

—Secretary of State Dean Rusk said Wednesday that two or more Soviet antiaircraft missile sites may now be under construction in north Vietnam.

He called this a deepening Soviet commitment to Hanoi.

Rusk told a news conference that "missile associated equipment" was believed to be present at one of the sites.

He did not report that any missiles themselves were at the sites, but he said it was to be presumed the sites would not remain empty.

Earlier this year, administration officials disclosed that one SAM missile site had been under construction in the Hanoi area. The initials stand for "surface to air missile."

Rusk said Wednesday there *(Continued on Back Page, Col. 4)*

American Dies, 1 Lost In Ambush

SAIGON (AP)—One American was killed, another was wounded and a third was missing Wednesday following a Viet Cong ambush 60 miles northwest of Saigon.

In the air war, U.S. warplanes battered military installations and transport facilities in north Vietnam on a round-the-clock basis.

The Americans were ambushed Tuesday as they were traveling in a jeep from the special forces camp at Ben Soi to Tay Ninh.

An irregular South Vietnamese strike force made contact with the Viet Cong, and a regional company accompanied by two *(Continued on Back Page, Col. 1)*

Typhoon Hits Japan Coast, Nears Tokyo

TOKYO (S&S) — Typhoon Amy, with 75 m.p.h. center winds, was forecast to lash Tokyo Thursday after slamming into the Izu Peninsula some 90 miles southwest of the city.

The U.S. Air Force Weather Central at Fuchu AS, Japan, said Amy's force was expected to diminish rapidly after hitting the coast around noon but that Tokyo could expect winds gusting up to 50 m.p.h. and heavy rain.

An Air Force spokesman said planes were being evacuated from Tachikawa AB Thursday morning. Tokyo International Airport officials said most flights had been canceled.

Weathermen said Amy had been forecast to skirt southern Japan but early Thursday changed her course and sped toward the coast at 40 m.p.h.

The fringes of the storm Wednesday brought 50 m.p.h.

winds to southern Japan and heavy rains to most of the southern and central part of the country.

A total of 3.12 inches of rain was reported at Tachikawa AB on the outskirts of Tokyo Thursday morning.

The heavy rains triggered floods and landslides in Japan. Police reported hundreds of homes flooded, roads blocked and scores of trains canceled.

The wind and rain in southern Japan grounded planes and halted ferry boats.

At least two persons were reported dead as the result of the floods and three fishermen missing after their boat capsized in heavy seas.

Amy was first spotted off Guam Sunday and threatened the island Monday. But the storm swerved toward Okinawa, sparing the island.

Weather

Tokyo Area Forecast

Thursday Night: Partly cloudy, Low Mid 50s

Friday: Fair; High Mid 70s

Wednesday's Temperature: Low 61, High 69

(USAF Weather Central, Fuchu AS)

Pound Vietnam Coast

NAVY GUNS OPEN FIRE

PACIFIC
STAR AND STRIPES

AN AUTHORIZED PUBLICATION OF THE
U.S. ARMED FORCES IN THE FAR EAST

10¢ DAILY
15¢ WITH SUPPLEMENTS

Vol. 21, No. 148 **FIVE-STAR EDITION**

昭和三十四年一月二十二日國鉄東局特別扱承認新聞紙第175号（日刊）
（昭和34年4月21日第3種郵便物認可）

Saturday, May 29, 1965

SAIGON (AP) — U.S. ships have entered the Republic of Vietnam ground war by firing at land targets in coastal provinces along the South China Sea, a U.S. spokesman said Thursday.

Four U.S. destroyers have fired shells on six missions against Viet Cong targets in the coastal areas of Binh Dinh, Binh Tuan and Phu Yen provinces since May 20, the spokesman said.

They have been credited with thwarting at least one Viet Cong attack on a Vietnamese district headquarters, the U.S. spokesman said.

The disclosure of Navy participation in the Vietnam war was made during a press briefing Thursday in which the death of U.S. Navy Seaman Jimmy C. Stinnett, of Cartersville, Va., was announced.

The U.S. spokesman said Stin-
(Continued on Back Page, Col. 3)

Kill 85 VC Near Da Nang

GIANG HOI, Republic of Vietnam (AP)—U.S. Army armed helicopters and South Vietnamese troops turned an apparent Viet Cong officers' convention into a turkey shoot Thursday, with the communists as both the targets and prizes.

"When the ground troops pushed the Viet Cong into the river, it was just like shooting sitting ducks for us," said Pvt. James E. Horner, a helicopter gunner from Lockbourne, Ohio.

About 85 Viet Cong were killed in the action, 25 miles south of Da Nang. All but about 25 of them were killed by American gunships, as the armed helicopters are called. Vietnamese marines also captured 27 Viet Cong suspects.

One U.S. helicopter gunner was wounded slightly, and Vietnamese government casualties were one killed and three wounded.

The operation kicked off near dawn, when U.S. Marine Corps
(Continued on Back Page, Col. 1)

Queen Elizabeth II with her husband Prince Philip beside her, drives along the West Berlin side of the wall bordering communist east Berlin. The Queen later stopped the auto to view the wall dividing east and West Berlin. (AP Radiophoto)

East Berlin Joins In Cheering Queen

HANOVER, West Germany (UPI)—Hundreds of thousands of West Berliners—and a sprinkling of defiant East Berliners—cheered Queen Elizabeth II Thursday on a triumphant tour of the Berlin Wall.

More than 500,000 West Berlin men, women and children waved, shouted and cheered the visiting monarch who, in the words of Mayor Willy Brandt, captured the city's heart with her dignity and charm.

A number of East Berliners followed her six-hour visit to this outpost city on western television—and a brave 250 even attempted to see her across the wall.

Communist police had to use force to push the East Berliners back from Brandenburg Gate when they refused to disperse.

The action-packed visit behind the Iron Curtain began and ended with a flight in the Berlin-Hanover air corridor, one of the three 20-mile wide Berlin air lanes above East Germany. Never before had a British monarch flown over communist territory.

The Queen never has a fighter escort and she did not have one Thursday.
(Continued on Back Page, Col. 4)

Margaret To Visit U.S.

LONDON (UPI) — Princess Margaret will tour the United States for three weeks in November, it was announced Thursday, thus achieving an ambition which she first expressed as a teenager. She will be accompanied by her husband, the Earl of Snowdon.

An announcement said the princess and her husband would visit San Francisco, Los Angeles, Washington and New York. The tour is expected to start about Nov. 4.

For many years, the princess, now 34, has been trying to get permission to go to the U.S.—first from her father, the late King George VI, and then from her sister, Queen Elizabeth.

Permission was always refused before her marriage on the ground public interest in her might present American authorities with a crowd problem.

Ad Sign Of the Times

WASHINGTON (AP)—A young man appeared in front of the White House Thursday carrying a sign.

It said, "Rent a Protest Marcher, $2 Per Hour."

2 Senators Given Medals

WASHINGTON (UPI) — The Defense Department has given medals to two senators for visiting U.S. bases in the antarctic.

The Antarctic Service Medal was awarded to Sens. Frank E. Moss (D-Utah), and Ernest Gruening (D-Alaska), who visited Antarctica earlier this year at the Navy's invitation.

Living Costs Hit New High

WASHINGTON (UPI) — The cost of living climbed by three-tenths of one per cent in April to a record high, the Labor Department reported Thursday.

Higher prices for gasoline, fresh fruits and vegetables, eggs, tobacco and consumer services contributed to the biggest monthly increase since last July.

Factory workers' take-home pay fell about $1.25 a week and their buying power declined 1.5 per cent from the record levels of March.

The Labor Department said its consumer price index climbed to
(Continued on Back Page, Col. 3)

New Strife Erupts in Bolivia

LA PAZ, Bolivia (AP)—Dynamite explosions and gunfire erupted Thursday morning in La Paz, injuring at least three persons and interrupting electric power.

It was not known immediately how the violence would affect a cease-fire agreed to Tuesday by the military junta and the Central Bolivian Workers Association. The truce came after a ten day general strike called by the union to protest government deportation of Juan Lechin, a union official and former vice president.

Sixteen persons were reported arrested in connection with the explosions.

Two explosions early Thursday morning erupted in the suburb of San Pedro and Chijini. There were reports that caches of dynamite had been placed in industrial zones north of here.

Another explosion damaged the large water duct which carried the Chaqueri River through this capital city. This explosion also wrecked several homes in a low cost public housing area.

Three wounded persons, including a woman, were hospitalized.

The government moved troops into several zones on the outskirts of the city.

Meanwhile, factories continued working normally and the majority of tin miners went back to work. Early in the week tin miners and troops clashed at several mines.

With the end of resistance to
(Continued on Back Page, Col. 4)

Weather

Tokyo Area Forecast
Friday Night: Partly cloudy; Low Near 60
Saturday: Partly cloudy; High Near 80
Thursday's Temperatures: Low 60, High 79
(USAF Weather Central, Fuchu AS)

Scotsman Wins 500—Page 22

2 HANOI BATTALIONS REPORTED IN SOUTH

PACIFIC STAR AND STRIPES

AN AUTHORIZED PUBLICATION OF THE
U.S. ARMED FORCES IN THE FAR EAST

10¢ DAILY
15¢ WITH SUPPLEMENTS

Vol. 21, No. 152 FIVE-STAR EDITION

昭和三十四年一月二十二日國鉄東局特別扱承認新聞紙第176号（日刊）
（昭和34年4月21日第3種郵便物認可）

Wednesday, June 2, 1965

Gemini-4 Gets A Green Light

CAPE KENNEDY, Fla. (UPI)—Troubles with the Gemini-4 spacecraft were cleared up Monday and technicians were given the go-ahead to proceed with final preparations for man's most ambitious venture into space Thursday.

A three-day series of preparations for the final countdown began as a special team of forecasters reported weather conditions in the area were expected to be good.

The spacecraft's latest problem, a water "leak" that turned out to be a result of human error, was solved early Monday and a break in an undersea communications cable linking the cape and tracking stations was bypassed with a commercial cable leased by the Air Force.

The water "leak" problem turned out to be a valve that had been turned in the wrong direction.

More than 100 pounds of liquid oxygen, to be converted to breathing and pressurization gas during the flight, was pumped into special tanks of the 7,200-pound spacecraft.

Some test cables were unhooked from the capsule and a space agency spokesman said "a lot of little details were cleaned up."

Rookie astronauts James McDivitt and Edward White were set to undergo physical examinations Tuesday for the four-day flight.

McDivitt and White, wearing the silvery white spacesuits that will protect them during their voyage, spent most of the morning rehearsing various details of their

(Continued on Page 6, Col. 3)

Derailed Gas Cars Peril Area

GREENVILLE, S.C. (UPI) — Almost half the cars in a 150-car freight train derailed near a trestle high over the Saluda River Monday and two butane gas cars began leaking.

About 10 families and hundreds of onlookers were evacuated. Police blocked all roads leading into the area.

One of the five engines pulling the Southern Railway freight burned white-hot about 200 yards from the leaking gas cars until late in the day. It was balanced precariously on the trestle 150 feet over the water.

Railroad engineers feared its heat would buckle the steel beams of the trestle.

There were no injuries. The crew of the train scampered off the trestle, leaving all five engines balanced and derailed. The rest of the cars were at the edge of the trestle.

The train derailed when one engine hit a bulldozer owned by Southern Railway that was working near the tracks. The bulldozer operator also jumped to safety.

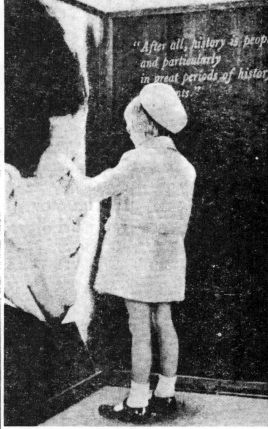

Mary Kerry Kennedy touches a portrait of her slain uncle, President John F. Kennedy, at the U.S. pavilion of the World's Fair in New York. Her father, Sen. Robert F. Kennedy (D-N.Y.), took his family to the exhibit. (UPI Radiophoto)

Eager Crowd Knocks RFK Off Feet

NEW YORK (AP)—Sen. Robert F. Kennedy (D-N.Y.) was knocked off his feet by an enthusiastic crowd Monday as he unveiled a Brooklyn memorial to his brother, the late President Kennedy. He was unhurt.

An unidentified woman went down with the senator and he helped her up. Kennedy shrugged off the incident, saying it had happened to him before in outdoor campaigning.

Six mounted policemen and a wedge of patrolmen got Kennedy and his wife, Ethel, out of the crowd of some 30,000 at Brooklyn's Grand Army Plaza.

The memorial is a white stone monument with a bronze profile of the President, who was assassinated in Dallas Nov. 22, 1963. It was in Grand Army Plaza that Kennedy delivered one of his main addresses while running for president in 1960.

QUANG NGAI, Republic of Vietnam (AP) — Senior U.S. military sources said Monday that they had confirmed the presence of two battalions of north Vietnamese troops in the Quang Ngai Province area where an estimated two regiments of the Viet Cong launched a series of weekend attacks.

U.S. sources said two battalions of north Vietnamese troops were reported in an area 15 miles west of Quang Ngai City and that they were believed to have taken part in an attack on a Special Forces camp at Ha Thranh.

A U.S. military spokesman in Da Nang said Sunday that two north Vietnamese battalions were

(Continued on Back Page, Col. 2)

8 MIGs Flee U.S. F-105s

SAIGON (AP) — Eight Soviet-built MIG fighters attempted to move in on a formation of U.S. Air Force jets Monday while the American planes were bombing an ammunition depot 45 miles southwest of Hanoi.

The MIGs jettisoned their fuel tanks and fled when the American planes moved in to make contact, however, and no shots apparently were exchanged. The MIGs reportedly got away in rain clouds obscuring the area.

A U.S. official said it was not known what model MIGs had been involved or whether the MIGs were north Vietnamese.

The sighting of MIGs was the first time in more than one month that enemy planes have turned out in force to meet American raiders over north Vietnam. In earlier encounters MIGs shot down four American planes and lost one of their own.

The sighting occurred during one of three U.S. and Republic of

(Continued on Back Page, Col. 1)

Weather

Tokyo Area Forecast
Tuesday Night: Partly cloudy with showers; Low Mid 50s
Wednesday: Partly cloudy with showers; High Mid 70s
Monday's Temperatures: Low 56, High 76
(USAF Weather Central, Fuchu AS)

U.S. STEPS UP COMBAT ROLE

WASHINGTON (UPI) —President Johnson has authorized U.S. troops in the Republic of Vietnam to drop their advisory role under certain conditions and battle the communist Viet Cong in direct combat.

The decision was revealed Tuesday by the State Department, which said the troops would go into action only upon request by South Vietnam military leaders, and only in conjunction with South Vietnam troops.

Senate minority leader Everett M. Dirksen (R-Ill.) said he feared the move would "transform this into a conventional war." He added, however, "I'm afraid circumstances may compel it."

Military sources in Washington applauded the move as the only way communist guerrilla units can be destroyed "where they live."

"There is no way to kill guerrillas if you wait for them to come

(Continued on Page 6, Col. 3)

PACIFIC
STAR AND STRIPES

AN AUTHORIZED PUBLICATION OF THE
U.S. ARMED FORCES IN THE FAR EAST

10¢ DAILY
15¢ WITH SUPPLEMENTS

Vol. 21, No. 160 FIVE-STAR EDITION 昭和三十四年一月二十二日國鐵東局特別承認新聞紙第175号（日刊）
（昭和34年4月21日第3種郵便物認可）

Thursday, June 10, 1965

FINEST U.S. SPACE HOUR

Astronauts Feel Fine; Big Welcome Readied

ABOARD USS WASP AT SEA (UPI)—The happy astronauts, James McDivitt and Edward White, headed toward dry land and home Tuesday to be honored by America as space heroes who squared the cosmic race with Russia.

They shot into the heavens last Thursday as a pair of clean-shaven rookie trainees. They returned safely from space aboard a tiny Gemini-4

Related stories, Page 5. More pictures, Pages 12 and 13.

capsule Monday as grizzled, bewhiskered veteran astronauts, co-owners of every U.S. space record in the books and short only the 119-hour Russian endurance record.

Tuesday, the two college chums who never flagged once in the spotlight of their nation's finest hour in space, relaxed aboard this aircraft carrier as it steamed off the Florida coast toward the mainland. They were resting for what astronauts who have gone before them have called the greatest ordeal of all—the hero's welcome that awaits them at home.

(Plans call for the Wasp to circle off Florida until released from Gemini duty Wednesday night or Thursday morning AFRTS
(Continued on Page 7, Col. 3)

Stock Market Tumbles in U.S.

NEW YORK (AP)—The stock market slid to one of its worst losses of 1965 Tuesday. The Dow Jones Industrial average was off 13.10—its worst loss since the assassination of President Kennedy. Details, Page 14.

Walk That Left the World Breathless

Astronaut Ed White comes into full view of fellow astronaut James McDivitt's camera as White climbs out of the Gemini-4 spacecraft during his 20-minute walk in space over the United States last week. The astronauts were relaxing Tuesday aboard the aircraft carrier Wasp as the ship headed for Florida where a huge reception awaited them. They are scheduled to go to Texas later in the week for a meeting with President Johnson.
(NASA Photo via AP)

Weather

Tokyo Area Forecast
Wednesday Night: Partly cloudy; Low Mid 50s
Thursday: Cloudy With rain; High Near 60
Tuesday's Temperatures: Low 62, High 73
(USAF Weather Central, Fuchu AS)

FIVE STAR EDITION

PACIFIC
STARS AND STRIPES

1Cc DAILY
15c WITH SUPPLEMENTS

昭和三十四年一月二十二日国鉄局特別扱承認新聞紙第175号（日刊）

（昭和34年4月21日第3種郵便物認可）

Vol. 21, No. 165 — AN AUTHORIZED PUBLICATION OF THE U.S. ARMED FORCES IN THE FAR EAST — Tuesday, June 15, 1965

Dong Xoai Area

U.S. TROOPS MOVE IN

U.S. paratroopers leap a trench as they take up positions around the Phuoc Vinh airstrip near Dong Xoai. They were moved into the area Sunday. (AP Radiophoto)

SAIGON (AP)—American paratroopers were rushed to a major airstrip near embattled Dong Xoai Sunday after a Vietnamese paratroop battalion was decimated in a Viet Cong ambush Saturday night.

The Americans, numbering about 600 combat troops and 300 artillerymen, flew into Phuoc Vinh, 40 miles north of Saigon, in big U.S. Air Force C-123s.

They immediately began digging in around the airport which is the main supply point for military installations throughout the special Phuoc Binh Thanh zone.

The U.S. paratroopers began arriving at Phuoc Vinh early Sunday afternoon.

The movement of the U.S. unit came when the enormity of the Saturday ambush against the Vietnamese 7th Paratrooper Bn. became known.

The ambush was the latest in a series of major Viet Cong thrusts against government units around Dong Xoai. The Viet Cong destroyed the 1st Bn. of

Other Vietnam news, Page 6.

the 7th Regt. Thursday, mauled the 2d Ranger Bn. Thursday night and continued harassing government posts and units Friday.

Latest reports indicate that 250 men from the 400 strong Vietnamese paratroop battalion are missing, believed killed or captured. From the Saturday action only 150 men, 20 of them wounded, have returned to Dong Xoai from the ambush point.

The paratroopers were reportedly ambushed at 5:10 p.m. Saturday night as they moved into Thuan Loi village four miles north of Dong Xoai.

The Viet Cong reportedly struck from the north and west, sealing off the paratroopers rear. The fight raged on into the night. (Continued on Back Page, Col. 4)

2 Swept Through Dam; 1 Dies

IONE, Wash. (AP)—A 14-year-old Explorer Scout drowned and a motorboat operator survived as they were swept through an open spillway of the Box Canyon Dam here late Saturday.

Two other men saved themselves by grabbing the spillway gate assembly and climbing out of the Pend Oreille River, swollen to a torrent by a heavy spring runoff.

Boats and shore parties searched Sunday for the body of Robert Ulrich, whose lifejacket was torn off as he and Robert Haney, about 24, were carried through the gate and into the foaming spillway pool 20 feet below. Haney suffered shock and bruises.

Roy Madsen, a powerhouse operator at the hydroelectric dam, and Lt. David K. Johnson, of Larson AFB at Moses Lake, caught the gate frame and pulled themselves to safety.

The trouble developed when the outboard motor of Haney's 14-foot boat failed as he was towing four canoes upstream, away from the dam. Approximately a dozen persons in the other canoes safely reached shore and did not go through the spillway.

3 Marines Die, 19 Hurt in Blast

DA NANG, Republic of Vietnam (AP)—An explosion aboard a truck killed three marines and wounded 19 others Sunday at Chu Lai beachhead, 53 miles south of Da Nang.

A U.S. spokesman said the explosion occurred as men were boarding the truck after taking showers near the beach.

Cause of the explosion was not immediately known. The spokesman said the men were returning to their unit.

Eight of the marines were reported in serious condition. Ten others were reported in good condition and another was returned to duty after treatment.

The explosion occurred at noon when the beach is normally crowded with U.S. personnel.

OFF AUSTRALIA

U.S. Skipper, All-Girl Crew Rescued as Ship Rams Ketch

SYDNEY, Australia (AP) — American adventurer Lee Quinn and his crew of three women were rescued Sunday after their ketch was sliced in two by a collision with a 4,000-ton coastal freighter.

They were saved by the freighter's lifeboat after spending half an hour in the water.

During the last 30 months Quinn has visited dozens of South Pacific spots with his ketch Neophyte. A total of 42 girls have served as crew members.

As the ketch cruised around the South Australian coast Sunday, it became involved in a head-on collision with the Australian freighter Woomera.

The Neophyte was cut in two and sank immediately.

Quinn and one girl jumped overboard. The two other girls were trapped among floating bits of wreckage but managed to fight their way clear before the lifeboat drew in to pluck all four from the sea.

The Neophyte was sailing from Hobart to Sydney when the collision occurred in darkness, a

mile from Sydney harbor's entrance.

Helena Anderson, 18, of Hobart, was on watch alone when Quinn heard her cry out a warning.

Quinn said he raced on deck and shouted to Barbara Sodt, 29, of the United States, and Jennifer Shaddock, 22, of Tasmania—who were sleeping below.

He told Helena to jump overboard. As he dived he heard the freighter hit the ketch.

He said Barbara told him later she raced on deck, then returned (Continued on Back Page, Col. 5)

$6-Million Lumber Fire

SUSANVILLE, Cal. (UPI)—A fire raged for seven hours through the huge Eagle Lake Lumber Co. Sunday. A spokesman estimated damage at $6 million.

A complex of five interconnected buildings was leveled and millions of board feet of kiln-dried lumber destroyed. The fire raced through 40 acres of buildings and yards.

Weather

Tokyo Area Forecast
Monday night: Cloudy; Low Near 60
Tuesday: Partly cloudy; High Near 70
Sunday's Temperatures: Low 62, High 73
(USAF) Weather Central, Fuchu AB

84 KILLED IN MATS CRASH

EL TORO, Cal. (AP)— A military jet loaded with marines bound for Okinawa crashed after takeoff Friday, killing 84 persons.

An observer who flew over the scene said the four-engine C-135 cut a 100-yard swath as it skidded up a slope, exploded and burned. Burned bodies and wreckage were widely scattered.

The Military Air Transport Services plane took off for Honolulu at 1:44 a.m. in a drizzle and almost immediately disappeared from the radar screen at this Marine air base 40 miles southeast of Los Angeles.

The plane crashed at the 600-foot level in foothills of the Santa Ana Mountains, which border the field.

The 72 marines aboard were mostly enlisted men, from bases around the country. The plane and its crew of 12 were from the 18th Air Transport Sq. at McGuire AB, N.J.

A fireman from the State Division of Forestry said the plane struck on a ridge and slid uphill, scattering wreckage, then went over the top and down the other side.

Much of the wreckage was blackened. Few of the bodies were intact. Scores of sea bags were burst open.

Gen. Howell M. Esters Jr., commander of the Military Air Transport Service, was flying here with three aides to investigate the crash.

There was no indication of what went wrong.

Because it is isolated, with few
(Continued on Back Page, Col. 2)

Millionaire Briton, U.S. Teen Wed

PHILADELPHIA (AP) — A judge disclosed Friday that on May 6 he married a 16-year-old girl and a Londoner, 46, reported to be worth $60 million.

The bride is Roslyne Rothchild, of suburban Rydal, and the bridegroom Charles Dormer, of Alford House, London.

Judge Joseph E. Gold, who performed the service in city hall, said "it was a valid marriage," adding, "I understand this fellow is worth about $60 million in cold cash."

The judge said Dormer told him he is in charge of Shell Oil Co. transportation on the continent.

The judge said he was asked to marry the couple by the
(Continued on Back Page, Col. 1)

PACIFIC
STAR AND STRIPES

AN AUTHORIZED PUBLICATION OF THE
U.S. ARMED FORCES IN THE FAR EAST

10¢ DAILY
15¢ WITH SUPPLEMENTS

Vol. 21, No. 177   FIVE-STAR EDITION   昭和三十四年一月二十二日國鉄東京局特別扱承認新聞紙第175号（日刊）
（昭和34年4月21日第3種郵便物認可）   Sunday, June 27, 1965

Terror Bombs Rip Saigon Restaurant; 25 Killed, 33 Hurt

The story in pictures, Pages 12-13.

Compiled From AP and UPI

SAIGON — Two terrorist bombs ripped through a floating restaurant on the Saigon River Friday night, killing 25 and wounding dozens of diners.

Of the dead, nine were Americans, five of them U.S. servicemen. Eleven Americans were among the wounded.

U.S. military authorities listed 25 persons killed and 33 wounded. They added that they expected these figures to change as more casualties were found in hospitals and clinics scattered throughout the city.

Unofficial sources said the death toll probably will be 30 or more and that the wounded were expected to exceed 100, including those cut
(Continued on Page 6, Col. 4)

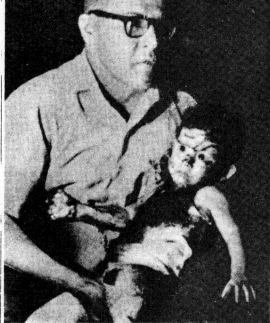

A child injured during terrorist bombing of Saigon restaurant is carried to an ambulance.   (AP Radiophoto)

LBJ Calls on U.N. For Peace Efforts

SAN FRANCISCO (AP)—President Johnson marked the 20th birthday of the United Nations Friday, calling on the U.N. to help promote peace in Vietnam and establish an "alliance for man" to fight poverty, the arms race and the population explosion around the globe.

Johnson, addressing a special U.N. convocation in the city where the organization's charter

Related stories, Page 2.
Text of address, Page 18.

was signed in June, 1945, said "clear and present dangers in Southeast Asia cast their shadow across the path of all mankind." Declaring "The United Nations must be concerned," he said:

"I call upon this gathering of the nations of the world to use their influence, individually and collectively to bring to the tables
(Continued on Back Page, Col. 4)

Viet Cong Execute U.S. Army Sergeant

SAIGON (UPI)—The U.S. Embassy here said Friday that the Viet Cong had announced the execution of U.S. Army Sgt. Harold George Bennett in retalia-

Related stories, Page 5.

tion for the firing squad execution of condemned communist terrorist Tran Van Dang last Tuesday.

The execution of Bennett, 25, of Perryville, Ark., was reported both by Radio Hanoi and the official communist Vietnam news

agency (VNA). Radio Hanoi identified the soldier only as "Bennett" but VNA gave his full name and serial number.

Bennett was listed as missing and presumed captured Dec. 29, 1964, in the bloody battle for Binh Gia, a Catholic refugee center 25 miles south of Saigon in Phuoc Tuy Province.

A U.S. Embassy spokesman said if the reported communist execution of the American is confirmed then "it is obviously a wanton act of murder."

(In Washington, the State De-

partment also condemned as "a wanton act of murder" the reported Viet Cong reprisal killing of an American serviceman, AP said.

(Press officer Robert J. McCloskey said that "this matter is one of very serious concern for us, quite obviously, because it concerns the lives of American citizens.")

Radio Hanoi announced the execution took place Thursday somewhere in the Republic of Vietnam.

It was the first time the com-

munists have announced such an execution, though they have threatened to kill American captives in the past.

Bennett was one of two U.S. Army sergeants reported captured when the 170-man Vietnamese Ranger force they were accompanying was overrun by communist guerrillas. Both men were advisers to the unit, which was attempting to relieve the village during a week-long battle.

The Rangers were airlifted into the battle but were caught in a
(Continued on Back Page, Col. 1)

Weather

Tokyo Area Forecast
Saturday Night: Cloudy; Low Near 70
Sunday: Cloudy with rain showers; High Mid 70s
Friday's Temperatures: Low 66, High 81
(USAF Weather Central, Fuchu AS)

FIVE STAR EDITION

Pacific STARS AND STRIPES

10c DAILY
15c WITH SUPPLEMENTS

昭和三十四年一月二十二日国鉄東京管特別扱承認新聞紙第175号（日刊）

（昭和34年4月21日第3種郵便物認可）

Vol. 21, No. 181   AN AUTHORIZED PUBLICATION OF THE U.S. ARMED FORCES IN THE FAR EAST   Thursday, July 1, 1965

U.S., AUSSIE TROOPS JOIN VIET CONG HUNT

American helicopters leave the landing zone in the D zone, 30 miles north of Saigon, as paratroopers of the U.S. 173d Airborne Brigade move out through tall grass at the beginning of an operation against the Viet Cong. Australian and Republic of Vietnam troops also took part in the operation.   (AP Radiophoto)

4 Marines Killed, 9 Injured In Chu Lai, Da Nang Action

Compiled From AP and UPI

DA NANG, Republic of Vietnam—Four U.S. marines were killed and nine others were wounded Tuesday in action against the Viet Cong in the Chu Lai and Da Nang areas, a U.S. military spokesman said.

Four of the marines were killed and four wounded in the Chu Lai area. Two of the wounded were reported in serious condition, the other two were listed in good condition.

The spokesman said 14 Viet Cong were killed and 43 suspects were detained in a day-long Marine sweep operation between the South China Sea and the Song Tra Bong River.

Communist guerrillas had been reported building up in the area.

Three companies of marines took part in the operation. They were lifted into the area in helicopters and one company acted as a blocking force for the assault.

U.S. Marine Corps Phantom jets provided close air support during the operation. The spokesman said seven of the Viet Cong were killed by artillery fire when they were caught on a sand bar along the river.

The other five marines were wounded Tuesday morning when

an explosion hit elements of a routine marine patrol 5½ miles southwest of Da Nang.

A U.S. Marine Corps spokesman (Continued on Back Page, Col. 1)

SAIGON (UPI) — U.S. paratroopers and Australian infantrymen converged in a giant pincer movement in War Zone D, 30 miles north of Saigon, Tuesday in the biggest allied troop offensive since Korea.

They were working with two Republic of Vietnam battalions in an effort to trap a large guerrilla force which overran Dong Xoai two weeks ago.

As of early Wednesday, however, the guerrillas appeared to be successfully eluding the net and only light contact was being reported.

The 1st Bn. Royal Australian Regt., commanded by Lt. Col. I. R. Brumfield, was helilifted into the combat zone, north of Bien Hoa late Tuesday after being held in reserve for a day.

They occupy the right flank in

The 173d Airborne Brigade sounds its battle cry—the story in pictures, Pages 12-13.

Related stories Pages 2, 6.

the combined task force of more than 2,000 troops.

The offensive was launched Monday into the communist-infested Viet Cong D Zone with a massive helilift by more than 120 U.S. Army choppers and 10 Vietnamese helicopters carrying elements of the 173d U.S. Airborne Brigade and Vietnamese paratroopers.

American and Vietnamese (Continued on Back Page, Col. 3)

$220,000 MISSING

Okinawa Payroll Looted

S&S Okinawa Bureau

SUKIRAN, Okinawa — Nearly a quarter million dollars was stolen from the American Express military banking facility on Okinawa Tuesday during a daylight motor vehicle currency shipment from Naha city to the bank's branch office at Sukiran.

The $220,000 was part of $927,600

which was withdrawn from the Bank of the Ryukyus shortly before noon to be used for military payday transactions.

"A shipment of $927,600 was counted, placed in five bags, signed for and placed in the vehicle to be transported to the military banking facility at Sukiran," (Continued on Back Page, Col. 1)

Weather

Tokyo Area Forecast

Wednesday Night: Partly Cloudy; Low Mid 70s

Thursday: Mostly fair; High Near 90

Tuesday's Temperatures: Low 68, High 89

(USAF Weather Central, Fuchu AS)

ADD 50,000 TROOPS, DOUBLE DRAFT CALL

PACIFIC
STAR AND STRIPES

AN AUTHORIZED PUBLICATION OF THE
U.S. ARMED FORCES IN THE FAR EAST

10¢ DAILY
15¢ WITH SUPPLEMENTS

Vol. 21, No. 210   FIVE-STAR EDITION   昭和三十四年一月二十二日国鉄東京局特別扱承認新聞紙第175号（日刊）
（昭和34年4月21日第3種郵便物認可）   Friday, July 30, 1965

PRESIDENT JOHNSON GESTURES AS HE ANNOUNCES STEPPED-UP U.S. PARTICIPATION IN VIETNAM.   (UPI RADIOPHOTO)

House OKs Bill Backing Union Shop

WASHINGTON (UPI) — The House Wednesday approved by a 221-203 roll call vote legislation that would nullify "right to work" laws in 19 states and open the way for labor in all states to bargain for union shop contracts.

The bill now goes to the Senate, where its chances for passage are considered good.

The bill would repeal Section 14-B of the 1947 Taft-Hartley Law. The section, a source of controversy for 18 years, authorizes states to outlaw labor-management agreements which required employes to join a union. Nineteen Southern and Western states have laws based on Section 14-B.

Passage of the bill was a triumph for organized labor, which threw all of its considerable lobbying strength into the battle. It also was another congressional victory for President Johnson, who gave the repeal bill only lukewarm support at first, but plunged into the fray with a will in its last days.

Weather

Tokyo Area Forecast
Thursday Night: Fair; Low Mid 70s
Friday: Fair; High Mid 90s
Wednesday's Temperatures: Low 76, High 86
(USAF Weather Central, Fuchu AS)

Text of Statement

Not long ago I received a letter from a woman in the Midwest. She wrote: "My dear Mr. President, in my humble way I am writing to you about the crisis in Vietnam . . . I have . . . a son who is now in Vietnam. My husband served . . . in World War II . . . Our country was at war, but now this time it's something I don't understand. Why?"

I have tried to answer that question a dozen times and more. I have discussed it fully in Baltimore in April, in Washington in May, and in San Francisco in June. Let me now discuss it again. Why must young Americans —born into a land exultant with hope and golden with promise—toil and suffer and sometimes die in such a remote and distant place?

The answer, like war itself, is not easy. But it echoes clearly from the painful lessons of half a century. Three times in my lifetime—in two World Wars and in Korea— Americans have gone to far lands to fight. We have learned —at a terrible and brutal cost—that retreat does not bring safety, or weakness peace.

It is this lesson that has brought us to Vietnam. This is a different kind of war. There are no marching armies or solemn declarations. Some citizens of South Vietnam at times with understandable grievances have joined in the attack on their own government. But we must not let this mask the central fact that this is really war.

It is guided by north Vietnam and it is spurred by communist China. Its goal is to conquer the south, to defeat American power, and to extend the Asiatic domination of communism.

And there are great stakes in the balance.

Most of the noncommunist nations of Asia cannot, by themselves, resist the growing might and grasping ambition of Asian communism. Our power is a vital shield. If we are driven from the fields in Vietnam, then no nation can ever again have the same confidence in our promise of protection. In each land the forces of independence would be

Continued on Page 4, Col. 1

LBJ Picks Fortas for High Court

WASHINGTON (UPI) — President Johnson announced Wednesday he will appoint Abe Fortas, a longtime friend and Washington attorney, to the Supreme Court to succeed Arthur J. Goldberg.

Johnson said Fortas was his first choice for the high tribunal.

Goldberg resigned to become U.S. ambassador to the United Nations after serving three years following his selection by the late President Kennedy.

The naming of Fortas continues the 50-year-old tradition of having a Jewish justice. The practice began with the selection of Louis Brandeis in 1916.

The White House said only Tuesday that Fortas had twice declined high government posts and (Continued on Back Page, Col. 5)

WASHINGTON (AP)— President Johnson announced Wednesday he was adding 50,000 troops to U.S. forces in Vietnam, doubling the draft call and asking the United Nations to start a new search for peace in the Southeast Asian war.

Johnson said at a news conference:

1. The monthly draft call will jump from 17,000 to 35,000.

2. U.S. military forces in the Republic of Vietnam will increase from 75,000 to 125,000 men.

3. Ambassador Arthur J. Goldberg had been directed to go to New York immediately and to present to the United Nations' secretary general "a letter from me requesting that all the resources, energy and immense prestige of the United Nations be employed to find ways to halt aggression and bring peace in Vietnam."

(Continued on Back Page, Col. 2)

Adlai's Chair Is 'Retired'

WASHINGTON (AP) — Adlai E. Stevenson's chair in the White House Cabinet room has been sold for $134.50.

The purchasers are President Johnson, Vice President Hubert H. Humphrey and members of the Cabinet, with whom Stevenson sat as ambassador to the United Nations.

Following an old tradition, the late ambassador's associates bought the chair from the government at its replacement price to give it to Stevenson's family.

Hard-Luck Boston Teen Breaks Reattached Arm

BOSTON (AP)—Everett Knowles, 15, has broken one of the most important right arms in medical history.

The frisky, freckle-faced teenager, whose arm was cut off more than three years ago by a wheel of a train but was successfully reattached, fell recently from a stone wall—and landed on the arm.

The boy was rushed to Massachusetts General Hospital, where some of the surgeons who performed the original operation re-examined the arm.

They worked late into the night (Continued on Back Page, Col. 1)

New Mars Secrets Bared

Pictures Pages 14-15

WASHINGTON (AP)—Latest pictures of Mars disclosed Thursday that the planet may be pockmarked by up to 10,000 craters, and that it appears to be more like the Moon than the Earth in its surface features.

This was disclosed by scientists in a report delivered personally to President Johnson at the White House. The report covered findings on 18 previously unpublished photographs taken by Mariner-4 on its voyage to the planet.

The scientist who made the main report said the findings "will profoundly affect scientific views about the origin of the solar systems," and may shed new light on the history of the earth.

Dr. Robert Leighton of
(Continued on Page 6, Col. 3)

PACIFIC
STAR AND STRIPES
AN AUTHORIZED PUBLICATION OF THE U.S. ARMED FORCES IN THE FAR EAST

10¢ DAILY
15¢ WITH SUPPLEMENTS

Vol. 21, No. 211   FIVE-STAR EDITION

昭和三十四年一月二十二日国鉄東京局特別扱承認新聞紙第175号（日刊）
（昭和34年4月21日第3種郵便物認可）

Saturday, July 31, 1965

3,700 PARATROOPS ARRIVE IN VIETNAM

CAM RANH BAY, Republic of Vietnam (AP) — American troops of the 101st Airborne Div. began landing Thursday at Cam Ranh Bay, 180 miles northeast of Saigon, to bolster U.S. combat forces in Vietnam.

The troop transport General Le Roy Eltinge brought the 3,700 paratroopers into the deep-water bay where the U.S. is building a major base. The men were transferred to landing craft for the trip ashore.

Among the first ashore was the commander of the 1st Brigade of the 101st, Col. James Timothy, who said his men were "capable of deploying anywhere in the **(Continued on Back Page, Col. 4)**

FLAGS OF 1ST BRIGADE, 101ST AIRBORNE DIV., ARE DIPPED IN SALUTE AS TROOPS ARRIVE AT CAM RANH BAY.

AP Radiophoto

Combat Pay Hike Proposed

WASHINGTON (UPI) — Sen. Richard B. Russell (D-Ga.) Thursday proposed an increase in combat pay for U.S. troops in Vietnam. The Pentagon said it would not object.

Russell, chairman of the Senate Armed Services Committee, predicted his group would vote a "substantial increase" in military pay generally, and said he would like to add a provision to boost the combat pay.

Norman S. Paul, assistant defense secretary for manpower who was testifying on the pay bill, told Russell the Pentagon "certainly would not object" to raising the $55-a-month combat pay. Russell mentioned a "token" increase of perhaps $10.

B-52s Bomb Reds, U.S. Troops Move In

SAIGON (AP)—Strategic Air Command B-52 bombers staged their sixth raid on suspected Viet Cong positions Thursday as U.S. Army paratroopers began an extensive sweep through Viet Cong-infested hills 35 miles southeast of here.

About 30 of the big jets flew from Okinawa to dump 500 tons of bombs, a U.S. spokesman reported. The paratroopers then began combing an area nearby for the enemy.

The huge operation, involving several thousand U.S. paratroopers, had established no important contact with the enemy by late Thursday. One Viet Cong was reported killed and another captured from a hiding place in a hollow tree. A spokesman said there were no U.S. casualties.

The operation was aimed at clearing out a portion of Phuoc Tuy Province, in which the Viet Cong recently cut strategic Route 15 to the sea.

Results of Thursday's B-52 raid could not be immediately assessed. Normally, B-52s stage their flights over South Vietnam from Guam, but a U.S. spokesman said Thursday's flight was staged from Okinawa because of a typhoon in the Guam area.

The B-52s returned to Okinawa from the latest raid and were to leave Friday for Guam.

In another major ground action which began Wednesday night, a U.S. Marine Corps spokesman said U.S. and Vietnamese marines were conducting their first joint battalion-strength operation of the war.

The operation, near the big U.S. Marine beachhead at Chu Lai, had resulted by late Wednesday night in 26 Viet Cong killed and nine suspected Viet Cong captured. **(Continued on Back Page, Col. 3)**

Weather

Tokyo Area Forecast
Friday night: Partly cloudy; Low Mid 70s
Saturday: Partly cloudy with scattered rain showers; High Mid 80s
Thursday's Temperatures: Low 75, High 91
(USAF Weather Central, Fuchu AS)

VC Batter Armored Supply Column

By PETER ARNETT

VAN TOUNG, Vietnam (AP) —The mission of Supply Column 21 was simple: get to the beachhead, resupply a U.S. Marine company and return to the Seventh Fleet mother ship anchored one mile out in the bay.

The Marine supply group figured they had an easy run. They had heard that line companies landed earlier Wednesday were getting heavy fire from Viet Cong positions on the peninsula.

But Supply Column 21 was a formidable force made up of five steel-shod "amtraks"—35-ton amphibious vehicles — to carry the food and ammunition, and two M-48 tanks to escort them when they arrived on shore.

The Viet Cong would hesitate to tangle with this, the men told themselves as they surged toward the beachhead.

They didn't know it at the time, but the biggest American battle of the war was shaping up.

This group of 30 men was to become deeply involved in one of the most vicious encounters of the war.

Supply Column 21 fulfilled only one of its objectives. It got to the beachhead.

It did not resupply the Marine company, and it did not return.

The paths that led the column to its destruction were paved more with confusion that anything else. First, they failed to locate the company, so they set out to look for it.

The amtraks, once out of the water, were unwieldy. They flopped from one rice paddy to another, calling at one battalion and then the next. No one seemed to pay much attention to it.

This proved fatal.

At 11 a.m. Wednesday, Supply Column 21 was about 400 yards

(Continued on Page 6, Col. 4)

PACIFIC STARS AND STRIPES

AN AUTHORIZED PUBLICATION OF THE ARMED FORCES IN THE FAR EAST

FIVE-STAR EDITION

昭和三十四年一月二十二日国鉄東局特別扱承認新聞紙第175号（日刊）
（昭和34年4月21日第3種郵便物認可）

10¢ DAILY
15¢ WITH
SUPPLEMENTS

Vol. 21, No. 232   Saturday, August 21, 1965

Marine Assault Kills 552 VC, Wounds 1,000

CHU LAI, Vietnam (AP)—The U.S. Marines reported Thursday they had smashed a big Viet Cong concentration on the Van Tuong Peninsula, inflicting bloody losses on the communist forces.

Marine spokesmen said 552 Viet Cong bodies had been counted. Marine casualties were officially called "light," but a U.S. military spokesman in Saigon said the Americans had suffered their heaviest loss of any single engagement of the Vietnamese war.

Security rules prohibit the disclosure of American losses.

A U.S. spokesman in Saigon said

(Continued on Back Page, Col. 1)

WOUNDED MARINE IS HELPED TO EVACUATION HELICOPTER NEAR VAN TUONG DURING BATTLE WITH VIET CONG.   AP Radiophoto

Rioting Mars Sato Visit

S&S Okinawa Bureau

NAHA, Okinawa — An angry mob of some 30,000 Okinawan leftists protesting U.S. and Japanese policies on Okinawa and the war in Vietnam forced visiting Japanese Prime Minister Eisaku Sato to seek refuge in the Japanese liaison office here Thursday night.

The demonstrators barricaded the highway leading to the Ryukyu Tokyu Hotel, where the prime minister is staying during his

(Continued on Back Page, Col. 5)

Gemini Shot Postponed

CAPE KENNEDY, Fla. (AP)— Stormy weather and troubles in the spacecraft washed out Thursday's effort to launch the Gemini-5 space mission. Another try was scheduled for 9 a.m. (2300 JST) Saturday.

The 3.12-million-mile voyage was called off after a losing battle with a thunderstorm and the

(Continued on Back Page, Col. 3)

Boy, 2 Kittens Sail 2,400 Mi.

HONOLULU (AP) — Sixteen-year-old Lee Graham—with only two kittens as companions—completed a 2,400-mile voyage from California to Honolulu Wednesday night and described the trip as "pretty easy."

Docking his 24-foot sailboat, the Dove, at Ala Wai Yacht Harbor in Waikiki, the teen-ager said, "I had no trouble."

The California-to-Hawaii voyage was the first lap of a proposed two-year solo trip around the world.

Graham, of Honolulu, entered the harbor nearly 24 hours earlier than expected.

The Dove was at the end of a Coast Guard towrope. Young Graham said he had accepted the tow "for safety's sake."

The youth said he hadn't wanted to be "riding around there (off Diamond Head) in the dark."

He described the trip from San Pedro, Cal., as "pretty easy" for 23 of the 25 days. He said he was a little seasick the first two days.

"But then I got the trades (prevailing northeasterly trade winds) pretty well all the way," he said.

Lee said his two frisky kittens, Suzette and Joliet, will continue with him on his world trip, which he plans to resume in two to four weeks.

Lee said he plans to sail from Hawaii to the Phoenix Islands

(Continued on Back Page, Col. 4)

Weather

Tokyo Area Forecast

Friday Night: Partly cloudy; Low Near 70

Saturday: Partly cloudy; High Near 90

Thursday's Temperatures: Low 78, High 90

(USAF Weather Central, Fuchu AS)

PARATROOPS FIND RUSS RIFLES

Marines Sweep Peninsula

PACIFIC

STARS and STRIPES

AN AUTHORIZED PUBLICATION OF
THE ARMED FORCES FAR EAST

10¢ DAILY
15¢ WITH SUPPLEMENTS

Vol. 21, No. 270   FIVE-STAR EDITION   Tuesday, Sept. 28, 1965

SAIGON (AP)—A U.S. Marine amphibious task force assaulted a peninsula on the central Vietnamese coast and paratroopers uncovered a cache of Soviet-made rifles in large-scale operations reported Sunday by a U.S. military spokesman.

The marines stormed ashore Saturday at Vung Mu Peninsula in Operation Dagger Thrust launched from Seventh Fleet ships 15 miles south of Qui Nhon, 270 miles northeast of the capital. They made no major contact with the Viet Cong.

Striking from helicopters in four waves, the marines swept the eight-mile-long peninsula and destroyed Viet Cong bunkers and tunnels before returning to their base at sea. One Viet Cong was killed and 20 suspects were captured. Light marine losses were suffered from punji traps, sharpened bamboo stakes with poisonous tips.

The first waves of helicopters carrying the marines dropped leaflets over the peninsula. The leaflets explained that the marines' mission was to kill Viet Cong and they warned civilians not to become involved in the fighting.

Viet Cong aboard junks fired at the helicopters and U.S. planes from the carrier Bon Homme Richard fired back. Several junks were damaged.

The amphibious assault was limited in size and had the single objective of securing the north end of the Peninsula. A reinforced battalion, possibly 1,200 marines, took part in the offensive.

Paratroopers of the 173d Airborne Brigade uncovered the Soviet-made sniper rifles. It was the first time the weapon was found in use in South Vietnam. The spokesman said 62 of the rifles, the basic sniper weapon of the Soviet Army until the end of World War II, had not been used.

The weapons were packed in

(Continued on Back Page, Col. 3)

Twins Win the Pennant

The Minnesota Twins celebrate their clinching of the American League pennant Sunday by pouring champagne on star outfielder Harmon Killebrew. Minnesota defeated Washington 2-1 for its first league championship. Details Pages 18-19.
(AP Radiophoto)

Report 2 Advisers Executed

SAIGON (UPI)—The Viet Cong executed two captive American servicemen Sunday morning, the clandestine Liberation Radio said late Sunday night.

The communist radio identified the two Americans as Capt. Albert Rusk Joseph and Sgt. Kenneth Morabeth (as received phonetically).

American authorities in Saigon were comparing the names with a list of missing American servicemen to determine if any such individuals were, indeed, communist captives.

The reported executions came less than three days after the Vietnamese government's execution of three convicted Viet Cong terrorists in Da Nang.

In revenge for the last previous execution of a Viet Cong by the government, the communists announced that they had executed Sgt. Harold G. Bennett, of Arkansas, on June 24.

Pro Scores

Details, Page 18

NFL

St. Louis	49
Cleveland	13
Dallas	17
Washington	7
New York	16
Philadelphia	14
San Francisco	27
Pittsburgh	17
Los Angeles	30
Chicago	28
Detroit	31
Minnesota	29
Green Bay	20
Baltimore	17

AFL

Buffalo	33
New York	21
Oakland	21
Houston	17
Kansas City	10
San Diego	10

New Fighting Erupts Over Kashmir

NEW DELHI (UPI)—India and Pakistan Sunday reported sharp fighting between their armed forces in defiance of the 4-day-old cease-fire in their war over Kashmir.

Radio Pakistan said Pakistani troops fought a night-long battle with Indian forces and drove them out of the Fazilka sector, about 80 miles southwest of Lahore. It said 90 Indians were killed, 94 others taken prisoner and four Indian tanks destroyed.

Radio Pakistan also quoted a claim by the rebel Voice of Kashmir radio that 200 Indian troops had been killed by Kashmir rebels in the past 24 hours near Gulmarg, west of Srinagar.

The Pakistanis charged Indian troops attacked with armor and artillery Saturday afternoon in violation of the cease-fire. It said the Indians finally withdrew at dawn.

In two other regions, the Indian spokesman said, Pakistani infiltrators withdrew from Indian-held territory after local commanders threatened to open fire.

Inside Kashmir, an Indian communique said, Indian forces opened fire twice on 100 alleged

(Continued on Back Page, Col. 5)

No Pullback Yet, Thant Says

UNITED NATIONS, N.Y. (AP)—U.N. Secretary General U Thant reported Sunday that the 4-day-old India-Pakistan cease-fire "is not holding" and that both sides are stalling on withdrawal of troops.

Thant sent the two-page situation report to the Security Council under its resolution of last Monday demanding that India and Pakistan order a cease-fire and the subsequent withdrawal of their

troops to Aug. 5 positions.

The report was based on information from Australian Lt. Gen. Robert H. Nimmo, chief U.N. observer.

The secretary general said:

"In the Lahore (Pakistan) sector, particularly, the cease-fire is not holding as of Sept. 26."

India and Pakistan issued cease-fire orders effective Wednesday and the council intended the withdrawal of troops to follow.

But Thant disclosed that India had ignored and Pakistan had rejected requests for withdrawal orders sent by Nimmo Saturday after each side had accused the other of advancing its lines.

He quoted Nimmo as saying of two such appeals to India:

"Replies have not been received yet to either of these requests, and there has been no indication of withdrawals anywhere."

(Continued on Back Page, Col. 5)

BULLETIN

DAHLGREN, Va. (AP)—A spokesman at the U.S. Naval Weapons Laboratory said Sunday night a report had been received that a plane—believed to be a commercial airliner—had crashed in the Potomac River.

LBJ WILL UNDERGO ABDOMINAL SURGERY

PACIFIC

STARS STRIPES

AN AUTHORIZED PUBLICATION OF THE ARMED FORCES IN THE FAR EAST

FIVE-STAR EDITION

昭和三十四年一月二十二日国鉄東京局特別扱承認新聞紙第175号（日刊）

（昭和34年4月21日第3種郵便物認可）

10¢ DAILY
15¢ WITH
SUPPLEMENTS

Vol. 21, No. 279   Thursday, Oct. 7, 1965

Viet Cong Hide Behind Children, Then Shoot Them

By AL KRAMER
S&S Staff Writer

SAIGON—The Viet Cong used a group of children as shields Friday during a military operation. Then another group of Viet Cong opened fire on the children.

Marine Maj. B. H. Mann reported Tuesday that he witnessed the incident, which occurred Friday during a Marine amphibious and helicopter assault against the Viet Cong near the coastal city of Qui Nhon, 260 miles north of here.

U.S. Plane Shot Down, Peking Says

TOKYO (AP)—Communist Chinese Air Force planes shot down a U.S. fighter plane over the China mainland Tuesday afternoon, Peking Radio claimed Tuesday.

A Chinese-language broadcast monitored here said the plane was one of four U.S. aircraft which "intruded" into Kwangsi province, southeast China, at 12:28 p.m.

Chinese Air Force planes took off to intercept the planes, shooting down one of them, the broadcast said.

The Chinese said the three planes "fled in dismay when they found the situation unfavorable" and accused the planes of "military provocation."

(In Washington, the Pentagon (Continued on Back Page, Col. 5)

Mann, flying in a copter from the helicopter assault ship Iwo Jima, was asked by a forward air controller to check a group of 18 people near a stream.

As Mann neared the group he saw children among them and ordered the forward air controller to hold fire. The group then got into a boat to cross the stream. The men in the group sat in the boat and held the children on their laps as two persons poled the boat to the other side, Mann said.

As they approached shallow water on the other shore the men threw the children into the water and ran ashore.

As soon as the men had cleared the area, guerrillas on the penin-
(Continued on Back Page, Col. 1)

PRESIDENT JOHNSON TELLS NEWSMEN ABOUT HIS SURGERY.
UPI Radiophoto

WASHINGTON (UPI)—President Johnson disclosed Tuesday he will have his gall bladder removed Friday.

The Chief Executive told reporters he has been having stomach pains since Sept. 7, and that a series of examinations indicated his gall bladder was to blame.

During the period he is under anesthesia, and at any other time when he is unable to make presidential decisions, Vice President Hubert H. Humphrey will be in charge under an agreement Johnson and Humphrey have had since the inauguration last year.

The operation will be performed at Bethesda Naval Hospital, near Washington, by Dr. George Aaron Hallenbeck, one of the ranking surgeons of the Mayo Clinic, Rochester, Minn.

Hallenbeck told reporters: "The risk to a normal person of the President's age is very low indeed."

Hallenbeck also said that after the operation Johnson should have "full intellectual capability" to carry out his job, although physically he might tire more
(Continued on Back Page, Col. 3)

Senate OK's $3 Bil. for Foreign Aid

WASHINGTON (UPI)—The Senate completed congressional action Tuesday on a compromise $3.22-billion foreign aid money bill.

By a vote of 40-to-23, senators sent the measure to President Johnson.

The House passed the compromise Friday. It was worked out last week by House-Senate conferees and provides money for one year of military, economic and technical assistance to scores of countries.

The Senate action ended the annual bumpy journey through Congress of the controversial aid program. The $3.22 billion was only $160 million below Johnson's request, which was the lowest Administration request in the history of the program.

The compromise money figure was $75 million above the figure voted by the Senate and $67 million less than the House total.

ON RETURN TO ROME

Pope Proclaims Peace Goal for Church

VATICAN CITY (UPI)—Pope Paul VI returned to the Vatican Tuesday from his visit to New York City and told the Ecumenical Council that the Catholic Church "has taken on a greater obligation to serve the cause of peace . . ."

The 68-year-old pontiff flew to the United States Monday on a "mission of peace" which took him to the United Nations, St.

Patrick's Cathedral, Yankee Stadium and the New York World's Fair. He also met President Johnson.

The Pope radioed his warm

Related stories, Page 6.

thanks and "heartfelt gratitude" to President Johnson from the plane carrying him back to Rome.

"We thank the Lord, venerated

brothers," Pope Paul told the 2,000 council fathers assembled in St. Peter's Basilica, "that we were privileged to announce the message of peace, in a sense, to all men on earth."

The Pope said, "A serious consequence springs from the fact that we announced peace: We now must be, more than before, workers of peace. The Catholic Church has taken on a greater

obligation to serve the cause of peace because through our voice it solemnly advocated its cause.

"It is certainly not our task, nor could it be our intention, to enter the fields of politics or of economics, where that temporal order which constitutes civil peace is directly built. But we can and must help also the construction of civil peace through
(Continued on Back Page, Col. 5)

Weather

Tokyo Area Forecast

Wednesday Night: Partly cloudy; Low Mid 50

Thursday: Mostly fair; High Mid 70s

Tuesday's Temperatures: Low 50, High 78

(USAF Weather Central, Fuchu AS)

'No Joy, No Joy,' Gemini Fails

CAPE KENNEDY, Fla. (UPI) — History's first attempt to couple two craft in space failed Monday when the target rocket, a 26-foot Agena, failed to go into orbit.

The mishap left Gemini-6 on the launch pad.

There were radar indications that the Agena broke into five pieces over the Atlantic shortly after launch. But officials emphasized it would take several days to determine exactly what happened.

The failure meant the attempt to link up spacecraft in orbit— a maneuver vital to the Apollo moon landing project—will have to be postponed until early 1966.

The Agena, boosted by an Atlas first stage, soared skyward in what looked like a perfect launch four seconds after the planned liftoff time of 10 a.m. EST. The

(Continued on Page 5, Col. 1)

PACIFIC STARS AND STRIPES

AN AUTHORIZED PUBLICATION OF THE U.S. ARMED FORCES IN THE FAR EAST

10¢ DAILY
15¢ WITH SUPPLEMENTS

Vol. 21, No. 299   FIVE-STAR EDITION

昭和三十四年一月二十二日第三種郵便物認可 第175号 (日刊)
(昭和34年4月21日第3種郵便物認可)

Wed., Oct. 27, 1965

Plei Me Siege Broken By Viet, 1st Cav. Troops

PLEIKU, Vietnam (AP)—A Vietnamese regiment led by armor reached the beleaguered outpost of Plei Me Monday night without encountering any significant Viet Cong opposition, a U.S. military spokesman said.

He said the relief column was just outside the Special Forces compound and the only reason elements of the column did not enter the camp was because there was no room.

The spokesman said that on the basis of incomplete reports the Viet Cong apparently offered no opposition from its dozen or more machine gun emplacements around the camp.

Elements of the 1st U.S. Cav. Div., (Airmobile), including strong artillery units, joined the Vietnamese in

(Continued on Back Page, Col. 2)

Astronauts Walter Schirra (left) and Thomas Stafford look downcast as they leave the Gemini-6 spacecraft. Their flight was canceled because the Agena "chase" rocket failed to orbit. (UPI)

Cannon Bandits Grab $400,000

SYRACUSE, N.Y. (AP)—A 20-mm cannon was used to blast open a foot-thick vault inside the Brink's Co. branch office here and an estimated $400,000 in cash, checks and securities was reported missing Monday.

Frank Steier, the office manager, said only about one-fourth of the loot was negotiable. Seventy-five per cent was in checks.

He said no one was in the office between 4 p.m. Saturday and 8 a.m. Monday, when he arrived at work.

Police and FBI agents sealed off the area. Authorities refused to disclose more than scant details of the crime.

One spokesman said, however, that a tripod used to mount a light cannon and "quite a few" shell casings, along with a gas torch, were found near the vault.

Detectives said the vault had been lined with mattresses, apparently to muffle the sound of the firing.

A check of the office's burglar alarm system showed it had been

(Continued on Back Page, Col. 4)

India Quits U.N. Parley

UNITED NATIONS, N.Y. (UPI)—India Monday night walked out of an emergency Security Council meeting called to hear Pakistani charges that India has no intention of seeking a political settlement of the Kashmir dispute.

India Foreign Minister Swaran Singh refused to return to the council chamber after a brief recess despite efforts by U.S. Ambassador Arthur J. Goldberg.

India contends the council has no right to consider the situation in Kashmir.

Hershey Calls Pacifist Program a Flop

WASHINGTON (UPI) —The head of America's Selective Service system says that an attempted draft-evasion movement among young Americans has been "a complete flop."

Lt. Gen. Lewis B. Hershey said that while he is disturbed by the anti-draft demonstrations, he doesn't think they are likely to have any effect on future military manpower pools.

The 72-year-old general, who has headed the draft program since 1940, said in an interview, his "real concern is that some local boards may react to all of this agitation by canceling student deferments."

"I hope that won't happen," he added.

He said that of two million college boys who are continuing their studies under student deferments, "Only a tiny fraction of 1 per cent have been involved in staging protest parades, burning draft cards or other demonstrations of unwillingness to serve in the armed forces."

"If I were the people who are trying to promote this movement, I'd feel it had been a complete flop," Hershey declared. "The effect on our ability to meet draft calls has been negligible, and I am confident it will remain negligible.

"If anything, the agitators may make my job easier. There is always a patriotic counter-reaction to this kind of thing — especially when it happens at a time when casualty lists are coming in from a war front in Vietnam."

He said there have already been some intimations from various parts of the country that the

(Continued on Back Page, Col. 1)

Weather

Tokyo Area Forecast

Tuesday night: Fair; Low Near 50
Wednesday: Fair; High Near 70
Monday's Temperatures: Low 53. High 68

(USAF Weather Central, Fuchu AS)

JOHNSON OKS HIKE IN VIETNAM TROOPS

PACIFIC

STARS AND STRIPES

AN AUTHORIZED PUBLICATION OF THE ARMED FORCES FAR EAST

10¢ DAILY
15¢ WITH SUPPLEMENTS

Vol. 21, No. 316   FIVE-STAR EDITION   Saturday, Nov. 13, 1965

JOHNSON CITY, Tex. (AP)—President Johnson Thursday authorized the sending of additional U.S. troops to fight in the Republic of Vietnam.

Defense Secretary Robert S. McNamara said Johnson instructed him to meet the requests of U.S. commanders in Vietnam for additional personnel.

McNamara did not estimate how many more troops would be sent to augment the 160,000 already there, saying this country does not want to tip off the communists in advance as to what forces they would face in the future.

McNamara and Secretary of State Dean Rusk spoke with newsmen at Bergstrom AFB near Austin after they and other top-level advisers had conferred for hours with Johnson at his ranch near here on a wide variety of world events. These ranged from the old Vietnam problem to the new one in Rhodesia.

McNamara said the South Vietnamese, with the help

(Continued on Back Page, Col. 4)

Rhodesia Pulls Out, Britain Retaliates

Rhodesia declares its independence from Britain.

Britain retaliates, expelling Rhodesia from the sterling area, banning exports and ending all British aid.

Britain asks for a meeting of the United Nations Security Council.

U.S. deplores Rhodesian action, will consult with Britain.

SALISBURY, Rhodesia (AP)—Prime Minister Ian Smith declared Rhodesia independent Thursday, the first such declaration against Britain since the American colonies broke away in 1776.

Britain retaliated swiftly, in effect outlawing Rhodesia. Prime Minister Harold Wilson declared in the House of Commons that Smith and his ministers had been fired—an action which will be ignored in Rhodesia. Wilson asserted his government will have no dealings with the Rhodesian regime.

Wilson expelled Rhodesia from the sterling area, banned exports, including British purchases of Rhodesia's $112-million-a-year tobacco crop, ended all British aid and halted trading preferences.

Britain embargoed the shipment of all arms to the central African country.

In New York, Britain called for an urgent meeting of the United Nations Security Council to consider Rhodesia's move.

(UPI reported British sources said they hoped the council could meet Friday morning.)

The Organization of African Unity (OAU) also requested a Security Council meeting.

Diallo Telli of Guinea, secre-

(Continued on Page 6, Col. 3)

GROUND CREWS LOOK OVER THE ILYUSHIN-28 JET BOMBER FLOWN TO TAIWAN BY THREE DEFECTING CHINESE.

AP Radiophoto

35 Killed in Utah Jet Crash

SALT LAKE CITY (UPI) — A United Airlines 727 jet with 88 persons aboard crashed and burned Thursday night while landing at Salt Lake Municipal Airport. At least 35 persons were killed.

Local officials said there were "at least 35 bodies in the plane—

all badly burned and mutilated." They said the FBI had been called for assistance in identifying the victims.

The plane, en route from New York to San Francisco with four intermediate stops, carried 82 passengers and a crew of six.

There were several survivors.

One Salt Lake hospital reported eight injured passengers had arrived by ambulance from the airport.

A witness to the crash, private pilot Don Cecala, said just as the plane touched down there was a "muffled explosion," then a big ball of fire appeared.

He said the blaze seemed to be coming from the rear of the plane and spraying toward the front. The flames seemed to die out briefly, then ignited again, Cecala said.

The plane was piloted by a 25-year flying veteran Gale C. Kehmeier, 47, of Denver. His family in the Colorado city said he was reported "okay."

It was the third 727 to have crashed since production of the triple jet craft was started by Boeing, and it was the second crash in a week.

The plane came to a halt on

(Continued on Back Page, Col. 5)

3 Defect To Taiwan

By ANDREW HEADLAND JR.
S&S Taiwan Bureau Chief

TAIPEI—Three airmen defected from Red China in an Ilyushin-28 light jet bomber and crash landed Thursday at an undisclosed air base on Taiwan.

One of the crewmen, a radioman identified as Lien Pao-sheng of Hopeh Province, was said to be seriously injured in the landing and was immediately hospitalized.

(UPI reported that "some

(Continued on Back Page, Col. 1)

Air Strikes Batter VC Force

By JOE SCHNEIDER
S&S Vietnam Bureau Chief

SAIGON—A government force Thursday killed 131 Viet Cong in an action about 60 miles southeast of Saigon, a U.S. military spokesman said here.

U.S. and Vietnamese Air Force planes flew nearly 30 sorties in support of the friendly troops. It was estimated that 100 of the Viet Cong dead were killed by air strikes, the spokesman said.

In other action, U.S. and Vietnamese marines who churned ashore in amphibious landing crafts Wednesday to launch an operation 18 miles northwest of Chu Lai, had netted two Viet Cong killed, two weapons captured and 18 Viet Cong suspects detained.

This was the first joint U.S.-Vietnamese amphibious assault of the war.

Further to the south, a govern-

ment regional force Wednesday found six secret shelters containing a large arms cache.

The cache included 1,200 rounds of submachine gun ammunition, two 60mm mortar rounds, two 57mm recoilless rifle rounds, 120 hand grenades, 90 cases of small arms ammunition, 140 antitank mines, 140 bangalore mines and 33 homemade claymore mines.

Government army units, taking

(Continued on Back Page, Col. 4)

CAV. KILLS 869 REDS

PACIFIC STARS AND STRIPES

AN AUTHORIZED PUBLICATION OF THE ARMED FORCES IN THE FAR EAST

FIVE-STAR EDITION

昭和三十四年一月二十二日国鉄東局特別扱承認新聞紙第175号（日刊）
（昭和34年4月21日第3種郵便物認可）

Vol. 21, No. 321   Thursday, Nov. 18, 1965

10¢ DAILY
15¢ WITH SUPPLEMENTS

RICE, FOODSTUFFS

Cambodians Aid VC, 3 PWs Say

By A3C BOB CUTTS
S&S Staff Correspondent

SAIGON—Three north Vietnamese hard-core communist prisoners taken near the Plei Me Special Forces camp revealed that Viet Cong fighting in the Republic of Vietnam are getting "substantial material aid" both from pro-Red Cambodian forces and from local Vietnamese villagers.

The trio, all soldiers of the People's Army of Vietnam (PAVN), were interviewed at a press conference here Tuesday. One man, Tran Ngoc Luong, 20, was captured by American paratroopers at a VC aid station near the Plei Me battle area, and two others, Huong Van Chung, 27, and Nguyen Xuan Lien, 25, voluntarily surrendered.

Lien told newsmen that Viet Cong forces traveling on the Ho Chi Minh trail supply route running from north Vietnam south to the republic, often received help, mainly in the form of rice and foodstuffs, from Cambodian militia forces.

He said the VC had established stopping points along

(Continued on Back Page, Col. 2)

By JOE SCHNEIDER
S&S Vietnam Bureau Chief

SAIGON — Enemy dead littered the battlefield Tuesday as communist troops launched a series of counterattacks on a brigade of

Related stories, Page 6

U.S. 1st Cav. Div. (Airmobile) troops near Plei Me.

The latest confirmed body count was 869 enemy killed, with 15 captured, a U.S. military spokesman said here.

(Continued on Back Page, Col. 3)

LBJ to Seek Law For Negro Justice

WASHINGTON (AP) — President Johnson said Tuesday night he will ask Congress in January for legislation "to prevent injustice to Negroes at the hands of all-white juries."

"We intend to make the jury box, in both state and federal courts, the sacred domain of justice under law." Johnson said.

He spoke to delegates here to plan for a White House civil rights conference next spring.

Johnson described the jury as "the cornerstone of our system of justice," adding:

"If its composition is a sham, its judgment is a sham. And when that happens, justice itself is a fraud, casting off the blindfold and tipping the scales one way for whites and another way for Negroes."

Johnson also said he will ask the civil rights commission Wednesday "to turn its careful attention to problems of race and education in all parts of the country."

"I am asking them to develop a firm foundation of facts on which local and state governments can build a school system that is color blind." he said.

Johnson noted that the government has already moved to join
(Continued on Back Page, Col. 1)

A member of the 1st Cav. Div. (Airmobile) rushes to pick up a fallen American as helicopter waits to fly the men out despite heavy fire during the battle against communist forces near Plei Me.
(UPI Radiophoto)

Youth Lunges At Rusk

MONTEVIDEO, Uruguay (UPI) —A teen-ager broke through police lines and attempted to attack Secretary of State Dean Rusk Tuesday but was subdued by police a few feet from Rusk.

The incident occurred during wreath-laying ceremonies at the monument to Jose Artigas, a hero of the Uruguayan independence. Security officers grabbed the youth, identified as Jesus Politano Roland Rojas, 18, as he ran toward Rusk.

Officials said the youth was not armed and attempted to spit on Rusk. Rusk is here for conferences with Uruguayan Foreign Ministry officials before the Inter-American Foreign Ministers Con-
(Continued on Back Page, Col. 5)

Rome Council Backs Ban on Birth Control

VATICAN CITY (UPI) — The Ecumenical Council Tuesday overwhelmingly approved provisions for tightening observance of the Catholic ban against artificial birth control.

A move by conservative bishops to win a condemnation of communism failed, but the council approved a strong statement against racial discrimination.

The developments emerged during near-final voting on the council's key decree charting the role of the church in the modern world.

More than two-thirds of the council fathers voted approval of the schema chapter on atheism in its current form, which does not specifically mention communism. This majority was big enough to block a last-minute conservative effort to insert a detailed denunciation of communism by name.

The document's section on racial discrimination was adopted by an almost unanimous vote, 2,015-35.

This section was recently strengthened to say that all forms of discrimination must be "crushed and removed."

By votes of 2,106-19 and 2,052-91, the bishops adopted amendments to a section of the decree dealing with marriage and conjugal love. The decree previously had left considerable latitude to the private consciences of married couples in the question of family planning.

The new formula spells out that

"the sons of the church are not to enter into ways of conjugal love which have been reproved by the teaching authority of the church."

The emphasis is on stricter obedience to church discipline, which some theologians feel has been put in doubt by current controversy on the matter. The new formula means that Catholics must comply with the present church ban on all artificial birth
(Continued on Back Page, Col. 1)

PACIFIC

STARS STRIPES

AN AUTHORIZED PUBLICATION OF THE ARMED FORCES IN THE FAR EAST

FIVE-STAR EDITION

昭和三十四年一月二十二日国鉄東局特別扱承認新聞紙第175号 (日刊)
(昭和34年4月21日第3種郵便物認可)

10¢ DAILY
15¢ WITH
SUPPLEMENTS

Vol. 21, No. 333   Tuesday, Nov. 30, 1965

'WAS FIGHT TO FINISH'

VC, Viet Toll High In 'Fiercest' Battle

SAIGON (AP) — Relief troops Sunday carefully picked their way across a devastated rubber plantation littered with scores of Vietnamese dead. A U.S. military spokesman said government casualties were heavy

* * * * *

in the action which took place about 45 miles north-northwest of Saigon. An infantry regiment was hit by human waves of Viet Cong in the Michelin rubber plantation early Saturday. The headquarters unit and two battalions were overrun and massacred.

The casualties could be the highest in any single action of the war.

The Vietnamese regimental commander and his American adviser were killed. Casualties among the Americans also were reported to have been heavy.

A U.S. spokesman said Vietnamese troops reported counting 300 enemy dead.

There was still no full account by late Sunday of what took place during the battle Saturday. A U.S. spokesman said "there is still a lot of understandable confusion up there"

There was little doubt, however, that the communists planned and executed the devastating attack with precision, coordination and fearlessness, the spokesman said.

Associated Press photographer Horst Faas visited the battle ground Sunday and reported that the area was reoccupied by government forces at noon.

Faas found Vietnamese and Americans lying dead in their fox-holes surrounded by spent cartridges, attesting to a fight to the finish. Faas saw rubber trees, pierced by bullets and shrapnel, dripping latex.

Among the government dead were some troops who appeared
(Continued on Back Page, Col. 4)

Red Base In Baltic Blasted

STOCKHOLM (UPI) — An explosion has destroyed a Russian military base in southern Estonia, the provincial newspaper Eskilstuna-Kuriren reports.

Eskilstuna-Kuriren said "the number of injured personnel at the base was so great that the equipment of the hospitals in Parnu was not sufficient. Blood donors were recruited from villages around the base."

The base was built a few years ago and all civilians were evacuated from the area, the paper said.

The Soviet Union has built a number of bases for rockets along the Estonian coast.

Eskilstuna-Kuriren, which has a close contact with Estonians in Sweden and carries daily news in Estonian, says visitors who recently returned from Estonia reported the explosion.

Report LBJ Thinking of Viet Trip

NEW YORK (UPI)—Newsweek magazine, in its "Periscope" column in its latest edition, said that President Johnson may visit the Republic of Vietnam during the Christmas season. Said the magazine:

". . . Reasons offered by proponents of the trip: 1) The visit would reaffirm in a most concrete and unmistakable way the determination of the U.S. to remain in Vietnam until some satisfactory solution to the war is found; 2) It would boost the morale of the troops (about which no complaint has been made); 3) It would give added support to the present regime in South Vietnam; 4) Were the trip coupled with another strong offer to negotiate, Hanoi might respond and relax the intransigent position it has long maintained.

". . . Opponents argue: 1) The trip would be a serious drain on the energies of the President, still recovering from a major operation; 2) Security arrangements could not eliminate all risk, 3) The President
(Continued on Back Page, Col. 1)

McNamara Opens Talks in Saigon

SAIGON (AP)—Defense Secretary Robert S. McNamara arrived in Saigon Sunday. He told newsmen he was surprised by the intensity and scale of Viet Cong and north Vietnamese attacks in recent weeks.

McNamara, who arrived with General Earle G. Wheeler, chairman of the Joint Chiefs of Staff, warned that "these actions will require counter action."

He declined to specify what that might be.

Asked if there will be a further increase in the U.S. military buildup in Vietnam, McNamara said: "I cannot discuss this with you until after the briefings and conference I will hold with officials while I am here."

Later in the day McNamara attended over five hours of briefings on the war.

Then he went off to dinner with top U.S. military and civilian men here, where more informal talks were held on the same subject.

The official word was that McNamara was making another of his periodic visits to get firsthand information on the current situation; that no hard recommenda-
(Continued on Page 6, Col. 1)

'Fare' Play, U.S. Style

CLIFTON, N.J. (UPI)—An official of a bus company that transported demonstrators to Washington for the anti-Vietnam march Saturday said the company will donate the protesters' travel fees to the American Legion.

John Gallagher, secretary-treasurer of the Community Bus Lines of Clifton, said the American Legion will use the money to buy Christmas presents for U.S. servicemen fighting in Vietnam. He estimated that $1,000 would be given to the legion.

Defense Secretary Robert S. McNamara and General Earle Wheeler, chairman of the Joint Chiefs of Staff, are accompanied by Lt. Gen. Nguyen Huu Co, Vietnamese defense minister, as they inspect a Vietnamese honor guard on their arrival Sunday at Saigon's Tan Son Nhut Airport. (UPI Radiophoto)

P.I. to Send Troops To Vietnam

WASHINGTON (UPI) — Philippine President-elect Ferdinand Marcos said in an interview published in the Washington Post Sunday that he plans to send Philippine troops to the Republic of Vietnam after his inauguration next month.

The Post quoted Marcos as saying he would recommend to Congress that 2,000 Philippine soldiers be sent to Vietnam to join the fight against the Viet Cong.

Washington Post correspondent Stanley Karnow, who interviewed Marcos in Manila, said "it is understood" that the United States would provide the major part of the $6 million initially
(Continued on Page 6, Col. 5)

Weather

Tokyo Area Forecast

Monday night: Cloudy with rain; Low Mid 40s

Tuesday: Partly cloudy becoming fair; High Mid 50s

Sunday's Temperatures: Low 35, High 57

(USAF Weather Central, Fuchu AS)

PACIFIC STAR STRIPES

AN AUTHORIZED PUBLICATION OF THE ARMED FORCES IN THE FAR EAST

FIVE-STAR EDITION

昭和三十四年一月二十二日國鉄局特別扱承認新聞紙第175号（日刊）

（昭和34年4月21日第3種郵便物認可）

10¢ DAILY
15¢ WITH SUPPLEMENTS

Vol. 21, No. 334   Wednesday, Dec. 1, 1965

Tide Has Turned But End Not Near, McNamara Says

By SSGT. JACK BAIRD
S&S Staff Correspondent

SAIGON — Defense Secretary Robert S. McNamara said here Monday night that "we have stopped losing the war." But he added that it will be a long struggle.

McNamara, flanked by General Earle G. Wheeler, chairman of the Joint Chiefs of Staff, and U.S. Ambassador Henry Cabot Lodge, made the statements during an airport press conference minutes before his departure from Vietnam for Guam and the U.S.

The defense secretary said his most vivid impression of his two-day visit in the Republic of Vietnam was that "we have stopped losing the war." He said "the very substantial increase in strength here of U.S., Australian, New Zea-

Related story, picture, Page 6.

land and Republic of Korea forces has denied the Viet Cong any victories they wanted during the recent monsoon season."

McNamara said the nine regiments of north Vietnam forces that have moved into South Vietnam "more than offset the losses they have suffered." Hanoi has escalated their level of infiltration.

The defense secretary said that an increase in friendly forces is required in South Vietnam. "Tactics we follow will be dictated by actions of the Viet Cong," he said.

McNamara said V i e t n a m e s e forces have dismembered many of north Vietnam's battalions and **(Continued on Back Page, Col. 1)**

DEFENSE SECRETARY MCNAMARA AND AMBASSADOR LODGE ADDRESS NEWSMEN JUST BEFORE MCNAMARA LEFT SAIGON.

AP Radiophoto

U.S. Patrol Fired On Near DMZ

SEOUL (S&S) — Elements of wo U.S. Army units continued search operations Monday night, but found no trace of unidentified assailants who reportedly fired on a U.S. Army patrol Monday near the DMZ.

The incident reportedly occurred at 2:40 a.m. Monday when the patrol was fired on between Libby and Freedom Bridges, near the DMZ along the south bank of the Imjin River. Members of the patrol observed movement in the bushes, and were fired on when they attempted to investigate.

Blast Wrecks Negro Grocery

VICKSBURG, Miss. (UPI)—An explosion Monday injured at least three persons, heavily damaged a Negro grocery and shattered windows in several nearby stores and homes.

Civil rights leaders called for a thorough investigation.

Humphrey Urges U.N. Peace Force

WASHINGTON (UPI) — Vice President Hubert H. Humphrey called Monday for new peacekeeping machinery both in the United Nations and locally in the American hemisphere.

Humphrey, opening a three-day White House conference on international cooperation, said creation of a permanent peacekeeping force should be "high on the agenda" of the United Nations.

Such a force was called for in the U.N. charter but never came

Related story, picture, Page 2.

into being, although some countries have earmarked their own forces for possible United Nations use.

Humphrey also u r g e d that peacekeeping machinery be established regionally as part of the inter-American system. Apparent-

ly referring to dispatch of U.S. troops to the Dominican Republic last April, Humphrey said "No American nation desires unilateral intervention in the affairs of another."

(Continued on Back Page, Col. 3)

Good Reason To Hustle

SAN FRANCISCO (UPI) — Toll collector Allen Davis thought it was funny when a truck driver paid his quarter on the Bay Bridge, then sped off without stopping for the safe that fell out the end of his meat truck.

Now Davis knows why. Police said the still-locked safe was stolen, as was the meat and the truck.

U.N. OKs World Talk On Arms

UNITED NATIONS, N.Y. (AP) —The United Nations General Assembly approved without a dissenting vote Monday a proposal for a world disarmament conference to which communist China and other countries outside the United Nations would be invited.

By a vote of 112-0 with one abstention, the Assembly adopted a resolution urging the establishment of a preparatory committee to work out details for holding the conference not later than 1967.

The United States joined with the Soviet Union and Britain in voting for the resolution. The United States has expressed willingness to enter into negotiations with Peking and other nations on **(Continued on Back Page, Col. 1)**

Pain Sends LBJ to Bed

JOHNSON CITY, Tex. (UPI)— President Johnson felt pain on the right side of his back Sunday night and was spending part of Monday in bed.

Vice Adm. George R. Burkley, the President's personal physician, attributed the discomfort to muscles irritated by the Oct. 8 gallbladder-kidney stone operation.

Johnson flew to Houston Sunday to hear evangelist Billy Graham, and the trip reportedly tired him.

He awoke at dawn Monday to go over some government documents, but returned to bed in midmorning "just to get a little rest."

Princess Michiko Has 6.6-Pound Boy

TOKYO (UPI)—Crown Princess Michiko gave birth to a 6.67-pound baby boy early Tuesday morning at the Imperial Household Hospital, the Imperial Household Agency reported.

The announcement said both the mother and baby are in excellent condition.

Crown Prince Akihito was given the happy news at the Togu Palace, the couple's imperial residence. He did not go to the hospi-

tal immediately.

Their majesties, Emperor Hirohito and Empress Nagako, were informed of the birth by the imperial chamberlain at the Imperial Palace.

Princess Michiko felt birth pains around 11:30 a.m. Monday and after an examination by her chief physician, Dr. Takashi Kobayashi of Tokyo University, entered the Imperial Household Hospital at 8:30 p.m.

She was seen off at the Togu Palace by Crown Prince Akihito and her son, Prince Hiro.

Her parents, Mr. and Mrs. Eizaburo Shoda, visited the hospital about an hour after she was admitted there.

The princess was transferred to the maternity room at 11:10 p.m. Kobayashi said the baby was 20.07 inches tall and weighed 6.67 pounds.

The doctor said the delivery

was two days ahead of schedule.

Prime Minister Eisaku Sato will call at the Imperial Palace at 3 p.m. Tuesday to offer congratulations to emperor and the empress on the birth of their grandchild.

The general public will offer felicitations by registering at the Imperial Palace from noon until 3 p.m.

The christening ceremony will take place at the Imperial Palace Dec. 6.

Weather

Tokyo Area Forecast

Tuesday Night: Mostly cloudy: Low Near 40

Wednesday: Mostly cloudy; becoming fair; High Mid 50s

Monday's Temperatures: Low 42, High 59

(USAF Weather Central, Fuchu AS)

N-Carrier Jets in 1st Strike; 2 Lost

By JOE SCHNEIDER
S&S Vietnam Bureau Chief

ABOARD THE CARRIER ENTERPRISE — A nuclear-powered ship was used in combat for the first time in history Thursday as jet fighter-bombers from this Seventh Fleet carrier struck enemy targets in the Republic of Vietnam.

Pilots, many making their first combat strike, reported successful hits on suspected Viet Cong troop concentrations.

(Two jets from the Enterprise were lost, AP reported, but all four pilots were rescued.

(One of the planes, an F4B Phantom, was shot down by ground fire 50 miles north of Saigon. The other plane, also a Phantom, plunged into the sea
(Continued on Back Page, Col. 5)

PACIFIC
STAR AND STRIPES

AN AUTHORIZED PUBLICATION OF THE
U.S. ARMED FORCES IN THE FAR EAST

10¢ DAILY
15¢ WITH SUPPLEMENTS

Vol. 21, No. 337   FIVE-STAR EDITION

昭和三十四年一月二十二日国鉄局特別扱承認新聞紙第175号（日刊）
（昭和34年4月21日第3種郵便物認可）

Saturday, Dec. 4, 1965

U.S. BACKS BID ON PEACE TALKS

JOHNSON CITY, Tex. (AP)—Secretary of State Dean Rusk said after a conference with President Johnson Thursday that the United States is willing to attend a conference on Southeast Asia of the sort proposed by British Foreign Secretary Michael Stewart.

Speaking with newsmen at Bergstrom AFB near Austin, Rusk was asked his reaction to Stewart's proposal in Moscow Thursday.

"We have indicated for some time that we will be willing to attend a conference on Southeast Asia or any part of it," Rusk said.

Rusk said more may be heard about Stewart's proposal in a matter of days.

In Moscow, Stewart called on the Soviet Union to join with Great Britain in calling a conference to arrange a cease-fire in Vietnam and bring about a peace-
(Continued on Back Page, Col. 1)

A NAVY JET TAKES OFF FROM THE DECK OF THE CARRIER ENTERPRISE TO BEGIN MISSION OVER VIETNAM.

AP Radiophoto

Gemini-7 Ready, Astronauts To Get Day's Grace in Space

CAPE KENNEDY, Fla. (UPI) —Space officials said Thursday Gemini-7 astronauts Frank Borman and James Lovell, set for launch Saturday on a 14-day flight, may be kept in orbit an extra day to better chances for a historic space rendezvous.

Everything was progressing smoothly for the scheduled 2:30 p.m. EST Saturday (4:30 a.m. Sunday JST) opening of the Borman-Lovell portion of the spectacular Gemini doubleheader.

The astronauts were so confident of the mission that they passed up a review session Thursday with top space officials for a three-mile run in blue coveralls.

The only hint of possible trouble came with a weatherman's report that a rainy area over Texas was expected to move into Florida by Saturday.

Astronauts Walter Schirra and Thomas Stafford are scheduled to be rocketed in pursuit of Gemini-7 on Dec. 13 to attempt an unprecedented meeting in space.

But William Schneider, Federal Space Agency mission director, said there could be a delay in the launch of Schirra and Staf-
(Continued on Page 6, Col. 4)

SAM Sites Blasted

By A3C BOB CUTTS
S&S Staff Correspondent

SAIGON—Air Force F-105 Thunderchief pilots used swarms of air-to-ground rockets to pound north Vietnamese surface-to-air missile sites in two simultaneous raids near Hanoi late Wednesday.

The fighter-bomber fliers struck one site 35 miles northeast of the north Vietnamese capital and another five miles further northeast.

Only 2.75 inch rockets were used against the missile complexes, according to a U.S. spokesman here.

Light flak was encountered, but all the jets returned safely. No damage estimate could be made because of dust and smoke
(Continued on Back Page, Col. 2)

Space Chief Dryden Dies

WASHINGTON (AP)—The man who has been deputy administrator of the Federal Space Agency since it was created by Congress in 1958—Dr. Hugh Dryden—died Friday at 67. Dryden died of cancer at the National Institute of Health.

He had been ailing for several years but entered the hospital only recently. In addition to his responsibilities for the space program under NASA, Dryden had several government advisory posts—advising the Defense Department among others.

Weather

Tokyo Area Forecast

Friday night: Mostly fair: Low Mid 30's
Saturday: Cloudy with Rain: High Mid 40's
Thursday's Temperatures: Low 36, High 55
(USAF Weather Central, Fuchu AS)

No Bunny for B Co.

CHICAGO (UPI)—Playboy magazine had bad news Thursday for B Co.—no bunny.

B Co., 2d Bn., 503d Inf., 173d Airborne Brigade, now stationed in the Republic of Vietnam, bought a lifetime subscription to the magazine, because an advertisement said that such subscriptions' first copy is delivered personally by a Playboy bunny.

So they subscribed and asked the magazine "how about it?"

Said Playboy today: "We can't send a girl."

Yule in Vietnam—Will the VC Hit?

By A3C BOB CUTTS
S&S Staff Correspondent

TUYEN NHON, Special Forces Camp, Vietnam—Christmas Eve, 1965, in the Mekong Delta. Eight Americans all wearing the green berets of the Army Special Forces, wait, watch and listen through a long, quiet darkness.

Maybe tonight. Maybe not. Only the slow passage of the endless hours will tell whether the cease-fire will last the night.

Eight Americans, each with his own thoughts of Christmas and home. Each far away from snow, silver bells, Christmas carols and Santa Claus. Each wondering if this Christmas Eve is the night Charlie will pick to unleash the death and

destruction the soldiers know is waiting out there.

Christmas is something that is far away this year. There isn't much time for it. But each man gives it a thought between rounds of checking the compound, loading weapons, and trying to catch a few hours sleep. It's all the Christmas they'll get tonight.

There's Capt. Ronald T. Shelton, a West Point graduate and advisory team leader. It's his first day in the outpost He got to Vietnam just two weeks ago. First Lt. Jack McDaniels is executive officer, a veteran of nine months in the camp.

Team sergeant SFC Lester Parish, spent most of the day checking two out-

posts that had been under attack the night before.

There's SFC Rudolph Cooper, intelligence officer, who's getting "short" and who had just brought back reports that an entire Viet Cong battalion has moved into the area with the purpose of attacking the camp within the next two weeks. Maybe tonight.

There's Sgt. Jerry Rainey, one of the team's two medics.

There are others. SFC George Yara and SSgt. James Chapnan. Both just returned from R&R in Saigon.

There's Sgt. Larry Lusar, the radio operator and SSgt. Robert Ollie, a munitions repairman and two others, SSgt. Lander Pierce, and SP5 Jimmy Strahan, spending a lonely Christmas Eve in the

two small outposts that were attacked the night before.

The plan for the night is discussed— who will get to sleep, who will stand guard, who will monitor the radio. The attack procedure is reviewed carefully, to make sure everyone knows what to do if tonight is the night.

Some of the men haven't slept much in the past two days, but they seem a little reluctant to go to bed. Maybe they're thinking about Charlie's habit of attacking between 10 p.m. and 3 a.m. in a light probe or attacking in strength before 9 p.m. if it's an all out battle for the camp.

At any rate, those who get to sleep tonight head for their bunks at 9, loading their weapons before turning in.

PACIFIC STARS STRIPES

AN AUTHORIZED PUBLICATION OF THE ARMED FORCES IN THE FAR EAST

FIVE-STAR EDITION

昭和三十四年一月二十二日國鉄東局特別扱承認新聞紙第175号（日刊）
（昭和34年4月21日第3種郵便物認可）

10¢ DAILY
15¢ WITH
SUPPLEMENTS

Vol. 21, No. 359   Sunday, Dec. 26, 1965

A Mostly Silent Night As Truce Calms Viet 1st Time in 5 Years

SAIGON (UPI)—The American and Republic of Vietnam 30-hour Christmas cease-fire went into effect Friday night and up to 8 a.m. Saturday the communists were abiding by the temporary halt in the war.

So, for the first time in five years, peace prevailed throughout the country.

But there was no assurance the Reds would go all the way with the Americans and the South Vietnamese troops over the 30-hour stretch in the peace. At least they have not said they would.

The communists offered to stop fighting for 12 hours, beginning at 6 p.m. Christmas Eve. That period expires at 6 a.m. Christmas day and there was a possibility they may resume violence then.

Allied forces are under strict order not to open fire until their 30-hour cease-fire is up unless the communists resume fighting.

The Viet Cong violated the cease-fire within hours after it started by lobbing seven mortar shells at U.S. Marine positions near the Chu Lai AB south of Da Nang, a military spokesman **(Continued on Back Page, Col. 3)**

No Letup For LBJ

AUSTIN, Tex. (UPI) — President Johnson kept hopeful watch on the Christmas truce in Vietnam Friday and celebrated the holiday with his family at the hearth of the LBJ Ranch.

The President was awake early to hear intelligence reports from all over the world—and the quiet Vietnam battlefield — from Col. James U. Cross, his armed forces aide.

He also checked with McGeorge **(Continued on Back Page, Col. 1)**

Bus Flips, 12 Killed In Oregon

MEDFORD, Ore. (AP)—A Greyhound bus overturned on an icy highway, killing 12 holiday-bound passengers and injuring 26 other persons late Thursday night.

State police said the bus, bound from Spokane, Wash., to San Francisco, plunged from Interstate Hwy. 5 between the southern Oregon cities of Grants Pass and Medford.

Nine persons were dead at the scene, state police said. One was dead on arrival at a hospital and two others died later.

Ambulances and emergency vehicles from surrounding communities took the injured to hospitals in the two cities.

Erving Carew, Greyhound superintendent at Medford, said there were 33 persons on the bus when it left Portland, 250 miles to the north.

The driver, Joseph Bailey of Battle Ground, Wash., told police he was traveling about 45 m.p.h. **(Continued on Back Page, Col. 1)**

Bob Hope is greeted at Tan Son Nhut airport by comedienne Martha Raye. Miss Raye had just returned from a Christmas Eve show for the Seventh Fleet. (UPI Radiophoto)

2,000 Hear Cardinal In Silent War Zone

SAIGON (UPI)—Francis Cardinal Spellman of New York celebrated Midnight Mass before more than 2,000 Americans and Vietnamese Saturday morning in an open air service on the outskirts of Saigon.

Comedian Bob Hope stood and knelt among the other worshipers, in the grassy soccer field at Tan Son Nhut AB.

Vietnamese children lined up with husky American soldiers to receive communion under the starry sky. Floodlights glittered on the gun barrels of men just back from guarding the jet fighters on the Tan Son Nhut runway.

Spellman assured the fighting men that there was no conflict between the message of the Prince **(Continued on Back Page, Col. 3)**

Hope Troupe Boffo in Saigon

By WALLACE BEENE
S&S Vietnam Bureau Chief

SAIGON — "You've seen some of those demonstrators, haven't you? Aren't you glad they're not on our side."

The old pro Bob Hope left them laughing—about 8,000 of them— at Tan Son Nhut Air Base Christmas Eve as he belted out the one-liners.

Despite a fall from the stage in Thailand the day before, which **(Continued on Back Page, Col. 3)**

Major, NCO Come Up With a Winning Gift

VINH LONG, Vietnam (S&S)—When a CO and his topkick look around for something to give their men at Christmas time, the choice isn't too great in a Mekong Delta outpost such as this.

MSgt. Jimmy Reed and Maj. Samuel Vincent of the 502d Aviation Bn. hit upon the answer—they gave the men a night off.

Since someone had to fly a recon mission to check the perimeter, Reed volunteered to serve as observer in the plane piloted by Vincent.

Calm Reigns in Battle-Torn Vietnam

By WALLACE BEENE
S&S Vietnam Bureau Chief

SAIGON—The war in Vietnam halted Thursday.

Despite the confusion between the various time zones about when cease-fires were to go into effect and the number of countries involved, the fighting stopped.

The only incident involving U.S. troops came about noon Thursday when the cease-fire went into effect. It occurred seven miles west of Tuy Hoa on the central coast when the VC fired on the 1st Brigade of the 101st Airborne. The troopers returned fire and one VC was killed before the enemy fled.

The Vietnamese reported only one clash after the halt in hostilities. It was a minor action lasting less than a half hour.

U.S. planes and troops continued their operations up until midday, then pulled back in keeping with the promise to observe the Vietnamese holiday season of Tet. The cease fire is supposed to last until 6 p.m. Sunday.

A U.S. spokesman said American forces are maintaining a full alert and planes are making surveillance flights.

Also, operations such as the Market Time blockade of the Vietnamese coast are continuing without interruption.

When asked if the U.S. might extend the cease-fire as was attempted during the Christmas lull, the spokesman said full operations are scheduled to resume Sunday evening, "and this includes offensive action."

During the Christmas truce, U.S. Forces received an addition-**(Continued on Back Page, Col. 3)**

New India Leader to Visit LBJ

NEW DELHI (AP)—President Johnson Thursday invited India's new prime minister, Mrs. Indira Gandhi, to visit him in Washington soon to discuss the "many momentous problems we both face" and Mrs. Gandhi told newsmen she had accepted.

She did not say when she would make the trip.

Johnson messaged his good wishes to Mrs. Gandhi Thursday and pledged "friendship and cooperation."

Mrs. Gandhi's predecessor, the late Prime Minister Lal Bahadur Shastri, had been scheduled to visit the United States Feb. 1.

The President said he would be "delighted" if Mrs. Gandhi could make it then, but acknowledged her pressing duties might make this difficult.

Johnson's message, made public by Mrs. Gandhi's office, congratulated her on her election as leader in Parliament of India's governing Congress Party. The election automatically elevated her to prime minister.

Johnson's letter was delivered by U.S. Ambassador Chester Bowles during a 25-minute call on Mrs. Gandhi. He also delivered a letter from Vice President Hubert H. Humphrey which said the **(Continued on Back Page, Col. 1)**

PACIFIC STAR AND STRIPES

AN AUTHORIZED PUBLICATION OF THE
U.S. ARMED FORCES IN THE FAR EAST

10¢ DAILY
15¢ WITH SUPPLEMENTS

Vol. 22, No. 21 **FIVE-STAR EDITION** 昭和三十四年一月二十二日国鉄東京特別扱承認新聞紙第175号（日刊）
（昭和34年4月21日第3種郵便物認可） **Saturday, Jan. 22, 1966**

83 and Set To Fight

PHOENIX, Ariz. (AP)—As a new citizen, and on his birthday, Hanna Sahhar made a wish Thursday:

"I hope the President of the United States will read this and will grant me _permission to serve in Vietnam. I am strong as a boy of 18."

Sahhar is 83.

Hanoi Avoids Peace In Hope U.S. Will Quit, Johnson Says

INDEPENDENCE, Mo. (UPI) — President Johnson said Thursday north Vietnam was holding up peace in Southeast Asia because of the "mistaken view" that the United States might abandon her allies, yield to pressure and get out of the Vietnam war.

Johnson, speaking at ceremonies honoring former President Harry S Truman, added a major section to his prepared text dealing with his current peace offensive in Southeast Asia.

The addition to the text was particularly significant, since it was drafted as Johnson flew from Washington to Missouri after conferring early Thursday with Secretary of State Dean Rusk and roving ambassador Averell Harriman, who returned Wednesday night from extensive peace missions around the world.

Johnson said his peace envoys reported this morning:

"In all the capitals they visited, the government leaders recognized the United States' genuine desire for peace in the world."

"Of this I am sure," Johnson added emphatically. ". . . The door of peace must be kept wide open to avoid the scourge of war, but the door to aggression must **(Continued on Back Page, Col. 4)**

President Johnson speaks at Independence, Mo., ceremony establishing the Harry S. Truman Center for the Advancement of Peace in Israel. **Seated behind the President are (from left) Chief Justice Earl Warren and Mr. and Mrs. Truman. Truman also spoke.** (UPI Radiophoto)

Taipei Boat Routs Pack

TAIPEI (AP)—A Chinese Nationalist warship repelled six Chinese communist torpedo boats in a short action Tuesday in the Taiwan Strait, the official Central News Agency reported Thursday.

The agency gave these details:

The action occurred 35 miles northeast of the Nationalist-held island fortress of Matsu and lasted three minutes.

The torpedo boats approached the warship from three directions in an attempt to encircle it.

When they came within 4,500 yards, the captain of the warship gave orders to fire. The torpedo boats retreated.

The type of the warship involved in the action was not stated, but most probably it was a patrol craft.

GETS CARD NO. 1

HST Is 1st in Medicare

INDEPENDENCE, Mo. (AP)—Harry Truman got Medicare card No. 1 personally from President Johnson Thursday and the President signed the application card as a witness.

"When the fellows at the Social Security Office heard I was coming here they asked me to bring you your new Medicare card," said Johnson.

Johnson signed the Medicare Bill in the same Truman Library auditorium, July 30, 1965.

"No. 1 is for you and No. 2 is for Mrs. Truman," Johnson said. "If you want to get the voluntary insurance you must sign the application and I must sign as your witness. You are getting the jump on the rest of the folks who won't get theirs until the end of the month."

Johnson said it was one more way of the American people telling Truman that they have not forgotten that it was he who proposed the Medicare program in his administration.

The Medicare program involving 19 million Americans begins July 1.

F-105 Rams Thai Village

BANGKOK (AP)—A disabled U.S. Air Force F-105 crashed into an isolated village in northeastern Thailand Thursday and first reports said at least 16 persons were killed.

The pilot, however, ejected from the aircraft and was rescued uninjured by a helicopter. He was flown to Nakorn Panom, about 18 miles north of the crash site.

U.S. Embassy officials said they were waiting for further information on the mishap.

First reports said the F-105 Thunderchief crashed into Sam **(Continued on Back Page, Col. 4)**

FIVE STAR EDITION

PACIFIC
STAR AND STRIPES

昭和三十四年一月二十二日國鉄東局特別承認新聞紙第175号（日刊）

10c DAILY
15c WITH SUPPLEMENTS

(昭和34年4月21日第3種郵便物認可)

Vol. 22, No. 22 — AN AUTHORIZED PUBLICATION OF THE U.S. ARMED FORCES IN THE FAR EAST — Sunday, Jan. 23, 1966

VC SHATTER TRUCE

By WALLACE BEENE
S&S Vietnam Bureau Chief

SAIGON—Some 400 Viet Cong troops overran a Republic of Korea Marine outpost in a bloody battle early Friday as the Vietnam ceasefire exploded into armed clashes throughout the country.

A U.S. spokesman said 50 VC violations of the ceasefire involving armed attacks had been reported, "and I'm sure there will be others." So far 15 of the assaults have involved Vietnamese units; the others were against other Free World forces.

"There have been U.S. casualties," the spokesman added.

(The Associated Press reported two U.S. Marine sergeants were killed when guerrillas caught a Leatherneck platoon on a security patrol in a cross fire as it struggled through the mud of a flooded rice paddy seven miles south of Da Nang.)

The clash between the VC and the ROK marines took place near Tuy Hoa, on the central coastal plain shortly after 1 a.m. in the rain.

Using local VC troops dressed in black pajamas and native hats as a human shield, the regular VC forces were able to get within about 10 yards of the ROK marine platoon guarding the perimeter of its headquarters area.

The VC opened up from three sides and overran the post, but the marines rallied and staged a counterattack which ended in hand-to-hand fighting, while their artillery opened fire on the enemy.

At daylight the marines counted 46 VC dead and three suspects detained. The Marine casualties were listed as moderate. First reports indicated the VC had used civilians for their human shield. (Continued on Back Page, Col. 3)

U.S. Military Police search debris in room in billet damaged by Viet Cong terrorist bomb early Saturday. An American sergeant was killed and two Americans were wounded. (AP Radiophoto)

Italian Premier Resigns

ROME (AP) — Premier Aldo Moro resigned Friday after an undercover rebellion in his own Christian Democrat Party and shaken confidence of his Socialist allies weakened his two-year-old center-left government.

Moro's resignation was triggered by an embarrassing defeat in the chamber of deputies Thursday on his bill to set up state nursery schools. He had described the measure as a key reform that the Socialists demanded when entering the coalition in December 1963.

The premier's decision to step down was taken after a meeting with his cabinet Friday.

After the surprise defeat over the nursery school bill, Moro's Socialist, Democratic Socialist, and Republican coalition partners advised him to quit.

He called an emergency meeting of his cabinet. It lasted only five minutes. When Moro walked out, he told newsmen, "the government decided to resign."

President Giuseppe Saragat reserved decision on the resignation and asked Moro to stay on in an interim capacity until a new government could be formed. This is the usual formula and left the president free to call on any political leader, including Moro, to form a new government.

The resignation plunges Italy into unexpected political crisis. Only a few weeks ago, it had appeared Moro probably would be able to hold his coalition government together until the next national parliamentary elections in 1968.

Moro had won two parliamen- (Continued on Back Page, Col. 1)

VC Bomb U.S. Billet, Kill NCO

SAIGON (AP) — A Viet Cong terrorist bomb exploded at a U.S. servicemen's billet shortly before dawn Saturday, and killed a U.S. sergeant, mortally wounded a woman in a nearby building and injured several other persons.

The bomb, estimated to have weighed about 25 pounds, was carried on a bicycle that was leaned against the American billet about a mile from Saigon's Tan Son Nhut Airport.

The American sergeant was asleep in a room that took the full force of the blast. He died immediately. Other U.S. servicemen in the room were wounded.

A Vietnamese woman and two (Continued on Back Page, Col. 4)

Hotter Red Action After End Of Holiday Likely, Rusk Says

WASHINGTON (AP) — Secretary of State Dean Rusk said Friday "there is every indication" that the communist side in Vietnam would intensify its activity after the Lunar New Year holiday.

Rusk told a news conference that President Johnson's peace offensive had failed to get "any positive and encouraging response" from the Vietnamese communists.

Otherwise, he said, it had drawn an "overwhelmingly favorable response" throughout the world.

His words indicated that the peace drive and the pause in bombing north Vietnam have come to the end of a phase, but he avoided saying so directly. He refused to say whether or when the United States would resume bombing the north.

Asked about the war outlook he said:

"There is every sign that the other side is going to intensify its activity after the Tet (Lunar New Year) period."

Concurrently with Rusk's report, the White House said instructions given American troops in the Republic of Vietnam to fire only when fired on cover the period of the current ceasefire.

That was Press Secretary Bill D. Moyers' response when asked how long U.S. forces would continue their strictly defensive stance.

At the time of the Christmas ceasefire, the troops reportedly had orders to try to maintain the (Continued on Back Page, Col. 5)

Firecrackers Spark 'Battle' in Saigon

SAIGON (UPI)—Anyone coming upon the scene on Saigon's Hai Ba Trung Street — a few hundred yards from U.S. Ambassador Henry Cabot Lodge's home—might have thought they had walked into the midst of a battle.

It was in fact almost that.

Three truckloads of Korean troops, members of the Korean engineering battalion based at Di An, 10 miles northeast of Saigon, were on their way to Tan Son Nhut Airport and home to Seoul.

It was in the midst of the lunar new year celebration in downtown Saigon and someone apparently set off a string of firecrackers. The Koreans mistook the exploding crackers for Viet Cong automatic-weapons fire.

They jumped from their trucks and set up defensive positions.

A convoy of trucks carrying American soldiers was heading down Hai Ba Trung about the same time. When the Americans saw the Koreans, they jumped from their trucks and also set up positions.

It was then that one Korean noncommissioned officer fired a shot into the air in an attempt to draw what he thought was enemy fire.

About this time, a Vietnamese policeman came along. He saw the two groups of soldiers lined up ready for battle. He quickly explained the situation to both Koreans and Americans.

No one was injured by the Korean sergeant's shot.

Weather

Tokyo Area Forecast

Saturday Night: Fair; Low Near 20
Sunday: Fair; High Near 50
Friday's Temperatures: Low 29, High 45

(USAF Weather Central, Fuchu AS)

U.S. BOMBS NORTH, ENDS 37-DAY LULL

★ ★ ★ ★ ★ ★ ★ ★ ★ ★ ★ ★ ★ ★ ★

LBJ Calls On U.N. to Seek Peace

PACIFIC STARS AND STRIPES

AN AUTHORIZED PUBLICATION OF
THE ARMED FORCES FAR EAST
昭和三十四年一月二十二日国鉄東局特別取扱新聞第175号

10¢ DAILY
15¢ WITH SUPPLEMENTS

Vol. 22, No. 32   FIVE-STAR EDITION   Wednesday, Feb. 2, 1966

WASHINGTON (UPI) — President Johnson called Monday for an immediate meeting of the United Nations Security Council in a new effort to bring the Vietnam war to the conference table.

The Chief Executive made the request during a brief, televised report on his deci-

Related stories and text of President's statement, Page 3.

sion to resume U.S. bombing raids on communist north Vietnam.

In New York, the Security Council was summoned to meet on Vietnam at 10:30 a.m. Tuesday (12:30 a.m. Wednesday Japan Time) in response to the President's request.

Johnson said resumption of the raids, which had been suspended since Christmas Eve, was necessary because of continued communist aggression.

He said the United States and others working for peace had met

(Continued on Back Page, Col. 1)

Rooney's Wife, Actor Found Shot

HOLLYWOOD (AP) — Mickey Rooney's estranged fifth wife and an actor, Milos Milocevic, were found dead Monday. Police said it appeared to be a murder-suicide.

The scene was Rooney's home in West Los Angeles.

Last Friday Rooney filed a document in Superior Court alleging that his wife, Barbara, was living in the home with Milocevic.

He asked the court for custody of his four children and to order the actor from the premises.

The Rooneys were married Dec. 1, 1958.

Milocevic was a young Yugoslavian actor who had been in this country about a year.

Police said Milocevic apparently shot Mrs. Rooney, then himself.

A chrome-plated revolver was found on the bathroom floor with the bodies, police said. Both bodies were clothed.

Officers said Mrs. Rooney, 29, was shot in the lower jaw. Milocevic, 25, was shot in the temple

(Continued on Back Page, Col. 3)

Weather

Tokyo Area Forecast
Tuesday Night: Cloudy; Low Near 30
Wednesday: Cloudy: High Near 50
Monday's Temperatures: Low 32, High 50
(USAF Weather Central, Fuchu AS)

Jelly Bean Bandit Hits

PUEBLO, Colo. (UPI) — The jelly bean bandit of Parkview Episcopal Hospital is loose again.

Police said the hospital's only jelly bean machines was taken from the ground floor to the sixth floor, where it was broken open and robbed of an undetermined number of pennies.

Hospital superintendent Frank Creshin said because the machine has been tapped several times before, he's thinking about replacing the jelly beans with jawbreakers.

Snow, Gales Whip East for 2d Day

Compiled From AP and UPI

A wild winter storm thrashed the eastern U.S. for the second straight day Monday. Gales lashed coastal communities and the south froze under the deepest snows of the century.

A new storm centered in Colorado moved eastward.

Heavy snow fell through the night in New England and blizzard conditions were forecast for much of New York State.

Nine inches of snow fell at Buffalo, N.Y., and four in northeastern Ohio. Greenville and Rumford, Me., reported snowfalls of 46 inches.

The worst snowstorms were in Delaware, Maryland, the District

Story in pictures, Pages 12-13.

of Columbia and Virginia, where snowdrifts piled up to 15 feet deep.

The number of storm-connected deaths since Thursday climbed to at least 84, 50 of them in the south, including 13 who froze to death or died from exposure.

Chattanooga, Tenn., equalled its all-time low when the mercury plunged to 10 degrees below zero. Bristol, Tenn., had 15 below.

Muscle Shoals, Ala., had 5 below and temperatures plunged below freezing over much of Florida. Farmers faced major losses of fruit and vegetable crops. Heavy damage was reported to tomatoes, corn and sugar cane.

Florida Citrus Mutual in Lakeland estimated that 15 million boxes of oranges and 15 million boxes of grapefruit would have to be picked immediately for processing because of frost damage.

Strong winds added to the problem in the northeast. Winds of 30 to 50 m.p.h. lashed most of the area and gusts were a problem as far south as the Virginias.

The western storm dropped two inches of snow in Colorado and in parts of Arizona. The

(Continued on Page 5, Col. 2)

Peronists Win In a Landslide

BUENOS AIRES (UPI) — Peronists won a smashing victory Sunday in local elections in Jujuy Province, nearly complete official returns showed Monday.

The Peronists won the gubernatorial and vice-gubernatorial posts as well as 17 seats in the provincial legislature.

Their total vote — some five Peronist factions were involved — exceeded 42,000 votes compared with 13,717 votes for the government's Peoples Radical Party. The government party, runnerup in the election, won only 6 legislative seats.

By WALLACE BEENE
S&S Vietnam Bureau Chief

SAIGON — U.S. Air Force and Navy planes blasted targets in north Vietnam Monday, ending the 37-day halt in air strikes that began Christmas Eve.

The announcement came at 3 p.m. when a special press briefing was called to release a one paragraph statement:

"The prime minister of

Editorial, Page 8.

Vietnam and the American ambassador to Vietnam announce that U.S. aircraft today attacked targets in designated areas in north Vietnam."

Heavy antiaircraft fire was reported and one plane was lost as reports came in on the first four targets hit.

While only four strikes were listed in the initial report, an Air Force spokesman said other attacks were under way Monday. Reports of the strikes, which be-

(Continued on Back Page, Col. 4)

President Johnson strides along a White House corridor, past a bust of Abraham Lincoln, on his way to a studio from which he addressed the nation on the resumption of the bombing of north Vietnam.
(AP Radiophoto)

FIVE STAR EDITION

PACIFIC
STARS AND STRIPES

10c DAILY
15c WITH SUPPLEMENTS

昭和三十四年一月二十二日国鉄東局特別扱承認新聞紙第175号（日刊）

（昭和34年4月21日第3種郵便物認可）

Vol. 22, No. 37   AN AUTHORIZED PUBLICATION OF THE U.S. ARMED FORCES IN THE FAR EAST   Monday, Feb. 7, 1966

FRESH TROOPS POUR IN

Allies in Largest Push to Date

By JO3 GARY M. COOPER
S&S Staff Correspondent

SAIGON — The bloody fighting north of Bong Son has developed into the largest military operation of the Vietnam war as thousands of fresh troops poured into the battlefield.

Operation White Wing—previously called Masher—55 miles north of Qui Nhon in the Bong Son area, "has been reinforced by other elements of the 1st Cav. and is now a multi-brigade operation," a military spokesman said Saturday.

The operation, which involves Vietnamese army units and the Korean Tiger troops, was described as a "continually expanding three-country operation."

With the increase to multi-brigade size, Maj. Gen. Harry W.O. Kinnard, leader of the 1st Air Cav., has assumed command.

When questioned about operation Double Eagle, the marine amphibious landing 20 miles to the north of White Wing, the spokesman explained that there has been no pincer-type movement but that the two units are coordinating their actions. He added the marines are moving toward the 1st Cav. troops as the operation continues.

White Wing had little contact Friday, as the 1st Cav. continued to search for the Viet Cong. They have killed 518 Viet Cong, captured 120 and detained 582 suspects since the operation began Jan. 25.

Nine minor contacts were reported in Double Eagle, with 25 enemy killed by air, ground and artillery fire. Enemy casualties
(Continued on Back Page, Col. 4)

President Johnson and Katherine Westmoreland, 17-year-old daughter of General William C. Westmoreland, commander of U.S. Forces in Vietnam, wave goodby as they board a helicopter at the White House for Andrews AFB, Md., where they took the President's jet for Hawaii. Katherine went along to visit her parents, who are in Honolulu.
(UPI Radiophoto)

Warships Collide Off Viet

By WALLACE BEENE
S&S Vietnam Bureau Chief

SAIGON — The guided missile destroyer Waddell and the destroyer Brinkley Bass collided in the South China Sea a few minutes before midnight Friday.

Both ships were heavily damaged but only one man was injured. A crewman on the Bass received a shoulder injury.

(Three sailors were lost, however, AP reported, when a helicopter from the carrier Ranger crashed in the sea as they were returning from repair work on the two destroyers.

(The Navy said the three, from the fleet oiler USS Navasota, are missing.

(A second helicopter, also from the Ranger, was forced down at sea by mechanical problems but all its passengers and crew were rescued. Among the passengers were five from the first crash.)

The Bass reported damage to her bow. The right side of the Waddell was hit.

The collision occurred at 11:45 p.m. but no details were released.

Several Seventh Fleet units are standing by to aid to the damaged ships, if necessary.

The 4,500-ton Waddell is com-
(Continued on Back Page, Col. 5)

LBJ Speeding to Hawaii for Viet Talks

EN ROUTE TO HONOLULU (UPI) — President Johnson sped toward Hawaii Saturday with his chief military and diplomatic advisers for a historic meeting with leaders of the Republic of Vietnam and the U.S. high command in Southeast Asia.

The Chief Executive's five-day trip began at midday in Washington when he boarded a jet transport for a nonstop flight to Honolulu, where he will meet Premier Nguyen Cao Ky of South Vietnam and General William C. Westmoreland, commander of U.S. Forces in Vietnam.

Flying with Johnson were Secretary of State Dean Rusk, Defense Secretary Robert S. McNamara, General Earle G. Wheeler, chairman of the Joint Chiefs of Staff, and Westmoreland's daughter Katherine.

Another large American delegation, including Agriculture Secretary Orville L. Freeman and Welfare Secretary John W. Gardner, will join Johnson Sunday.

(News Secretary Bill Moyers said Johnson had learned that Katherine was a senior at the National Cathedral School for Girls in Washington and that Mrs. Johnson's news secretary, Elizabeth Carpenter, called the youngster and invited her to make the trip, AP reported.

(Moyers commented:

("She seemed to be very happy about it.")

Premier Ky, a 35-year-old air vice marshal, was flying to Hawaii with his chief of state, Nguyen Van Thieu, and Henry Cabot Lodge, U.S. ambassador to Saigon.

Their talks with Johnson and his advisers were expected to begin shortly after they arrived in Honolulu Sunday. Westmoreland was in Hawaii ahead of Johnson's arrival.

Talks dealing extensively with health, education and agriculture projects in South Vietnam as well as the military situation, were expected to last through Tuesday. Johnson was due back in Washington some time Wednesday.

Selection of Hawaii as the site of the meetings was to cut down on distance for the principals
(Continued on Back Page, Col. 1)

Luna-9's Signals Hint Moon Blast-Off Try

JODRELL BANK, England (UPI) — New, mysterious signals from the Russian Luna-9 moon station following completion of its announced "set program" Saturday night caused British scientists to speculate the Russians might be planning its blast-off from the moon.

"It is possible, perhaps, that they are going to lift it off for some purpose such as orbiting around the moon," Prof. Sir Bernard Lovell, director of the Jodrell Bank radio telescopic observatory, told reporters.

Lovell voiced his speculation
(Continued on Back Page, Col. 1)

Related stories, picture Page 3.

Safe's Safe All Around

PHILADELPHIA (AP) — Two men bent on robbery battered and hacked and pounded away at a 1,500-pound safe in the Debbie Sales Co. store early Saturday, but couldn't open it before police arrived.

The owner, Maurice Cramer, said he was disappointed.

He told police he'd been trying to get the safe open ever since he took over the store, safe and all, two years ago. He said he had always wondered what was inside. Locksmiths, he said, had wanted $200 to open it and change the combination.

Weather

Tokyo Area Forecast

Sunday Night: Fair; Low Near 20
Monday: Fair; High Mid 50s
Saturday's Temperatures: Low 39.
High 47
(USAF Weather Central, Fuchu AS)

U.S. HIKING VIET TROOPS BY 20,000

PACIFIC
STAR AND STRIPES

AN AUTHORIZED PUBLICATION OF
THE ARMED FORCES FAR EAST

10¢ DAILY
15¢ WITH SUPPLEMENTS

Vol. 22, No. 62   FIVE-STAR EDITION   Friday, March 4, 1966

WASHINGTON (AP)—Defense Secretary Robert S. McNamara said Wednesday he has authorized an increase in U.S. forces in the Republic of Vietnam to 235,000 men. He said this strength could be boosted to over 350,000 without calling reservists to active duty.

McNamara told a news conference another 20,000 troops have been ordered to Vietnam, on top of the 215,000 now there.

This was the first public disclosure that U.S. armed strength in Vietnam had reached 215,000.

McNamara also said the United States has the capability to send 21 more battalions to Vietnam within the next 90 days, if such action should be required.

The defense secretary said, however, that based on his present assessment, such action is not likely.

McNamara made the disclosures in connection with a report on U.S. readiness in which he said that despite stationing about 300,000 U.S. fighting men in Vietnam and elsewhere in Southeast Asia "we are fully capable of meeting our commitments elsewhere in the world."

(Continued on Back Page, Col. 5)

N-Bombs 'Burst,' U.S. Says

WASHINGTON (AP) — Two nuclear bombs were blown apart by their conventional explosive charges when a U.S. B-52 bomber crashed near Palomares, Spain, Defense Department officials said Wednesday.

But there was no nuclear explosion, a spokesman said.

The State Department also acknowledged that a third bomb is missing and that the search is continuing.

The Defense Department officials made their report after the State Department said that some plutonium and uranium—elements of a nuclear bomb—were scattered over the ground around the crash scene.

The State Department's announcement was the first acknowledgment that some nuclear material was scattered in the crash 44 days ago.

A Pentagon official said four nuclear bombs were aboard the craft.

The State Department said there has been "no evidence of a health hazard" as a result of the accident.

Nevertheless, he said, the Atomic Energy Commission is preparing to remove hundreds of

(Continued on Back Page, Col. 2)

Baby Born On the Street

TRENTON, Mich. (AP) — A baby was born in the middle of this Detroit suburb's main street Wednesday.

Mrs. James E. Sullivan, 18, was crossing the street when she called for help. The police station is directly opposite. Officers, waving down traffic, rushed to Mrs. Sullivan's aid.

The baby was a 6-pound 6-ounce boy. A crowd of spectators cheered.

Defense Secretary Robert McNamara (left) tells reporters in Washington that U.S. forces in Vietnam will be increased to 235,000 men. With him is Cyrus Vance, under secretary of defense.
(AP Radiophoto)

Nkrumah Flies Into Guinea; Report He's Asked Red Help

Compiled From AP and UPI

Kwame Nkrumah, ousted president of Ghana, flew to Guinea Wednesday and announced he is on his way back to Ghana. He was reported planning to ask the Soviet Union and communist China to help return him to power.

Meanwhile, more than 200 Russian aid specialists left Ghana Tuesday and Wednesday aboard Ghana Airways' Russian-built Ilyushin transports and by commercial flights.

A chartered French UTA DC-8 jet arrived Wednesday to transport the first contingent of departing Chinese to Karachi. Another UTA plane was expected to fly out Thursday. Both aircraft were booked for 125 passengers.

Diplomatic sources in Ghana do not expect a break in relations between Accra and Moscow and Peking. But one Ghanaian Foreign Ministry source said such action was imminent.

Nkrumah told a crowd in Conakry, capital of Guinea, "I came here so as to tell the world that I will very soon be back in Accra."

Nkrumah's remarks were carried by the Conakry Radio and heard in Dakar, Senegal. Nkrumah arrived by plane earlier in the day at Conakry airport and was greeted by Guinean President Sekou Toure with honors befitting a chief of state.

Toure escorted Nkrumah to the Conakry stadium in an open car through cheering crowds, the radio said.

Nkrumah was in Peking when the coup occurred and went from there to Moscow.

He had been accompanied to Red China by his foreign minister.

(Continued on Back Page, Col. 3)

Weather

Tokyo Area Forecast

Thursday night: Cloudy; Low Mid 50s
Friday: Cloudy; High Mid 60s
Wednesday's Temperatures: Low 42, High 66
(USAF Weather Central, Fuchu AS)

VC Caught Returning For Dead

By JOE GARY COOPER
S&S Staff Correspondent

SAIGON—Viet Cong, returning to the scene of a recent battle to pick up their dead, joined the ranks of their slain comrades, it was revealed Wednesday.

Intelligence sources felt the Viet Cong had left a major portion of their dead behind when they clashed with Vietnamese government troops about 55 miles east-northeast of Saigon Feb. 28.

Consequently, a watch was posted over the area to check for returning VC.

Tuesday night, a Vietnamese spotter over the area saw numerous small lights and radioed for flare ships and air strikes.

The lights reportedly were flashlights held by guerrillas returning to carry off their dead comrades.

(Continued on Back Page, Col. 1)

BULLETIN

SAIGON (AP)—A Vietnamese force in a mop-up operation in An Xuyen Province at the tip of the Mekong Delta killed 17 Viet Cong, a government military spokesman said Thursday. The operation began Wednesday morning in the Quan Long area about 155 miles southwest of Saigon and continued until about dusk.

Clay-Terrell Fight Moved to Montreal P. 18

PACIFIC STARS AND STRIPES

AN AUTHORIZED PUBLICATION OF THE ARMED FORCES IN THE FAR EAST

FIVE-STAR EDITION

昭和三十四年一月二十二日国鉄東局特別扱承認新聞紙第175号（日刊）
（昭和34年4月21日第3種郵便物認可）

10¢ DAILY
15¢ WITH
SUPPLEMENTS

Vol. 22, No. 69   Friday, March 11, 1966

2 Days Without A Smoke

By SUSAN DIBBLE
S&S Staff Writer
Second of a Series

Last night we saw a movie. It was about a hard-smoking newspaperman who had lung cancer. It was in Technicolor, and when they cut him up, the blood looked red.

Right then I got nervous and wanted a cigaret. It was only the second day of the five-day plan —and I was weakening.

But I just kept breathing deeply, as we had been advised to do when temptation strikes, and repeating, "I choose not to smoke." It was a good start. And I hope the 150 others watching the show were able to do the same.

SUSAN

After the movie, Paul Eldridge, associate director of the Five-Day-Plan, who has traveled from Singapore to present the program here, told us that in case we had any doubts about the matter, smoking was indeed a form of drug addiction and that nicotine was indeed a very strong drug.

But in addition, he said, it was a neuromuscular habit, the same kind of thing that makes you open

(Continued on Back Page, Col. 4)

Paris Snubs Any Reform Of NATO

PARIS (AP) — France said Wednesday that reform of the North Atlantic Treaty Organization is impossible and that President Charles de Gaulle's government is going ahead with plans to get out.

But the government expressed a willingness to talk over other mutual defense arrangements with NATO Allies.

A spokesman said after the weekly cabinet meeting that France intends to take whatever measures it deems necessary concerning foreign military bases on French soil. He added that France is willing to discuss the consequences of such a move.

The statement outlining the French position was read to newsmen by Yvon Bourges, secretary of state for information.

The announcement seemed to represent a further stiffening of the French attitude. For several years, De Gaulle has been insisting that NATO must be revised.

Sources said that France does not intend to take advantage of the clause permitting denunciation of the NATO Treaty on April 4, 1969. De Gaulle has always distinguished between the Atlantic

(Continued on Back Page, Col. 2)

BULLETIN

GOTEMBA, Japan (AP)—The flight recorder aboard a British Overseas Airways Corp. jetliner that crashed into Mount Fuji has been found, but police said Wednesday that it was too badly damaged to be of use.

Lone Survivor Radios

REDS OVERRUN 312-MAN CAMP

By SSGT. JACK BAIRD
S&S Staff Correspondent

DA NANG, Vietnam—The radio operator at the As Hau Special Forces camp reported early Thursday that he was the "lone survivor"—shortly before the camp was apparently overrun by the Viet Cong.

The message was the last received from the camp which was defended by 300 Montagnard soldiers and 12 U.S. Army Special Forces advisers, according to AP.

It followed earlier messages which reported the camp, 30 miles southwest of Hue and a scant 1½ miles from the Laotian border, was under full attack. The messages told of hand-to-hand fighting along the barbed wire covered walls of the fortress-like camp and a last ditch stand in the camp's communications bunker.

Up until 3 a.m. Thursday the defenders had reported they were in good shape even though they were under small arms and mortar fire.

At 3:25 a.m. the radio operator reported the camp was under full attack.

A half hour later he reported the camp walls had been breached and the camp split in half by the attackers.

The message from the radio operator that he was the "lone survivor" at the camp came at 4:25 a.m. and was the last radio message.

A flare-drop plane later reported the camp appeared to have been overrun but there were signs

(Continued on Back Page, Col. 1)

Has Anyone Seen Zaza?

CHICAGO (UPI) — Zaza, a white toy poodle, was supposed to make a surprise visit to her owner Sunday, but apparently was stolen about 50 miles from her destination.

Mrs. Frank Pontillo said she arrived from Naha, Okinawa, a week ago to visit her mother-in-law, Mrs. Constance Pontillo, in Kenosha, Wis.

Her husband, a businessman on Okinawa, shipped Zaza by air as a surprise. Sunday night she received word from Northwest Orient Airlines that the dog was missing.

Railroad workers begin repairs on tracks wrecked Wednesday when a boxcar carrying ammunition blew up near Corning, Ark. The blast left a crater 50 feet long and 15 feet deep.
UPI Radiophoto

Ammo Boxcar Blows Up in Arkansas

CORNING, Ark. (AP)—A railroad car loaded with 175mm artillery shells mysteriously exploded near here Wednesday with a force felt in three states.

The predawn blast gouged a crater 50 feet long and 15 feet deep in a railroad siding 3 miles north of this town of 2,565.

The explosion, felt in Arkansas, Missouri and Tennessee, ruptured a natural gas line and forced the evacuation of several hundred Corning residents before the gas was shut off.

One house was demolished by the explosion and fire. Walls of two others were caved in. Only one person was injured, not seriously.

John Hutchinson, secretary of the Corning Volunteer Fire Department, said the fear of more explosions kept firemen from battling the fire in the wreckage.

The gas leak, which existed for about two hours, could not be repaired because it, too, was near the fire, Hutchinson said.

Deputy Sheriff Jess Watson said

the artillery shells exploded as the car stood on the siding to which it had been pulled to clear the main line for another train.

The car was one of 80 in a Missouri Pacific Lines freight hauling ammunition to the Red River Arsenal at Texarkana on

(Continued on Back Page, Col. 2)

TO PROTECT SHIPPING

Marines in 1st Delta Assault

PACIFIC
STARS AND STRIPES
AN AUTHORIZED PUBLICATION OF
THE ARMED FORCES FAR EAST

10¢ DAILY
15¢ WITH SUPPLEMENTS

Vol. 22, No. 86   FIVE-STAR EDITION   Monday, March 28, 1966

By JOHN K. BAKER
S&S Vietnam Bureau Chief

LONG THANH PENINSULA, Vietnam—U.S. marines landed only 30 miles southeast of Saigon Saturday to open a drive aimed at halting Viet Cong sabotage along the major river channel between the South China Sea and the capital.

It was the farthest south U.S. troops have operated in any numbers since the beginning of the Vietnam war.

Some 1,200 Leathernecks poured ashore from Seventh Fleet ships by landing boat and helicopter shortly after daybreak and immediately began sweeping this rugged stretch of delta land, which guards the east side of the entrance to the Long Tau River.

The river is the only waterway into Saigon big enough to handle most of the huge military and commercial deep-draft cargo ships. One source estimated that 60 per cent of all cargo to Vietnam travels up the Long Tao.

The Viet Cong recently have stepped up harassment along the channel including at least five attempts since late last year to sink ships and block the vital passageway.

The over-all objective of the operation—dubbed Jack Stay—is to clear the Reds from the area and secure the river against future attacks.

The immediate goal of the ma-
(Continued on Back Page, Col. 1)

TWO COLUMNS OF MARINES WADE THROUGH SHALLOW WATER TOWARD BEACH AT LONG THANH PENINSULA, VIETNAM.   AP Radiophoto

Anti-Viet Marchers Heckled

By United Press International

Tens of thousands of demonstrators protesting America's role in the Vietnam conflict marched through city streets from New England to California Saturday, dodging rotten eggs, beer cans and fists.

Massed police in the large cities prevented protestors and hecklers from clashing during the second of the "international days of protest."

Eggs were hurled by hecklers in New York, Boston and Oklahoma City. Spectators in Boston tossed beer cans at the marchers.

Three persons were arrested by police breaking up fist fights between protestors and hecklers in Detroit's Kennedy Square when 30 members of "Break Through," a conservative group, attacked marchers.

Seven persons were arrested in
(Continued on Back Page, Col. 4)

Crippled Vet Must Return $78

MIAMI (AP)—Charles Cole, 74-year-old disabled war veteran, must return $78.75 his nation paid him by mistake five years ago.

Cole, once Calvin Coolidge's chauffeur, has 30 days to get started.

He can repay in a lump sum or use the Veterans Administration's installment plan.

"We are sorry for the necessity of taking this action," said the VA letter. "It was an erroneous payment."

"I don't have the money to pay it back," Cole said. "I draw $100 a month pension, my rent is $75.
(Continued on Back Page, Col. 1)

BULLETIN
Race details, Page 18

SEBRING, Fla. (AP) — A race car smashed through a fence during the Sebring 12-hour sports car race Saturday, killing three persons. First reports indicated the car was a Porsche.

Astronauts Tell How 'Thrill' Became Brush With Death

HOUSTON, Tex. (UPI) — Astronauts Neil Armstrong and David Scott said Saturday they began their emergency dash home from space when they feared an out-of-control jet might cause their Gemini-8 ship and an Agena satellite to break apart in orbit.

The pilots, facing newsmen for the first time since their March 16 voyage, told a fascinating story of a flight that ranged from the "greatest thrill" of a rocket blastoff to the problem seven hours later that forced them to one "drastic step" after another.

Eventually, they came home safely from a close brush with death 185 miles deep in space—but after completing only one-seventh of an intended 71-hour journey.

Gemini-8 had accomplished an historic linkup with the Agena when a short circuit evidently locked the No. 8 thruster wide open and threw the ship into a violent bucking, rolling motion.

First, they said, they thought the trouble was in the 26-foot-long Agena locked to the nose of Gemini-8. They tried various controls, attempting to pinpoint the difficulty.

Still the rolling continued. "When it became obvious that this was not effective," said Armstrong, "we began to consider that some sort of spacecraft system was involved."

Furiously working at the controls, the Astronauts alternately kept the ship steady and then felt it slipping again.

"We began to think we had the
(Continued on Back Page, Col. 5)

Marine Dies to Save a Buddy

DA NANG, Vietnam (AP)—A young U.S. marine smothered an enemy hand grenade with his body to save the life of a foxhole mate he scarcely knew.

Because James R. Reilly, 19, sacrificed his life, Edward E. Burgess, 20, survived a Viet Cong attack March 17.

The two were manning a machine-gun position southwest of Da Nang.

Burgess, interviewed near the same foxhole where he almost died, described the incident:

"I came on watch to relieve Reilly and he said he couldn't sleep and would stay around and talk for awhile. I don't remember what we talked about. We just talked. The VC had probed a couple of times earlier and we talked low.

"We were sitting on the upper half of the hole—I guess you could call it a split level hole," Burgess grinned slightly.

"Then Reilly yelled 'My God

Burgess get down in the hole. It's a grenade.'

"I fell down expecting him to follow. But he dove toward the grenade and he must have landed right on it. It seemed like it took a long time to go off and I thought he must be joking. Then it exploded.

"He saved my life."

Company Commander Capt. R. L. Woodward said Reilly would be recommended "for one of the highest combat decorations possible to get."

CAV. UNIT MAULED; 5 COPTERS DOWNED

PACIFIC
STARS AND STRIPES

AN AUTHORIZED PUBLICATION OF
THE ARMED FORCES FAR EAST

10¢ DAILY
15¢ WITH SUPPLEMENTS

Vol. 22, No. 90   **FIVE-STAR EDITION**   Friday, April 1, 1966

SAIGON (UPI)—A 1st Air Cav. Div. reconnaissance unit dropped in the midst of a north Vietnamese regiment Wednesday and fought for their lives along the base of Chu Pong mountain, southwest of Pleiku.

The ground fire was so intense that five helicopters, including one of the big Chinooks, were shot down. Several other choppers were badly shot up, but managed to limp back to base.

The fight erupted less than one mile from the Cambodian border just to the south of the mountain, about 210 miles northeast of Saigon.

A second unit was sent in to help the first, but it was pinned down by such heavy fire that it could not be withdrawn. Night closed in and the unit was surrounded by north Vietnamese.

Air Force fighter-bombers hammered the communist troops with rockets, napalm and bombs. Transport planes dropped flares to illuminate the perimeter of the surrounded unit.

The Americans shortly after dusk called for more ammunition and it was sent.

The unit held out through the night. Early Thursday Chinook helicopters moved an artillery company into place, and the 105mm guns opened up to give

(Continued on Back Page, Col. 1)

Wilson Favored 25 to 1

LONDON (UPI)—Betting odds on a Laborite victory jumped another five points to 25-1 Wednesday just 24 hours before Britons vote in national parliamentary elections.

Meanwhile, Conservative Party challenger Edward Heath at his final news conference lambasted Prime Minister Harold Wilson and his Laborite government for letting "the price dam burst" and opening the way for another upward surge in living costs.

The government's Iron and Steel Board Tuesday night approved a 4 per cent boost in maximum prices of all steel products effective April 1—the day after the election.

Experts estimated this would add another 36 million pounds ($100,800,000) to the price of a huge range of manufactured goods.

"The price dam has now burst." Heath charged.

"Now the truth is out." he said. "Everyone can see just what we have been saying is right—that the cost of living is going to go up again."

Heath spoke to newsmen at Conservative Party headquarters.

Lord Byars, chairman of the third-running Liberal Party, asserted that the Conservatives in the new Parliament "will be even more impotent" against Wilson than in the last one.

As zero hour approached, Heath

(Continued on Back Page, Col. 4)

Soldiers of the 1st Air Cav. Div. blaze away at communist positions during fierce battle that developed when a cavalry reconnaissance unit dropped into the midst of a north Vietnamese regiment at Chu Pong Mountain Wednesday.
(UPI Radiophoto)

Chutist Dragged 7 Minutes

FORT CAMPBELL, Ky. (AP)—After flying like a kite behind a plane traveling 135 m.p.h., a young paratrooper freed himself and landed safely.

"It was like getting a second chance," said PFC Michael A. McDonald, 17, of Missoula, Mont.

McDonald, a member of the 101st Airborne Div. here, landed in a pine tree after freeing himself from tangled parachute lines during a training exercise Tuesday. He was apparently unhurt, the Army said.

The static line connecting his parachute to a C-119 transport failed to disconnect during the practice assault, the Army said, and McDonald was dragged through the air for about seven minutes.

Crewmen on the plane were unable to haul in McDonald. He finally cleared his arms, the static line snapped and his reserve parachute opened as he fell free.

Yes, Sgt. Keehn, There Is a Santa Claus

EL TORO MCAS, Cal. (UPI)—The newspaper advertisement read simply enough:

"For sale: 1961 Simca, $50. Husband in Vietnam. Real good tires. Stupid car won't run . . ."

The results were amazing.

So surprised was the advertiser, Mrs. Chris-Celia Keehn, of nearby Huntington Beach, wife of Marine Sgt. Ronald Keehn, currently in Vietnam, that she wrote the following letter to Maj. Gen. Frank G. Tharin, commander of this base:

"Dear Gen. Tharin: The enclosed ad was in our newspaper over a month ago and I am still receiving many calls—but not to buy my car. People from all over Orange County have called offering to fix my car and pay for all the necessary parts.

"That was only the beginning. Many people have called just to offer their assistance and car for whenever I need them.

"They have told me that nothing is too small a task in helping me. And do you know why, sir? Because they believe in the job my husband is doing and this is their way of thanking all those who have suffered and given their most precious possession—their life.

"With Americans like that backing up our servicemen, it makes me feel good inside and full of pride for our countrymen."

Weather

Tokyo Area Forecast
Thursday night: Cloudy with rain; Low Mid 40s.
Friday: Cloudy with rain; High Near 50
Wednesday's Temperatures: Low 44, High 56
(USAF Weather Central, Fuchu AS)

Storm Splits Tanker, 11 Stranded

HONOLULU (UPI) — Planes and ships fought a furious Pacific storm Tuesday in an effort to rescue 11 crewmen believed stranded on the stern of an American tanker which broke apart 600 miles northwest of Midway Island.

A Navy seaplane arrived on the scene in the afternoon. It reported a "tremendous storm" in the area and was unable to communicate with the ship, Comet Commander, which split apart Monday night.

The plane said huge swells prevented a landing.

A Japanese fishing vessel rescued 31 of 42 men aboard the Liberian-registered, American-owned ship but heavy seas and fierce winds prevented contact with the other crewmen.

(Most of the crewmen were Chinese. Those rescued were reported in good condition, AP reported.)

The Coast Guard in Honolulu, 1,700 miles away, also dispatched a plane to the ship.

A British merchant ship, the Marabank, and a Japanese fishing vessel, the Kagasami Maru, changed courses in mid-ocean and were expected to arrive by daybreak.

(The Comet Commander was en route from the United States to Yokohama, Japan, with a cargo of oil, AP reported.)

Lloyd's Registry in London listed the Comet Commander as a 10,000-ton tanker.

The Japanese fishing vessel on the scene, Yayoi Maru, indicated that the fore section of the ship had sunk.

First reports of the incident came from the maritime safety agency in Kagoshima, Japan, which relayed the information to the Navy in Honolulu.

PACIFIC STARS AND STRIPES

AN AUTHORIZED PUBLICATION OF THE
U.S. ARMED FORCES IN THE FAR EAST

10¢ DAILY
15¢ WITH SUPPLEMENTS

Vol. 22, No. 96   FIVE-STAR EDITION

昭和三十四年一月二十二日国鉄東局特別扱承認新聞紙第175号（日刊）
（昭和34年4月21日第3種郵便物認可）

Thursday, April 7, 1966

Da Nang Clash Averted; U.S. Pulls Out Advisers

WASHINGTON (AP) — American advisers have been pulled out of opposing Republic of Vietnamese forces at Da Nang to avoid U.S. involvement in the internal political conflict, the State Department said Tuesday.

Press Officer Marshall Wright also said Saigon leaders are meeting now on means to move faster toward a constitutional government.

The sum-up of the turbulent political scene in South Vietnam given to newsmen here reflected a belief by many U.S. officials that a dangerous phase of the crisis has passed, though much remains to be threshed out.

The American advisers pulled out of opposing Vietnamese units had been assigned to I Corps units at Hue and Da Nang and to the three battalions flown to **(Continued on Back Page, Col. 5)**

A Vietnamese soldier patrols outside the Da Nang City Hall, headquarters of Mayor Nguyen Van Man. Prime Minister Nguyen Cao Ky vowed Sunday to have Man executed. (AP Radiophoto)

DA NANG, Vietnam (AP) — Republic of Vietnam Prime Minister Nguyen Cao Ky and opposition elements in this northernmost I Corps area appeared Tuesday night to have worked out a compromise to avert possible bloodshed in a clash within the South Vietnamese army.

Ky flew here early Tuesday and held day-long talks with Maj. Gen. Nguyen Van Chuan, newly named I Corps commander.

After the talks were over and Ky had taken off to return to Saigon, Chuan told newsmen the prime minister had agreed that about 4,000 Vietnamese Marines who landed overnight at Da Nang air base would remain on base and would not seek to enter the city of Da Nang.

He said elements of the 11th Ranger Bn. that he had ordered to Da Nang were sent back to their station at Hoi An, south of Da Nang.

Chuan added that he had pledged to control the antigovernment demonstrations that have swept Da Nang and would try to halt expressions of anti-Americanism here.

Chuan said the Vietnamese Marines flown here on orders of the Saigon government would remain at the air base "to provide security." He said he and Ky had agreed they would not be moved into Da Nang.

Last Sunday Ky charged that Da Nang was in control of communist elements and said the government would launch military operations to bring this to an end.

Chuan told newsmen there was a misunderstanding over the statement Ky made Sunday. He said the prime minister meant that Da Nang was more heavily infiltrated by the Viet Cong than any other area, but did not mean **(Continued on Back Page, Col. 3)**

River on Rampage In Minn., Canada

GRAND FORKS, N.D. (AP) — Rampaging flood waters in the agriculturally rich Red River Valley of Minnesota and North Dakota eased Tuesday at critical points in the United States as Canadians braced for the surge of the rapid spring runoff.

Emphasis in the flood watch shifted to southern Manitoba Province in Canada, where the blasting of a dike on the international border sent flood water spreading over thousands of acres of Canadian farmland.

Already under water on the American side of the border are hundreds of square miles of lush farmland from Grand Forks to the Canadian border 75 miles to the north.

A dispute over the dynamiting of the dam near Emerson, Man., reached the provincial legislature. Manitoba Agriculture Minister George Hutton promised an investigation.

The Canadians said an American crew apparently blasted the Canadian dike near Emerson sometime Monday, sending waters backed up in North Dakota fields spilling into Manitoba farmland.

Hutton said he didn't think the blasting did any more than to speed the overflow into Canada, but said many Canadian farmers were not yet prepared for the influx of water and still had grain and livestock unprotected.

The Red River Valley is a big growing area for sugar beets, wheat and potatoes.

No damage estimates have been offered by official agencies **(Continued on Back Page, Col. 1)**

NO SHOW AT LATIN QUARTER

Chorus Girl Strike Shakes Up Broadway

NEW YORK (AP) — A Broadway chorus line took to the sidewalks Tuesday for a traffic-stopping picket line in a dispute over wages, hours and working conditions.

The shapely showgirls, trooped around the block — when they could fight their way through the crowd.

The girls walked out before Monday night's performance at the Latin Quarter and showed up Tuesday for picket duty.

The chorines were joined by other members of the floor show. They voted unanimously to strike the club when it refused to sign a contract negotiated last November, said Dick Jones, national administrative secretary of the American Guild of Variety Artists.

The performers did not appear Monday night and patrons received a 50 per cent reduction in their dinner checks because of no shows. The club closed at 10 p.m., several hours earlier than usual.

A club spokesman said, "We had a very good house, and the patrons took it very nicely."

Jones said the Latin Quarter made the girls work seven days a week, did not contribute to their welfare fund, and provided inadequate toilet facilities. He said the girls were paid $122 for a basic six-day week.

A spokesman for owner Elias Loew said the dispute centered about "defining terms . . . the union and Mr. Loew just don't seem to agree on them."

VC HIT SAIGON AB, 7 KILLED, 155 HURT

PACIFIC
STARS AND STRIPES

AN AUTHORIZED PUBLICATION OF
THE ARMED FORCES FAR EAST

10¢ DAILY
15¢ WITH SUPPLEMENTS

Vol. 22, No. 103   FIVE-STAR EDITION   Thursday, April 14, 1966

SAIGON (AP)—The Viet Cong attacked Saigon's Tan Son Nhut AB with mortars early Wednesday, killing 7 Americans and wounding 155 other persons.

The American dead included six soldiers and one sailor.

Among the wounded were 20 Air Force men, 77 other U.S. servicemen, and 58 Vietnamese. It was the first mortar attack on the base, where 10,000 U.S. servicemen are stationed and which houses the residence of Prime Minister Nguyen Cao Ky. The base is about four miles from the heart of Saigon.

Five U.S. aircraft were damaged. They included F-100 fighter-bombers and one TVC121. The latter is the craft that provides television relay to Saigon. The television plane was described as badly damaged.

Two Vietnamese C-47 cargo planes also were damaged and a fuel storage installation was set ablaze.

The huge fuel tanks set ablaze **(Continued on Back Page, Col. 5)**

FIREMAN LEANS FROM WINDOW OF USAF TRUCK THAT IS POURING WATER ON BLAZING OIL TANK AT TAN SON NHUT AB.

AP Radiophoto

Air Tanker Overdue Off Viet

WASHINGTON (AP)—The Defense Department said Tuesday a Navy tanker plane is overdue after flying from the Philippine Islands toward the carrier Kitty Hawk cruising off South Vietnam.

The announcement that a Navy KA3B is overdue came several hours after the New China News Agency claimed an A3B heavy attack plane was shot down Monday (Tuesday in the Far East) by communist Chinese Air Force planes over southeast China.

The Pentagon statement did not refer to the communist Chinese claim. Nor did it acknowledge that the KA3B is lost.

Defense sources said the tanker plane was being ferried back to the carrier on which it was based. The mission of such planes normally is to refuel fighter bombers when they are mounting air strikes against communist targets.

The KA3B is a tanker version of the A3B, a turbojet-powered airplane which normally carries a three-man crew.

A Navy official said the tanker version normally carries only two **(Continued on Back Page, Col. 2)**

Giants Win N.L. Opener

Compiled From AP and UPI

Willie Mays and Len Gabrielson hit home runs Tuesday to power the San Francisco Giants to a 9-1 victory over the Chicago Cubs in their National League opener.

Rain halted the New York Mets and Cincinnati for the second straight day, while the other three N.L. games were at night.

Sandy Valdespino's single in the ninth inning drove in the winning run as the defending champion Minnesota Twins edged Kansas City 2-1.

Detroit pushed across its deciding run in the ninth as the Tigers nipped New York, 2-1. It took 14 innings for Chicago to top California, 3-2, and 13 innings for Baltimore to nip Boston, 5-4.

Details Page 18.

Weather

Tokyo Area Forecast
Wednesday Night: Mostly cloudy; Low Mid 40s
Thursday: Cloudy with rain; High Mid 50s
Tuesday's Temperatures: Low 45, High 60
(USAF Weather Central, Fuchu AB)

1st Inf. Div. Unit Hit Hard By Viet Cong Near Saigon

By JOHN K. BAKER
S&S Vietnam Bureau Chief

SAIGON—A badly outnumbered U.S. company Monday suffered heavy casualties during a bitter 3-hour battle with the Viet Cong in heavy jungle 40 miles east of Saigon, it was reported Tuesday.

The battle started when the Reds hit the company from all sides with mortar and small arms fire.

The enemy force was estimated at about a battalion—about 500 troops. About 180 U.S. infantrymen, part of the 1st Inf. Div. taking part in Operation Abilene, were involved.

The U.S. troops had been running into enemy small arms fire throughout the day as they pushed across the rugged terrain.

At 5:30 p.m. the VC opened up from all directions and pinned the outmanned and outgunned U.S. unit down. The battle raged until 8:30 when the VC pulled back. The Americans had called on artillery to help beat off the attack.

U.S. casualties in the battle were described as heavy by an American spokesman.

There was no report on Viet Cong casualties, but they were presumed to be high since the VC were forced to retreat.

A 1st Inf. engineer unit moved **(Continued on Back Page, Col. 1)**

Voiceprint Admitted as Evidence in N.Y.

WHITE PLAINS, N.Y. (UPI)—The voiceprint, which may eventually rival the fingerprint as a method of identification, was introduced Tuesday as evidence in a court trial for the first time in history.

A recording of a person's voice on paper by means of an electronic device was introduced as evidence against George Straehle of New Rochelle, N.Y., a detective accused of lying to a grand jury about his alleged warning of a candy store owner of an impending gambling raid.

The store owner, George Rispole, also is on trial.

During Tuesday's proceedings, Lawrence G. Kersta, a retired Bell Telephone Laboratories physicist who developed the voice recording technique, showed jurors prints obtained in witnessed conversations with Straehle and prints of matching words obtained from a wire-tapped telephone call allegedly made by the defendant to Rispole.

Kersta testified that sound in the alleged warning call matched sounds uttered by Straehle in known conversations. He displayed spectrographic pictures of words used for purposes of comparison, explaining that the voice of each person is unique and cannot be mistaken for someone else's voice.

The words portrayed were: I, you, know, Christ, all right and okay. The sounds were extracted from wiretap tapes provided by the state investigation commission.

The suspects have denied making the call.

Judge Robert Dempsey, in a historic decision Monday, ruled that the state could use the new form of "positive identification" despite defense counsel protests **(Continued on Back Page, Col. 1)**

Ky Planes Hit Da Nang Rebels; Police Battle Mobs in Saigon

SAIGON (AP) — Riot police Friday night beat back seven assaults by screaming, rock hurling Buddhist demonstrators demanding the ouster of the military government.

Saturday morning, thousands of Buddhist monks and nuns and their followers crowded into Saigon's main Buddhist Institute to begin a sit-down and hunger strike. There were rumors that student demonstrators joining the crowds might try to march on Premier Nguyen Cao Ky's office and the U.S. Embassy.

Friday night, the rioters ex-
(Continued on Back Page, Col. 1)

PACIFIC STARS STRIPES

AN AUTHORIZED PUBLICATION OF THE ARMED FORCES IN THE FAR EAST

FIVE-STAR EDITION

昭和三十四年一月二十二日国鉄東局特別扱承認新聞紙第175号 (日刊)
(昭和34年4月21日第3種郵便物認可)

10¢ DAILY
15¢ WITH
SUPPLEMENTS

Vol. 22, No. 141   Sunday, May 22, 1966

Compiled From AP and UPI

DA NANG, Vietnam—Premier Nguyen Cao Ky's troops battled rebel forces in the heart of Da Nang Saturday and his planes strafed, bombed and rocketed antigovernment positions on the outskirts of the city.

Automatic weapons and small arms fire erupted about 10 a.m. near the rebels' pagoda pocket in the city.

Ky's all prop-driven Skyraiders earlier swooped down on the rebels across the river from town.

During the night three mortar rounds smashed into the suburban U.S. air base. The only damage was a jeep splattered with shrapnel, a U.S. military spokesman said.
(Continued on Back Page, Col. 1)

A government soldier fires a tank-mounted machine gun toward a pagoda in Da Nang where rebel troops were firing on the government forces. Firing erupted again Saturday morning in the city.
(AP Radiophoto)

No Shift In Plans: Wheeler

By The Associated Press

The chairman of the Joint Chiefs of Staff said Thursday that the civil unrest in the Republic of Vietnam has had no effect on United States military operations in the country.

"It is too early to change any programs and plans," General Earle G. Wheeler said in a news confe·ence in Houston, Tex., following a speech to a Chamber of Commerce committee.

Wheeler said he could not forecast the length of the war in Vietnam, but that 10 years is "far too long."

He praised the efforts of the fighting men there saying they were "well trained, well disciplined and well led."

In Washington, officials said Friday that the United States is in urgent touch with government and rebel leaders in South Vietnam's intensifying civil conflict and is trying to help work out a solution.

Although the effect of the strife so far has been virtually to remove South Vietnamese forces in the Hue-Da Nang area from the war against the communists, high
(Continued on Back Page, Col. 4)

Israel to Buy U.S. Planes

Compiled From AP and UPI

JERUSALEM, Israel — The United States has agreed to sell American "tactical" military aircraft to Israel, the government announced Friday.

It was the first time the United States has sold warplanes to the largely French-equipped Israeli Air Force. The sale was apparently undertaken to meet increased Soviet assistance to Arab nations during the last decade.

The government announcement did not mention the type or number of American warplanes involved in the deal.

A Washington correspondent for the New York Times identified the planes as older models of the A-4 Skyhawk, a lightweight attack bomber that has been a mainstay of the U.S. Navy's carrier strike force in Vietnam.

In Cairo, the Egyptian newspaper Al Ahram reported in a dispatch from New York that a number of swept-wing F-111 jet bombers and 80 F-104 jet fighters were included in the sale. The
(Continued on Back Page, Col. 3)

Ex-GOP Aide Guilty In N.Y. Bribe Case

NEW YORK (AP) — Former New York State Republican Chairman L. Judson Morhouse was convicted Friday of helping arrange a bribe to aid the Playboy Club in obtaining a liquor license.

A jury in New York City found him guilty on two counts, both involving a reported $25,000 payment in 1962 to Martin Epstein, then chairman of the State Liquor Authority.

One count charged Morhouse with helping arrange a bribe. The other accused him of taking unlawful fees. He was found innocent on four other counts.

The maximum penalty on the two counts on which he was convicted is 7 years in jail and a $9,000 fine.

He helped launch the political career of Gov. Nelson Rockefeller in 1958. He resigned as party chairman in 1962, at the time a scandal was developing in the state liquor authority.

Young Girl Gets Change

CINCINNATI, Ohio (AP) — The excitement of Playland at the Cincinnati Zoo proved too much Friday for 11-year old Vickie Jackman.

Vickie threw her hand over her mouth during the excitement of a ride.

The result? She swallowed a fist full of nickels, dimes and at least one quarter.

She was taken to a hospital and reported in good condition.

2d Heart-Implant Patient Dies

HOUSTON, Tex. (AP)—Walter L. McCans, the second patient to undergo a partial artificial heart implant in Methodist Hospital here in recent weeks, died Friday.

Doctors blamed a persistent bleeding condition in the chest.

McCans, 61, died nearly three days after undergoing surgery at Methodist Hospital. The plastic pump that assisted his heart was removed 27 hours after surgery and the hospital indicated his damaged heart chamber had shown signs of repairing itself.

The first hospital bulletin Friday said the probable cause of death was pulmonary insufficiency.

A second bulletin released an hour later said a cardiovascular team had determined the cause as "hemorrhagic diathesis, which persisted and was uncontrollable."

"Mr. McCans' cardiac condition seemed to be satisfactory until time of death," the second bulletin said. "However, his hemorrhagic diathesis caused lung complications."

A diathesis is a body condition that causes an organ to malfunction.

McCans underwent surgery Tuesday and the pulmonary disturbance and bleeding condition was first reported 24 hours later. He was returned to surgery twice to have fluids removed from his lungs.

Weather

Tokyo Area Forecast

Saturday night: Cloudy rain; Low Near 60

Sunday: Cloudy rain; High Mid 50's

Friday Temperatures: Low 56. High 78

(USAF Weather Central, Fuchu AS)

S&S Staffer Flies Over N. Vietnam

By A2C BOB CUTTS
S&S Staff Correspondent

North Vietnam.

There it was below me as I sat, cramped and hot, in the Skyraider's cockpit—the first correspondent ever to fly in an air strike over that well-known yet unknown land above the 17th Parallel.

With the engine throbbing around me and the crackle of radio voices in my earphones, I was physically as detached from that shrouded land as if I were watching a movie in a theater.

But I know no American could fly over north Vietnam as an enemy and not feel affected by it in some way—even though it could have been a raid anywhere in this war.

I had casually asked the pilot, a World War II fighter veteran, if I could go on his next raid north.

Lt. Col. Dick Willsie stared at me. "Are you sure you really want to?"

"Well, if you've taken chances all these years, I guess I can take one," I said.

Now I wondered.

As we circled over north Vietnam, Willsie was tight-lipped, drawn-faced and grim, and I wondered why I was here.

But, nearing our target, I began to realize that just by my presence, by my being an American, I was here to kill or be killed. I was part

(Continued on Page 6, Col. 3)

PACIFIC STARS AND STRIPES
AN AUTHORIZED PUBLICATION OF THE ARMED FORCES IN THE FAR EAST
FIVE-STAR EDITION
10¢ DAILY
15¢ WITH SUPPLEMENTS
昭和三十四年一月二十二日国鉄東局特別扱承認新聞紙第 175 号 (日刊)
(昭和 34 年 4 月 21 日第 3 種郵便物認可)
Vol. 22, No. 195 Friday, July 15, 1966

2 CZECH ENVOYS TRIED TO 'BUG' U.S. STATE DEPT.

WASHINGTON (AP)—Two communist Czechoslovakian diplomats tried to wiretap the U.S. State Department building with a hidden electronic listening device, the department charged Wednesday.

The department announced that one of its officials, acting as a "double agent" for more than four years, went along in the Czech efforts climaxed by an attempt to listen in on conversations inside the main State Department building.

The announcement said the double agent, Frank John Mrkva, was acting with the knowledge of the FBI.

Late in May, the department said, the Czechs supplied Mrkva with a tiny microphone-transmitter to be installed in the office of a senior State Department officer.

An effort was made to test the "bug" and shortly thereafter the U.S. counter-intelligence agents decided to put an end to the communist spy attempt.

The Czechs apparently got no information of any significance.

The department announced that one of the two Czechs involved has been declared persona non grata, not acceptable to the U.S. government, and has been order

(Continued on Back Page, Col. 1)

Frank John Mrkva, a State Department employe, displays a listening device two Czech diplomats attempted to use to "bug" the department. Mrkva helped foil the attempt. (UPI Radiophoto)

Heat Toll Hits 26 in St. Louis

By The Associated Press

Summer's longest heat wave gripped most of the eastern two-thirds of the United States Wednesday causing widespread misery and inconvenience.

The Weather Bureau said the oppressive heat and humidity was expected to continue for several days, with possibly minor relief in some areas.

Temperatures have soared to 100-plus for five straight days in parts of the Midwest and in the South.

The number of deaths attributed to the heat wave climbed to 26 in the metropolitan St. Louis area and one official expressed fear the toll would go higher.

Mrs. Helen Taylor, St. Louis coroner, said the bodies of 53 persons were brought to the morgue Wednesday "whereas we normally receive five or six."

She said tests, which have not been completed, had shown that heat was the contributing factor in the deaths of five, bringing to 20 the number of persons in the

(Continued on Back Page, Col. 1)

GI Pay Hike Signed by LBJ

WASHINGTON (AP) — President Johnson signed into law Wednesday the 3.2 per cent pay raise for the Armed Forces and the $17.4 billion military buying authorization passed by Congress Tuesday.

He took the unusually speedy action without comment, merely announcing it through the White House.

The authorization to buy, build and develop weapons of war includes a number of items put in by Congress over the opposition of Defense Secretary Robert S.

(Continued on Back Page, Col. 2)

U.S. Jets Down MIG Over North

SAIGON (AP) — Four U.S. Navy jets tangled with six communist MIG-17s over north Vietnam Wednesday and shot down one of the MIGs, the U.S. announced.

The dogfights took place 23 miles southeast of Hanoi, a spokesman said.

The F4B Phantoms, from the aircraft carrier Constellation were flying cover for other planes attacking rail and highway bridges. All four Navy planes returned to the Constellation without damage.

Sinatra, 50, Engaged to Mia Farrow, 21

NEW YORK (AP) — Frank Sinatra's engagement to 21-year-old Mia Farrow was announced Wednesday by her mother, actress Maureen O'Sullivan.

No wedding date is set, Miss O'Sullivan said, but the couple is expected to marry just before Christmas.

Sinatra, 50, gave Miss Farrow a nine-carat diamond engagement ring just before he left Tuesday for London to film a movie.

"I couldn't be more delighted," Miss O'Sullivan said of her daughter's decision to marry Sinatra. "Frank is a wonderful person and I know they'll be very happy together."

Sinatra, with a 25-year career as an entertainer and recording star, has been married twice. He was divorced from his first wife, Nancy, in 1959. A stormy marriage to Ava Gardner also ended in divorce.

In recent years, Sinatra has squired various screen and television beauties around Hollywood and New York.

In 1962, he was engaged for six weeks to leggy, red-haired Juliet Prowse, then 25. He gave her an engagement ring almost identical with the one Miss Farrow is now wearing.

Miss Farrow met Sinatra when she visited his movie set while he was making "Von Ryan's Express." She was working in the television series "Peyton Place" on a nearby set.

The pretty blonde found herself instantly captivated by the personable Sinatra and later confided:

"I feel more at ease with Frank than with any boy my own age."

Marriage rumors flew last sum-

(Continued on Back Page, Col. 1)

SEEKS NO WIDER WAR

U.S. Rejects Ky Call to Invade

PACIFIC
STAR AND STRIPES
AN AUTHORIZED PUBLICATION OF
THE ARMED FORCES FAR EAST

10¢ DAILY
15¢ WITH SUPPLEMENTS

Vol. 22, No. 208   FIVE-STAR EDITION   Thursday, July 28, 1966

WASHINGTON (AP)—The United States disassociated itself Tuesday from a call by Republic of Vietnam Premier Nguyen Cao Ky for a military confrontation now with communist China.

A State Department spokesman declared: "Our position of not seeking any wider war has been repeatedly made clear and remains our position."

Ky had proposed in an interview that "it is better to face them (the communist Chinese) right now than in 5 or 10 years." He also suggested an allied invasion of north Vietnam to smash the source of communist aggression against South Vietnam.

Ky's remarks brought a storm of objection in the Senate Tuesday. Senate Majority Leader Mike Mansfield (D-Mont.) called on the Johnson Administration to disassociate itself from the Ky declarations.

The Administration decided, it was learned, to deal as softly as possible with what was clearly a sharp division between the policy line projected by the South Vietnamese leader and the policies being followed by President Johnson.

State Department Press Officer Robert J. McCloskey told a news conference, in response to questions, that he did not want to comment directly on Ky's statement, but then added:

"I would say our position of not seeking any wider war has been (Continued on Back Page, Col. 4)

Senate OKs Aid Measure

WASHINGTON (AP) — The Senate passed a $2.06 billion economic foreign aid authorization Tuesday after slashing the total, raising interest rates on development loans and balking at long-term commitments.

The 66-27 vote wrapped up a bill far different from what the Johnson Administration requested and what the House passed.

However, on the basis of past experience, as Sen. J. W. Fulbright (D-Ark.), floor manager for the bill, noted, a Senate-House conference is expected to work out a compromise that will revise some of the Senate changes.

The Administration asked $2.47 billion plus $892 million for military aid for the year that started July 1, with a 5-year authorization. The House lumped the economic and military aid together with a 2-year authorization of $4.1 billion for each year.

The Senate, after wrapping up the economic assistance, plunged immediately into the military aid portion. Thus, it went along with the Administration request that (Continued on Back Page, Col. 2)

Girls Burn; Mother Unaware

PRINCETON, W.Va. (AP) — Two young sisters burned to death in the back seat of their mother's car as she drove along unaware of a fire engulfing the back seat of the car, state police said.

The victims were Lisa Kay Meadows, 2, and her sister Lana Elaine Meadows, 4, of Columbus, Ohio.

State police said their father, Eugene Meadows, 30, was following in another car Monday and had honked the horn repeatedly in an effort to get his wife to stop the car, burning from the rear.

Once stopped, 29-year-old Betty Meadows pulled another 7-month-old daughter from the front seat. Then the parents tried to reach the two girls in the back seat, but they couldn't be reached from inside and the rear doors were locked.

No explanation was given for the cause of the fire.

Help on Way for Wounded Marine

A Navy corpsman is lowered by cable from a helicopter to the hilltop position of I Co., which suffered 71 casualties in a battle with the north Vietnamese in Operation Hastings just south of the DMZ. Wounded man on stretcher in the foreground will be lifted out by cable. Little contact with the north Vietnamese force is now reported. More details, Page 6.   (AP Radiophoto)

Gunmen Grab $60,000

BOSTON (AP) — Two guards were shot Tuesday by three armed gunmen who robbed an armored car of $60,000 in cash as it was stopped outside a Veterans Administration hospital here.

Neither of the guards, shot in the legs, was wounded seriously.

Witnesses said the masked gunmen opened fire on the guards as the men were walking toward the hospital.

The ambush was the second of an armored car in four days in greater Boston. Last Friday, three masked gunmen, toting machine guns, fled with some $130,000 from a Brink's crew at an electronics firm in Bedford, 15 miles north of Boston.

The robbery and shootings Tuesday were witnessed by hospital personnel and patients sitting at windows in the building.

Police said two of the robbers carried what appeared to be machine guns. One was wearing a (Continued on Back Page, Col. 5)

BULLETIN

YADKINVILLE, N.C. (AP)— A plane believed to be a four-engine military jet crashed in a wooded area near Courtney, five miles south of here Tuesday night.

Early reports did not indicate whether there were casualties.

There were reports one man parachuted from the plane.

The area is 25 miles west of Winston-Salem.

Pilot Tells of Prison Camp Ordeal

SAN DIEGO, Cal. (AP) —A German-born U.S. Navy flier who escaped a north Vietnamese prison camp said Tuesday prisoners were beaten, shot at and hung upside down from trees with ants put on their faces.

The apparent aim of the captors, said Lt. (jg) Dieter Dengler, was to persuade American war prisoners to sign statements condemning U.S. actions in Vietnam.

Dengler, 28, of Pacifica, Cal., described his ordeal at a news conference.

Dengler's remarks were censored at times when they touched on areas of security. A Navy spokesman said the value of Dengler's debriefing is "extremely helpful," in training pilots who will fly in Vietnam.

Dengler's first words at the conference were: "Man, it's great to be alive—alive and free."

Dengler was rescued July 20, six months after his plane crashed on his first flight over north Vietnam. He said it came down near the north Vietnam-Laos border. He crawled from the wreckage and evaded the enemy for a day, then was captured.

He escaped after six days, was
(Continued on Back Page, Col. 1)

Wilson Faces Crisis

LONDON (AP)—A major crisis Tuesday night split the British Commonwealth after Prime Minister Harold Wilson rejected 17-nation demands that legal independence be given to a Rhodesia ruled only by Africans.

In a take-it-or-leave-it mood, nonwhite leaders at the 22-nation Commonwealth Conference also called for a total compulsory United Nations embargo on all trade with Premier Ian Smith's breakaway regime — complete with powers of enforcement.

A statement presented to a secret session of presidents, premiers and ministers here insisted on the immediate release of African political prisoners in Rhodesia as soon as the Smith regime is toppled.

The British had sought to defer this move until a transitional caretaker government is formed.

The group of African, Asian and Caribbean states, which claim the backing of Cyprus and Canada, urged the introduction of a one-
(Continued on Back Page, Col. 1)

PACIFIC
STAR STRIPES

AN AUTHORIZED PUBLICATION OF THE
U.S. ARMED FORCES IN THE FAR EAST

10¢ DAILY
15¢ WITH SUPPLEMENTS

Vol. 22, No. 257   FIVE-STAR EDITION   昭和34年1月22日国鉄●信吉方俗承通期新聞紙第175号 (日三)　(昭和34年4月21日第3種郵便物認可)   Thursday, Sept. 15, 1966

CRY FROM SPACE: RIDE IT, COWBOY

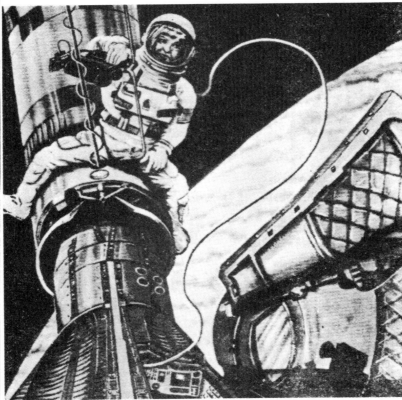

Artist's drawing illustrates how astronaut Richard Gordon rode the Agena rocket during his walk in space Tuesday. Gordon also attached a towing cord to allow the spacecraft to fly in formation, but he was forced to cut the walk short. (AP Radiophoto)

CAPE KENNEDY, Fla. (AP) — Astronaut Richard F. Gordon got out of the Gemini-11 spacecraft Tuesday and mounted the Agena rocket attached to his ship — riding it like a cowboy.

He was forced, however, to cut his space walk short when "he got so hot and sweaty he couldn't see."

Gordon, husky, 36-year-old Navy lieutenant commander, remained outside Gemini-11 only 44 minutes of the planned 115-minute excursion.

It was the third straight time
(Continued on Back Page, Col. 4)

Vorster Succeeds Verwoerd

CAPE TOWN, South Africa (UPI)—Balthazar Johannes Vorster, avowed advocate of rigid racial segregation, became South Africa's second Republican premier Tuesday.

He succeeds the assassinated Dr. Hendrik Verwoerd.

Vorster was formally summoned into the presence of President Charles Swart and officially appointed prime minister.

Vorster, detained for his pro-Nazi activities during World War II and the "iron man" justice minister in Verwoerd's cabinet, immediately pledged he would follow the path of his predecessor—and hinted he might go further.

"My aim is to walk further along the path on which Dr.
(Continued on Back Page, Col. 3)

President Signs Base Projects Bill

WASHINGTON (AP)—President Johnson signed the $1 billion military construction bill Monday.

He objected to a provision in the bill that requires that Congress be notified before a military base is closed and said he will seek to have this feature revised if it proves to be necessary to the national interest.

Seabee Wins Posthumous Medal of Honor

Compiled From AP and UPI
WASHINGTON — President Johnson made a posthumous presentation of the Medal of Honor Tuesday to Navy Seabee Marvin G. Shields of Port Townsend, Wash. It was the fifth Medal of Honor given for bravery in Vietnam.

Shields' daughter, Barbara Diane, 2, was too young to understand the solemnity of the award ceremony in President Johnson's office.

She romped about in the office, dropping and picking up her small pocketbook, until Johnson picked her up, placed her on his desk, and put an arm around her.

Navy Secretary Paul R. Nitze read the citation before Shields' closest relatives, military officials, and members of Congress.

Also present was 1st Lt. Charles Williams of Varce, S.C., who was awarded the Medal of Honor — America's highest military decoration for heroism—June 23 for the same action in which Shields lost his life.

Johnson said Shields, by his heroism in a 14-hour battle at Dong Xoai on June 10, 1965, saved the lives of many of his comrades.

Although twice wounded, the citation said, he continued to supply his fellow Americans with needed ammunition and to return the enemy fire for hours.

Johnson took occasion to describe the war in Vietnam as one of limited objectives.

"It is a war fought, not to gain territory or dominion, but to prove that despots cannot work their will by spreading the fires of violence," Johnson said.

"In this war, the battle lines are not clear. But our goals are very clear.

"We intend to prevent the success of aggression.

"We intend to make it possible for a young nation to begin its experiment with democracy without staring down the barrel of an aggressor's gun."

Johnson said he does not know when victory will come "but surely the first long mile was reached on Sunday when more than 4.2 million South Vietnamese citizens —more than 80 per cent of that country's registered voters— marched to the polls without fear to elect members of their Constituent Assembly. They gave us a lasting lesson in democracy."

Would Halt Raids, U.N. Told

U.S. BIDS FOR PEACE

UNITED NATIONS, N.Y. (UPI)—The United States formally offered Thursday to end the bombing of north Vietnam and withdraw its forces from the Republic of Vietnam if the communists take corresponding action.

Furthermore, U.S. Ambassador Arthur J. Goldberg said in a speech to the General Assembly, the question of Viet Cong participation in Vietnam peace talks would not be "an insurmountable problem."

Goldberg said the United States still was ready to negotiate a Vietnam settlement on the basis of the 1954 and 1962 Geneva accords, "and we will support a reconvening of the Geneva conference, or an Asian conference, or any other generally acceptable forum."

Soviet Ambassador Nikolai T. Fedorenko said after the assembly meeting that Goldberg's speech was "a set of declarations and words—familiar old sounds and tunes."

Goldberg put three concrete proposals to the north Vietnam regime and said more may follow from the "not inflexible" position of the United States.

"We do not ask of north Vietnam an unconditional surrender or indeed the surrender of anything that belongs to it," Goldberg said. "Nor do we seek to exclude any segment of the South Vietnamese people from peaceful participation in their country's future.

"—We want a political solution, not a military solution, to this conflict. By the same token, we reject the idea that north Vietnam has a right to impose a military solution.

"—We seek to assure for the people of South Vietnam the same right of self-determination —to decide their own political destiny, free of force—that the U.N. charter affirms for all.

"—And we believe that re-unification of Vietnam should be decided upon through a free choice by the peoples of both the (Continued on Back Page, Col. 2)

U.S. Ambassador to the United Nations Arthur Goldberg makes a new Vietnam peace offer during General Assembly speech.
(AP Radiophoto)

PACIFIC STAR AND STRIPES

AN AUTHORIZED PUBLICATION OF THE ARMED FORCES IN THE FAR EAST

FIVE-STAR EDITION

10¢ DAILY
15¢ WITH SUPPLEMENTS

昭和34年1月22日 第三種郵便物認可新聞紙第175号 (B刊)
(昭和34年4月21日第三種郵便物認可)

Vol. 22, No. 266   **Saturday, Sept. 24, 1966**

U.S. to Buy 280 Extra Warplanes

WASHINGTON (AP) — Defense Secretary Robert S. McNamara announced Thursday the United States will increase its planned production of warplanes by approximately 280 aircraft at a cost of $700 million.

McNamara said the additional order for fighter and attack aircraft was prudent, in view of the long lead time—between design and production—involved in getting planes off the production line for war use.

The defense chief said, "I have come to the conclusion that it is wise to place on order aircraft that may be required to support operations beyond June 30, 1967."

This is the end of the current fiscal year, the arbitrary time point MacNamara has used in military planning.

The announcement thus placed American war planning into fiscal 1968, at least on a procurement basis.

McNamara will not announce what types of planes would be added to the purchase order until the manufacturers themselves are told.

He did say, however, that most would be for the Navy.

Pentagon spokesmen indicated, however, that a large number of the extra planes might be the Navy's new A7, a subsonic aircraft used for low-level bombing. The other aircraft, they said, quite likely would be the F4 Phantom, a fighter-bomber which escorts the slower A7 bombing craft.

In response to questions at a news conference, McNamara said (Continued on Back Page, Col. 5)

Hertz to Buy 90,000 Autos

NEW YORK (UPI)—The biggest single planned commercial purchase of motor vehicles in history—90,000—was announced Thursday by Hertz Corp.

The retail value of the planned purchase will run to about $314 million and will include cars and trucks for Hertz rental and leasing operations. Of the total, 83 per cent will be acquired for Hertz corporate branches in the United States and abroad, the rest for Hertz domestic and foreign licensees.

House Unit Strips Powell of Power

WASHINGTON (AP) — The House Education and Labor Committee voted overwhelmingly Thursday to strip controversial chairman Adam Clayton Powell of much of his power to direct the committee's business.

The vote was 27 to 1, according to Rep. Dave Martin (R-Neb.), a member of the committee.

The action came at a meeting from which another Republican member emerged to charge that Democrats were trying to lynch Powell, a Democrat and a Negro.

Powell agreed to go along with the rebellious majority of his committee, and thus averted a bitter fight that had headed toward a showdown over new rules.

Only Rep. William H. Ayers of Ohio, the senior Republican committeeman, voted against the new rules.

Powell indicated he views the outcome as a victory. Puffing a cigar and smiling at the huge (Continued on Back Page, Col. 1)

BULLETIN

SAIGON (AP) — American infantrymen accidentally detonated four land mines in their own minefield Thursday and killed seven U.S. soldiers and wounded 14, the U.S. military command said Friday.

ROK Cabinet Quits in Shocking Incident

SEOUL (UPI) — The Korean government resigned en masse Thursday night after a critical legislator tossed a bucket of human waste on the prime minister in parliament.

The incident occurred during debate on a smuggling case involving a fertilizer plant owned by the wealthiest businessman in Korea Byung Chul Lee.

Sources said, however, that President Chung Hee Park was unlikely to accept the resignation of Premier Il Kwon Chung, although he might replace Finance Minister Chang Yun Kim.

The firm, which has a $60 million government-backed plant under construction in Ulsan is accused of importing about $100,-000 worth of saccharine for sale on the black market, on import licenses authorizing shipment of construction materials from Japan.

The Customs Department, which falls under Kim's ministry, investigated the case last spring and fined Lee's fertilizer firm a small amount.

The waste was thrown Thursday afternoon by Rep. Doo Han Kim, an independent member of the body, while the assembly was in the middle of debate on the issue.

Kim was given the floor, and when he came to the speaker's rostrum he carried with him a half-gallon can.

As Kim took the rostrum he announced that the can "contains material evidence" in the issue. He then proceeded to make 10-minute speech denouncing the government.

At the end of it, he turned toward the table behind him at which Premier Chung, Deputy Premier Key Young Chang and (Continued on Back Page, Col. 3)

ALLIES OFFER HANOI 6-POINT PEACE PLAN

PACIFIC STAR STRIPES

AN AUTHORIZED PUBLICATION OF
THE ARMED FORCES FAR EAST

10¢ DAILY
15¢ WITH SUPPLEMENTS

Vol. 22, No. 299   FIVE-STAR EDITION   Thursday, Oct. 27, 1966

MANILA (UPI)—The Vietnam Allies offered north Vietnam a six-point plan for peace Tuesday night, including a pledge to withdraw all foreign troops from South Vietnam within six months after the communists withdraw.

President Johnson and the six other national leaders insisted, however, that any peace arrangements and subsequent Allied withdrawals would depend on "effective international guarantees" and supervision to insure that the communists live up to their side of the deal.

The members of the Asian summit conference also issued a four-point document entitled "Goals of Freedom," in which they declared their deter-

Related stories, pictures on pages 5, 12, 13. Partial text of summit communique on page 18.

mination to seek for Vietnam and other Asian and Pacific areas these rights:

—"To be free from aggression."

—"To conquer hunger, illiteracy and disease."

—"To build a region of security.

(Continued on Back Page, Col. 3)

President Johnson (left) and Republic of Vietnam Premier Nguyen Cao Ky (right) sign communique at the end of the Manila summit conference Tuesday in Malacanang Palace. Looking on are U.S. Secretary of State Dean Rusk (second from left) and Vietnamese Chief of State Lt. Gen. Nguyen Van Thieu (second from right).   (AP Radiophoto)

Charge N. Korea In Killings

S&S Korea Bureau

PANMUNJOM, Korea—The United Nations Command Tuesday charged north Korea with killing "several" Republic of Korea soldiers in the deliberate ambush of an unarmed ration truck south of the Military Demarcation Line last Friday evening.

Marine Maj. Gen. Joseph O. Butcher, senior UNC member to the Military Armistice Commission, told the commission here that the incident was "the worst to date of several over the past two weeks."

According to the UNC charges, soldiers in north Korean Peoples Army (KPA) uniforms waited for and ambushed the ration truck 1,500 feet inside the South Korean half of the Demilitarized Zone.

The ambush took place approximately 24 hours after the last (Continued on Back Page, Col. 2)

Speck Can Stand Trial, Doctors Say

Compiled From AP and UPI

CHICAGO — A court-appointed psychiatrist said Tuesday he and five colleagues have determined that Richard Speck is mentally competent to stand trial on charges he killed eight student nurses.

Dr. Edward J. Kelleher, a psychiatrist for Chicago's Municipal Court, said the panel of six psychiatrists have unanimously agreed that Speck could cooperate with his attorney and stand trial.

As to whether Speck was sane at the time of the slayings last July, Kelleher said the panel reached a unanimous finding on this question also. But he said he was committed to secrecy and could not discuss this decision.

Kelleher said the panel concluded its study Saturday. He said that Criminal Court Judge Herbert C. Paschen, who will hear the case, the Cook County State Attorney's Office, and (Continued on Back Page, Col. 1)

Subandrio Guilty, Gets Death; Only Appeal Is to Sukarno

JAKARTA, Indonesia (UPI)— The former No. 2 man of Indonesia, Dr. Subandrio, was sentenced to be shot by a firing squad by a military tribunal here Tuesday night.

The former foreign minister and vice premier was convicted of aiding the armed communist rebellion against the government which took place just over a year ago.

He has 30 days to appeal the conviction and the sentence. He must appeal to Sukarno, the man whose testimony helped to seal his fate.

The sentence came after a long summation of the charges by the members of the 9-man tribunal.

Chief Judge Lt. Col. Ali Said announced the sentence, which he said had been decided Sunday.

In a climax to the month-long trial, he droned the court's verdict: "Defendant named Suban-

drio, born in Kependjen (east Java), male, etc. etc., religion Moslem, detained since March 18, 1966, is guilty of the following crimes:

"He aided others to execute a coup against the state. He had prior knowledge of an armed rebellion. He had acted in undermining the government's prestige."

Subandrio's medals would be (Continued on Back Page, Col. 4)

Special Reserve to Be on Call Till Mid-'67

WASHINGTON (AP) — The Pentagon plans to maintain the nation's Selected Reserve Force (SRF) in a high state of readiness at least until mid-1967 as a hedge against any required mobilization.

Maj. Gen. Winston P. Wilson, head of the National Guard Bureau, disclosed this Tuesday in assessing the progress of the

150,000-man force, organized a year ago as a first-line backup for the Regular Army.

"The results have been fantastic," Wilson said, pointing out that 86 per cent of 423 SRF units tested during the summer passed Regular Army battalion-level examinations. Sixty which failed are being retested.

The National Guard forms the

bulk of the Selected Reserve Force with 131,000 men, compared with the Reserve's 19,000.

Defense Secretary Robert S. McNamara set up the Selected Reserve Force a year ago during the Vietnam buildup as an alternative to ordering to active duty Army Reserve or National Guard units

The objective of the select units

in the past year has been attained —getting in shape to be able to arrive at a mobilization station on seven days' notice, then undergo eight weeks of brigade and division-level training before deployment overseas.

During the Berlin crisis, it took five months for a Guard division to achieve deployment status. In past wars it took a year or more.

LBJ FLIES TO VIET, DINES WITH TROOPS

PACIFIC
STARS STRIPES

AN AUTHORIZED PUBLICATION OF THE
U.S. ARMED FORCES IN THE FAR EAST

10¢ DAILY
15¢ WITH SUPPLEMENTS

Vol. 22, No. 300 FIVE-STAR EDITION

昭和34年1月22日国鉄 ● 将特別扱承認新聞紙第1776号（日刊）
（昭和34年4月21日第3種郵便物認可）

Friday, Oct. 28, 1966

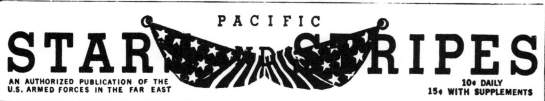

CARRIER HEADS FOR R.P.

Oriskany Fire Kills 43

By WALLACE BEENE
S&S Vietnam Bureau Chief

SAIGON — An explosive fire broke out aboard the aircraft carrier Oriskany Wednesday morning. The Navy reported 43 men killed and 16 injured.

The flames started in the forward bay of the hangar deck where flares are stored as the carrier with its crew of 3,500 was on station in the Gulf of Tonkin.

There was no indication of what might have set off the flares in the crowded hangar deck where planes, bombs, rockets and other armaments are stored before being lifted up to the flight deck.

The first blaze broke out at 7:45 a.m. and was brought under control in about an hour, but flash fires continued to erupt during the morning and early afternoon. The final blaze was not extinguished until 3:23 p.m., the Navy reported.

The carrier operates about 70 planes.

(Two helicopters were destroyed and four A4E Skyhawk jet fighter-bombers were damaged, AP reported. The Navy also reported extensive damage to overheads and bulkheads.

(The Oriskany was sailing under her own power Thursday for the Philippines to undergo repairs at the U.S. Naval Base at Subic Bay.

(The 42,000-ton carrier will be replaced at her station in Tonkin Gulf by either the Intrepid or the Coral Sea, Navy officials announced.)

Doctors, hospital corpsmen and chaplains were rushed to the Oriskany from the carrier Constellation, which was standing by.

The seriously injured were
(Continued on Back Page, Col. 4)

Nervous? Not a Bit

PORTSMOUTH, Va. (AP) — "Don't get nervous," the armed bandit told restaurant waitress Pauline Smith Wednesday as he announced a stickup.

She didn't. She threw a cup of steaming coffee in his face and he fled.

AP Radiophoto

A GI RUNS TO SHAKE HANDS WITH PRESIDENT JOHNSON AT CAM RANH BAY, VIETNAM.

CAM RANH BAY, Vietnam (AP) — President Johnson made a top-secret flight to Vietnam Wednesday and told the American fighting men "we depend on you."

Johnson spent 2 hours and 24 minutes on Vietnamese soil and capped his historic visit by exhorting General William C. Westmoreland and his top field commanders to "come home with that coonskin on the wall."

The President—who got closer to battlefield than any President since Abraham Lincoln—ate with the troops, visited the wounded, pinned medals on the brave, signed scores of autographs, shook hundreds of hands and delivered an emotional speech.

Troops in battle dress—there are several thousand of them at the base—grinned broadly and cheered as Johnson moved among them

Related stories, pictures on pages 5, 12-13.

both on foot and standing in an open jeep, holding onto a roof brace.

The soldiers, who got almost no advance notice of Johnson's visit, sometimes appeared at a loss about how to react.

Some seemed to think he should be treated like a general—until he extended his hand. Then they rushed forward, almost like any streetcorner crowd back home.

Johnson left Manila secretly in mid-afternoon and flew back there after dark.

The President was to fly to
(Continued on Back Page, Col. 3)

NATO Votes to Quit Paris

PARIS (AP)—The North Atlantic Alliance voted Wednesday to shift its political headquarters from Paris to Brussels.

The unanimous decision was made by the 15 ambassadors on the North Atlantic Treaty Organization (NATO) Council.

It capped months of intense lobbying by the United States and Britain, who argued against keeping the NATO political directorate in a country where Allied troops are not welcome.

President Charles de Gaulle has withdrawn French forces from NATO's military command and has set an April 1, 1967, deadline for Allied troops and headquarters to leave his country.

The resolution adopted Wednesday noted the transfer of Supreme Headquarters Allied Powers in Europe (SHAPE) to Belgium and said:

"Considering that the proper functioning of the alliance requires the council to be located
(Continued on Back Page, Col. 3)

CANCER-RIDDEN RUBY DIES OF BLOOD CLOT

PACIFIC
STAR ⋆ ⋆ ⋆ RIPES

AN AUTHORIZED PUBLICATION OF THE
U.S. ARMED FORCES IN THE FAR EAST

10¢ DAILY
15¢ WITH SUPPLEMENTS

Vol. 23, No. 4   FIVE-STAR EDITION   昭和34年1月22日西独 電電特別掲示 認新聞紙第17ヶ号(日刊) (昭和34年4月21日第3種郵便物認可)   Thursday, Jan. 5, 1967

12-14 MINUTE DOGFIGHT

Ace Describes Epic MIG Battle

By
ANDREW HEADLAND JR.
S&S Vietnam Bureau Chief

SAIGON — "To make a long story extremely short, they lost."

With this sentence Col. Robin Olds, a Seventh Air Force fighter wing commander, summed up the swirling air battle in which Air Force Phantom jets knocked seven MIG-21s out of the sky Monday northwest of Hanoi.

Olds, 44, gave details of the war's biggest aerial battle at Tan Son Nhut AB.

The battle raised to 34 the total of MIGs downed by U.S. pilots in the Vietnam War.

No U.S. planes were lost, to the MIGs' missile and cannon fire.

Olds said his flight was attacked "very aggressively" by an unknown number of MIGs while making the sweep over north Vietnam.

The seven downed MIG-21s were shot down by air-to-air missiles.

Olds downed his first MIG during the battle. The kill brings his total of enemy planes to 25. He flew P-38s and P-51s in World War II.

Olds said one MIG got up behind him. "It wasn't the first time I have had someone behind me who was angry," he said. "I didn't worry too much, though, knowing that my flight was there providing protection."

At one point he had two MIGs in front and another on his left. He rolled up behind the MIG on his left, flying upside down until he lined up the enemy jet.

He fired a missile and saw a tremendous orange flash. One wing of the MIG flew off. The plane went out of control and plunged to earth.

Olds said, "I was elated. I was glad they tangled with us. It was
(Continued on Page 5, Col. 1)

750 License Tags —All the Same

KINGMAN, Ariz. (AP) — The city bicycle-licensing ordinance in Kingman has run into trouble. When Police Chief Carl Fisher opened the package of license tags, all had the same number —1—750.

Fisher sent an emergency order back to the manufacturer explaining he wants the plates all to be different—with numbers running from one to 750.

Col. Robin Olds (left) tells Brig. Gen. Edward A. McCough how he downed a communist MIG-21 over north Vietnam Monday. McCough is combat operations director at Tan Son Nhut AB.

AP Radiophoto

DALLAS (AP) — Jack Ruby, 55, the slayer of accused presidential assassin Lee Harvey Oswald, died Tuesday in Parkland Memorial Hospital, where he had been suffering from cancer since Dec. 9.

Dr. Eugene Frenkel said an autopsy showed the immediate cause of death was a blood clot that broke loose in Ruby's right leg and coursed into a lung.

Ruby insisted until the end that he was part of no plot, that he

Pictures, Pages 12-13

acted alone, that an accident of timing and a surge of blinding passion caused him to shoot Oswald, accused killer of President Kennedy.

A tough from Chicago's South Side. Ruby died after more than three years in jail—and only a month or so short of a second trial.

Because of his death. District Atty. Henry Wade said he would dismiss the murder charge against Ruby.

"Of course Jack died not a con-
(Continued on Back Page, Col. 2)

U.S. Nabs 70 in Haiti Plot

KEY WEST, Fla. (AP)—Seventy Latin and American commandoes were arrested Monday night at a remote Florida beach. One of the Latins said Tuesday the arrests stopped an invasion of Haiti.

However, one boatload of commandoes got away before U.S. customs agents and local officers moved in, according to Rolando Masferrer, a former Cuban senator.

"It's in international waters." he said. "It's free and clear. Nothing can be done about it."

He said 50 heavily armed men were aboard the ship. They were to have rendezvoused with two other boatloads of invaders in
(Continued on Back Page, Col. 1)

Royal Divorce Shakes British Society

LONDON (UPI) — A cousin of Queen Elizabeth II, who is 18th in line to the British throne, announced Monday that his wife is divorcing him and that he wants to marry the woman whose baby he fathered in 1964.

The announcement by the Earl of Harewood, 43, through his lawyers, was the biggest royal scandal since the abdication of King Edward VIII in 1936. It will be the first royal divorce since the turn of the century.

Harewood said he wants to marry a former Australian fashion model and violinist. Patricia Tuckwell, known as Bambi. She was formerly his secretary and has one 16-year-old son by a former marriage to Melbourne photographer Athol Smith.

Harewood admitted fathering her child, Mark, born in July, 1964.

The earl, son of the late Princess Royal and Viscount Lascelles, was married in a royal wedding attended by King George and Queen Elizabeth in 1949. He met Miss Tuckwell during a visit to Australia several years ago.

The official announcement of what society gossips had been expecting since Harewood and his wife, former concert pianist Marion Stein, split up 16 months ago. also posed a constitutional problem.

Under the Royal Marriages Act Queen Elizabeth II now must give her permission for Harewood to marry again after the divorce, which he said he will not defend.

If the queen decided to oppose the marriage, Harewood would have to seek permission from the Privy Council and wait 12 months. But parliament could forbid the wedding.

Not since Princess Marie Louise and Victoria, granddaughters of Queen Victoria, were involved in divorces at the turn of the century has anyone so closely related to the reigning monarch been involved in divorce.

Experts said tonight the child born to Miss Tuckwell would have no rights to his father's title or to a place in the line of succession to the throne even if
(Continued on Back Page, Col. 5)

NORTH VIET BUILDUP

★ ★ ★ ★ ★ ★ ★ ★ ★ ★ ★ ★ ★ ★ ★

Supplies Spotted Flowing South From Hanoi

PACIFIC
STAR ~~~~ RIPES

AN AUTHORIZED PUBLICATION OF THE
U.S. ARMED FORCES IN THE FAR EAST

10¢ DAILY
15¢ WITH SUPPLEMENTS

Vol. 23, No. 42 FIVE-STAR EDITION 昭和34年1月22日（略）中部地域郵便認可第1回号（七…）
（昭和44年4月1日第3種郵便物許可…） Sunday, Feb. 12, 1967

Kosygin Hails Struggle Against 'Dictator Mao'

LONDON (AP)—Soviet Prime Minister Alexei Kosygin Friday night came out in support of those communist Chinese "struggling against the dictatorial regime of Mao Tse-tung."

Kosygin's blast against Mao was unprecedented for a Soviet statesman visiting a foreign capitalist state.

The Soviet leader said an end of American military action against north Vietnam could lead to "the ending of the Vietnam conflict" and would be "the most correct solution."

Earlier Kosygin had completed the formal phase of his world-ranging talks with Prime Minister Harold Wilson with one slender agreement over Vietnam: The war should be ended through political, not military action.

But the two men remained divided over how to launch a peace negotiation.

In a television interview broadcast by Britain's main networks, Kosygin, speaking through an interpreter, with Kenneth Harris, disclosed he has had a full exchange with Wilson on the China upheaval.

This, in itself, was a rare admission because heretofore, with the British at least, Soviet leaders have refused to discuss the feud with China.

Kosygin called it "a state of aggravation." It had come about, he asserted, through no fault of Russia:

"It is entirely the fault of the Chinese state," he said.

"We should like to have good relations with the Chinese government and with the Chinese Communist Party which we hold in high regard.

"We are aware there are today (Continued on Back Page, Col. 5)

Peking Jails 2 A-Spies

TOKYO (AP)—The first atomic spy case in Red China—which has detonated five nuclear bombs since 1964—was reported Friday by a Japanese correspondent in Peking.

The Mainichi Shimbun, quoting a newspaper loyal to Chinese chairman Mao Tse-tung—the "Revolutionary Workers Daily"—said two armed men in the chemical industry ministry have been arrested on a charge of stealing atomic secrets.

The accusation was posted on the capital's walls.

The implication was that the arrested men, one of them identified only as an official named Ting Tieh-sheng, were supporters of President Liu Shao-chi.

Security Minister Hsieh Fu-chih, a Mao ally, personally made the arrest, said the paper, organ of the Peking workers revolutionary rebel headquarters. He found seven pistols, two of them on the alleged spies.

The paper said Hsieh was probing to discover whether any of the information—of an unspecified nature—had sifted into a foreign country.
(Continued on Back Page, Col. 5)

Indira in Hospital

NEW DELHI (AP)—Prime Minister Indira Gandhi has entered a local nursing home for the "correction of a minor displacement of her nose and tooth," an official medical bulletin said Friday. It said an X-ray had revealed a fracture of the nasal bone with slight displacement.

A pedestrian doesn't quite make it over a pile of snow in New York City. (AP Radiophoto)

(Continued on Back Page, Col. 2)
(Continued on Back Page, Col. 5)

SAIGON (AP) — The U.S. command Friday reported a massive supply buildup in north Vietnam during the first three days of the Lunar New Year truce and the suspension of American bombing raids.

U.S. officials said the 4-day cease-fire proclaimed by the Republic of Vietnam government remains in effect, but they would not rule out the possibility that air strikes against north Vietnam might be ordered before the truce ends Sunday should the communist buildup reach levels considered "intolerable" by the U.S. command.

The north Vietnamese movement of supplies southward is "not technically a violation of the stand-down," these sources said, but it was obviously long planned and "creates doubts as to north Vietnamese sincerity about the truce."

American sources said in Saigon that "the volume, scope and direction" of the shipments "creates hazards for our military which cannot be overlooked."

During the first three days of the truce, American reconnaissance has counted more than 900 communist cargo boats and barges moving in the gulf or on inland waterways. This is about five times the normal traffic, sources said.

In addition, hundreds of trucks are on the go all over north Vietnam, moving equipment and supplies into the southern area toward the demilitarized zone.

The increased supply work was first noted in north Vietnam Tuesday night before the truce period began. Military sources said 112
(Continued on Back Page, Col. 2)

Train Hauls 'Snow Job'

MEMPHIS, Tenn. (UPI) — Officials of the Illinois Central Railroad have sent more than a million pounds of unwanted snow farther south.

The snow arrived here Thursday in 14 hopper cars from Chicago.

"We'll send it on south to McComb, Miss., and New Orleans," said A. W. Pirtle, Memphis yardmaster, "It'll just melt away."

"They . . . sent it south to melt," explained J. H. Jefferson, assistant general yardmaster.

Snow-Lashed East Gets 13 More Inches

Compiled From AP and UPI
NEW YORK — A new snowstorm struck the already blizzard-ravaged Eastern Seaboard Friday with up to 13 inches of additional snow that tangled transportation and played havoc with thousands of commuters.

The storm hit Virginia and the Carolinas, then swept northward into New Jersey, New York and New England, where millions were still digging out of Tuesday's blizzard that dumped up to 16 inches of snow, took lives and cost millions of dollars in business losses and snow-removal expenses.

Swirling out of the Appalachian Mountains Thursday, the storm dumped heavy snow inland and whipped exposed coastal points with winds of gale force.

The storm, spawned in the South, moved quickly up the East Coast and by mid-morning was over southern New England.

Thirteen inches of snow was recorded at the Atlantic City, N.J., airport, 12 inches on Cape Cod in Massachusetts and 10 inches in the Carolinas.

New York City got away with only two inches of snow.

The gale-whipped storm also spared other big eastern cities most of its punch. Philadelphia received only three inches of snow and Washington two.

In the Midwest, meanwhile, a low pressure system brought rain, snow and gale winds to the Great Lakes.

In Los Angeles, International Airport was closed early Friday when heavy fog reduced visibility.

A spokesman for the airport, which has been forced to close frequently because of fog in recent weeks, said incoming flights were being diverted to airports in Burbank, Ontario and other outlying areas.

U.S. Peace Bid Rejected

LBJ, HO EXCHANGE NOTES ON VIET WAR

PACIFIC STARS AND STRIPES

AN AUTHORIZED PUBLICATION OF
THE ARMED FORCES FAR EAST

10¢ DAILY
15¢ WITH SUPPLEMENTS

Vol. 23, No. 81   FIVE-STAR EDITION   Thursday, March 23, 1967

By The Associated Press

TOKYO—President Johnson wrote to President Ho Chi Minh of north Vietnam early in February suggesting "direct talks" for peace in Vietnam but Ho rejected the offer, it was announced Tuesday.

In Washington, Tuesday night, after returning from the conference at Guam, Johnson declared he will continue to seek an honorable peace in Vietnam despite Ho's "regrettable" rejection of his offer.

Until his efforts are successful, Johnson said, "we shall of course do our duty in Vietnam."

The north Vietnamese Foreign Ministry, in a statement monitored in Tokyo, said Ho sent his reply to Johnson Feb. 15, the day after the United States resumed air raids against north Vietnam following the lunar New Year pause.

Ho said in his reply, "In your message, you suggested direct talks between the Democratic Republic of north-Vietnam and the United States."

Turning down the offer. Ho said, "if the U.S. government really wants these talks, it must first of all stop unconditionally its bombing raids and all other acts of war" against north Vietnam.

The United States has already made it plain it will not de-escalate the war unless the communists respond with matching action.

Ho went on to say it is only

LBJ's Letter

WASHINGTON (UPI)—Text of a letter sent by President Johnson to north Vietnamese President Ho Chi Minh.

Dear Mr. President:

I am writing to you in the hope that the conflict in Vietnam can be brought to an end.

That conflict has already taken a heavy toll—in lives lost, in wounds inflicted, in property destroyed, and in simple human misery. If we fail to find a just and peaceful solution, history will judge us harshly.

Therefore, I believe that we both have a heavy obligation to seek earnestly the path to peace. It is in response to that obligation that I am writing directly to you.

We have tried over the past several years, in a variety of ways and through a number of channels, to convey to you and your colleagues our desire to achieve a peaceful settlement.

For whatever reasons, these efforts have not achieved any results.

JOHNSON

It may be that our thoughts and yours, our attitudes and yours, have been distorted or misinterpreted as they passed through these various channels. Certainly that is always a danger in indirect communication.

There is one good way to overcome this problem and to move forward in the search for a peaceful settlement.

(Continued on Back Page, Col. 1)

Ho's Reply

TOKYO (AP)—Text of Ho's reply to President Johnson, broadcast by the Vietnam News Agency:

To His Excellency Mr. Lyndon B. Johnson,

President,

United States of America.

Your Excellency,

On Feb. 10, 1967, I received your message. This is my reply.

Vietnam is thousands of miles away from the United States. The Vietnamese people have never done any harm to the United States.

But contrary to the pledges made by its representative at the 1954 Geneva conference, the U.S. government has ceaselessly intervened in Vietnam.

It has unleashed and intensified the war of aggression in South Vietnam with a view to prolonging the partition of Vietnam and turning South Vietnam into a neo-colony and a military base of the United States.

HO

For over two years now, the U.S. government has, with its air and naval forces, carried the war to the Democratic Republic of Vietnam, an independent and sovereign country.

The U.S. government has committed war crimes, crimes against peace and against mankind.

In South Vietnam, half a million U.S and

(Continued on Back Page, Col. 5)

Premier Ky announces his government made fresh peace proposals to Hanoi several days ago, Page 6.

Text of joint communique summarizing Guam talks, Page 6.

after his conditions are met that north Vietnam and the United States "could enter into talks and discuss questions concerning the two sides."

In his reply—of which the full text was released by the Foreign Ministry—Ho declared, "the Vietnamese people will never submit to force, they will never accept talks under the threat of bombs."

In Washington Tuesday, Johnson said, "during my flight home I learned that Hanoi had made public an exchange of letters between me and Ho Chi Minh.

"His reply to me of mid-February and his earlier public reply to His Holiness, the Pope, were regrettable rebuffs to a genuine

(Continued on Back Page, Col. 2)

$280 Mil. Air Shield For NATO

LONDON (UPI) — The United States and five Allied countries have formed a six-nation corporation to build a $280 million air defense early warning system for Western Europe, it was announced Tuesday.

The other countries are Britain, West Germany, France, Italy and the Netherlands.

The system is to be known as "NADGE," standing for "NATO Air Defense Ground Environment."

Although French President Charles de Gaulle has withdrawn his country from virtually all other military cooperation with the North Atlantic Treaty Organization (NATO), he has left it in the "NADGE" project, which is

(Continued on Back Page, Col. 4)

B-52s Flee Gale off Guam

TOKYO (S&S)—Tropical storm Theresa, with center winds of 52 m.p.h., was reported 333 miles northeast of Guam Wednesday morning, according to Air Force Weather Central at Fuchu AS.

An Air Force spokesman at Kadena AB, Okinawa, said about 30 B-52 bombers were flown to Kadena from Guam to avoid possible damage. The spokesman said it was a "normal typhoon evacuation flight."

The Air Force said some of the B-52s flew back to Guam Tuesday and the rest were returning Wednesday.

Weathermen said Theresa is moving east-northeast at 17 m.p.h. The storm is not expected to hit any land areas.

Point-Blank Artillery Kills 423 Reds

By SP4 ALLEN FASOLDT
S&S Staff Correspondent

SOUI DA, Vietnam—The communists suffered their worst defeat of the war in terms of deaths Tuesday when more than 423 Reds were killed during a battle 17 miles northeast of Tay Ninh City.

Troopers of the 3d Bn., 4th Inf. Div. serving under the 25th Div. task force cut down human wave attacks of 200 and 300 men by firing artillery flat out with cannister loads.

(The Americans were running low on ammunition when a column of 113 armored vehicles, including 33 tanks, clanked to the rescue, AP reported.)

Capt. George Shoemaker, company commander, said "as the Reds were cut down, they would fall back and patch up the wounded before launching a fresh assault." Many of the dead were wearing fresh bandages, he reported.

Lt. Col. John A. Bender, battalion commander, said the fighting was more savage than anything he had seen in World War II or Korea.

The fighting broke out in the dense jungle around the 3d Bn.,

4th Div., artillery post when a patrol spotted forces of the 272d VC Regt.

Artillery, air strikes and armed helicopters took a tremendous toll of the attacking forces, but it was direct fire from artillery at the camp that was credited with turning back the assaults.

(Of 18 howitzers that the enemy attacked with rockets and mortar shells, 11 were knocked out, AP said. Repairs by the artillerymen, however, put all but four of these back in working order after the battle.

(These guns, making up three

batteries of the 2d Bn., 27th Arty. Regt., sat in the middle of a half-mile-wide landing zone established about 70 miles northwest of Saigon to support the month-old Operation Junction City.)

U.S. losses in the fierce fighting throughout the day were 30 killed and 109 wounded.

The 423 VC death toll reported includes only bodies found in the immediate vicinity of the artillery camp.

While the enemy troops were identified as part of the 272d VC Regt., there were also reports

(Continued on Back Page, Col. 2)

OUTNUMBERED GIS CUT DOWN 581 VC

PACIFIC

STARS AND STRIPES

AN AUTHORIZED PUBLICATION OF
THE ARMED FORCES FAR EAST

10¢ DAILY
15¢ WITH SUPPLEMENTS

Vol. 23, No. 92   FIVE-STAR EDITION   Monday, April 3, 1967

By SP5 GERARD FORKEN
S&S Staff Correspondent

SROC CON TRANG, Vietnam — Outnumbered U.S. troops cut down waves of Viet Cong attackers Saturday in a battle that killed at least 581 communists and left only nine Americans dead.

The one-day toll was the highest ever suffered by the VC. Bodies of fallen VC soldiers were still being counted at dusk Saturday, even as the battered enemy force struck again at U.S. defenses.

Thirty-two Americans were wounded.

The communists were overrun after they tried to trap a battalion of the 1st Inf. Div. 6 miles from the Cambodian border in Tay Ninh Province.

Outnumbered more than three to one, troops of the 1st Bn., 26th Inf., fired from log-covered bunk-

Quick action when VC mortar rounds started falling kept U.S. casualties low. Page 6

ers as an entire Viet Cong regiment charged their position.

The attack followed a pre-dawn communist mortar barrage of more than 300 rounds. As the last round exploded, regulars from the 271st VC Regt. ran from the north and east across a clearing and smashed into the U.S. lines.

At one point, the attackers
(Continued on Back Page, Col. 3)

Kidnaped Girl OK; Man Held

CHICAGO (AP) — Carrie Stephens, 8, who was abducted Monday, was found alive Saturday.

The child was taken to Swedish Covenant Hospital, according to a spokesman for the deputy superintendent of police, who said a man was being questioned in connection with the girl's disappearance.

Apparently information received by a policeman, Anthony Ruh, sent a task force of searchers into an apartment building on the north side, where the girl was found. Details were not immediately available.

A hospital official said that the girl was brought there for a
(Continued on Back Page, Col. 2)

Freighter In Danger

MIAMI (UPI) — The Swedish freighter Andrew Salmon was reported listing dangerously Saturday in 30-foot seas about 20 miles east of San Salvador Island in the Bahamas.

The Coast Guard here said the 300-foot ship, with a crew of 18 aboard, reported by radio that its copper cargo had shifted, causing the vessel to list 15 degrees to port.

The wind-swept Atlantic is causing the vessel to roll to a dangerous 60 degrees, the Coast Guard said. A merchant ship, the Pioneer Contractor, about 40 miles away was speeding to the scene.

A wounded U.S. Army sergeant clings to the back of a medic as he is carried to safety. The NCO was hit by Viet Cong fire Friday while trying to silence an enemy position with a mine during action in War Zone C near the Cambodian border. (AP Radiophoto)

Truckers Voting On Strike

WASHINGTON (UPI) — Thousands of truck drivers began voting Saturday in a poll that is expected to authorize the Teamsters Union to call a strike against 1,500 U.S. trucking firms.

The strike vote was expected to be completed by Sunday night and a strike deadline set possibly as early as Monday.

The union's contract with Trucking Employers Inc. (TEI) ended at midnight Friday. Negotiations on a new three-year pact continued Saturday, but with little hope for settlement before a strike deadline could be set by the union.

A TEI spokesman in Washington said the truckers and the union still were more than half a
(Continued on Back Page, Col. 1)

Demo Leads In House Race

PROVIDENCE, R.I. (UPI) — Democratic state Sen. Robert Tiernan of Warwick held a slim 410-vote lead Saturday as election officials continued counting absentee ballots in the race for the congressional seat of the late Rep. John Fogarty (D-R.I.).

Precinct returns in Tuesday's election gave Tiernan a 521-vote lead over his Republican opponent, Cranston Mayor James Di Prete Jr.

Tabulation of the 1,899 absentee ballots began Friday.

Percy Wedding Clouded by 2d Death

CHICAGO (AP) — John D. (Jay) Rockefeller IV and Sharon Percy exchanged wedding vows Saturday in a ceremony saddened by a sudden death in the Percy family.

While a 72-bell Carillon tower resounded across the University of Chicago campus, the 22-year-old bride was given in marriage by her father, Sen. Charles Percy (R-Ill.), during a 15-minute double ring ceremony in the Gothic Rockefeller Memorial Chapel. More than 1,200 guests attended.

Sharon, whose twin sister, Valerie, was stabbed to death by an unknown assailant in the Percy home in September, wasn't informed until shortly before the wedding that her step-grandmother, Mrs. Emily Guyer, had died of a heart attack just hours before.

Mrs. Guyer, a widow, fainted Friday in the Chicago Art Institute during presentation of a print by New Trier High School classmates and friends in Valerie's memory. Mrs. Guyer took

a turn for the worse during the night in the senator's suburban Kenilworth home and was rushed by ambulance to an Evanston hospital where she died.

Mrs. Guyer was the mother of the senator's second wife.

Chicagoans watched the ceremony on color television Saturday night.

Forty minutes before the ceremony, the chapel was searched after an anonymous telephone call to police that an explosive had been hidden in the building.

None was found.

Several hundred onlookers lined the sidewalk outside the chapel in the misty rain, some equipped with camp stools. There were cheers as some of the guests arrived.

Gov. and Mrs. George Romney of Michigan evoked a wave of cheering. Another echoed for New York's Mayor John Lindsay and his wife, and yet another when French actor Maurice Chevalier stepped jauntily from his limousine.

RAID AT HAIPHONG
SEATO Council Backs Bombing

WASHINGTON (AP) — The Southeast Asia Treaty Organization Foreign Ministers Council Thursday supported the U.S. refusal to end the bombing of North Vietnam unless there is also a scaling down of military action by the communist side in the Vietnam war.

A communique issued by the council, concluding its 12th annual meeting declared that "reciprocity is an essential element of any
(Continued on Back Page, Col. 1)

PACIFIC
STARS AND STRIPES

AN AUTHORIZED PUBLICATION OF THE ARMED FORCES IN THE FAR EAST

FIVE-STAR EDITION

10¢ DAILY
15¢ WITH
SUPPLEMENTS

Vol. 23, No. 111   **Saturday, April 22, 1967**

SAIGON (UPI) — Navy jet raiders in two waves Thursday flew through missiles, anti-aircraft fire and aerial mines to bomb only a little over a mile from the port city of Haiphong for the first time.

The strike, with the reported personal approval of President Johnson, knocked out both of the city's power plants and plunged the vital port into darkness.

The jets, from the Seventh Fleet carriers Kitty Hawk and Ticonderoga, slashed through the heaviest ground defenses the communists had to offer. But they hit the targets and returned without a loss.

Only one plane was damaged. It had nine holes in it from one of the flurry of Russian-built surface to air (SAM) missiles hurled at the attacking Navy jets.

Military headquarters in Saigon said the targets were located 1.1 miles northwest and 2.1 miles northeast of Haiphong.

A spokesman said all raids within 10 miles of Haiphong and Hanoi, the capital, must have White House approval.

It was assumed that President Johnson personally approved the strikes.

The first wave of jets swept off the decks of the two carriers shortly before noon.

Those from the Kitty Hawk swept in from the sea and up the Cau Cam River. They wheeled in on the thermal power plant known as Haiphong West.

Ten minutes later, the jets from the Ticonderoga moved in further to the east, and ham-
(Continued on Back Page, Col. 3)

126 Die in Cyprus Air Crash

CYPRIOT PRESIDENT MAKARIOS (LEFT) SURVEYS TWISTED WRECKAGE OF AIRLINER NEAR NICOSIA. (AP RADIOPHOTO)

Darwin Gains in Tennessee

NASHVILLE, Tenn. (AP) — In an atmosphere akin to a religious revival, the Tennessee Senate passed a bill Thursday to permit teaching Charles Darwin's theory of evolution — but not as fact.

State law since 1925 has prohibited public school teachers from telling students of Darwin's theory, but opponents of the law said it has been violated daily for 42 years.

The House voted last week for outright repeal of the controversial law, but the Senate deadlocked 16-16 on that bill Thursday and instead passed, 23-19,
(Continued on Back Page, Col. 2)

Carson Returns To 'Tonight' Show

NEW YORK (AP) — The National Broadcasting Co. and lawyers for Johnny Carson announced late Thursday that the entertainer will resume appearances on the "Tonight" show Monday. The announcement said all disputes have been satisfactorily resolved. Carson announced during the recent performers strike against the networks that he considered his contract broken because NBC used reruns of some of his old shows.

NICOSIA, Cyprus (AP) — Rescuers collected 126 burned, broken bodies Thursday on the slopes of a hillock where a chartered Swiss airliner crashed during a thunderstorm.

Four survivors were taken to a hospital where three remained on the danger list.

The four-engine turboprop Bristol Britannia airliner crashed near here as it attempted a night landing. There were re-
(Continued on Back Page, Col. 3)

Paula Mae Hogs Beauty Title

MURFREESBORO, Tenn. (AP) — With five pretty coeds to choose from, students at Middle Tennessee State University elected a pig as May Queen on a write-in vote.

Paula Mae Pigg, one month old, 15 pounds, and measuring 20-22-20, got 786 votes, to 112 for the nearest human challenger in Wednesday's election.

There was talk of a runoff, or a new election on the grounds that Paula Mae is not a student, but the other contestants withdrew because "we don't feel the student body should be taught a lesson at the candidates' expense.

"We were all treating it lightly, but after the pig got 700 votes, we felt it had gone too far."

Traditionally the May Queen reigns over the annual junior-senior prom.

A group of student leaders said they entered the pig in protest to student apathy toward the elections and prom.

Miss Kitten McCreary, second in the voting, said the five coeds withdrew because "we don't feel the student body should be taught a lesson at the candidates' expense.

WESTY CHARTS PATH TO VICTORY IN VIET

PACIFIC STARS AND STRIPES

AN AUTHORIZED PUBLICATION OF THE ARMED FORCES IN THE FAR EAST

FIVE-STAR EDITION

10¢ DAILY
15¢ WITH
SUPPLEMENTS

Vol. 23, No. 119   Sunday, April 30, 1967

WASHINGTON (AP)—Gen. William C. Westmoreland told Congress Friday that only "unrelenting — but discriminating — military, political and psychological pressure" can defeat the Communist foe in Vietnam.

The commanding general in Vietnam carried to House and Senate a vow of military determination in the field and a request for solid support at home. But Westmoreland's call for mili-

Text of General Westmoreland's Address to Congress, Page 4.

tary pressure was tempered by his use of the word "discriminating," one of his few departures from his speech text.

His pledges of determination, nationally televised, were applauded by members of a Congress which has been marked by angry debate recently over the course of the war—and over Westmoreland's personal mission to Washington.

Applause interrupted Westmoreland 19 times in the

(Continued on Back Page, Col. 1)

Criticism, Praise in Congress

WASHINGTON (AP)— Here are examples of reaction among members of Congress and others Friday to General William C. Westmoreland's address to a joint meeting of Congress on the war in Vietnam.

House Speaker John W. McCormack, D-Mass., said he is confident "the people of America will strongly support General Westmoreland and our fighting forces."

Sen. John G. Tower, R-Tex., said:

"The general has quite properly pointed out that the Communists continue to fight and believe they can win because they think America's domestic will is weak."

Rep. Gerald R. Ford of Michi-

(Continued on Back Page, Col. 2)

Clay Spurns Induction

HOUSTON, Tex. (AP) — Heavyweight champion Cassius Clay refused Army induction Friday and faced a possible five-year prison sentence and loss of his title.

Lt. Col. J. D. McKee, commandant of the Houston Induction Center, announced that Clay, who contends he spends 90 per cent of his time as a Black Muslim preacher, had refused to take the traditional step forward symbolizing entrance into the armed services.

U.S. Atty. Morton Susman said he would begin immediate criminal action, but estimated that legal procedures would take from 30 to 60 days even to get an indictment.

"Even then it may be two years before this can be fought out in the courts," Susman said. "Meanwhile, Clay, or Muhammad Ali if you wish, will be free to keep on fighting and preaching."

In New York, the influential State Athletic Commission an-

(Continued on Page 18, Col. 1)

GEN. WESTMORELAND SALUTES VICE PRESIDENT HUMPHREY AND HOUSE SPEAKER JOHN MCCORMACK.

AP Radiophoto

Goes Down With His Car

SAN FRANCISCO (AP) — Sitting proudly at the wheel of his new car Thursday, Roy E. Rosencutter turned on to what he assumed was a freeway near Polk Street.

It wasn't a freeway but was the Aquatic Park ramp and shortly Rosencutter's shiny car bump-bump-bumped down six stone steps into a lagoon. A bystander yelled for Rosencutter to get out of the car.

"This is my new car and if it goes down, I go with it," said the soggy Rosencutter. Police begged him to get away from the car. Finally, an hour later, he waded ashore.

Coppolino Guilty of Murder; Sentenced to Life in Prison

NAPLES, Fla. (UPI) — Dr. Carl A. Coppolino was found guilty Friday of second degree murder for the death of his first wife. The state charged him with giving her a fatal drug injection.

The all-male jury returned the verdict shortly after resuming deliberation Friday morning of the charge that the retired anesthesiologist killed his wife,

Carmela, with an overdose of an exotic drug.

Circuit Court Judge Lynn N. Silvertooth pronounced sentence immediately, ordering Coppolino to Raeford, Fla., prison "for the remainder of your natural life."

The verdict was objected to by the defense. Coppolino's Attorney F. Lee Bailey said "the set of facts did not warrant that verdict."

Coppolino himself hesitated when the decision was announced, then whispered something into Bailey's ear.

It was Coppolino's second trial on murder charges. The first time, Bailey won an acquittal, clearing the doctor of a charge of killing Ret. Army Lt. Col. William E. Farber, the husband

(Continued on Back Page, Col. 4)

BULLETIN

SAIGON (AP)—U.S. Air Force pilots fought six aerial duels with MIGs over North Vietnam Friday and reported shooting down two of them. The dogfights took place while Air Force F-105 Thunderchiefs bombed the Hanoi railroad car repair shops only 2½ miles from the center of the city.

N. Viet Hopes Die on Hill 881

KHE SANH, Vietnam (UPI)—North Vietnamese dreams of a second Dien Bien Phu ended Tuesday on Hill 881.

The 3rd Marines in a bloody week-long battle threw back the Communists attacking this mountain stronghold in the northwest corner of South Vietnam about seven miles from the Laotian border.

Marines said a total of 726 "well-disciplined" North Vietnamese troops were killed in the series of hill fights. 270 of them by body count.

(Military officials at headquarters in Saigon put the North Vietnamese casualty figure at 333.)

The Marine casualties were 369—96 of them killed—in the costliest battle since Operation Hastings last summer.

Marines said they encountered only light resistance, however, when they moved along half-mile-high ridgelines and took the hill early Tuesday.

Col. John Lanigae of London, **(Continued on Back Page, Col. 2)**

U.S. MARINES CHARGE UP HILL 881 TO BATTLE ENTRENCHED NORTH VIETNAMESE FORCES.   AP Radiophoto

PACIFIC
STAR AND STRIPES

AN AUTHORIZED PUBLICATION OF THE ARMED FORCES IN THE FAR EAST

FIVE-STAR EDITION

10¢ DAILY
15¢ WITH SUPPLEMENTS

昭和四十二年、日本の（ ）新聞（日 ）
（昭和四十二年 日本 第 ）

Vol. 23, No. 123   Thursday, May 4, 1967

Plan NATO Cut
U.S. TO PULL OUT 35,000 TROOPS

WASHINGTON (AP)—The United States will withdraw up to 35,000 troops and almost 100 airplanes from West Germany next year, saving an estimated $100 million spent abroad, under an agreement reached last week among this country, Great Britain, and West Germany.

The agreement, announced Tuesday, was reached after five months of negotiations on the crucial issue of keeping as many American troops in Germany as possible while cutting back on the drain of America's gold reserve.

According to the announcement Britain will withdraw about 5,000 soldiers and about 20 planes from West Germany.

President Johnson was deeply involved in the five-month-long negotiations, officials said.

The agreement was welcomed by Sen. Mike Mansfield, D-Mont., an advocate of substantial troop reductions in Europe, who described the pact as a "sound foreign policy decision — an initial step in the adjust- **(Continued on Back Page, Col. 3)**

$1.6 Mil. Heist From Jet Fails

CHICAGO (UPI)—A policeman who noticed a service truck "out of place" on a O'Hare International Airport runway Monday night arrested two men moments after they had stolen $1.6 million in negotiable bonds from the baggage compartment of an airliner.

The men were charged with stealing a Brinks, Inc., bag containing the negotiable bonds and $600,000 in nonnegotiable bonds from the baggage compartment of an American Airlines Boeing 707 jet while it was waiting in line to take off for New York City.

One of the men told police they had worked out the scheme in detail for six months.

But not only did their big job fail, they missed an additional $10 million in four other money bags on the plane, Brinks officials said.

Charles E. Perce, a plainclothes policeman who checks the cargo areas at O'Hare, said he spotted a service truck on an airplane taxiway leading over an overpass across an expressway. He said he at first thought they were going to steal a rental car.

"This one just seemed out of place," he said, so he followed **(Continued on Back Page, Col. 2)**

Senate Republicans Back LBJ on Viet

WASHINGTON (AP) — Senate Republicans pledged their "wholehearted support" Tuesday of President Johnson in his conduct of the Vietnam war.

The Senate minority leader, Everett M. Dirksen of Illinois, read reporters a statement he said represented a consensus of members in a closed session of the GOP Policy Committee, in which a staff report critical of Johnson's course was debated.

The staff report, issued Monday night, charged that the President had assumed enormous discretionary powers in the conduct of the war and that he sought congressional approval only after he had acted.

In the statement, which Dirksen said he personally drafted Tuesday morning before leaving Walter Reed Army Hospital, the Republicans said:

"Preserving wholly the right of full and fair inquiry and criticism, we reiterate wholehearted support of the commander in chief of the armed forces and reaffirm our position of standing foursquare behind him and our field, air and sea commanders in Southeast Asia, along with support of our superb fighting men in their fight to win over Communist aggression."

Dirksen had been in the hospital for treatment of infectious pneumonia.

Dirksen appeared to disagree in part with Sen. George D. Aik- **(Continued on Back Page, Col. 4)**

Love Finds a Way to U.S.

NEW YORK (UPI) — Sandra Hilder, who made headlines when she sneaked aboard the U.S. missile cruiser Long Beach in Sydney, Australia, in a vain attempt to reach California to see her boyfriend, arrived here Tuesday.

The 20-year-old Australian told newsmen that "someday" she and her boyfriend, seaman Bernard "Bud" Brewer, 23, would get married.

Brewer might wish to finish college when he leaves the service in September, she remarked.

The Australian governess flew in here from San Francisco. She is scheduled to make several TV appearances here and then will head for Las Vegas, for a reunion with Brewer, of Fort Lauderdale, Fla.

She said she wanted to marry Bud, but must wait for him to ask.

Why did such a beautiful young woman pick out an American over all those surfboard-riding men from down under?

"American men are more refined. They open doors for a girl when she gets into a car. Australian men think that sort of thing is sissy."
(Continued on Back Page, Col. 1)

Russ Clip U.S. Destroyer Again

WASHINGTON (AP) —The United States charged Thursday that a Soviet warship ran into a U.S. destroyer for the second time in two days. It called on Russia to "take prompt steps" to halt what it called harassment of U.S. naval vessels.

The Pentagon reported that an unidentified Soviet destroyer "turned into and toward" the U.S. Navy destroyer Walker despite six short horn blasts signaling danger. The incident, at 1:33 a.m. EDT, occurred in the Sea of Japan where the Walker was scraped by another Soviet vessel on Wednesday.

Wednesday's incident occurred about 275 miles due east of Vladivostok. Thursday's encounter occurred 210 miles southeast of Vladiovostok.

The Soviet ship, not identified by name, was described as a destroyer of the Krupnyv class. This type ship is equipped with 16 57mm antiaircraft guns, two surface-to-surface guided missile launchers and two trip-tube torpedo launchers. The 453-foot ship can travel at 34 knots.

The Pentagon said no Americans were hurt but did not preclude the possibility that Soviet crewmen may have been injured. A spokesman said merely that there was no knowledge of any Russian casualties.

Damage to the ships was described as light.

The State Department followed up with what a spokesman called a severe protest, demanding an end to the dangerous situation.

The Walker had just warned the Soviet ship "do not cross my bow," according to State Department information.

By early Thursday afternoon three protests had been made involving the two accidents and a fourth was in preparation.

The first, an oral protest was delivered early Wednesday aft- (Continued on Back Page, Col. 1)

Tot Cheats Icy Stream

SAN BERNARDINO, Calif. (AP) — For nine hours, a 2-year-old boy bobbed in an icy mountain stream Wednesday, clinging to a partly submerged car.

The child's father, called away from his job to search for his missing family, found the youngster clinging to the car. Inside, were the bodies of James Lawson's wife Patsy, 36, and daughter Susan, 5.

Lawson pulled his son, Gerald, from the water and drove him to St. Bernardine's Hospital. The boy was later reported in (Continued on Back Page, Col. 4)

PACIFIC STARS STRIPES

AN AUTHORIZED PUBLICATION OF THE U.S. ARMED FORCES IN THE FAR EAST

10¢ DAILY
15¢ WITH SUPPLEMENTS

Vol. 23, No. 132 **FIVE-STAR EDITION** 昭和34年1月22日 第三種郵便物認可第175号 (日刊)
(昭和34年4月21日第3種郵便物認可)

Saturday, May 13, 1967

VIET CONG SHELL 2 U.S. AIRFIELDS

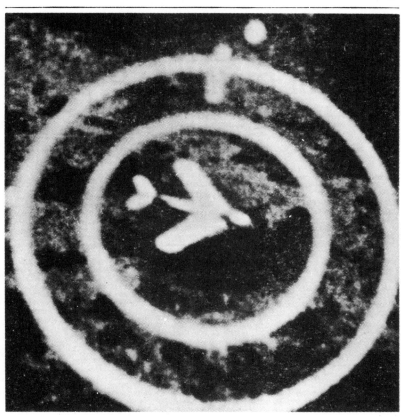

MIG in a Gunsight

While flying his F-105 Thunderchief on a strike mission over north Vietnam, Maj. Frederick G. Tolman saw this MIG-17 in his sight and shot the picture with his gun-mounted 16mm movie camera. (AP Radiophoto)

SAIGON (UPI)—Viet Cong guerrillas early Friday launched coordinated attacks on two U.S. airfields north of Saigon, military spokesmen said.

They hit the Bien Hoa airfield with heavy mortar, rocket and recoilless rifle attacks 16 miles north of the city and about an hour later struck at Phuoc Vinh 18 miles further north.

U.S. spokesmen said the attack on Bien Hoa, the sprawling air base where more than half of all U.S. and Vietnamese air strikes in South Vietnam are flown from, came at 1 a.m.

Guerrillas lobbed in about 125 rounds of 140mm rockets along with mortars and recoilless rifle fire.

They killed six American Air (Continued on Back Page, Col. 2)

Westy's Duties Expanded

SAIGON (AP)—U.S. Ambassador Ellsworth Bunker Thursday announced a sweeping change in the American pacification effort in South Vietnam by handing full control of the previously civilian programs to General William C. Westmoreland.

Speaking at a news conference, the newly arrived ambassador ended a controversy over whether civilians or soldiers should run the program, sometimes called "the other war". (Continued on Back Page, Col. 1)

Couple Sees Son Wounded on TV Film

LA GRANGE, Ga. (AP) — Mrs. A. Landon Morrow Sr. was watching a late news program on television and a film report on fighting in Vietnam caught her attention. Suddenly there was a familiar face in battle gear.

She looked, then shouted: "Come quick, Landon. Here's our son."

The camera had focused briefly on Spec. 4 Landon Morrow Jr., a radio operator, as the televison newsman described fighting in "Operation Manhattan."

As the La Grange couple listened and watched, the newsman described an explosion that had wounded a captain and a radio operator. Then there was a film close-up of a soldier lying on the ground.

"We knew then that was our son," said Mrs. Morrow. "We didn't see the explosion but the next time they put the camera on him he was lying on the ground. There were two or three working on him. We could tell he was wounded."

The next day the Morrows and their daughter-in-law re- (Continued on Back Page, Col. 3)

LBJ Wins on Draft

WASHINGTON (UPI) — The Senate voted Thursday to give President Johnson a four-year extension of his authority to draft men into the armed services.

The roll call vote was 70 to 2 with Sen. Wayne Morse, D-Ore., and Sen. Ernest A. Gruening, D-Alaska, voting against.

ALLIES SWEEP DMZ

MARINE COLUMN STRETCHES TO HORIZON AS THE LEATHERNECKS MARCH TOWARD DONG HA TO BOARD HELICOPTERS FOR THE DMZ.

AP Radiophoto

PACIFIC
STARS AND STRIPES

AN AUTHORIZED PUBLICATION OF THE ARMED FORCES IN THE FAR EAST

FIVE-STAR EDITION

昭和44年1月20日第三種郵便物認可 (日刊)
(昭和34年4月5日第2540号)

10¢ DAILY
15¢ WITH
SUPPLEMENTS

Vol. 23, No. 140   **Sunday, May 21, 1967**

U.N. Withdraws From Gaza Strip

By The Associated Press

The withdrawal of the U.N. emergency force from its front line positions in the Gaza Strip and the massive Egyptian buildup in the Sinai Peninsula brought the Middle East closer to war Friday night.

U.N. Secretary General U Thant told the General Assembly in New York Friday morning that he was bowing with grave misgivings to a United Arab Republic demand that the UNEF be withdrawn from the Gaza Strip and Egyptian territory.

Israeli Prime Minister Levi Eshkol, expressing his surprise in Tel Aviv, Israel at the hasty U.N. agreement to withdraw its 3,400-man force from Gaza, vowed, however, that Israel would take care of itself.

All-out mobilization had not been announced, but it was apparent that a number of Israeli reservists had been called up.

In London, it was reported that quiet warnings have reached Britain and other western powers that Israel will fight any Egyptian move blocking Israel's Gulf of Akaba outlet to the Red Sea.

(High sources also said the situation in and around the Gulf of Akaba at the apex of the Sinai Peninsula, is likely to become the focus of the developing Israeli-Egyptian confrontation. U.N. Security Council intervention was said to be probable.

At outposts along the Gaza Strip the U.N. flag came down at 4 p.m. Friday.

The event was marked by a simple ceremony at the U.N.
(Continued on Back Page, Col. 3)

By TOM DREILING
S&S Staff Correspondent

ONE MILE BELOW THE DMZ, Vietnam—U.S. Marines and South Vietnamese troops launched a massive assault on the DMZ Thursday.

It was the first time Allied forces had crossed into the buffer zone created when Vietnam was divided 13 years ago.

The three-pronged drive, by a multi-battalion force, is named Operation Hickory Nut. It is an attack against North Vietnamese "who have been violating the rules and using the DMZ as a sanctuary," a Marine commander said.

"They have been hitting our bases with rockets, mortars and artillery and then going back into the DMZ. We got sick of it, and we're going in to get them."

A Marine spokesman said at least two North Vietnamese regiments are being tracked down by the allied troops sweeping a 20-mile strip along the southern half of the zone.

U.S. aircraft hammered North Vietnamese artillery positions Thursday, destroying at least 10 guns able to fire into South Vietnam.

Seven of the gun sites were along the northern boundary of the DMZ.

At least 23 North Vietnamese guns have been knocked out near the DMZ since Tuesday, U.S. sources said.

North Vietnamese shore guns hit the Marine special landing force as the Leathernecks hit the beaches Thursday morning while more Marines were lifted
(Continued on Back Page, Col. 1)

U.S. and South Vietnamese troops hit the DMZ in a three-pronged attack. Marines landed by helicopter and landing craft on the south bank of the Ben Hai River (1) while another Marine battalion moved to the southern bank of the river north of Con Thien (2). Vietnamese troops moved to the Ben Hai bridge (3) and fanned out east and west.

'Defense Action' In DMZ

WASHINGTON (AP)—The United States said Friday the new U.S. military thrust into the Demilitarized Zone in Vietnam is a purely defensive measure against the buildup of North Vietnamese forces.

"It is not in any sense an invasion of North Vietnam," a State Department spokesman declared.

He also asserted that the United States is prepared to consider any possible solution for restoring the zone as a demilitarized barrier between North and South Vietnam under international supervision.

"Meanwhile," press officer Robert J. McCloskey said at a State Department news conference, "we have no choice but to take the necessary military measures to counteract the buildup by North Vietnam in the southern portion of the zone."

The zone is six miles wide, three miles being southern territory and three being North Vietnamese territory.

McCloskey refused to say that the current timing of the joint U.S.-South Vietnamese operation into the zone was aimed at frustrating an expected massive
(Continued on Back Page, Col. 1)

TV Robbery Is Fake, But Cops Real

DETROIT (UPI)—A crew of bogus bank robbers filming a television commercial ran into a crew of real-life cops Thursday in a Mack Sennett style mixup which could have ended in mayhem.

"I can't think of a better way to get killed," said a veteran police sergeant, surveying the sheepish crew of actors. Patrolman James Faytek said the TV boys looked like something "out of the 1920s."

"What the heck," said actor David McLaughlin, alias Willard Mack, a Capone-era tommy gunner in the television plot. "I almost got shot."

The commercial was being filmed outside a bank building and the unwanted extras, real cops in blue suits and genuine FBI men, arrived with sirens screaming and guns drawn after a passerby saw the old-fashioned bandits and telephoned police.

There stood McLaughlin, brandishing a submachine gun and dressed in a dark suit, black turtleneck sweater, sunglasses and a dark hat. Another actor sat at the wheel of a big black getaway car.

Five squad cars blocked off the streets. FBI men and police rushed the bank door.

"We're only acting," McLaughlin shouted, lowering his gun hastily, his holdup bungled the wrong way. He was supposed to ruin the robbery by lighting a cigarette, the prospective sponsor's product, instead of fleeing from the scene.

A film company, Photography Center, Inc., set up the holdup as a commercial to present to a prospective client. The film company wanted realism and asked Detroit Bank & Trust Co. if the filming could be held outside a bank before business hours.

Robert Langley, manager of the bank branch, said the film company promised to notify the police. Harry Kokyer, a partner in the film company, said he thought the bank had notified the cops.

TOLL ON FORRESTAL: 71 DEAD, 112 MISSING

PACIFIC STARS AND STRIPES

AN AUTHORIZED PUBLICATION OF THE ARMED FORCES IN THE FAR EAST

FIVE-STAR EDITION

昭和54年1月22日 ... 第175号（日刊）
（昭和54年4月21日第3 ... ）

10¢

Vol. 23, No. 212   Tuesday, Aug. 1, 1967

How Fire Started

S&S Vietnam Bureau

SAIGON—A freak chain of events apparently touched off Saturday's disastrous fire on the carrier Forrestal.

According to eyewitnesses, an A4 Skyhawk near the center of the flight deck started "hot" just before launch and shot a long tongue of flame toward 16 planes parked in a horseshoe on the aft deck.

The hot start apparently was caused by excess fuel in the jet's engine, which creates a burst of flame much like an overfilled cigarette lighter.

The flame ignited a Sidewinder missile under the wing of an F4 Phantom on the starboard side.

The missile streaked across the deck and blew up a 400-gallon belly tank on a parked Skyhawk. Aviation gas spilled from the tank, spreading the fire to other planes.

Capt. John K. Beling, the Forrestal's skipper, said Sunday "no human error was involved. This is one of those things that happen in a war."

Hot starts occur about once a week on carriers. The flame from the Skyhawk was described as three times as long as the burst from normal hot starts.

By DAVE PRESTON
S&S Staff Correspondent

SAIGON—The burned and battered carrier Forrestal sailed out of the Tonkin Gulf Sunday for Subic Bay in the Philippines with 71 of her crew known dead, 78 injured and 112 missing.

A search was still going on in the ripped and seared fantail compartments between flight and hangar decks, where exploding bombs and burning fuel from launch-ready jets Saturday trapped most of the missing. Officials said there was little hope of finding any survivors.

Anyone caught in the area, they said, would almost certainly have died in the fire or been asphyxiated.

Fires, fed by clothing and bedding in the two-deck berthing spaces, continued smouldering until Sunday. Holes were being cut through bulkheads and decks in an attempt to get

Related stories, pictures, pages 5, 6, 12 and 13.

into the area, but searchers were severely hampered by compartments flooded with water from fire hoses, debris and chlorine gas from water-soaked storage batteries.

The compartments were still so hot, steam fogged gas masks worn by the rescue parties.

Some of the missing will never be accounted for. Bombs blew

(Continued on Back Page, Col. 1)

Chaplain (Lt. Cmdr.) Geoffrey E. Gaughan conducts a memorial mass on the hangar deck of the carrier Forrestal for the men who were killed when fire and explosions hit the ship Saturday. (AP Radiophoto)

Predict 300 Dead In Quake

CARACAS, Venezuela (AP)—Officials predicted Sunday the death toll would reach 300 in the massive earthquake that struck Venezuela's capital region Saturday night. Fifty bodies were recovered by Sunday afternoon.

Raul Valera, governor of the federal district (Caracas and environs) told newsmen he expected the dead to number 300 by the time workers finished dragging bodies from collapsed buildings.

He spoke just before joining an emergency session of the cabinet called by President Raul Leoni. Earlier, Leoni declared three days of national mourning.

Authorities said five buildings in east Caracas toppled to the ground. A number of other buildings in the area suffered heavy damage in what was

(Continued on Back Page, Col. 5)

Troopers Leave Detroit

Compiled From AP and UPI

DETROIT — Federal paratroopers withdrew Sunday from Detroit's riot areas, leaving scaled-down National Guard patrols on duty.

Cyrus Vance, President Johnson's representative in Detroit, said the men of the 82nd and 101st Airborne divisions were

(Continued on Back Page, Col. 2)

Swordfish Gets the Point: Don't Mess With Tiny Subs

WOODS HOLE, Mass. (UPI)—In a true life Jules Verne adventure, an angry 200-pound swordfish attacked a 16-ton scientific submarine craft earlier this month and forced it to surface before its mission was completed.

The strange episode came to light this week when Vice President Hubert H. Humphrey visited the Woods Hole Oceanographic Institution and spent a night aboard the marine center's research ship, Atlantis II.

As related to Humphrey by a research specialist, Dr. Edward F. K. Zarudski, the incident occurred July 6 during a research dive in the Atlantic about 140 miles east of Charleston, S.C.

Zarudski and two operators of the capsule were lowered from the submarine, the Alvin, to a depth of 2,000 feet for a six-hour study of underwater phenomena.

After they had been down about an hour, the eight-foot swordfish swam into view, nosed about the craft, then began thrashing and bumping the capsule.

"We could feel him bouncing us around and feel him hitting us," Zadruski, a 51-year-old

(Continued on Back Page, Col. 3)

Boy's 24-Hour Terror in Cave-In

LENORE, W.Va. (AP) —A 15-year-old boy was pulled from an old well in relatively good spirits Saturday after being trapped 14 feet underground by a cave-in for nearly 24 hours.

Leonard Boyce, scratched, bruised and haggard looking, was rushed to a hospital at Williamson, about 15 miles from here near the West Virginia-Kentucky border.

Boyce was trapped by falling rock about 5:15 p.m. Friday and was freed at 5:07 p.m. Saturday.

A feverish rescue operation was hampered by other small cave-ins.

Earth-moving machines finally dug a deep trench alongside the old well and Boyce was pulled out feet first. The well is in an isolated mountain area about 70 miles southeast of Huntington.

The youth was stiff and blue from the cold, rescue workers said. But he was conscious when

(Continued on Back Page, Col. 2)

PACIFIC

STARS STRIPES

AN AUTHORIZED PUBLICATION OF THE U.S. ARMED FORCES IN THE FAR EAST

10¢

Vol. 23, No. 225 FIVE-STAR EDITION 昭和34年1月22日国鉄東局特別扱承認新聞紙第175号（日刊）（昭和34年4月21日第3種郵便物認可） Monday, Aug. 14, 1967

U.S. DISCLOSES LAOS BOMBING

SAIGON (UPI)—The U.S. Air Force revealed officially Sunday for the first time that American warplanes are bombing communist targets in Laos, Vietnam's neighbor to the west.

The U.S. fighter-bombers are conducting air raids "at the request of the Royal Laotian government," a spokesman for the Air Force in Saigon said Sunday.

The Air Force confirmed that American warplanes have been running "armed reconnaissance" missions over Laos, and have been for more than three years. "We are looking for targets and we bomb at the request of the Royal Laotian government," the spokesman said.

The spokesman was unable to list the exact targets, nor would he say how many American planes had been shot down over Laos.

It was reported the main target is the so-called "Ho Chi Minh Trail" that runs from North Vietnam through Laos into South Vietnam.

The trail is a supply route so elaborate, sources in Laos say that it includes a two-lane, all-weather, surfaced road and carries five-ton Czechoslovakian-made trucks loaded with war supplies.

When asked about the loss of U.S. aircraft over Laos, another spokesman for the U.S. Military Assistance Command in Vietnam (MACV) said tersely, "we don't report anything but

(Continued on Back Page, Col. 2)

Rescue workers extend their trench into the side of well where Leonard Boyce, 15, was trapped for 24 hours. The boy was pulled from the well late Saturday. (AP Radiophoto)

Insurance Bill Vetoed By LBJ

WASHINGTON (UPI)—President Johnson Saturday vetoed a government employe life insurance bill and warned Congress against raising federal pay scales more than he recommended.

Johnson used his veto message on a relatively minor bill to deliver advice to Congress about going beyond his budget recommendations on some programs.

He had recommended that the government share of life insurance programs for federal employes be raised by $13 million from its present level of $63 million. The bill passed by Congress would have increased the government contributions by $61 million during the first year.

Johnson said he was returning the bill without his signature because it would set "an unwise

(Continued on Back Page, Col. 3)

Winter in U.S.

NEW YORK (AP) — Record-shattering cold nipped a huge area Saturday. The mercury dropped to the freezing level in Pellston, Mich. Low marks for Aug. 12 were equaled or broken in 39 cities. Temperatures fell into the 30s in Pennsylvania, Michigan, Wisconsin and Minnesota.

300 Rescued as Ferry Runs Aground

ALERT BAY, B.C. (AP) — Nearly 300 persons, most of them American tourists, were rescued Friday from a Canadian ferry that ran aground 3½ miles from this Vancouver Island community.

Passengers, many of them in night clothes, scrambled into lifeboats when the Queen of Prince Rupert, $6.5-million flagship of the British Columbia government-owned fleet, ran up on a reef in Broughton Strait about 6:15 a.m.

A fleet of small boats from Alert Bay picked up the passengers and towed lifeboats to this town of 825 persons 180 miles northwest of Vancouver, B.C.

"I woke up with a start," said Dean Jennings, 42, of Sausalito, Calif., who was returning with his wife from a trip to Alaska.

"Bells were ringing all over the place. Suddenly a voice crackled over the speaker system: 'All hands on deck! All hands on deck!'

"I'd felt no bump and I didn't know what was happening. I thought maybe it was an exercise. About 20 minutes later the loudspeaker said, 'All passengers on deck, please. Immediately.'"

Efforts to salvage the 87 vehicles and baggage aboard got under way immediately.

The ferry was en route from Prince Rupert, on the northern British Columbia Coast to Kelsey Bay, about 40 miles south of here. The overnight trip is a popular tourist route from Alaska.

Bill Weston, operations manager for the ferry authority,

(Continued on Back Page, Col. 5)

ELECTRONIC 'WALL' TO SPAN VIETNAM

PACIFIC
STARS AND STRIPES

AN AUTHORIZED PUBLICATION OF THE ARMED FORCES IN THE FAR EAST

FIVE-STAR EDITION   10¢

Vol. 23, No. 251   Saturday, Sept. 9, 1967

Romney Charge Snowballs Into Campaign Issue

Compiled From AP and UPI

WASHINGTON—Michigan Gov. George Romney's charge that he had been "brainwashed" when he visited Vietnam in 1965 contains all the makings of a major issue in next year's presidential campaign.

The administration wasted no time in firing back at Romney, a leading but still unannounced Republican candidate for the presidency.

The controversy began earlier this week when Romney said in an interview he had been "brainwashed" during a 1965 tour of Vietnam. Romney said he had been given a thorough and distorted favorable impression of the U.S. effort in Vietnam.

Asked about the statement at a news conference late Wednesday, the governor said, "If you want to get into a discussion of who's been brainwashing whom I suggest you take a look at what the administration has been telling the American people. The information has not been accurate."

He quoted Defense Secretary (Continued on Page 5, Col. 3)

6 NASA Data Tapes Stolen

DALLAS (AP)—A $150 reward was offered Thursday for missing magnetic computer tapes containing $100,000 worth of data. Owners of the tapes said they were almost valueless to anyone else. Three of the tapes belong to the Swedish Government.

The disappearance of the six computer tapes, representing 3½ years of work, was reported Wednesday by George W. Crawford, a physics professor at (Continued on Back Page, Col. 3)

Extradition for Brown

RICHMOND, Va. (AP) — Virginia Gov. Mills E. Godwin Jr. signed an extradition order Thursday for the return of Black Power advocate H. Rap Brown to Maryland to face charges of inciting to riot and arson. Brown reportedly is in New York, where he is free on bail on a federal charge of transporting firearms across a state line while under indictment.

McNAMARA POINTS TO VIETNAM MAP DURING NEWS CONFERENCE

AP Radiophoto

Quake Wakes California

SAN FRANCISCO (AP) — A wake-up earthquake aroused sleepers in a 90-mile sector from San Francisco to Hollister at 5:39 a.m. Thursday. More than an hour later, a Nevada underground nuclear test deluded seismologists into thinking there was a second quake.

The real one caused no damage but gave thousands a decided jolt.

The measurement on the Richter scale—based on the amount of energy released—was 4.7.

The nuclear test shock at 6:45 a.m. measured 5.5.

WASHINGTON (AP)—Defense Secretary Robert S. McNamara Thursday ordered a barbed wire and electronic barrier laid across South Vietnam to cut the infiltration of North Vietnamese soldiers and supplies across the Demilitarized Zone.

Experts indicated it would be an early warning system rather than a solid barrier, although barbed wire and other obstacles might make the crossing tougher and possibly slow it down.

McNamara's first Pentagon news conference in two months also produced the defense secretary's opening shot of the 1968 presidential campaign.

In tones of irritation, McNamara said Gov. George Romney of Michigan "appears to be blind to the truth" in claiming the Johnson administration put out inaccurate information on the Vietnam war.

"I don't think Gov. Romney can recognize the truth (Continued on Back Page, Col. 1)

160,000 Ford Workers Walk Off Job

DETROIT (AP) — Some 160,000 United Auto Workers Union members walked off their jobs at Ford Motor Co. Thursday, launching a strike which some fear might last until Christmas.

As picket lines formed at plant gates in 25 states, assembly lines came to a halt and Ford's production of 1968 models slowed to a trickle.

Only in Canada, where Ford turns out a small number of Falcons and pickup trucks, did the company continue to operate. And even there, a parts

Photos on Page 12-13

shortage was expected to halt production in about two weeks.

Meanwhile, Ford's chief competitors—General Motors and

Chrysler—kept their assembly lines rolling. Workers stayed on the job even though the two companies refused to extend their labor contracts beyond their Wednesday midnight expiration.

In contrast to previous strikes where mass picketing was the rule and violence was commonplace, only token picket lines were reported at most Ford

plants and there was only one incident of minor shoving and shouting—at the Ford Parts Depot in the Detroit suburb of Redford Township.

The UAW permitted two Ford plants in Mount Clemens, Mich., to continue operating. The plants make paint and vinyl trim for GM's Ternstedt Division (Continued on Back Page, Col. 1)

MARCH ON PENTAGON

PACIFIC

STARS AND STRIPES

AN AUTHORIZED PUBLICATION OF THE ARMED FORCES IN THE FAR EAST

FIVE-STAR EDITION   10¢

Vol. 23, No. 295   Monday, Oct. 23, 1967

Mob Hurled Back By GIs, Marshals

WASHINGTON (AP)—Thousands of youthful antiwar demonstrators, some waving Viet Cong flags, tried to storm the Pentagon Saturday but were thrown back by soldiers and U.S. marshals.

At least one round of tear gas was fired during one melee in the driveway leading to the Pentagon mall.

The violence broke out after demonstrators marched on the U.S. military nerve center following a mass rally at the Lincoln Memorial where Dr. Benjamin Spock, baby spe-

A nationwide program of vigils, religious services and demonstrations begins in support of Americans in Vietnam. Page 24.

President Johnson signs legislation imposing sharp new penalties on those who demonstrate near the Capitol Building. Page 24.

Anti-Vietnam war protesters march in Europe and Asia. Page 5

cialist, author and outspoken war critic, charged President Johnson is "the enemy."

U.S. park police estimated the number of demonstrators that (Continued on Back Page, Col. 1)

U.S. MARSHALS AND SOLDIERS FORM SECURITY LINES AS DEMONSTRATORS SURGE TOWARD MALL ENTRANCE TO PENTAGON.   AP Radiophoto

Judge Jails Own Son

ST. PETERSBURG, Fla. (UPI) — Associate Municipal Court Judge George S. Saltsman sentenced his 19-year-old son to 10 days in city jail Friday for driving a motor vehicle while his driver's license was revoked.

John Saltsman began serving the sentence Friday night.

"I couldn't ask the other judges to do this, I had to do it myself and clear the matter up before John reports Nov. 5 for duty in the Navy," Judge Saltsman said.

Israeli Destroyer Sunk; Egyptian Missiles Blamed

TEL AVIV (AP) — The Israeli destroyer Eilat was sunk off the northern Sinai coast, 14 miles from Port Said Saturday night by Egyptian missiles, the Israeli army said.

It was believed hit by missiles from an Egyptian cruiser anchored in Port Said harbor, a spokesman said.

The Eilat was on patrol several miles off the desert coast when hit, the spokesman said.

"It sank at 10 p.m. and the crew abandoned ship," he said.

It was not known how many of the 250 crewmen survived. The spokesman said "tens" of survivors had been picked up by helicopters and rescue boats. The Beersheba military hospital was alerted to receive them, the spokesman said.

"The situation is very confused," he said. "We have no idea of casualties . . . but it

looks as though they may be heavy."

U.N. military observers have confirmed the sinking of an Israeli vessel in the Mediterranean and "have intervened to prevent further incidents," a U.N. spokesman said Saturday night in New York.

"This attack is the most serious escalation since the war," the Israeli spokesman said. (Continued on Back Page, Col. 2)

Scores

Details in Sports Section

Army	14
Rutgers	3
★ ★ ★	
William & Mary	27
Navy	16
★ ★ ★	
Southern Cal	23
Washington	6
★ ★ ★	
Oregon St.	22
Purdue	14
★ ★ ★	
UCLA	21
Stanford	16
★ ★ ★	
Colorado	21
Nebraska	16
★ ★ ★	
Tennessee	24
Alabama	13
★ ★ ★	
Georgia	56
VMI	6
★ ★ ★	
Houston	43
Miss. St.	6
★ ★ ★	
Wyoming	30
Wichita St.	7

THANKSGIVING:

Time Out for Turkey in Vietnam; A Counting of Blessings in U.S.

SAIGON (UPI)—Most of the half-million American troops in Vietnam enjoyed a traditional Thanksgiving Day turkey feast Thursday. But the band of weary soldiers who captured the summit of Hill 875 mostly gave thanks just to be alive.

The men who took the hill Thursday in the central highlands

also had a turkey dinner. It was airlifted in by helicopters and eaten in the abandoned ruins of a North Vietnamese command post.

It was their first hot meal in 12 days.

Col. James Johnson, commander of the 4th Bn., 503rd Airborne, 173rd Airborne Brigade, made a
(Continued on Back Page, Col. 3)

By United Press International

Most of the 200 million Americans observed Thanksgiving in traditional pursuits of pleasure—family get-togethers, turkey and trimmings, and watching parades and football games on television.

For the vast majority of Americans, it was a stay-at-home holiday.

It also was a day of prayers for

peace, for an end to the war in Vietnam, and for spoken and unspoken thoughts of gratitude for the bountiful blessings of most Americans.

The traffic toll mounted slowly, as it usually does on Thanksgiving, when the National Safety Council does not keep a tally of highway
(Continued on Back Page, Col. 4)

PACIFIC STAR AND STRIPES

AN AUTHORIZED PUBLICATION OF THE ARMED FORCES IN THE FAR EAST

FIVE-STAR EDITION

昭和34年1月26日 第三種郵便物認可第1758号 (日刊)
(昭和34年4月21日第3種 (郵便物認可))

10¢

Vol. 23, No. 328   Saturday, Nov. 25, 1967

Red Losses Climb

GIs Take Hill 875 After 5-Day Fight

SAIGON (AP)—Battle-weary U.S. paratroopers captured Hill 875 Thursday—Thanksgiving Day—after five days of bitter fighting. The victorious American commander claimed Allied forces had killed at least 2,500 to 3,000 enemy in the 21-day Dak To campaign.

Maj. Gen. William R. Peers, commander of the U.S. forces in the Dak To battle, said the

---
Related story, photo on Pages 6, 12
---

combined toll of North Vietnamese troops killed by U.S. and South Vietnamese forces was 1,250 by actual body count.

"And we probably killed at least 2,500 or 3,000, and maybe far more," Peers added. The U.S. Command in Saigon had given the 1,250 figure earlier Thursday.

The U.S. force launched its final assault on the last ridgeline held by the North Vietnamese at 11:30 a.m.

Pounded incessantly before-
(Continued on Back Page, Col. 1)

Weather Fouls U.S. Travelers

By The United Press International

Snow hampered holiday travel in many parts of the nation Wednesday and tornadoes raked the South.

Travel warnings were up in parts of New Mexico, Utah, Idaho, Arizona, Wyoming, Montana, North Dakota, Minnesota, Maine, Vermont and New Hampshire.

In northern New England, freezing rain atop a snow blanket several inches deep made highway travel difficult.

Tornadoes struck along the Georgia-Alabama line, near Anniston, Ala., Bremen, Ga., and Villa Rica, Ga. Two
(Continued on Back Page, Col. 1)

SHOUTING "WE WANT WAR," 15,000 TURKS MARCH IN ISTANBUL IN REACTION TO CRISIS OVER CYPRUS

(UPI Radiophoto)

An Arresting Head Pain

CHESAPEAKE, Va. (AP) — A headache for which Frederick O'Neil West III, 26, was treated last May has led to his conviction for statutory burglary.

Prosecution witnesses testified in court Wednesday that a doctor removed a bullet from West's head when he sought treatment for a headache.

During West's burglary trial, an FBI ballistics expert testified the bullet was fired from the gun of William Rustin, a restaurant owner, who said he shot at two men rifling his cash register on May 6.

Turkish Jets Streak Over Cyprus as Tension Mounts

Compiled From AP and UPI

NICOSIA, Cyprus — Overflights by Turkish jets, plus another killing, fed tension on Cyprus Thursday after a respite caused by diplomatic efforts to avert war over the island.

Turkish Cypriots in Nicosia hastily threw up barricades in the Turkish quarter of the divided city.

Three flights of Turkish air force jet fighters zoomed over Famagusta on the east coast

and Morphou on the northwest. It was widely believed that if Turkey invaded the troops would land at those two points to form a pincer movement on Nicosia.

Police reported another Greek Cypriot had been shot to death near a Turkish Cypriot village, Ambelikou.

He was the second Greek Cypriot killed in three days, bringing the current death roll to 24 Turkish Cypriots and four Greeks.

Two loud explosions shook the Greek sector within half an hour Thursday night.

The first was caused by a bomb planted outside the permanent Soviet trade showroom. The second went off outside a tailor's shop near the new British-owned Chartered Bank of the Middle East. Neither explosion caused casualties.

Earlier Thursday another bomb exploded by the garden
(Continued on Back Page, Col. 1)

Snake Bites Handler

MIAMI (AP)—Bill Haast, a professional snake handler who has survived 101 bites from poisonous snakes, was bitten Thursday by an Australian tiger snake as 50 tourists watched him milk the reptile for its venom. Haast was reported in critical condition at a Miami hospital.

FIVE STAR EDITION

PACIFIC STAR & STRIPES

10¢

昭和34年1月22日国鉄東局特別扱承認新聞・成第175号（日刊）

(昭和34年4月21日第3種郵便物認可)

Vol. 23, No. 333 — AN AUTHORIZED PUBLICATION OF THE U.S. ARMED FORCES IN THE FAR EAST — Thursday, Nov. 30, 1967

MCNAMARA IS SET TO QUIT PENTAGON

ROBERT S. MCNAMARA

Compiled From AP and UPI

WASHINGTON—The World Bank confirmed Tuesday night that Defense Secretary Robert S. McNamara had been nominated as its new president.

Pentagon sources had indicated there would be no formal announcement of McNamara's resignation until the directors of the 106-member bank voted his selection.

When McNamara would leave the Pentagon remained a question. It could be fairly soon or several months away.

The White House, still withholding confirmation or denial of the open secret, said Tuesday that McNamara's departure would mean no change in the conduct of the Vietnam war.

It denied there was any rift between McNamara and the President over bombing policy.

Some observers expressed concern that a major pre-election escalation of the war might be in the offing. Senate Democratic Leader Mike Mansfield felt that the shift in defense leadership would remove a powerful voice of military restraint from the President's inner circle of advisers.

"I hope his successor will be somewhere nearly as strong as he has been (and) will continue to exercise

Related Stories, Page 3

civilian control as he is mandated to do under the Constitution," Mansfield said.

There was a wall of silence at the White House and the Pentagon on a successor to McNamara, who has ruled the Defense Department with a firm hand for nearly seven years.

Some suggested Johnson might want to tap a Republican as defense secretary, with the 1968 presidential campaign ahead and the certainty that the war in Vietnam will be the most important issue.

Others speculated that Johnson might bring in a leading industrialist in the mold of the management-minded McNamara.

Still others felt Johnson might promote from within the top hierarchy of the Pentagon, drawing on the experience of seasoned McNamara subordinates.

Among those mentioned prominently as possibilities were:

—Charles B. (Tex) Thornton, board chairman of Litton Industries Inc. Thornton, of Los Angeles, has been a close friend of McNamara's at least as far back as World War II. They served in the Air Force together.

—Cyrus Vance, presidential trouble shooter in Cyprus and previously special Johnson representative in the Dominican Republic during the 1965 crisis there.

Vance worked with Johnson in the President's Senate years and was deputy secretary of defense until last summer. He has worked more closely with McNamara than possibly anybody else. He has an ailing back, a factor against his assuming the enormous work

(Continued on Back Page, Col. 1)

Peking Denied U.N. Seat

UNITED NATIONS (AP) — The U.N. General Assembly voted decisively Tuesday to keep Communist China out of the United Nations for another year.

The 122-nation Assembly defeated by a vote of 45-58 a resolution by Communist Albania and 11 other nations that would have given the Chinese seat to Peking and expelled Nationalist China from the world forum. There were 17 abstentions.

It marked the 18th year that the United States and its supporters have turned back efforts by Communist and nonaligned nations to bring the Chinese Reds into the U.N.

The action came after six days of debate which made clear that no major shift had taken place. The vote found the western allies split once more, with Britain and France supporting the seating of the Chinese Communists and the United States leading the fight against it.

The Soviet Union showed no great enthusiasm for the Albanian resolution although it gave its endorsement.

The China question first came up in 1950 after the Communists had seized the China mainland. From then until 1960, it was decided at each session to shelve the representation issue.

The issue has been put to a vote in the assembly since 1961. Peking came closest in 1965 when the balloting resulted in a 47-47 tie.

They're Not Junkmen

TURIN, Italy (UPI)—Judges are considering the prosecution's charges that three postal carriers regularly took advertising mail, postcards and other mail they judged "nonessential" and burned it in a suburban meadow.

Russ Drug, Search U.S., British Aides

MOSCOW (AP)—The top Army attaches of the U.S. and British embassies in Moscow were drugged, forcibly held down and searched in violation of diplomatic immunity, the two embassies have protested to the Soviet government.

The Soviet reply to the protests "was not considered satisfactory," an American spokesman said Tuesday.

Further protests are being considered in both Washington and London.

The two were British Brigadier C. A. Des N. Harper and American Col. William J. Spahr. Both head the Army attache offices attached to their embassies.

They were visiting the Soviet provincial capital of Kishinev near the Romanian border when the incident occurred Nov. 17.

Five or six men reportedly invaded the two officers' hotel room after they had gone to bed sick from apparently drugged wine. Holding the officers down, the men seized papers from their money belts and read them.

All papers were returned and the men left after about an hour. The officers suffered no lasting injuries, the U.S. spokesman said.

The incident was similar to several druggings and searches which Western embassies have charged occurred in the Soviet Union in recent years to military attaches.

The trip to Kishinev, capital of Soviet Moldavia, was made with the required Soviet permission, according to the U.S. Embassy and a British Foreign Office statement.

In Kishinev, a guide for the government tourist agency Intourist suggested Harper and Spahr visit an experimental wine-making farm. There the two sampled apparently drugged wine.

"On returning to their hotel room," the British statement said, "they both suffered a violent attack of vomiting and retired to their beds." Medical tests later indicated drugging.

About four hours later, the Soviet men invaded their room,

(Continued on Back Page, Col. 3)

Frantic Battle Saves U.S. Embassy

PACIFIC

STAR STRIPES

AN AUTHORIZED PUBLICATION OF THE ARMED FORCES IN THE FAR EAST

FIVE-STAR EDITION   (10¢)

Vol. 24, No. 32   Friday, Feb. 2, 1968

SAIGON (AP)—For the handful of Americans inside the glossy white U.S. Embassy, the fight that began at 2:54 a.m. Wednesday was one of survival.

The 19 Viet Cong commandos who blasted their way through the embassy's ornate concrete outside wall with explosive charges made it clear early that they intended to stay until they were killed, and to take as many Americans with them as they could.

For the young soldiers of the 716th Military Police Bn., crawling along the exposed gutters and sidewalks toward the besieged embassy, the mission was to clean out the enemy before he could get inside the building.

The Viet Cong planned the embassy attack well.

They dressed some of their commandos in the black pajamas of the Vietnamese peasant, others in the white shirts of the Saigon white collar worker. All carried perfectly forged curfew passes.

When the attack began, those in white shirts fastened the top button as a mark of identification. Those in peasant garb pulled red armbands up their sleeves.

At the designated time, enemy mortars and rockets began crashing down on the capital.

The Communist commandos sprinted down the wide treelined boulevard, dodging

---
Photos on Pages 12, 13
---

from trunk to trunk. The Vietnamese guards outside the embassy were crouched down to avoid the incoming shells. The Viet Cong laid the charge in an instant. The loud explosion blew in the northern corner of the embassy outer wall and they were inside.

The first shell fired against Saigon sent window glass spraying over the bed of

(Continued on Back Page, Col. 1)

Total for 54 Hours

5,000 REDS DIE IN RAIDS

UPI Radiophoto

AMERICAN MP'S LEAD A VIET CONG AWAY FROM THE U.S. EMBASSY DURING WEDNESDAY'S ATTACK IN SAIGON.

SAIGON (AP)—Nearly 5,000 Communists have been killed in 54 hours of savage fighting that has swept across South Vietnam, the U.S. Military Command said Thursday.

The soaring casualty toll was announced as sharp firefights erupted again Thursday in outlying sections of Saigon and heavy action was reported in other areas of the country.

Command spokesmen said 4,959 enemy were killed in action during the period from 6 p.m. Monday to midnight Wednesday. Another 1,862 persons were seized as Viet Cong suspects.

U.S. casualties for the period were listed at 232 killed and 929 wounded. South Vietnamese government casualties were 300 killed and 747 wounded, spokesmen said. Other Allied casualties were put at three killed and 22 wounded.

The bloodiest general fighting of the war broke out after the enemy launched a series of devastating lunar new year (Tet) attacks on South Vietnam's major cities and on key Allied air-

(Continued on Back Page, Col. 1)

80,000 Stage Anti-Red Rally in Seoul

By SPEC. 4 CRAIG GARNER
S&S Korea Bureau

SEOUL — Thousands of angry Korean students and citizens burned an effigy of North Korean Premier Kim Il Sung in City Hall Plaza and loudly denounced the hijacking of the Pueblo and the Communist attempt to assassinate ROK President Chung Hee Park.

The 10-foot image was splashed with gasoline and set ablaze after 80,000 persons, mostly industrial workers and black-clad middle and high school students, crowded Seoul Stadium to hear Mayor Kim Hyun Ok and other speakers assail the ship seizure and the assassination attempt that ended with most of the would-be killers dead.

Other exhorted the crowd in frigid Seoul Stadium to prepare both the South Korean populace and military to repulse further attacks that might include an all-out North Korean invasion.

They demanded that the four remaining infiltrators of the 31 discovered near Park's residence at Blue House Jan. 21 be tracked down and killed.

Three ROK Army veterans of Vietnam slashed their fingertips and scrawled in blood on banners: "Kill Kim Il Sung" and

(Continued on Back Page, Col.

"Fight for Reunification."

Hundreds of colored banners called for the return of the Pueblo and her crew, the defection of North Koreans, the death of the remaining infiltrators and for citizens to steel themselves for a second invasion and another war.

The Seoul rally marked the fifth day of demonstrations all over the republic. It fitted the

At Glance

PACIFIC STAR STRIPES

★★ ★★★ EDITION

昭和34年1月22日第三種郵便物認可毎週水曜日発行第1253号（日刊）

（昭和34年4月21日第3種郵便物認可）

10¢

Vol. 24, No. 37　　AN AUTHORIZED PUBLICATION OF THE U.S. ARMED FORCES IN THE FAR EAST　　**Wednesday, Feb. 7, 1968**

REDS OPEN UP ON KHE SANH

Tourist Tax Bid By LBJ

WASHINGTON (UPI) —The Johnson administration asked Congress Monday to impose a tourist tax on Americans traveling overseas. A tax of 15 to 30 per cent would be imposed on all spending in excess of $7 a day outside the western hemisphere.

Tourists would have to pay at least a part of the tax even before they leave. It was part of a package of proposals unveiled by the administration to reduce the $3.6 billion balance of payments deficit.

The American tourist would be required to estimate in advance—and pay—the amount of tax he will owe for a trip abroad. The tax plan would run through this year's and next year's tourist seasons, expiring Oct. 1, 1969.

Treasury Secretary Henry H. Fowler outlined to the House Ways and Means Committee a package of travel taxes to cut into the $2 billion President Johnson has estimated is the difference between the amount American tourists spend overseas and foreigners spend in this country.

Fowler said American tourists would have to report the amount of funds they were taking with them. When they returned home, they would be required to make a statement on how much they have left and give this information to customs officials.

A formal tax return would be required within 60 days after return and travelers would be required to pay any new tax to the Internal Revenue Service.

Fowler described the balance- **(Continued on Back Page, Col. 3)**

Marines supported by tanks battle in the streets of Hue, Vietnam, for control of the southern approach to the bridge across the Perfume River. **(AP Radiophoto)**

SAIGON (AP)—Communist forces pushed their seven-day offensive Monday with heavy artillery and ground attacks on the U.S. Marine bastion at Khe Sanh. U.S. headquarters disclosed it had moved 3,500 crack Army paratroopers to the critical northern sector "to be prepared for any contingency."

Some of the 3,500 paratroopers, a brigade from the U.S. 101st Airborne Div., are currently on an operation against Communist forces in the northern sector.

The new fighting at Khe Sanh came as the week-long Communist offensive on South Vietnamese cities continued in many areas, including Saigon and the old imperial capital of Hue far to the north.

The ground attack at Khe Sanh by an estimated 200 to 300 North Vietnamese troops armed with Bangalor torpedoes, explosive charges and bazooka-type rockets was directed at a company of Marines defending Hill 861A.

The hill is a bald patch of scarred earth that dominates the combat base's northwestern approaches 3 miles away.

Associated Press correspondent John T. Wheeler reported from Khe Sanh that the Marines crushed the attack with the help of artillery and jet strikes that sent the Communist assault waves reeling back.

Six North Vietnamese bodies were found inside the company's perimeter and about 150 **(Continued on Back Page, Col. 1)**

U.S. Balks at Apology Over Pueblo

WASHINGTON (AP) — The United States appeared to be balking Monday at demands by North Korea that an apology be made in advance as the price for release of the 82 surviving crew members of the U.S. Navy intelligence ship Pueblo.

At the same time, the State Department cautioned against any premature hopes of the U.S.-North Korean negotiators in Panmunjom being on the verge of a settlement leading to speedy release of some or all of the American crew.

The fact that talks were continuing was the only thing that could be considered progress, a spokesman said. Earlier, Assistant Secretary of State William P. Bundy deflated optimistic reports from Seoul that some agreement had been reached in principle for the release of the Pueblo crew.

Bundy, in charge of East Asian affairs, said he had no confirmation of the reports of a settlement, that he did not know the basis for them and that he could not report any progress at this time.

Press officer Robert J. McCloskey, at his midday news conference, recalled that U.S. Ambassador Arthur J. Goldberg had told the U.N. Security Council Jan. 26 that it was "incontrovertible" that the Pueblo when first approached "was **(Continued on Back Page, Col. 5)**

Girl's 'Two Bits' Put in Smog Fight

PORTLAND, Ore. (AP)—Amy Steinback, 9, was so concerned about smog in Portland that she sent her 25 cents allowance to Gov. Tom McCall to help fight air pollution.

The third-grader wrote, "I am . . . very sorry that the air was ever dirty. Last night it was so thick you couldn't see the street light. The paper said that ours is thicker than New York. Here is 25 cents to help you."

3 U.S. Pilots Released by Hanoi

LT. (JG) DAVID MATHENY

CAPT. JOHN BLACK

VIENTIANE, Laos (UPI) — Three American pilots were released by North Vietnam Friday after about six months in captivity.

They arrived here Friday night aboard an International Control Commission aircraft and almost immediately boarded a U.S. military DC3 to fly to an airbase at Udorn, Thailand.

(In Washington the Pentagon said the men had arrived at the Udorn Royal Thai Air Force Base and were undergoing physical examinations, AP reported.)

Maj. Norris M. Overly, senior among the three officers, speaking for the group, said, "Physically, after boarding a U.S. plane I am a little weary but mentally I feel totally unreal. I have the feeling I'm on the outside looking in at myself in a mirror."

Overly, 39 of Wheeling, W.Va., Capt. John David Black, 30, Johnson City, Tenn., and Lt. (jg) David T. Matheny, 24, of South Bend, Ind., touched down at 10:25

(Continued on Back Page, Col. 2)

MAJ. NORRIS OVERLY

PACIFIC STARS AND STRIPES

AN AUTHORIZED PUBLICATION OF THE ARMED FORCES IN THE FAR EAST

★★★★★ EDITION

10¢

昭和34年1月22日国鉄第三種郵便物認可 第1755号 (日刊)
(昭和34年4月1日付 乙第一種郵便物認可)

Vol. 24, No. 47   Sunday, Feb. 18, 1968

Trowbridge Quits

LBJ Raps Move To Oust Westy

WASHINGTON (AP)—President Johnson announced Friday the resignation of Alexander B. Trowbridge as secretary of commerce and named as his successor—C. R. Smith, chairman of the board of American Airlines.

This was the kick-off for a news conference ranging over major matters of the moment.

For one thing, Johnson said that General William C. Westmoreland has his complete con-

Related Story, Page 3

fidence as commander in Vietnam and said there had been something of a conspiracy among other countries to undermine him.

"I do think it is in the nation's interest and your inter-

(Continued on Back Page, Col. 1)

---

10 Killed In Taipei Jet Crash

TAIPEI (AP) — A Civil Air Transport jet from Hong Kong with 63 persons aboard crashed near Taipei Friday night, killing 10 as it tried to make an emergency landing in bad weather. CAT said 40 others were known to have survived.

The Boeing 727 with 52 passengers and a crew of 11 crashed, broke apart and burst into flames.

CAT said it was not known whether the fatalities included two reported killed on the ground. Police reported two Chinese were killed on the ground, one when the plane hit and leveled his home and the other was walking on a highway.

The plane crashed about 9 p.m. local time Friday.

A passenger manifest listed 39 Chinese, 13 aliens.

Muddying the Waters

CHARLESTON, W.Va. (AP)—Engineers preparing to build a flood control dam in the West Virginia hamlet of Pullman may have trouble finding the spot. The state contract describes the location this way: The north fork of the left fork of Slab Creek, which flows into the south fork of the Hughes River.

Soviet Bear Off Greenland

The Pentagon Friday identified this plane as a Soviet Bear long-range bomber and said it was the type spotted 70 miles off the North American coastline last week. American jets intercepted two of the Russian planes. Story, page 24.

(AP Radiophoto)

TOKYO (S&S) — We're sorry, No *Pacific Stars and Stripes* was printed Friday because, for the first time in our 23-year history, we were snowed under and frozen out.

Happened this way: The worst snowfall to hit Tokyo in 17 years closed out incoming aircraft and heaped ice and snow on the runways at Tachikawa AB and Yokota AB where *Stars and Stripes* is flown out after being printed in Tokyo.

Nothing, including almost 15 tons of newspapers, got out Thursday night. And a plane that would have flown the papers from Tachikawa Friday was stuck in Taipei because the storm shut out flights to Tokyo.

We had to make a hard decision. No paper Friday.

We were back in business Saturday with all the news — including the news you, our readers and game subscribers, have missed.

Senate Probers Bare Secret Message on Tonkin Incident

P A C I F I C

STARS AND STRIPES

AN AUTHORIZED PUBLICATION OF THE ARMED FORCES IN THE FAR EAST

★★★★★ EDITION 10¢

昭和44年1月22日国鉄中号第2字3号承認第175号（日刊）
（昭和34年4月21日第3種郵便物認可）

Vol. 24, No. 53   Saturday, Feb. 24, 1968

WASHINGTON (UPI)—The Senate Foreign Relations Committee said Thursday it has a secret U.S. Navy message supporting Sen. Wayne Morse's contention that the American destroyers involved in the 1964 Gulf of Tonkin incident provoked an enemy attack.

Morse told the Senate Wednesday that t h e destroyer Maddox was "a spy ship" that incited a North Vietnamese attack on it and a sister destroyer, the Turner Joy, Aug. 4, 1964. He disputed Defense Secretary Robert S. McNamara's statement that the ships were on a routine, nonhostile patrol.

A spokesman for the committee said its staff report includes a classified Navy cable suggesting that the destroyers were trying electronically to lure Communist naval vessels away from a South Vietnamese bombardment mission in the gulf.

The committee, headed by Sen. J. William Fulbright, D-Ark., is investigating circumstances surrounding the Tonkin incident, which prompted President Johnson to request and receive overwhelming congressional approval

(Continued Back Page, Col. 1)

Surgery Again for Lurleen

MONTGOMERY, Ala. (AP)—Gov. Lurleen Wallace, fighting perhaps against a third outbreak of cancer, was stricken early Thursday and taken to a hospital for emergency surgery.

An aide said the 41-year-old governor, who had undergone two previous cancer operations in two years, was suffering from "an intestinal obstruction."

The latest surgery removed a tumor.

Lt. Gov. Albert Brewer gave that report about four hours after Mrs. Wallace entered surgery at Montgomery. He said members of the family had told him that a pelvic tumor had been removed and that Mrs. Wallace was doing well.

The decision to send Mrs. Wallace to surgery again came after seven hours of tests and diagnostic examinations at St. Margaret's Hospital. She was taken to the hospital in an ambulance at 5:30 a. m.

Her husband, former Gov. George Wallace, canceled a speech at Cape Kennedy, Fla., and remained at her bedside. Wallace, a third party candidate for president, was to have outlined his space program in the speech.

Whether there was any direct relation between the intestinal ailment and the governor's battle against cancer was not divulged. She has had malignant

(Continued on Back Page. Col. 5)

Old Glory Keeps Flying High off Hue

The American flag flutters from the mast of a U.S. Navy landing craft in the Perfume River. In the background, fire and smoke pour up from a burning boat and from an embattled sector of the Hue Citadel. Related stories on Pages 6 and 24.

(AP Radiophoto)

Coin Legend All Wet?

HAGERSTOWN, Md. (AP) — The Hagerstown Herald decided to test the legend of Washington's tossing a silver dollar across the Potomac.

Two young pitchers — Tom Elgin and Chris Raemer — were staked to $1.50 worth of Kennedy half dollars each and taken to the Potomac River at Williamsport, Md.

Elgin, who has just been signed by the Washington Senators, and Raemer, a star high school pitcher, made the attempts at a point where the Potomac is 600 feet wide.

That's narrower than the Rappahannock at Fredericksburg, Va., where Washington is supposed to have performed the feat as a boy.

Both pitchers succeeded in lofting the coins about 450 feet — but no farther.

A New Kind Of Stamp Act

CRESTWOOD, Mo. (AP) — Loren Greason dropped a quarter into a stamp machine Wednesday and the machine kicked out 632 25-cent stamps worth $158.

"Stamps just kept coming out," said Greason. "It didn't seem like it would ever stop. I just remember a string of green."

He said he was so excited he didn't remember whose picture was on the stamps. A postal clerk who put them back in the machine said it looked like Paul Revere.

LBJ Drafts 10-Year Program For 26 Million New Homes

AUSTIN, Tex. (AP) — President Johnson asked Congress Thursday to "set a far-reaching goal" to build 26 million new homes and apartments during the next 10 years.

This was the dramatic centerpiece of Johnson's longest special message to Congress this year, labeled "The Crisis of the Cities."

Johnson said the housing and urban development act he seeks would, among other things, re-

place six million "shameful substandard units of misery where more than 20 million Americans still live."

In the first five years of the program, Johnson said he wants $2.34 billion of contracting authority to build or rehabilitate nearly 2.5 million housing units.

Some other key points in the cities program were proposals to:

—Authorize adjustment of FHA interest rate ceilings "to

reflect the economic realities of the financial markets." Similar to a recent administration call for flexible VA home loan interest the upshot would be to raise the FHA rates in this period of tight money.

—Establish a cooperative federal-state industry program to reinsure property insurance policies in high-risk city areas—notably those that might be targets of urban rioting—by char-

(Continued Back Page, Col. 3)

Certain Reds Struck First In Tonkin, McNamara Says

PACIFIC

STARS STRIPES

AN AUTHORIZED PUBLICATION OF THE
U.S. ARMED FORCES IN THE FAR EAST

10¢

Vol. 24, No. 55 ★★★★★ EDITION 米国防総省 1月22日印刷★ 新聞協会月刊 米国防総省... (日刊)
(昭和24年4月20日第 3 種 郵便...)

Monday, Feb. 26, 1968

By WALTER R. MEARS and ROBERT T. GRAY

WASHINGTON (AP) —On a murky, fateful night in the Gulf of Tonkin, the commander of the destroyer Maddox cabled his superiors that "freak weather and an over-eager sonar man" could have contributed to reports that American vessels had just been attacked by North Vietnamese torpedo boats.

But Defense Secretary Robert S. McNamara said in testimony made public Saturday he issued orders which withheld retaliatory American air raids "until we were damned sure the attack had taken place."

McNamara said Capt. John J. Herrick, who sent the cable on Aug. 4, 1964, swiftly resolved his

(Continued on Page 5, Col. 1)

Allies Mopping Up in Hue

MARINES USE A STONE WALL FOR COVER DURING THE BATTLE FOR CONTROL OF HUE.

UPI Radiophoto

HUE, Vietnam (AP) — Allied forces slugged away at remaining pockets of resistance in the Hue citadel late Saturday, while other units moved outside the city to cut off Communist approach routes.

South Vietnamese troops took over the old imperial palace grounds in the citadel early in the day. Commanders termed the remaining action in the citadel a process of "mopping up."

In one of the sweeps outside the city, Associated Press Correspondent George McArthur reported that a battalion of U.S.

(Continued Back Page, Col. 1)

Thant Convinced Peace Talks Would Follow Bombing Halt

UNITED NATIONS (UPI) — Secretary General U Thant said Saturday he was "more than ever" convinced that meaningful peace talks would begin a few days after an unconditional end of U.S. bombing of North Vietnam.

He said he was assured by Nguyen Hoa, Hanoi's consul general in New Delhi, that North Vietnam "would hold talks with

Washington on all relevant matters at an appropriate time after the unconditional cessation of bombing and of all other acts of war" against it.

Thant said Mai Van Bo gave him further official assurance in Paris of the North Vietnam government's willingness to hold talks under such conditions. He said, "The United States could bring up any matter for discus-

sion in the same way as the Democratic Republic of Vietnam (North Vietnam) could bring up any matter."

Thant gave no information of the U.S. views expressed during his private conversations with President Johnson and Secretary of State Dean Rusk at Washington except to say that the President emphasized his "San

(Continued Back Page, Col. 2)

Rocky: I'll Run If Drafted

DETROIT (AP) — Gov. Nelson A. Rockefeller of New York said Saturday that he would run for President if drafted by the Republican national convention.

Aides of the New Yorker reported it was the first time he had said flatly he would run if drafted and that previously he had said only "I'd face it" if a convention draft came.

Rockefeller reiterated, however, he has no desire to be President and does not anticipate being drafted.

He was in Detroit to plump for presidential campaign funds for Michigan's Gov. George Romney, the New Yorker's avowed favorite over former Vice President Richard M. Nixon.

Expressing confidence Romney would be the convention choice, Rockefeller told a news conference, however, that if Nixon were nominated he would

(Continued Back Page, Col. 3)

Police Dog Objects

PHILADELPHIA (AP) — A policeman — Charles Stewart — limped into a hospital after being bitten by a police dog named "Wolf." It seems he had committed a cardinal sin that no dog will let a man get away with, even if it's a policeman. Stewart had accidentally stepped on Wolf's tail.

PACIFIC STARS AND STRIPES

AN AUTHORIZED PUBLICATION OF THE ARMED FORCES IN THE FAR EAST

★★★★★ EDITION

10¢

昭和34年1月22日国鉄事務特別第2種新聞物に承認5号（日刊）
(昭和34年4月21日第3種郵便物認可)

Vol. 24, No. 61   Sunday, March 3, 1968

Attack in Fog

KHE SANH RAID FAILS

SAIGON (AP) —

Charging through a natural camouflage of predawn fog, more than 500 North Vietnamese infantrymen drove to the barbed-wire ring around the U.S. fortress at Khe Sanh Friday.

South Vietnamese Rangers and giant Air Force B52 bombers crushed the attack, the heaviest mounted yet against the 500 Rangers and 5,000 U.S. Marine defenders.

Associated Press correspondent Peter Arnett reported from Khe Sanh that the eight-engine B52 Stratofortresses, flying in direct support of infantrymen at Khe Sanh for the first time in more than 1,000 sorties, rained tons of explosives only 750 yards in front of the Rangers' lines.

Arnett said that the North Vietnamese troops lost 70 dead. Casualties among the Allied defenders in the ground attack and an earlier heavy shelling of the fortress were reported as "very light."

The attack was launched on the eastern perimeter of the two-square-mile base held by (Continued Back Page, Col. 1)

With President Johnson looking on and Mrs. Clifford holding the Bible, Clark Clifford takes the oath of office as secretary of defense from Chief Justice Earl Warren in ceremony in the White House East Room Friday.   (AP Radiophoto)

Clifford Takes Oath

WASHINGTON (UPI)—President Johnson welcomed Clark M. Clifford to the cabinet as secretary of defense Friday with a renewed pledge that control of American military might would "firmly and forever" reside in civilian hands.

Clifford took the oath of office in a ceremony in the White House East Room. The oath was administered by Chief Justice Earl Warren.

Before Clifford took the oath Johnson praised the new cabinet officer's role in helping develop a unified Defense Department.

Shortly after World War II as (Continued on Back Page, Col. 4)

Amen

FT. LEWIS, Wash. (UPI)—As Brig. Gen. Robert L. Ashworth was presenting officers diplomas for a course in work simplification, he asked Maj. Walter R. Laubscher, a chaplain, "Does this mean you've found a short-cut to heaven?"

"No sir," replied Laubscher, "just shorter prayers."

Hundreds Injured in Rome As Students Battle Police

ROME (AP) — Downtown Rome was paralyzed Friday by rioting Rome University students who battled thousands of helmeted policemen.

The police used clubs and tear gas.

About 150 police and scores of passers-by were hurt. More than 150 students were arrested.

Midcity bus and taxi service halted. Shopkeepers shuttered their stores. Passers-by and school children fled as the rioting spread.

Students screaming "Revolution! Revolution!" bombarded police with stones ripped up from the streets. They overturned and set fire to police cars and buses. Ambulances with sirens screaming raced through the streets.

It was the most violent clash in the city since students began occupying university buildings three weeks ago in a campaign for more say in school administration and more modern teaching methods.

A parade of 3,000 students formed in Piazza di Spagna and marched to the School of Archi-

tecture to fight with police guarding the building.

Groups of shouting students surrounded a policeman, disarmed him and set fire to two empty police trucks, a jeep, a police car and a fireman's car.

The rioting came a day after police, summoned by Giovanni D'Avack, university rector, moved onto the main campus

and dragged hundreds of students from buildings they had been occupying since early February.

Demonstrations originally began as part of a national student move to force a series of reforms. But the movement quickly took on a political tone. Many of the demonstrators were (Continued Back Page, Col. 2)

$150-Million Mistake Keeps Bouncing Along

RICHMOND, Va. (AP)—The Fidelity Bankers Life Insurance Co. in Richmond as a promotional gimmick mailed out $150 million in make-believe checks to insurance brokers last year.

By design, the checks—each for $15,485—looked real. Far too real, in fact. And to complicate matters, Fidelity bankers forgot one detail—it forgot to mark them non-negotiable. All 10,000 of them.

So far, a score or so have turned up at banks around the

nation. Company officials' faces now are the color of the red banknote paper on which the checks were printed. They admit a couple have even cleared Richmond banks and gone as far as regional Federal Reserve clearing houses.

The checks were mailed out to emphasize to insurance brokers how they could increase their commissions by selling the new Fidelity Bankers policy.

The checks, all numbered (Continued Back Page, Col. 3)

Blizzard Paralyzes Northeast

Compiled From AP and UPI

Heavy wet snow, riding on winds up to 45 miles an hour, swept across New England Friday with the total fall in some sections reported at 15 inches.

In New York City heavy snow accompanied by high winds snapped power lines in three of the city's boroughs, blacking out numerous residential areas and playing havoc with the fire department alarm system.

Police said the snow had particularly affected fire alarm lines in Brooklyn, Queens and Staten Island.

The sanitation department had 1,500 men spreading salt and said that if the snow continued (Continued on Back Page, Col. 5)

Topless Triple Exposure

HANFORD, Calif. (UPI)—Two women, aged 22 and 21, were charged with indecent exposure in the first raid on a topless nightclub in Kings County. The arrests came after five county investigators gathered evidence by watching the show—three times.

LBJ WON'T RUN
Halts Bombing North of DMZ

PACIFIC
STARS AND STRIPES

AN AUTHORIZED PUBLICATION OF
U.S. ARMED FORCES IN THE FAR EAST
昭和34年1月22日国鉄東局特別扱承認新聞紙第175号（日刊）
（昭和34年4月21日第3種郵便物認可）

10¢

Vol. 24, No. 91　　★★★★★ EDITION　　Tuesday, April 2, 1968

AP Radiophoto

CAPT. ROBB KISSES WIFE LYNDA GOODBY AT NORTON AFB, CALIF.

A Parting Kiss for Lynda Bird, And Robb Is Off to Viet War

NORTON AFB, Calif. (AP)— President Johnson's eldest daughter, Lynda Bird, stood composed Saturday as her husband, Marine Capt. Charles S. Robb, departed for 13 months' duty in Vietnam.

After embracing her husband, Lynda Bird told a wife of another departing Marine, "I hope I can be as brave as the rest of you women here."

The couple arrived at the base shortly before 6 and stayed together in a room separate from the rest of the departing servicemen.

They emerged from a hall leading to the gate, faced newsmen silently and then walked to the gate.

"I do not know what duty I will have in Vietnam. I expect to be there a full 13 months," said the tall, handsome former White House aide.

He asked for a moment alone with Lynda and they embraced each other, saying nothing.

Again they headed for the gate, Robb was dressed smartly in his greens. He carried no baggage.

Neither offered any comment, but when asked Lynda Bird said she planned to return to Washington "on the next commercial flight."

Robb, an infantry officer, boarded the jet liner with 165 other Marines.

The plane lifted off the ground. Lynda watched, her face composed and then turned on her heel for a waiting limousine.

The Robbs were married in December. They stayed in the San Clemente, Calif., area while he underwent four days of intensive training for combat that ended Friday at Camp Pendleton, Calif.

Meanwhile in Da Nang, South Vietnam, Marine Corps officials said Capt. Robb will be assigned to the 1st Marine Div.

Robb, arrived in Naha Okinawa, early Monday. He will spend two or three days at Camp Butler getting processed for Vietnam, officials said.

He is expected to arrive in Da Nang in two or three days. On arrival he will be interviewed by the division's personnel section, then assigned according to the "needs and availability in his field," Marine officials said.

WASHINGTON (AP)—President Johnson said Sunday, "I shall not seek and I will not accept the nomination for another term as president."

He said he does not believe that with war in Vietnam he should "devote an hour or a day of my time" to any partisan cause.

Johnson made his dramatic withdrawal at the end of a nationally broadcast speech in which he disclosed he is ordering a halt in nearly all air and sea action against North Vietnam in a move to bring peace talks.

Johnson recalled that 52 months and 10 days ago he came into the Presidency through the tragic death of President John F. Kennedy.

Now he said there is divisiveness in the country and made an appeal for unity.

"I would ask all Americans to guard against divisiveness and all its ugly consequences."

In announcing the Vietnam moves, Johnson said there will be a pause in air attacks on North Vietnam, except in the area near the demilitarized zone.

He called this "the first step to de-escalate" the war, saying the U.S. will substantially reduce "the present level of hostilities."

Johnson appealed anew for immediate peace talks, saying: "There is no need to delay the talks that could bring an end to this long and bloody war."

The chief executive called on the Soviet Union and Great Britain, as co-chairmen of the Geneva confer-

(Continued on Back Page, Col. 1)

N. VIET DECLARES IT'S READY TO TALK

LBJ, Aids to Confer in Honolulu

PACIFIC STAR STRIPES

AN AUTHORIZED PUBLICATION OF THE U.S. ARMED FORCES IN THE FAR EAST

10¢

Vol. 24, No. 94 ★★★★★ EDITION Friday, April 5, 1968

WASHINGTON (UPI)—The United States and North Vietnam took a small but enormously significant step Wednesday toward preliminary diplomatic discussions that could lead to an end of the Vietnam war.

First, the Hanoi government declared in a radio broadcast its willingness to meet with American representatives to discuss "the unconditional cessation of the United States bombing raids and all other acts of war against the Democratic Republic of Vietnam so that talks may start."

Then President Johnson told newsmen at the White House he was accepting Hanoi's offer.

He announced that the United States "will establish contact with the representatives of North Vietnam. Consultations with the government of South Vietnam and other allies are now taking place."

The President also said he would fly to Honolulu, Hawaii, late Thursday evening for a long weekend of conferences with American officials from South Vietnam.

The Pentagon said Defense Secretary Clark Clifford and Gen. Earle G. Wheeler, chairman of the Joint Chiefs of Staff, would accompany the President to Hawaii.

State Department officials said they expected Secretary of State Dean Rusk would join the Presidential group in Honolulu. Rusk is now in Wellington, New Zealand, for talks with U.S. allies in the Far East.

Johnson did not say when, where or how contact would be made with North Vietnam.

(Continued on Back Page, Col. 1)

McCarthy, Nixon Sweep Wisconsin

MILWAUKEE, Wis. (AP)—Sen. Eugene J. McCarthy, propelled by a landslide, 57 per cent showing in Wisconsin's presidential primary, went to work Wednesday to enhance his Democratic fortunes in contests he acknowledged may prove more difficult.

The Minnesota senator swept to a Wisconsin primary victory Tuesday. President Johnson, whose Sunday rejection of candidacy stripped the primary of its major contest, drew 35 per cent of the Democratic vote.

Richard M. Nixon captured 80 per cent of the smaller Republican turnout. He said it showed (Continued on Back Page, Col. 1)

Stocks Shatter Trading Mark

NEW YORK (AP) — Trading volume on the New York Stock Exchange soared to a record 19,290,000 shares Wednesday in a powerful reaction to Hanoi's broadcast offer to talk with the United States about a complete halt of the bombing of North Vietnam.

The total topped the record of 17.73 million shares set Monday. Before this week's hectic trading, the previous mark of 16.41 million shares had stood since Oct. 29, 1929, the day of the great market crash.

(Details on Page 8.)

Sen. Eugene McCarthy smiles as he is surrounded by well-wishers and campaign workers Tuesday night in Milwaukee.
(AP Radiophoto)

LBJ Sees Humphrey, Bobby Separately

WASHINGTON (AP) — President Johnson met Wednesday for about an hour each with Vice President Hubert H. Humphrey and Sen. Robert F. Kennedy, D-N.Y.

The two meetings were separate and the White House had almost nothing to say about either one. It indicated it would maintain silence.

Kennedy and Humphrey are possible finalists in the showdown for the Democratic presidential nomination, along with Sen. Eugene J. McCarthy of Minnesota.

Kennedy is actively campaigning now and Humphrey is expected to say within a week or two whether he will run.

White House press secretary George Christian said he knew of no plans for Johnson to confer with McCarthy and was unaware of any request from McCarthy for a conference.

Kennedy had asked for a meeting with Johnson, and Humphrey had announced he planned to see the President, too—obviously about what may happen now in the wake of Johnson's renunciation of any attempt for a second full term.

Kennedy was first in, at 10 a.m. EST, for a talk with John-(Continued on Back Page, Col. 2)

Allied Force Pushes Toward Khe Sanh

SAIGON (UPI) — Columns of allied tanks and infantrymen covered by swarms of helicopters inched along Highway 9 toward Khe Sanh Thursday to relieve the threatened Marine garrison there.

For the first time since last September, American forces traveled the twisting mountain road that links the 6,000 Leathernecks at Khe Sanh with coastal supply areas.

The going was slow. At least 17 bridges were knocked out and mines and booby traps turned up about every 100 yards.

By dusk Wednesday, the column was still about three miles from the besieged base, which is surrounded by North Vietnamese troops.

The move down Route 9, a dust-choked road that is little more than a trail, was a massive allied thrust code-named Operation Pegasus and involving about 10,000 troops.

It was aimed at seizing control of Highway 9 and taking (Continued on Back Page, Col. 1)

LBJ CANCELS TRIP; CONGRESS TALK SET

Troops Called to Curb D.C. Violence

WASHINGTON (AP)— President Johnson Friday proclaimed a "condition of domestic violence and disorder" in the nation's capital, and regular Army troops quickly were deployed in small numbers in the downtown area with more available.

The President's action came as vandalism spread in the District of Columbia and across the nation in the angry aftermath of the assassination of Dr. Martin Luther King.

Mayor Walter E. Washington clamped down a daily 13-hour curfew in the capital until further notice. The curfew will run from 5:30 p.m. to 6:30 a.m.

The curfew bans from the street all persons except law enforcement officers, firemen, physicians, nurses and medical **(Continued on Back Page, Col. 3)**

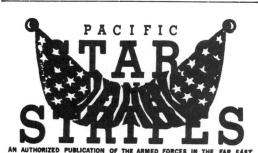

PACIFIC

STARS AND STRIPES

AN AUTHORIZED PUBLICATION OF THE ARMED FORCES IN THE FAR EAST

★★★★★ EDITION 10¢

昭和34年1月22日国鉄東局特別扱承認新聞紙第175号 (日刊)
(昭和34年4月21日第3種郵便物認可)

Vol. 24, No. 96   Sunday, April 7, 1968

Arrest Is Close, Clark Says

MEMPHIS, Tenn. (UPI) — Atty. Gen. Ramsey Clark said Friday evidence indicates the assassination of Dr. Martin Luther King was "perpetrated by one man" and that authorities are "very close" to making an arrest.

"The investigation has spread some several hundred miles from the borders of Tennessee at this time," said Clark. He flew here on orders from President Johnson to help with the investigation and to express to King's widow the "very deep regret" of the President and the cabinet "at the loss of this great American."

Clark said FBI agents were pursuing the investigation "in several sections of the country," and that "large numbers of items of evidence have been uncovered, and a number of out-of-state leads have been developed."

A short, balding white man was taken into custody Friday **(Continued on Back Page, Col. 4)**

Reward for Killer Reaches $155,000

MEMPHIS (UPI) — Rewards for information leading to the arrest and conviction of the killer of Dr. Martin Luther King Jr. now total at least $155,000.

The Memphis City Council met Friday and guaranteed a minimum reward of $100,000.

Earlier the Memphis Commercial Appeal offered a $25,000 reward. Other Scripps-Howard newspapers added $25,000 and Lewis Hutchinson, president of Dwight and Co., a management consultant firm in Greenwich, Conn., said he would add $5,000.

WASHINGTON (AP) — President Johnson told the nation Friday he plans to address a joint session of Congress to deal with the problems stemming from the assassination of Dr. Martin Luther King. The session was promptly set for 9 a.m. EST Monday night.

Johnson canceled plans to fly to Hawaii for conferences with American leaders in Vietnam as a preliminary to possible peace talks with the North Vietnamese.

Gen. William C. Westmoreland, commander of U.S. forces in Vietnam, is coming to Washington to confer with Johnson Saturday.

The White House announced Westmoreland's trip here instead of the meeting in Hawaii which was planned before the assassination of Dr. King.

There was still no further word on plans for the President to confer with other U.S. officials from Saigon who had been scheduled to meet with Johnson in Honolulu this weekend.

Somberly, Johnson asserted that "the fiber and the fabric of America" are being tested.

He said he wants to give Congress new recommendations and suggestions for easing the plight of the Negro.

Related Stories, Photos, Pages 2-4, 12.

But Whitney Young, director of the National Urban League, said he expects Johnson to ask Congress to expedite legislation already pending. Congressional sources said this would include **(Continued on Back Page, Col. 1)**

Khe Sanh Siege Lifted

KHE SANH, Vietnam (AP)— The 76-day enemy siege of Khe Sanh was lifted Friday and U.S. Marines and Army units struck out through the hills looking for vanishing North Vietnamese.

A 20,000-man allied relief column that approached almost unopposed to within less than a mile of the combat base made no attempt to enter as enemy gunners zeroed in with 110 rounds of artillery and mortar fire.

While the possibility of another battle was not excluded, it appeared the enemy had abandoned any attempt to wipe out the base astride an invasion route from Laos.

U.S. officers said the North Vietnamese force around Khe Sanh, once estimated at 20,000, had been reduced to about 7,000.

The big relief force, which started its drive Monday, appeared to be hunting the enemy in the hills north and south of Khe Sanh.

Saying "the basic concept of **(Continued on Back Page, Col. 1)**

President Johnson and Justice Thurgood Marshall, the first Negro ever to sit on the Supreme Court, listen solemnly at White House conference Friday. **(AP Radiophoto)**

U.S., HANOI AGREE ON PARIS FOR TALKS

PACIFIC

STARS STRIPES

AN AUTHORIZED PUBLICATION OF THE
U.S. ARMED FORCES IN THE FAR EAST
昭和34年1月22日国鉄東局特別扱承認新聞紙第175号 (日刊)
(昭和34年4月21日第3種郵便物認可)

10¢

Vol. 24, No. 124 ★★★★★ Sunday, May 5, 1968

84 Die as Plane Explodes, Crashes in Texas Storm

DAWSON, Tex. (AP) — A Braniff International Electra exploded while flying in a rainstorm Friday, scattering bodies and wreckage over a half-mile square area.

Braniff said there were 84 persons aboard—79 passengers and five crew members. No survivors were found at the scene.

The plane fell about one mile east of this small central Texas farm community. Dawson is about 25 miles southeast of Corsicana and about 90 miles south of Dallas.

The flight was Braniff 352 en route from Houston to Dallas. It was due in Dallas at 4:58 p.m., and was to have gone on to Tulsa, Fort Smith, Little Rock and Memphis.

Jerry Strader, publisher of the Corsicana Sun, was one of the first at the scene.

"I saw no survivors, no bodies intact," he said. "At least 50 per cent of the bodies appeared to be burned.

"The pieces of the plane were just fragmentary. The largest piece I saw was just a portion of the landing gear."

Strader said he found what appeared to be an engineer's flight plan and turned it over to a Texas Department of Public Safety officer.

"You couldn't tell whether it was a plane crash or a train wreck— pieces of wreckage were so small," Strader said.

Rain fell heavily as ambulance drivers and other rescue workers picked up pieces of bodies and wrapped them in sheets.

Witnesses said the plane ex-

ploded in the air and plummeted through the storm like a ball of fire.

Dean Montgomery saw the plane blow up as he drove with his wife and two children about two miles east of Dawson.

He said the plane exploded once and then a second time.

An Electra is a four-engine turbo prop plane, meaning that it uses a combination of jet engines and propellers.

Braniff lost one Electra previously, in 1959, when an airlin-
(Continued on Back Page, Col. 2)

Ike Doing Well

MARCH AFB, Calif. (AP)— Former President Dwight D. Eisenhower, hospitalized Monday after a mild heart attack, is feeling well enough to do some reading. A condition report Friday said he is in excellent spirits.

Celtics Win

INGLEWOOD, Calif. (UPI)— The Boston Celtics recaptured the National Basketball Association championship Thursday night with a 124-109 victory over the Los Angeles Lakers. Details on Page 17.

WASHINGTON (UPI)—The United States and North Vietnam agreed Friday to meet in Paris late next week to start discussing conditions for possible Vietnam peace talks.

President Johnson announced at a nationally televised and broadcast news conference: "I have sent a message informing Hanoi that the day of May 10 and the site of Paris are acceptable to the United States."

The President's statement came shortly over an hour after a Hanoi Radio broadcast proposed Paris as "an appropriate venue for the formal bilateral talks." The North Vietnamese broadcast said talks should begin "on May 10 or a few days later."

In Paris, the South Vietnamese consulate said representatives of their government "will sit in on" the talks.

Johnson told newsmen he was informed of Hanoi's willingness to meet in Paris "about one o'clock this morning.

"As all of you know, we have sought a place for these conversations in which all of the parties would receive fair and impartial treatment," Johnson said. "France is a country where all countries should expect such treatment."

The President expressed "hope that this agreement on initial contact will prove a step forward and can represent a mutual and a serious movement by all parties toward peace in Southeast Asia.

"I must, however, sound a cautionary note," Johnson said. "This is only the very first step, and there are many, many

Related stories Pages 4 and 5.

hazards and difficulties ahead.

"I assume that each side would present its viewpoint in these contacts.

"I have never felt that it was useful for public officials to confuse delicate negotiations by detailing personal views or suggestions, or elaborating on positions in advance."

The President promised that the United States will "continue in close consultation at all stages with our allies." He noted that all of them have representation in the French capital.

Paris is also an adequate location from the North Vietnamese point of view. Hanoi maintains a mission there, headed by a senior diplomat, Mai Van Bo, and Communist China is also represented in Paris.

In Paris, the South Vietnamese consulate said Consul
(Continued on Back Page, Col. 1)

UPI Radiophoto

PRESIDENT JOHNSON ANNOUNCES PEACE TALKS WILL BE HELD IN PARIS.

New Heart Transplants in Texas, U.K.

By The Associated Press

Three middle-aged men, two in the United States and one in London, fought to survive Friday night after heart transplants—the second, third and fourth in a week. All three were reported doing well.

Transplants were performed Friday in Houston, Tex., and

London, following by less than 24 hours a transplant operation in Stanford, Calif. A heart transplant was performed in Paris Saturday, but the patient died Tuesday.

In Houston, doctors said that Everett Claire Thomas, 47, an accountant from Phoenix, Ariz., was "doing fine" after receiving

the heart of Mrs. Charles L. Martin III, 15, who died of a gunshot wound to the brain. Surgeons said Thomas was awake three hours after the operation and that he had shown no sign of rejecting the new heart.

Doctors in London did not identify the recipient of the heart in Britain's first trans-

plant operation except to say the patient was a man of 45. Newspapers identified the donor as Patrick Ryan, 26, a building worker who was killed in an accident. The doctors said the patient's condition was "entirely satisfactory."

The third patient, Joseph Ri-
(Continued on Back Page, Col. 1)

Both Sides Urge De-Escalation As Peace Talks Open in Paris

PACIFIC STAR AND STRIPES

AN AUTHORIZED PUBLICATION OF THE ARMED FORCES IN THE FAR EAST

★ ★ ★ ★ ★

10¢

Vol. 24, No. 134   Wednesday, May 15, 1968

Thousands Join Anti-De Gaulle March in Paris

PARIS (AP)—A mammoth protest parade against the De Gaulle regime surged through the heart of Paris Monday in the climax of a day of general strikes and demonstrations across France.

Hundreds of thousands—workers, students, people of all ages and classes—marched for three miles amid chants for De Gaulle to resign and cries of "De Gaulle assassin! De Gaulle assassin!"

It was the biggest people's parade through Paris in memory and the strongest demonstration of feeling against President Charles de Gaulle's 10-year-old Fifth Republic.

It went off peacefully into the Left Bank but armed police in

Picture on Page 24

battle dress massed at bridges crossing the Seine.

The work stoppage, called by the country's four major labor unions to support student protests against police action during the past week of rioting in the Latin Quarter, was a near failure.

Organizers had hoped for nationwide paralysis. But despite appeals by the unions and student groups for a total walkout of French workers, work stoppages were so spotty it was difficult to tell a strike was on except for minor disruptions in transport and electric power.

Shots Follow Panama Vote

PANAMA (AP)—Violence exploded in the heart of Panama Monday in the wake of a hotly contested presidential election. Two persons were shot dead and at least five wounded in clashes between rival political factions.

The apparent closeness of the results of Sunday's balloting, in which the major contending factions claimed victory, honed tempers among activists on both sides and led to clashes in various parts of the city.

In the most prolonged fight, rock-throwing opposition partisans battled government party followers armed with what sounded like machine pistols. One three-story building was set afire in this battle which raged
(Continued on Back Page, Col. 3)

U.S. delegates Averell Harriman (left) and Cyrus Vance confer as preliminary peace talks between the U.S. and North Vietnam get under way in Paris. (AP Radiophoto)

PARIS (AP)—The United States and North Vietnam challenged each other Monday to take new steps to scale down the war in Southeast Asia, and both pledged serious efforts to find some basis for a peaceful settlement.

Ambassador Xuan Thuy of North Vietnam, who spoke first, called on the United States to end the rest of the bombing and "all other acts of war" against his country, but did it in softer words than expected. He did not threaten to break off the talks if the demand is not quickly granted.

President Johnson's envoy, Ambassador W. Averell Harriman, asked for some sign of military "restraint" by

Pictures on Page 12

North Vietnam that would meet Johnson's request for a de-escalation response to his March 31 partial bombing ban. What actually has happened, Harriman charged, is that North Vietnam has moved "substantial and increasing numbers of troops and supplies from the north to the south" since March 31.

Thuy made the opening statement at the first session of the talks, a U.S. spokesman said, after Harriman sug-
(Continued on Back Page, Col. 1)

Johnson Silent On Paris Talks

AUSTIN, Tex. (AP) — President Johnson received direct reports from U.S. negotiators in Paris, but had no comment from his Texas ranch Monday on the Vietnam talks.

His press secretary, George Christian, said no comment is to be expected, though the President will continue to keep in close contact with Ambassador W. Averell Harriman and Cyrus R. Vance, his two chief negotiators in Paris.

Walt W. Rostow, presidential assistant for national security affairs was at the ranch with the President, keeping close tabs on developments in Paris, Christian said.

The President received cabled reports through the weekend and Rostow was in telephone contact with the U.S. delegation in Paris, Christian said.

Johnson came to his ranch over the weekend for rest and relaxation.

Poor Settle in D.C. to 'Plague' Congress

WASHINGTON (AP) — The Poor People's Campaign raised its wooden camp on a lawn by the Lincoln Memorial Monday to begin what its leaders say will be a summer-long siege of Congress.

The Rev. Ralph David Abernathy promised protesters, "We're going to plague the pharaohs of this nation, with

Pictures on Pages 4, 12

an unannounced number of troops in what it termed "a state of readiness," there were

plague after plague, until they agree to give us meaningful jobs and a guaranteed annual income.

Although the Pentagon placed

no incidents of any type reported.

Abernathy drove the first nail for the tent-shaped plywood dwellings that will house the throng of marchers converging on the nation's capital.

Abernathy, leader of the campaign planned by the late Dr. Martin Luther King Jr., said, "We're going to stay here until

the Congress acts or the Congress adjourns, and then we will go on wherever Congress goes."

The first marchers arrived by bus from Mississippi and Tennessee Sunday. Other regiments wound their way toward the capital Monday through Michigan, South Carolina and New Jersey. March leaders pre-
(Continued on Back Page, Col. 1)

North Viets May Be Using Copters

Compiled From UPI and S&S Vietnam Bureau

SAIGON — Unidentified aircraft—believed to be enemy helicopters—have been spotted and fired on by U.S. Navy vessels near the eastern end of the Demilitarized Zone, the U.S. military command in Vietnam said Monday night.

If they are enemy copters, it marks the first time they have been used in the war.

The report comes on the heels of rumors that a Communist copter gunship was responsible for the sinking of a Navy Swift boat, the PCF 19, at 1:30 a.m. Sunday a few miles below the DMZ.

It was the first U.S. gunboat lost in the war. Early reports on the sinking indicated it was the work of Communist shore batteries above the DMZ. The boat went down about a mile offshore, four miles below the DMZ. Five of the seven crewmen were listed as missing. The other two were picked up.

A South Vietnamese general said Monday U.S. warplanes shot down seven North Vietnamese copters from the skies around the DMZ.

Lt. Gen. Hoang Xuan Lam, commander of South Vietnam's (northern) I Corps, said two of the copters were shot down over South Vietnam and five more over the north in two separate night-

(Continued on Back Page, Col. 1)

PACIFIC STARS STRIPES

AN AUTHORIZED PUBLICATION OF THE
U.S. ARMED FORCES IN THE FAR EAST

10¢

Vol. 24, No. 169   Wednesday, June 19, 1968

Night Assault

Last VC Holdouts Routed in Saigon

SAIGON (AP) — Grenade-hurling Vietnamese Special Forces troopers, racing from bunker to bunker, wiped out the last Viet Cong stronghold in Saigon's suburbs in face-to-face fighting that ended at dawn Monday.

The elite soldiers, brought to Saigon specifically to wrench free a hamlet held by the Viet Cong for two weeks, killed 30 guerrillas and drove 100 others fleeing into rice paddies along the Saigon River. Fifteen prisoners were taken.

Only a few of the Vietnamese
(Continued on Back Page, Col. 4)

Ike's 5th Attack 'Major'

WASHINGTON (UPI) —Army doctors said Monday the heart attack suffered by former President Dwight D. Eisenhower Saturday night was "major," but that "no signs of heart failure have appeared."

Doctors at Walter Reed Army Medical Center, where Eisenhower was recovering from his fourth heart attack when he was seized by his fifth, said examinations "indicate that the general has sustained another major heart attack."

However, they said the 77-year-old general "has been comfortable for the past 24 hours and his vital signs remained stable...No signs of heart failure have appeared. He has remained alert and in good spirits."

A spokesman said Mrs. Eisenhower has visited him frequently and that his son, John, and the general's brothers have been kept fully informed of his condition.

Mrs. Eisenhower has remained at the hospital since her husband was brought there May 14 from California, where he suffered his fourth heart attack

(Continued on Back Page, Col. 4)

A South Vietnamese Special Forces trooper shouts to his buddies for fire cover as he leads a prisoner from a bunker in the Saigon suburb of Gia Dinh. The Viet Cong was left behind and disarmed by his fleeing mates after he was wounded.   (AP Radiophoto)

Striking Actors Dim Broadway

NEW YORK (UPI)—The actors' union struck nationwide Monday closing down Broadway's "Great White Way" and roadshows in major cities and cancelling auditions and rehearsals for next season's productions.

The strike was announced by the executive council of Actors Equity Association (AEA) after a four-day break in negotiations with the League of New York Theaters, the producers' organization. It idled 500 Equity mem-
(Continued on Back Page, Col. 5)

Hot and Cold Soda

MAXWELL, N.M. (AP)—Early morning risers found pink water coming out of their faucets. Then city employe Jeff Barlett arrived at work and discovered someone had put several packages of instant sweet drink in a 40,000-gallon storage tank.

Dog's Life Now One of Luxury

CHICAGO (UPI) — The independent pet industry trade show is showing umbrellas that attach to dog collars, wall-to-wall carpeting for canine cottages, mouth sprays to eliminate doggy halitosis, stereo records to train talking birds, cashmere sweaters for birds and colonial and provincial beds for pets.

There also is Irish beef kidney stew, which one firm said, may be eaten by the dog or his owner.

LBJ Vows Support to Berlin In Latest E. German Squeeze

AUSTIN, Tex. (UPI)—President Johnson Monday charged the East German squeeze on Berlin travel is "totally unprovoked and unjustified aggravation" and said United States' support of free Berlin "remains as firm as ever."

In a message to West German Chancellor Kurt Kiesinger, Johnson said the United States and West Germany are consulting with the British and the French on the new crisis involving communist restrictions on surface travel between West Germany and West Berlin.

"I want to express to you on this 'Day of Germany unity' that our support of Free Berlin and the goal of a German people united in peace remains as firm as ever," Johnson said in a brief two-paragraph message on the 15th anniversary of the 1953 East German uprisings.

"It is a matter of great regret to me that while the federal republic and we are pursuing objectives that I believe all mankind shares, namely to live in peace with our neighbors, Berlin is once again threatened."

The West German government is deeply concerned with the latest rupture in West-East German relations and the new Berlin crunch.

The United States, Britain and France have protested the East German regulations, which include passports by July 15 for
(Continued on Back Page, Col. 2)

LBJ Asks Vote for 18-Year-Olds

WASHINGTON (UPI)—President Johnson, terming the ballot box "the great anvil of democracy," asked Congress Thursday to approve a constitutional amendment granting 18-year-olds the right to vote in federal elections.

Johnson, in a message to Congress, said "The time has come to grant our youth what we ask of them but still deny to them—full and responsible participation in our American democracy."

The amendment would require two-third approval in both the Senate and the House and ratification by three-

(Continued on Back Page, Col. 4)

PACIFIC
STAR STRIPES

AN AUTHORIZED PUBLICATION OF THE
U.S. ARMED FORCES IN THE FAR EAST

10¢

Vol. 24, No. 179   Saturday, June 29, 1968

Agree to Discuss Cutback

RUSS OK ARMS TALK

MARINES FILL UP TRENCHES AND BUNKERS WITH BULLDOZER WHILE OTHERS EMPTY SANDBAGS AT KHE SANH.

AP Radiophoto

MOSCOW (UPI) — The Soviet Union Wednesday accepted an American appeal for talks on calling off the costly anti-ballistic missile race. The Russians also agreed to discuss reducing offensive weapons.

Foreign Minister Andrei Gromyko, in a report to the Soviet Parliament, answered President Johnson's recent bid for better U.S.-Soviet relations by declaring, "We see no reason for conflict with the United States . . . if the U.S. respects the security of others."

In Washington, both a White House spokesman and Vice President Hubert Humphrey welcomed Gromyko's offer to confer.

George Christian, White House press secretary, said, "We welcome the indication that the Soviet Union is prepared to discuss the limitation of offensive and defensive missile systems." He declined to disclose whether President Johnson had been advised in advance of the Gromyko speech.

Humphrey said Gromyko's offer was "good news for all of us who have worked for peace. We have been trying very hard for 15 months to discuss with Soviet leaders the subject of both offensive and defensive weapons."

Gromyko said, "One of the untouched problems in this field is the mutual limitation and later reduction of strategic weapons, both offensive and defensive, including antimissile missiles."

In February, 1967, Johnson
(Continued on Back Page, Col. 3)

A Stinging $1 Mil. Suit

GARDEN GROVE, Calif. (UPI) — Seven couples here Wednesday filed a $1 million lawsuit claiming they were "stung" in their purchase of apartment houses.

The couples' lawsuit against everybody involved in building and selling the four-unit apartments opened Tuesday in Superior Court.

The couples purchased the apartments in 1963 so they could live in one unit while renting out the other three for invest-
(Continued on Back Page, Col. 1)

Marines Leaving Khe Sanh; Red Shift in Tactics Cited

SAIGON (AP)—The U.S. Marines are pulling out of the Khe Sanh combat base on the northern frontier, where they weathered a 77-day siege last winter with 2,500 casualties. The U.S. command, announcing the move Thursday, cited mounting enemy pressure as part of the reason.

"There have been two significant changes in the military situation in Vietnam since early this year," the command said,

"An increase in friendly strength, mobility and firepower and an increase in the enemy's threat due to both a greater flow of replacements and in a change in tactics."

During the long winter siege, senior U.S. officers called the base in South Vietnam's northwest corner indispensable. They said it would be held at any cost. But the pullout decision apparently had already been

made by the time a division-plus relief force arrived at Khe Sanh in April.

The new western anchor of American bases along the Demilitarized Zone apparently was to be Landing Zone Stud, about 10 miles to the east. It has been supporting the eight battalions operating around Khe Sanh since the siege was lifted.

Khe Sanh is the first major
(Continued on Back Page, Col. 1)

Little Delinquent Getting to Work

WASHINGTON (AP) — Eddie LeBaron, former football star who is directing a government-sponsored program to aid juvenile delinquents this summer, was late getting to work Thursday.

He explained to his staff that juvenile delinquents had stolen two wheels from his car.

Captives 'Roughed It' With Russ

By CAUSA E. BERRY
S&S Japan Bureau Chief

YOKOTA AB, Japan — The 214 American servicemen aboard a Seaboard World Airlines jet forced down in the Kurile Islands by the Russians were well treated, but they were happy to get back to non-Communist soil.

Seaman Mike Casey of Wilkes-Barre, Pa., may have stated the feelings of many of them.

"Sarge," he told a Yokota AB NCO when the big DC8 landed here for servicing, "When they said 'Born Free' they weren't kidding.

"When you see the way those poor bastards live up there. . . ."

Most of the servicemen aboard the plane painted a bleak picture of conditions on Iturup Island, where the plane was forced to land by Russian MIGs.

"All they had was a bunch of black and brown shacks and a few 1939 vintage automobiles running around," said Pfc. An-
(Continued on Back Page, Col. 2)

PACIFIC

STARS STRIPES

AN AUTHORIZED PUBLICATION OF THE
U.S. ARMED FORCES IN THE FAR EAST

10¢

Vol. 24, No. 185   Friday, July 5, 1968

HANOI TO RELEASE 3 DOWNED PILOTS

TOKYO (AP)—North Vietnam said Wednesday it is releasing three more U.S. pilots but did not give their names or say when and where they will be freed.

Only once before have the North Vietnamese released American fliers captured on missions over the North. It freed three on Feb. 16 as a gesture for the Vietnamese Lunar New Year. In exchange, the United States released three North Vietnamese sailors a month later.

Hanoi Radio's brief announcement Wednesday said: "Proceeding from the humanitarian and lenient policy of the government of the Democratic Republic of Vietnam, the general political department of the Vietnam People's Army has decided to release three U.S. pilots captured in North Vietnam."

In Washington, U.S. officials said they were gratified by North Vietnam's decision to free the three pilots. Indications were that the United States, in response, would soon free three captured North Vietnamese.

The officials said Ambassador Averell Harriman was speaking for the U.S. government when he thanked Hanoi's envoy at the Paris peace talks. (See Story, Page 5.)

Before the release of the three fliers in February, nine servicemen had been released by the Viet Cong in three years.

Some 700 American servicemen, mostly airmen, were listed in May as missing or captured in North Vietnam. The exact number held prisoner is not known because Hanoi has refused to supply names.

USAF Photo by Sgt. Paul J. Harrington

U.S. SERVICEMEN ON A PLANE WHICH WAS HELD BY THE RUSSIANS APPEAR HAPPY TO BE BACK IN THE FREE WORLD.

Quake Rocks Tokyo

TOKYO (S&S)—A sharp earthquake shook Tokyo and Yokohama at 9:35 a.m. Thursday. A spokesman for the Central Meteorological Agency said the tremor, centered in the ocean off the Boso Peninsula east of Tokyo, registered three on the Japanese scale of seven in Yokohama. The reading in Tokyo was two.

LBJ Watches 'Westy' Become Chief

WASHINGTON (AP) — President Johnson made a surprise visit to the Pentagon Wednesday and watched smilingly as Gen. William C. Westmoreland was sworn in as the Army's 25th Chief of Staff.

Johnson, dressed in a snappy, light brown suit, stepped into the office of Secretary of the Army Stanley R. Resor just as Westmoreland, former U.S. military commander in Vietnam, was about to take the oath.

"Mr. President, golly, you're always surprising me," West-

moreland commented as he stepped forward to shake hands with his commander-in-chief.

The ceremony also was attended by several congressional figures, all of the Joint Chiefs of Staff and three other military figures closely associated with Vietnam: Retired Army Gen. Lawton Collins, former ambassador to Vietnam Gen. Maxwell D. Taylor, and former Army Chief of Staff Gen. George H. Decker.

Also present was former Illinois Gov. Otto Kerner, who as a

major served as then-Lt. Col. Westmoreland's executive officer in North Africa and Sicily from 1942 to 1944.

Westmoreland took the oath, standing straight, chin out, right hand raised. His wife Katherine in a rose linen dress was at his left side.

"Westy," as he is known to many, said he accepted the Army's top uniformed job with "pride and humility."

Paying tribute to the men who served under him during his 4½ years in Vietnam, he said, "The

recognition given to me this morning is in large measure a result of their steadfast effort."

He thanked his predecessor, Gen. Harold K. Johnson, who retired Tuesday, and the Joint Chiefs of Staff for their support during the war and concluded: "To the authorities over me and to the troops under me I pledge my loyalty."

After the oath was administered and Westmoreland had spoken, the President stepped
(Continued on Back Page, Col. 1)

Diners Flee N.Y. Skyscraper Fire

NEW YORK (UPI)—More than 500 persons, including 250 patrons of the elegant 48th floor Tower Suite restaurant, were safely removed from the Time-Life Building Sunday when a fire broke out on the 11th floor, filling the skyscraper with dense smoke.

Although most of the offices in the building, home of the Time Inc. publishing company, were closed for the weekend, both the Tower Suite and another restaurant on the ground floor were serving Sunday diners.

About two dozen persons were **(Continued on Back Page, Col. 4)**

PACIFIC STAR AND STRIPES

AN AUTHORIZED PUBLICATION OF THE U.S. ARMED FORCES IN THE FAR EAST

10¢

Vol. 24, No. 210

Tuesday, July 30, 1968

232 Red Boats Bagged As Navy Jets Set Mark

SAIGON (AP) — An armada of U.S. Navy warplanes destroyed or damaged 232 Communist supply boats in the largest single day's catch of the war, military spokesmen announced Sunday.

At the same time, other U.S. warplanes maneuvered through Communist surface-to-air missiles and heavy antiaircraft fire to pound the North Vietnamese panhandle with 130 air strikes, heaviest total in two weeks.

The 130 air strikes over the North Saturday were concentrated on the scores of canals and highways that wind through the southern half of North Vietnam below the 19th parallel. Headquarters said nearly 200 Navy fighter-bombers from three carriers off the coast of North Vietnam destroyed or damaged the 232 supply boats in sweeping raids over an area stretching from the 19th parallel 75 miles south to Cape Mui Ron.

A spokesman called it "the largest bag of boats for the war." He said that repeated air strikes on roads, bridges and truck parks had forced the North Vietnamese to switch to the waterways in efforts to push arms and ammunition into the south for an anticipated countrywide offensive.

"Certainly there has been an increase in waterborne traffic because roads are being cut, **(Continued on Back Page, Col. 1)**

A GI, suffering from heat exhaustion, is carried to a waiting helicopter during a sweep in the Mutters Ridge area in the central portion of the Vietnam DMZ. Temperatures daily soar over 100 degrees. (AP Radiophoto)

Bitten Diver Outwits Shark

BODEGA BAY, Calif. (UPI)—A skin-diver attacked by a man-eating shark was in good condition Sunday after he "played dead" until the fish let go.

Frank Logan, 25, Placerville, Calif., was ripped and slashed on his back, shoulders and chest during the grim encounter Saturday. Hospital authorities said he had 18 separate wounds that required 200 stitches.

Logan had gone hunting for abalone near Bird Rock in Bodega Bay and was about a mile offshore when the shark attacked.

He said he was swimming on the ocean bottom, in 18 feet of **(Continued on Back Page, Col. 1)**

Czechs On Way to Parley With Politburo in Railway Car

PRAGUE (AP)—Members of the Czechoslovak Communist party's presidium arrived by plane Sunday night in Kosice, about 25 miles from the Soviet border, then left by train for a meeting Monday with Soviet leaders.

Reliable sources said the talks would be held in a railroad car.

The meeting, which may decide the future of Prague's liberalization drive, was expected to begin at 9 a.m. in the special train that was bringing the Soviet politburo to Czechoslovakia, the sources said.

The Czechoslovak delegation arrived in two planes, one from Prague and the other from Bratislava, the official news agency CTK reported.

President Ludvik Svoboda was an occupant of the Prague plane and the only official mentioned by name.

Speculation about the site of the meeting centered on two railway junctions in eastern Slovakia—Cierna or Presov.

Unconfirmed reports from the region spoke of heavy security precautions along the nearby Czechoslovak Soviet border.

An official announcement said the flight carried "some members and alternate members" of the party presidium and that "other members will join the main part of the delegation on the spot."

The leaders traveled to the airport in suburban Ruzyne in a fleet of official black limousines. One of them, National Assembly Chairman Josef Smrkovsky, was seen waving at television cameramen posted outside the restricted area.

Strict secrecy on location and date of the meeting complies with a Soviet request.

Informants here have predicted that the meeting will be a short affair, probably not longer than a day or so. Ro- **(Continued on Back Page, Col. 1)**

And Took Away His Surfboard

HONOLULU (UPI) — Tiny Mauna Olu College on the island of Maui with 250 students boasts that it has no student riot problem.

"Well, that's not quite true," admitted Richard L. Taylor, dean of the college. "We had one about a year ago, but we sent him home."

'No Man Can Predict Pullout'

NO BOMB HALT: LBJ

PACIFIC
STARS STRIPES
AN AUTHORIZED PUBLICATION OF THE
U.S. ARMED FORCES IN THE FAR EAST
10¢

Vol. 24, No. 254   Thursday, Sept. 12, 1968

NEW ORLEANS (AP)—President Johnson Tuesday again rejected a complete halt to bombing in North Vietnam and said that events in Eastern Europe make it clear "we are still a long way from the kind of peaceful world we all wish to see."

"The message out of Czechoslovakia," Johnson said, "is plain; the independence of nations and the liberty of men are still under challenge. And the free parts of the world will survive only if they are capable of maintaining their strength and building their unity."

Yet Johnson said that the United States will continue in every honorable way open to move toward more normal relations with Russia and other Communist countries.

The chief executive made the remarks in a keynote address to the American Legion's 50th annual national convention. His stand against a complete cessation of bombing North Vietnam echoed what he had told the convention of the Veterans of Foreign War in Detroit on Aug. 19.

(At another point the President said "no man can predict when the day will come" that the United States can bring some of its troops home, according to UPI.

(Vice President Humphrey had forecast Monday that some U.S. forces could be withdrawn from Vietnam in late 1968 or early 1969.)

As commander-in-chief of the armed forces, Johnson went over some of the hard facts he confronts and listed three choices on what could be done.

He said the first would be to invade North Vietnam, overrun military positions and throttle supply routes in the country and "this we do not wish to do."

Retreat, he said, would be the second choice—the withdrawal

(Continued on Back Page, Col. 3)

School Accord In N.Y.

NEW YORK (UPI) — The striking New York City teachers union and school officials reached tentative agreement Tuesday on the racially tense issues which touched off a paralyzing two-day school strike. The agreement is subject to ratification by the 55,000 union members.

The tentative settlement came during a sometimes stormy meeting between Schools Superintendent Bernard B. Donovan and Albert Shanker, president of the United Federation of Teachers.

The strike had meant an extra two days of vacation for most of the city's 1,129,000 public school students who had been scheduled to return to classes Monday.

At issue was job security for teachers as control of the schools is given to 30 locally elected school boards. The strike was precipitated by the dismissal of 10 white teachers by the Negro and Puerto Rican administrators of the Ocean Hill-Brownsville district in Brooklyn.

Mrs. Rose Shapiro, outgoing president of the Central Board (Continued on Back Page, Col. 2)

Crime Pays —For Victim

SYRACUSE, N.Y. (UPI)—A young bandit confronted the angry daughter of his elderly victim Monday became so flustered that he not only returned his loot but his own wallet, an additionnal $1.80 and what is believed to be a photograph of himself.

The young man had forced his way into the West Side home of Mrs. George Laughlin, 76, who gave him the small amount of cash she had under the threat of death. The bandit fled just before Mrs. Laughlin's daughter, Mrs. Mary Telp, arrived.

When Mrs. Telp heard the holdup story, she became so enraged she set off after the bandit in her car and caught up with him a short way down the road. She hopped out of the car and demanded the money. The young man handed it over, along with his wallet with his picture and his money, and fled.

AP Radiophoto
PRESIDENT JOHNSON GESTURES EMPHATICALLY DURING LEGION SPEECH.

BULLETIN

SAIGON (AP) — Communist troops invaded Tay Ninh City in strength Tuesday night and heavy fighting was underway Wednesday for control of the city of 200,000 which lies on a major invasion route to Saigon.

N. Korea Asks More Than Apology: Rusk

WASHINGTON (AP) — Secretary of State Dean Rusk indicated Tuesday that North Korea is demanding not only an apology but a promise that U.S. ships will stay out of the Sea of Japan as the price for release of the USS Pueblo and her crew.

"It is not just a question of an apology." Rusk said.

"It is my understanding they have asked for a good many things including commitments about further action that would involve the high seas in the Sea of Japan."

Rusk made the disclosure at about the same time the State Department, in a carefully considered statement, declared the seizure of the Navy intelligence ship seven months ago was an illegal act which does not call for an apology.

There have been repeated reports that the United States planned to apologize and the statement was in response to these.

The State Department spokesman, press officer Robert J. McCloskey, said that if negotia-

tions to obtain the release of the crew of 82 and the ship are to prove successful "we have an obligation to keep the negotiations private."

However, Rusk shed a little more information on the negotiations, which have been stalemated since last January.

State Department officials related his remarks to North Korea's repeated and insistent demands for three actions by the United States.

They are: an admission that the Pueblo was guilty of violat-

ing North Korea's territorial waters; an apology; and a promise that there would be no violations in the future.

He told them there is no independent evidence whatsoever that the Pueblo violated its sailing orders on Jan. 23. Those orders were to remain outside of the 12-mile limit.

North Korea has claimed the Pueblo moved within seven miles of the nearest land, the port of Wonsan, when it was seized by armed North Korean patrol craft.

30th Win For Denny

Story on Page 17

PACIFIC

STAR STRIPES

AN AUTHORIZED PUBLICATION OF THE
U.S. ARMED FORCES IN THE FAR EAST

10¢

Vol. 24, No. 258   Monday, Sept. 16, 1968

By Land, Sea and Air

ALLIES SWEEP DMZ

VIETNAMESE PARATROOPERS DISARM A NORTH VIETNAMESE SOLDIER CAPTURED NEAR TAY NINH.

AP Radiophoto

By
SPEC. 4 RANDY WOODS
S&S Staff Correspondent

SAIGON — U.S. and Vietnamese troops, backed by aircraft, naval gunfire and tanks, went into the Demilitarized Zone Friday after dug-in North Vietnamese troops.

The allied force reported 158 Reds killed in a day-long battle.

Elements of the U.S. Army's 5th Mechanized Div.; the 3rd Marine Div. and the South Vietnamese 1st Inf. Div. attacked the fortified enemy position two miles northeast of Gio Linh in the southern portion of the DMZ.

Backed up by Marine tanks, Air Force jets, naval gunfire and Army artillery, the ground troops drove the Communists from their bunkers.

U.S. casualties were 22 wounded, all Army. No Americans were killed. Vietnamese losses were reported light.

After completing a sweep of the battle area, the Allies returned to their bases in Quang Tri Province.

Near Loc Ninh, 80 miles north of Saigon, 1st Inf. Div. troops killed 38 Communists Friday, bringing to 167 the enemy's losses in a savage series of fights that began early Thursday. Three U.S. troopers were killed and nine wounded in Friday's fighting.

Fighting continued around Tay Ninh City as Vietnamese forces pursued the fleeing remnants of a Communist battal-

(Continued on Back Page, Col. 1)

Not Big Man On Compass

MARQUETTE, Mich. (UPI)—A new freshman standing in line during registration at Northern Michigan University found out he was standing in the wrong line. He missed by 550 miles.

Jack Kunkel, assistant director of housing at the university, said he was working on housing for incoming freshmen when a young man came up and said, "Sir, can you help me with this card?"

"This is my first semester at Eastern," the young man explained.

"Did you say Eastern?" Kunkel asked. "This is Northern Michigan University."

"Oh my God," the youth said. "I've made a horrible mistake."

Eastern Michigan Univeristy is in Ypsilanti, near Detroit, 550 miles to the southeast.

Nixon Challenges Hubert On Who Is Blocking Fortas

CLEVELAND, Ohio (AP) — Richard M. Nixon challenged Vice President Hubert H. Humphrey Friday night to recruit from the Democrats the support needed for U.S. Senate confirmation of Abe Fortas as chief justice of the United States.

Strongly replying to his Dem-

ocratic opponent's charge that he is working to block Fortas' nomination, the Republican presidential candidate said: "I suggest that before he looks at our party, he take a look at his own."

Nixon said in a televised question and answer session that 12

★ ★ ★ ★ ★

Says 6 Steps Trip HHH

CLEVELAND (AP) — From Robert Ellsworth, political director for Republican presidential nominee Richard M. Nixon:

"Mr. Hubert H. Humphrey is now perfecting the technique of the six-step statement. This consists of (1) a lengthy opening statement, (2) his objection to its misinterpretation, (3) a further clarification, (4) an explanation of his running mate's disagreement, (5) a tortured denial that it really differs from administration policy, (6) a plea that it was only something that he read in the newspaper and wasn't really anything new in any case."

Republicans are backing Fortas. Among them, he said, are some of his own strongest supporters such as Sen. Edward Brooke of Massachusetts and Hugh Scott of Pennsylvania.

Nixon said that if Humphrey could round up the support of enough Democrats, Fortas would get confirmation.

Some Southern Democrats are opposing Fortas.

The Democrats hold the majority in the Senate.

Nixon, in an interview later, accused Humphrey of "rather silly name calling."

Referring to the vice president's charges on the Fortas matter, Nixon said "some of this business lately of 'Fearless Fosdick' and all that is kind of a

(Continued on Back Page, Col. 2)

Vance May Sub For Harriman

PARIS (AP)—Ambassador Cyrus R. Vance will probably head the U.S. delegation to this Wednesday's session of the peace talks with North Vietnam, the American delegation reported Saturday.

Vance will take over in absence of W. Averell Harriman, chief of the delegation, who is leaving Sunday for New York to attend the funeral, on Monday, of his mother-in-law, Mrs. Sheridan S. Norton, who died at the age of 91.

WILLING TO CALL OFF BOMBING, HHH SAYS

PACIFIC STARS STRIPES

AN AUTHORIZED PUBLICATION OF THE U.S. ARMED FORCES IN THE FAR EAST

10¢

Vol. 24, No. 274   Wednesday, Oct. 2, 1968

SALT LAKE CITY, Utah (AP) — Hubert H. Humphrey said Monday that if elected President he would be willing to stop the bombing of North Vietnam — thus dramatically moving away from the Johnson administration war policy.

Humphrey, in a half-hour speech on foreign policy at a critical time in his presidential campaign, said North Vietnam has contended it would promptly conduct "good faith negotiations if we stop the present limited bombing of the north."

Humphrey told a nationwide television audience:

"As President, I would be willing to stop the bombing of the north as an acceptable risk for peace because I believe it could lead to success in the negotiations and a shorter war. This would be the best protection for our troops."

Humphrey repeated, however, an earlier statement that neither he nor anyone else had control over the Vietnam war while President Johnson remained in office.

Humphrey also said if Hanoi showed bad faith, "I would reserve the right to resume the bombing."

Humphrey said he would not unilaterally withdraw American troops. He said this "would be an open invitation to more violence, more aggression, more instability."

Nor, added Humphrey, would he "escalate the level of violence in either North or South Vietnam. We must seek to de-escalate."

Humphrey also proposed once more an immediate cease-fire with United Nations or other international supervision and withdrawal of all foreign forces from South Vietnam.

Humphrey also called for ratification of the nuclear non-proliferation treaty. He also expressed belief the United States "must have the courage to talk with the Soviet Union as soon as possible about a freeze and reduction of nuclear missile systems."

Discussing his proposal if elected President, Humphrey said "in weighing that risk—and before taking action—I would place key importance on evidence direct or indirect, by deed or word—of Communist willingness to restore the demilitarized zone between North and South Vietnam."

Humphrey also said he would take a second step which would involve "the risk that the South Vietnamese would meet the obligations they say they are now ready to assume in their own self defense."

Humphrey said another risk he would be willing to take would be "free elections, including all people in South (Continued on Back Page, Col. 3)

New Jersey's Debut Is a Blockbuster

By S.SGT. DAVE PRESTON
S&S Staff Correspondent

ABOARD THE USS NEW JERSEY—The U.S. battleship New Jersey made her long-awaited debut in the Vietnam War Monday, blasting deep into North Vietnam to demolish a storage area and knock out Communist guns menacing Allied troops and aircraft.

The New Jersey, which displaces 56,000 tons and is the only battleship in service today, prowled 1,600 yards off the Ben Hai River marking the demilitarized zone. At 7:32 a.m., one of her nine 16-inch guns roared and sent a 2,700-pound projectile 12 miles into a Communist supply dump on the northern fringes of the zone.

LBJ Acts To Block Dock Tieup

WASHINGTON (UPI) — President Johnson invoked the Taft-Hartley Law Monday in an effort to block a threatened midnight strike by 75,000 longshoremen at ports from Maine to Texas.

Johnson signed an executive order setting up a board of inquiry to determine whether a settlement of the dispute between the International Longshoremen's Association and management was likely. After the board review, the next step would be for the President to direct the attorney general to seek an injunction halting a work stoppage for an 80-day cooling-off period.

The White House said Johnson acted after the Administration determined that the strike would be "dangerous to the national health and safety."

Presidential aide Joseph Califano said government economists estimated that a strike would cost about $70 million a day in terms of lost imports and exports.

Califano said a strike might jeopardize some shipments of supplies to U.S. troops in Vietnam.

It was the first shot fired on an enemy target by a battleship since 1953, when the New Jersey pounded Red targets in Korea. Fifteen years and 66 days later, she was still a destructive giant which in three and a half minutes can equal the devastation of 60 bombers.

Communist radar tracked the New Jersey as she swung down the coast in range of 100mm shore batteries. She was not fired upon. Far ahead of the battleship, an aerial spotter hovered over the first target and watched the first shell raise a billow of dust and flame. Five more shells smothered the supply dump.

"Right on the money," radioed the spotter. "Scratch off the target. It isn't there anymore."

Then, a mile from that target, bursts of antiaircraft fire began to explode around the spotter plane. The New Jersey turned her guns on them. Six rounds later, four of the anti-aircraft emplacements were demolished.

A third barrage erased a Communist artillery position that has been menacing forward outposts at Gio Linh and Con Thien (Continued on Back Page, Col. 5)

The veteran battleship New Jersey made her debut in the Vietnam War Monday as she opened up with her powerful 16-inch guns on enemy targets deep in North Vietnam. (UPI)

Reds Still Threaten Thuong Duc Camp

By BILL COLLINS and SPEC. 5 RANDY WOODS
S&S Vietnam Bureau

THUONG DUC, Vietnam —Elements of three Communist regiments were still threatening the Thuong Duc Special Forces camp Monday, and a North Vietnamese battle flag was reported still flying from a group of villages a mile from the camp,

despite two days of Allied efforts to drive the Reds out.

Fighting broke out around two outposts of the camp early Saturday. A North Vietnamese attacking force was beaten back by government troops who killed 39 enemy troops.

But another Communist force occupied a complex of small villages across a nearby river at

the same time and the Special Forces troops battled them through Sunday night.

Many of the villagers fled across the river into the district headquarters which is protected by the Special Forces camp.

About 100 South Vietnamese troops assaulted the village complex from the east Sunday and

managed to fight their way inside the hamlets, but heavy enemy fire pinned them down. They slipped out of the complex in the dark and returned to the main camp.

Thuong Duc Camp was still under siege late Monday by large elements of three Communist regiments. The camp was (Continued on Back Page, Col. 5)

NLF to Join Paris Talks

BOMBING HALT

PACIFIC **STAR AND STRIPES**

AN AUTHORIZED PUBLICATION OF THE
U.S. ARMED FORCES IN THE FAR EAST

10¢

Vol. 24, No. 305   Saturday, Nov. 2, 1968

WASHINGTON (UPI) — President Johnson Thursday night ordered a total halt to the bombing of North Vietnam and said the Saigon government and the National Liberation Front would be brought into broadened and "intensive" peace talks in Paris on Wednesday.

The President said in a nationwide television address that he had reason to expect that North Vietnam would begin "prompt, productive, serious and intensive negotiations in an atmosphere that is conducive to progress" when the broadened talks start.

But American officials announced while Johnson was speaking that North Vietnam understands that the bombing halt would be broken if prompt and useful talks were not initiated in Paris.

The officials said that no ceasefire in South Vietnam had been agreed upon. They said the (Continued on Back Page, Col. 1)

Lost N-Sub's Debris Spotted

AP Radiophoto

WRECKAGE OF NUCLEAR SUBMARINE SCORPION HAS BEEN LOCATED BY NAVY RESEARCH SHIP MIZAR (ABOVE)

WASHINGTON (AP)— After a five-month search, the Navy announced Thursday it has spotted pieces of the vanished nuclear-powered submarine Scorpion about two miles down on the floor of the Atlantic.

Adm. Thomas H. Moorer, chief of naval operations, said "objects identified as portions of the hull of the submarine USS Scorpion have been located about 400 miles southwest of the Azores in more than 10,000 feet of water."

The find was reported Wednes- (Continued on Back Page, Col. 3)

Silent Film Idol Novarro Beaten to Death in Home

HOLLYWOOD (UPI)—Ramon Novarro, matinee idol of silent and early sound movies, was found beaten to death in his Hollywood Hills home where he lived alone Thursday. The star of the first "Ben Hur" was 69 years old.

Forty years ago Novarro was a dark-haired, dashing leading man who wooed Hollywood's glamor girls on the screen and off.

Novarro, a life-long bachelor, was another in the mold of Rudolph Valentino as one of the flickering screen's great Latin lovers. He successfully made the transition from silent movies to talkies.

Hollywood chief of detectives

Robert A. Houghton said the actor's pajama-clad body was discovered at approximately 8:30 a. m. by his male secretary, Ed Weber. Officers said Novarro's glasses were broken and furniture overturned, indicating a struggle.

Houghton said Novarro ap- (Continued on Back Page, Col. 1)

6th Death Spurs Bonn Spy Probe

BONN, Germany (AP) — The body of a defense ministry clerk was found floating in the Rhine River Thursday, raising to six the number of mystery deaths in West Germany's widening espionage probe.

The senior clerk, Gerhard Boehm, 61, missing since Oct. 21, was officially declared a suicide. An autopsy has been ordered.

The intensified investigation of spying activities in Bonn began when Rear Admiral Herman Luedke was found dead of gunshop wounds Oct. 8.

Boehm was a senior clerk in the defense ministry's administrative and legal section. Officials said investigation has revealed no evidence of breaches of security by Boehm.

They said he had no direct access to classified or defense papers but part of his job was to carry documents from room to room in sealed containers.

He left behind a suicide note (Continued on Back Page, Col. 2)

Papandreou Dies

ATHENS (UPI) — Former Greek Prime Minister Georges Papandreou died early Friday. He was 80.

NORTH VIET AGREES TO EXPLORE PEACE

PACIFIC
STARS STRIPES

AN AUTHORIZED PUBLICATION OF THE U.S. ARMED FORCES IN THE FAR EAST

10¢

Vol. 24, No. 306   Sunday, Nov. 3, 1968

Hanoi Must Make Next Move: Rusk

WASHINGTON (UPI) —U.S. Secretary of State Dean Rusk Friday challenged those who have demanded a halt in bombing of North Vietnam to now make good their promise that "something good would happen" toward ending the war.

"We think the move is up to Hanoi" and those who can influence the North Vietnamese, Rusk told a news conference eight hours after the United States stopped all air, sea and artillery bombardment of North Vietnam in the hope of prompting serious peace talks in Paris.

Besides putting the burden of action on Hanoi, Rusk also sought to assure South Vietnam of full U.S. support at the delicate stage in events and to put an end to speculation that the timing of President Johnson's decision was politically motivated.

Evidently referring primarily to the Russians, Rusk said:

"Some governments and leading personalities have over many months undertaken to tell us that something good would happen if we would only stop the bombing of North Vietnam.

"It is now incumbent upon all of those who have taken that view to make a maximum effort to insure that their advice has substance in it.

"We have our own reasons to
(Continued on Back Page, Col. 1)

It's Bonnie and Floyd

HOBBS, N.M. (AP) — Bonnie Hisey, a candidate for the New Mexico House of Representatives, has a problem. Voters who don't know him think he's a lady candidate. The Hisey family has to live with this problem and one other—Bonnie Hisey's wife's name is Floyd.

An American airman in Saigon tries to explain a headline in a capital newspaper, "LBJ Orders Bomb Halt," to a Vietnamese girl as the news broke Friday.
(AP Radiophoto)

Many Are Concerned

Troops in Saigon Skeptical

S&S Vietnam Bureau

SAIGON — "There's no point in stopping the bombing unless you're going to pull the troops out. This way, it's not getting us anywhere. The NVA aren't going to stop just because we quit bombing."

The young soldier was getting a shoeshine at the Saigon USO and giving his verdict on the latest U.S. bid for peace, the bombing halt—a bid which could ultimately affect the men here in South Vietnam whom the interdiction bombings in North Vietnam were protecting.

Almost none of the GIs questioned on Saigon street corners the morning of the announcement and shortly before had any clear idea where the halt would lead, but they had opinions. Most were skeptical.

"It will definitely hurt us," says Spec. 4 Rudolph Meeks, 23. "I don't think Hanoi will stop the war because of the bomb halt. The NVA will be able to move in more supplies and set up more artillery and rocket sites in North and South Vietnam."

(Continued on Back Page, Col. 2)

PARIS (UPI)—North Vietnam said Friday it has agreed to attend broadened peace talks in Paris, including the National Liberation Front (NLF) and the Saigon regime.

In a terse, three-paragraph statement a North Vietnamese spokesman said his delegation, headed by Minister Xuan Thuy, had been informed on Oct. 30 of President Lyndon Johnson's decision to stop the bombing and shelling and "all other acts of war" against North Vietnam.

The statement said, "in order to find a peaceful settlement of the Vietnam problem, a meeting including the representatives of the democratic Republic of Vietnam, the South Vietnam National Liberation Front, the United States and the Republic of Vietnam will be held in Paris not earlier than Nov. 6, 1968."

President Johnson in announcing the total bombing halt, Thursday night already set the date of the broadened talks as starting next Wednesday.

In a printed statement, the North Vietnamese spokesman said Thuy has relayed the com-

Related stories and photos on Pages 2, 5, 6, 12, 13

munication of the United States delegation headed by Ambassador Averell Harriman to Hanoi. The spokesman refused to elaborate on whether his statement meant that Hanoi was prepared to enter extended peace negotiations.

Thuy refused to say why his statement was referring to "a meeting" while President Johnson had flatly announced that the Paris talks were entering a new phase.

In spite of the apparent inconsistency of the Hanoi delegation statement, Harriman earlier flatly announced the opening of a new phase of the talks Wednesday.

Harriman warned, however, that Saigon may not be represented at Wednesday's first meeting because it may take them time to organize a delegation.

Well-informed Communist diplomatic sources said Hanoi did not commit itself immediately to prolonged talks for three main tactical considerations.

— North Vietnam, sources said, will insist immediately at the first meeting of the extend-
(Continued on Back Page, Col. 5)

Street Without Joy

S&S Vietnam Bureau

SAIGON — President Johnson's bombing halt brought no apparent joy to Saigon.

The Presidential Palace was silent Friday. So was the rest of South Vietnamese officialdom. President Nguyen Van Thieu was scheduled to make a televised speech Saturday.

In a curt statement issued Friday afternoon, Thieu strongly indicated he had not willingly agreed to the cessation of all bombardment of North Vietnam.

"This morning at 9 a.m.," he said, "the American government has unilaterally decided to halt the bombing of North Vietnam as of 9 p.m. the same day.

"The Republic of Vietnam did not see any solid reasons to join the decision of the United States on this matter," Thieu's communique said.

"The Republic of Vietnam has reminded its allies of the harmful acts by which North Vietnam can profit through the cessation of the bombing, so precautionary measures have been taken and have been applied by the Republic of Vietnam and its allies."

Thieu did not spell out what the "precautionary measures"
(Continued on Back Page, Col. 5)

Cites Hero's Courage

WASHINGTON (UPI)—Army Secretary Stanley R. Resor Thursday praised the "surpassing act of personal courage" of an Army first sergeant — the newest Medal of Honor winner— who shielded his buddies from a grenade blast with his body and died wiping out a Viet Cong machine gun position.

Resor presented the 56th Medal of Honor of the Vietnam war at a Pentagon ceremony to Mrs. Janis A. Yabes of Lafayette, Colo., widow of 1st Sgt. Maximo Yabes.

In presenting the nation's highest military award to Mrs. Yabes, Resor said many men have "made that sacrifice but few have coupled with it the kind of surpassing act of
(Continued on Back Page, Col. 2)

Foe Moves Troops in Buffer Zone

By
SGT. ROGER NEUMANN
S&S Staff Correspondent

SAIGON — North Vietnam has used the Demilitarized Zone five times this week to move troops, equipment and to fire at U.S. reconnaissance planes, the American command said Thursday.

In four of the incidents, occurring Wednesday, U.S. artillery and ships fired back at the Communists, spokesmen said. The fifth incident occurred Monday.

The spotter planes, none of which was reported hit in the exchange of fire, directed U.S. counter-barrages and reported at least 35 secondary explosions and several fires.

A Marine tank battalion sighted the headlights of 10 vehicles moving through the buffer zone northeast of Con Thien, spokesmen said, but the targets were not fired on.

Communist troops also stepped up their attacks against South Vietnamese villages and Allied camps Tuesday. One shelling came possibly from within the Demilitarized Zone.

Twenty settlements or bases had been assaulted in the past 24 hours, military spokesmen said Wednesday, the greatest number since President Johnson called the bombing halt.

It was first reported that a South Vietnamese fire support base had been mortared from North Vietnamese positions within the buffer zone early Tuesday. But officials said later there was a possibility the Red gun sites were within South Vietnam. The incident was being investigated.

The Reds shelled U.S. Marine outposts five times Sunday from the DMZ, the first time since Johnson stopped attacks on the north.

Johnson had demanded the withdrawl of all Communist troops from the buffer strip in exchange for the bombing halt. The U.S. Command here has not commented on either of the attacks.

The South Vietnamese fire support base, four miles north-
(Continued on Back Page, Col. 2)

House IS a Home for GI

MEDINA, Ohio (AP) — Pfc. William G. Batchelder III is being discharged from the Army now that he has been elected to the Ohio House of Representatives.

A provision in the draft law exempts legislators from military service.

Batchelder, drafted last April and stationed at Ft. McPherson, Ga., was elected to the Ohio General Assembly last week. His father, William G. Batchelder Jr., said he had talked with his son on the telephone Tuesday and was informed that his application for discharge is being processed.

Batchelder filed his petitions for the primary before he was drafted. He won the Republican nomination in a four-man race in May and went on to defeat his Democratic opponent in absentia in the Nov. 5 general election.

PACIFIC

STARS STRIPES

AN AUTHORIZED PUBLICATION OF THE
U.S. ARMED FORCES IN THE FAR EAST

10¢

Vol. 24, No. 318   **Friday, Nov. 15, 1968**

Wet Side Story

These New Yorkers suddenly found themselves in "Venice" after knee-deep floodwaters inundated a section of the Battery, the lower tip of Manhattan. In left foreground is a stalled truck. The rain was dumped on the city by a violent storm which struck the U.S. East Coast and Canada, leaving at least 25 persons dead. Story on Page 3.   (AP Radiophoto)

U.S. WARNS REDS ON DMZ ATTACK

WASHINGTON (AP)—The United States is-sued a new warning Wednesday that "serious talks" could not be conducted with North Vietnam if the demilitarized zone dividing North and South Vietnam were violated by North Vietnamese attacks from the zone on allied forces.

The State Department said in a statement that U.S. representatives in Paris have called the attention of North Vietnamese representatives there "forcefully" to firing on allied forces "from positions within the DMZ" by North Vietnamese since Nov. 9.

The statement stopped short of declaring that these attacks were violations of the understanding with North Vietnam on the basis of which President Johnson ordered a halt to the bombing of North Vietnam on Oct. 31. The halt became effective Nov. 1.

The statement also covered two points of the understanding now in controversy with North Vietnam:

1. It denied the claim made by North Vietnam that the United States had agreed to "a four-sided or four-party conference" in the Paris peace talks and said the United States had proposed and still considers that it would be a conference of two sides, with the United States and South Vietnam constituting one side and North Vietnam and the National Liberation Front the other.

2. It denied that continuing reconnaissance flights over North Vietnam violate understandings reached before Johnson ordered the bombing stopped.

"The activities that we undertook to stop," the statement
(Continued on Back Page, Col. 1)

War Tour Is Ending For F111

By
S.SGT. JOHN HUBBLE
S&S Staff Correspondent

SAIGON—The controversial F111 fighter-bombers, brought into the war to deliver devastating strikes against Communist targets, are being sent home.

U.S. Air Force officials here announced Wednesday that a detachment of the super-sophisticated planes stationed at Takhli Royal Thai Air Base, Thailand, will be returned to Nellis Air Force Base outside Las Vegas, Nev., within the next two weeks.

F111s flew only slightly more than 50 attacks against Red targets during their deployment to the fighting. The swing-wing, $7 million jets flew their first mission March 26, their last May 1.

Three of the swift all-weather, low-altitude attackers were lost
(Continued on Back Page, Col. 1)

Negro Leader Slain By Negro Bandits

BOSTON (AP) — Five men burst into the headquarters of a civil rights group Wednesday shot the founder and two other men dead, then escaped, police said.

Two others wounded were hospitalized. All the victims and all the assailants were Negro, officers said.

One victim was identified as Guido St. Laurent, the blind founder and executive director of the New England Grass Roots Organization (NEGRO). St. Laurent was characterized by a city official as "a responsible militant."

St. Laurent's guide dog, a black Belgian Shepherd, re-mained at the victim's side as police closed off the three-story brick building on Blue Hill Avenue in the Roxbury section, a predominantly Negro area.

One of the others killed was identified as Carnell Eaton of Boston. The third victim was tentatively identified as Harold King of Cleveland, Ohio.

Police Supt. William Bradley said St. Laurent, 38, and Eaton were on parole.

The state Department of Corrections said the two were codefendants in a case in which they were convicted of armed robbery while masked. The case in-
(Continued on Back Page, Col. 4)

5 Win Medal of Honor

WAR NOT OVER: LBJ

PACIFIC
STARS ✦ STRIPES

AN AUTHORIZED PUBLICATION OF THE
U.S. ARMED FORCES IN THE FAR EAST

10¢

Vol. 24, No. 324   Thursday, Nov. 21, 1968

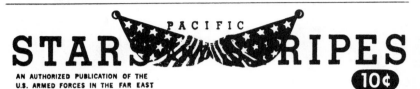

WASHINGTON (UPI) — President Johnson said Tuesday only "the possibility of peace" has been achieved in the Paris talks on Vietnam and that "bitter days and battles lie ahead."

At a White House ceremony honoring five new Medal of Honor winners, for heroism in Vietnam, Johnson said the United States is doing everything possible to attain a peaceful settlement at the conference table.

"All of our efforts are bent to that pursuit."

However, he added, "other bitter days and battles lie ahead" before a permanent settlement is reached.

Johnson was somber —he did not smile once —during the medals ceremony. "I cannot emphasize strongly enough that we have not attained peace...only the possibility of peace," he said.

Turning to the five Army men, including the first chaplain to receive America's highest military decoration, Johnson said "other brave men will be called upon for other brave acts" before peace is reached at the conference table.

On this occasion the nation's highest honor went to:

Sgt. Sammy L. Davis, 22, of Martinsville, Ind.; Capt. James A. Taylor, 31, Ft. Knox, Ky.; Spec. 5 Dwight H. Johnson, 21, Detroit; Spec. 4 Gary G. Wetzel, 21, Oak Creek, Wis.; and Capt. Angelo J. Liteky, 37, a chaplain, a native of Washington, D. C., whose mother lives in Jacksonville, Fla.

The men's citations listed these acts of heroism: Davis: Singlehandedly manned a howitzer and repeatedly fired into enemy positions Nov. 18, 1967, at a remote fire support base west of Cai Lay. While still under heavy enemy fire managed to float himself across a deep nearby river to rescue three wounded comrades—despite his inability to swim. Wounded in the attack on his base, ignored his wounds and returned to the battle to help another howitzer crew until the enemy force gave up.

Taylor: On Nov. 9, 1967, singlehandedly rescued wounded crew members from a burning assault vehicle after it had been ambushed west of Que Son. Taylor personally rescued five wounded persons from the vehicle despite heavy enemy fire and exploding ammunition from the burning vehicle.

After completing the rescue Taylor was painfully wounded by a bursting mortar round but
(Continued on Back Page, Col. 2)

Five heroes of Vietnam war wear Medals of Honor presented by President Johnson. From left: Capt. James A. Taylor, Spec. 4 Gary G. Wetzel, Sgt. Sammy L. Davis, Spec. 5 Dwight H. Johnson and Chaplain Angelo J. Liteky.   (AP Radiophoto)

Defiant Czechs

PRAGUE (UPI) — Tens of thousands of students and journalists raised new opposition Tuesday to the restrictive provisions of the Czechoslovak Communist Party's new party line.

A lengthy resolution approved in a meeting of the full Czechoslovak party Presidium Monday replaced the April "Action Program" and became the new guiding policy of the party.

Not far from the Bratislava meeting, students at Comenius University occupied their class buildings to back demands for more political freedom.

Tens of thousands of students in other cities participated in the (Continued on Back Page, Col. 4)

Alas, It's a Lad

HOUSTON (UPI) — Chivalry isn't dead but it got lost somewhere among the bangles and beads. When a long-haired hippie boarded a Houston Rapid Transit Co. bus, a male passenger got up to give the newcomer his seat. He lost his seat because what he thought was a girl turned out to be a boy.

U.N. Rejects Peking Seat Bid; Support for Chiang Grows

UNITED NATIONS (UPI) — The General Assembly Tuesday night defeated a move to expel Nationalist China and seat the Chinese Communists. The vote was 58-44 with 23 abstentions.

The 14-vote margin was the largest in favor of Nationalist China since 1963, when the Assembly voted 57-41 for the Taiwan government. The result put 56.8 per cent of the expanding U.N. membership behind the Nationalists, compared with 56.3 per cent last year.

The vote came after a week and a half of debate on the issue which is hotly contested in the U.N. each year.

It was the 19th year the China representation issue was before the Assembly. Each year, except for 1964 when paralysis over the financial crisis prevented a vote, the Assembly has voted in favor of Nationalist China.

Last year's vote was 58-45 with 17 abstentions.

Albania, with support from Cambodia, Cuba and several other powers, has been the main proponent of seating the Peking regime in recent years. The Soviet Union, as it has for several years, gave little more than lip service to the Peking cause, announcing that it supported the move to give the U.N. seat to Communist China "as a matter of principle."

Before the principal vote, on a resolution sponsored by Albania and 15 other sponsors which would have expelled Generalissimo Chiang Kai-shek's regime and opened the seat to the Chinese Communists, the Assembly approved a U.S.-backed resolution making the issue an "important question" requiring a two-thirds majority for approval. The vote on the procedural resolution was 73-47 with 5 abstentions.

Saigon Still Balks at Talks

Compiled From AP and UPI
PARIS — The United States, in spite of redoubled efforts, has failed to break down South Vietnam's boycott of the scheduled broadened Paris talks. There would be no meeting Wednesday, the past regular meeting day, high allied sources said Tuesday night.

An official with direct access to the negotiations said, "We can report no progress in our effort to reach an accord with Saigon on terms of reference that would overcome their hostility to the presence of the National Liberation Front (NLF)."

But, the source said, hopes remained high that President Nguyen Van Thieu will soon work out a formula with U.S. Ambassador Ellsworth Bunker permitting him to send a delegation to Paris shortly.

Meanwhile, in Saigon, some South Vietnamese sources close to the government indicated that the principle of dispatching a delegation to the French capital had been decided. There was a "50-50 chance" it would be led by Vice President Nguyen Cao Ky.

Lending support to suggestions there has been a softening (Continued on Back Page, Col. 1)

Marines Repel Human Waves

RED SUICIDE ATTACK

PACIFIC
STARS AND STRIPES

AN AUTHORIZED PUBLICATION OF THE
U.S. ARMED FORCES IN THE FAR EAST

10¢

Vol. 25, No. 57   Thursday, Feb. 27, 1969

Nixon Sees Royalty And Commons, Too

LONDON (UPI)—President Nixon lunched with the queen, sipped tea with a "cross-section" of commoners and discussed politics with the prime minister in a series of meetings Tuesday.

In between, the President found time to pay an unscheduled visit to the "Mother of Parliaments," so far as is known the first visit by a U.S. president to the House of Commons while it was sitting.

Nixon smiled his way through the toughest day yet of his eight-day schedule. His security guard and the London bobbies assigned to him were thrown into confusion several times when he stepped into crowds to shake hands and chat.

Protest plans by the "Hot Reception for Nixon Committee"— which vowed to dump the President physically on the "first plane back to the United States" — fizzled miserably. Only a score of long-haired youths turned up to shout "down with Nixon" and toss two rotten apples in the direction of his passing limousine. They missed.

Nixon opened his day by meeting with Conservative Party leader Edward Heath to hear the opposition viewpoint. Then he went to No. 10 Downing Street for more than two hours of formal discussions with Prime **(Continued on Back Page, Col. 5)**

Ike Progress 'Remarkable'

WASHINGTON (AP) — Former President Dwight D. Eisenhower continued to recover from abdominal surgery Tuesday and doctors called his progress "little short of remarkable."

An evening medical bulletin from doctors attending the 78-year-old general at Walter Reed Army hospital said Eisenhower has progressed to the point where he "read for a brief period this afternoon."

"Gen. Eisenhower has spent a comfortable day. His cardiovascular status is remaining stable. Mrs. Eisenhower has visited him frequently during the day. He asked for his glasses and read for a brief period this afternoon," the bulletin said.

Queen Elizabeth escorts President Nixon on a tour of Buckingham Palace as the President arrives for lunch.   (AP Radiophoto)

Compiled From AP and UPI

SAIGON—North Vietnamese infantrymen, attacking behind suicide volunteers who turned themselves into human bombs, slashed into two U.S. Marine outposts near the Demilitarized Zone early Tuesday but were driven out in vicious hand-to-hand fighting.

As the smoke of battle cleared, the Marines counted their losses—36 killed and 97 wounded in the biggest of a series of attacks launched by the Communists Sunday.

Fifty-six Communist soldiers were known dead, their bodies sprawled inside the perimeters or on the barb wire. The Marines had yet to make a sweep of the fog-shrouded battlefields.

Sandal-clad Communist sappers carrying tiny flashlights and with explosive satchel charges strapped to their bodies attacked the two outposts, four and nine miles west-northwest of the geographical designation called "The Rockpile" about 4 a.m.

The Communists attacked the bases in two 200-man waves, UPI's David Lamb reported from the scene. Mortar rounds thudded into the outposts as the assaults began, Lamb reported.

The Communists blazed away

Related Stories, Page 6

with automatic weapons fire and tossed their satchel charges into Marine bunkers, penetrating the barb wire perimeter of both camps and forcing the Leathernecks to call in artillery barrages on their own positions.

One Marine killed five Communists with a knife in hand-to-hand combat. Another beat one to death with a hand grenade.

The Leatherneck commander at Fire Base Russell, just two miles below the DMZ, reported to Marine headquarters in Da Nang that enemy sappers taped 25-pound bundles of TNT on their backs, wrapped the detonating cord around their chests, and then charged to blast lanes through the Marine defenses.

The commander, who was not identified, was quoted as saying:

"At least two were wounded as they reached the lines of the perimeter and became entangled in the wire. When Marines went toward them at first light they pulled the detonating device and blew themselves up."

The Marines on the hilltop **(Continued on Back Page, Col. 3)**

6 Killed In Calif. Deluge

Compiled From AP and UPI

Thousands of Californians fled floods and earthslides Tuesday as a record rain poured down.

At least six persons were dead. An estimated 6,000 persons were evacuated in six counties from Fresno south.

Four persons were killed and a fifth injured Tuesday when a wall of mud and water crushed the walls of their cabin in a tiny village at the lower slope of 8,500-foot Mt. Baldy.

Killed at Mt. Baldy Village were Donald J. Stewart, 50, his daughters Denise, 16, and Ann, 12, and son David, 6. His wife and four other children survived although one daughter was injured, the San Bernardino County coroner's office said.

Several automobiles were reported buried by mud in the mountain resort area 40 miles east of Los Angeles. Several hundred persons were evacuated from their flood-threatened homes in nearby Cucamonga.

The wall of a fire station in Orange County being used as an evacuation center collapsed, killing at least one other person, the coroner's office said. Eleven other persons in the building are **(Continued on Back Page, Col. 1)**

Airborne 'Assault' To Make History

By S&S Washington Bureau and Associated Press

WASHINGTON — About 2,500 Army paratroopers will be flown to South Korea next month for maneuvers the Pentagon called "the longest airborne assault operation in history."

Paratroopers of the 82nd Airborne Div. will join other U.S. and South Korean troops in a joint training exercise, called "Focus Retina." The operation will be held under simulated conditions of enemy attack.

The paratroopers will be flown 8,500 miles from Ft. Bragg, N.C., to the maneuver area.

The U.S. Strike Command at

MacDill AFB, Fla., will direct the movement of stateside forces by military aircraft from Pope AFB, N.C., to Korea where they will take part in ground landings and parachute drops during the exercise.

The exercise will be held about 40 miles southeast of Seoul.

The general concept of operations will see a Strike Command brigade of two battalions and full combat supporting equipment—the Second Brigade of the 82nd—fly to Korea on C141 transports of the Military Airlift Command and C130's of the Tactical Air Command.

In Korea between March 15 **(Continued on Back Page, Col. 2)**

Air-Land Duel Rages Along Suez

Compiled From AP and UPI

JERUSALEM — Egyptian and Israeli artillery batteries opened fire Saturday in an intensive five-hour duel along the Suez Canal.

Earlier in the day Egyptian and Israeli jets exchanged fire over the Sinai Desert and each side claimed to have downed one of the other's planes.

An Israeli spokesman said four Egyptian MIGs had entered Israeli airspace and were intercepted in the sky. He said one MIG was downed during a dogfight. The pilot bailed out and was captured by Israeli ground forces and taken to a hospital. The spokesman claimed all Israeli planes returned safely to base.

An Egyptian military spokesman acknowledged over Cairo Radio that a MIG was lost but he claimed an Israeli Mirage fighter also was shot down. The

(Continued on Back Page, Col. 1)

PACIFIC
STARS AND STRIPES

AN AUTHORIZED PUBLICATION OF THE
U.S. ARMED FORCES IN THE FAR EAST

10¢

Vol. 25, No. 68   **Monday, March 10, 1969**

GIs Hurl Back Charge By N. Viet Battalion

By JO2 DAVE WARSH
S&S Vietnam Bureau

SAIGON — A battalion of well-equipped North Vietnamese soldiers — some of them carrying flame-throwers — charged an isolated U.S. landing zone early Saturday but crumbled as the little camp's howitzers were fired at them like rifles.

The attack on the 1st Air Cav. Div.'s Landing Zone Grant, about 45 miles northwest of Saigon, was coupled with two other unsuccessful assaults on American bases along Communist corridors to the capital.

Meanwhile, Communist gunners opened up overnight on some 50 targets scattered throughout Vietnam. Most of the shellings were aimed at small military units, U.S. spokesmen said. Few casualties and only light damage was reported.

Some larger units also were hit, the spokesmen said, and the Communists apparently reserved the heaviest of their shellings for the U.S. Marine combat base at An Hoa, about 20 miles southwest of Da Nang. About 135 mortar and rocket rounds hit the camp, causing light casual-
(Continued on Back Page, Col. 3)

An Israeli soldier inspects a missile taken from the wreckage of an Egyptian MIG downed during a dogfight over the Sinai Desert Saturday with Israeli jets. Egypt claimed an Israeli plane also was shot down, but the Israelis denied this. (AP Radiophoto)

Focus on Earth's Riches

Astronauts Turn 'Space Prospectors'

SPACE CENTER, Houston (AP) — Their dangerous test-piloting over, the three Apollo 9 astronauts took on a new job Saturday. They prospected the earth for hidden riches from more than 100 miles in space.

With special cameras aimed precisely at special ground targets, the astronauts hope to pick up clues to mineral resources, water, timberlands, and fishing grounds by the special light radiations they emit.

But they ran into small difficulties on their first attempt because of an error by mission control.

As Air Force Cols. James A. McDivitt and David R. Scott and civilian Russell L. Schweick-art trained their filtered cameras on the American Southwest, they noticed the automatic pilot was turning the ship the wrong way.

Mission control quickly gave permission for manual flight, and after checking, sheepishly reported it had given the wrong autopilot information.

But before they turned to their task, they took time off to sing "Happy Birthday" to the flight operations director, Christopher Columbus Kraft Jr., the man in mission control who has shepherded every U.S. manned flight.

As the astronauts sped into the last and easiest half of their 10-day mission, they asked Kraft to be put on the line to hear their belated greeting. He turned 45 on Feb. 28, the day the Apollo 9 launch was originally scheduled.

At 2:27 p.m. EST the astronauts gave their spaceship a small backwards burst with their powerful rocket engine, lowering their orbit slightly to an elipse ranging from about 138 to 121 miles above the earth. This normal and planned adjustment allows the astronauts to use their small attitude control rockets to break their speed and come home if an emergency occurs. The shot had been delayed about 90 minutes because of a faulty computer reading

The prospecting experiment consists of four small cameras mounted on a ring that fits over one of the Apollo windows to be aimed at earth.

With the information Apollo 9 obtains, scientists hope to devise satellites that can inventory the world's resources, find underground water supplies, tell the difference between diseased and healthy crops, locate schools of fish, and tally the board feet of timber in forests.

The cameras will be able to see chlorophyll in plants, and even underwater food supplies. They may be able to detect warm water currents, and locate the oil slick fish give off.

St. Pat's Pat On 5th Ave.

NEW YORK (AP) — Mayor John V. Lindsay promised 1,000 Irishmen that the St. Patrick's Day parade "will always be on Fifth Avenue."

The mayor addressed the installation ceremony of the grand marshals for this year's parade on March 17.

Harking to a suggestion by some residents and businessmen that parades be abolished on Fifth Avenue and moved to Central Park, Lindsay said:

"Any mayor who tried to move the St. Patrick's Day parade to Central Park would probably wind up in the pond."

Japan Says U.S. Envoy Named

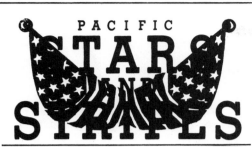

PACIFIC STARS AND STRIPES

AN AUTHORIZED PUBLICATION OF THE
U.S. ARMED FORCES IN THE FAR EAST

10¢

Vol. 25, No. 117   Monday, April 28, 1969

Compiled From AP and UPI

TOKYO—The United States has appointed Armin H. Meyer, currently ambassador to Iran, as ambassador to Japan, a Foreign Ministry spokesman said Saturday.

The Japanese government has agreed to accept Meyer, he said.

The spokesman said President Nixon will announce formally the appointment of Meyer to the post, vacated in January when Ambassador U. Alexis Johnson left here to assume his new position as State Department under secretary for political affairs.

In Tehran, Meyer expressed surprise over the Japanese reports.

"I honestly know nothing about it and have received no official notice relevantly," Meyer said.

"Anything like that, about appointments, must come from the White House and I have not received it," he said.

In Washington, the White House would neither con-
(Continued on Back Page, Col. 2)

ARMIN H. MEYER

At Cambodia Border

REDS BUSHWHACKED

By JO2 DAVE WARSH
S&S Staff Correspondent

SAIGON — One American soldier was wounded early Saturday when 213 Communists died in a battle so lopsided it wasn't worth the name.

U.S. cannons fired into Cambodia to silence Red mortars threatening the defenders of "Frontier City," a tiny circle around some 200 GIs less than a mile from the border.

Machine gun-firing helicopters began picking off Communists about 10 p.m. Friday as the Reds hustled into place. The enemy troops hid in groves of trees and behind sun-baked paddy dikes on the broad plain 35 miles west of Saigon.

The camp's defenders, members of C Co., 4th Bn., 9th Inf. of the 25th Inf. Div. watched on radar scopes or peered through $35,000 telescopes that allowed them to see in the dark while about a battalion of Red troops —most of them North Vietnamese—prepared for a charge.

At division headquarters 15 miles away, commanders shrugged off an apparent diversionary move by a platoon of Communists against nearby patrol base Diamond and pointed cannons, helicopters and jet bombers at Frontier City.

A half-hour after midnight, the Reds were ready.

Nearly 300 mortar rounds and a score of powerful 107mm rockets fell on the camp but
(Continued on Back Page, Col. 1)

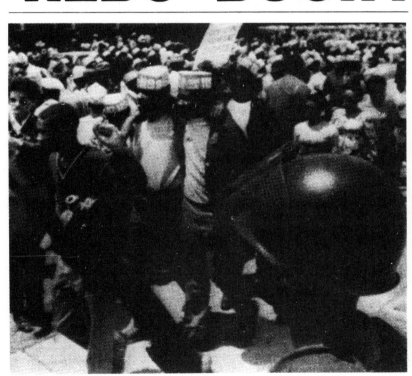

AP Radiophoto
NATIONAL GUARDSMAN WATCHES STRIKERS MARCH IN CHARLESTON, S.C.

It's Over And Out For Haney

WASHINGTON (AP) — Paul Haney, once the "voice" of the U.S. manned spaceflight program, has announced he is resigning from the National Aeronautics and Space Administration.

Haney, formerly director of public affairs at the Manned Space Flight Center in Houston, Texas, had been relieved of that post.

Space agency officials said they were making a change and had offered Haney another post at Washington headquarters of the agency.

The one-time Washington newsman whose voice was familiar to millions of people throughout the country as the commentator for major space shots in recent years, told a reporter, "I'm quitting."

He said his decision followed a three-hour, "fairly moderate" discussion with Julian Scheer, NASA's public affairs chief, that "found no area of accommodation at all."

He said Scheer had offered him a post in Washington but that he had turned it down.

$12.2 Billion Deficit

WASHINGTON (UPI) — The Treasury Department said Friday the federal budget showed a deficit of $12.2 billion at the end of the third quarter of fiscal 1969.

2nd Negro Mass Arrest

CHARLESTON, S. C. (UPI)— About 75 negroes were taken into custody Saturday in the second mass arrest in as many days after staging a four-hour demonstration in support of striking hospital workers and the jailed Rev. Ralph D. Abernathy.

Abernathy and 100 others were arrested Friday for illegal
(Continued on Back Page, Col. 5)

29-Warship U.S. Armada Shifting to the Yellow Sea

WASHINGTON (UPI) —The 29-warship U. S. armada formed in the Far East to protect intelligence flights is leaving the Sea of Japan, the Defense Department announced Saturday.

The department said the task force, led by the nuclear-powered aircraft carrier Enterprise, will continue operations in the Yellow Sea on the opposite side of the Korean peninsula.

The ships were ordered on station in the Sea of Japan after North Korea shot down an American EC121 reconnaissance plane.

No reason was given for the shift. But it was assumed the task force would continue the protective mission assigned to it after the Navy's plane was shot down by North Korean MIG jets with a loss of 31 lives April 14.

Asked whether intelligence
(Continued on Back Page, Col. 3)

REDS SHELL, ATTACK 159 U.S., VIET SITES

PACIFIC STARS STRIPES

AN AUTHORIZED UNOFFICIAL PUBLICATION
FOR THE U.S. ARMED FORCES OF THE PACIFIC COMMAND

10¢

Vol. 25, No. 133   Wednesday, May 14, 1969

By JO2 DAVE WARSH
S&S Staff Correspondent

SAIGON — Communist gunners and troops struck overnight at 159 targets in South Vietnam —including almost every major U.S. headquarters in the country— raising speculation that a new Red offensive was in the works, military spokesmen said Monday.

The wave of attacks was the biggest since the Communists' 1968 Tet offensive, U.S. spokesmen said, but only 70 of the attacks caused casualties or damage.

About 100 Americans are believed to have died in the assaults across the country. Forty-eight of the Reds' attacks were directed at U.S. installations, including a handful of determined assaults on small outposts, which were turned back.

The headquarters of five of nine U.S. divisions in Vietnam were targets. Included were of the 1st, 9th and 25th Inf. Divs.; the 1st Air Cav. Div. and the 3rd Marine Div. headquarters at Dong Ha. The huge army command complex at Long Binh was also hit.

Other targets were air bases at Da Nang, Chu Lai, Phan Rang, Bien Hoa and the Marine airstrip at Marble Mountain near Da Nang. A delayed report said Pleiku AB in the central highlands took about five 122mm rockets early Sunday.

About five 107mm rockets hit near the runways at Tan Son

(Continued on Back Page, Col. 2)

Facts About Fortas Handed to Warren

WASHINGTON (AP)— Atty. Gen. John N. Mitchell acknowledged Monday that he passed on "certain information" to Chief Justice Earl Warren last week concerning the controversy surrounding Justice Abe Fortas.

Earlier, Newsweek magazine reported that Mitchell had asked Warren to urge that Fortas resign from the court.

A Republican senator said Monday that he has been told Fortas will resign this week.

In a terse statement in response to inquiries, Mitchell said:

"At my request, the chief justice was kind enough to see me in his chambers last Wednesday, May 7, 1969, at 11:30 a.m.

"As a courtesy to the chief justice, I felt it incumbent upon me to inform him of certain information known by me which might be of aid to him."

After Mitchell issued his statement, a Justice Department spokesman said there would be no further comment.

Newsweek said that Mitchell visited Warren on orders of President Nixon but the White House press secretary, Ronald L. Ziegler, said Monday:

"The President did not direct the attorney general to discuss

(Continued on Back Page, Col. 1)

Fumes Fell 42 Workers

KANSAS CITY, Mo. (AP) — At least 42 persons were hospitalized with carbon monoxide poisoning incurred at a federal government building in suburban Grandview, Mo., Monday.

Capt. James Collier of the Grandview Fire Dept. said an air conditioning unit was not ventilating properly. The carbon monoxide was drawn into the system from a hot water heater's exhaust flue.

The building is occupied by the Internal Revenue Service and the General Services Administration.

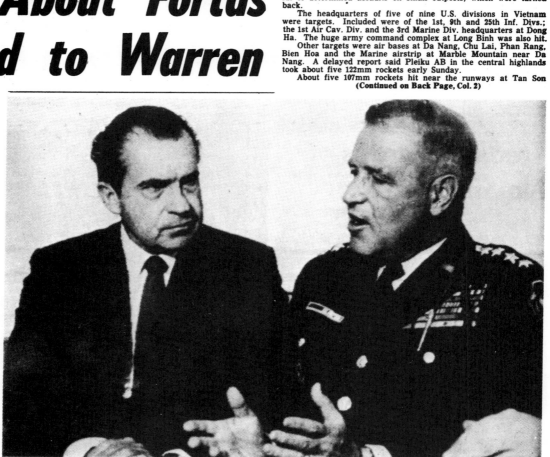

PRESIDENT NIXON DISCUSSES THE VIETNAM WAR SITUATION WITH GEN. CREIGHTON ABRAMS.   AP Radiophoto

Nixon to Address Nation on Viet Outlook

WASHINGTON (AP) — President Nixon conferred Monday with the U.S. military commander in Vietnam, Gen. Creighton Abrams, and will address the nation Wednesday on prospects of peace as he sees them.

But he is not expected to announce any major breakthrough in the Paris talks or any U.S. troop withdrawals from Vietnam.

Abrams flew in from Vietnam Sunday and returned Monday afternoon.

Monday morning he met with Nixon, Secretary of Defense Melvin R. Laird, Gen. Earle G. Wheeler, chairman of the Joint Chiefs of Staff, and the President's national security adviser, Henry A. Kissinger.

White House press secretary Ronald L. Ziegler said this first meeting between the President and the top U.S. military man in Vietnam was a review of the situation there, with three factors uppermost.

Nixon sought Abrams' views on enemy military activity, including the possibility of new offensive actions.

He wanted information on the state of training of the South Vietnam army.

And he wanted to discuss the level of U.S. forces in Vietnam.

On the latter point, Ziegler said he wanted to emphasize that any decision on force levels will be made on the basis of the three criteria he said Nixon has

mentioned on numerous occasions:

1. "The ability of the South Vietnamese to defend themselves in the areas we now are defending them.

2. "Progress of the Paris talks.

3. "The level of enemy activity."

Abrams will report on these and other matters again after his return to Saigon.

Officials underscored repeat-

(Continued on Back Page, Col. 5)

Draft Destroyer Caught in the Act

PACIFIC STARS & STRIPES

AN AUTHORIZED UNOFFICIAL PUBLICATION
FOR THE U.S. ARMED FORCES OF THE PACIFIC COMMAND

10¢

Vol. 25, No. 141   Thursday, May 22, 1969

In top photo, Charles Friend (left), 22, and Walter Skinner, 25, watch as fire consumes records taken from Los Angeles Army induction center. Skinner looked down to discover his clothes afire. Below, Friend and a passerby roll Skinner on pavement to douse flames. Police later arrested Skinner, unhurt, and Friend on burglary charges.   (AP Radiophoto)

10-Day Fight Over
'HAMBURGER HILL' TAKEN

Compiled From S&S and AP

SAIGON — American paratroopers and South Vietnamese infantrymen, in a four-pronged assault, Tuesday seized "Hamburger Hill," a 3,000-foot North Vietnamese mountaintop fortress along the rugged Laotian frontier. It was the 10th day of heavy fighting for the position.

Spokesmen for the 101st Airborne Div. said the reinforced Allied force, which was doubled overnight to include more than 1,000 paratroopers and 400 South Vietnamese infantrymen, stormed the Dong Ap Bia mountain from four sides.

Sharp fighting was reported, however, between the mountain and the Laotian border, less than two miles away. The North Vietnamese troops were said to be trying to move back into base sanctuaries in Laos.

But one battalion of paratroopers, part of the assault force, ran into the retreating North Vietnamese and maneuvered to try to trap them between the Allied forces. Helicopter gunships firing rockets and machine guns raked the retreating Communist soldiers.

Military spokesmen said the Communists lost 426 men killed in the battle for the mountain, while U.S. casualties were put at 39 killed and 273 wounded.

Tuesday's push hit the hill's defenders from all sides as the 101st's 3rd Bn., 187th Inf. was joined by the 1st Bn., 506th Inf.; the 2nd Bn., 501st Inf. and the 3rd Bn. of the Vietnamese 1st Div.

The ground assault came after heavy artillery and air bombardment. The 3,000-foot peak fell into Allied hands as A and C Companies of the 3rd Bn., 187th Inf., secured the crest on the northwest side and the Vietnamese took the southeastern knoll.

''The men moved right along,'' said Capt. Gerald R. Harkins, A Co. commander. "We started 300 yards from the top and used the treeline and fallen trees for cover."

The Reds, protected by heavily fortified bunkers on the steep slope, answered with small arms and rocket grenades. But
(Continued on Back Page, Col. 1)

Apollo's Jolly Trio Hit of Show

Compiled From AP and UPI

SPACE CENTER, Houston — With the moon pulling them closer and their arrival less than a day away, Apollo 10 astronauts did homework Tuesday for their hazardous close-view trip and once more gave a televised travelogue of the now-small earth.

They had a long quiet period, with little talk to the ground, in which they studied the intricate maneuvers that lie ahead — where any misstep could mean death on the barren lunar surface.

If they were apprehensive they didn't show it.

Navy Commander Eugene
(Continued on Back Page, Col. 2)

Nixon, Thieu Set Talks on Midway

WASHINGTON (UPI)—President Nixon will meet June 8 with President Nguyen Van Thieu of South Vietnam on Midway Island to discuss the war and how to end it, the White House announced Tuesday.

Both the White House and Republican congressional leaders sought to squelch speculation that the conference was arranged hurriedly because of pressure from Thieu, who publicly called for such a meeting. Thieu is known to differ with Washington on where the road to peace lies and how to travel it.

The White House announcement said the two leaders had wanted to get together as soon as feasible to exchange views. The statement stressed in advance of the meeting that it would be an occasion to affirm the "unity of purpose" between Washington and Saigon.

House Republican Leader Gerald R. Ford said after Tuesday's weekly meeting of GOP legislative leaders with Nixon that the Nixon-Thieu conference was "anticipated from the outset of this Administration."

Nixon will have with him at the meeting such top advisers as Secretary of State William P. Rogers, Defense Secretary Melvin R. Laird, his national security adviser, Henry A. Kissinger, and his ambassador to Saigon, Ellsworth Bunker.

Mystery Blasts Jolt Ore. Town

EUGENE, Ore. (UPI)—Hit-run saboteurs dynamited a bank, church, newspaper, university admissions office and a shop near state police headquarters Monday night and early Tuesday.

The 114-member police department in this city of 77,000 was placed on extra shifts as officers sought an explanation for the six mystery blasts which shattered windows and caused moderate damage to the five buildings.

Four other blasts occurred on city streets, apparently from explosives tossed from an automobile. No injuries were reported.

No arrests were made and no one was questioned except possible witnesses, said Police Capt. William Smith. Officials refused to speculate on the reason or those responsible for the dynamitings.

The only clues were a piece of fuse from a similar explosion
(Continued on Back Page, Col. 5)

1st Combat Troops Arrive Home

PACIFIC

STARS AND STRIPES

AN AUTHORIZED UNOFFICIAL PUBLICATION
FOR THE U.S. ARMED FORCES OF THE PACIFIC COMMAND

10¢

Vol. 25, No. 190   Thursday, July 10, 1969

Compiled From S&S, AP and UPI

MCCHORD AFB, Wash. —The first of 25,000 U.S. troops President Nixon is taking out of Vietnam landed at this sunswept air base Tuesday and stepped smiling to American soil as welcomers waved a sign reading "Welcome Home—Thank You for Keeping America Free."

Gen. William C. Westmoreland, their former commander in Vietnam and now Army chief of staff, told the returning veterans: "I want to convey to you the appreciation of our nation — appreciation for a job well done."

Westmoreland warned the troops that they "will be confronted by those who will degrade your performance in Vietnam."

But he told them they would find themselves "more mature, more dedicated to the service of others, more compassionate, more responsible, more realistic and more practical" than their contemporaries who have not served.

The Vietnam veterans stepped out of their C141 transport plane loaded down with souvenirs, (Continued on Back Page, Col. 1)

Damascus Disputes Claim

7 Syria Jets Downed In Dogfight, Israel Says

TEL AVIV (AP) — Israeli jets shot down seven Syrian MIG fighters over the occupied Golan Heights Tuesday, an Israeli military spokesman said.

The Syrian radio countered with a claim that four Israeli jets were destroyed and only three Syrian planes were lost in the battle.

An Israeli Army announcement said their sets intercepted the MIGs and a 30-minute dogfight took place at altitudes ranging from 10,000 to 20,000 feet.

The MIGs crossed into Israeli held territory near Quneitra in the highlands taken from Syria by the Israelis in the 1967 war, the spokesman said.

It was the biggest single score claimed by Israeli pilots since the six-day 1967 war, and was one of the largest dogfights in the Middle East since the war.

News of the battle was announced in parliament by Prime Minister Golda Meir, who sent her congratulations.

Israeli soldiers stationed near Quneitra said they saw part of the fight. "At times the battle was very high above the ground, other times it was so low we could see our planes chasing the Syrian aircraft," said one.

"We heard explosions at great height, but we saw no planes falling," said another.

The Damascus communique said two Syrian pilots bailed out safely but a third was killed. It added the battle lasted 70 minutes and that the four Israeli planes downed fell into Israeli-held territory.

The communique accused the Israeli planes of intruding into Syrian air space. The Israelis admitted no losses.

The Israeli announcement brought to 10 the number of Syr-(Continued on Back Page, Col. 1)

AP Radiophoto

Gen. William C. Westmoreland, Army chief of staff, at left, and Brig. Gen. Arthur W. Cruikshank, commander of the 62nd Military Airlift Wing, rejoin reviewers at McChord AFB, Wash., after greeting the troops returning from the Republic of Vietnam.

Astromonk Bonny Dies

HONOLULU (UPI) — Bonny the astromonk died Tuesday 12 hours after an emergency splashdown in the Pacific three weeks ahead of schedule. Investigators said the space capsule may have been too cold.

The 14-pound pigtail monkey was brought down near here Monday and rushed to an intensive care unit at Hickam AFB where scientists at first said he (Continued on Back Page, Col. 2)

Bombing Halt Has Let North Repair Supply Net: McConnell

WASHINGTON (UPI)—North Vietnam has rebuilt all the bridges, highways, and trans-shipment points that were destroyed by U.S. planes before the Oct. 31 suspension of bombing, according to Air Force Chief of Staff John P. McConnell.

"Practically everything in North Vietnam has been rebuilt," McConnell testified. "All the highways, the bridges, the trans-shipment points that were destroyed, and what little industry they have, which is not much.

"But everything is operating up there now very nearly as if it had not been even touched," McConnell said. "I would say the repair is 75 per cent completed."

McConnell's assessment was given to the Senate Armed Services Committee in closed session April 16. It was released Monday.

McConnell said that since the bombing halt, "supplies now enter North Vietnam without (Continued on Back Page, Col. 5)

Forecast: Riots, Brawls

WASHINGTON (AP)—You can now "dial-a-disturbance," or at least information about one here. The Pentagon has set up a recorded phone message to inform its employes about any civil disturbances going on.

Ted to Run Again in '70; Won't Enter '72 Campaign

—Page 24

PACIFIC

STAR AND STRIPES

AN AUTHORIZED UNOFFICIAL PUBLICATION
FOR THE U.S. ARMED FORCES OF THE PACIFIC COMMAND

10¢

Vol. 25, No. 212 — Friday, Aug. 1, 1969

'It's Up to Reds'

NIXON VISITS GI'S IN VIET

BANGKOK (AP) — President Nixon swept in and out of South Vietnam Wednesday, saying: "We have gone as far as we can or should go in opening the door of negotiations which will bring peace."

Nixon made his statement at Independence Palace in Saigon where he conferred with President Nguyen Van Thieu.

Recounting the peace offers made by the allies at the Paris talks, Nixon said it is now time

Related stories, photos on Pages 6, 12, 13

for the North Vietnamese and the Viet Cong "to sit down with us and talk seriously about ways to stop the killing."

Later at a combat base near Saigon, he told U.S. infantrymen: "Out here in this dreary, difficult war, I think history will record that this may have been one of America's finest hours, because we took a difficult task and we succeeded."

Nixon dashed to nearby Vietnam and back before heading for India Thursday on his round-the-world tour.

Nixon's noon arrival at Saigon's Tan Son Nhut airport and (Continued on Back Page, Col. 3)

PRESIDENT NIXON MINGLES WITH 1ST INF. DIV. TROOPS AT DI AN, VIETNAM. — AP

Nixon Forces 'Bend' on Surtax
—Page 2

Mars Photos Show Some New Features
—Page 3

Soviet Author Skips to Britain
—Page 24

PACIFIC
STAR STRIPES

10¢

Vol. 25, No. 225   AN AUTHORIZED UNOFFICIAL PUBLICATION FOR THE U.S. ARMED FORCES OF THE PACIFIC COMMAND   Thursday, Aug. 14, 1969

Reds Attack 16 Camps

Heavy Battles Flare Throughout S. Viet

Troops of the 1st Air Cav. Div. prepare to board helicopters to go to the aid of a base camp 25 miles north of Tay Ninh which was attacked by Communists. It was one of a series of Red assaults launched around Vietnam Tuesday.

UPI Radiophoto

By SPEC. 5 ERIC JOHNS
S&S Staff Correspondent

SAIGON — Massive Communist shelling and ground attacks raged throughout South Vietnam Tuesday in the heaviest outbreak of enemy-initiated actions in three months.

The Reds assaulted at least 16 Allied camps and let loose with 137 rocket and mortar barrages. The enemy rammed their way into three of the camps' perimeters, but were driven back or withdrew in each case.

Military reports listed 447 Communists and 52 Americans killed in the incidents. The U.S. command declined to characterize the outbreak of action as the start of a new offensive.

(The Associated Press said more than 800 Communist soldiers were reported to have been killed in the fighting.)

The heaviest fighting centered around An Loc, 60 miles north of Saigon. Communists attacked U.S. and Vietnamese troops within five miles of the Binh Long Province capital five times, and hit Americans within five miles of Loc Ninh, 12 miles farther north, three more times.

All eight battles began between 1:30 and 3 a.m. Tuesday and ended with the Reds pulling back before daybreak.

The fiercest clash came four miles northeast of An Loc as North Vietnamese battered for two hours at the headquarters base of the 1st Cav. Div.'s 3rd Brigade, which also houses 11th Armored Cav. Regt. troops.

The camp was hit by 107mm rocket fire in the midst of the fighting, and enemy soldiers carrying satchel charges pushed through the perimeter in at least three places. But fire from tanks, helicopter gunships and point-blank artillery pushed the Communists back.

Forty-eight Reds were found dead.

Seven GIs died and 45 others were injured.

Seventy-five NVA died in a charge on a 11th Armored Cav. Regt.-ARVN 5th Inf. Div. landing zone, four miles southwest of An Loc. An attack on a nearby 11th Armored Cav. fire base cost the Reds 32 more men, and 23 other NVA died after about 100 enemy encountered an American patrol five miles east of the city.

U.S. losses in the three engagements were four killed and 35 injured. Vietnamese casualties were termed light to moderate.

About 20 miles west of An Loc, North Vietnamese troops tried to overpower the 1st Cav. Div.'s Landing Zone Becky for the second morning in a row. A 50-minute fight, seven miles southeast of Katum, left 59 Communists dead. Thirteen Americans were killed and 39 others were wounded.

Farther north, three Americal Div.

(Continued on Back Page, Col. 2)

HO CHI MINH DIES

PACIFIC STARS STRIPES

AN AUTHORIZED UNOFFICIAL PUBLICATION
FOR THE U.S. ARMED FORCES OF THE PACIFIC COMMAND

10¢

Vol. 25, No. 247   Friday, Sept. 5, 1969

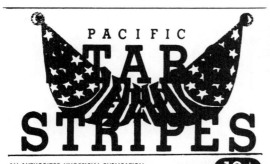

Heart Stroke Fatal To N. Viet Ruler

SAIGON (UPI)—Radio Hanoi Thursday said President Ho Chi Minh is dead. A Vietnamese language broadcast from the North Vietnamese capital said Ho died at 9:47 a.m. Wednesday.

The communique read over Radio Hanoi said:

"The Central Committee of the Lao Dong (Communist) party, the current affairs committee of the National Assembly, the Council of Ministers and the Front of the Fatherland are very pained to inform the people of Vietnam that Ho Chi Minh, president of the Democratic Republic of Vietnam, died at 9:47 (Hanoi time) on 3 September, 1969, as the result of a heart stroke."

Radio Hanoi said North Vietnam would observe a week of mourning Sept. 4-10.

"His death is a heavy loss to the Vietnamese people and country," it said.

Death came to the goateed North Vietnamese president after a day of rumors and report that he lay on his death bed.

The son of a middle class family, Ho was educated partly in Paris but returned to the Indochina peninsula to help organize and lead a revolution against French rule.

For 25 years he led first the Viet Minh against the French and later supported the Viet Cong against the South Vietnamese regime and later against U.S. Forces in almost continuous fighting that tore Vietnam apart.

Diplomatic circles speculated on the course North Vietnam would follow in the Vietnam peace talks and on its policy toward the two Communist giants which supported the Viet Cong—China and the Soviet Union.

Diplomats at Paris said Ho's death would not affect North Vietnamese policy in any way.

As the Vietnam war became the target for Pacific forces Ho became a symbol of revolution throughout the world and the chant "Ho, Ho, Ho; Ho Chi Minh" was heard at almost every antiwar rally.

Ho Chi Minh was not his real name. His actual age was equally

(Continued on Back Page, Col. 1)

Ho Chi Minh (left in both pictures) smiles during a banquet in Peking with Chinese Communist Premier Chou En-Lai (top). At bottom, Ho turns to chat with former Indonesian President Sukarno at Tjipanas, Indonesia.   (AP Radiophoto)

8 BERETS FREED; CHARGES DROPPED

Army Acts as CIA Shuns Trial

PACIFIC

STAR  RIPES

10¢

AN AUTHORIZED UNOFFICIAL PUBLICATION
FOR THE U.S. ARMED FORCES OF THE PACIFIC COMMAND

Vol. 25, No. 273   Wednesday, Oct. 1, 1969

WASHINGTON (UPI) — The Army Monday dropped all charges against six Green Beret officers accused of murdering a Vietnamese counter-spy, explaining that the Central Intelligence Agency (CIA) had refused to let its agents testify at their trial.

Army Secretary Stanley R. Resor ordered the action on grounds that the six Special Forces officers accused of killing alleged double agent Thai Khac Chuyen could not get a fair trial without CIA testimony.

When Armed Services Committee Chairman L. Mendel Rivers announced Resor's action on the floor of the House of Representatives, members broke into applause. About a dozen congressmen then spoke in praise of Resor's decision. None criticized it.

The six men, including the former Green Beret commander in Vietnam, Col. Robert B. Rheault, could have been sent to prison for life if they had been convicted at their courts-martial.

The secretary said all the men would be reassigned outside Vietnam.

Two other Green Berets, both enlisted men, against whom charges had been held in abeyance, were also freed by Resor's order.

Controversial from the start, the decision to prosecute the men had been appealed all the way to President Nixon by irate congressmen.

At the White House, Press Secretary Ronald Ziegler said as far as he knew President Nixon had nothing to do with Resor's decision. "This is a matter that has remained in the jurisdiction to which it appropriately belongs," Ziegler said.

Resor did tell Defense Secretary Melvin R. Laird (Continued on Back Page, Col. 1)

Power Play on In Bonn

Compiled From AP and UPI

BONN, Germany — West Germany's two major political parties jockeyed for power Monday with Social Democrat Willy Brandt trying to become the first Socialist chancellor of Germany since 1930.

The government, meanwhile, freed the mark to find its own level.

Neither major party won a clear mandate in Sunday's federal elections. The Christian Democrats of Chancellor Kurt Georg Kiesinger and Foreign Minister Brandt's Social Democrats each need the 30 parliamentary seats won by the small Free Democratic party in order to dominate the next government.

The two major parties now are joined in a ruling government coalition.

While top party officials analyzed election results, the government loosed the mark from its fixed exchange rate in an effort to halt speculation against an increase in value.

The present government stays in office until Oct. 19.

Speculators betting the German mark would be revalued upward following Sunday's election had poured more than $563 (Continued on Back Page, Col. 4)

COL. ROBERT B. RHEAULT

CAPT. ROBERT F. MARASCO

CAPT. BUDGE E. WILLIAMS

MAJ. DAVID E. CREW

MAJ. THOMAS C. MIDDLETON

CAPT. LELAND J. BRUMLEY

Antique Sale A Greek Myth

IRAKLION, Crete (AP) — Summer tourists grabbed at bargains in antiques on the Aegean island of Crete, including vases, jewelry and statuary represented as originals of the Minoan era— 3,000 B.C. And they paid fancy prices—about $330,000.

Now the Greek authorities call it all a fake. Forty so-called antique dealers have been arrested, charged with having replicas of archaeological objects manufactured in secret workshops and representing them as the real thing.

While Russia Keeps Building

Many U.S. Warships Obsolete: Expert

LONDON (AP) — Hundreds of American warships are now so old they are becoming a liability to the United States Navy, Raymond V. B. Blackman, a world authority on naval power, warned Monday.

He said Russia was ahead in new construction and had built a navy "to be reckoned with."

Blackman, writing in the annual "Jane's Fighting Ships," which he has edited for 21 years, said:

"The U.S. Navy is the only navy of any consequence which has had recent experience of operating warships in real war conditions. So qualitatively and quantitatively the U.S. Navy ought to be first and foremost among the top navies for several years to come.

"All the same, prodigious though the recent shipbuilding effort has been, especially in the fields of nuclear powered submarine construction and guided missile development, the U.S. Navy still has not overcome its block obsolescence problem.

"Most of the United States aircraft carriers, cruisers, destroyers, escorts and minesweepers, refitted or not, are a quarter of a century old. War potential though they could still just be, they are becoming a liability."

Blackman noted that the American taxpayer is "not very enthusiastic about paying for the building of new ships" and referred to statistics showing the Soviet Union has outpaced the United States in new construction.

The Soviet Navy is reported as (Continued on Back Page, Col. 2)

Lodge Tables Talks

PARIS (AP) — Ambassador Henry Cabot Lodge refused to speak at Thursday's session of the Vietnam peace talks, complaining "the other side's invective has created an atmosphere in which it is impossible to conduct serious negotiations."

When it came his turn to speak, he said, he simply asked for an adjournment, requesting that next week's session, the 40th where all four parties are involved, take place as usual next Thursday.

This action was unprecedented in any of the formal meetings on Vietnam since preliminary negotiations began in May, 1968.

Lodge reported this as he left the conference hall after a session which lasted for 4 hours and 25 minutes.

Saigon's Ambassador, Pham Dang Lam, said no progress toward peace had been made because "the Communist side hasn't given the least sign of a desire to conduct serious negotiations."

Xuan Thuy, Hanoi's emissary,

(Continued on Back Page, Col. 2)

'Phantom' Of Zodiac Calls Belli

SAN FRANCISCO (UPI) — A troubled man claiming to be the "Zodiac" killer of five persons has again tried repeatedly to set up a secret meeting with attorney Melvin Belli, the lawyer said Thursday.

Belli said the man, who pleaded for help and cried out "I've got to kill" during a series of bizarre conversations on a television talk show Wednesday, called his home and office several times during the night.

State agents turned to recent Dick Tracy comic strips about a "Zodiac gang" to see if they contained a clue to the killer's identity, while baffled police investigators reported all leads to the suspected slayer of five persons remained negative.

Belli said the caller, who failed to appear at two earlier rendezvous, wanted to meet at the lawyer's home. Belli attended the opening of the San Francisco International Film Festival and didn't learn of the latest calls until reaching his office Thursday.

"He called my home twice

(Continued on Back Page, Col. 2)

PACIFIC
STARS STRIPES
AN AUTHORIZED UNOFFICIAL PUBLICATION
FOR THE U.S. ARMED FORCES OF THE PACIFIC COMMAND

10¢

Vol. 25, No. 297

Saturday, Oct. 25, 1969

4 NCOs Take 5th; Wooldridge Relieved

Listening to testimony at a Senate investigations subcommittee hearing on alleged irregularities in operation of servicemen's clubs are (left to right), Sgt. Maj. William Wooldridge, Sgt. Narvaez Hatcher, ret., and Sgt. William Higdon. (UPI)

Senate OKs GI Bill Boost

WASHINGTON (AP) — The Senate passed Thursday a bill to raise veterans' education benefits by 46 per cent, despite hints that President Nixon might veto it as inflationary.

The vote on passage was 77-0.

Sen. Jacob K. Javits, R-N.Y., supporting the bill, mentioned the possibility of a veto, and warned that Nixon will have to cut federal spending elsewhere to balance the added expense of the veterans bill.

His amendment would have cut the education benefit boost from 46 per cent to 27 per cent.

WASHINGTON (AP)—Four Army sergeants invoked the 5th Amendment more than 100 times Thursday as Senate investigators sought to connect them with irregularities possibly running into millions of dollars.

One of them, Sgt. Maj. William O. Wooldridge, was promptly stripped of his rating as a command sergeant major.

Wooldridge is a former sergeant major of the Army and until his refusal Thursday to answer questions he had been command sergeant major at the White Sands Proving Ground in New Mexico.

This action by the Army does not affect his pay or title as a sergeant major and he will remain at White Sands in a different assignment.

Joining Wooldridge in refusing to testify before the Senate's permanent investigating subcommittee were Sgt. William Higdon and former Sgts. Narvaez Hatcher of Pensacola, Fla., and Seymour Lazar, Anaheim, Calif.

The questions they refused on advice of counsel to answer were concerned mainly with what one witness called systematic thefts from noncommissioned officers'

(Continued on Back Page, Col. 1)

Bulletin

TEXAS CITY, Tex. (AP) — Two gigantic explosions rocked the Union Carbide plant in Texas City Thursday night.

The explosions, about ten minutes apart, rattled windows and doors 25 miles away.

There was a huge roar and what sounded like a tremendous escape of gas. Flames leaped from the massive plant 100 feet into the air.

Ambulances and all types of emergency vehicles rushed to the scene.

At Galveston County Memorial Hospital, the emergency ward swung into feverish activity.

At Clear Lake City, near the Manned Spacecraft Center, a witness said the sky turned "almost clear white."

Texas City is south of Houston and north of Galveston.

In April, 1947, the French freighter Grand Camp exploded near a Texas City dock. That blast set off fires that caused one of the greatest holocausts in world history, killing more than 500 persons.

Beckett Wins Nobel Literature Prize

STOCKHOLM (UPI) — Dublin-born novelist, playwright and poet Samuel Beckett Thursday won the 1969 Nobel Prize for literature.

The announcement was made by the Swedish Academy.

The prize carried a cash award of $72,000.

The academy announcement said Beckett got the prize "for his writing, which — in new forms for the novel and drama — in the destitution of modern man acquires its elevation."

(Beckett's Paris publishing agent, Jerome Lindon said he did not know how he could advise the Irish-born writer that he had won the prize because Beckett was abroad on a trip and had not left word where he would be.

(Lindon said he thought Beckett could be on a cruise in the Mediterranean, in Italy, or even in the United States.)

The 63-year-old writer and philosopher, who lives in France and writes in the French language, has been a candidate for many years.

Beckett's possibly best known and most perplexing work is "Waiting for Godot," which won international acclaim when published in 1953.

Literary experts have noted that the academy has had a tendency to take geography into consideration when awarding the Nobel Prize.

In 1967 Latin American writer Miguel Angel Asturias was recognized. Last year Japanese author Yasunari Kawabata got the prize.

A total of 64 prizes in literature have been distributed since the first was awarded to

(Continued on Back Page, Col. 2)

LET US BE UNITED FOR PEACE—NIXON

PACIFIC STARS AND STRIPES

AN AUTHORIZED UNOFFICIAL PUBLICATION
FOR THE U.S. ARMED FORCES OF THE PACIFIC COMMAND

10¢

Vol. 25, No. 308   Wednesday, Nov. 5, 1969

WASHINGTON (AP)—President Nixon told the nation Monday night he has a secret timetable for withdrawing all U.S. ground combat forces from South Vietnam but declared Hanoi could sabotage it by stepping up military pressure.

At the same time, in a nationwide television-radio address, Nixon disclosed a hitherto secret exchange of correspondence last summer with the late President Ho Chi Minh of North Vietnam which he said bolsters his contention that Hanoi is blocking the road to peace.

The Nixon address broke no new ground in the realm of peace initiatives. It added up to a carefully-prepared appeal for homefront support of the administration's Vietnam policies.

"I have chosen a plan for peace," he said. "I believe it will succeed . . .

"Let us be united for peace. Let us also be united against defeat. Because let us understand: North Vietnam cannot defeat or humiliate the United States. Only Americans can do that."

Declaring that he would not reveal any details, Nixon talked about his withdrawal program in these words:

"We have adopted a plan which we have worked out in cooperation with the South Vietnamese for the complete withdrawal of all U.S. ground combat forces and their replacement by South Vietnamese forces on an orderly scheduled timetable."

The chief executive said that if enemy infiltration and the current battlefield lull continues, withdrawals probably could be speeded. But he said should Hanoi step up military pressure and jeopardize U.S. forces in Vietnam, "I shall not hesitate to take strong and effective measures to deal with that situation."

As he spoke, dispatches from South Vietnam told of increasing pressure by a force of about 5,000 North Vietnamese troops in the central highlands.

Administration officials declined to specify what counter steps Nixon might employ. They also said they could not

(Continued on Back Page, Col. 5)

Out of the Volley of Death

U.S. troops from Firebase Anne look relaxed as they head for helicopter to take them to Bu Prang Special Forces camp. The men left Firebase Anne after it came under heavy mortar, rocket and artillery attacks. (Story, Page 6.)   (AP)

Skyjack Trial Set for 1 of 6

AUGUSTA, Ga. (UPI) — The trial of the first of six hijackers to return to the United States from Cuba is scheduled Dec. 1, according to the FBI.

Robert Lee Sandlin, 19, accused of hijacking a Delta flight to Cuba last March, is to stand trial in federal district court on charges of air piracy and kidnaping, the FBI said.

Sandlin was one of six hijackers who returned to the United States Sunday, apparently disillusioned with the regime of Fidel Castro in Cuba.

K.W. Whittaker, special agent
(Continued on Back Page, Col. 3)

Marine Faces 8 Charges In Italy, Possible 30 Years

ROME (UPI) — An Italian prosecutor filed three more charges Monday against plane hijacker Raffaele Minichiello and said he was sure the American would be tried first in Italy.

If the 20-year-old skyjacker is tried here and convicted of all eight charges made against him, he could spend as long as 30 years in Italian prisons before American authorities could lay hands on him.

Assistant Prosecutor Massimo Carli called on Minichiello at Rome's Queen of Heavens jail Monday night to inform him of the three new charges against him — kidnaping and private violence against the Trans World Airlines crew he forced to fly him from California to Rome, and violence against a public official.

The last charge referred to Rome airport police chief Pietro Guli, forced by Minichiello to drive him at gunpoint from the airport Saturday into the Roman countryside, where the air pirate was captured.

Maximum sentences on the eight charges add up to 31 years and six months, but under Italian law the most time a person can serve in prison short of life imprisonment is 30 years.

Minichiello, who hijacked the plane in California last Friday and forced the pilot to fly it to Rome, faces a possible death
(Continued on Back Page, Col. 2)

Oldest GI, 72, Retires

COLUMBUS, Ohio (UPI)— Howard R. Davis of Columbus, who was the oldest enlisted man on active duty in any of the nation's armed forces, has retired after serving his country since 1916.

Davis, 72, who reached the rank of Army Sergeant First Class, earned two Silver Stars, a Purple Heart and numerous other citations. His retirement became official last Saturday.

He served for 35 years in active and inactive capacities, beginning with World War I and continuing with service in World War II, the Korea War, Hawaii, briefly in 1959 on the Pacific atoll of Eniwetok and for the last 15 months at Fort Hayes here.

New Offensive?

REDS ATTACK SAIGON, BASES

PACIFIC STARS AND STRIPES

AN AUTHORIZED UNOFFICIAL PUBLICATION
FOR THE U.S. ARMED FORCES OF THE PACIFIC COMMAND

10¢

Vol. 25, No. 312   Sunday, Nov. 9, 1969

S&S Vietnam Bureau

SAIGON—Communist troops launched their first attacks on Saigon since 1968 and the heaviest enemy shellings throughout Vietnam in more than two months were reported early Friday as top Allied military men said the Reds may be ready to begin a winter offensive.

Later Friday evening Communists fired more than 100 rocket and mortar rounds into a U.S. artillery base 60 miles northwest of Saigon and early Saturday morning launched a ground attack on another U.S. camp 83 miles north of the capital, military spokesmen said.

The barrage caused light casualties but no one was killed at the 1st Cav. Div.'s fire support base Ike 15 miles northeast of Tay Ninh. U.S. artillery and helicopter fire hit suspected enemy positions around the camp, but Communist losses were unknown.

U.S. and Vietnamese Civilian Irregular Troops at fire support base Jerry north of Saigon near the Cambodian border drove back an hourlong assault on the 1st Cav. Div. camp Saturday morning. Seven GIs were wounded and Vietnamese casual-

Related Story Page 6

ties were also light. Enemy losses were again unknown.

The fighting in Saigon started just after midnight Thursday, according to Vietnamese National Police. It marked the first time the Viet Cong had attacked the capital since May 1968.

Three Viet Cong and one Na-
(Continued on Back Page, Col. 1)

Apollo 12 Takes Aim

CAPE KENNEDY, Fla. (AP) — The week-long countdown began Friday for America's second moon landing expedition as the three Apollo 12 astronauts met with geologists to learn what lunar features they should look for during their ambitious 10-day mission.

The launch team started the countdown clock exactly on time at noon and began preparing the towering moon rocket for an 11:22 a.m. lift-off next Friday for Navy Cmdrs. Charles "Pete" Conrad Jr., Richard F. Gordon Jr., and Alan L. Bean.

Electrical power was turned on for several rocket and moonship systems, fuel lines were inspected for leaks and the Saturn 5's first-stage engines were checked to assure they will generate the desired 7.6 million pounds of lift-off thrust.

Altogether, the countdown will take 98 hours. It was spread out over a week, however, and will be interrupted by four planned
(Continued on Back Page, Col. 2)

Vietnamese Special Forces troopers and U.S. artillerymen watch white phosphorous bombs, dropped by U.S. jet fighter-bombers, explode in the jungle just outside the perimeter of the Duc Lap Special Forces camp.   (S&S Photo by Spec. 4 Bob Hodierne)

NCO Finds a Bride in Amputee Ward

NEW YORK (AP) — When Vietnam veteran Albert Nirenstein and Nancy Dunker met in the amputee ward at Valley Forge Army Hospital about a year ago—he a patient and she the new head nurse—they never dreamed they would someday be man and wife.

And even in their wildest dreams they never imagined the kind of wedding they'd have—a party in a $600-a-day hotel penthouse, champagne, pheasant, beef Wellington and all the trimmings—and honeymoon in Hawaii. Fifty other Vietnam amputees will attend the wedding.

"It will be as elaborate as it would be for a visiting head of state," said an official of the New York Hilton, where Al and Nancy will be married Sunday night. The Disabled American Veterans group is sponsoring the affair.

Nancy, 26, a captain in the Army Nurse Corps who is retiring to become a housewife in Stamford, Conn., admits she
(Continued on Back Page, Col. 4)

250,000 TURN OUT FOR PROTEST IN D.C.

PACIFIC
STARS STRIPES

AN AUTHORIZED UNOFFICIAL PUBLICATION
FOR THE U.S. ARMED FORCES OF THE PACIFIC COMMAND

10¢

Vol. 25, No. 320   Monday, Nov. 17, 1969

WASHINGTON (UPI) — Shouting, paint-throwing extremists staged a wild demonstration at the Justice Department Saturday and police retaliated with tear gas.

The melee came after an estimated 250,000 persons had conducted a peaceful mammoth peace march and rally through the streets of the city.

A throng of several thousand later swarmed in front of the Justice Department as dusk fell, shouting slogans and protesting the trial of "the Chicago Eight" for conspiring to cause violence at last summer's Democratic National convention.

A barrage of rocks and bottles from demonstrators smashed windows in the building.

At one point, the protesters hauled down the American flag from a six-story high pole and sought to run up the Viet Cong

Related stories on Page 2

banner. Police blocked the attempt when the Communist flag had been raised about three-fourths of the way up.

Shortly after, a smoke bomb went off in the area and red paint bombs were hurled against the building, spattering the exterior walls.

A marshal representing the peace march organizers used a bull horn to appeal for an end of the demonstration. Some of them responded by calling him a "pig."

A line of patrol cars moved down the street to reinforce the officers who had ringed the Justice Department building.

Finally, police headquarters announced that officers at the scene fired tear gas at 4:50 p.m. EST in an effort to break up the tense scene.

The crowd —including contingents of Yippies and other ultra-extremists —retreated up

(Continued on Back Page, Col. 1)

PEACE DEMONSTRATORS RALLY AT FOOT OF WASHINGTON MONUMENT BEFORE STARTING MARCH   *AP Radiophoto*

Scores

Pittsburgh	15
Army	6
Syracuse	15
Navy	0
Stanford	47
Air Force	34
Ohio State	42
Purdue	14
Texas	69
TCU	7
Mississippi	38
Tennessee	0
Arkansas	28
SMU	15
Penn State	48
Maryland	0
Southern Cal	16
Washington	7
UCLA	13
Oregon	10

Need Rockets Now to Return

Astros Take Better Aim on Moon

SPACE CENTER, Houston (AP) — More than halfway to target, the Apollo 12 pilots gave their spaceship a rocket-kick ahead Saturday, surrendering a safety factor that guaranteed their return to earth if trouble bars them from the moon.

Under the eye of their color television camera, Charles Conrad Jr., Richard F. Gordon Jr. and Alan L. Bean fired their main rocket motor for 8.8 seconds at 6:15 p.m.

It tightened their aim on the moon, cutting the miss distance to just 69 miles from more than 800 miles.

But it also put them on a "no return" course that will require rocket power to bring them home again. Their previous course would have brought them home automatically after a long loop around the moon. The new course, if not altered later by rocket firings, would carry them out into the solar system and into fatal orbit with no chance whatever of returning.

But as much as it spoke for the confidence in the Apollo 12 engines, the new maneuver was also necessary if the astronauts are to land where they want to, some 200 miles south of the lunar equator on the eastern shore of the Ocean of Storms.

That moment came less than an hour and a half after they woke up after eight hours sleep in a 10-hour sleep period.

Before the rocket burn, Conrad told Mission Control what they would be doing in the immediate hours afterward.

"After the burn," he said, (Continued on Back Page, Col. 3)

How Could a Massacre Happen?

Allegations that American GIs massacred South Vietnamese civilians during a raid on a village complex last year have stunned the United States. How could it happen? is the most frequently asked question. In the following analysis, John T. Wheeler, who reported the war in Vietnam for the Associated Press for several years, gives an insight into the conditions of a strange war in which anything can happen.

By JOHN T. WHEELER
Associated Press Writer

To try to understand the alleged massacre by American GIs of civilians at My Lai it is necessary also to understand the atmosphere of a war which has led many U.S. fighting men to feel they are as much at war against Vietnam as for it.

While the communiques speak of battles involving companies and battalions—the clash of professional soldiers doing their grim job—each GI carries with him the certain knowledge that in any village there may be men, women, and even children who are also the enemy, waiting for the time and place to attack him.

Brutality, and indifference to human life, are commonplace in Vietnam. Even the disfigurement of dead GIs is common.

In Vietnam the killing of civilians was a practice established by the Viet Cong as a major part of the war long before the first U.S. ground troops were committed in March 1965.

By official count, more than 20,000 civilians had been murdered by that time in enemy executions aimed at so thoroughly terrorizing the countryside that none would resist. The total now is more than 3,000 killed by the enemy in Hue when they held part of that city for 2½ weeks. At Hue, the victims were predominantly civilians of all ages. Many were killed simply by tying their hands behind their backs, shoving them into a trench and burying them alive.

It was into this conflict that the American troops were plunged. They had been told to kill the Viet Cong who were bad and woo the peasant who only aided the enemy because he had no choice. Given a chance, the official line went, Vietnam wanted to be free and democratic just like America.

But the GIs found a war of sundered families, and divided allegiances to any regime, either Viet Cong or Saigon.

The infantry came to know that the farmer, who might be a friend by day, could become a guerrilla by night who killed just as surely and just as ruthlessly as

(Continued on Back Page, Col. 1)

Benefits Boost OKd By Senate

WASHINGTON (UPI)—Over the Nixon Administration's opposition, the Senate Friday approved a 15 per cent increase in Social Security benefits and raised the minimum payment to $150 a month for a married couple.

The proposal, to go into effect Jan. 1 and benefitting 25 million elderly Americans, is even more generous than legislation which comes up for a vote in the House of Representatives next week.

It will cost $6.2 billion a year.

The House bill also provides for a 15 per cent across-the-board increase in benefits but does not carry a special provision in the Senate measure granting a substantial boost in minimum payments.

Minimum benefits are now $55 a month for a single person. A single person would receive $100 a month under the Senate provision and a married couple would get $150 monthly. About 3.5 million Americans now collect the minimum benefits.

The provision increasing the minimum benefits was offered as an amendment by Senate Democratic leader Mike Mansfield and Sen. Robert Byrd, D-W.Va., and adopted by a 48 to 41 vote. It would be financed by

(Continued on Back Page, Col. 1)

★ ★ ★ ★ ★ ★ ★ ★ ★ ★

2 Lawyers Named

ARMY HEARS LT. CALLEY

WASHINGTON (AP)—Two New York lawyers were assigned Friday to an Army probe of investigative aspects of the alleged My Lai massacre while the only man charged in the case underwent Pentagon questioning.

First Lt. William L. Calley Jr., accused of murdering 109 Vietnamese

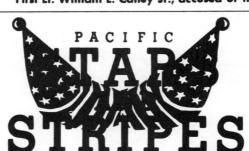

PACIFIC

STARS AND STRIPES

AN AUTHORIZED UNOFFICIAL PUBLICATION FOR THE U.S. ARMED FORCES OF THE PACIFIC COMMAND   10¢

Vol. 25, No. 340   Sunday, Dec. 7, 1969

civilians, arrived tight-lipped at the Pentagon where the Army hearing is being held.

The Army panel is seeking to learn whether field officers tried to cover up any mass killings in their initial investigation shortly after the March 1968 My Lai operation.

The New York attorneys, Robert MacCrate and Jerome K. Walsh Jr., were named to add a nonmilitary viewpoint to the work of the group headed by Lt. Gen. William R. Peers.

A spokesman said Secretary of the Army Stanley R. Resor wanted the outside counsel to insure "objectivity and impartiality" to the Peers investigation, separate from the over-all criminal probe of My Lai.

Calley was flown in from Ft. Benning, Ga., where he awaits court-martial early next year.

Accompanied by his military lawyer, Maj. Kenneth A. Raby, the young lieutenant was hustled into the Pentagon and down to the Army's secret operations center shortly after noon.

Newsmen tried to ask Calley questions but he looked straight ahead and said nothing.

Calley was leader of a platoon which went into My Lai as part of a company commanded by Capt. Ernest Medina.

Medina told reporters Thursday he neither ordered a massacre nor saw nor heard of one.

A brigade investigation after the My Lai operation concluded that only a few inadvertent civilian deaths occurred and that

(Continued on Back Page, Col. 2)

Mighty Mo A Safe Port

BREMERTON, Wash. (AP) — The battleship Missouri, on which the Japanese surrender documents were signed, has been designated a public nuclear blast fallout shelter.

The Missouri, which can accommodate 2,200 persons, has been stocked with medical and sanitary supplies, food, water and radiological monitoring instruments. The Navy cooperated with state Civil Defense officials in the project.

When the Missouri was mothballed here, former President Harry Truman complained about locating her "in a closet." Contacted about her latest duty, he wrote expressing "hope that the USS Missouri may never be called upon to be so used."

1st Lt. William L. Calley (center), arrives at the Pentagon to testify at an inquiry into the alleged mass killing at My Lai, Vietnam. He is flanked by his military counsel, Maj. Kenneth A. Raby (left), and Maj. Jeffrey L. Scribner (right), information officer. (AP Radiophoto)

Big Red 1 Leads Phase III Cutback

By PFC. JACK FULLER
S&S Staff Correspondent

SAIGON — The U.S. Army's "Big Red One," the first American infantry division to land in Vietnam, and the Marine Corps' 26th Regimental Landing Team are going home before mid-April.

The U.S. military command announced Monday which units would leave Vietnam under President Nixon's "phase III redeployment." Along with the 1st Inf. Div. and the Marine landing team, the withdrawal will include the 3rd Brigade of the 4th Inf. Div. and three tactical fighter squadrons from the Air Force's 12th Tactical Fighter Wing.

Nixon said Dec. 15 that the authorized strength of 484,000 men in Vietnam would be cut back to 434,000 by April 15, 1970.

The scheduled withdrawal includes about 29,500 Army spaces, 12,000 Marine Corps spaces, 5,600 Air Force spaces and 2,000 Navy spaces.

As in past troop withdrawals, "short-timers," men with little time left in their one-year Vietnam tour, will return to the United States with their units while men who have just recently arrived in Vietnam will be reassigned to other units here.

(In Washington, the Pentagon announced the 1st Div. would return to Fort Riley, Kan., and to Europe, replacing the 24th Inf. Div. (Mech.) which will be inactivated.

(The Pentagon said the 1st Div. will be mechanized and replace the 24th in its NATO and U.S. Army Europe role. The 3rd Brigade of the 24th is now in West Germany and the balance of the division is at Fort Riley.)

On July 12, 1965, the 1st Div.'s 2nd Brigade landed at Cam Ranh Bay and Vung Tau — the first element of a U.S. infantry division in Vietnam.

Only eleven days later, the unit fought its first major battle in the Vietnam war, tackling an estimated Viet Cong regiment along Highway 13, 30 miles north of Saigon.

The division's biggest single battle victory in Vietnam was at Ap Gu at the end of March, 1967, when the 1st Bn., 26th Inf., killed 609 enemy in two days of fierce combat.

During its time in Vietnam, the Big Red One took part in 15 major operations. During the Tet offensive of 1968 it was called upon to secure the critical Saigon Air Base at Tan Son Nhut.

In September, 1969, its commanding general, Maj. Gen. Keith L. Ware, was killed by enemy gunfire when his helicop-
(Continued on Back Page, Col. 1)

WASHINGTON (AP)—The son of Air Force Chief of Staff General John Ryan — 29-year-old Capt. John Ryan Jr.—has been killed in a plane crash off California. He and another man were killed Monday when their F4 fighter-bomber crashed into San Pueblo Bay. They had just taken off from California's Hamilton AFB.

PACIFIC
STARS AND STRIPES

AN AUTHORIZED UNOFFICIAL PUBLICATION FOR THE U.S. ARMED FORCES OF THE PACIFIC

10¢

Vol. 26, No. 13 **Wednesday, Jan. 14, 1970**

BIAFRA GIVES UP; MASSIVE AID SET

Airmen load medical supplies into a Hercules transport plane of the Royal Air Force at Lyneham Station, England. The plane is to fly to Lagos with 10 tons of supplies for defeated Biafra, the first of several U.S. and British mercy flights planned for this week. (UPI)

LAGOS, Nigeria (AP) — Biafra surrendered Monday, ending a 30-month war of secession that wiped out nearly a generation of Ibo tribe children — perhaps two million lives overall — and shattered black Africa's most promising nation.

Maj. Gen. Philip Effiong, a minority Efik tribesman left in charge when Biafra's leader, Gen. C. Odumegwu Ojukwu, caught one of the last flights out, capitulated in a broadcast at 4:40 p.m. He agreed to discuss terms in the framework of a United Nigeria.

Maj. Gen. Yakubu Gowon accepted Biafra's surrender in a midnight broadcast and asked all Nigerians to welcome the former rebels as brothers.

He said army units accompanied by police would establish "effective federal presence" in the enclave.

"They will take all care . . . and shoot only if they encounter resistance," Gowon said.

He said there would be a general amnesty "for all those misled into attempting to disintegrate the country."

Effiong ordered his troops disengaged and appealed to the federal leader, Gowon, to cease
(Continued on Back Page, Col. 1)

N. Viet Radiomen Break U.S. Codes

By SPEC. 4 PHILIP MCCOMBS
S&S Staff Correspondent

SAIGON — Communist radio operators speaking fluent English recently sent a message to an Allied fire support center calling for artillery to pound another Allied position, U.S. military sources disclosed Monday.

The ruse failed, the sources said, but an extensive campaign is now under way in the provinces surrounding Saigon to counter code-breaking operations by the enemy.

These security-tightening efforts followed the discovery three weeks ago of an underground enemy communications center where English-speaking North Vietnamese soldiers had intercepted and broken codes on hundreds of Allied radio communications, the sources said.

Troopers from the 25th Inf. Div. uncovered the communications center and captured 12 enemy soldiers, killing another one, during an operation about 35 miles north of Saigon.

The enemy soldiers, who speak fluent English, are still being interrogated, according to the sources.

Their bunker contained what the sources described as "crude" radio receivers, including modified Sony radios, captured American equipment, radios of Chinese Communist manufacture and homemade sets.

More than 1,400 separate radio transmissions written out in longhand in English were found, according to the sources.

"Every place a homemade or illegal code was used, they had penciled in the coordinates," said the sources. "They had bro-
(Continued on Back Page, Col. 3)

The Longest Days—POW's 2,000

LT. ALVAREZ' WIFE WAITS, AND WAITS, AND WAITS . . .

UPI Radiophoto

WASHINGTON (UPI)—This is the 2,000th day Navy Lt. Everett Alvarez Jr. has spent in captivity in North Vietnam. In all American history no man has ever been held a prisoner of war so long.

On Aug. 5, 1964, Alvarez was among the first pilots attacking North Vietnam in retaliation for reported torpedo boat attacks on American ships in the Gulf of Tonkin. He never made it back to his ship.

Alvarez had been married only two months when he was captured.

His wife Tangee, 29, lives—and waits—in an apartment in Lafayette, Calif. "Five years," she said recently, gazing solemnly at a photograph of a young naval officer receiving his wings. "Five years—how much can a man take?"

Shortly after their marriage, Alvarez, now 32, was assigned to the aircraft carrier Constellation.

"It never crossed my mind that something like this could happen," Tangee said. "If only I had thought of it before—maybe we could have said something to each other, talked it over before in case something happened.

"But it never entered my mind—and I don't think it did his either."

Alvarez is one of 430 men identified by the Defense Department as prisoners in Southeast Asia. They have

(Continued on Back Page, Col. 1)

PACIFIC STAR AND STRIPES

AN AUTHORIZED UNOFFICIAL PUBLICATION
FOR THE U.S. ARMED FORCES OF THE PACIFIC COMMAND

10¢

Vol. 26, No. 25   Monday, Jan. 26, 1970

Russians Form A 'Red NATO'

MOSCOW (UPI)—The Soviets Saturday disclosed the formation of a new multinational Communist land, sea and air force opposed to NATO.

A long article in the army newspaper Krasnaya Zvezda (Red Star) —written by the new commander of the force—said the joint force was established during a Warsaw Pact summit in Budapest in March 1969.

The article was written by General of the Army Sergei M. Shtemenko, identified as the chief of staff of the joint force.

Previously, Shtemenko had been the deputy chief of staff of the Soviet armed forces.

"At present the joint armed forces includes land forces, air forces, naval forces and also antiaircraft defense forces," Krasnaya Zvezda said.

But at the same time it indicated that the Soviets will retain exclusive control over nuclear rocketry and will not put such weapons under the joint command.

"Of significance is the fact that guarding the security of the Socialist Communists is the rocket nuclear power of the armed forces of the Soviet Union," the article said.

Shtemenko's report was the first public disclosure of the creation of such a force within the Warsaw Pact.

A loose joint command has existed since the pact was formed but in the past the seven nations (Continued on Back Page, Col. 3)

Ammo Truck Blast Kills 18 Israelis

Compiled From AP and UPI

An Israeli Army truck laden with explosives blew up on the quayside of the Red Sea port of Elath Saturday. Israeli spokesmen said 18 persons were killed and 42 injured, many critically.

Two Palestinian guerrilla organizations claimed responsibility for the explosion. The Palestine Armed Struggle Command and the Popular Democratic Front for the Liberation of Palestine both claimed in Amman, Jordan, that guerrillas from their organizations infiltrated Elath and planted the explosives.

Meanwhile, Egyptian planes struck at Israel Saturday with four air assaults on army strongpoints along the Suez Canal.

Israeli Defense Minister Moshe Dayan warned Egyptians to expect more strikes inside their territory.

The Elath explosion was one of the worst disasters in the 22-year history of the Jewish state.

One resident who rushed to the military port after hearing the explosion said:

"We saw a huge black mushroom of smoke. There were dozens of bodies strewn over a hundred yards. It was the most horrifying thing I have ever seen."

An Israeli military spokesman said there was no immediate evidence that the blast was caused by Arab saboteurs. "All the signs point to an accident," he said.

The blast occurred at 4:30 p.m. in Elath's naval port. Throughout the city of 13,000 people, houses shook and windows rattled.

Casualties were rushed to Elath's only hospital by ambulances.

One unconfirmed account said the truck was disembarking from a transport ship which had (Continued on Back Page, Col. 2)

'Driving Half My Life'

LINCOLN, Neb. (UPI) — "There's no problem" the young driver told police after they curbed his small imported car. "My parents know I drive —I've been doing it since I was 5 years old." There was a problem: the driver was 10.

Financier Wolfson To Leave Prison

PENSACOLA, Fla. (UPI)— Millionaire financier Louis E. Wolfson will be freed Monday —two days before his 58th birthday —from the federal government's honor prison at nearby Eglin Air Force Base.

Wolfson, whose income was estimated at $2 million a year before he went to prison, is finishing a one-year sentence given him in 1967 for selling unregistered stock in a Florida firm he controlled, Continental Enterprises, Inc.

Wolfson still faces an 18-month term given him on a second conviction, for conspiring to obstruct justice and filing false reports with the Securities and Exchange Commission in connection with stock transactions. Wolfson is appealing the second conviction.

Wolfson began serving his one-year term last April 25. He is getting out early, according to the Justice Department in Washington, because of time earned for good behavior.

Wolfson served his time in a fenceless prison that has no bars, but is located amid the 297,000 acres of the huge military reservation, 18 miles from the nearest road.

At the prison, Wolfson became known by fellow inmates as "Mr. W." and was sought out for business advice. Wolfson, a one-time pro boxer and a former University of Georgia football player, has financial arrangements with former U.S. Supreme Court Justice Abe Fortas which resulted in Fortas resigning from the court.

Girl, 13, Lost 52 Days, Found Starving

HONOLULU (AP) — A 13-year-old girl, found Friday in an unused section of a large warehouse, was too ill Saturday to tell authorities where or how she spent the nearly two months since she disappeared from her Army base home.

Mary Annette Washington, daughter of WO Alexander Washington, was in serious condition at Tripler Hospital suffering from severe malnutrition and dehydration.

Two soldiers handling mail in the used part of the warehouse at Schofield Barracks heard a noise at about 3 a.m., investigated and found the girl, an Army spokesman said.

"From the time she disappeared until we found her we don't have any idea of where she's been or how she stayed alive," the spokesman said. He said the case is being investigated, but that the girl was too ill to be questioned.

The girl was last seen when she left her home Dec. 2 to attend her seventh grade classes at nearby Wheeler Intermediate School.

Her disappearance touched off an intensive statewide search.

Her father, stationed in Vietnam, was due back in Hawaii Saturday night on emergency leave for a second time, officials said. Washington returned from the war zone when his daughter disappeared to aid in the search.

The girl's mother is to arrive from Florida Monday on a flight being arranged by the Red Cross.

Nixon: Russ Missiles Threat To U.S.; Peace Up to Hanoi

WASHINGTON (AP) —President Nixon told Congress Wednesday the key to peace in South Vietnam lies in Hanoi's willingness to conduct serious give-and-take negotiations leading toward a compromise settlement.

"Hanoi will find us forthcoming and flexible," he declared in his first State of the World report on U.S. foreign policy for the 1970s.

Nixon announced the formation of a high-level Vietnam spe-
(Continued on Back Page, Col. 3)

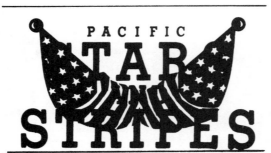

PACIFIC
STAR
STRIPES

AN AUTHORIZED UNOFFICIAL PUBLICATION
FOR THE U.S. ARMED FORCES OF THE PACIFIC COMMAND

10¢

Vol. 26, No. 50   Friday, Feb. 20, 1970

WASHINGTON (AP)—Surveying the world situation, President Nixon reported Wednesday the Soviet Union's missile buildup "raises serious questions about where they are headed and the potential threats we and our allies face."

By year's end, Nixon said, Russia is expected to have 236 more ocean-spanning, landbased nuclear missiles than the United States, a reversal of the status of the 1960s.

When submarine-launched rockets are counted, this country will still hold a 1,710 to 1,590 lead in missiles, he said.

Nevertheless, Nixon found the situation disturbing enough to proceed with expansion of the Safeguard anti-ballistic missile (ABM) system, a revamped program he approved in 1969.

"I believed then, and I am even more convinced today, that there is a serious threat to our retaliatory capability . . ." the chief executive declared.

The uncertainty of Russian aims stood out in Nixon's State-of-the-World message to Congress, a 119-page document he hailed as the most comprehensive document of its type ever given by a President.

In it, Nixon also:

—Expressed hope the Strategic Arms Limitations Talks can bring a curb on nuclear weaponry. He said the Soviets have been "serious and businesslike" in preparatory negotiations.

—Said there is little the Big Powers can do to solve the Middle East crisis. He urged Egypt and Israel to show "mutual willingness to compromise."

The 40,000-word message offered a global look at the past year and projected a future in which "partnership" and "military strength" will be the key words in American foreign policy.

Nixon reaffirmed this intention to go on reducing U.S. involvement in the affairs of other lands, attempting in the process to negotiate peace-preserving agreements with the Soviets and eventually Red China.

Nixon styled his presentation "United States Foreign Policy for the 1970s ... A New Strategy for Peace," but it seemed to (Continued on Page 5, Col. 1)

Convict 5 of 'Chicago 7'

CHICAGO (AP)—Five men were convicted Wednesday of inciting violence during the week of the 1968 Democratic National Convention but they and two codefendants were acquitted of conspiracy.

Those convicted after 40 hours' deliberation by a U.S. District Court jury were David T. Dellinger, 54; Jerry C. Rubin, 31; Abbott "Abbie" Hoffman, 31; Thomas E. Hayden, 30, and Rennard C. "Rennie" Davis, 29. They were found guilty of having crossed state lines to provoke rioting.

John R. Froines, 31, and Lee Weiner, 31, were acquitted of inciting violence. The jury found them innocent of teaching the use of an incendiary device. They also were acquitted of conspiracy.

All seven men have been in jail since the weekend on contempt sentences imposed for causing courtroom disturbances and other misbehavior during their trial. The contempt terms range from 2½ months to 2½ years.

The five convicted men were denied release on bond after the verdict was handed in. Judge (Continued on Back Page, Col. 2)

Youths try vainly to pry the U.S. Seal from the wall of the U.S. Embassy in Manila during violent demonstrations in the city. About 2,000 broke into the embassy compound (AP)

Love Is a Many Vendored Thing

COLUMBUS, Ohio (AP) — A 19-year-old sophomore at Ohio Dominican College is only 13,800 pop bottles away from a Hawaiian reunion.

Dee Hudson is collecting the bottles to finance a trip to the island and a visit with her fiance in the Army. She's collected 1,200 bottles so far, refundable at two cents a bottle.

2,000 Manila Youths Storm, Firebomb the U.S. Embassy

MANILA (AP) — A mob of Filipino youths hurling stones, sticks and fire bombs broke inside the U.S. Embassy compound Wednesday night and shattered windows in the main office building before U.S. Marine guards drove them out with tear gas.

An embassy spokesman said an emergency staff on duty moved to a boat landing ready to escape when the youths burst through the gates. They went back to their desks when the Marines forced out the invaders. The embassy is located on Manila Bay.

U.S. Ambassador Henry Byroade, who was absent from the compound at the time of the attack, assailed the lack of Filipino police protection and praised the American Marines.

The youths, numbering up to 2,000, shouted slogans against "U.S. imperialism" and accused President Ferdinand E. Marcos of "fascism."

Even after they were routed from the compound, the youths threw stones and missiles at the embassy for nearly an hour before Manila riot police arrived and dispersed them. They then (Continued on Back Page, Col. 2)

'Flower Power'

SAN BERNARDINO, Calif. (AP)—Beverly Duval and her teen-age daughter stumbled on "this big piece of junk" last summer on a Southern California beach. They hauled it home, intending eventually to paint it pink and use it as a pot for petunias.

And there it sat in the backyard, while they waited for some free moments to start the project.

Then Mrs. Duval saw a television program in which the U.S. Navy warned about explosive devices inadvertently lost at sea in recent months.

A Navy demolition team, arriving in response to her telephone call, hauled it away . . . for explosion under controlled conditions. It was a fully loaded depth charge minus the detonator, said the experts—designed to blow up an enemy submarine.

ACCUSE 14 OFFICERS
My Lai Charges Hit 2 Generals

PACIFIC STARS STRIPES

AN AUTHORIZED UNOFFICIAL PUBLICATION
FOR THE U.S. ARMED FORCES OF THE PACIFIC COMMAND

10¢

Vol. 26, No. 77   Thursday, Mar. 19, 1970

Lt. Gen. William R. Peers (left), Secretary of the Army Stanley A. Resor, and Army Chief of Staff Gen. William C. Westmoreland announced the findings of a probe headed by Peers into the alleged My Lai massacre. Fourteen officers have been charged as a result of the probe. (AP)

Cambodians Call For Viet's Help In Border Clash

CHAU DOC, Vietnam (AP)—Cambodian troops attempted to push a Viet Cong battalion back across the border into South Vietnam in a major military operation Sunday and Monday, and called in South Vietnamese artillery fire to help, highly reliable informants reported Tuesday.

A Cambodian officer was in radio contact with the chief of South Vietnam's An Phu District, adjoining Cambodia, during the entire operation, these informants said. He directed 105mm artillery fire from the district's guns into both sides of the border where the Viet Cong were moving.

American officials in Chau Doc Province, where the incident took place, said it was the first time they knew of Cambodians and South Vietnamese working together so openly to fight the Viet Cong.

The Cambodian military operations was the second known to
(Continued on Back Page, Col. 2)

Americans Evacuate Laos Base

VIENTIANE, Laos (UPI) — The U.S. administered hospital at Sam Thong was evacuated Tuesday and most of the U.S. personnel at an adjoining logistics base were flown out to safety in the face of advancing North Vietnamese troops.

Civilian refugees in the area began streaming to the south and west.

AP reported sources on the scene, about 80 miles north of Vientiane, said about 2,000 Laotian civilians and refugees were
(Continued on Back Page, Col. 1)

BULLETIN

UNITED NATIONS (UPI) — The United States cast its first veto in United Nations history Tuesday night to kill an African resolution calling on Britain to use force to overthrow the white supremacy regime of Southern Rhodesia.

Accused Bids Sad Farewell

WEST POINT, N.Y. (AP) — Maj. Gen. Samuel W. Koster bade an emotional farewell to the 3,700-member Corps of Cadets at the U.S. Military Academy Tuesday. When he concluded, they sprang to their feet to cheer him for 1½ minutes.

"My appearance before you today is the most difficult I have ever had to meet," Koster told the Corps at lunchtime formation in the vast West Point dining hall.

"I want you to be among the first to know that I will soon leave West Point," continued the 50-year-old officer, who has
(Continued on Back Page, Col. 4)

WASHINGTON (UPI)—The Army Tuesday instituted court-martial proceedings against 14 top ranking officers, including the present superintendent of West Point for allegedly covering up "a tragedy of major proportions" at My Lai.

Maj. Gen. Samuel W. Koster, who was commander of the American Division in Vietnam at the time of the reported My Lai massacre, was accused of "dereliction in the performance of his duties" and "failure to obey lawful regulations." He is now superintendent of the U.S. Military Academy at West Point, N.Y.

The same charges were filed against Brig. Gen. George H. Young, Jr., the assistant division commander, and Col. Oran K. Henderson, who was commanding the division's 11th Inf. Brigade.

In addition, Henderson was accused of "false swearing" and "making a false official statement."

The charges were announced at a Pentagon news conference at which results of an inquiry conducted by Lt. Gen. William R. Peers were released.

The Peers inquiry was ordered Dec. 24. In closed hearings beginning Dec. 2, it took 20,000 pages of testimony from 400 witnesses.

Peers told the news conference that his investigation "clearly established that a tragedy of major proportions occurred there at My Lai on that date."

Until Tuesday, 10 military men had been charged in connection with the actual incident, three captains, one lieutenant and six enlisted men.

The most serious charges have been brought against 1st Lt. William L. Calley, 26, leader of the platoon that swept through My Lai in search of Viet Cong snipers on the day of the massacre. Calley is accused of premeditated murder of 102 South Vietnamese civilians.

Calley is scheduled for court-martial trial starting May 18 at Fort Benning, Ga.

Among others charged is Capt. Ernest L. Medina, 33, commander of Company C, of which the Calley platoon was a part. Charges were brought against Medina last week. He is accused
(Continued on Back Page, Col. 1)

Many Marines Due Early Out

WASHINGTON (UPI) — Many Marines will be discharged as much as a year before their enlistments expire to carry out President Nixon's order of an 18 per cent cut in the ranks of the corps, the Senate Armed Services Committee was told Tuesday.

Marine Commandant Leonard F. Chapman Jr., said the cutback would create "unusual turbulence and undesirable instability" but that it also would help improve the quality of the corps in the long run.

The administration's budget for the 12 months starting July 1 calls for a 53,000-man cut in Marine strength, from 294,000 to 241,000.

Chapman said recruitment of officers and men would be "significantly" lower and that the corps probably will no longer use the draft.

The cutback also will be carried out by "allowing many enlisted Marines to voluntarily leave the corps up to 12 months before their enlistments expire," Chapman said.

"Certain effects of this decrease will have an adverse impact on our units and on our individual Marines," he said.

But, he added, fewer recruitments and elimination of the
(Continued on Back Page, Col. 2)

Plans Exile Regime

CAMBODIA ENDS SIHANOUK RULE

PRINCE SIHANOUK
Given the boot

PACIFIC
STARS ✦ STRIPES

AN AUTHORIZED UNOFFICIAL PUBLICATION
FOR THE U.S. ARMED FORCES OF THE PACIFIC COMMAND

10¢

Vol. 26, No. 78   Friday, Mar. 20, 1970

Compiled From AP and UPI

SAIGON — Prince Norodom Sihanouk's rule in Cambodia was ended Wednesday by a rebellious Parliament.

The lawmakers may have acted at the instigation of a general who quarreled with the chief of state over North Vietnamese and Viet Cong occupation of border provinces.

The Radio Phnom Penh announcement of his ouster reached Sihanouk in Moscow, where he had stopped on his way home from a vacation in Paris. Before he left Moscow for Peking, he talked with the staff of the Cambodian embassy.

An American Broadcasting Co. correspondent in Moscow said Sihanouk told the staff he would form a government in exile if the Russians and Chinese do not recognize the new regime. But if recognition comes from the two big Communist powers, he added, this would be the end of him.

Soviet Premier Alexei N. Kosygin was the first to tell Sihanouk of his ouster, Sihanouk said Wednesday.

He disclosed Kosygin himself told him of the decision of the Cambodian National Assembly.

(Continued on Back Page, Col. 2)

Bloody Gunfight on Plane

BOSTON (AP) — A pilot shot in both arms landed an airliner with 71 persons aboard after a mile-high cockpit struggle Tuesday night which left the copilot dead and a passenger seriously wounded. The passenger was charged with murder.

East Boston Municipal Court issued a murder complaint Wednesday against John J. DiVivo, 27, of West New York, N.J., in the death of James E. Hartley, 31, of Fort Lee, N.J., the slain copilot. He died of a bullet wound in the chest.

Hartley was fatally wounded, but managed to wound his assailant in the wild cockpit struggle, the wounded pilot said.

DiVivo was reported in satisfactory condition at Massachusetts General Hospital, where he underwent emergency surgery for bullet wounds in the chest, arm and abdomen. He was under police guard.

An Eastern Airlines spokesman said a struggle for the gun broke out after the passenger entered the cockpit and told the pilot, Captain Robert Wilbur Jr., 35: "Take me east."

The plane was then a mile high over the town of Franklin, about 30 miles south of Boston, making its final approach to Lo-
(Continued on Back Page, Col. 4)

The body of James Hartley of Fort Lee, N.J., slain copilot of an Eastern Airlines plane, is removed from Massachusetts General Hospital in Boston.
(AP Radiophoto)

Hot Off the Press

NEW YORK (S&S) — There have been 1,231 bomb scares in New York since March 12. On Wednesday, the 1,232nd scare brought the *Stars and Stripes* news transmission from New York to a temporary halt when the building was evacuated. Staffers returned 15 minutes later, although police checked for more than two hours for explosives.

Denies Aid To Cambodia

By SPEC. 5 JOE KAMALICK
S&S Staff Correspondent

CAN THO, Vietnam — A highly placed American official here has categorically denied a report a Cambodian officer asked for and received Vietnamese artillery fire in support of operations by Cambodian troops against North Vietnamese army soldiers inside Cambodia.

The official said, however, there is some indication the NVA may soon follow Cam-
(Continued on Back Page, Col. 5)

Order Striking Mailmen Back on Feet

NEW YORK (AP) — A federal judge ordered striking government letter carriers back to work Wednesday, after their illegal walkout halted all mail deliveries in metropolitan New York, the business and financial capital of the world.

Gus Johnson, president of Branch 36, AFL-CIO National Association of Letter Carriers in Manhattan and the Bronx, publicly appealed to his members to go back to work.

But Jack Levanthal, president of the union's 3,900-member local in Brooklyn, said, "I'm not going to appeal to my members

to respect any injunction." He said he would wait to hear from Johnson before deciding on a final course of action.

Other union officials reported a defiant attitude among the rank and file and said the tieup threatened to spread across the nation.

The Manhattan-Bronx and Brooklyn locals started the strike at midnight Tuesday.

"The men I spoke to will defy any injunction—they will stay out until hell freezes over," said Herman Sandbank, the branch executive vice president. "If the strike accelerates at the present

rate, in 48 hours there will be no mail service in the United States."

In Washington, Postmaster General Winton M. Blount ordered that the strikers forfeit their pay while they are idle. He declined to speculate on further steps that would be taken if the injunction was defied.

Blount told a news conference that he and President Nixon "are deeply concerned about this situation, since the mail system is the life blood of the economy and millions of Americans rely on it for their very survival."

At the heart of the dispute involving 50,000 postal workers in this area was congressional deferment of long-sought wage increases. Union officials claimed low wages have forced many postmen to seek welfare benefits.

All across the country, a national embargo diverted tens of millions of items of New York-bound mail into storage in post offices for the duration of the strike, the first of its magnitude in American history.

The New York City Commerce and Industry Association
(Continued on Back Page, Col. 2)

Had Her Fill of Music?
You Said a Mouthful

DAYTONA BEACH, Fla. (AP)—It's midnight and you're sound asleep. Suddenly you're blasted awake by a rousing rendition of "Battle Hymn of the Republic."

Annoying? Yes, and especially when no radio or phonograph is turned on in your house or the neighbor's.

A Daytona Beach housewife, who agreed to talk about it only if her name was not publicized, has been receiving the music through her dental fillings and crowns since the night of March 16.

She was sitting with her family in the living room when an orchestra began blaring, "It's a Long Way to Tipperary."

The woman asked one of her children to turn off the radio. He replied that it
(Continued on Back Page, Col. 1)

PACIFIC

STARS AND STRIPES

AN AUTHORIZED UNOFFICIAL PUBLICATION
FOR THE U.S. ARMED FORCES OF THE PACIFIC COMMAND

10¢

Vol. 26, No. 88   Monday, Mar. 30, 1970

Reds Advance on Capital

CAMBODIA MOBILIZES

PHNOM PENH, Cambodia (UPI)—The government announced mobilization of all veteran soldiers Saturday to boost the armed forces in face of a reported advance by four Viet Cong columns on Phnom Penh.

Cambodian veterans were ordered to report to their nearest army, air force and navy posts while Cambodian regulars were dispatched to counter the Viet Cong movements.

National Assemblyman Trinh Hoan said three Viet Cong columns of 1,000 men each had pushed to within 50 miles of the capital from their base camps in the Vietnam border area, northeast of the city. Another column is moving in from the east with 600 troops, Trinh said.

There was no word of any Cambodian clashes with the Viet Cong columns, but unofficial reports said the Cambodian armed forces threw in tanks to counter a Viet Cong attack on the Koh-Ky area on the Mekong River 12 miles from Phnom Penh.

The reports said at least 10 persons were killed.

Both the Viet Cong and the North Vietnamese government have pledged support for the comeback bid of deposed chief of state Prince Norodom Sihanouk, reported in exile in Peking.

It was discontent with Sihanouk's policy of permitting an estimated 40,000 to 60,000 Viet Cong troops to camp permanently in Cambodia's border area with South Vietnam that led to his overthrow by the government of Premier Lon Nol March 18.

Nol again Saturday appealed for calm and warned the popu-
(Continued on Back Page, Col. 1)

The Border Patrol

Men of the 25th Inf. Div. at Phuoc Chi prepare for a three-day patrol just east of the Cambodian-Vietnamese border. The adjacent Cambodian area is heavily infiltrated by enemy. Soldier in center holds a rifle with a night vision sniperscope.
(AP Radiophoto)

Controllers Face Suit By Airlines

By United Press International

Striking air controllers tightened their squeeze on operations at New York airports Saturday and caused flight delays and cancellations from coast-to-coast. The airlines announced they would sue for damages on Monday.

The air controllers already have defied a Federal Aviation Administration ultimatum to return to work by Saturday morning and a restraining order against the walkout issued by a U.S. District Court in Washington, D.C.

The Air Transport Association said it would file a damage suit in New York City Monday against the Professional Air Traffic Controllers Association (PATCO), its officers and members because of "an illegal strike that is causing extreme damage to passengers and shippers and to the airlines."

The association had no exact figures but said the airlines had suffered "millions of dollars of extra cost because they have had to cancel flights, reschedule flights and pay heavy overtime charges."

An ATA spokesman said the airlines had cancelled 827 flights since the strike began Wednesday morning. The daily total of scheduled airline flights averages about 7,000 a day.

The control tower at Chica-
(Continued on Back Page, Col. 3)

A Fortune At His Door

AKRON, Ohio (UPI) — For several years a 14-inch statue had been used as a doorstop in the home of the late Leo Carey of nearby Green Township.

It was not until Carey's estate was appraised recently that it was discovered the statue is a miniature of Rodin's classic sculpture "The Thinker" created in the 19th Century. The miniature was valued at $16,500.

The statue was removed to a bank vault.

Postal Pay Boost Triggers Federal Workers' Rumble

WASHINGTON (UPI) —The strike by postal employes and prospects that they may get a quick and generous settlement of their wage demands is causing rumblings among other federal employe unions.

Before the postal workers were all back on the job, air traffic controllers, who also work for the government, began calling in sick, causing a slowdown in air traffic. They were careful to deny they were on strike, however.

Officials of the major unions say wildcat strikes in other government departments have become a real threat. This may explain why Congress and the Administration are considering including other federal workers in any pay raise for postal employes.

"We have a lot of repercussions," says John Griner, president of the American Federation of Government Employes (AFGE) which claims 350,000 members. "I have some situations where it is pretty hard to hold members in line."

The AFGE represents white and blue collar workers in the lower grades, most of them in
(Continued on Back Page, Col. 3)

Bandit Afraid to Teller

PIKESVILLE, Md. (AP) — A would-be bandit went into the Woodmere National Bank with a note demanding money but fled with only a red face after a woman teller simply took the note and walked away.

REDS STEP UP WAR; U.S. GENERAL SLAIN

PACIFIC STARS AND STRIPES

AN AUTHORIZED UNOFFICIAL PUBLICATION
FOR THE U.S. ARMED FORCES OF THE PACIFIC COMMAND

10¢

Vol. 26, No. 92   Friday, April 3, 1970

SAIGON (AP)—Brig. Gen. William R. Bond, commander of the U.S. 199th Light Infantry Brigade, was killed by enemy small-arms fire Wednesday. He was the fifth American general killed in action in the Vietnam war—the previous four died in aircraft crashes.

Bond, 51, of Portland, Maine, was hit in the chest by a single bullet along the (Continued on Back Page, Col. 1)

BRIG. GEN. BOND

Compiled from AP and S&S Saigon Bureau

SAIGON — North Vietnamese and Viet Cong forces attacked more than 100 military bases and towns across South Vietnam Wednesday in the heaviest coordinated shellings and ground assaults since September of last year.

American casualties were more than 40 killed and 190 wounded, including 24 troops slain and 54 wounded in a fierce sapper attack on a firebase near the Cambodian border.

The total of U.S. casualties was the most sustained in a one-day period since last Aug. 13, when 80 Americans died during a similar upsurge in fighting.

Field reports indicated the casualty figures would rise as later reports reached U.S. Command headquarters in Saigon.

Initial reports indicated South Vietnamese losses were at least as high as those suffered by the Americans.

More than 300 Communists were claimed killed.

Firebase Illingworth, a 1st Air Cav. Div. battalion headquarters and artillery base, five miles from the border, was pounded (Continued on Back Page, Col. 1)

100 Captives Given Food

Jet Holdout Continues

SOUTH KOREAN TROOPER OBSERVES THE HIJACKED JAL AIRLINER THROUGH A TELESCOPE AT KIMPO AIRPORT.   (AP)

Compiled from AP, UPI, S&S
Korea Bureau

SEOUL — North Korea has pledged to guarantee the safety of 93 passengers and seven crewmen aboard a hijacked Japan Air Lines plane if they and the leftist students who seized the craft fly to Pyongyang.

At 10 a.m. Thursday, the plane and passengers had been held by the hijackers for 50 hours. At about that same time, the air- (Continued on Back Page, Col. 1)

Kuhn Suspends McLain
Until July 1—Story P. 17

Truck Strike Spreads

WASHINGTON (AP) — Spreading Teamsters Union strikes crippled or slowed trucking in at least 22 cities Wednesday but industry negotiators went back to national wage talks pledging they would not retaliate with a nationwide lockout.

"The industry intends at this moment to take no retaliatory action," said Trucking Employers Inc., the management group that three years ago closed down virtually the entire nation's trucking industry in response to scattered strikes before a settlement was finally reached.

Chief industry negotiator Ray F. Beagle said the current strikes are "massive," compared with the walkouts during the 1967 negotiations.

However, it appeared most of (Continued on Back Page, Col. 3)

News Strike Looms

NEW YORK (UPI)—Negotiators for the city's four major newspapers and 10 unions wrestled Wednesday with thorny contract issues in an effort to avert a strike to which four of the unions are pledged if their leaders deem it necessary.

U.S. War Role in Laos Disclosed for First Time

PACIFIC STAR AND STRIPES

AN AUTHORIZED UNOFFICIAL PUBLICATION
FOR THE U.S. ARMED FORCES OF THE PACIFIC COMMAND

10¢

Vol. 26, No. 110   Tuesday, April 21, 1970

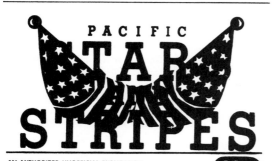

Compiled From AP and UPI

WASHINGTON — A secret anti-Communist military operation in Laos has been directed by the U.S. Embassy in Vientiane for the past four years unknown to Congress and the American people, it was disclosed Sunday.

The existence of the operation, called "Project 404," was disclosed in testimony taken last fall by the Senate subcommittee on security agreements and commitments abroad. The testimony was released for the first time Sunday.

About 200 Americans have been killed and about 200 more are missing or prisoners as the result of the clandestine war in Laos between 1962-69, according to the secret testimony.

The figure contrasted with an earlier White House announcement that American civilians and military assigned to the U.S. mission in Laos who lost their lives as the result of Communist action totaled fewer than 50.

"In this case, the White House did not have the
(Continued on Page 5, Col. 1)

★ ★ ★

Nixon, McCain Mull Cut

HONOLULU (AP) — President Nixon called the Pacific commanders into consultation Sunday to discuss pulling more troops from Vietnam.

Nixon held a breakfast table session at his hotel with Adm. John S. McCain Jr., commander in chief Pacific, and some of his top assistants to review the outlook in their theater in advance for an updated presidential report to the country Monday night on prospects in Vietnam.

Nixon is to announce on national radio and television networks his decision on a fourth round of U.S. troops withdrawals.

Although the U.S. Joint Chiefs of Staff have some obvious misgivings, there has been persistent speculation that the President would authorize pulling out another 50,000 men—for a total of 165,000. That would bring the presently authorized force level of 434,000 down to 384,000.

A year ago the ceiling was about 550,000.

The President flew back to his San Clemente, Calif., home Sunday from where he will address the nation.

Tornado Rips Miss., 5 Killed

Compiled From UPI and AP

Five persons were killed when a tornado ripped through a residential area of Corinth, Miss., Sunday. In Texas, police reported Saturday's tornado toll rose to 26 dead in a 200-mile strip of the Texas Panhandle.

At least 100 homes were damaged in the powerful storm which struck Corinth and there were more than 50 injuries.

Broken gas lines were reported leaking in some areas, and utility company crewmen were called in to close off the lines.

National Guard units were called in from throughout northeast Mississippi to assist local authorities.

Communications with the stricken city were cut off tempo-
(Continued on Back Page, Col. 5)

Honolulu Is Snug Harbor for Astros

The Apollo 13 astronauts receive warm welcomes from their families in Honolulu. At right John L. Swigert Jr. embraces his mother, Mrs. J. Leonard Swigert. Fred W. Haise Jr. kisses his wife, at left, and James A. Lovell Jr. and his wife embrace in background. After a short stop in Hawaii the astronauts and their families headed for Houston and home. (Story on Page 24.)   (UPI)

'Aided by 2 U.S. Agents'
Author Claims Czar, Family Escaped

NEW YORK (UPI)—Newfound evidence indicates Czar Nicholas II and his family were spirited from Russia safely with the aid of two American secret agents and the collusion of high Bolshevik officials, according to a book published this month.

"The Hunt for the Czar," written by veteran journalist Guy Richards, discloses for the first time the existence of an account of the dramatic escape which was covered by a "hoax"

execution arranged by the Bolsheviks. The escape may have been sponsored by George V of England and Kaiser Wilhelm II, both cousins of the czar and czarina.

The account is contained in an anonymous privately printed volume published in San Francisco in 1920 entitled "Rescuing the Czar." The manuscript was given the printer by the White Russian consul. Richards contends it was printed to leak the news of

the Czar's survival without divulging many of the factual details.

It took Richards, who was city editor of the defunct New York Journal-American, several years of sleuthing to identify the editor and translator of this book as William Rutledge McGarry III, attorney of San Francisco and New York and economic and financial adviser to many foreign governments before his death in 1942. According to the National

Cyclopedia of American Biography he did intelligence work for the Department of State in World War I.

The other agent was a friend of McGarry's, Charles James Fox, who apparently wrote the diary account of the rescue contained in "Rescuing the Czar." Fox was the American owner of the North China Star in Tientsin, China, a friend of ex-Chinese emperor Henry Puyi who later put up $50,000 for
(Continued on Back Page, Col. 2)

Cops Run In Trackmen

AKRON, Ohio (AP)—As fans gathered for a track meet here they were surprised to see one of the high school teams arriving in paddy wagons. It seems the school's bus broke down and the police obligingly took the team the rest of the way so they could get to the meet on time.

150,000 CUTBACK
'Just Peace' in Sight—Nixon

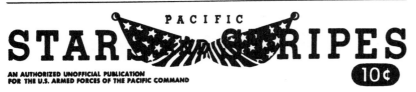

PACIFIC

STARS AND STRIPES

AN AUTHORIZED UNOFFICIAL PUBLICATION
FOR THE U.S. ARMED FORCES OF THE PACIFIC COMMAND

10¢

Vol. 26, No. 111   Wednesday, April 22, 1970

Hopes for SALT Success

Laird: Russ Threat Too Big To Delay Nuclear Systems

NEW YORK (AP) — Secretary of Defense Melvin R. Laird said Monday "we are literally at the edge of prudent risk" in postponing decisions on major new offensive nuclear weapons to give U.S.-Russian arms limitation talks maximum chance for success.

Claiming a steadily rising Russian missile threat, Laird said that "if the Soviet strategic offensive buildup continues, the risk to our nation will become too great to sustain without major offsetting actions."

In a major speech prepared for the 70th annual meeting of the Associated Press, the Pentagon chief expressed hope for success at the strategic arms limitation talks—SALT— which have just opened a hard-bargaining phase in Vienna.

But Laird rejected arguments that the United States should, at the outset of the negotiations, unilaterally hold up impending deployment of multiple independently targetable warhead missiles (MIRVs) and expansion of the Safeguard missile ABM system.

"The place to resolve these issues is at the conference table with the Soviets," he said.

"Let us try to find out at the conference table the meaning of the Soviet Union's increased weapon deployments and let us conduct these important negotiations with full recognition of these continuing Soviet deployments."

Laird said the risks in deferring "hard decisions" on whether to go ahead with advanced missiles and bombers are acceptable only if the United States proceeds with the long-planned MIRV deployment and what he called a "minimal addition" to the Safeguard system.

Disputing critics who contend MIRV and ABM systems spur the arms race, Laird asserted these weapons are essential to preserve the U.S. nuclear force that deters Russian attack—the ABM by saving land-based U.S. missiles and bombers from surprise knockout and the MIRV by assuring that land-based and submarine-launched missiles can overwhelm formidable Soviet defenses.

The defense secretary said the United States seeks "no more than a posture of effective deterrence" and that "we obviously could recognize as legiti-

Relates story, Page 4

mate a Soviet desire for a comparable deterrent to protect its interests."

However, he said that Russia for the past five years "has engaged in a major effort to change the balance of power" and added that "a clear strategic superiority on the part of the Soviet Union would affect our interests and our obligations throughout the world."

Since 1965, he said, "The United States has virtually been in neutral gear in the deployment of strategic offensive forces, while the Soviet Union has moved into high gear in both deployment and development of

(Continued on Back Page, Col. 5)

MELVIN LAIRD
Sees growing risk

Carswell Quits Circuit Court To Seek Florida Senate Seat

MIAMI (AP) — Judge G. Harrold Carswell announced Monday he will run for the U.S. Senate, which two weeks ago rejected his nomination as an associate justice of the Supreme Court.

Florida Lt. Gov. Ray Osborne made the announcement at a news conference attended by Carswell, his wife Virginia, Gov. Claude Kirk and U.S. Sen. Ed Gurney, R-Fla., and other top party leaders.

Osborne, who entered the Senate race several months ago,

said he was withdrawing in favor of the Tallahassee judge.

Carswell said he had just resigned from the U.S. 5th Circuit Court of Appeals to seek the seat being vacated by retiring U.S. Sen. Spessard Holland, a Democrat.

"The Republican party today offers the best chance for the conservative government that our people want," Carswell told the packed news conference at a Miami hotel.

"It is the same sort of devotion to duty that inspired me

through 17 years as a prosecutor that has led me to run in the Senate race," he said.

Carswell and his party left the conference immediately after the brief announcement, refusing to elaborate.

On April 8, the U.S. Senate voted 51-45 against Carswell's nomination to the U.S. Supreme Court.

In Washington Holland, who learned of Carswell's announcement from a newsman, said he is sorry to see Carswell leave

(Continued on Back Page, Col. 2)

SAN CLEMENTE, Calif. (UPI) — President Nixon Monday night ordered a 150,000-man pullout of U.S. troops from South Vietnam within the next year and promised "with confidence" that all American troops will be withdrawn in an unspecified future.

"We finally have in sight the just peace we are seeking," Nixon said in a nationwide report on Vietnam.

"We can now say with confidence that pacification is succeeding. We can say with confidence that the South Vietnamese can develop the capability for their own defense. We can say with confidence that all American combat forces can and will be withdrawn," Nixon said.

Nixon conceded that the reduction he was ordering "clearly involves some risks," especially in view of the Communist escalation in Laos and Cambodia and the surge in fighting in South Vietnam this month. But he added:

"I again remind the leaders of North Vietnam that while we are taking these risks for peace they will be taking grave risks should they attempt to use the occasion to jeopardize the security of our remaining forces in Vietnam by increased military action in Vietnam, in Cambodia or in Laos."

The 150,000-man reduction would reduce U.S. troop levels in South Vietnam to 284,000 by May, 1971. The timing of the additional withdrawals was left purposely vague and will be determined by continual reassessments of the military and diplomatic situation.

According to White House officials familiar with the President's thinking, the rate of U.S. troop withdrawals would remain virtually the same as it has been since last December —approximately 12,000 men per month. The officials said the advantage of announcing the larger withdrawal figure over a longer period of time was that it put the government of President Nguyen Van Thieu on notice of America's intentions.

The officials said the American pullback possibly would be accompanied by minor reductions in the troop commitments of the five U.S. and South Vietnamese allies in Vietnam.

The new announcement means that by May, 1971, a total of 265,000 U.S. troops will have been pulled out of South Vietnam since President Nixon ordered the initial cutback on June 8, 1969 during his meeting with President Thieu on Midway Island.

The President made his 15-minute address over national television from the Western White House atop a bluff overlooking the Pacific. He sat at his desk before a blue velvet drape flanked on one side by the American flag and on the other by the Presidential flag.

Nixon said his decision to reduce the American commitment was based entirely on the progress made by South Vietnamese armed forces in taking on a greater portion of the war. He reported with regret that

PRESIDENT NIXON
Faces the nation

no progress had been made at the negotiating table but reiterated that the overriding U.S. objective was "a political solution that reflects the will of the South Vietnamese people and allows them to determine their future without outside interference."

He called on Hanoi to enter into meaningful negotiations that would produce fairly apportioned political power in South Vietnam.

And in what appeared to be a significant portion of his address, he said: "A fair political solution should reflect the existing relationship of political forces."

White House sources, amplifying the President's remarks, stopped short of saying that the current balance of political forces that now exist in South Vietnam would be acceptable. The sources said simply that the United States was willing to accept any solution acceptable to South Vietnam.

BULLETIN

SAIGON (AP)—Two thousand South Vietnamese troops, tanks and armored personnel carriers crossed into Cambodia Monday in a third major offensive across the border in the past week and killed 144 North Vietnamese and Viet Cong troops, informed sources said Tuesday. Related story, page 6.

ARVN Push 3-Prong Drive

By SGT. PHIL MCCOMBS
and
SPEC. 4 JACK FULLER
S&S Staff Correspondents

CHIPUH, Cambodia — Three columns of South Vietnamese tanks, armored personnel carriers and infantry pushed through North Vietnamese Army base camps and quiet villages Thursday, 25 miles inside Cambodia.

Along the way the columns—the equivalent of three brigades—built artillery positions and rear

Related stories, Page 6

guard posts as this action inside Vietnam's neutralist neighbor crashed farther and farther up the Parrot's Beak 60 miles northwest of Saigon.

Two American advisers are on the ground inside Cambodia with each battalion involved in the battle, according to the U.S. Command, and American heli-
(Continued on Back Page, Col. 1)

Nixon Orders Sweep

GI'S ATTACK IN CAMBODIA

PACIFIC
STARS STRIPES

AN AUTHORIZED UNOFFICIAL PUBLICATION
FOR THE U.S. ARMED FORCES OF THE PACIFIC COMMAND

10¢

Vol. 26, No. 121   Saturday, May 2, 1970

WASHINGTON (AP) —President Nixon announced Thursday night that American ground troops have attacked—at his order—a Communist base complex extending 20 miles into Cambodia.

Nixon told a radio and television audience that he would stand by his order, certain to provoke controversy, even at the risk of becoming a one-term president.

"This is not an invasion of Cambodia," he asserted. "The areas in which these attacks will be launched are completely occupied and controlled by North Vietnamese forces. Our purpose is not to occupy the areas. Once

Related stories, Page 4

enemy forces are driven out of these sanctuaries and their military supplies destroyed, we will withdraw."

The attack, commanded by American officers and augmented by units of the South Vietnamese army, began about 7 p.m., about two hours before Nixon addressed the United States and about one hour before he met with Democratic and Republican leaders of Congress to discuss his decision.

A White House source, who declined to be quoted by name, said several thousand U.S. combat troops were involved in the operation, which he said is expected to last six weeks to two months.

This official said the new move would not affect Nixon's
(Continued on Back Page, Col. 5)

South Vietnamese armored personnel carriers and troops gather in a field near the Cambodian border at sunset before pushing across the border. The operation is being supported by U.S. helicopter gunships and advisers. (AP Radiophoto)

Troops Alerted for Conn. Panther Trial

Compiled From AP and UPI

WASHINGTON — The Defense Department announced Thursday that 4,000 Army airborne troops and Marines will be moved to New England to stand by in case of trouble at a rally for the Black Panthers Friday in New Haven, Conn.

Connecticut Gov. John Dempsey requested the troops in a message to Atty. Gen. John N. Mitchell, and Mitchell asked the Defense Department to send

them "as a precautionary measure."

Dempsey placed the entire Connecticut National Guard on

Related stories, Page 3

alert for possible duty in New Haven.

Thousands of activists from throughout the nation are traveling to New Haven for the demonstrations on the New Haven Green, across the street from the

courthouse where Black Panther National Chairman Bobby G. Seale and seven other Panthers are to be tried on charges of slaying a fellow Panther.

"The federal troops will be available to respond if required to assist local law enforcement officers," a Defense Department announcement said.

It said Army troops of the 2nd Brigade, 82nd Airborne Division would be flown from

their base at Ft. Bragg, N.C. to Westover Air Force Base, Mass.

Marines of the 1st Regiment of the 2nd Marine Division were to be flown from Camp Lejeune, N.C. to Quonset Point Naval Air Station, R.I. Both units were scheduled to arrive Thursday night.

"It is emphasized that these troops will remain on federal property as a purely precau-
(Continued on Back Page, Col. 3)

Inger Stevens Dies at 35

HOLLYWOOD (UPI)—Inger Stevens, the statuesque blonde actress who played the beguiling housekeeper on "The Farmer's Daughter" television series, was found dead in her home Thursday at the age of 35.

The coroner said death was from "acute barbiturate poisoning." Tests are under way to determine if the death will be ruled a suicide, Coroner Thomas T. Noguchi said.

In 1959, the Stockholm-born actress was found unconscious
(Continued on Back Page, Col. 1)

PLOW INTO CAMBODIA

★ ★ ★ ★ ★ ★ ★ ★ ★ ★ ★ ★ ★ ★ ★

Allied Tanks, Troops Slug Enemy

PACIFIC STAR AND STRIPES

AN AUTHORIZED UNOFFICIAL PUBLICATION
FOR THE U.S. ARMED FORCES OF THE PACIFIC COMMAND

10¢

Vol. 26, No. 122   Sunday, May 3, 1970

President, Congressmen In Showdown

WASHINGTON (AP)— The Senate Foreign Relations Committee unanimously demanded Friday a face-to-face discussion on the foray into Cambodia with President Nixon who reacted by calling for meetings Tuesday with four Senate and House groups concerned.

White House press secretary Ronald L. Ziegler said he had shown the President a telegram from the Senate committee seeking a meeting with Nixon on the Cambodian issue and remarked:

"We saw the story on the wire and the President thought it would be a good thing."

In addition to the request from the Foreign Relations Committee, senators reacting in frustration against the new military combat operation in Cambodia introduced a censure resolution against Nixon and talked of cutting off Vietnam war funds eventually.

The bid for a committee meeting with the President was the first since debate over joining the League of Nations 51 years ago.

Chairman J.W. Fulbright, D-Ark., and other senators questioned the legal and constitutional power of the President— even as commander in chief—to send troops into a neutral nation.

Some hours later, after Nixon and his family had left for Camp David in Maryland to spend the weekend, the White House announced arrangements for the Tuesday meetings.

The complete membership of four committees have been invited—the Senate Foreign Relations and House Foreign Affairs Committee members for 5 p.m. and the members of the Senate and House Armed Services Committees for 8:30 a.m.

Asked whether this was Nixon's response to the action of the Foreign Relations Committee, Ziegler said:

"This is what the President has determined to do, inviting down all the members of the appropriate committees of Congress."

Ziegler said he was sure Nixon would be willing to discuss not only Cambodia on Tuesday but other foreign affairs matters also.

In one of the moves critical of
(Continued on Back Page, Col. 1)

A Viet Cong prisoner, captured during the early hours of move into Cambodia, is led to an interrogation point at Katum, Vietnam, by a U.S. trooper.   (AP Radiophoto)

By SPEC. 4 BILL TOLIVER & SPEC. 4 JOHN CODY
S&S Staff Correspondents

QUAN LOI, Vietnam—Thousands of allied soldiers, including American armored cavalry and foot soldiers, drove into Cambodia 65 miles north of Saigon Friday morning in an attempt to squeeze the life out of the Communists' command headquarters for the Vietnam war.

Tanks from the 11th Armored Cav. Regt. slogged their way toward the headquarters all day Friday through mud from early monsoon rains, crashing through dense jungles and crushing enemy troops in bunkers and trench lines, according to military sources here.

Meanwhile, to the south a Vietnamese tank column

Related stories, P. 4, 6 — Nixon's text, P. 11

thundered up Route 1 Friday to meet Cambodian troops at the town of Svay Rieng.

The Vietnamese unit, by agreement with the Cambodians, stopped at the edge of the town.

The drive against the Communist headquarters, ordered by President Nixon Friday, met very little enemy
(Continued on Back Page, Col. 1)

Prayer Day For POWs

WASHINGTON (UPI)—President Nixon Friday declared Sunday a national day of prayer for all American prisoners of war and missing servicemen. He said the United States is making every effort "to alleviate the anxiety of the families" of prisoners.

"One of the cruelest tactics of the war in Vietnam is the Communists' refusal to identify all prisoners of war, to provide information about them and to permit their families to communicate with them regularly," Nixon said in the proclamation.

Nixon urged all Americans "to offer prayers on behalf of these men, to instill courage and perseverance in their hearts and the hearts of their loved ones and compassion in the hearts of their captors."

Nixon Praises GIs, Hits Campus 'Bums'

WASHINGTON (AP) — President Nixon expressed pride in the nation's young fighting men Friday and contrasted them with "these bums blowing up the campuses."

The comments came as he talked informally with a group of Pentagon employes following a visit there for a briefing on the war situation in Southeast Asia.

"You finally think of these kids out there," he said. "I say kids, I've seen them. They're the greatest.

"You know, you see these bums, you know, blowing up the campuses. Listen, the boys on the college campuses today are the luckiest people in the world —going to the greatest universities—and here they are burning up the books. I mean storming around about this issue, I mean you name it, get rid of the war, there'll be another one.

"And then, out there, we've got kids who are just doing their duty. And I've seen them, and they stand tall and they're proud.

"I'm sure they're scared—I know I was when I was there— but when it really comes down
(Continued on Back Page, Col. 5)

New Air Raids on N. Viet Halted

WASHINGTON (AP) — The Pentagon announced Monday an end to a series of heavy U.S. air attacks against North Vietnamese missile and anti-aircraft installations but said such raids may be resumed if necessary.

Daniel Z. Henkin, calling the attacks "reinforced protective reaction strikes," said the missions were successful in knocking out a number of antiaircraft facilities that had endangered unarmed U.S. reconnaissance planes.

Henkin is assistant secretary of defense for public affairs. His words supported the Nixon administration's contention that the air raids against North Vietnam, like the attack by U.S. ground forces into Cambodia, are not an escalation of the Southeast Asia war.

"I want to inform you that these reinforced protective reaction strikes, which were all that were planned, have been terminated," Henkin told Pentagon newsmen.

The announced end to the raids, at least temporarily, came after North Vietnamese delegates at the Paris peace

Related stories, Page 4

talks complained that the attacks violated the American commitment to halt all bombing of Vietnamese territory in November 1968.

Asked whether the U.S. decision to end the attacks was influenced by North Vietnam's criticism, Henkin said "I have no knowledge of that at all."

At the White House, press secretary Ronald L. Ziegler said he understood the operation of U.S. troops in Cambodia was proceeding as planned, and that significant amounts of supplies and equipment were being seized.

He passed along reports that 25,000 pounds of enemy ammunition had been discovered, including 20,000 pounds of rockets. Other finds included 500,000 pounds of rice, 1,500 rifles, other weapons, and vast medical and other supplies, Ziegler said.

He emphasized the contention that the air strikes were "not a resumption of the bombing of North Vietnam," but were intended only for protection of U.S. fighting men.

The air strikes, which followed U.S. offensive operations in Cambodia, were directed against three target areas along the Laos-North Vietnam border "from which there has been fir-

(Continued on Back Page, Col. 2)

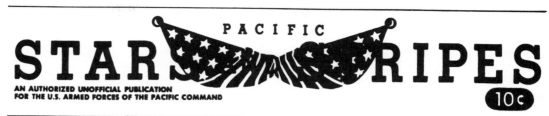

PACIFIC
STARS STRIPES

AN AUTHORIZED UNOFFICIAL PUBLICATION
FOR THE U.S. ARMED FORCES OF THE PACIFIC COMMAND

10¢

Vol. 26, No. 125   Wednesday, May 6, 1970

4 DIE IN CLASH ON OHIO CAMPUS

KENT STATE COED SCREAMS AS CLASSMATE LIES DEAD, SHOT DURING CAMPUS VIOLENCE

Copyright Valley Daily News
(AP)

Compiled From AP and UPI

KENT, Ohio—Four Kent State University students were shot to death Monday in a football field gun battle between National Guardsmen and 3,000 rioting students. At least 15 students and two Guardsmen were injured.

The gun battle broke out after the antiwar protesters defied an order not to assemble and rallied on the commons at the center of the tree-lined campus. Guardsmen moved in and began tossing cannisters of tear gas at the assembled

(Continued on Back Page, Col. 1)

Big Catch in the Fishhook: 500 Huts, Tons of Rice, Arms

By SPEC. 4 JOHN CODY & SPEC. 4 JACK FULLER
S&S Staff Correspondents

WITH AMERICAN ARMOR IN THE FISHHOOK, Cambodia —American 11th Armored Cav. units burst through jungle and dashed eight miles up Highway 7 Monday to join 1st Air Cav. Div. troops who had discovered two massive Communist depots hidden under a blanket of thick forest near a day-old American landing zone 80 miles north of Saigon.

The largest of the two depots, dubbed "The City" by military sources, is said to be the size of Quan Loi, headquarters of the 3rd Brigade of the 1st Air Cav. Div. and the 11th ACR.

Helicopter pilots reported seeing at least 500 hootches in the two-square mile area, rice in 250 lb. bags stacked eight feet high along the hard-packed trails which honeycomb the depot and numerous long wire radio antennae.

The other depot is said to be a major weapons transfer point where more than 700 rifles were

(Continued on Back Page, Col. 1)

Protests Shut 136 Colleges

By The Associated Press

Approximately 136 colleges across the nation were officially closed Wednesday because of antiwar activities. At many others, classes were curtailed or canceled because of student strikes, marches, sit-ins and, in some cases, violence.

President Nixon held a conference with eight uni-

Related stories on Pages 2, 3

versity presidents to explore the causes of "student frustrations and unrest."

At the same time, Yale University President Kingman Brewster Jr. called for a nation-wide effort by college students and teachers "to put pressure on the Nixon administration to

(Continued on Back Page, Col. 4)

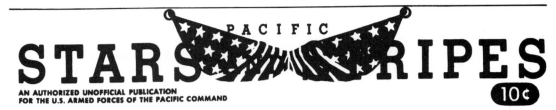

PACIFIC STARS STRIPES

AN AUTHORIZED UNOFFICIAL PUBLICATION
FOR THE U.S. ARMED FORCES OF THE PACIFIC COMMAND

10¢

Vol. 26, No. 128   Saturday, May 9, 1970

GI'S CAPTURE 'MAJOR BASE'

WASHINGTON (AP) —The White House announced Thursday American troops in Cambodia have captured "a major sophisticated base complex" that possibly could be the supreme Communist headquarters designated as the goal of the American attack in that country.

Press secretary Ronald L. Ziegler said that he could not say for certain this was the chief headquarters, adding that the headquarters in many ways depends upon a group of men who move from spot to spot.

However, he said that in terms of construction and communications facilities, the bastion in the Fishhook area of Cambodia was the largest yet uncovered by allied troops in that country.

Ziegler spoke to newsmen shortly after Edmund A. Gullion, acting as spokesman for

(Continued on Back Page, Col. 2)

S&S Radiophoto by Spec. 4 Jack Fuller

U.S. TROOPS TAKE LUNCH BREAK IN SNUOL, CAMBODIA, AS FLAMES FROM EARLIER BOMB STRIKE BURN IN BACKGROUND.

Comb Massive NVA Camp

S&S Vietnam Bureau

WITH AMERICAN INFANTRY AT LZ PHILLIPS, Cambodia — American 4th Div. infantrymen began Thursday to comb what is thought to be a North Vietnamese army regiment or division base camp here after driving off its defenders with massive air and artillery bombardments, while American and Vietnamese soldiers just inside the eastern edge of Cambodia rooting out enemy stores at various points along a 250-mile arc of border country.

To the south, in the Fishhook, 1st Air Cav. Div. troopers continued a painstaking search of an enemy supply and communications complex so large American officers call it "the

(Continued on Back Page, Col. 1)

Epitaph for a Soldier—LZ Phillips

By SPEC. 4 STEVE WARSH
S&S Staff Correspondent

WITH AMERICAN INFANTRY AT LANDING ZONE PHILLIPS, Cambodia — Wednesday afternoon this place didn't even have a name.

Wednesday night, a soldier — a company commander — died, and it did.

The "higher-ups" didn't pick the name. The 50-odd 4th Inf. Div. GIs who spent their first night in Cambodia here did.

There wasn't a formal vote. It

was just one of those things you do, like packing up your rucksack and moving out when the word comes.

That's what the men did. Only they thought they would have more friendly company.

They had company but it wasn't exactly the friendly kind.

Trouble started early in the day Wednesday. First, an earlier landing site was scratched due to stiff Communist ground fire.

No sweat — an alternative

drop zone was not far away. Ground commanders were told of the switch and an armada of UH1 choppers packed with men and rucksacks headed for Cambodia.

Infantry first, support troops next and then the forward command post — one, two, three — or so the Cambodia-bound troops thought.

But, instead of a textbook operation, it turned out to be a long, hard pull.

Shortly after noon, the first

chopper in the first wave of troops made it in. No ground fire. Good — a "cool" landing zone — maybe.

The second chopper wasn't so lucky. Sniper fire flashed from the 200-foot-high treeline to the southwest. The chopper went down upright and would sit intact in the stump-studded, trench-lined, dusty clearing until it could be lifted out Thursday.

Not so with a later helicopter — it soaked up bullets and

(Continued on Back Page, Col. 1)

60,000 Tell White House: 'Peace Now' in Indochina

PACIFIC STARS AND STRIPES

AN AUTHORIZED UNOFFICIAL PUBLICATION
FOR THE U.S. ARMED FORCES OF THE PACIFIC COMMAND

10¢

Vol. 26, No. 130   Monday, May 11, 1970

ANTIWAR DEMONSTRATORS GATHER IN THE ELLIPSE IN WASHINGTON. WHITE HOUSE IS AT RIGHT REAR.   (AP)

U.S., Viet Forces Make New Stab Into Cambodia

By SPEC. 4 DAVE OSTWALD
S&S Staff Correspondent

THIEN NGON, Vietnam — A fresh brigade of American 25th Inf. Div. soldiers stormed across the Cambodian border north of the "Dog's Face" region 80 miles northwest of Saigon Saturday morning and a joint Vietnamese-U.S. riverine force penetrated the border 100 miles west of Saigon and began moving north on the Mekong River.

Meanwhile, 1st Air Cav. Div. troopers found 3.7 million rounds of .51-caliber machine gun ammunition as they continued Saturday sifting through Commu-

nist Base Area 351 in Cambodia, 95 miles north-northwest of Saigon — a storage complex so gigantic that it rivals "The City" 50 miles to its southwest as the largest Red cache unearthed in the war.

The Delta riverine operation was announced Saturday by the Vietnamese Ministry of Defense in Saigon to be 18 miles northeast of Chau Doc — about five miles inside Cambodia. The operation included Vietnamese navy, marine, infantry and armored columns, it was announced.

U.S. forces — including 30

Navy boats — are supplying combat support for the operation, including resupply, medical evacuation and helicopter gunships plus tactical air support as requested by the Vietnamese, according to a U.S. spokesman in Saigon.

The spokesman said U.S. forces are not authorized to go further than 21.7 miles into Cambodia — the limit set by President Nixon May 5. The Cambodian capital of Phnom Penh is 45 miles north of the closest point in South Vietnam.

In the Dog's Face region, 1,000
(Continued on Back Page, Col. 4)

WASHINGTON (UPI)—Thousands of America's young vented their frustration over the Indochina war Saturday at a three-hour rally in sweltering heat, then surged around barricades surrounding the White House shouting "Peace Now!"

Police restraint and the pleas of the demonstrators' own marshals for order appeared to have averted a violent confrontation. After two hours of milling around the bumper-to-bumper wall of buses sealing off the White

Related stories on Pages 2, 3

House for a block on every side, many protesters drifted away.

Police reported 15 arrests by early evening. Eight, described as members of the American Nazi Party, were charged with disorderly conduct. Two demonstrators frolicking in the Reflecting Pool on the Mall to cool off were accused of indecent exposure, three were held for crossing police lines and two others on minor charges.

The early afternoon rally in a park just south of
(Continued on Back Page, Col. 1)

ALL COMBAT GI'S OUT BY JUNE '71: LAIRD

PACIFIC STARS STRIPES

10¢

AN AUTHORIZED UNOFFICIAL PUBLICATION
FOR THE U.S. ARMED FORCES OF THE PACIFIC COMMAND

Vol. 26, No. 133   Thursday, May 14, 1970

WASHINGTON (UPI) — Defense Secretary Melvin R. Laird said Tuesday the Vietnamization program is going so well that the United States will have no ground fighting forces in the war after June 30 of next year.

"At the end of this next fiscal year there will be some ground forces in Vietnam but they will not be assigned to combat missions," he said.

Laird made the prediction in public testimony before the Senate Armed Forces Committee during which he also said the United States already has pulled "several thousand" troops out of the offensive against Communist strongholds in Cambodia.

The secretary, calling President Nixon's program for turning the war over to South Vietnam "the most credible" to date, said:

"Every timetable we've set, every troop withdrawal, has been met. Every single public announcement, every timetable, has been met. Each time . . . from the first withdrawal announcement at Midway, every pledge has

(Continued on Back Page, Col. 2)

Tex. Town Crippled By Killer Tornado

LUBBOCK, Tex. (UPI) — A tornado that struck again and again along an eight-mile path of death and destruction in this west Texas city Tuesday left a skyscraper teetering near collapse, as many as 1,000 persons injured and another 10,000 homeless.

A body count showed 20 dead from the twister that spewed out of a spring thunderstorm.

Lubbock's tallest structure, the 20-story Great Plains Life Building, stood pocked and battered, wobbling in Tuesday's breeze. Police said it was unsafe because part of its brick foundation was sheared away.

Fearing it would collapse, officers roped off two blocks around the building as it swayed gently back and forth.

The tornado touched down at (Continued on Back Page, Col. 1)

WRECKED PRIVATE PLANES AND HANGARS AT LUBBOCK AIRPORT MARK TORNADO'S PATH.   (AP)

Blackmun Approval Unanimous

WASHINGTON (AP) — The Senate, which rejected President Nixon's first two choices to fill a year-old vacancy on the Supreme Court, unanimously confirmed Tuesday his nomination of Judge Harry A. Blackmun of Rochester, Minn.

There was little debate before the 94-0 vote, but Sen. Ernest F. Hollings, D-S.C., and other

Related Story, Page 4

Southern senators said that in Blackmun's case the Senate was applying a different standard of judicial ethics than it did in rejecting Judge Clement F. Haynsworth Jr.

Haynsworth, whose home is in Greenville, S.C., was the first of two Southern judges nominated by Nixon for the post, both of (Continued on Back Page, Col. 5)

6 Die, 60 Hurt in Georgia Race Riot

AUGUSTA, Ga. (AP) — Racial violence which left six persons dead, more than 60 injured and widespread property damage in this east Georgia city was brought under control Tuesday as 1,000 National Guardsmen patrolled the streets.

The violence, which included firebombings, sniper fire and window smashing, erupted late Monday after the death of a teen-age Negro prisoner who police said was beaten by other Negro inmates.

At midday Tuesday, there was still no official count on the number of persons arrested. Officers said the number may be as high as 200, but it was difficult to compile because many of those arrested were being released on bail throughout the day.

Even as the outburst was brought under control, city officials and Negro leaders met to discuss the situation and try to restore calm.

Gov. Lester Maddox, who ordered guardsmen and state troopers into the city, prepared to fly to Augusta Tuesday afternoon for a personal check on conditions.

Maddox said about 1,000 guardsmen have been sent to the area and the situation "is now under control." He added that additional troops were sent in early Tuesday "just to make sure the situation stays under control."

Maddox said guardsmen were under orders to control the situation. "We've got the guns and the equipment. Those sniping at our guardsmen—we're not going to ask them to stop. If they continue that, they'd better be prepared to meet their maker."

The governor said he did not think the death of the youth caused the riot. He said he believes it was a planned thing, "a Communist conspiracy."

At Tuesday's meeting, members of the city's black community charged that racism exists in the city and mentioned specifically that jobs are needed for Negroes.

Mayor Millard Beckum told the group that guardsmen and state police would be kept in the city "as long as necessary to keep the peace and protect the lives and property of this community, regardless of race, creed or color."

Officials said after the meet-(Continued on Back Page, Col. 1)

Crown Miss U.S.A.

MIAMI BEACH (UPI) —Debbie Shelton, a statuesque green-eyed beauty from Virginia, won the Miss USA title over 50 other contestants Saturday night to earn a berth in the Miss Universe pageant.

Miss Shelton, a 21-year-old, 5-foot-8-inch brunette with measurements of 39-24-36, earlier had been chosen the most photogenic contestant by news photographers. She received her crown from another Miss Virginia, Wendy Dascomb, who won the title last year. Miss Dascomb's home is New Orleans.

Vickie Lynn Chester, Miss South Carolina, was first runnerup. Miss Nevada, Sharon Lee Schruhl, was second runnerup, followed by Miss Tennessee, Donna Marie Ford, and Miss Georgia, Cherie Stephens.

Miss Shelton, daughter of a Norfolk, Va., dentist, won a (Continued on Back Page, Col. 3)

Reinforce Key Town
3 Viet Divs. Cross Line, Link With Cambodians

By SPEC. 4 SETH LIPSKY
S&S Staff Correspondent

PACIFIC STARS AND STRIPES

AN AUTHORIZED UNOFFICIAL PUBLICATION
FOR THE U.S. ARMED FORCES OF THE PACIFIC COMMAND

10¢

Vol. 26, No. 138   Tuesday, May 19, 1970

TAKEO, Cambodia — In a massive sweep beginning early Sunday, nearly three divisions of South Vietnamese armor and infantry pushed across the border on the Cambodian flatlands west of the Mekong River. By midafternoon, ARVN infantrymen had linked up with Cambodian troops holding this key provincial town 25 miles northwest of the Vietnamese city of Chau Doc.

To the southwest, 21st ARVN Div. armor and infantry units battled an estimated enemy battalion Sunday morning while other armored elements with the 9th ARVN Div. pushed to within 15 miles of Takeo, according to Allied officers with the operation.

Meanwhile, Vietnamese naval elements backed the operation from off the Cambodian coast and from the inland waterways northwest of here, military sources said. Other ARVN units crossed the border several miles from the coast, informed sources said.

According to the operation's commander, Maj. Gen. Ngo Dzu, large weapons caches as well as enemy troops are believed to be in the area.

The 9th Inf. Div.'s 14th ARVN Regt. air-assaulted to within several miles of Takeo just after dawn Sunday and battled two small enemy units to the east and southeast before it sent troops into town to link up with the Cambodians, sources said.

U.S. Cobra gunships blasted the enemy units in at least one of the contacts, sources here

Pictures on Page 12-13

said. Enemy dead were put at 10, and friendly casualties were said to be several wounded.

Takeo itself, which has been the scene of recent fighting between Cambodian and Communist forces, was quiet Sunday afternoon, and its wide, clean streets appeared nearly deserted.

Cambodian and Communist forces have been fighting for control of Takeo for several weeks, officers here said. On the outskirts of town several dozen substantial buildings were re-(Continued on Back Page, Col. 4)

South Vietnamese sailors pass a baby down the gangplank as they load a landing craft in Cambodia with war refugees. The South Vietnamese government, following the military sweep into Cambodia, has offered to repatriate Vietnamese refugees. (AP)

Get Foreign Troops Out: Asia Parley

JAKARTA (UPI) — The foreign ministers conference on Cambodia jointly called Sunday for the cessation of hostilities and withdrawal of all foreign military forces from that embattled Southeast Asia nation.

Eleven Asian and Pacific nations said in their joint communique at the end of a two-day conference here that a special commission was being appointed to place the Cambodian crisis before the United Nations Security Council and Secretary General U Thant.

The conference nations — Indonesia, Malaysia, Singapore, Thailand, South Vietnam, South Korea, Australia, New Zealand, Laos, the Philippines and Japan — also charged the special commission with pressing the Geneva Conference cochairmen for reactivation of the International Control Commission to oversee Cambodian neutrality.

Indonesian Foreign Minister Adam Malik, Japanese Foreign Minister Kiichi Aiichi and Malaysian Deputy Premier Tun Abdul Razak were chosen to carry out the missions at the United Nations and with the Geneva Conference countries.

In their communique the Jakarta conference countries said that primary responsibility for dealing with regional problems rested with the countries of that region.

"We have tried our best to get maximum results at this meeting," Malik told newsmen after the closing session Sunday afternoon.

"We hope that all powers large and small will take into account the results of this meeting," Malik said.

The 11-nation communique made the following "emphatic" points for solution of the Cambodian crisis:

— That all acts of hostilities (Continued on Back Page, Col. 1)

Trash Can? It's Adorable

ST. LOUIS (AP) — "Get that nonsense out of this office," Mayor A. J. Cervantes growled when the city trash can color controversy was submitted to him for binding arbitration.

The 275 trash cans in the downtown area are a light green and street director Paul Spelbrink wanted them to stay that way.

But a Cervantes aide and Harvard art graduate, Edward A. Ruesing, said he thought orange would be a nice color.

Spelbrink offered the opinion that painting the cans orange would make them "look like hell."

The City Beautification Commission recommended that the cans be painted beige.

With the mayor out of the picture, Spelbrink, generous in triumph, agreed to paint 10 of the cans orange "on an experimental basis."

PACIFIC
STAR ☆ ☆ ☆ RIPES

10¢

Vol. 26, No. 159   AN AUTHORIZED UNOFFICIAL PUBLICATION FOR THE U.S. ARMED FORCES OF THE PACIFIC COMMAND   **Tuesday, June 9, 1970**

CIA Cover-up in Laos Admitted

☆ ☆ ☆ ☆ ☆ ☆ ☆ ☆ ☆

JOHN A. HANNAH

WASHINGTON (AP) — Foreign-aid **chief John A. Hannah** acknowledged Sunday that the U.S. aid program is being used as a cover for CIA operations in Laos. He said President Nixon may propose **divorcing** such intelligence work from overseas economic assistance in the future.

"Well, I just have to admit that that is true," Hannah said when asked if the program of his aid-administering Agency for International Development, "is being used as a cover for CIA operations in Laos."

Hannah was questioned on the Metromedia Radio News program "Profile."

Central Intelligence Agency and other U.S. activities in Laos were aired recently in a Senate inquiry headed by Sen. Stuart Symington, D-Mo. but it is rare for an executive branch official to acknowledge publicly that his organization is being used for undercover work abroad.

Nixon spelled out U.S. aid in Laos in a March 6 statement which did not mention the CIA. U.S. activities there previously had been kept hush-hush to avoid impairing the Vientiane government's neutral status.

Hannah made plain he disapproves of the CIA's use of his agency. He said Laos is the only place this is being done, and that it stems from a 1962 decision that such activity was in the U.S. national interest.

"Certainly, our preference is to get rid of this kind of operation," he said.

Hannah said he is sure that Nixon will include such a recommendation in the foreign-aid reorganization ideas the President plans to present soon for congressional discussion.

"I hope it is going to be in the (Continued on Back Page, Col. 2)

THAIS PAID BY U.S. FOR VIET TROOPS

UPI Radiophoto

MONK LOOKS AT ENDANGERED 1,000-YEAR-OLD TEMPLE AT ANGKOR WAT

WASHINGTON (AP) — The United States has paid **Thailand** more than $200 million under a **secret agreement** providing that Bangkok **would send** up to 10,000 troops to fight in Vietnam, it was disclosed Sunday.

A heavily censored summary of the Nov. 9, 1967, secret agreement was made public in the 310-page transcript of hearings conducted by a Senate Foreign Relations subcommittee on U.S. security agreements and commitments abroad.

At the same time, Sen. Stuart Symington, a Missouri Democrat who heads the subcommittee, called on Secretary of State William P. Rogers to tell how much more aid—directly and indirectly—is being given to the Thai government for agreement to send troops to Cambodia.

Under the agreement reached at the ambassadorial level, the United States absorbed the costs for sending a Thai combat division to Vietnam and to maintain and improve the defense capability of Thai forces remaining at home.

The United States agreed to fully equip and provide logistic support for the forces going to Vietnam, pay overseas allowances, assume the costs of preparing and training and also (Continued on Back Page, Col. 3)

Heated Wage Demand

CHELSEA, Mass. (UPI)—Chelsea firemen want heat pay.

The firemen, members of Firefighters Local 937, are negotiating with the city for a new contract. One of their demands is for an extra day's pay when the temperature goes above 90 degrees.

Reds Seize Airport Near Angkor Wat

Compiled From UPI and AP

SAIGON — A Cambodian airport near the provincial capital of Siem Reap and the tourist mecca of Angkor Wat fell to Communist command forces Sunday, raising further the possibility of troop help from Thailand for Cambodia's government.

Fighting continued around Siem Reap itself, and informants said that if that capital should fall, the Communists would score a major propaganda coup because it is just six miles south of Angkor Wat, site of major historical ruins.

A government spokesman in Phnom Penh reported there was some fighting going on in the streets of the town itself.

The Communist attempt to seize Siem Reap also suggested the Communist command was trying to cut the highway between that city and the border of Thailand. Earlier reports had said that Thailand would send in troops as part of its efforts to aid the Cambodian government of Premier Lon Nol.

Siem Reap is 80 miles east of the Thai border and 185 miles northwest of the Cambodian capital, Phnom Penh.

Siem Reap is said to be well-defended by government troops, but the highway leading from there to Phnom Penh has been cut by Communist forces for more than a week.

A battle also was reported still going on for control of Kompong Thom, a provincial capital 80 miles north of Phnom Penh.

All tourists have been evacuated from Angkor Wat.

The spokesman in Phnom Penh said all civilian communications between the capital of Phnom Penh and Siem Reap had been cut.

According to the spokesman, North Vietnamese and Viet Cong soldiers first attacked the town Friday night. Siem Reap is famous for the ancient temple complex of Angkor Wat, which (Continued on Back Page, Col. 5)

Senate Votes to Repeal Gulf of Tonkin Resolution

PACIFIC
STARS STRIPES
AN AUTHORIZED UNOFFICIAL PUBLICATION
FOR THE U.S. ARMED FORCES OF THE PACIFIC COMMAND
10¢

Vol. 26, No. 176   Friday, June 26, 1970

WASHINGTON (UPI)—The Senate voted 81 to 10 Wednesday to repeal the controversial 1964 Gulf of Tonkin resolution which authorized a big U.S. buildup in Vietnam.

Sen. J. William Fulbright, a caustic critic of the resolution, wound up voting against the repealer.

The repealer was written into a $300 million foreign military sales bill that will require approval by the House and the President's signature.

Because administration forces sponsored the amendment, Fulbright and other antiwar senators contended the action violated normal Senate procedure.

Asserting he wished to "preserve the integrity" of the Senate, Fulbright voted no on the repeal of the resolution he has condemned in recent years.

The Arkansas Democrat said he would vote for repeal later when a resolution of his own is brought to the floor.

Fulbright has fought the Tonkin resolution steadfastly for the last several years, contending Congress was duped into giving former President Lyndon B. Johnson a blank check for the Vietnam war.

When the original resolution was adopted, Fulbright voted for it as only two votes were registered in opposition.

Besides Fulbright, those who voted against the repealer were Sens. James B. Allen, D-Ala.; Henry Bellmon, R-Okla.; James O. Eastland, D-Miss.; Sam J. Ervin Jr., D-N. C.; Ernest F. Hollings, D-S. C., Russell B. Long, D-La., John L. McClellan, D-Ark., Gale W. McGee, D-Wyo., and John C. Stennis, D-Miss.

The repealer was mainly symbolic and was instigated by Republicans since the Nixon administration already had renounced the resolution and is not using it for the legal authority to remain in Vietnam.

The Tonkin resolution gave the President permission to "take all necessary steps, including the use of armed forces" to protect American forces in South Vietnam and to aid Vietnam and other U.S. allies in Indochina.

President Johnson interpreted the resolution as sweeping congressional backing for his subsequent decisions that swelled U.S. troop strength in South Viet-

(Continued on Back Page, Col. 5)

Goldberg Wins Close N.Y. Primary

ALBANY, N.Y. (UPI)—Arthur J. Goldberg, seeking his first elective office, won the Democratic nomination for governor Tuesday night over Howard Samuels, the millionaire inventor of plastic sandwich bags, in a close primary election.

Rep. Richard L. Ottinger, heir to a plywood fortune who spent an estimated $1 million on television advertising, beat organization candidate Theodore C. Sorensen, for the Senate nomination.

Sorensen, a former Kennedy aide, ran third in the race behind Paul O'Dwyer, the unsuccessful 1968 Senate nominee and Rep. R.D. "Max" McCarthy came in last.

Goldberg will oppose Gov. Nelson A. Rockefeller, who is seeking an unprecedented fourth term. Samuels refused to concede defeat as midnight passed.

Samuels' press secretary told supporters the contest was still a "horse race."

"He'll have to ask for a recount, I think," the press secretary said.

Goldberg's running mate for lieutenant governor will be state Sen. Basil A. Paterson, the first Negro to seek the post. He easily defeated his opponent, a little known township supervisor.

With all but 2,000 of the state's 13,735 districts counted, (Continued on Back Page, Col. 1)

ARTHUR GOLDBERG

Powell Upset In Harlem

NEW YORK (AP) — Rep. Adam Clayton Powell, for 24 years Harlem's flamboyant voice in the House of Representatives, was narrowly defeated for renomination in a major upset in Tuesday's Democratic primary.

Powell, 61, lost to state Assemblyman Charles Rangel, 40, in a five-man race. The final unofficial tally gave Rangel, also a Negro, 7,804 votes to Powell's 7,599. Rangel also has the Republican nomination.

Powell was not available for comment after it became clear he had lost while supporters at Rangel's headquarters were jubilant. Newsmen asked Rangel if he thought Powell would ask for a recount.

"I think Adam withdrew from this race a long time ago," he said, adding that Powell "was not servicing the people and the overwhelming number wanted a change."

There was a long time when that was not true. For years Powell's constituents thought he could do no wrong.

As recently as two years ago he could truthfully boast, "I could be re-elected with Mickey Mouse as my campaign manager." He won handily then even while he was excluded from the House for alleged misuse of funds.

Powell fought the exclusion in the Supreme Court and (Continued on Back Page, Col. 1)

ADAM CLAYTON POWELL

Tonkin: What It's All About

WASHINGTON (AP)— Here at a glance is the Gulf of Tonkin resolution which the Senate voted to repeal Wednesday:

What it is: The Gulf of Tonkin resolution was requested by former President Lyndon B. Johnson in 1964, based on two alleged North Vietnamese attacks on U.S. intelligence ships oÑ the Vietnamese coast. It was passed by Congress by votes of 88 to 2 in the Senate and 416 to 0 in the House.

What it does: The key provision "approves and supports the determination of the President, as commander in chief, to take all necessary measures to repel any armed attack against the forces of the United States and to prevent further aggression."

How it was used: Though senators denied any such purpose was intended, the resolution was subsequently used by the Johnson administration as partial legal basis for dispatch of more than 500,000 U.S. troops to Vietnam.

Why is it controversial: Later accounts have questioned whether the Tonkin Gulf incidents occurred as reported and Sen. J. W. Fulbright, D-Ark., who steered the measure through the Senate, has charged it was obtained by fraud and deception.

Why repeal it? War critics have urged its repeal as part of the clearing away of "cold war debris" and the Nixon administration has taken the position it is no longer relevant.

Prospects? The amendment approved Wednesday will go to Senate-House conference on the military sales bill with a good chance it will be approved and be included in the final legislation. The Senate will consider the matter again later on a resolution approved in April by the Foreign Relations Committee.

Dear Senator: In Other Words

WASHINGTON (AP) — Sen. Stephen M. Young, D-Ohio, a man who takes pride in answering letters from constituents, admitted Tuesday he got one that stumped him.

It read: "Unfortunately you have that type of ineptitude and multitudinous instability that terminates in inconceivable and ill-considered opinions."

Bouton's Controversial 'Ball Four' Starts Today

A series of excerpts from Houston Astros pitcher Jim Bouton's highly controversial and much-publicized book, "Ball Four," begins on Page 9 in today's *Pacific Stars and Stripes*.

Sports buffs and general readers alike will find Bouton's spectacular book engrossing. This is the inside story of salary hassles, what goes on in spring training camps, of the pill-popping that occurs before the signal to "play ball," and of what kind of personality the clean-cut baseball hero has when he's off the field. "Ball Four" tell this story and much more. It has already resulted in a reprimand for the author from Baseball Commissioner Bowie Kuhn, which brought cries of "repression" and "intimidation" in the U.S. Congress.

OUT OF CAMBODIA— RIGHT ON SCHEDULE

PACIFIC STARS STRIPES

AN AUTHORIZED UNOFFICIAL PUBLICATION
FOR THE U.S. ARMED FORCES OF THE PACIFIC COMMAND

10¢

Vol. 26, No. 181   Wednesday, July 1, 1970

SAIGON (AP)—The last American combat troops pulled out of Cambodia Monday, leaving only a handful of U.S. advisers due to return to South Vietnam before President Nixon's deadline of midnight Tuesday.

As the Americans withdrew, Viet Cong and North Vietnamese troops renewed their assault on the Cambodian munitions depot at Long Vek, 23 miles north of Phnom Penh, the capital, and shelled Cambodian troop positions in the Siem Reap-Angkor area in the northwest.

Last to leave Cambodia were 1,800 men of the U.S. 1st Air Cav. Div., thus was ended a 60-day drive that overran huge Communist stores of munitions, food and supplies.

Bravo and Delta Companies of the 2nd Bn., 12th Cav., weary and worn, were the last to leave.

Delta Co. was lifted out by helicopter, and Bravo walked back into South Vietnam on a rope bridge that spanned the Dak Huyt River on the border, Associated Press Correspondent Willis Johnson reported from the field.

The American pullout does not preclude the possibility that U.S. air and arillery would continue to pound the border base areas from which the ground troops withdrew.

American guns already have
(Continued on Back Page, Col. 3)

An armored column of the U.S. 11th Armored Cav. Regt. moves back into South Vietnam south of Mimot, Cambodia. The regiment was among the first U.S. units to go into Cambodia May 1. They left before the June 30 deadline set by President Nixon.

Senate Tables Peace Bill

WASHINGTON (AP) — The Senate voted Monday to table a proposal that all funds for fighting in Southeast Asia be cut off by June 30, 1971.

Tabled was an amendment by Sen. Gordon Allott, R-Colo. He was opposed to it but introduced it last week in an effort to force a showdown with administration critics now on a device they planned to use to prolong debate on the war.

The tabling motion, offered by Majority Leader Mike Mansfield, was approved 62 to 29.

By tabling the amendment, known when it was first proposed under the liberal flag as the "Amendment to End the War," administration critics prevented a straight up or down vote that might have killed it for good.

"By bringing this up out of order, the sponsors of this amendment are confusing the debate, confusing the public and preventing any kind of serious de-
(Continued on Back Page, Col. 1)

A Nervous Wreck

HARRODSBURG, Ky. (AP)—The only two police cruisers in Harrodsburg were rushing to answer a shooting call when they collided at an intersection. The officers were not injured but both cars were wrecked.

Nasser, Russ Set to Talk

By The Associated Press

Egyptian President Gamal Abdel Nasser arrived in the Soviet Union Monday and was expected to discuss with Soviet leaders the new American Middle East peace proposals and his country's defense needs.

The Arab leader's visit came in the wake of statements by Palestinian guerrilla leaders that they would sabotage any effort at reaching a political settlement between Arab governments and Israel.

On the battle fronts, Israeli warplanes raided Jordan and southeast Lebanon Sunday in retaliation for Arab guerrilla attacks that killed one civilian and wounded two civilians and two policemen. The Israeli Air Force also kept up its day-and-night attacks on Egyptian posts
(Continued on Back Page, Col. 5)

U.S. Planes, Thai Troops To Hit Sanctuaries: Rogers

SAN FRANCISCO (AP) — Secretary of State William P. Rogers declared Monday that the United States will not send American ground troops into Cambodia again but will continue to use air power to disrupt Communist sanctuaries in that country.

He told a national foreign policy conference of editors and broadcasters that it is American policy to replace U.S. troops with Asian troops in the Indochina conflict.

He spoke after a morning conference with President Nixon at the Western White House at San Clemente, and just before taking off for Southeast Asia meetings in Manila and Saigon.

Rogers said that in the future, Communist forces in Cambodia will have to face Thai troops and South Vietnamese troops as well as the interdiction by American air power of supply and communications lines.

It was the first official reference to Thai troops taking part in the Cambodian conflict and indicated some decision may have been reached on the extent of U.S. military aid for Thailand in the Cambodian operation.

Rogers stressed that the Communist forces no longer would be able to use Cambodia as a base for operations against South Vietnam and a place of safety for retreat.

Rogers also said he thought it possible that Communist forces in South Vietnam may decide to negotiate an agreement which gives them representation pro-portionate to their numbers.

"We have sought serious negotiations in several ways and we have welcomed the effort of third parties to get them started," he said.

Noting that he is on his way to Asia where he will have talks with South Vietnam President Nguyen Van Thieu and with other leaders about future plans, Rogers added:

"President Nixon has asked me to report to him on the results of these discussions when I return so that he may consider whether there are further initiatives for peace that might usefully be undertaken."

Rogers did not elaborate on the kind of proportional representation that could be negotiated with the Communists.

Orphans Slain in Attack by NVA

**By PFC. DAN EVANS and
SGT. RICH LIEFER**
S&S Staff Correspondents

AN HOA, Vietnam
—About 30 uniformed North Vietnamese soldiers attacked a Buddhist orphanage complex on the outskirts of An Hoa early Sunday morning, killing 12 civilians and wounding more than 50, most of them children.

After hitting the orphanage with more than 15 rounds of B40 rocket and 82mm mortar fire at about 1:15 a.m., the NVA soldiers, wearing packs and helmets, came out of the jungled hills to the northeast and systematically blasted the children's dormitories with hand grenades.

A Buddhist monk in a temple that is part of the orphanage (Continued on Back Page, Col. 2)

PACIFIC
STARS STRIPES

AN AUTHORIZED UNOFFICIAL PUBLICATION
FOR THE U.S. ARMED FORCES OF THE PACIFIC COMMAND

10¢

Vol. 26, No. 243

Tuesday, Sept. 1, 1970

REDS IN CAMBODIA CHECKED—AGNEW

BODIES OF VICTIMS OF RED ATTACK ARE LAID OUT AT BUDDHIST ORPHANAGE NEAR AN HOA, VIETNAM.

AP Radiophoto

HONOLULU (AP) — Vice President Spiro T. Agnew said Sunday "somewhere in excess of 50 per cent of all the Viet Cong and North Vietnamese forces in Cambodia have been eliminated" and he said there is no need at the present time for the return there of U.S. troops.

Talking with reporters aboard Air Force Two on his way home from Asia, Agnew praised Cambodian Premier Lon Nol. said Thai, Cambodian and South Vietnamese forces are working well together and pictured the Communist failure to take the Cambodian capital of Phnom Penh as a sign of weakness.

"I think that the Communists would take Phnom Penh in a minute if they thought they could," he said, adding that he expects the major Communist effort in the next few months to (Continued on Back Page, Col. 1)

Tokyo to Say SayonR&R

S&S Vietnam Bureau

SAIGON — Geisha and the Ginza. Get them while they last.

After Sept. 30 American servicemen in Vietnam will no longer be able to take rest and recuperation leave in Tokyo, according to a U.S. military spokesman.

That also means that GIs hoping to fly standby on R&R flights to Tokyo when they take their seven-day leaves will also be out of luck come October.

The reason for the cut, the spokesman said, is "the redeployment of U.S. forces from the Republic of Vietnam has necessitated a realignment of the R and R program to meet adjusted requirements."

Still available for that vacation after Sept. 30 will be Bangkok, Sydney, Hawaii, Hong Kong and Taipei.

U.S. Violence Fatal to 2

By United Press International

At least two persons were killed and 70 more injured during a weekend of violence that included the bombing of two Washington foreign missions, the assassination of a Philadelphia policeman and a clash between Mexican-Americans in Los Angeles that resulted in the death of a noted journalist.

Ruben H. Salazar, 41, news director of KMEX-TV, a Spanish-language television station, was killed late Saturday (Continued on Back Page, Col. 1)

Egypt Takes Dim View
Israelis Clash on Policy

By The Associated Press

The Israeli cabinet, gripped with internal discord, failed to reach agreement Sunday on how to approach the U.N. peace talks with the Arabs. Egypt claimed the Israelis were preparing the world for their eventual withdrawal from the talks.

Yosef Tekoah, Israel's ambassador to the United Nations and alternate delegate to the talks, attended the seven-hour cabinet session. A spokesman said he would remain for another meeting Tuesday.

This means a full-scale resumption of the talks is unlikely until the middle of the week at the earliest. Tekoah flew to Israel from New York after two meetings with U.N. Middle East special envoy Gunnar Jarring. Tekoah and Foreign Minister Abba Eban reported to the cabinet about indirect talks under Jarring with Egypt and Jordan.

Related story on Page 4.

At the Sunday cabinet session, Defense Minister Moshe Dayan and chief of staff Lt. Gen. Haim Bar-Lev presumably presented the military's case against continuing Egyptian missile deployment in the Suez Canal ceasefire zone. Dayan met twice with Premier Golda Meir over the weekend, apparently to press for a firmer Israeli attitude toward (Continued on Back Page, Col. 5)

OSU Bowls Over Mich.

Details on Sports Pages

Colorado	49	Nebraska	28	Tennessee	45	Long Beach St.	27	Northwestern	23
Air Force	19	Oklahoma	21	Kentucky	0	San Diego St.	11	Michigan St.	20
★ ★ ★		★ ★ ★		★ ★ ★		★ ★ ★		★ ★ ★	
Notre Dame	3	Arkansas	24	California	22	Dartmouth	28	Penn St.	35
LSU	0	Texas Tech	10	Stanford	14	Penn	0	Pittsburgh	15

U.S. BOMBS NORTH
★ ★ ★ ★ ★ ★ ★ ★ ★ ★ ★ ★ ★ ★ ★ ★
Retaliation for Recon Attacks

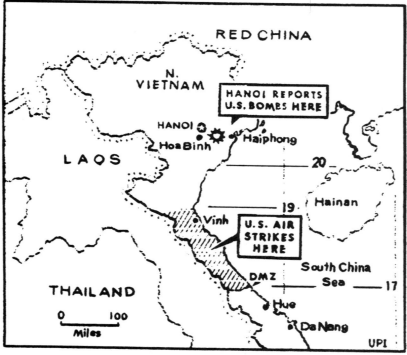

HANOI REPORTS U.S. BOMBS HERE

U.S. AIR STRIKES HERE

UPI

PACIFIC STARS AND STRIPES

AN AUTHORIZED UNOFFICIAL PUBLICATION
FOR THE U.S. ARMED FORCES OF THE PACIFIC COMMAND

10¢

Vol. 26, No. 326   Monday, Nov. 23, 1970

Compiled From AP and UPI

SAIGON—U.S. warplanes, retaliating for attacks on unarmed reconnaissance aircraft, bombed deep inside North Vietnam Saturday in the heaviest raids on the North in seven months.

Radio Hanoi denounced the new air raids on North Vietnam as a "serious act of war." It said there were two waves of attacks, including strikes in the morning in the vicinity of Hanoi and the port of Haiphong.

Defense Secretary Melvin R. Laird, however, said in Washington the planes were restricted to south of the 19th Parallel, 150 miles north of the Demilitarized Zone dividing Vietnam. Hanoi and Haiphong are more than 100 miles north of the 19th Parallel.

Laird also said the raids were ending at 7 a.m., 29½ hours after Hanoi said they began.

He added that the United States would continue to use such measures "as necessary to protect the pilots of our unarmed reconnaissance planes."

U.S. officials declined to comment on Hanoi's claim that five jets and a helicopter were shot down.

Laird described as false Hanoi's claim that a prisoner of war camp was struck by bullets and a number of captive U.S. pilots were injured.

A North Vietnamese radio broadcast said there were "a number of U. S. prisoner of war casualties" at a POW camp, but no location was given for the camp.

Challenging the Hanoi claim, Laird said: "I have noted erroneous reports from Hanoi that, in connection with our protective reaction strikes, we have bombed prisoner of war camps.

"Such reports are false. We will continue to hold the other (Continued on Back Page, Col. 1)

Cops Kill Ex-Con Kidnaper

COVINGTON, Va. (UPI)—An ex-convict who took seven hostages in a wild, three-day spree stretching from Cleveland to this mountain community, was shot and killed Saturday in a woods where police had cornered him.

James E. Kelley, 42, had a woman hostage with him when he died, but she was unharmed. He had previously released the others.

Police said Kelley, who evaded one of the largest police dragnets in northeastern Ohio history, had the IQ of a genius.

He was shot in the head by police. He had at least three guns with him when he was killed.

Kelley took his last hostages, two women, Saturday morning. They were seen driving along Interstate Highway 64. Kelley was in the back seat with one of the women and the other woman was driving.

Later he abandoned the car and freed one of the women, Donna Ayers, unharmed. He took her mother, Mrs. Thomas Ayers, into a wooded area about 1,000 feet off the highway.

Covington is in the western sector of the state, near the Vir- (Continued on Back Page, Col. 3)

This Takes the Cake

BINGHAMTON, N.Y. (UPI) —The State University at Binghamton chapter of the radical Students for a Democratic Society is raising money on campus for its activities. How? A cupcake sale.

Raids Could Prolong War—Mansfield

WASHINGTON (AP) — Senate Democratic Leader Mike Mansfield of Montana said Saturday U.S. bombing attacks on North Vietnamese targets mean a resurgence of activity that could delay settlement of the war.

Sen. George McGovern, D-S.D., called the American air raids almost beyond belief.

Republican Sen. Mark O. Hatfield of Oregon said he is concerned that the bombing "could jeopardize chances for successful negotiations."

Sen. Edmund Muskie, D-Maine, said the raids evidently were "far more intense and extensive" than those ordered previously in retaliation against enemy attacks on U.S. recon-

naissance flights. He said this indicated "our policy has taken a new turn, with renewed reliance on military pressure to force a settlement on the other side" but that "the net effect is likely to be more fighting and killing, not less."

Secretary of Defense Melvin R. Laird announced that U.S. jets had hit missile and antiair-

craft installations in response to "attacks on our unarmed reconnaissance aircraft." He termed them "limited duration protective reaction air strikes."

Mansfield said, "This is a type of renewed involvement. No matter how you look at it, it means a resurgence of activity, a renewed involvement, (Continued on Back Page, Col. 5)

RAID ON POW CAMP

PACIFIC
STARS AND STRIPES

AN AUTHORIZED UNOFFICIAL PUBLICATION
FOR THE U.S. ARMED FORCES OF THE PACIFIC COMMAND

10¢

Vol. 26, No. 328   Wednesday, Nov. 25, 1970

But GIs Find Prison Near Hanoi Is Empty

WASHINGTON (AP)—Secretary of Defense Melvin R. Laird disclosed Monday that a small force of U.S. soldiers landed 20 miles west of Hanoi in an attempt to rescue American prisoners of war while U.S. fighter planes bombed enemy gun and missile sites in North Vietnam over the weekend.

Laird said the task force, made up of Army and Air Force volunteers, landed in helicopters at a prisoner of war camp which was found to be abandoned. The mission, Laird said, had been planned for months and was carried out with the approval of President Nixon.

This was "the only operation that took place north of the 19th parallel this past weekend," Laird told a news conference.

Earlier, Pentagon spokesman Jerry W. Friedheim had filled newsmen in on details of the weekend air strikes but made no mention of the prisoner rescue effort described by Laird.

Friedheim also refused under persistent questioning to state whether U.S. planes had struck targets in the Hanoi-Haiphong area.

Laird said the special task force was launched early Friday morning Washington time and was undertaken only in the face of "continued adamant refusal" by the North Vietnamese to abide by the Geneva Conventions regarding prisoners of war or to participate in negotiations for the release and treatment of POWs.

After being unable to find prisoners, Laird said the volunteer team flew out of the camp.

One helicopter was destroyed intentionally on the ground by the team after it made what he called a controlled crash landing.

Laird said that the action was spurred largely "by a recent report of prisoners dying in their

(Continued on Back Page, Col. 1)

Army Col. Arthur Simons (left) reports at a Pentagon news conference how he led a band of men into a POW camp near Hanoi. With him (from left) are Defense Secretary Melvin Laird, Adm. Thomas Moorer, chairman of the Joint Chiefs of Staff, and Brig. Gen. LeRoy Manor, who was in overall charge of the task force that carried out the operation.   (AP Radiophoto)

Senate Backs Nixon's Veto Of Campaign Broadcast Bill

WASHINGTON (AP) — The Senate upheld Monday President Nixon's veto of a bill sharply limiting campaign spending for radio and television broadcasting.

The roll call vote that sustained the veto killed the bill.

The tally was 58 to override the veto, to 34 to sustain it. The vote to override was 4 short of the two-thirds necessary.

Senate Republican Leader Hugh Scott said he will propose next year a more comprehensive campaign reform bill.

On Sunday Scott released a letter from Nixon supporting its plan to introduce a broader bill.

In the letter, Scott said, Nixon pledged to work closely with Congress and the governors "to arrive at a bill which will deal with all problems of political campaigns, including spending

limitations in a direct, effective and enforceable manner . . . ."

Speaking of the two-thirds Senate vote needed to override Nixon, Scott said it would be "as close as a senator's whisker"—within one or two votes either way.

Senate Democratic Leader Mike Mansfield agreed with Scott that odds were slightly in favor of upholding the veto.

Scott and Mansfield appeared on ABC's Sunday interview program "Issues and Answers."

The Senate originally passed the bill 60 to 19. Democrats said before this afternoon's vote they were counting on 61 solid votes to override and looking for more from a bloc of about 10 undecided senators.

In vetoing the bill Nixon said reform should be across the board, not be limited to a single

avenue of political advertising.

"The problem with campaign spending is not radio and television," he said, "the problem is spending. This bill plugs only one hole in a sieve."

Nixon argued the broadcast limit might lead to increased spending as candidates shifted their advertising to other, less effective and therefore more expensive avenues to the voter.

Some Democrats have charged Nixon vetoed the measure because Republicans are in good shape financially, while Democrats are deeply in debt.

Scott said the vetoed bill discriminated against the radio and television industry, and favored incumbent candidates because it set few limitations on expenditures during primary elections.

LAIRD: GI'S TO STAY TILL POWS GO FREE

PACIFIC
STAR AND STRIPES
AN AUTHORIZED UNOFFICIAL PUBLICATION
FOR THE U.S. ARMED FORCES OF THE PACIFIC COMMAND

10¢

Vol. 26, No. 346   Sunday, Dec. 13, 1970

1968 Derby Ruling Upset
— Page 17

A Jackpot For Lemons
— Page 12

'Significant' POW News
— Page 21

FLAMES ROAR FROM RYAN'S CAFE IN DOWNTOWN MANHATTAN.   (UPI)

WASHINGTON (UPI) — Defense Secretary Melvin R. Laird said Friday the United States would remain in Vietnam until U.S. prisoners of war are freed.

"Vietnamization cannot be completed as far as I'm concerned until these prisoners are freed," Laird told the Senate Foreign Relations Committee.

Laird testified on a proposal to pump $255 million in foreign aid into Cambodia, acknowledging that "a commitment" had already been made to Vietnam's embattled neighbor.

But most of the two-hour hearing was devoted to the prisoner-of-war issue and the circumstances surrounding the abortive Nov. 21 commando mission to rescue some of them from a camp near Hanoi.

Laird denied Chairman J. William Fulbright's charge that the Central Intelligence Agency (CIA) had not been consulted about the issue. He bitterly assailed Fulbright for spreading "innuendo" that the administration knew in advance no prisoners would be found.

It was left to Sen. Claiborne Pell, (D-R.I.,) to raise the question about overall policy regarding prisoners. He reasoned that, since the Vietnamization program is the alternative to a negotiated settlement, he could not see how it would ever lead to the release of prisoners—since Hanoi refuses to let them go until the fighting ends.

"This is one of the major concerns we have," Laird said.

(Continued on Back Page, Col. 1)

Bush Named Envoy to U.N.

WASHINGTON (UPI) —President Nixon Friday personally announced the appointment of Rep. George H. W. Bush, R-Tex., to be U.S. Ambassador to the United Nations, replacing Charles W. Yost.

The President, appearing at a White House news briefing, praised Yost as having served with "great distinction" as the

(Continued on Back Page, Col. 3)

Rainy Day Gift Is Noah Sale

DALLAS, Tex. (AP) — Noah's ark is still for sale.

Stanley Marcus of the Neiman-Marcus Department store in Dallas — noted for offering extravagant and eccentric Christmas gifts—said Wednesday not a single ark had been sold yet.

The ark carries a price tag of $588,247, is 80 feet long and has space for 92 pairs of mammals and 31 pairs of reptiles. Delivery time is four years.

In its catalogue, the store said the ark was for pessimists.

Blast-Fire Rips Bar Near N.Y. City Hall

NEW YORK (AP) — An explosion and fire ripped through a tavern opposite City Hall Friday. Authorities said between 40 and 50 persons were injured, 11 of them seriously.

The five-alarm fire spread to several adjoining structures and forced the evacuation of nearby stores and buildings.

Police, firemen and passersby formed a human chain to pull injured and bleeding men from the Tavern, Ryan's Bar and Grill, as flames engulfed the interior. Pieces of glass and furnishings littered the sidewalk outside.

Fire Commissioner Robert O. Lowery attributed the explosion to illuminating of natural gas. It was believed to have occurred in the kitchen.

There were no reports of fatalities, but Lowery said, "At this time we still don't know if there are persons or bodies in the ruins."

Joe La Femina, treasurer of the Uniformed Firefighters Association, with headquarters less than 300 feet away, said "The blast was so strong it knocked the air-conditioner, the cigarette machine and other furnishings across the street."

Rescue and firefighting efforts were hampered by a crowd which gathered to watch. Over 40 pieces of apparatus and 200 firemen rushed to the scene.

Mayor John Lindsay, surrounded by bodyguards, watched firemen fight the blaze. Lindsay said he heard the explosion while sitting in his office at city hall.

Truce Stills War Action

A Silent Night in Vietnam

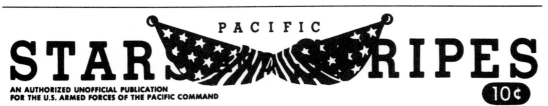

PACIFIC STARS STRIPES

AN AUTHORIZED UNOFFICIAL PUBLICATION
FOR THE U.S. ARMED FORCES OF THE PACIFIC COMMAND

10¢

Vol. 26, No. 359   Saturday, Dec. 26, 1970

A Hint Of Peace At Yule

By The Associated Press

Christians around the world were doing their best Thursday to forget war, politics and economic troubles long enough to enjoy a merry Christmas and follow it up with a happy New Year.

In the Middle East, with a cease-fire keeping the Arab-Israeli conflict in check for the first time since the 1967 war, some 10,000 Christians from all over the world poured into Bethlehem, the town where Christ was born.

As usual, Arab guerrillas threatened terrorist attacks, and Israeli police and troops were out in force. Tourists and pilgrims with special passes were the only outsiders allowed in the picturesque little town in the Judean hills on the Israeli-occupied West Bank of the Jor-

(Continued on Back Page, Col. 1)

Thief Can't Steal Spirit

HARTFORD, Conn. (AP) — Santa Claus came early for Betty Bryant and her children.

Someone broke into her house Monday and stole the presents for her three children and a nephew from under the Christmas tree. Mrs. Bryant, a welfare recipient, didn't know how she was going to replace them.

After a story about the incident was published Wednesday, clothing, toys and money came from all over the state. At last count, cash and gift certificates totaling some $700 had been sent to the Bryant home.

Bob Hope displays a copper bracelet bearing the name of Cmdr. Charles Lee, a U.S. Navy pilot being held captive in North Vietnam. The bracelets, each bearing the name of a different POW, are being worn by all members of Hope's troupe during their Christmas tour. (UPI)

Hope Wows Men at Da Nang

By SPEC. 5 STEVE KROFT
S&S Staff Correspondent

DA NANG — Nearly 20,000 GIs packed a hillside here Christmas Eve to watch the military's answer to Woodstock: the Bob Hope Christmas Show.

The audience, U.S. servicemen from southern Military Region I, cheered enthusiastically throughout the two-and-one-half hour performance.

"I'd like to thank Brig. Gen. Arthur Sweeney of the Da Nang Support Command for the use of this pasture," quipped the 67-year-old entertainer, obviously pleased with the huge crowd that overflowed the Freedom Hill amphitheater and spilled out onto the neighboring hillside.

Hope sang, strolled through a soft shoe routine with actress-dancer Lola Falana, and rattled off one-line jokes like a smoking minigun.

This was the second Vietnam performance of Hope's Christmas tour. He entertained troops

(Continued on Back Page, Col. 2)

SAIGON (AP)—U.S. and South Vietnamese forces joined the Viet Cong and North Vietnamese in a Christmas ceasefire Thursday night, and the U.S. Command announced the lowest weekly death toll in more than five years.

The Americans and South Vietnamese suspended offensive combat operations throughout South Vietnam for 24 hours, beginning at 6 p.m. Saigon time. But American bombers continued to hit targets in Cambodia and Laos, where the truce did not apply.

A Viet Cong cease-fire went into effect at 1 a.m. Saigon time Thursday and was to last 72 hours. The allied commands reported only two enemy attacks in the first hours of the Com-

Picture on Page 6

munist cease-fire, both against South Vietnamese forces. One South Vietnamese soldier was reported killed.

The U.S. Command announced that 23 Americans were killed in action in Indochina last week, the lowest toll since 14 combat deaths were reported Oct. 17-23, 1965. Another 46 Americans died last week of nonhostile causes, including accidents and illness; 160 were wounded, the lowest total in six weeks, and 1,431 are missing or captured, the command said.

The report brought total American casualties in the war to 44,167 killed in action, 8,900 dead from nonhostile causes, and 293,077 wounded.

South Vietnamese headquarters reported 266 of its troops

(Continued on Back Page, Col. 3)

Happy Holiday, Somebody . . .

FARGO, N.D. (AP) — A soldier, apparently feeling the pangs of loneliness, mailed his Christmas card from Vietnam — to "Anyone in the United States."

Spec. 4 Michael Smith, A Co., 23rd Bn., Americal Div., was the sender.

The card, a blue one with a picture of a church and a mountain in the background, arrived at the Fargo post office Tuesday. Postmaster Don Fraser had no explanation as to why Fargo got it.

---

50 Nations Draft Skyjack Treaty
— Page 2

2 Soviets to Die For Air Piracy
— Page 4

Big Gains Seen In U.S. Economy
— Page 5

Major U.S. Combat Role In Vietnam to Cease May 1

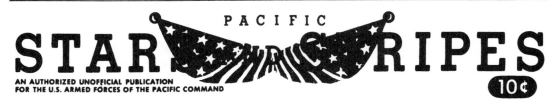

PACIFIC STAR STRIPES

AN AUTHORIZED UNOFFICIAL PUBLICATION
FOR THE U.S. ARMED FORCES OF THE PACIFIC COMMAND

10¢

Vol. 27, No. 8   Saturday, Jan. 9, 1971

A Record 41 Hours, 30 Minutes

Around World on Day Off

SAN FRANCISCO (UPI)—Maurice Rosen arrived home Thursday on time to go to work after traveling around the world in record time on his day off.

"It's good to get away from home for a day," said Rosen, who managed to read only 75 pages of a book on the life of Beethoven that he had taken along.

The 55-year-old businessman spanned the globe in 41 hours and 30 minutes aboard regularly scheduled airliners, changing planes at London, Moscow and Tokyo before getting back to San Francisco aboard a Pan American Airways flight.

According to unofficial records the previous record was 43 hours and 31 minutes, set by Harry Martin, a San Diego disc jockey in 1969.

Rosen's wife and two daughters picked him up at the airport at 7:20 a.m., in plenty of time to open his bar stool business at Millbrae, Calif., just across the freeway from the airport. He flew around the world on Wednesday because that is the day his store is closed.

He said he may go around the world again next week on his day off.

"I had a ball. I recommend it to anyone," Rosen told a dozen (Continued on Back Page, Col. 2)

Maurice Rosen sits in his office in a San Francisco suburb and talks by phone with a friend after completing a round-the-world flight on commercial airlines.   (AP Radiophoto)

Next Challenge: Coming Down to Earth

By HAL DRAKE
S&S Staff Writer

TOKYO — "How can I ever go back to a mundane existence selling barstools?" Maurice Rosen chuckled to himself Thursday as he prepared to take a headlong plunge through the International Dateline on his way to a round the world flying record.

After landing in San Francisco Rosen planned to work an eight-hour day — on Thursday morning.

Confused? No less than the 55-year-old Rosen is, after a whimsical, tiring odyssey that has taken him past airports in London, Moscow and Tokyo but nowhere near Big Ben, the Kremlin or the Imperial Palace.

Rosen left San Francisco at 1:45 p.m. Tuesday aboard a Trans World Airlines plane that had him in London at 11:30 a.m. Wednesday; there he boarded Japan Airlines Flight 442 at 2:20 p.m., touching down at Moscow before he arrived here at 12:37 p.m. Thursday.

Buffeted by time zone changes and hours of sleepless travel, the alert and talkative Rosen figured he had used up 32 hours of his travel time when he boarded Pan American World Airways Flight 846 at 2:45 p.m., this one bound for San Francisco.

Rosen told *Pacific Stars and Stripes* he wasn't out to set a record — only to make a point. Happened this way: Rosen,

who had never been out of the U.S., decided to take a world trip on his day off. A gray-haired, mustached man, he runs a bar supply business in Millbrae, just outside San Francisco Airport. Rosen does most of his business with young couples who want bar fixtures in their home; for this reason, he stays open on weekends, closing on Wednesday.

"We've closed on Wednesday for years," he said, "and come back on Thursdays to find forehead marks on the window. People would come from 60 miles around and say, 'We saw your ad.'" Rosen said he tried radio and television announcements and even bigger ads to tell people he worked a six-day

week and closed on Wednesdays. Nothing worked — and the idea of going around the world on his day off "occurred eight or 10 years ago."

"Setting the record is incidental," Rosen said. "I just wanted to show people in a very public way that I'm closed that day."

His wife, Rosen relates, thought he was out of his mind. His 15-year-old daughter, more of a romanticist, said: "Great! Right on!"

And so away Rosen went on what might be described as a non-world trip. Getting only flash impressions of airports, he could recall that it was "dis-(Continued on Back Page, Col. 1)

(Continued on Back Page, Col. 2)

WASHINGTON (UPI) — U.S. troops will cease to play a major combat role in Vietnam after May 1, but the Pentagon said Thursday that more than 100,000 combat troops will remain there in a security role.

A Pentagon spokesman, Jerry W. Friedheim, mentioned the figure after Defense Secretary Melvin R. Laird said in Bangkok, Thailand, Thursday that by May 1 "a major portion of our combat forces that have a combat responsibility or a combat assignment within the country will have been withdrawn."

Friedheim said that the present force level of 335,000 U.S. troops in Vietnam would be cut to about 285,000 as of May 1, and that more than 100,000 of these will be combat troops.

Other U.S. officials said the role of the remaining combat troops will be to supply the South Vietnamese with air and artillery support, logistics and security. They said the troops might be sent out on patrol as part of their security role.

As withdrawals continue after May 1, Friedheim said, combat troops will still constitute 40 to 50 per cent of the force remaining in Vietnam.

Those that remain, Washington sources said, will be used as advisers with South Vietnamese units or will be kept in a reserve status to cope with any emergency situations posing a threat to the security of other American personnel.

During an interview by four television network representatives Monday, Nixon spoke only in general terms of a continued measured withdrawal. In Paris on Tuesday, Laird mentioned a mid-summer goal of ending U.S. combat responsibilities. This and his reference Thursday to May 1 represented the first move by the administration toward a scheduled withdrawal timetable.

The May 1 date has been set, government sources said, unless the administration's troop withdrawal plans are upset by some (Continued on Back Page, Col. 2)

Johnny Cash 'Moonlights'

TUCSON, Ariz. (AP) — Apollo 14 astronauts will be listening to Johnny Cash's country music on their way to the moon.

Cash, in Tucson to film a one-hour television special, said Wednesday he taped eight songs for the astronauts with the understanding they would be played during the Apollo flight scheduled to blast off Jan. 31.

Astronauts making the moon flight are Stuart A. Roosa, Alan B. Shepard Jr., and Edgar D. Mitchell.

GIANT ALLIED PUSH NEAR LAOS BORDER

* * * * * * * * * * * * * *

U.S. May Use 'Alternatives'

PARIS (AP) — The United States Thursday warned the Vietnamese Communists that until they agree to "engage in genuine negotiations" the United States and South Vietnam "will carry out alternative solutions to the conflict."

"The choice remains in your hands," U.S. Ambassador David K. E. Bruce told the Vietnam peace conference.

Bruce did not spell out what he meant by "alternative solutions" to the war, but he apparently was referring to Vietnamization of the conflict and related military action to insure the safety of

(Continued on Back Page, Col. 1)

PACIFIC STARS AND STRIPES

AN AUTHORIZED UNOFFICIAL PUBLICATION
FOR THE U.S. ARMED FORCES OF THE PACIFIC COMMAND

10¢

Vol. 27, No. 36   Saturday, Feb. 6, 1971

By CAUSA E. BERRY
S&S Vietnam Bureau Chief

SAIGON — Nearly 30,000 U.S. and South Vietnamese troops have thrust into the western part of South Vietnam's two northernmost provinces to eliminate a North Vietnamese buildup along the Laotian frontier that responsible officials term a serious threat to the U.S. withdrawal from Vietnam.

The drive began shortly before midnight Jan. 29, but details of the operation were not released until Thursday by the U.S. Command for security reasons.

Much of the drive, according to informed sources, will center around the old abandoned

(Continued on Back Page, Col. 1)

ARVN TROOPS FILE FROM CHINOOK HELICOPTER AT MAI LOC, VIETNAM, HEADING FOR ROUTE 9 TO KHE SANH.

Astros Skim Moon, Fasten Seat Belts

SPACE CENTER, Houston (UPI)—The excited crew of Apollo 14 skimmed the craters of the moon in the lowest lunar orbit ever flown Thursday before setting out to explore the dusty surface.

"We're here!" exclaimed lunar module pilot Edgar D. Mitchell moments after the

Kitty Hawk command ship swooped to a height of about 10 ½ miles, only a few thousand feet higher than the normal

Related stories Page 3

cruising altitude of the big commercial jets.

Alan B. Shepard, America's 47-year-old space pioneer who

waited 10 years for a moon flight, was duly impressed. "Wow, it's really wild up here. It has all the grays, browns, white and dark craters that everybody's talked about."

Apollo 14 is America's fourth moon landing mission, and the first since April when an explosion ripped the Apollo 13

spacecraft and sent it scurrying for home without ever attempting a landing.

Shepard and Mitchell plan to spend 33½ hours on the lunar surface, from 4:17 a.m. EST Friday until 1:47 p.m. Saturday, while the third astronaut, Stuart A. Roosa, orbits the

(Continued on Back Page, Col. 1)

Illegal Driver Courts Arrest

PITTSBURGH (UPI)—Charles Jones, 32, dutifully headed downtown recently to face trial on his sixth arrest for driving without a license.

The trial was postponed. On the way to court, Jones was detained by police, after his seventh arrest for driving without a license.

LAOS THRUST LIMITED, STATE DEPT. DECLARES

PACIFIC

STARS AND STRIPES

AN AUTHORIZED UNOFFICIAL PUBLICATION
FOR THE U.S. ARMED FORCES OF THE PACIFIC COMMAND

10¢

Vol. 27, No. 40   Wednesday, Feb. 10, 1971

WASHINGTON (AP)—The United States declared Monday that the South Vietnamese-U.S. strike against Communist bases in Laos will be limited in "time and area" and will protect American lives in the course of further troop withdrawals.

"This limited operation is not an enlargement of the war," the State Department said in a policy statement.

Press officer Robert J. McCloskey said his understanding is that the operation in which the United States is supplying air support for thousands of South Vietnamese troops, will be limited to the area between the 16th and 17th parallel. That would keep it within the southern Laos panhandle and the region of the Communist supply center of Sepone.

McCloskey declined to define the time limitation. Under questioning he said that the limits determined by South Vietnamese President Nguyen Van Thieu would apply to U.S. air support also.

The White House said the decision to launch the strike into Laos goes back to January, when there were consultations between commanders of the army of Vietnam and U.S. forces. Press secretary Ronald L. Ziegler said President Nixon approved the operation then but Ziegler did not pin the timing down any more definitely.

From then on, there was continued reassessment, however, Ziegler told reporters. At no time, he said, was there any holdup of approval.

And the final assessment was made prior to this weekend, the press secretary reported.

"Did the President decide to delay the operation until Sunday?" a reporter inquired.

"There were no stops or starts in this operation," Ziegler replied.

At another point, Ziegler said that the administration regards the Laotian operation as definitely consistent with international law and the charter of the United Nations.

President Nixon made the basic decision on striking at the North Vietnamese sanctuaries **(Continued on Back Page, Col. 1)**

U.S. Will End 17-Year Vigil On Korean DMZ

By M.SGT. JIM FREELAND
S&S Korea Bureau

SEOUL—South Korean troops will assume responsibility for guarding the entire 155-mile-long Demilitarized frontier with the cutback of American troops, President Park Chung Hee said in a special message to the Korean people Monday.

Park announced that, with the withdrawal of 20,000 U.S. troops, Republic of Korea forces would take over the 18-mile sector of the DMZ which has been guarded by U.S. army units since the signing of the Korean Armistice in July 1953.

The U.S. 2nd Inf. Div. is presently deployed along this sector of the 4-kilometer-wide no-man's-land that separates the Republic from the Communist north.

Following Park's message, Presidential Press Secretary Yun Chu explained that the narrow perimeter surrounding the truce conference site at Panmunjom would still be controlled by the United Nations Command.

Park further said that the announcement came as a result of the completion of negotiations between the two countries Feb. 6, which called for the reduction of 20,000 U.S. troops and provided for modernization of ROK armed forces through the provision of additional Military Assis- **(Continued on Back Page, Col. 5)**

Nixon: Up War on Pollution

WASHINGTON (AP) — President Nixon proposed Monday strong new enforcement powers for the Environmental Protection Agency to combat water pollution, ocean dumping, excessive noise, and the misuse of pesticides and other poisons.

Enforcement recommendations were coupled with proposals to tax air-polluting sulphur in fuels and lead in gasoline, evidence of Nixon's stated goal of making market forces work against pollution.

He called also for a national land-use policy designed to encourage the states to set up environment-protecting programs.

The chief executive gave no over-all cost estimates for his comprehensive package.

Nixon's program, outlined in a special presidential message to Congress, would require pas- **(Continued on Back Page, Col. 1)**

Market Sales Set Record

Page 8

A U.S. Army demolition man ducks as he triggers the explosion (background) of an old shell at Khe Sanh. Teams are busy clearing up old U.S. mines around the reoccupied base.   (AP Radiophoto)

Viets Drive Into Laos Along 4 Routes

By SPEC. 4
HOWARD LAVICK
S&S Staff Correspondent

AT THE LAOTIAN BORDER, Vietnam — An initial task force of nearly 60 tracked vehicles carrying South Vietnamese airborne and armored cavalry soldiers clattered without resistance across the Laotian border at 7 a.m. Monday in one finger of a four-pronged assault to clear out Communist strongholds along the Ho Chi Minh Trail.

Simultaneously, South Vietnamese troops were airlifted into Laos along three parallel lines north and south of Route 9, according to Col. Dui Le Dung, commander of the land assault.

At 11 a.m. Monday, American artillerymen opened up from the Vietnam side of the border with eight-inch howitzers at an estimated 50 to 100 North Vietnamese spotted near a bunker complex inside Laos — the first U.S.

heavy artillery support for the Vietnamese push.

The operation has been dubbed Lam Son 719 by the South Vietnamese.

South Vietnamese convoys had been massing along Route 9 between Khe Sanh and Lang Vei in

northwestern Quang Tri Province for three days before Monday's thrust across the border.

The Army of the Republic of Vietnam (ARVN) troops appeared nonchalant about the assault, relaxing on their person- **(Continued on Back Page, Col. 1)**

British Approve, Soviets Blast Push

Compiled From AP and UPI

The South Vietnamese drive into Laos brought a mixed reaction from Congressional leaders in Washington Monday, while other countries responded to the news with statements ranging from a Soviet charge of criminal

aggression to a British announcement of support.

Senate Democratic leader Mike Mansfield said the invasion of Laos could lead to circumstances that would force reversal of the present U.S. policy

of withdrawing forces from Southeast Asia.

The Montana senator said that if the attempt to cut Communist supply lines and infiltration routes failed, "It would create a situation which would be ex- **(Continued on Back Page, Col. 2)**

PACIFIC
STARS AND STRIPES
10¢

Vol. 27, No. 89 — AN AUTHORIZED UNOFFICIAL PUBLICATION FOR THE U.S. ARMED FORCES OF THE PACIFIC COMMAND — Wednesday, March 31, 1971

CALLEY CONVICTED

MP'S ESCORT LT. WILLIAM CALLEY TO FT. BENNING STOCKADE.

AP Radiophoto

FT. BENNING, Ga. (AP)—Lt. William Calley was convicted Monday of the premeditated murder of 22 Vietnamese civilians at My Lai three years ago. He is the first American veteran of Vietnam to be held responsible in the My Lai massacre.

Calley stood ramrod straight as the verdict was read, then did an about face. He was flanked by his military and civilian lawyers.

A half-hour after the verdict was announced, military police escorted him to the post stockade. "Take my word for it, the boy's crushed," his civilian attorney, George Latimer, said as they left the courtroom.

He was placed in quarters separate from those of enlisted men, and will be returned to the courtroom at 9 a.m. Tuesday when the sentencing phase of the court-martial begins.

Calley was convicted of killing one person at a trail intersection, 20 at a ditch where he admitted firing six or eight bullets, of the death of a man in white and of assault on a child believed to be about 2 years old.

He had been charged with the deaths of 102 Vietnamese men, women and children.

Calley was notified that a verdict was ready by an Army officer who went to his bachelor apartment on the post. "They're finally ready," he said. He was tense when he arrived at the courtroom, but smiled at newsmen.

"We're with you Calley" shouted a young blonde teenager in the crowd of about 100 persons who watched Calley escorted to the two-room cell at the stockade.

Capt. Ernest Medina, Calley's superior officer at My Lai who also faces court-martial on murder charges, could not be
(Continued on Back Page, Col. 1)

Death in Gas Chamber Edict for Manson Family

CHARLES MANSON

LOS ANGELES (AP)—A jury—ignoring defense pleas for a "gift of life"—decreed death in San Quentin Prison's gas chamber Monday for Charles Manson and three women followers convicted of the seven savage Sharon Tate murders.

None of the defendants faced the jurors during the action. All were thrown out for shouting derogatory comments.

Manson was first out before any verdicts were read. He muttered: "I don't see how you can get by with this. You don't have no authority over me. You're not nearly as good as me. This is not the people's courtroom."

The judge first ordered him to be quiet, then ordered him out. The three women, their formerly long hair cropped close to their heads, sat silent until the first verdict of death was pronounced for Manson. Then Patricia Krenwinkel, 23, spoke to jurors: "You've all just judged yourselves."

Then Susan Atkins, 22, shouted angrily, "It's gonna come down hard. Lock your doors, protect your kids." When the judge ordered her out, she wrenched from a bailiff and shouted at the judge, "Remove yourself from the face of the earth. You're all fools."

She was led out followed by Miss Krenwinkel, who muttered, "The whole system is a game." Last to go was Leslie Van Houten, who also muttered: "You've all just judged yourselves."

The same seven men and five women who convicted the four of first-degree murder and conspiracy last Jan. 25 chose the death penalty over the only alternative, life imprisonment with the possibility of parole after seven years.

The state had demanded death, terming the de-
(Continued on Back Page, Col. 3)

Tanker Sinks; 13 Rescued

PORTSMOUTH, Va. (UPI)—A merchant vessel pulled two crewmen from the cold Atlantic Monday to bring to 13 the number of survivors of a tanker that snapped in two and went down in heavy seas with 44 men aboard.

Eleven of the crewmen were picked up from life rafts Sunday by the Liberian tanker Sasstown.

Coast Guard and merchant vessels churned through a massive oil slick Monday in a continuing search for the other 31 men from the 661-foot Texaco Oklahoma which sank
(Continued on Back Page, Col. 3)

NIXON TO PULL OUT 100,000 MORE GI'S

PACIFIC STAR AND STRIPES

AN AUTHORIZED UNOFFICIAL PUBLICATION
FOR THE U.S. ARMED FORCES OF THE PACIFIC COMMAND

10¢

Vol. 27, No. 98   Friday, April 9, 1971

WASHINGTON (UPI)—Declaring that "our goal is no American fighting and dying any place in the world," President Nixon announced Wednesday night he will withdraw an additional 100,000 U.S. troops from Vietnam by Dec. 1.

While ordering American troop strength in Southeast Asia reduced to 184,000 men — its lowest point since November, 1965 — Nixon rejected persistent demands by Democrats that he set an early deadline for a total U.S. pullout.

But in response to growing pressure from Republicans as well as Democrats, the President asserted no less than four times during his 20-minute address to the nation that "American involvement in Vietnam is coming to an end."

In a speech broadcast around the world from his White House office, Nixon said the success of the Cambodian and Laotian operations permitted him to increase the rate of U.S. troop withdrawals from 12,500 to about 14,300 men a month starting May 1, the end of the previous withdrawal phase.

The pullout of 100,000 men between May 1 and Dec. 1 will reduce the authorized troop strength by two-thirds from the peak of 549,500 when Nixon took office in January, 1969.

The President again urged North Vietnam to enter serious peace negotiations and appealed in particular for "the immediate and unconditional release of all prisoners of war throughout Indochina."

He made no direct mention of criticism against him by Capt. Aubrey M. Daniel III, the Army prosecutor of Lt. William L. Calley Jr. who accused Nixon of intervening in the case and undermining military justice.

But the President noted public reaction to "reports of brutalities in Vietnam" and "atrocity charges" and took the occasion to defend the 2.5 million Americans who have fought in Vietnam with "courage" and "self-sacrifice."

"We can and should be proud of these men," Nixon said. "They deserve not our scorn but our admiration and our deepest appreciation."

Nixon dismissed demands by the House Democratic membership and several of his potential Democratic opponents for re-election in 1972 that he set a deadline of December, 1972, for
(Continued on Back Page, Col. 1)

Daley Wins Again

By The Associated Press

Richard J. Daley has swept to a fifth consecutive term as mayor of Chicago while a self-styled radical coalition won three seats on the Berkeley, Calif., City Council but failed in its bid to take control of that body. A proposal to split Berkeley's police department into three departments was defeated.

Daley pulled in 70 per cent of the votes and won 48 of the city's 50 wards Tuesday in a convincing demonstration that he is still the nation's most successful big city organization politician.

"The overwhelming vote was a mandate to us to make Chicago a better city for all the people," the 68-year-old Democratic power declared in a victory speech.

Republican Richard E. Friedman, 41, a bachelor who switched parties to take on Daley, expressed pride in his campaign and said, "We made some waves today, and they're going to be hitting shore."

The final tally showed Daley won by a margin of 735,787 to 318,059. The turnout 'was the lightest in a Chicago mayoral election in 36 years.

An estimated 80 per cent of the voters in Berkeley turned out in the hard-fought contest that saw councilman Warren Widener, who supported the
(Continued on Back Page, Col. 2)

U.S. Table Tennis Team Will Play in Red China

Rufford Harrison (foreground), leader of U.S. table tennis team, sits with Lu Ting (center background) and Kinkazu Saionji (left) in Nagoya, Japan. Saionji is a Japanese who lived in Peking until last year. Lu Ting is principal of the Peking Athletics School. (AP)

Compiled From AP and UPI

NAGOYA, Japan — An American table tennis team of 16 players and officials leaves Friday for Peking as guests of Communist China, the first such visit by Americans since the Communist takeover in 1949.

Graham B. Steenhoven, president of the U.S. Table Tennis Federation, said the Chinese issued a formal invitation for the visit Wednesday, and the Americans accepted.

The gesture came on the final day of the 1st World Table Tennis Championships in this Japanese city 180 miles south of Tokyo.

"The Chinese didn't seem surprised at hearing our acceptance of their invitation," Steenhoven said. "We are certainly happy to have this chance to visit mainland China and we are going at their expense."

Steenhoven said the Chinese will pay the Americans' travel costs from Tokyo to Peking via Hong Kong, and their return flight to Tokyo.

"We won't be able to stay there too long — probably five to six days — because we are committed to go back to the United States within this month," Steenhoven said.

The American paddlers, like most other Americans, have been legally free to visit Communist China since December, 1970, when President Nixon withdrew a long-standing restriction barring American nationals from the Chinese mainland.

The visit to Peking will take the Americans to a country where five of their countrymen,
(Continued on Back Page, Col. 1)

Laird Orders Tighter Army CID Control

WASHINGTON (AP) — Secretary of Defense Melvin R. Laird has ordered the Army's Criminal Investigation Division brought under tighter Pentagon control in the wake of a congressional probe of corruption in military PXs and servicemen's clubs.

Laird, in an unpublicized memo March 17, directed Secretary of the Army Stanley R. Resor "to develop a CID agency which has vertical control of all CIDs worldwide" and to be similar in structure to the Air Force's Office of Special Investigations.

"One top cop or chief detective would be in charge of CID investigations worldwide and assure that people here would be aware of what's going on in the field," an Army spokesman said.

CID detachments now take orders from local commanders. Air Force criminal investigators are directed by OSI headquarters in Washington.

The Senate Permanent Investigations subcommittee's hearings into alleged kickbacks and bribes in operation of the PXs and servicemen's clubs system brought charges the CID was unable to coordinate investigations between major commands.

Sen. Abraham Ribicoff, D-Conn., heads the panel.

Some senators said evidence suggested a series of high-level coverups in local commands to protect senior officers and high-ranking enlisted men. Because of the CID's structure, the senators said, local commanders were able to quash investigation or suppress findings.

Reacting to another area of
(Continued on Back Page, Col. 1)

Spiro Can Hear Favorite Talker

DENVER (UPI) — Vice President Spiro T. Agnew said Tuesday he was always glad to visit Colorado.

"There is one point overlooking a valley that I've been to in the Rockies where you can actually create an echo of your own voice," he told Colorado legislators. "To me that's very good. It's the only place I know of where I can make a speech and hear the words come back exactly as I said them."

PACIFIC
STARS & STRIPES 10¢
AN AUTHORIZED UNOFFICIAL PUBLICATION
FOR THE U.S. ARMED FORCES OF THE PACIFIC COMMAND

Vol. 27, No. 129   Monday, May 10, 1971

Kidney Victims' Fund

$53,888—That's Texas-Size Help

PHAN RANG, Vietnam (UPI)—A disease-stricken brother and sister in Austin, Tex., will receive more than a year of medical help because of donations from American, Australian and Vietnamese servicemen and civilians in South Vietnam.

A military spokesman said Saturday that a final accounting showed that $53,888 had been collected in a fund-raising drive at Phan Rang Air Base, 165 miles northeast of Saigon, on behalf of Paula Holt, 17, and her brother, Gary, 20.

They are victims of acute nephritis, a rare, hereditary kidney disease which requires them to spend 15 hours a week channeling their blood through a machine to stay alive. The machine, which processes the blood, consumes a non-reusable liquid chemical which costs the H.V. Holt family at least $360 a month for each person. The family was unable to meet the costs.

(Continued on Back Page, Col. 4)

15,000 at D.C. Win-War Rally

Compiled From AP and UPI

WASHINGTON—Win-the-war demonstrators paraded along misty Pennsylvania Avenue Saturday and rallied at the Washington Monument, where the Rev. Carl McIntire urged President Nixon to repent his South Vietnam policy and "use the sword as God intended."

Park police estimated the crowd at 15,000 while McIntire claimed his National March for Victory had drawn about 25,000 people from every state in the Union.

Washington police estimated 5,000 to 6,000 people were in the procession that paraded from the foot of Capitol Hill to the monument to the strains of "Onward Christian Soldiers" and "The Stars and Stripes Forever" played alternately by a 26-piece volunteer band. Many who attended the rally skipped the 90-minute parade.

At the monument grounds, they heard a series of speeches exhorting the United States to seek victory in Vietnam, before a late afternoon rainstorm sent much of the crowd seeking shelter.

The heavy rain came just as Gov. George C. Wallace of Alabama began addressing the rally by telephone from Dallas, Texas.

"I, like you and many others, have become very disenchanted with our government and its no-win policy," Wallace said. "I want out of Vietnam, but I want out of Vietnam with a victory that will mean our boys have not died in vain."

"Governor, they're cheering you here," said McIntire, holding the telephone. "I hope you can hear them."

McIntire urged President Nixon to "reverse your policy to give the world the leadership it needs in confronting and defeating communism."

The flag-waving, hymn-singing crowd cheered another telephoned greeting from Vice President Nguyen Cao Ky of South Vietnam and roared approval of (Continued on Back Page, Col. 1)

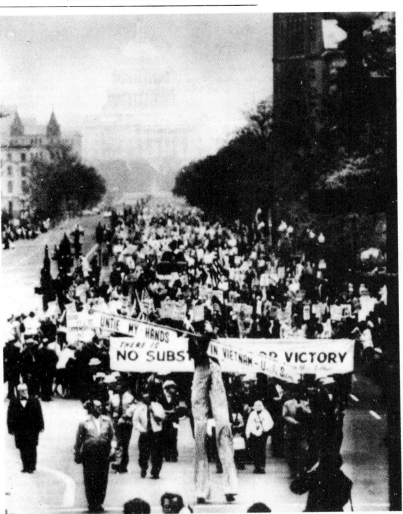

AP Radiophoto

VICTORY MARCHERS HEAD DOWN PENNSYLVANIA AVENUE.

Mars Shot Fails

CAPE KENNEDY, Fla. (AP) — The first attempt to send a spaceship to orbit the planet Mars failed Saturday night when the second stage of the booster rocket did not function properly.

An Atlas Centaur rocket blazed away from Cape Kennedy right on schedule at 9:11 p.m. EDT. The first stage fired properly for four minutes. A minute later the launch control center reported, "We appear to have a serious problem with the second stage."

A space agency spokesman said, "We don't know exactly what is wrong, we are receiving abnormal data from the second stage and it is not flying the prescribed flight path."

He said experts were studying (Continued on Back Page, Col. 4)

Beauty Is A Beast

WACO, Tex. (UPI) — Students at Baylor University have elected Miss Delilah Bear as spring holiday queen.

Miss Bear received twice as many votes as the other nine candidates combined. At her coronation, she received a case of soda pop.

The new queen is the school's mascot, a 3½-foot-tall bear cub.

SENATE OK'S $2.6 BIL. MILITARY PAY INCREASE

PACIFIC

STARS STRIPES

AN AUTHORIZED UNOFFICIAL PUBLICATION
FOR THE U.S. ARMED FORCES OF THE PACIFIC COMMAND

10¢

Vol. 27, No. 160   Thursday, June 10, 1971

WASHINGTON (UPI)—In an upset victory for advocates of an all-volunteer army, the Senate reversed itself Tuesday and approved a $2.6 billion military pay increase that would more than double the monthly pay of a raw recruit.

Approved by a 31-27 vote was an amendment sponsored by Sen. Gordon Allott, R-Colo., that would earmark three-fourths of the overall pay boost for enlisted men in their first and second years.

The amendment to legislation extending the draft for two years past June 30 is intended, like others of its kind, to induce enough voluntary enlistments through attractive pay to reduce the need for conscription.

A similar $2.6 billion pay raise already has been approved by the House, although Allott noted it would give lower-grade servicemen only 60 per cent of the total increase. Both the House and Senate versions far exceed President Nixon's request for $1 billion in volunteer-attracting pay raises.

Only last week, the Senate rejected, 42 to 31, a pay raise amendment sponsored by Sen.
(Continued on Back Page, Col. 3)

Price Falls, Seizures Soar

GIs Get Viet Heroin for $2 a 'Fix'

By SPEC. 4 DAN EVANS
S&S Staff Correspondent

PHU BAI, Vietnam — It's cheap and easy to buy all along Highway 1 from the Hai Van pass to the DMZ.

It is 95 per cent pure heroin,

Related Story on Page 6.
---

powdery and white. It looks something like laundry detergent, but you can tell it from soap by the taste. It is very bitter, and the white particles burn like acid on the tongue.

The amount of heroin seized by military police in this area has doubled every month since September

as drug prices have dropped, armed robberies have jumped and the number of drug users has increased, informed sources here said.

More than 500 vials, about 130 grams, of pure heroin were collected by the 504th Military Police Det. during the last monthly reporting period, the sources said.

More than 500 vials of heroin have been picked up in the first 12 days of the current monthly reporting period, and close to 1,000 empty vials with traces of heroin were found or seized, they said.

Another 2,000 vials of heroin were picked up by 101st Airborne Div. MPs during the last monthly reporting period.

The price of heroin in northern I Military Region has dropped since September from $5 a vial to $2 a vial or less in large quantities. A vial usually contains from one-eighth to one-fourth of a gram.

The clear plastic containers are about three-fourths of an inch long and half an inch in diameter.

One source estimated that 30,000
(Continued on Back Page, Col. 1)

Train Bugs To Turn On —And In

WASHINGTON (UPI) —Tiny lightning bugs are being trained to turn on to heroin, and the government is betting $29,012 this will help police nab users and pushers.

"The first tests have proved successful," Richard W. Velde, associate administrator of the Law Enforcement Assistance Agency, told Congress.

Velde's agency has a $29,012 contract with Huntington Laboratories, aimed at developing heroin-sensitive fireflies which
(Continued on Back Page, Col. 5)

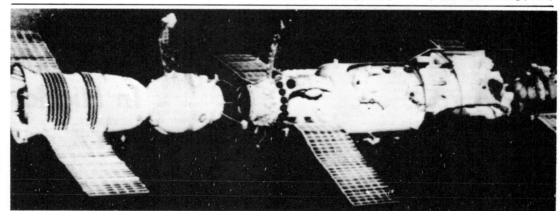

These models illustrate the Soviet "cosmodom" now orbiting the earth. In the mockup, the three-man Soyuz 11 (left) is about to link up with the space lab Salute. The actual link-up was made Monday by the three cosmonauts. (Tass Photo Via AP)

Latest N.Y. Woe: Sewage Disposal

NEW YORK (UPI)—New York City, plagued by an illegal strike of more than 8,000 municipal employes including refuse disposal workers, Tuesday began dumping 1.3 billion gallons of raw sewage daily into its waterways in violation of federal water standards.

The city's Environmental Department assured metropolitan area residents that there was no immediate health hazard, but Gerald Hansler, Federal Environmental Protec-

tion Administration (EPA) regional coordinator, disagreed.

"It is a threat to health and safety and is in violation of the federally approved water quality standards," he said, adding the main threat was to swimmers and to shell fish harvesting areas off the New Jersey coast. Contaminated shell fish can transmit hepatitis.

Hansler said the federal EPA could not act until it had given
(Continued on Back Page, Col. 1)

Russ Ask U.N. to Push Treaty For Peaceful Uses of Moon

MOSCOW (UPI) — Russia Tuesday unveiled a proposed treaty ensuring peaceful use of the moon by banning man's chief destructive tools: nuclear weapons, ecological abuse and disputed sovereignty.

Soviet Foreign Minister Andrei A. Gromyko asked U.N. Secretary General U Thant to put the draft treaty on the agenda of the 26th General Assembly session, Tass said.

The draft treaty would ban nuclear weapons, military bases

and "other weapons of mass annihilation" on the lunar body. It would forbid all weapons-testing and military exercises.

"The use of force and any other hostile actions, and also the use of the moon for committing such actions with regard to the earth, is barred," the draft said.

"The moon, as the only natural satellite of the earth, plays an important part in the exploration of outer space and should be used exclusively in the interests of peace and for the good of

all mankind," Gromyko told Thant.

Meantime, Russia hailed its Salute manned orbital laboratory as the first "cosmodom" (space house) Tuesday amid predictions it is the cornerstone of earth's first space colony and an eventual space city named "Cosmograd."

The three Soyuz 11 cosmonauts who boarded Salute after Monday's link-up drove the lab into a higher orbit Tuesday and
(Continued on Back Page, Col. 1)

'Greatly Concerned'

Nixon: Aid Jobless Viet Vets

★ ★ ★ ★ ★ ★

President, 6 Envoys Talk Drugs

WASHINGTON (AP)—President Nixon has summoned administration officials and U.S. ambassadors from six foreign countries to a Monday White House meeting to discuss ways to cope with the drug-abuse problem affecting American society.

Press secretary Ronald L. Ziegler said Sunday this meeting will climax a lengthy examination of the drug problem, including illicit traffic the wide-spread use among Vietnam servicemen and the growth of a youth drug culture in America.

Nixon expects to announce this week a government initiative to deal with the problem, the press secretary said.

The 10 a.m. Cabinet Room meeting will include Secretary of State William P. Rogers, Atty. Gen. John Mitchell, Treasury

Laird Sees Bigger Role For Viets

Compiled From AP and UPI

WASHINGTON — Defense Secretary Melvin R. Laird said Sunday the South Vietnamese military will take over ground-combat responsibility within the next few months but American troops will be engaged in some combat as long as Americans are in Vietnam.

The statement brought a call from Sen. Hubert H. Humphrey, D-Minn., for some "straight talk" by the Nixon administration about its plans in Southeast Asia.

Laird was interviewed on the CBS TV-radio program "Face the Nation" while Humphrey was questioned later on the similar ABC program "Issues and Answers."

Laird said "As long as there are Americans stationed in Vietnam and as we look forward to transfer of the air, the logistic, the artillery role to the South Vietnamese under the Vietnamization program, we will have combat forces stationed in a security role in Vietnam.

"These particular forces will carry on security missions and will be involved in combat." Laird declined to give a specific date for the transfer of combat responsibility, but replied "We are on schedule" when asked if he is sticking by his earlier statements that full ground-combat responsibility would be turned over this summer.

Humphrey called on the Nixon administration to tell the public (Continued on Back Page, Col. 2)

Related Story Page 6

Secretary John B. Connally as well as the U.S. ambassadors to Thailand, Mexico, France, Luxembourg, Turkey, South Vietnam and the United Nations.

All of these countries have been cooperating with the United States government in efforts to cope with the drug problem and the illicit traffic in narcotics and marijuana.

The drug session will launch a busy week for President Nixon in the wake of the weekend festivities in connection with the Saturday wedding of his daughter Patricia to Edward Cox.

A meeting of the top four presidential economic advisers, known as the quadriad, and a meeting with the Republican leadership of Congress is scheduled. And West German Chancellor Willy Brandt arrives for meetings with Nixon Tuesday.

The President has sent counselors Robert H. Finch and Donald Rumsfeld on a recent visit to countries in Europe and Africa to discuss drug-abuse prevention and control, and the problems of American citizens living and traveling abroad, including drug usage relating to military personnel in foreign countries. They are expected to be on hand for the session.

Already in this country for consultations and to attend a class reunion at Yale was U.S. (Continued on Back Page, Col. 1)

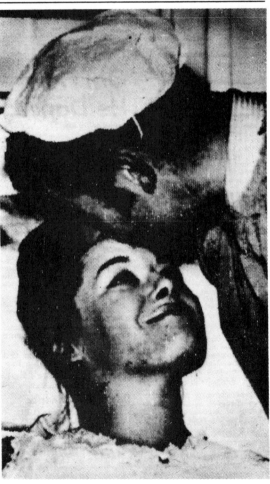

Geraldine Brodrick gets a kiss from husband Len in Sydney hospital after bearing nine babies. (AP Radiophoto)

WASHINGTON (AP) — President Nixon Sunday ordered highest priority for an "effective mobilization of federal resources" to place the growing number of unemployed veterans of the Vietnam era in jobs or training.

"I am greatly concerned at any denial of civilian job opportunities to these young men who have borne the burden of fighting," Nixon said in a letter giving "my personal mandate" to Secretary of Labor James D. Hodgson to head the effort.

"I am also deeply concerned at the evidence that the most serious problem is experienced by those with educational deficiences or other disabilities," Nixon said.

Hodgson told a White House news conference the new program calls for a total new effort that "expands current programs, creates new priorities and establishes mechanisms needed to do the job."

He said there are 370,000 Vietnam-era veterans now unemployed, a rate of 10.8 per cent of those between ages 20 to 29 compared with 8.4 per cent of those of the same age who did not serve in the military.

The President told Hodgson to coordinate his effort with Chairman James Oates of the Jobs for Veterans Committee which has been spotlighting the veterans' problems and declared "to speed action, I call upon all government agencies to draw fully upon resources at hand."

As for costs, Hodgson said an effort will be made to do the job with current resources but if this is not enough "we'll ask for more money . . . no matter what it costs" to achieve the goal.

Actually, he said, "it's a costs saving," for every veteran who gets employment gets off the unemployment compensation rolls.

Nixon directed Hodgson to draw upon the resources of the National Alliance of Businessmen, and the secretary noted that the alliance has been able to find employment for several hundred thousand disadvantaged people.

"I anticipate," he said, "an NAB pledge of a large number of veteran placements that will be in addition to that organization's present hiring pledge for the disadvantaged."

Symphony Goes Great Guns

PITTSBURGH (AP) — Two dozen National Guardsmen played cannon over the weekend with the Pittsburgh Symphony Orchestra.

The program was a salute to Tschaikovsky and six cannon were used in the climax of the 1812 Overture.

The salute was staged at Three Rivers Stadium and about 19,000 persons attended.

A spokesman said the police received several calls "from people wondering where the attack was coming from."

PACIFIC STARS AND STRIPES

AN AUTHORIZED UNOFFICIAL PUBLICATION FOR THE U.S. ARMED FORCES OF THE PACIFIC COMMAND

10¢

Vol. 27, No. 165   Tuesday, June 15, 1971

Only 4 of 9 Babies Are Alive Now

SYDNEY (UPI) — Three of the Brodrick nontuplets died during the night, leaving only four babies alive of nine delivered to their mother Sunday, a hospital spokesman announced.

The dead babies were all those previously reported as suffering from breathing problems. They were two boys — the fourth and fifth born — and a girl, the seventh born.

Spokesman said the condition of the first born girl was unchanged from satisfactory but he said the other three — a boy and two girls — were causing "some concern."

Fear that bad news was in the offing was expressed among newsmen waiting at Sydney Royal Women's Hospital when a scheduled 10 a.m. announcement on the condition of the children was delayed.

About 15 minutes later the hospital superintendent, Dr. John Greenwell, made the sad announcement.

He declined to elaborate and said nothing more would be released until 6 p.m.

Mrs. Geraldine Brodrick, 29, Canberra housewife and socialite, delivered the nine babies early Sunday morning. Two were stillborn. By Sunday evening three of the children had begun to falter in their breathing.

Mrs. Brodrick, mother of two other small daughters delivered (Continued on Back Page, Col. 2)

SUPREME COURT OK'S VIET DATA RELEASE

PACIFIC STARS AND STRIPES

AN AUTHORIZED UNOFFICIAL PUBLICATION
FOR THE U.S. ARMED FORCES OF THE PACIFIC COMMAND

10¢

Vol. 27, No. 182   Friday, July 2, 1971

Russ Space Crew Dies Mysteriously

The Soviet cosmonauts posed in their capsule before their ill-fated flight. From left are Lt. Col. Georgy Dobrovolsky, Viktor Patsayev and Vladislav Volkov.   (UPI Radiophoto)

Situation at Glance

Here are highlights of Wednesday's developments pertaining to the Pentagon papers and disclosures from newly released sections of the Vietnam war study:

—The Supreme Court, in a 6-3 decision, upheld the right of the New York Times and Washington Post to resume publication of stories based on the Pentagon papers.

—Sen. Mike Gravel, D-Alaska, released a major portion of the study saying there is no justification for keeping it from the American public.

—Senate Republican Leader Hugh Scott of Pennsylvania called on Senate Democrats to determine whether Gravel violated chamber rules in releasing parts of the Pentagon study.

—The Pentagon papers disclosed early, high-level U.S. talks about using nuclear weapons in the Vietnam war if Red Chinese forces joined the fighting.

—The war study said that the night before President Lyndon B. Johnson announced cessation of the bombing of North Vietnam in his successful 1968 bid to get peace talks started, the State Department notified U.S. war allies that the move probably would fail.

—The Christian Science Monitor reported that although the State Department had no evidence of a link between Ho Chi Minh and Moscow, it refused eight direct appeals for aid from Ho shortly after the end of World War II.

—The Pentagon papers disclosed that former Secretary of Defense Robert S. McNamara, as early as November 1961, raised with President John F. Kennedy the possibility of attacking North Vietnam.

WASHINGTON (AP) — The Supreme Court on a 6 to 3 vote Wednesday permitted the New York Times and the Washington Post to publish stories based on the secret Pentagon study of the Vietnam War.

The majority's opinion said the government had not met the burden of showing justification for a restraint. Chief Justice Warren E. Burger and Justices Harry A. Blackmun and John M. Harlan dissented.

The decision affirmed the judgment of the federal

Related Stories on Pages 2-3
---

appeals court here allowing the Post to publish, and reversed the judgment of the federal appeals court in New York that had prevented the Times from printing material to which the government objected.

In addition to the short, unsigned majority opinion
(Continued on Back Page, Col. 1)

MOSCOW (AP) — The three Soyuz 11 cosmonauts died Wednesday as their space ship brought them back to earth from the world's first manned orbital space laboratory and a record of nearly 24 days in space.

An official announcement said the three spacemen — Lt. Col.

More Photos on Pages 12-13

Georgy Dobrovolsky, Flight Engineer Vladislav Volkov and Test Engineer Viktor Patsayev — completed their flight program Tuesday and communicated with ground control on the way down. Soyuz 11 made a smooth landing where it was (Continued on Back Page, Col. 2)

It's Final: 18-Year-Olds Get the Vote

COLUMBUS, Ohio (AP) — The voting age in all elections was lowered to 18 years Wednesday night when Ohio ratified the 26th amendment to the U.S. Constitution, fulfilling the requirement that 38 states do so to make it law.

The Ohio house, with 99 members, ratified the amendment 81-9, one day after the Senate passed it 30-2.

House Speaker Charles Kurfess had to rule out of order fellow Republican Rep. Jim Thorpe, who loudly objected to the quick action as the vote was taken electronically.

North Carolina and Alabama legislatures approved the amendment earlier in the day.

It took only three months—record time—for 38 states to ratify the amendment, making it law. The process normally takes about 15 months.

Both the Republican and Democratic parties are already at work devising strategies to win support of the 11 million voters under age 21 who are eligible to vote for the first time.

Congress passed a law last year lowering the voting age to 18 but the Supreme Court held it valid only for federal elections. The new amendment gave the vote to 18-year-olds in state elections as well.

The 18-year-old vote amendment is the fourth since the electorate since the constitution was originally adopted. The 14th Amendment gave the vote to Negroes, the 19th to women, and the 23rd permits voting for president in the District of Columbia.

The new amendment reads: "The right of citizens of the United States, who are 18 years of age or older, to vote shall not be denied or abridged by the United States or by any state on account of age."

According to Census Bureau statistics, about half of the 11 million new American voters are receiving some type of higher education, about three million are working full-time and 1.4 million are in the armed forces. About half are married.

These new voters, along with others who are at least 21 but who were too young to vote in 1968, mean more than 25 million Americans under age 25 will become potential voters for president for the first time in the 1972 election.

No GI Pay Raises Before Nov. 13

WASHINGTON (UPI) — The White House said Wednesday President Nixon intends to delay military pay raises provided by the draft extension law until after the wage-price freeze expires Nov. 13.

The draft measure, which won final congressional approval Tuesday after months of legislative wrangling, provided that the increases take effect Oct. 1.

Gerald Warren, deputy White House Press Secretary, told newsmen: "It is our intention that the increase not be applicable during the period of the freeze."

Some legal experts on Capitol Hill argued that the draft legislation would take precedence over the law authorizing the freeze, and that if Nixon signs the bill as expected, the pay increases of $2.4 billion a year would have to take effect Oct. 1.

Warren said the White House was studying ways in which the boost could be legally deferred until the wage-price moratorium is lifted.

Nixon originally proposed the military pay hikes as an inducement toward his goal of achieving an all-volunteer military force, thus doing away with the draft.

Meantime, the Defense Department went to work Wednesday to decide how many men would be included in next week's draft call, the first since the old conscription (Continued on Back Page, Col. 1)

PACIFIC STARS AND STRIPES

AN AUTHORIZED UNOFFICIAL PUBLICATION
FOR THE U.S. ARMED FORCES OF THE PACIFIC COMMAND

10¢

Vol. 27, No. 266   Friday, Sept. 24, 1971

57-Min. Deliberation

Medina Innocent On All Charges

Capt. Medina dashes down the steps from Pershing Hall toward the courtroom at Ft. McPherson to hear his acquittal verdict. (AP)

FT. MCPHERSON, Ga. (UPI) — Capt. Ernest L. Medina, the last officer charged in the massacre at My Lai, was cleared of all counts Wednesday by a court-martial jury that deliberated 57 minutes.

One other officer, Col. Oran K. Henderson, is on trial at Ft. Meade, Md., but he is accused of covering up the massacre, and not with the actual killings.

Twenty five officers and men originally were charged in the March 16, 1968 incidents, 12 with participating in the actual killings, 12 with covering up, and one with both. Of that number five were tried, four were acquitted, one was convicted, and the charges against all others were dismissed.

The verdict in the Medina case came at 4:19 p. m., and the speed with which the jury reached the decision was in sharp contrast to the 13 days which another panel at Ft. Benning, Ga. took in returning the only conviction in the case —that of Lt. William L. Calley Jr.

Calley, like Medina, was charged with 102 murders at My Lai, and was convicted of 22 of them. He has his 20 year sentence under appeal.

All but one of the murder charges against Medina had (Continued on Back Page, Col. 1)

U.N. Voting: U.S. Wins 1, Then Loses 1

Compiled From AP and UPI

UNITED NATIONS — The United States won endorsement of the U.N. General Assembly's steering committee Wednesday night for a full hearing on its "two-China" policy.

It lost another test, however, when the 25-nation committee rejected a U.S. proposal that the two-China formula be discussed concurrently with a rival plan to give China's U.N. seat to Peking alone.

In Tokyo, meanwhile, Japanese Prime Minister Eisaku Sato announced that his government would co-sponsor both U.S. resolutions on the China issue. One resolution would designate The ouster of Taiwan, an important question, requiring a two-thirds vote for passage, and the other would recommend seating (Continued on Back Page, Col. 1)

Just One Of Life's Reversals

OXNARD, Calif. (UPI) — Merv Griffith drove into a service station Wednesday morning. He left the motor running, got out and slammed the door. The jolt locked the door. It also jarred the gears into reverse. The 1970 auto backed out of the filling station on its own, hit a divider and then went into a circular pattern in reverse, in the center of one of the busiest intersections in Oxnard.

Griffith, 30, ran wildly in pursuit of his errant automobile as it circled over and over again in the street, occasionally bouncing off a curb and back into the same pattern.

Motorists came to a screeching halt and stared in amazement at Griffith trying to stick a key in the lock of a gyrating door.

For what seemed hours but was only a few minutes, Griffith ran with his auto. One impatient motorist took a chance and sped through the circle. He made it.

Someone handed Griffith a hammer. He smashed in a window, reached in and unlocked the door. He opened it, jumped in and cut the ignition. Honest.

BULLETIN

SEOUL (S&S) — Seventeen North Korean spies were arrested in various parts of the Republic of Korea last Friday, the ROK Army Security Unit announced Thursday.

Living Costs, Wages Rose in August

WASHINGTON (AP) — The government said Wednesday in its first consumer price report since President Nixon ordered the wage-price freeze that both living costs and wages rose in August.

Living costs increased three-tenths of one per cent, largely because of a sharp boost in gasoline prices, but the Labor Department's Bureau of Labor Statistics said the report did not reflect the price freeze because many of the figures were compiled before it was announced Aug. 15.

Wages of some 45 million rank-and-file workers rose two cents hourly and $1.43 weekly to $129 per week. Purchasing power after deduction for price increases was up seven-tenths of one per cent for the month and 1.1 per cent from a year earlier and was only five-tenths of one per cent under the 1968 all-time high, the report said.

The rise in living costs, slightly larger than in July, pushed the government's consumer price index up to 122.2 per cent of its 1967 base of 100. The figure means that it cost $12.22 last month for every $10 worth of typical family purchases four years ago.

On a seasonally adjusted basis, the August rise was four-tenths of one per cent, double the size of the July increase, but still well below the increases in May and June, the bureau said.

Grocery prices were unchanged in August, the first time since January there had been no increase.

In other major price categories, housing costs rose five-tenths of one per cent, transportation was up five-tenths, including a 3.7 per cent hike for gasoline, medical care increased five-tenths, and recreation rose one-tenth of one per cent.

Clothing prices declined three-tenths of one per cent but there was a rise of five-tenths of one per cent for shoes.

The bureau said future price reports during the freeze are likely to show change because some items are not frozen and others are not priced every month and will later show changes from before the freeze.

The bureau said fresh fruits and vegetables and eggs which (Continued on Back Page, Col. 5)

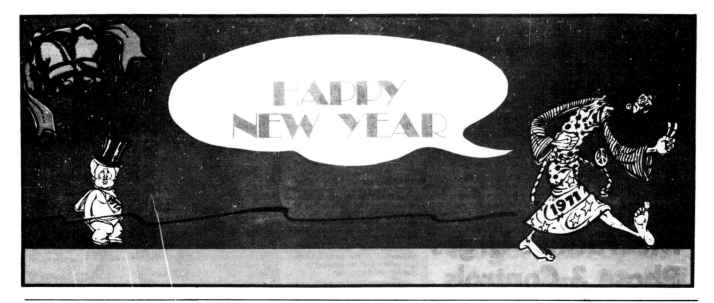

HAPPY NEW YEAR

1971

3 Jets Lost

5 DAYS OF RAIDS END

PACIFIC
STARS and STRIPES
AN AUTHORIZED UNOFFICIAL PUBLICATION
FOR THE U.S. ARMED FORCES OF THE PACIFIC COMMAND
10¢

Vol. 28, No. 1   Saturday, Jan. 1, 1972

By SPEC. 5 STEVE MONTIEL
S&S Vietnam Bureau

SAIGON—U.S. Air Force and Navy warplanes ended five days of blistering air strikes against North Vietnam Thursday, and the U.S. Command said three jets were lost during the raids.

Air Force and Navy pilots flew 1,000 sorties against assorted targets in North Vietnam during the heaviest bombing campaign in more than three years, spokesmen reported.

The "limited duration, protective reaction air strikes" ended at 3:36 p.m. Thursday, according to the command communique.

Targets of the air raids were airfields, supply depots, surface-to-air missile launchers, antiaircraft artillery and air-defense radar sites, spokesmen said.

Most of the strikes were within 90 miles of the Demilitarized Zone, but planes also bombarded airfields south of the 20th parallel, which is 75 miles south of Hanoi, spokesmen said.

Two U.S. Navy jets — an F4 Phantom and an A6 Intruder — crashed in North Vietnam Thursday, spokesmen said, and an Air Force F4 was lost on the first day of the raids last Sunday.

One crewman of the A6 was rescued, but the other five crew members of the three downed planes were reported missing. Each jet carried a crew of two.

Spokesmen said the specific causes of the jet crashes were unknown.

Another F4 fighter-bomber and a North Vietnamese MIG21
(Continued on Back Page, Col. 2)

Cushman: Will Keep MC Lean

WASHINGTON (AP) — Gen. Robert E. Cushman Jr. was sworn in as the 25th commandant of the Marine Corps Thursday.

Secretary of Defense Melvin R. Laird administered the oath of office in ceremonies at the Marine Barracks here.

Cushman succeeds Gen. Leonard F. Chapman Jr., who is retiring after 36 years in the Marines and four years as commandant.

Laird called Chapman a "close friend and key military adviser" and charged Cushman with "maintaining the fine edge of professionalism that is the United States Marine Corps."

Cushman promised to maintain that edge and said "I'd like to promise that the corps will be kept lean and mean and that we'll take care of our own."

Although Cushman received the corps battle colors and his fourth general's star at the ceremony, he will not take over command until Jan. 1.

Ellsberg, Russo Indicted For Pentagon Papers

LOS ANGELES (AP)— Dr. Daniel Ellsberg and Anthony J. Russo, former colleagues at Rand Corp., stood accused by a federal grand jury Thursday of conspiring to steal and distribute the Pentagon Papers.

It was the second indictment to be returned in the case against Ellsberg and the first against Russo.

The indictment, which replaces the earlier one against Ellsberg, was announced by the Justice Department in Washington. It was actually returned here Wednesday but was sealed while FBI agents were looking for Russo, who authorities said has not yet been arrested.

A Justice Department spokesman said the indictment was
(Continued on Back Page, Col. 1)

DANIEL ELLSBERG

ANTHONY J. RUSSO

Last 'Pure' Word in Computerization

MENLO PARK, Calif. (AP) — Computers now can do almost everything but carry on a conversation with humans.

Now scientists want to build one that does that.

The Stanford Research Institute announced Tuesday its researchers and others have launched a five-year program to develop a machine that can carry on an intelligent dialogue with any person who speaks "pure American male English" and limits himself to a specified 1,000-word vocabulary.

Bertram Raphael, manager of SRI's artificial intelligence program, said the computer could be used for such things as helping in repairs of broken household appliances.

He said the computer could be prestored with all the information necessary to fix an item like a television set and would respond to oral questions from a repairman such as "How do I remove a part?" or "How do I connect the replacement?"

The machine will be geared to understand only "pure American male English," Raphael said, explaining that women have a different way of speaking.

Stars & Stripes Takes a Holiday

Because of the Jan. 1 holiday, there will be no Pacific Stars & Stripes dated Jan. 2. This is the only day of the year on which the paper is not published. Normal schedules will be resumed with editions dated Monday, Jan. 3.

70,000 CUT IN VIET

★ ★ ★ ★ ★ ★ ★ ★ ★ ★ ★ ★ ★ ★ ★ ★

Allies Ask Talks on NVA Pullout

Pacific
STARS STRIPES
AN AUTHORIZED UNOFFICIAL PUBLICATION
FOR THE U.S. ARMED FORCES OF THE PACIFIC COMMAND
10¢

Vol. 28, No. 14   Saturday, Jan. 15, 1972

PARIS (AP) — The South Vietnamese government asserted Thursday that the withdrawal of all U.S. forces from South Vietnam depends on Communist willingness to negotiate the withdrawal of North Vietnamese troops as well as on the release of American prisoners of war.

The U.S. government endorsed this stand, which appeared to set a new condition for a total American withdrawal.

South Vietnamese representative Pham Dang Lam told the Communists at the 140th session of the Vietnam peace talks:

"Whether all the allied forces leave South Vietnam or there remains residual forces, and how long these forces will take to disengage, depends on whether or not you accept to negotiate seriously on the problem of troop withdrawal as part of an over-all settlement, as well as on the question of the release of prisoners of war."

U.S. Ambassador William J. Porter followed with a statement that "the representative of the government of the Republic of Vietnam has spoken for our side. I support his remarks."

Hanoi has never acknowledged the presence of North Vietnamese regular forces in South Vietnam and has always ignored demands to discuss their withdrawal.

President Nixon has said final withdrawal of U.S. forces depends on the release of the captive Americans and on the ability of the South Vietnamese government to survive without U.S. military support.

Lam gave notice that the Vietnamization program will remain the basis of allied strategy, telling the Communists: "It is necessary because of the fact that you continue to have recourse to force and violence and continuously increase your military potential with massive aid from the Communist bloc, instead of seeking (Continued on Back Page, Col. 1)

WASHINGTON (AP) —President Nixon announced Thursday that 70,000 more American troops will be brought home from Vietnam before May, reducing the U.S. military force there to the smallest in nearly seven years.

The new withdrawal order, stepping up the pace slightly, will bring the American commitment in Vietnam down to 69,000 men on May 1—a drop of 474,000 from the peak shortly after Nixon took office in early 1969.

Following Nixon's brief announcement, Secretary of Defense Melvin R. Laird fired what sounded like the opening volley of the President's re-election campaign with a sharp shot at Democratic White House hopefuls.

"Strangely enough, some of those individuals that are going around the country today criticizing the program to withdraw Americans from Vietnam were silent in 1968 and before when we were on the escalator going up, up, and up," Laird said.

"Now when we are going, down, down, down, it seems they have changed this position and are critical of the President and the program . . . to withdraw Americans from Southeast Asia and South Vietnam."

Laird named no names, but it was obvious he was referring to Sen. Edmund Muskie of Maine, currently rated the Democratic front-runner, and other Democratic contenders who have urged that Nixon set a specific withdrawal date and pull out all Americans.

Laird told White House reporters that: "We will always have a remaining presence in Vietnam until the POW problem has been resolved."

In this, Laird was echoing Nixon, who has indicated the United States will get down to a residual force of 25,000 to 35,000 men in Vietnam well before the November election and will retain some troops there until the North Vietnamese and Viet Cong have freed every American held captive.

Under questioning, Laird said, as he has before, that "we will continue to use American air power to protect the remaining forces."

However, he stressed that (Continued on Back Page, Col. 1)

A house trailer and a panel truck lie in a crumbled heap in Ft. Rucker, Ala., after a tornado ripped through the Army post Thursday. One hundred trailers were destroyed or damaged. (AP)

Tornado Rips Ft. Rucker; 4 Killed in GI Trailer Park

FT. RUCKER, Ala. (UPI)—A tornado spawned in the unseasonal, spring-like weather that covered much of the South ripped through this Army base and two nearby trailer parks crowded with GI families Thursday, killing 4 persons and injuring 79 others.

At least 50 trailers were destroyed, 50 others were heavily damaged. Cars, boats, power lines and trees were left stacked in hopelessly snarled piles of rubble.

Scores were left homeless and shelters were set up to house them.

Seven UH1 helicopters, each costing a half million dollars, were destroyed at Ft. Rucker, and eight other 'copters were damaged. In addition, two hangars were destroyed and both air strips hit.

The deadly funnel struck in the darkness without warning about 1 a.m. EST, dipping into Pinebrook and Dogwood Acres trailer parks, located about two miles west of the base.

A spokesman at Ft. Rucker, the Army's main helicopter training center, said the trailer parks were occupied almost exclusively by young soldiers and their families.

All four of the victims were Army dependents. One was seven-month-old Marshall Ladd whose mother and father made a frantic unsuccessful dash to reach him before the winds crushed the rear section of their trailer home.

Two other victims were identified as Ruth White, wife of 2nd Lt. William J. White, and Elaine Rice, wife of Sgt. David W. Rice. Rice was away on temporary assignment at Ft. Benjamin Harrison in Indiana.

The fourth victim was identified as Debbie Bennefield, wife of Pfc. Gary J. Bennefield. Permanent addresses of the servicemen were not available.

David Reno, a young soldier (Continued on Back Page, Col. 2)

Bungling Burglars

MARTINSVILLE, Va. (AP)— Some nights it's not such a good idea to go to work.

Burglars broke into a furniture store here to steal the safe.

They took the safe but someone forgot and left his pistol at the scene.

They stole the store's pickup truck to haul the safe away, but while making a getaway the safe fell off the back of the truck.

Police said the safe was recovered but they were still looking for the pickup truck and the burglars.

Enlistee Dropoff Worries DoD

WASHINGTON (AP) — Voluntary enlistments fell below the armed services objectives during the last half of 1971, a time when the draft was taking very few men.

This could spell trouble for Nixon administration hopes of ending the draft and changing to an all-volunteer force by mid-1973.

The coming months should indicate whether about $3 billion in new military pay boosts will attract enough additional volunteers. These boosts became effective too late to have any significant impact on recruitment totals in 1971.

Pentagon figures show that the services recruited 195,300 new men in the July-December period, about 17,000 fewer than their objective.

Selective Service calls totaled only 10,000 during that same six-month span, so there was only light draft pressure on young men to enlist in the service of their choice.

Some senior military officers and congressional critics of the concept contend an all-volunteer force is an impractical goal, that more money and im- (Continued on Back Page, Col. 5)

No More Concessions

NIXON WARNS HANOI

PACIFIC
STARS AND STRIPES

AN AUTHORIZED UNOFFICIAL PUBLICATION
FOR THE U.S. ARMED FORCES OF THE PACIFIC COMMAND

10¢

Vol. 28, No. 42   Saturday, Feb. 12, 1972

WASHINGTON (AP)—President Nixon said Thursday he has gone as far as he intends to go to entice the Communists to a negotiated settlement of the Vietnam war until Hanoi begins to negotiate seriously.

In an impromptu news conference at the White House, Nixon said the Communists had not yet responded formally to his Jan. 25 eight-point peace proposal and "there will be no further concessions on our part" until or unless the other side joins in genuine negotiations.

The President also announced that his historic journey to China would begin next Thursday. But he advised friends and critics alike not to expect too much from the trip. He said it would produce more talk than solutions.

Nixon said he favored prosecuting whoever leaked the secret White House documents on the India-Pakistan crisis but that there was not enough evidence yet to go to court.

He said that during the crisis he was not anti-India but rather "antiwar."

Presidential candidates have a right to criticize the incumbent, Nixon asserted, but they must bear the responsibility of what they say.

Nixon also said there would be no tax increase this year.

The President praised South Vietnam's President Nguyen Van Thieu as courageous and

Related stories Pages 2, 3

discounted speculation of a rift between Saigon and Washington.

Talking without interruption for about 15 minutes at the outset, Nixon said his meetings with Chinese leaders would represent more of a dialogue than negotiations because "we are in truth at a beginning."

The chief executive, standing behind the desk in his Oval Office, was asked if he felt it was fair to the voters and rival would-be presidential candidates to expect no presentation of alternatives to the eight-point Vietnam peace proposal he unveiled before a nationwide television audience Jan. 25.

Nixon responded: "All have a right to say what they want. They must decide if it is right to say it."

The chief executive said that while out of office, he had many objections to Vietnam policy but that as the Republican presidential candidate in 1968 he vowed he would say

(Continued on Back Page, Col. 1)

Invective At Paris Parley

PARIS (AP) — The United States Thursday refused to agree on the date for a new meeting of the Vietnam peace talks, in a storm of invective over an anti-war meeting scheduled for nearby Versailles this weekend.

U.S. Ambassador William J. Porter told the Communist side at Thursday's session of the peace talks that he would "not agree to a meeting next week" and added "we will notify you when we have determined how soon another meeting will be desirable."

The indefinite delay for the next meeting infuriated the Communists who "protested energetically" against the U.S. move. The North Vietnamese taxed the United States with the "intention of torpedoing the conference" and referred to the "arrogant attitude" of the Americans.

Porter said he acted because of the anti-war meeting set for Friday, Saturday and Sunday at Versailles. Organizers say the meeting is expected to attract about 1,200 delegates from 80 countries. It is formally called the "Paris World Assembly for Peace and Independence of the Indochinese Peoples."

Porter told the Communists that they had been "sabotaging" the talks from the beginning and "in fact ruined them as far as negotiations are concerned."

"Now," he said, referring to the Versailles meeting, "a horde of Communist-controlled agitators" is being brought in "for the purpose of harassing our effort to make peace."

Viet Cong delegate Nguyen Van Tien said Porter's remark was "insolent" and added that his "arrogance was absolutely unpardonable." He called Porter's attitude "unworthy of a

(Continued on Back Page, Col. 3)

BULLETIN

SAPPORO, Japan (AP) — Monika Pflug of West Germany won the women's 1,000 meter speed skating gold medal of the Winter Olympics Friday in 1:31.40, an Olympic record.

Atje Keulen-Deelstra of the Netherlands won the silver medal in 1:31.61. Anne Henning, 16-year-old star from Northbrook, Ill., took the bronze in 1:31.62.

Smile to Match

Golden Blades Anne

Anne Henning, 16, of Northbrook, Ill., proudly displays the gold medal she won by setting an Olympic record in the women's 500-meter speed skating event in Sapporo Thursday. Photos on Pages 12, 13, with further details on the sport pages.   (S&S Photo by Paul J. Harrington)

U.S. Freezes RR, Airline, Utility Rates

WASHINGTON (AP) — The Price Commission Thursday ordered a temporary nationwide freeze on rates charged by all privately owned utilities, railroads and airlines.

The commission said it will tighten up its instructions to regulatory agencies on what rate increases will be allowed in the future.

The commission will hold four days of public hearings later this month to gather infor-

mation that Chairman C. Jackson Grayson Jr. said will be used to sharpen utility rate rules.

The freeze does not affect publicly-owned utilities, such as municipal water operations. It does hit virtually all railroads, airlines, telephone and telegraph companies, electric utilities, gas companies and other private utilities.

The freeze will run as long as

to March 10, but could end sooner, Grayson said at a news conference. It suspends rate increases that would have gone into effect legally after midnight Wednesday.

Grayson said that in addition the commission is ordering a specific rollback of a $160 million rate increase that went into effect last Feb. 3 for the New York Telephone Co., on grounds it has an extraor-

dinarily large economic impact. That increase is the subject of a federal court lawsuit alleging that the company violated Price Commission regulations.

Otherwise all increases that went into effect before Wednesday midnight are not affected, except that the commission extended its time limit for reviewing utility rate increases which are now in effect but which the commission still could roll back.

PACIFIC STAR STRIPES

AN AUTHORIZED UNOFFICIAL PUBLICATION
FOR THE U.S. ARMED FORCES OF THE PACIFIC COMMAND

10¢

Vol. 28, No. 44   Monday, Feb. 14, 1972

Most in 1½ Years

200 Air Strikes Hit Red Buildup

CREWMEN LOAD BOMBS ON A JET ABOARD THE AIRCRAFT CARRIER CONSTELLATION IN THE TONKIN GULF.

AP

SAIGON (AP) — The United States has launched its biggest aerial campaign across South Vietnam in more than 18 months, hoping to crush a Communist buildup along South Vietnam's western border.

Ranging over jungled infiltration networks, supply routes, staging areas and storage sites, U.S. tactical fighter-bombers and B52 heavy bombers made about 200 strikes in northern and central South Vietnam Friday and Saturday.

Informants said a North Vietnamese buildup of troops and supplies was continuing in the regions along South Vietnam's western frontier with Laos, but said they did not anticipate a major offensive until after the Tet lunar new year celebrations which begin Tuesday.

The Viet Cong have announced a four-day cease-fire for Tet, beginning at 1 a.m. Saigon time Monday. The allies have said they will observe a 24-hour cease-fire effective at 6 p.m.

The U.S. command said Navy and Air Force fighter-bombers made 172 strikes in South Vietnam during the 24-hour period ending at dawn Saturday, the most in one day since September 1970. This raised to 356 the total number of strikes flown by U.S. fighter-bombers in Vietnam alone during the past three days, compared to an average of less than 10 a day during the past four months.

Other Air Force and Navy planes also kept up the pressure on the other side of South Vietnam's border. They made about 200 strikes against the Ho Chi Minh Trail supply network, which winds through southern Laos and into South Vietnam's northern provinces and central highlands.

The U.S. command also said B52 bombers flew 12 missions in South Vietnam, the highest number since January 1970.

The command does not disclose the specific number of B52 bombers on each mission, but it ranges from one to three. Most of the latest missions reported

(Continued on Back Page, Col. 4)

IRA Bullet Wrecks Wedding

BELFAST, Northern Ireland (UPI) — Bomb attackers invaded a Londonderry hotel during a Roman Catholic wedding celebration Saturday, shot and wounded the 17-year-old best man, and blasted the hotel, police said.

Best man Alphonsus Patton, 17-year-old brother of the groom, was shot in the head when he pleaded with bombers to remove the explosive device because children among the guests might be hurt, police said.

Patton was rushed to Altnagelvin Hospital where his condition was reported "very serious."

Three masked men stormed into Londonderry's Woodleigh Hotel, two carrying a bomb and the third brandishing a pistol. As they placed the bomb on the reception desk, the man with the pistol yelled a warning the
(Continued on Back Page, Col. 3)

Judge Reverses Ruling

Hughes 'Book' Excerpts OKd

NEW YORK (AP) — A New York State Appeals Court judge threw out an attempt Saturday to block Time Inc., from publishing excerpts from the purported Howard Hughes autobiography it has termed a hoax.

At his Manhattan home, Justice Theodore Kupferman, of the Appellate Division of the State Supreme Court, reversed an earlier order of the State Supreme Court enjoining the publication.

Kupferman said Time could print four passages from the book, but no more than a total of 1,000 words.

He scheduled a hearing of the case before the full five-man appeals court bench for Thursday.

Kupferman acted after hearing arguments for 80 minutes only hours after the lower court's injunction. Attorneys in the action said Kupferman decided against imposing prior restraint of publication on grounds of free speech rights.

Kupferman said he had decided also on the grounds that the number of words was limited and that parties opposing publication still had recourse to a law suit for damages.

State Supreme Court Justice Gerald P. Culkin ruled earlier that the material was not the magazine's property after hearing Time lawyer Alan J. Hruska argue, "We are attempting to publish passages in furtherance of the belief that the Irving text is a fake."

Hruska said after Kupferman's ruling, "I am very pleased, I am very happy."

Arrayed against Time were McGraw-Hill Inc., which contracted with author Clifford Irving for the book; Rosemont En-
(Continued on Back Page, Col. 1)

This Guy's a Credit To Art of Thievery

CHICAGO (AP)—A convict has told Illinois state officials investigating credit card fraud that his scheme was so successful that four companies once offered to pay him to stop cheating.

"They asked me to stop defrauding them and each company would pay me $150 a week," said Edmund Bryson in testimony before the Illinois Legislative Commission on Thursday.

"I knew their operation so well that they knew they couldn't stop me, and I guess they figured the $150 a week would be less than I would steal from them."

Bryson, 30, now serving a seven-year sentence for narcotics use, said he refused the companies' offer and lived very well for seven years exclusively through the use of fraudulent credit cards.

Politics Is No Picnic

OKLAHOMA CITY (UPI) — Sen. Phil Smalley Friday told his colleagues the most immediate problem facing the Legislature was the horde of ants in the Capitol Building.

"They're crawling all over the desks, all over the secretaries —and all over me," he said.

The Oklahoma Senate voted unanimously to ask the Public Affairs Board to hire an exterminator.

Nixon Suspends Paris Talks Until Reds Halt Propaganda

★ ★ ★ ★ ★ ★

POW-MIA Week Gets Under Way

TOKYO (S&S)—March 26 marks the beginning of a National Week of Concern for Prisoners of War/Missing in Action proclaimed March 10 by President Nixon to urge Americans to continue to work toward the release of

---

Related stories Page 6

---

the 1,623 U.S. servicemen and 50 American civilians missing or known to be captives of the North Vietnamese and their allies.

In his proclamation, which also designates March 26 a national day of prayer, Nixon pointed out that many American POW-MIAs in Southeast Asia are beginning

(Continued on Back Page, Col. 1)

PACIFIC STARS AND STRIPES

AN AUTHORIZED UNOFFICIAL PUBLICATION
FOR THE U.S. ARMED FORCES OF THE PACIFIC COMMAND

10¢

Vol. 28, No. 85   **Sunday, March 26, 1972**

WASHINGTON (AP) —President Nixon said Friday he personally ordered the suspension of Paris peace talks until the North Vietnamese quit using the conference as a pulpit for propaganda.

In a wide-ranging news conference Nixon also declared that he will take action if necessary to curb rising food prices. He indicated the action would be aimed at middlemen — not farmers.

The chief executive also defended as constitutional his move for a moratorium on busing to achieve school desegregation.

And he expressed confidence in Atty. General-designate Richard Kleindienst, predicting the Senate would confirm his nomination despite the controversy over Kleindienst's role in negotiations to settle an antitrust action against the International Telephone & Telegraph Co.

As he firmly defended settlement of the ITT case, he also rejected charges his administration is pro-business. "Nobody gets anything back ..." when they make campaign contributions to his reelection effort, Nixon said.

Standing behind his oval office desk, Nixon began the news conference by responding to a question on the U.S. moves which forced suspension of the Paris peace talks Thursday.

The decision that there would be no further meetings until the Vietnamese Communists showed willingness for serious discussion was made "under

(Continued on Back Page, Col. 1)

DEMOLISHED SCHOOL BUS SMASHED BY A PENN CENTRAL FREIGHT TRAIN IN CONGERS, N.Y.

UPI

Next: A Lady Admiral

CHICAGO (AP) — Secretary of Defense Melvin R. Laird repeated Friday that one of the things he will do before he leaves his post is appoint a woman admiral.

Laird was interviewed on a television talk show.

The defense secretary was interrupted Thursday when he was speaking at a businessmen's luncheon by five women who took over the rostrum.

The women were members of the Chicago chapter of National Organization for Women— NOW. After they left the speaker's table, Laird departed from his prepared text and talked about how his department has improved the position of women in the services.

He said there now are women generals and he added, "Before I end the job as secretary of defense, we will have our first woman admiral."

3 Die, 43 Hurt In School Bus

CONGERS, N.Y. (UPI) — A Penn Central freight train, its horn blowing frantically, ripped a school bus in half at an unguarded crossing Friday, killing three high school students and injuring 43. The train, which officials of the line said was traveling at 25 miles an hour, dragged part of the bus 1,000 feet, spilling injured children beside the tracks.

Ambulances from four communities near Congers, located 33 miles northwest of New York City, took the injured children to Nyack Hospital, just across the
(Continued on Back Page, Col. 2)

U.K. Takes Over Ulster Rule; Extremists Hint at Civil War

LONDON (AP) — Britain took over direct rule of Northern Ireland Friday in a dramatic pitch for peace, but alerted 4,000 more troops against the risk of civil war in the troubled province.

Demonstrations immediately broke out in Belfast, Northern Ireland's capital, where Prime Minister Brian Faulkner denounced Britain's move, saying it could be construed as a terrorist victory. But he agreed to stay in office until the British takeover.

Extremists among the Protestant majority of Northern Ireland and their chief antagonists, the outlawed Irish Republican Army (IRA), issued belligerent statements that raised the peril of civil war.

A grim Prime Minister Edward Heath announced the drastic development that breaks 50 years of Protestant mastery in the six-country province. He told a silent and solemn House of Commons that he was naming house floor leader, William Whitelaw, to rule the province with the new position of cabinet minister for Northern Ireland. Whitelaw pledged all-out war against guerrillas.

Whitelaw will be assisted by a commission of local residents, which will mean giving Catholics a voice in the government for the first time.

Heath's plan also includes a phasing out of the controversial
(Continued on Back Page, Col. 1)

2 More ARVN Bases Fall

REDS PUSH SOUTH

PACIFIC
STARS AND STRIPES
AN AUTHORIZED UNOFFICIAL PUBLICATION
FOR THE U.S. ARMED FORCES OF THE PACIFIC-COMMAND

10¢

Vol. 28, No. 94   Tuesday, April 4, 1972

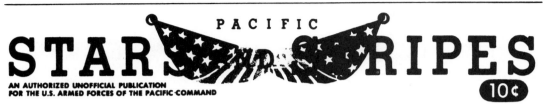

Berrigan Guilty On One Count; Jury Sent Back

HARRISBURG, Pa. (UPI)—A federal jury convicted the Rev. Philip F. Berrigan Sunday for smuggling a letter out of prison, but announced it was still unable to reach a verdict on conspiracy charges against the priest and other members of the Harrisburg Seven.

U.S. District Court Judge R. Dixon Herman accepted the verdict, which could result in a maximum 10-year prison sentence, but instructed the jurors to return to deliberations in an effort to arrive at a verdict on the other charges.

"Because of the length of this trial, its expense, its importance ... and the unlikelihood that we would get a better jury at another time, I'm going to ask you to go back and continue deliberations on the other counts of the indictment," Herman said.

The charge on which Berrigan was found guilty accused him of attempting to smuggle a letter out of Lewisburg Federal Penitentiary on May 24, 1970. This was about two weeks before Boyd F. Douglas Jr., the star government witness in the trial, became an FBI informant.

The principal charge against Berrigan and his six codefendants was conspiring against the government by plotting to kidnap presidential adviser (Continued on Back Page, Col. 1)

GIL HODGES

Baseball's Gil Hodges Dies at 48

WEST PALM BEACH, Fla. (AP) — Gil Hodges, manager of baseball's New York Mets, died Sunday in a hospital here after collapsing in his motel.

A spokesman at Good Samaritan Hospital said Hodges, 48, died of a heart attack. He had been stricken with a mild heart attack in 1968 but recovered and came back to manage the Mets to the World Series championship one year later.

An official at the Ramada (Continued on Back Page, Col. 2)

AP

Awards and a Nice Decoration
During an awards ceremony at McConnell AFB, Kan., it was obvious the male officers outnumbered the ladies—but viva the minority! She's WAF Lt. Kristie Reeves of Santa Barbara, Calif.

ITT Paid No Taxes in '71, Sen. McGovern Claims

MILWAUKEE, Wis. (UPI) — Sen. George S. McGovern said on nationwide television Sunday a federal report showed International Telephone and Telegraph Inc. paid no income taxes last year and listed a $400,000 contribution to the Republican National Convention as deductible. He later apologized, saying his statement about the deduction was "an honest mistake."

Appearing on a television interview show, McGovern said a Securities and Exchange Commission report not only "shows that they (ITT) paid no taxes at all last year, but it also shows that they listed as tax deductible the $400,000 they contributed to the Republican National Convention in San Diego this summer."

McGovern's office issued a statement a short time later affirming that ITT paid no taxes for 1970 but denying that SEC records show the huge firm deducted the $400,000 contribution.

"As to the payment of $400,000 for the Republican National Convention, that payment does not appear in the SEC reports," the statement said. "Senator McGovern's statement that it was included was based on statements by company officials that they considered it a proper business expense and that they would rely on the opinion of counsel to that effect ... and would apply it as a deductible offset against income."

McGovern was cornered by aides after the appearance on television and learned he had apparently misinterpreted his information. "It was an honest mistake," he said.

SAIGON (AP) — Spearheaded by tank columns, the biggest North Vietnamese drive since the 1968 Tet offensive chewed up large chunks of South Vietnamese territory Sunday, crushed two more bases and sent hundreds of government troops retreating in disarray.

At Camp Carroll, a regimental command post eight miles below the Demilitarized Zone, some of the battered South Vietnamese soldiers threw up the white flag of surrender. Some South Vietnamese soldiers appeared to be trying to mix in with thousands of civilians fleeing south from the DMZ fighting.

But the four-day North Vietnamese campaign appeared to be broadening to other fronts.

SAIGON (AP) — U.S. fighter-bombers launched heavy strikes against antiaircraft defenses inside North Vietnam Sunday, and four American aircraft were shot down while supporting South Vietnamese troops in the embattled sector below the Demilitarized Zone. Eight American crewmen were reported missing.

One tank column spearheaded a drive that overran Firebase Pace near the Cambodian border, only 85 miles northwest of Saigon, in the deepest southern penetration North Vietnamese armor has ever made in the Indochina war.

The fighting on the northern front continued to overshadow all other action, since North Vietnam has long desired to annex Quang Tri, South Vietnam's northernmost province bordering the DMZ on the north and Laos on west.

By dusk Sunday, the northernmost South Vietnamese de-(Continued on Back Page, Col. 3)

Winning Ticket

CLINTON, Iowa (UPI) — Mrs. John Ringsdahl flipped on her car radio Saturday just in time to hear the Clinton police chief draw the winning ticket for a 1972 automobile, in a contest run by station KCLN in Clinton.

The winner was Mrs. Ringsdahl.

In her excitement to notify her family and claim the car, she stepped on the gas — and was promptly arrested for speeding by a police officer traveling right behind her.

After posting a $15 bond on the speeding charge, Mrs. Ringsdahl drove slowly to the station and claimed her grand prize.

Nixon Maps Counter Strategy

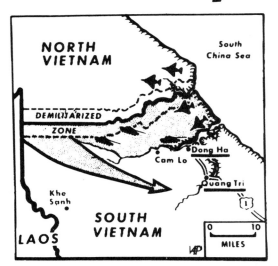

MAP LOCATES AREA OF INVASION.

★ ★ ★ ★ ★ ★ ★ ★ ★

Recalls 2 Carriers

U.S. READIES AIR ARMADA

SAIGON (AP)—The United States recalled two aircraft carriers to the Tonkin Gulf Monday to reinforce a massive air strike force preparing to hit back at an enemy offensive in South Vietnam's northernmost province.

PACIFIC

STARS STRIPES

AN AUTHORIZED UNOFFICIAL PUBLICATION
FOR THE U.S. ARMED FORCES OF THE PACIFIC COMMAND

10¢

Vol. 28, No. 95   Wednesday, April 5, 1972

WASHINGTON (AP)—President Nixon ordered his top advisers Monday to prepare recommendations for U.S. action to counter the rapid thrust of Communist forces into South Vietnam and a White House spokesman said "all options are open."

Presidential press secretary Ronald L. Ziegler refused under questioning by newsmen to rule out the possibility of U.S. air attacks on North Vietnam or the use of U.S. ground forces.

But he said several times that coping with the new North Vietnamese offensive was a "South Vietnamese operation." In saying that "all options are open," Ziegler referred to statements earlier in the day by State Department officials, saying they are "totally reflective of the overall administration view."

The State Department had branded the Communist action as an invasion which violated the 1968 agreement which led President Johnson to suspend bombing attacks on North Vietnam.

"We are watching the situation very closely," Ziegler said. He added that "this recent attack by North Vietnam has been anticipated ... now that it is beginning, the position we are in is to continue to evaluate it day by day."

"The exact effect and scope,"
(Continued on Back Page, Col. 4)

The 'Little Tramp' Is Back

NEW YORK (AP) — Charlie Chaplin, hailed by many critics as the greatest comedian of the 20th century, returned to the United States Tuesday 20 years after he left amid accusations of Communist associations and immorality.

"I am very happy to be in New York again," he said as he left the plane from Bermuda.

Although he walked slowly and unsteadily, Chaplin, who will be 83 April 16, waved and blew kisses to the throng of newsmen who greeted him at Kennedy Airport.

Slightly behind him, her hand on his shoulder, was his wife, the former Oona O'Neill, daughter of the famous playwright Eugene O'Neill, and mother of eight of his children.

David Rockefeller Jr., chairman of a "Salute to Charlie Chaplin" scheduled Tuesday
(Continued on Back Page, Col. 3)

Charlie Chaplin throws a kiss to newsmen as he arrives at Kennedy International Airport. (AP)

The carrier Kitty Hawk arrived in waters off Vietnam Tuesday and the Constellation was steaming in from Japan to join the Coral Sea and the Hancock. The four carriers and their some 275 warplanes, combined with 250 Air Force jets at bases in South Vietnam and Thailand, will form the biggest U.S. attack force since the 1968 bombing halt.

The U.S. Command strongly indicated massive air strikes are planned against North Vietnam to retaliate for the enemy offensive across the demilitarized zone and against enemy troops and materiel already engaged south of the zone.

U.S. pilots said targets inside North Vietnam would include long-range artillery guns bombarding South Vietnamese positions

---

Related stories, Pages 3 and 6.

---

tions across the DMZ and a reserve infantry division poised just north of the zone.

Other key targets will include tanks, self-propelled artillery pieces and other heavy equipment that North Vietnam is using more than ever before in the Indochina war.

Forecasters said they did not
(Continued on Back Page, Col. 1)

A Shot of Ol' Breakfast

LOUISVILLE, Ky. (AP) — Andrew Hastings' breakfast may be his secret for longevity.

He observed his 100th birthday Monday by eating two fried eggs, rolls with peanut butter spread on them, a steamy serving of sauerkraut and a can of beer.

And he finished it off with a shot of liquor.

Hastings, who spent most of his life working as a machinist, has a simple explanation for his choice of food and drink: "Water will rust your insides."

"He moved in with us in 1945," said Hastings' niece, Eunice Ollis. "He said that's what he wanted every morning, and that's what he's had."

Hastings' hearing has faded slightly and he walks with a cane, but Mrs. Ollis says he's no problem.

"Except when he eats that stuff," she says.

Critic of Fulbright Resigns USIA Post

WASHINGTON (UPI) — Bruce Herschensohn resigned as motion picture director of the U.S. Information Agency (USIA) Monday and charged that Sen. J. William Fulbright's criticisms of the last five U.S. Presidents "are only balanced by his words of praise for Ho Chi Minh and Khrushchev".

His resignation came after he said on a weekend television program sponsored by Sen. James T. Buckley, the New York Conservative, that Fulbright was "very simplistic, very naive and stupid" in his views about U. S. information efforts in other countries.

Herschensohn also said that Fulbright's views on the USIA "could be tragic for this nation and catastrophic for the peoples of other nations".

In a bitter attack on Fulbright, a critic of USIA operations as a relic of the cold war, Herschensohn told reporters that his description last week of the senator's views as "simplistic, naive and stupid" was inappropriate —but accurate.
(Continued on Back Page, Col. 2)

Reds Open 3rd Front

Battle 60 Miles From Saigon

PACIFIC STAR AND STRIPES

AN AUTHORIZED UNOFFICIAL PUBLICATION
FOR THE U.S. ARMED FORCES OF THE PACIFIC COMMAND

10¢

Vol. 28, No. 97   Friday, April 7, 1972

South Dakota Sen. George McGovern shows a smiling profile of confidence at a news conference Wednesday after his victory in the Wisconsin presidential primary. Details on Page 3.   (UPI)

SAIGON (AP)—North Vietnamese tanks and troops opened a third front Wednesday, slashing 20 miles across the Cambodian border to within 60 miles of Saigon.

On the major front south of the Demilitarized Zone, other North Vietnamese battled to cut off the provincial capital of Quang Tri from the south while advancing from the north and west on that city base 19 miles south of the DMZ.

Communist tanks were also on the attack in the Central Highlands.

(Pacific Stars nad Stripes correspondent Spec. 4 Allen Schaefer reported from the Central Highlands that the South Vietnamese have repulsed a tank-supported Communist drive against a string of seven fire bases about 15 miles west of Kontum, killing 350 Reds.)

Brig. Gen. Vu Van Giai, commander of the South Vietnamese 3rd Inf. Div. on the far northern

Related Stories, Page 6

front, told newsmen North Vietnamese MIG fighters appeared over South Vietnam for the first time in the war. He said two flew over his lines but did not attack.

Sources in Saigon denied the report, but three Americans in Quang Tri said they had seen MIGs over South Vietnam in the last few days.

In the new drive north of Saigon, South Vietnamese troops and eight U.S. advisers withdrew by helicopter from the big base camp at Quang Loi, 60 miles north of the capital after an attack.

Fifteen miles to the north, Communist infantrymen led by

(Continued on Back Page, Col. 1)

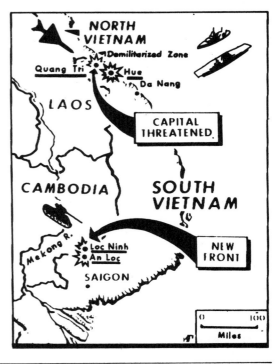

NORTH VIETNAM — Demilitarized Zone — Quang Tri — Hue — Da Nang — LAOS — CAPITAL THREATENED — CAMBODIA — SOUTH VIETNAM — Mekong R. — Loc Ninh — An Loc — SAIGON — NEW FRONT — 0 — 100 — Miles

---

Berrigan, Nun Convicted; Deadlocked Jury Frees 5

HARRISBURG, Pa. (AP) — The Rev. Philip Berrigan and a nun who served as his lieutenant in the antiwar movement were convicted Wednesday of smuggling letters in and out of a federal prison, but a jury deadlocked on charges that they conspired with five other defendants to kidnap presidential aide Henry Kissinger. The five were freed by the jury deadlock.

Berrigan could receive 40 years in prison, Sister Elizabeth McAlister 30.

"These verdicts are yours and yours alone, and you don't need to justify them or explain them to anybody," U.S. District Court Judge R. Dixon Herman told the nine women and three men as he dismissed them after their week-long quest for a verdict that ended with their split decision.

"There will be many, many people who disagree and there will be just as many who agree," added Herman, a bald 61-year-old jurist appointed to the bench in 1969.

At the heart of the government's case was a three-pronged conspiracy charge accusing the "Harrisburg Seven" of scheming to kidnap Kissinger, blow up government heating tunnels in Washington and vandalize draft boards in several Eastern cities.

But these went by the boards as a result of the jury's deadlock.

Instead, Berrigan and his assistant in the Catholic antiwar left, Sister McAlister, were convicted of smuggling half a dozen letters in and out of Lewisburg, Pa., federal penitentiary after the priest entered in 1970 to begin a term he still is serving.

The other five defendants were not involved in the letter smuggling, and thus not included in any way whatsoever in the verdict. It was returned at 4:09 p.m.

The five defendants on whom the jury could not agree were Eqbal Ahmad, 41; the Rev.

(Continued on Back Page, Col. 5)

Harlem's 'Voice' Adam Powell Dies at 63

MIAMI (AP) — Adam Clayton Powell, the flamboyant former congressman who swept through life with beautiful women on his arm, a sermon on his lips and an adoring Harlem at his feet, has died after a long illness. He was 63.

His death at Jackson Memorial Hospital Tuesday night was attributed to complications stemming from an earlier prostate operation.

He had been confined to the hospital's intensive care unit since he was airlifted by the U.S. Coast Guard from his Bimini, Bahamas retreat March 7.

The first black elected to Congress from the East, Powell

Related story, Page 9

also became the first congressman in modern times excluded by a vote of the House.

He was turned out in 1967 for misusing funds and defying the courts some 22 years after the tall, handsome preacher was first sent to Washington by New York constituents who packed his 10,000-member Abyssinian Baptist church on Sundays hearing him admonish, "Keep the faith, baby."

Powell was re-elected in a special election a month after his colleagues voted to deny him a congressional seat. However, he did not try to reclaim his seat.

In 1968, without making a single campaign appearance in Harlem, Powell was re-elected again, by a 7-1 majority—the same margin by which the Supreme Court ruled the following June that Congress had exceeded its constitutional power in barring him.

But he got neither the $55,000 in back pay nor restoration of the seniority that made him chairman of the House Educa-

(Continued on Back Page, Col. 4)

Windstorm Kills 7 in Wash. Town

VANCOUVER, Wash. (AP) — A violent wind, spawned by a thunderstorm, whipped through Vancouver Wednesday. Seven persons were reported to have died.

A spokesman at one hospital said at least a dozen persons were in the intensive care unit, indicating their injuries were serious. A check of two Vancouver hospitals indicated as many as 125 persons may have been injured.

B52S HIT VINH AREA

U.S. 'Insurance' Forces Readied

PACIFIC STARS AND STRIPES

AN AUTHORIZED UNOFFICIAL PUBLICATION
FOR THE U.S. ARMED FORCES OF THE PACIFIC COMMAND

10¢

Vol. 28, No. 102   Wednesday, April 12, 1972

WASHINGTON (AP) —Secretary of Defense Melvin R. Laird said Monday additional air and naval forces will be sent to Southeast Asia this week as part of the American buildup to counter the North Vietnamese offensive.

"They are the additional needed insurance showing the determination of the United States as this massive violation . . . has been undertaken by the enemy," Laird said.

Addressing a women's group at the Pentagon, he said these additional forces would be available to Gen. Creighton Abrams, the U.S. commander in Vietnam, later this week.

The buildup is intended, he said, to reflect the "determination and resolve of the United States government to continue our (troop) withdrawal program on schedule and to provide further withdrawals to go forward."

The defense secretary reiterated that Abrams is continuing to withdraw American ground troops each day and that he would meet or beat the 69,000-man troop ceiling set by President Nixon for May 1.

At least eight warships left Southern California naval bases Monday for undisclosed deployment. Sailors said they were going to Vietnam.

The U.S. Navy refused to comment on the departure of four warships from Long Beach, Calif., and four more from San Diego. They reportedly will rendezvous with the aircraft carrier Midway.

The Midway left its base at **(Continued on Back Page, Col. 2)**

Niagara Car Falls Apart

NIAGARA FALLS, Ont. (AP) — Tourists enjoying a sunny day found their attention diverted from the grandeur of the cataracts Sunday.

An unoccupied car, parked near the Horseshoe Falls, turned its lights on. Then the lenses shattered.

Then the horn began to blow.

The engine started.

The car burst into flames and the windshield exploded.

Firemen blamed the activity on a short-circuit.

SAIGON (AP)—U.S. B52 bombers returned to the air war over North Vietnam Monday for the first time in more than four years and hit targets around the big coastal city of Vinh, 145 miles northwest of the Demilitarized Zone. It was the deepest penetration of North Vietnam ever made by America's biggest warplanes.

Meanwhile, South Vietnam's commander on the northern front said his forces had crushed the spearhead of the 12-day-old Communist offensive across the DMZ and turned the tide of battle.

A senior U.S. officer in the northern front area said as a result of the latest battles the enemy "has kind of shot his wad" in the north. He said the North Vietnamese probably only have 50-60 tanks left in Quang Tri Province. The South Vietnamese claim to have destroyed 100 tanks in the area since the offensive began.

But there was no letup in the enemy attack north of Saigon and the South Vietnamese command ordered another 20,000 troops into the battle for An Loc, 60 miles north of the capital.

Official sources said the use of the eight-jet B52s over North Vietnam for the first time since Nov. 27, 1967, was a show of force by President Nixon.

The U.S. Command gave no details of the B52 operations, saying in a communique: "In

Related stories, Page 6.

response to the Communist invasion of South Vietnam through the Demilitarized Zone, U.S. air and naval operations continue south of, in and north of the DMZ. These operations include naval gunfire, tactical aircraft and B52s throughout the battlefield area."

The command said it now considers North Vietnam part of the battlefield area.

Other official sources said that because overcast skies for the third day curtailed raids by the smaller fighter-bombers over the North, the high-altitude B52s which fly above the clouds and bomb by radar were sent to hit rear bases at Vinh and supply routes leading south along Highway 1 to the DMZ.

When the B52s last flew over **(Continued on Back Page, Col. 1)**

South Vietnamese soldiers and civilians look over a captured North Vietnamese tank displayed in Quang Tri. The tank was captured in recent fighting near Dong Ha. **(AP)**

Red Sappers Hit Viet Ammo Dump

SAIGON (UPI) — Communist saboteurs slipped into a government ammunition dump just outside Saigon early Tuesday and planted an explosive charge that rocked the South Vietnamese capital.

U.S. and South Vietnamese officials said the ammunition dump about seven miles southeast of the capital near Cat Lai sustained 25 per cent damage in the 3:50 a.m. incident.

At least one of the sappers was killed, authorities said. Two South Vietnamese troopers at the facility were reported wounded.

Another Mafia Figure Gunned Down

NEW YORK (UPI)—Joseph "Crazy Joe" Gallo, the victim of a gangland-style execution last week, was buried Monday, hours after a Brooklyn restaurant owner, said to have been a bodyguard of Gallo rival Joseph Colombo, was gunned down outside his restaurant.

"If this isn't gang war I don't know what is," said a high police source after the latest killing, the fifth assassination of a reputed Mafia figure in two weeks.

Gallo, slain in an Italian restaurant early Friday by a middle-aged gunman as he celebrated his 43rd birthday with his bride and friends, was buried in Brooklyn's Greenwood Cemetery.

About 200 bystanders, including plainclothes policemen, watched as the gold-colored casket bearing Gallo's body was carried from a Brooklyn Catholic church after a 15-minute service.

Less than eight hours before Gallo was buried, Gennaro Ciprio, 30, a Brooklyn restaurant owner who was awaiting trial in Chicago on charges of transporting stolen securities, was shot in the head outside his restaurant.

Federal sources said Ciprio had been a bodyguard of Joseph Colombo Sr., who was critically wounded last June in an assassination attempt. Gallo had been among the underworld figures questioned by police after the Colombo shooting.

Police said there were no witnesses to Ciprio's shooting. He was found face down on the sidewalk by friends and relatives who rushed from the **(Continued on Back Page, Col. 5)**

BOMB HANOI AREA

Damage Is Heavy Near Capital, Port

SAIGON (AP) — The U.S. command reported Sunday's raids by hundreds of jets on North Vietnam caused heavy damage and left areas around Hanoi and Haiphong in flames.

U.S. pilots reported seeing fireballs and columns of black smoke rising into the sky from around the North Vietnamese capital and Haiphong, the seaport funnel for war materiel from abroad, chiefly from the Soviet Union.

A command spokesman, in confirming early Monday that areas near Hanoi had been bombed, said eight-jet B52 Stratofortresses hit Haiphong and smaller tactical jet fighter-bombers attacked near Hanoi.

The North Vietnamese claimed Hanoi itself was hit.

Late reports indicate that two tactical fighter-bombers were shot down and that all B52s returned safely, the command said. It reported the enemy fired thousands of rounds of antiaircraft shells and about 200 surface-to-air missiles—the Soviet-supplied SAMs that American pilots call flying telephone poles.

Two U.S. airmen were listed as missing and a third was reported rescued.

Hanoi claimed one B52 and 14 smaller planes were shot down.

Related stories, Pages 2 and 6.

Its official Vietnam News Agency said a Soviet ship was damaged and a crewman wounded in the attack on Haiphong.

The dispatch, distributed by the (Continued on Back Page, Col. 1)

PACIFIC STARS AND STRIPES

AN AUTHORIZED UNOFFICIAL PUBLICATION FOR THE U.S. ARMED FORCES OF THE PACIFIC COMMAND

10¢

Vol. 28, No. 108   Tuesday, April 18, 1972

Apollo Off and Right On

CAPE KENNEDY, Fla. (AP)—America's Apollo 16 explorers streaked toward the moon Sunday to search a rugged mountain plateau for ancient volcanoes and further evidence that the moon was once a dynamic, evolving planet like the earth.

Navy Capt. John W. Young, Air Force Lt. Col. Charles M. Duke Jr. and Navy Lt. Comdr. Thomas K. Mattingly II thun-

Pictures, Pages 12-13.

dered away from their home planet at 12:54 p.m. EST on the thrust of a 36-story Saturn 5 rocket.

CAPE KENNEDY, Fla. (AP) —America's Apollo 16 explorers reported a few hours after launch Sunday that insulation on the outside of their lunar lander was being stripped away. Mission Control engineers in Houston began studies to evaluate the potential problem.

After orbiting the earth for nearly three hours, the rocket's third stage re-fired to thrust the spacecraft out of orbit and rifled the astronauts accurately to-(Continued on Back Page, Col. 1)

King Hussein of Jordan (right with dark shirt) was among the spectators at the Apollo 16 launch. Also on the stand were Mrs. Spiro Agnew (next to Hussein), and in the row below, Mr. and Mrs. David Eisenhower. Mrs. Eisenhower is President Nixon's daughter. (AP)

Both Sides Claim An Loc

LAI KHE, Vietnam (UPI) — Two optimistic American generals said Sunday the siege of the battered province capital of An Loc had been lifted. Radio reports from commanders in the city however, said a sizable Communist force with 29 tanks carried fighting into a fourth consecutive night.

Both the Saigon government and the Viet Cong claimed An Loc, 60 miles north of Saigon, was in full control of their troops. Both, according to field reports, were wrong.

South Vietnamese commanders ordered another 1,000 government troops into the battle by helicopter, and the two battalions of former Green Beret mercenaries lifted to within a (Continued on Back Page, Col. 2)

BULLETIN

SAIGON (UPI) — U.S. jets shot down three Soviet-built North Vietnamese MIG21 jets in dogfights over Hanoi during Sunday's bombing of Hanoi and Haiphong, the U.S. Command announced Monday.

More F4s Headed for S.E. Asia

★★★ ★★★ ★★★ ★★★

Pullout to Continue

NIXON: WON'T HALT BOMBING

PACIFIC

STAR  **RIPES**

AN AUTHORIZED UNOFFICIAL PUBLICATION
FOR THE U.S. ARMED FORCES OF THE PACIFIC COMMAND

10¢

Vol. 28, No. 118   Friday, April 28, 1972

WASHINGTON (AP)—The United States is preparing to send another 36 F4 fighter bombers to Southeast Asia soon to strengthen further the already heavy U.S. air power trying to stem North Vietnam's offensive against South Vietnam.

Two squadrons of F4s are due to leave Florida bases in a few days for Thailand, Pentagon sources said.

This disclosure, coming ahead of President Nixon's report to the nation Wednesday night, indicated that he intends to maintain strong U.S. air power pressure against North Vietnamese troops, their supply routes and bases.

At the same time, it was learned that eight B52 heavy bombers, previously unreported, were sent from the United States to Guam in early April.

These moves bring to more than 200 the number of U.S. heavy bombers and fighter bombers flown to the war zone (Continued on Back Page, Col. 5)

WASHINGTON (UPI)—President Nixon, declaring he could "see the day when no more Americans will be involved," announced Wednesday night the withdrawal of 20,000 more U.S. troops from Vietnam by July 1. But he said U.S. planes would continue to bomb North Vietnam until Hanoi abandons its offensive in the south.

The President's announcement, delivered in a nationwide radio and television address from his White House office, meant that American troop strength would be down to 49,000 men within two months. The new rate of withdrawal was 10,000 a month, compared to about 23,000 per month under (Continued on Back Page, Col. 1)

Report Muskie Pullout

WASHINGTON (AP) — Sen. Edmund S. Muskie was reported ready Wednesday to pull out of the race for the Democratic presidential nomination.

The Mutual Broadcasting System quoted aides to the Maine senator as saying he will withdraw from the race Thursday morning.

Muskie's campaign headquarters said he is "evaluating the

Related stories, Page 2

political situation" and will hold a news conference at 10 a.m. EST Thursday.

Muskie, the 1968 Democratic vice presidential nominee once considered the frontrunner for the Presidential nomination but now battered by a string of primary defeats, canceled a scheduled campaign trip to Toledo, Ohio.

"Sen. Edmund S. Muskie is presently evaluating the political situation," his headquarters said in a brief announcement.

AMMUNITION TRUCKS EXPLODE AT KONTUM AIRPORT AFTER BEING HIT BY COMMUNIST ROCKETS.

AP

Red Drive Slowed in Viet Highlands

SAIGON (AP) — The North Vietnamese drive in the central highlands slowed Wednesday and South Korean troops to the east cleared the Communists from a vital pass that may open the way for resumption of convoys to the imperiled highland cities.

Another major threat developed in the coastal highlands behind the South Koreans, however. North Vietnamese troops swarmed out of the hills into the coastal Binh Dinh Province, seized one base and pushed into three populous districts.

The North Vietnamese are

Related stories, pictures, Pages 5, 6, 12-13.

north of Highway 19, where the South Koreans are operating at An Khe Pass. But should the Communists push south to Qui Nhon, the gateway to Highway

19, the route would be closed again.

In past offensives, the Communist goal has been to seize the highlands and Binh Dinh Province to sever South Vietnam at its waist. The objective in this spring offensive seems to be the same.

A Korean spokesman and John Paul Vann, the senior U.S. adviser in the highlands, announced that An Khe Pass had

been cleared after more than two weeks of sharp fighting.

Reports from Qui Nhon said the highway is still closed by destroyed culverts and damage to the roadway.

Unless the North Vietnamese return, repair work can be rushed so that the convoys can roll again. The highway runs from Qui Nhon to Pleiku, one of the two major cities in the highlands (Continued on Back Page, Col. 1)

Abandoned to N. Viets

QUANG TRI FALLS

★ ★ ★

350,000 Refugees On Move

SAIGON (AP) — More than 350,000 refugees are on the roads of South Vietnam, seeking escape from the thunderous fighting over the weekend in the northern provinces and central highlands.

American refugee workers in Saigon reported nearly a quarter of a million refugees are now on the move, trying to get to Hue and then on to Da Nang from Quang Tri, the fallen northernmost province capital.

Some 5,000 have boarded boats at Tam My, near Hue, to get to Da Nang by sea. The stream of refugees from Hue to Da Nang was halted for a time Monday when the road was cut by the Communists.

In coastal Binh Dinh, the nation's most populous province, welfare officials said there "has been so much fighting the people don't know which way to run." They estimated the flow of refugees on foot, by truck, on rickety province buses and motor bikes at 35,000, mostly from An Nhon and Binh Khe. Perhaps another 37,000 from Hoai An, now in enemy hands, had not made it so far to Qui Nhon City.

For the first time in more than two weeks, a rice air drop was made on An Loc, the embattled provincial capital in the rubber plantation country 70 miles north of Saigon.

War victims trying to flee the Communist columns moving on the highlands capital of Kontum from three directions were bottled up along Highway 14 by sporadic action in the Pleiku Pass, leading to Pleiku City.

A welfare worker just back from Kontum reported a trickle of families, carrying everything they had on their backs, were braving the pass and the sniper **(Continued on Back Page, Col. 1)**

The Last Laugh

LIVERPOOL, England (AP)— A man who set up a "Dial-a-Laugh" telephone service from his home has called it quits — because it got out of hand. The scheme became so popular that 600 people a day were calling him to listen to tape recordings of a man and woman laughing.

PACIFIC STAR AND STRIPES

AN AUTHORIZED UNOFFICIAL PUBLICATION FOR THE U.S. ARMED FORCES OF THE PACIFIC COMMAND

10¢

Vol. 28, No. 123   Wednesday, May 3, 1972

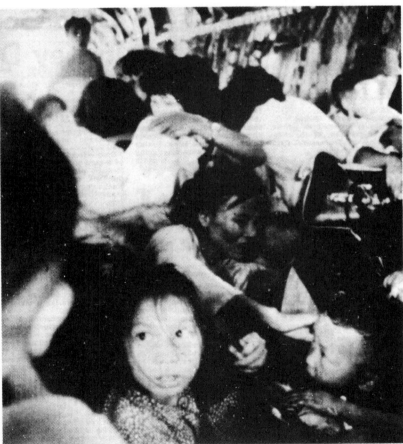

Refugees fleeing fighting around the central highlands city of Kontum crowd a helicopter carrying them to safety in Pleiku. Thousands more are fleeing on foot. **(AP)**

SAIGON (AP)—South Vietnam's first provincial capital was abandoned to the North Vietnamese Monday after five days of savage assaults in the northern sector by troops of four divisions, giving Hanoi its biggest victory of its current offensive.

South Vietnamese troops abandoned Quang Tri and into enemy hands went territory stretching from the demilitarized zone 27 miles to the south.

This May Day triumph followed the enemy's seizure of full control of the population and important rice crops along the central coast; the cutting of Highway 1 in crucial points north of Da Nang, site of the big U.S. air base, and renewed enemy pressure on Kontum, another provincial capital in the central highlands.

With the fall of Quang Tri, capital of the province of the same name, a threat became more imminent to the old imperial capital of Hue, now only 24 miles south of the northernmost defensive line of the South Vietnamese on Highway 1.

Field reports said some 5,000 South Vietnamese troops were trying to escape the fallen capi-

---

DA NANG, Vietnam (UPI)— Eighty American military advisers who were rescued Monday by helicopter from Quang Tri city said another 16 American fighting men stayed behind with South Vietnamese Marines.

---

tal as best they could. Most of the civilians had long since fled and only a very few remained.

Quang Tri had a population of about 27,000.

A mauled battalion of South Vietnamese rangers moving south from Quang Tri broke and fled after a day-long battle with troops of two North Vietnamese regiments near Highway 1.

But U.S. advisers said South Vietnamese marines moving north to link up with the rangers attacked a nearby regimental post and killed 160 enemy soldiers with help from U.S. bombing strikes. The marines were forced to pull back, however, when the rangers turned off the pressure from the north.

The enemy drive in the north-**(Continued on Back Page, Col. 1)**

Hawaii May Curb Cars

HONOLULU (UPI)—Hawaii may become the first state to limit the number of cars allowed in the state at one time. Such a measure awaits the signature of Gov. John A. Burns.

The bill, approved by the Legislature April 14, sets up an interdepartmental Transportation Control Commission which would have the task of setting a ceiling on the number of automobiles and other vehicles permitted in the state.

Burns, a Democrat, has not indicated whether he will sign the measure.

Hopes Rise for U.S.-Russ Missile Curb

WASHINGTON (AP) — The White House said Monday that President Nixon has had recent secret exchanges with Soviet Communist party chief Leonid I. Brezhnev which Nixon believes have substantially increased the possibility of a U.S.-Soviet missile-curb agreement.

Nixon has ordered Ambassa-dor Gerard C. Smith, top U.S. negotiator at the U.S.-Soviet Strategic Arms Limitation talks, to return to the Helsinki negotiations with new instructions.

The President was reported confident that the Soviet envoy to the SALT parley, Vladimir Semenov, also will receive from his government new in-structions which "can lead to an agreement which is mutually acceptable to both sides."

Presidential press secretary Ronald L. Ziegler announced this following a one-hour Nixon session with Smith and top administration diplomatic, military and intelligence officers.

Smith headed back to Helsinki Monday night, having ar-rived for Washington consultations last Wednesday.

Ziegler did not go into any details of the prospective U.S.-Soviet accord or say whether it would be reached before, during or after Nixon's May 22-29 visit to the Soviet Union.

The presidential spokesman said that a major advance to-**(Continued on Back Page, Col. 4)**

PRESIDENT ORDERS RED PORTS MINED

WASHINGTON (AP) —President Nixon announced Monday night he has o r d e r e d entrances to North Vietnamese ports mined to keep w e a p o n s and supplies from what he c a l l e d "the international outlaws."

Nixon said U.S. forces have been directed to take appropriate measures to interdict delivery of supplies by sea. He said rail and other lines of supply will be cut off, while air and naval strikes continue.

In a nationally broadcast address, Nixon said the measures he had ordered taken already were under way.

He spoke to the nation several hours after U.S. warplanes had returned to attacks in the Hanoi area after a three-week lapse. And he announced the decisions after he had worked over the plans in a three-hour session with the National Security Council.

Nixon never used the word blockade, but he said Hanoi must be denied weapons and supplies of war.

Nixon said that all Americans would be withdrawn within four months from South Vietnam, and the mining of North Vietnamese sea approaches halted at once if two conditions are met:

1. All U.S. prisoners of war are returned.
2. An internationally-supervised ceasefire is instituted.

Nixon said nations shipping supplies to North Vietnam have been notified they have three days to get their ships out, presumably from the port of Haiphong.

He said any ships entering North Vietnamese waters after that will do so at their own risk.

With that, he disclosed the steps taken to seal off North Vietnamese ports, actions that recalled the naval quarantine of Cuba during the crisis over Soviet missiles a decade ago.

Nixon prefaced his announcement by saying there appeared to be only three available courses of action: to withdraw U.S. forces immediately, to simply continue negotiations, or to take decisive military action.

But he said given the certain impact of the first two courses, **(Continued on Back Page, Col. 1)**

AN AUTHORIZED UNOFFICIAL PUBLICATION
FOR THE U.S. ARMED FORCES OF THE PACIFIC COMMAND

10¢

Vol. 28, No. 130   Wednesday, May 10, 1972

New Dispute Seen

Wage Panel Cuts Dockers' Raise

WASHINGTON (AP) — The Pay Board Monday night cut back pay raises for 50,000 East and Gulf Coast longshoremen, increasing the likelihood of renewed labor unrest on both East and Gulf Coast ports and West Coast ports.

By a vote of 6 to 1 the board rejected the International Longshoremen's Association, AFL-CIO, contracts covering North Atlantic ports, New Orleans and West Gulf ports.

These contracts contained straight-time pay increases of 70 cents an hour in addition to fringe benefits.

The board said it won't approve any more than 55 cents an hour. But it will accept all the fringe benefits won by the union.

This means the board will allow only a 12 per cent increase in straight-time hourly pay, rather than the 15 per cent negotiated by the union. When both straight-time pay and fringes are figured in, the way the Pay Board judges pay raises, different numbers result for different ports.

The ILWU and the PMA kept quiet about what action they would take while awaiting the Pay Board decision. There was no immediate response from either.

Harry Bridges, ILWU president, has said that if the Pay Board trims the ILA contract terms, joint action by the West Coast ILWU and the ILA might be taken to close down all U.S. ports. But ILA President Thomas W. "Teddy" Gleason has given no public sign he is agreeable to taking part in such a shutdown.

Bridges flew to Washington **(Continued on Back Page, Col. 3)**

BULLETIN

SAIGON (AP) — Rear Adm. Rembrandt C. Robinson, 47, commander of the Cruiser-Destroyer Flotilla 11, was killed in a helicopter crash in the Tonkin Gulf Monday night, the U.S. command announced Tuesday.

The command said two other high-ranking Navy officers, Capt. Edmund B. Taylor Jr., 40, chief of staff of Flotilla 11, and Cmdr. John M. Leaver, 38, the operations officer, are missing in the crash.

Robinson was the first Navy admiral killed in the war. Seven American Army, Marine and Air Force generals have been killed in the Indochina war.

Navy Planes Raid Camp Near Hanoi

Compiled from UPI and AP

U.S. Navy jets struck at a military base and training camp about 15 miles west of Hanoi Monday, the U.S. command announced. Radio Hanoi said two of the planes were shot down, but the command denied it.

A Defense Department spokesman in Washington said "several tens of strike aircraft" were involved in Monday's raid.

Related stories, Page 6.

"in the vicinity of Hanoi" and first reports indicated two or three Communist MIG fighters were shot down.

"This was the only strike in the vicinity of Hanoi and it was a g a i n s t military targets," spokesman Jerry W. Friedheim said when asked about reports from Radio Hanoi that U.S. planes bombed the Red River irrigation dikes 30 miles south of Hanoi.

"There's been no mentioning of any targeting of dikes," he said. However, Friedheim added that the attacking planes may have flown over the dikes to and from their targets in the Hanoi area.

Asked why the barracks and training area was attacked,

Friedheim replied that the North Vietnamese are training replacements for the battlefield and that this would have some effect on Hanoi's invasion force.

"Was the raid meant to be an object lesson?" a newsman asked.

Friedheim replied: "If the other side chose to take it as an object lesson and ceased its invasion we'd be delighted."

A U.S. command spokesman said, "Tactical aircraft of the U.S. Navy struck military targets approximately 15 miles west of Hanoi. There were no **(Continued on Back Page, Col. 1)**

Threaten to Blow Up Airliner, 100 Aboard

TEL AVIV (AP) — Despite a tipoff and security search, three armed Arabs hijacked an Israel-bound Belgian jetliner carrying 100 persons Monday. After landing in Tel Aviv, they threatened to blow up the plane and its passengers unless Israel freed 300 Palestinian guerrilla prisoners and flew them to Cairo.

A senior Israeli Army officer told the gunmen that freeing hundreds of prisoners within a few hours was impossible. The Israelis, speaking to the hijackers by radio, were reported to have offered to free 15 or 20 military prisoners of war "as a gesture of good will."

The gunmen set a deadline of 8 p.m. for Israel to make a deal, but the deadline passed with no explosion or other evident action.

Transport Minister Shimon Peres said 60 male passengers were captive aboard the jetliner, with 30 women or girls, and one child who had not been noted on the passenger list.

"They are all in satisfactory condition," the minister said.

Peres said the hijackers had given dozens of specific names of guerrillas they wanted released.

The leader of the hijacking trio identified himself as Capt. Rafah, the minister said. The men reportedly had explosives as well as grenades aboard the aircraft.

A statement issued in Beirut identified the hijackers as members of the Black September Organization, an underground Palestinian group named for the September 1970 Jordanian civil war in which King Hussein's forces all but destroyed guerrilla power in Jordan. It said the **(Continued on Back Page, Col. 4)**

GUN DOWN 7 MIGS

★ ★ ★   ★ ★ ★   ★ ★ ★   ★ ★ ★

Soviet Ship Turns Away—Laird

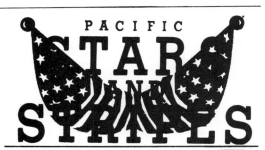

PACIFIC
STAR AND STRIPES

AN AUTHORIZED UNOFFICIAL PUBLICATION
FOR THE U.S. ARMED FORCES OF THE PACIFIC COMMAND

10¢

Vol. 28, No. 132   Friday, May 12, 1972

WASHINGTON (AP) —At least one Soviet ship heading for Haiphong has changed course since President Nixon ordered the sealing of North Vietnamese harbors, Secretary of Defense Melvin R. Laird said Wednesday.

The secretary said a Russian freighter had been scheduled to enter Haiphong "yesterday or today" but did not. He also indicated more ships may have changed course.

The defense chief also said in a 53-minute news conference in a crowded Pentagon press room "that all action will be taken that is necessary" to stop deliveries to North Vietnam, and he indicated this meant by air, sea or ground.

Laird appeared to have gone past presidential adviser Henry A. Kissinger's statements Tuesday in discussing what the United States might do to prevent supplies from reaching the North.

For instance, Kissinger had said no attempt would be made to prevent ships from entering the mined harbors, but Laird said Wednesday repeatedly that all steps necessary would be taken to stop deliveries.

He was emphatic in making this point and said "I consider the entire land mass of North Vietnam would be a delivery." This would seem to indicate any effort to fly supplies in would be met with American force.

Laird was asked in various ways what would happen to Soviet or other nations' ships which might try to deliver material and in every case his answer was typified by this response:

"We will take those steps that are necessary to prevent the delivery of supplies that can be used to help the North Vietnamese to carry out their military aggression in Southeast Asia.

"I don't know how I can be any more forthright or make it any clearer."

He also said there is no evidence the Soviets have tried to sweep the mines from the harbor entrances.

In noting "there is some evidence of some change of course" by Soviet ships, Laird said there is still a full period **(Continued on Back Page, Col. 1)**

Compiled From AP and UPI

SAIGON — U.S. warplanes shot down seven enemy MIGs Wednesday while carrying out the deepest and heaviest air strikes inside North Vietnam in more than four years, the U.S. Command announced.

The downing of seven MIGs in one day is a record for the Vietnam war.

The U.S. aircraft attacked both Hanoi and Haiphong, while hitting at widespread areas of North Vietnam, the command said.

It made no mention of any U.S. air losses.

The aircraft streaked to within 60 miles of the Chinese border to attack North Vietnam's northwest rail link to China.

Meantime, President Nguyen Van Thieu proclaimed a state of martial law throughout Vietnam effective at midnight Thursday, and the mayor of Saigon, Do Kien Nhieu, went on television to warn residents that an attack on the South Vietnamese capital was imminent.

Nhieu unveiled a new emergency plan for coping with a major attack, asked residents to sandbag their homes, and issued detailed instructions for personal safety during shelling and rocket attacks. Nhieu also said he was setting up classes to teach first aid and emergency evacuation procedures.

It was not immediately clear what the effect of the martial law proclamation would be, but

Related stories, Pages 5 and 6.

there has been discussion in the Vietnamese National Assembly for two days of giving Thieu "special powers."

There already have been widespread roundups in Hue and Da Nang of persons whose loyalty was considered suspect. Field reports said about 3,000 persons being held in Hue were transferred to Da Nang two days ago.

On the war front, military sources reported new attacks west of Hue near the government bases of King and Birmingham, and a brief but intense shelling attack with 130mm artillery against Marine positions along the My Chanh **(Continued on Back Page, Col. 5)**

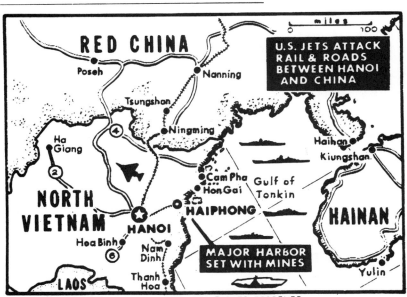

RED CHINA

Poseh   Nanning

Tsungshan

④ Ningming

Ha Giang

②   Haihan   Kiungshan

NORTH VIETNAM   Cam Pha   Gulf of Tonkin   HAINAN

HonGai

HAIPHONG

HANOI

Hoa Binh ⑥

Nam Dinh

Thanh Hoa

LAOS

Yulin

U.S. JETS ATTACK RAIL & ROADS BETWEEN HANOI AND CHINA

MAJOR HARBOR SET WITH MINES

miles
0   100

Shots May Have Hit Russian Ship

Compiled From AP and UPI

WASHINGTON — Pentagon sources said Wednesday at least one and possibly more Soviet ships in Haiphong Harbor may have been caught in a cross fire between U.S. mine-laying planes and North Vietnamese shore batteries.

"There was an awful lot of shooting going on from both sides," one well-placed source said.

Both the military sources and Pentagon officials speaking 'on the record' denied there had been any deliberate attacks on any ships in North Vietnamese ports. "There have not been any ships on the target lists," a spokesman said.

The White House said Wednesday it is thoroughly investigating China News Agency reports that U.S. planes hit two Chinese freighters in North Vietnamese waters.

Presidential spokesman Ronald L. Ziegler said "we are aware of statements from news reports" that the ships were hit.

He added, however, that the Defense Department is "not authorized" to target freighters of that country.

Ziegler also told reporters at a briefing that the White House has no report that a Soviet freighter was hit, as announced by the North Vietnamese News Agency.

Ziegler said, "U.S. aircraft are not authorized to target freighters of any other country."

He declined to amplify his remarks.

A North Vietnamese broadcast reported that two Soviet ships, the Babouchkine and the Pezeck, had been attacked by U.S. warplanes Tuesday and that four crewmen had been injured. The broadcast gave no further details.

Pentagon sources said that at least the Pezeck probably had been hit inadvertently during the mining operation Monday night.

Pentagon officials also denied persistent reports that two Soviet minesweepers were nearing Haiphong after setting out from the Soviet Union five days ago.

"We just have seen nothing that would support that," an official spokesman said. He said the closest Soviet minesweepers to North Vietnam were in port at Bangladesh, and had shown no signs of leaving.

"Meanwhile, reports were re- **(Continued on Back Page, Col. 1)**

Another Top General Fired by Thieu

SAIGON (AP) — President Nguyen Van Thieu fired his controversial commander in the central highlands Wednesday in the continuing high-level military shakeup resulting from battlefield setbacks.

Lt. Gen. Ngo Dzu, commander in the 2nd Military Region that includes the highlands, was replaced by Maj. Gen. Nguyen Van Toan, who had been deputy commander in the 1st Military Region.

The disclosure was made ahead of Thieu's own official announcement by John Paul Vann, senior U.S. adviser in the 2nd Region, in a news conference at Pleiku. He said Dzu's dismissal resulted from criticism of his forces for having lost four districts and a number of bases to the enemy.

He identified those who had pressured Thieu to fire Dzu as members of the National Assembly, especially in the affected areas.

"All distant critics like to see a scalp fall," said Vann, who publicly had defended Dzu against his critics.

"One senior military commander obviously bears responsibility for the defense or lack of defense of his areas," Vann said. Of Toan, he added: "Either he will be better or worse. I have no way of knowing which."

Dzu is said to be suffering from a mild heart ailment and reportedly asked Thieu for a **(Continued on Back Page, Col. 1)**

ERA ENDS: OKINAWA GIVEN BACK

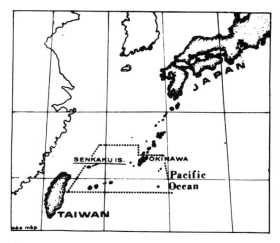

TOKYO (S&S)—The Ryukyu Islands reverted to Japan Monday after 27 years of American rule and Vice President Spiro Agnew said in a ceremony in Tokyo that the event marked a turning point in the relations between the two countries by resolving the last major issue of the war.

Agnew was participating in ceremonies along with Emperor Hirohito, Prime Minister Eisaku Sato and Lt. Gen. James Lampert, who was U.S. high commissioner of the islands until reversion came at one minute past Sunday midnight.

The vice president read President Nixon's proclamation, formally ending U.S. administration of the islands, and then went on to say that, being a legal document, the proclamation "does not begin to convey the real significance and emotional impact that this occasion holds for the people of Japan and Okinawa.

"Nor does it adequately reflect the feelings of the people of the United States."

But he said that "in a very real way, this ceremony marks a turning point in the relations between our two countries, for it resolves the last major issue of the war. It is the end of an era, but, more importantly, it is the beginning of a new one in which we can expect an even greater community of interests between our two great nations."

Agnew noted that Americans look back on the years of Ryukyus occupation "with considerable pride in the improvements we believe we have made in the well-being of the people of Okinawa. And we cherish the deep friendship and respect which have developed between the people of Okinawa and of the United States.

"We place the highest value on our relations with Japan. A balanced relationship between our two countries, based upon interdependence, equality and reciprocity, is essential—not only

(Continued on Back Page, Col. 1)

PACIFIC STARS AND STRIPES

AN AUTHORIZED UNOFFICIAL PUBLICATION
FOR THE U.S. ARMED FORCES OF THE PACIFIC COMMAND

10¢

Vol. 28, No. 136   Tuesday, May 16, 1972

TV's 'Hoss' Blocker Dies at 43

DAN BLOCKER

HOLLYWOOD (AP) — Dan Blocker, the hulking Texan who as Hoss Cartwright helped rule a television rangeland on the western epic "Bonanza," is dead at 43.

Blocker, whose 300 pounds and bouncer-style character made him a favorite with the series' millions of viewers in 70 nations, died in a hospital Saturday night of complications following an operation earlier in the month.

He had been released after surgery for a gall bladder problem May 1 but suffered a subsequent infection, a family spokesman said. He died of a blood clot in the lung after he had gone to the hospital in the morning complaining of shortness of breath. His wife and daughter were with him when he died.

The actor blended humor, sensitivity and powerfulness both on and off the television screen.

Raised in West Texas, where in Bowie County he was legend as the biggest baby ever born—14 pounds—he once observed

(Continued on Back Page, Col. 2)

U.S. Bombers Break The 'Dragon's Jaw'

SAIGON (AP) — U.S. warplanes have cut the heart of North Vietnam's supply network by destroying the Thanh Hoa "Dragon's Jaw" Bridge 80 miles south of Hanoi, the 7th Air Force announced Sunday. It said the bridge had stood for seven years, despite repeated air attacks, as "a symbol of invincibility and a challenge to U.S. pilots."

Officials also reported that North Vietnamese rail links with China had been cut in places and that a key railroad bridge on the edge of Hanoi had been wrecked by air strikes.

The aim of the attacks was to sever some of North Vietnam's land routes for supplies while its ports are mined in a U.S. effort to cut down supplies from across the sea.

On the ground in South Vietnam, fighting picked up in the central highlands and the northern sector, but eased up around An Loc, 60 miles north of Saigon.

Fighting was reported continuing around Kontum in the central highlands shortly before midnight, but the South Vietnamese said that North Vietnamese forces were being contained. North Vietnamese forces had launched heavy tank, infantry and artillery assaults just before dawn against the outer defenses of Kontum. The enemy shelled South Vietnam's northernmost front with heavy, long-range guns.

The renewed assaults could signal that the North Vietnamese are ready to launch the third phase of their 46-day-old offensive. Thousands of South Vietnamese reinforcements were rushed to the Kontum defense line, and pushed the North Vietnamese back about a mile. Kontum city and Hue, 20 miles below the northern defense line, are said to be key North Vietnamese objectives in the offensive.

The 7th Air Force said the destruction of the Thanh Hoa Bridge, 80 miles south of Hanoi, on Saturday "represents a significant air interdiction accomplishment."

"The combination railway and highway bridge spanned the Song Ma River and was a key link in the major North Vietnam supply line from the Hanoi-Haiphong area south to the DMZ," the announcement said.

"The destruction of the bridge yesterday cuts a major logistical route over which heavy and bulky enemy war material and equipment moved south by major rail and roadways to the Mu Gia and Ban Karai Passes and the DMZ for further transshipment to support the North Vietnamese invasion of the Republic of Vietnam."

The DMZ is the Demilitarized Zone between the two Vietnams.

Officials also reported that both the northeast and northwest rail lines linking Hanoi with China, a supplier of arms

(Continued on Back Page, Col. 4)

His Beak Is Top Banana

SORAGNA, Italy (UPI) — With measurements of 69-26-42 bricklayer Luigi Rossetti was the winner by a nose Sunday of the annual "King Big Nose" contest.

Those measurements, in millimeters, translate in inches to 2¾ by 1½ by 1⅝.

Rossetti, 50, came in second last year. He was helped to victory by the fact that last year's winner was home sick.

Meteorite Rattles Moon, Scientists

SPACE CENTER, Houston (AP) — A meteorite smashed into the moon early Saturday with a force equivalent to about 1,000 tons of TNT and carved out a crater as large as a football field, a space scientist said here.

Dr. Gary Latham of the Lamont-Doherty Geological Observatory at Columbia University said the impact of the meteorite was recorded by four seismometers left on the moon by Apollo missions.

The huge chunk of space debris, he said, hit "uncomfortably close" to the Apollo 14 nuclear powered science station.

The scientists said the impact seemed to have been only "a few tens of miles" from the Apollo 14 site, which is in the Fra Mauro formation of the moon.

The meteorite struck about 4:49 a.m. EDT.

Latham said it caused a rain of debris that was recorded on all four seismometers and which lasted about one minute.

There was no immediate indication that the debris damaged the Apollo 14 science station but officials feared dust may have collected on the instruments. If such is the case, a spokesman said, it could cause thermal damage when the site comes into the sun's rays.

All four Apollo landing sites were in the dark when the meteorite struck.

Latham said the seismic reverberations lasted for three hours and were so violent at the Apollo 14 site that the seismic instrument there went off scale high for 16 minutes until

(Continued on Back Page, Col. 2)

To Bomb N. Viet Industrial Plants

WASHINGTON (AP) —The Pentagon Tuesday signaled a widening of bombing targets in North Vietnam, saying that U.S. planes will hit industrial plants supporting the enemy's war effort.

Until now, the revived U.S. bombing of North Vietnam, ordered by President Nixon after North Vietnam opened its spring offensive against South Vietnam, has concentrated on petroleum storage depots and transportation facilities, including bridges, railroads and truck parks.

Pentagon spokesman Jerry W. Friedheim said these kind of attacks will continue on a major scale and that U.S. bombers "will be hitting some of the other targets such as power plants and some of the industrial facilities which support the military effort of the North."

Friedheim's words indicated that this was the beginning of a new phase in the bombing which will aim at some of North Vietnam's basic economic resources, as well as more directly military type targets.

During the 1965-1968 phase of the air war, U.S. bombers virtually knocked out about a dozen thermal power plants. Most have been rebuilt and some have been protected with blast walls to minimize damage from bombing.

Friedheim declined to go into any kind of detail on what kinds of plants will now be subject to U.S. bombing, but it appeared probable that the old target list from 1965-1968 bombing days will again be in use.

At another point, Friedheim said he "would not rule out any sort of industrial target" that supports the enemy's war effort.

Under questioning, Friedheim acknowledged that U.S. commanders now exercise more authority in carrying out bombing (Continued on Back Page, Col. 2)

New Skipper For 7th Fleet

ABOARD THE OKLAHOMA CITY (AP) — Vice Adm. James L. Holloway succeeded Vice Adm. William P. Mack Tuesday as commander of the U.S. 7th Fleet — the most powerful naval unit ever assembled in terms of firepower.

Mack will go from the Oklahoma City, off Vietnam, to Annapolis, Md., to take command of the U.S. Naval Academy.

The 7th Fleet has increased in size by almost 50 per cent since the start of the Communist enemy offensive March 30.

PACIFIC

STARS & STRIPES

AN AUTHORIZED UNOFFICIAL PUBLICATION
FOR THE U.S. ARMED FORCES OF THE PACIFIC COMMAND

10¢

Vol. 28, No. 145

Thursday, May 25, 1972

SIX RED BRIDGES, POWER PLANT HIT

White House secretary Elizabeth Murphree unrolls a 417-foot telegram sent to President Nixon from Denver. The telegram carries a message supporting Nixon's latest Vietnam war decisions and was signed by 15,012 people. **(UPI)**

BULLETIN

SAIGON (AP)—U.S. Air Force and Navy fighters shot down four Soviet-built MIG interceptors over North Vietnam Tuesday, U.S. military sources said Wednesday.

Compiled From AP and UPI

SAIGON — American warplanes attacked North Vietnam's Red River Valley, destroying six bridges on the northwest rail line linking Hanoi with China, and blowing up Hanoi's transformer station providing power for military installations in the Communist capital, the U.S. command announced Tuesday.

The command also announced that a total of more than 1,000 strikes were carried out by American bombers all across North Vietnam during the past three days, and that other positions were heavily shelled by 7th Fleet cruisers and destroyers.

The guided missile cruiser Providence was hit by Communist shore batteries Monday in the Gulf of Tonkin and sustained light shrapnel damage to a night

Related stories, Page 6.

observation post, the command reported. It said the officer manning the post was slightly injured.

The intensified raids, raised from an average of 250 a day to between 300 and 350 a day during the past week, are part of a campaign ordered by President Nixon to destroy rear bases and installations supporting North Vietnam's 55-day offensive in South Vietnam and to cut supply lines to the South.

The bridges, in an area generally 110 miles northwest of Hanoi and about 50 miles south of the Chinese border, were knocked out Monday by a relatively small force of Air Force (Continued on Back Page, Col. 1)

McGovern Wins R.I. Primary

By The Associated Press

Sen. George McGovern captured a victory in Rhode Island's Democratic presidential primary Tuesday.

Meanwhile, Oregon was voting, too, and most of the campaign emphasis shifted to the West Coast, where California offers the main event of the Democratic primary race in two weeks.

In Rhode Island, President Nixon was burying two Republican challengers, taking more than 90 per cent of GOP ballots.

McGovern's victory added 22 more delegates to his slate of convention delegates as he topped Sen. Hubert H. Humphrey, Sen. Edmund M. Muskie and Gov. George Wallace.

Here are the vote totals in the Rhode Island Democratic primary with 48 per cent of the 245 precincts reporting:

McGovern 5,745 — 42 per cent.
Humphrey 3,118 — 23 per cent.
Muskie 2,322 — 17 per cent.
Wallace 2,137 — 15 per cent.

In Kentucky, meanwhile, Republican voters chose former Gov. Louie B. Nunn as their nominee for a Senate seat. Walter Huddleston, a state senator, won the Democratic nomination in a primary that drew a sparse turnout.

Summit Moves to Big Issues

MOSCOW (AP) — President Nixon and Soviet leaders cleared a pair of modest bilateral agreements from their summit agenda Tuesday and moved on with talks ranging over such crucial issues as arms limitation and Vietnam.

Nixon sandwiched a pair of private talks with Communist Party Chief Leonid I. Brezhnev around ceremonies signing bilateral agreements on environ-

Related stories, Page 4.

mental protection and health.

They were the second and third sessions Nixon has had with Brezhnev since he became on Monday the first American President to set foot in Moscow.

The evening session turned into a night session, too, lasting nearly three hours until 10 p.m. Moscow time. Nixon then dined in his suite at the Kremlin Grand Palace.

In the gilded splendor of a vaulted Kremlin hall, Nixon signed with Soviet President Nikolai V. Podgorny a U.S.-Soviet agreement pledging a cooperative attack on water and air pollution.

This was followed with the signing by Secretary of State William P. Rogers and the Soviet health minister of an agree- (Continued on Back Page, Col. 1)

Connally Going on World Tour

KEY BISCAYNE, Fla. (AP)—President Nixon is sending outgoing Treasury Secretary John B. Connally on a 15-nation, month-long tour beginning Tuesday to discuss international economic matters and "any subject which his hosts wish to raise," the White House announced Monday.

Connally, however, will not go to North Vietnam to negotiate for the release of prisoners of war as was suggested by Sen. Hubert H. Humphrey, D-Minn., in the Democratic presidential candidates' debate Sunday in California.

He will travel to South America, the Far East, South Asia and Europe.

Details of the trip are not firm, said Ronald L. Ziegler, presidential press secretary, but Connally will go first to Venezuela and then to Colombia, Brazil, Argentina, Bolivia and Peru between June 6 and June 14 on the first leg of his journey.

He will depart Key Biscayne Tuesday and be in Caracas (Continued on Back Page, Col. 1)

PACIFIC
STARS & STRIPES

AN AUTHORIZED UNOFFICIAL PUBLICATION
FOR THE U.S. ARMED FORCES OF THE PACIFIC COMMAND

10¢

Vol. 28, No. 158

Wednesday, June 7, 1972

DESERTER'S INFO DEFEATS N. VIETS

SAIGON (UPI) — North Vietnamese troops retreated from embattled Phu My district capital on South Vietnam's central coast Monday, and a U.S. adviser claimed "quite a victory" for government soldiers.

Military sources said the greatest credit for the victory went to a double deserter who carried detailed plans for last Friday's Communist assault to South Vietnamese officers at Phu My, 280 miles north of Saigon.

The man had deserted from South Vietnam's army in April

Related stories, Page 6.

and was impressed into the Viet Cong, the sources said.

He then deserted from the Communists and fled to Phu My with full plans for the North Vietnamese attack.

"It was quite a victory," said Col. Phillip Kaplan, senior U.S. adviser to the South Vietnamese 22nd Inf. Div.

"They've withdrawn and pulled back. But they're still out there. I'll tell you, we're going to win this one."

Kaplan gave credit to the double defector for the victory, which resulted in an estimated (Continued on Back Page, Col. 5)

A North Vietnamese fishing boat (bottom center) brushes past the U.S. cruiser Newport News as she fires her eight-inch guns at Thanh Hoa, 75 miles south of Haiphong. The fishing vessel was not harmed during the firing run. (UPI)

True Believer

MILWAUKEE (UPI) — James Michalski would not give up his chance to become a Jesuit priest for half a million dollars.

When Michalski takes his vows Thursday, he will be giving up a family estate totaling almost that amount. His father, Leon G. Michalski, who died in 1968, offered his son the money in his will if he would leave the religious life.

"What's so surprising?" he said. "I don't see life in terms of money. I'm really very happy. I feel I can bring more love into the world in what I'm doing."

Laird: SALT Doesn't Mean a Cutback

WASHINGTON (UPI) —Defense Secretary Melvin R. Laird testified Monday the U.S.-Soviet strategic arms limitation agreements would produce net savings at most of $1 billion a year in U.S. defense costs —and it might not lead to any reductions at all.

Warning that "peace cannot be bought cheaply," Laird told a congressional committee that the United States must begin crash programs to develop new submarines and bombers to keep up with the Russians despite the Strategic Arms Limitation Talks (SALT).

He said there may be no net savings to the taxpayers at all from the accords if the Vietnam war continues at its current pace.

Pentagon critics, led by Sen. William Proxmire, D-Wis., immediately charged that the Nixon administration was depriving the U.S. taxpayer of the "dividend" from SALT by applying the savings to new, expensive weapons.

But Laird warned that deep reductions in the defense budget because of the agreement would put the United States behind the Soviets in the arms race. He said Russia has "far outstripped" the United States in the momentum of weapons construction.

He singled out Democratic presidential contender George S. McGovern for special criticism. On the eve of the California primary, where defense spending is a key issue, Laird said McGovern's pro- (Continued on Back Page, Col. 1)

5 GI Amputees Conquer a Mountain

BRETTON WOODS, N.H. (AP)—Five Vietnam veterans, all amputees, met the challenge of high winds, snow, ice and sheer rock walls to scale Mt. Washington.

Leon Dubay, a veteran climber who led the group, said he thought climbing the 6,288-foot mountain would be a real challenge for the men. But he didn't expect it to be as difficult as it was.

"I chose the Lion's Head (part of the headwall of Tuckerman's Ravine) because I thought it would be mostly trails. I was wrong," Dubay said. "It turned out to be one of the toughest places to climb.

"A lot of climbing was up sheer rock-face. We had stretches of 40 to 50 feet, straight up."

The amputees, accompanied by Dubay, a nurse, a cook, someone to mind the base

(Continued on Back Page, Col. 2)

PACIFIC STAR AND STRIPES

AN AUTHORIZED UNOFFICIAL PUBLICATION
FOR THE U.S. ARMED FORCES OF THE PACIFIC COMMAND

10¢

Vol. 28, No. 165   Wednesday, June 14, 1972

Unauthorized Raids on N. Viet

Lavelle: Tried to Stop Buildup

Retired Maj. Gen. John D. Lavelle (right) is seated with Air Force Chief of Staff Gen. John D. Ryan as they appear to testify before a House Armed Services subcommittee. (UPI)

WASHINGTON (AP) — Ousted air commander John D. Lavelle confirmed Monday he ordered unauthorized strikes against North Vietnamese airfields, missiles and artillery last winter in "trying to stop the buildup" for Hanoi's invasion of the South.

Retired Maj. Gen. Lavelle told the House Armed Services investigating subcommittee continuation of the strikes could not have prevented the offensive but "they could have made it more costly."

Lavelle said he ordered the strikes, begun in January, halted March 10 after he learned false reports on three of the missions had been sent to higher headquarters and he saw no way to continue the strikes without further inaccurate reports.

"If I had it to do over I would do the same thing," Lavelle told a congressman, "but I would check into the reporting procedure better."

Gen. John D. Ryan, Air Force chief of staff, told the subcommittee he fired Lavelle as commander of the 7th Air Force in Indochina because of 28 missions involving 147 planes he said violated rules prohibiting all but "protective reaction" strikes into North Vietnam, in line with the 1968 bombing halt.

Asked by a congressman if "forcing men to file these false reports" was a factor in La-

(Continued on Back Page, Col. 1)

Stalled Boxcars Bombed

Compiled From AP and UPI

SAIGON — U.S. jets left a 10-mile stretch of North Vietnam's northeast rail line to China and about 60 stranded freight cars in flames Sunday and shot down two more MIG jets, the U.S. Command announced Monday.

Large orange fireballs lit up the skies 25 miles south of the Chinese border after about 20

Related stories, Page 6.

Air Force F4 Phantoms attacked the rail line and a string of freight cars 50 to 60 miles northeast of Hanoi, pilots reported.

They told of one big explosion that sent an orange fireball 1,-600 feet in diameter rising 2,000 feet into the air. Flames shot up 500 feet from another huge fire.

Two Navy Phantoms from

(Continued on Back Page, Col. 1)

6-3 Decision by Top Court

Private Clubs Free to Bar Black Guests

WASHINGTON (AP) — The Supreme Court Monday upheld the right of private clubs to exclude Negroes as guests.

The 6 to 3 decision was delivered by freshman Justice William H. Rehnquist. It went against a black brought as a guest to the Moose Lodge in Harrisburg, Pa.

The black, Leroy Irvis, the majority leader of the Pennsylvania House, contended that since the club held a liquor license from the state it could not exclude blacks as members or as guests.

Monday's decision dealt directly with the exclusion of blacks as guests—and not with their exclusion as members.

Rehnquist said Irvis could not challenge the lodge's all-white membership policy since he had never applied for membership, but had only been brought to the club as a guest.

Rehnquist said the club's refusal to serve Negroes does not violate the Fourteenth Amend-

Related stories, Page 3.

ment even though the Moose Lodge gets its liquor license through the state.

"Since state-furnished services include such necessities of life as electricity, water, and police and fire protection, such a holding would utterly emasculate the distinction be-

tween private as distinguished from state conduct," he said.

Chief Justice Warren E. Burger and Justices Harry A. Blackmun and Lewis F. Powell, the three other Nixon administration appointees, lined up with Rehnquist, a former assistant attorney general. Justices Potter Stewart and Byron R. White also were in the majority.

Dissenting were Justices William O. Douglas, William J. Brennan Jr., and Thurgood Marshall, the court's only Negro member.

Brennan said Pennsylvania's liquor regulations plainly intertwined the state with the operation of the lodge's bar in a sig-

nificant way and lent the state's authority "to the sordid business of racial discrimination."

The ruling reverses a three-judge federal court in Harrisburg which held in 1970 that the Moose Lodge could not keep both its liquor license and its racially exclusive policy.

The lodge is across the street from the Pennsylvania state capitol. Irvis, an Allegheny county Democrat, had been brought to it for dinner and drinks by a white member.

The constitution that governs all Moose lodges provides that membership "be composed of male persons of the Caucasian

(Continued on Back Page, Col. 3)

BULLETIN

DETROIT (AP) — The Wayne County sheriff's department reported a bomb exploded in the baggage compartment of an American Airlines DC10 jet shortly after takeoff from Detroit Monday night.

It forced the plane to make an emergency landing.

Deputies say 11 persons were reported injured. None of the injuries was believed serious.

At least eight persons, including two stewardesses, were taken to Wayne County General Hospital.

An official in the air traffic control tower at Detroit's Metropolitan Airport said there apparently was no serious damage to the plane.

Weyand Is Top Viet Commander

WASHINGTON (AP) — President Nixon elevated Gen. Frederick C. Weyand to commander of U.S. forces in Vietnam Wednesday and announced a consolidation of Army and Air Force commands in the war zone.

The White House, after making the announcements, also disclosed that Nixon is dispatching Maj. Gen. Alexander M. Haig, No. 2 man to Henry Kissinger on the National Security Council, to South Vietnam and Cambodia on Thursday for a six-day fact-finding mission.

Weyand, a four-star general, will, as predicted widely, succeed Gen. Creighton Abrams as commander of the Military Assistance Command in Vietnam and as commander of the U.S. Army in Vietnam. He has been deputy commander of MACV since September, 1970, under Abrams, who was nominated by Nixon last week to be Army chief of staff.

White House press secretary Ronald L. Ziegler said Weyand's post as deputy commander of MACV will be taken by Air Force Gen. John W. Vogt, who also will retain his position as commander of the 7th Air Force, a post he recently was assigned.

Naming Vogt as deputy commander, rather than selecting an Army general, is part of the consolidation of U.S. operations in Southeast Asia ordered by Nixon.

(Continued on Back Page, Col. 5)

Only Draftee Vols to Viet

NIXON SLOWS PULLOUT

PACIFIC

STAR STRIPES

AN AUTHORIZED UNOFFICIAL PUBLICATION FOR THE U.S. ARMED FORCES OF THE PACIFIC COMMAND

10¢

Vol. 28, No. 181   Friday, June 30, 1972

WASHINGTON (AP) — President Nixon slowed the Vietnam withdrawal rate Wednesday—to 10,000 troops over two months—but said draftees no longer will be sent to the war zone unless they volunteer.

Nixon's action will cut U.S. force levels in South Vietnam to 39,000 by Sept. 1. This compares with a peak ceiling of 549,500 when he took office. The 39,000 figure does not take into account about 87,000 participating in the war from Thailand and the 7th Fleet off Vietnam.

In May and June, troops were pulled out at the rate of 10,000 a month, but with the remaining force getting ever smaller and Hanoi's army continuing its Southern offensive, Nixon opted for a go-slower approach at this time.

Press secretary Ronald L. Ziegler said some 4,000 draftees already in South Vietnam, or with those holding current orders to go there, would not be affected by Nixon's decision to restrict war-zone service to drafted volunteers and regulars.

The White House spokesman said he had nothing new to report on the search for a negotiated Vietnam settlement.

However, he announced that Nixon will hold a television-radio news conference in the East Room of the White House Thursday night—a session at which the subject is certain to arise.

The President's news conference is scheduled for 9 p.m. EDT Thursday. It will be his first such appearance before live cameras and microphones since June 1, 1971. On Nov. 12, 1971, he had a news conference

(Continued on Back Page, Col. 4)

Once a Marine . . .

A Marine honor guard removes the flags from coffins containing the remains of five Marines killed in 1942 on Guadalcanal as they are buried at Arlington National Cemetery. The remains were discovered in 1970. Story, Page 9. (AP)

A Soldier At 16

GREELEY, Colo. (UPI)—The Army is trying to decide what to do with a 16-year-old boy who ran away from home when his family moved to Greeley, altered his birth certificate and joined the service. The boy's mother knows what she wants to do.

Mrs. Delores Van Nostrand, relieved to learn her son, Arthur, was at basic training at Ft. Dix, N.J., and not missing, said she would be willing to sign a waiver letting him stay in the Army.

Arthur telephoned his mother after a radio station in Boston,

(Continued on Back Page, Col. 2)

Viets Battle to Retake Quang Tri

Compiled From AP and UPI

SAIGON — Thousands of South Vietnamese marines, paratroopers and armored cavalrymen punched into Quang Tri Province Wednesday in their first counteroffensive against North Vietnamese occupation forces.

Elements of four North Vietnamese divisions have had two months to consolidate their hold on the province since it fell May 1, but field commanders advancing along a broad front were confident of retaking Quang Tri.

Asked if he expected to seize the province capitol, Marine Commandant Brig. Gen. Bui The Lan replied: "Maybe not only Quang Tri, maybe further than that. Today is a good day, tomorrow may be better."

He added; "I hope we run into heavy contact. We have to destroy the enemy first. They are strong."

A South Vietnamese spokesman said two brigades of paratroopers and two brigades of marines, backed by at least a pair of tank squadrons, crossed the My Chanh River northern defense line before dawn and pushed by evening up to five miles into Quang Tri Province.

Military sources said many other government units joined the original 10,000-man force during the day, but the South Vietnamese command clamped an embargo on news about the additional units.

The U.S. command said about 75 Air Force B52 Stratofortresses, America's biggest bombers, dumped tons of bombs on Quang Tri Province just ahead of the advancing troops.

The command said 30 other B52s struck in Thua Thien Province below the My Chanh River to keep the Communists from skirting around and attacking the rear of the advancing troops.

A command communique said smaller Air Force, Navy and Marine tactical fighters flew 152 air strikes during the day over provinces on both sides of the My Chanh River to support the new push.

The command said 17 U.S. cruisers and destroyers from the 7th Fleet in the Gulf of Tonkin turned their big guns shoreward to batter Communists in Quang Tri Province.

Lt. Col. Do Dang Bo, government military spokesman in upper South Vietnam, reported 235 Communists killed during the drive across the river and up into Quang Tri Province.

Bo said seven government sol-

(Continued on Back Page, Col. 1)

N. Viet Dikes:

Waldheim Says They're Being Hit; Rogers Issues an Angry Rebuttal

·UNITED NATIONS (AP)—Secretary-General Kurt Waldheim says he has received information through private channels that U.S. bombs have damaged dikes in North Vietnam both by direct hits and by nearby explosions.

He told a news conference Monday he has been assured by the U.S. government that the dikes were not a target, but that he was deeply concerned by word received through sources he would not identify.

Waldheim noted that he had expressed concern during his Moscow visit about published reports on the alleged bombing of the dikes and had made an appeal for a halt.

"I am deeply concerned," he said, "and I now appeal again for the stopping of this kind of bombing."

He said his informants said some bomb explosions near the dikes had caused

(Continued on Back Page, Col. 4)

KURT WALDHEIM

WASHINGTON (AP)—U.S. Secretary of State William P. Rogers sharply criticized U.N. Secretary-General Kurt Waldheim Monday for repeating allegations of U.S. bombing damaging the dikes in North Vietnam.

In an unusual statement following a news conference by Waldheim, Rogers said, "We cannot consider helpful any public statements giving further currency to these reports."

Rogers said that he has instructed U.S. Ambassador to the United Nations George Bush to seek an early appointment with Waldheim "again to point out that the information he has received concerning alleged deliberate bombing to damage the dikes in North Vietnam is false—as President Nixon stated in his June 29 press conference."

Rogers said he has asked Bush "to

(Continued on Back Page, Col. 1)

WILLIAM P. ROGERS

Senate Antiwar Vote
POW—PULLOUT PLAN

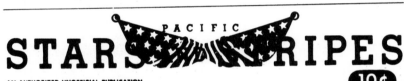

STARS PACIFIC STRIPES

AN AUTHORIZED UNOFFICIAL PUBLICATION
FOR THE U.S. ARMED FORCES OF THE PACIFIC COMMAND

10¢

Vol. 28, No. 207   Wednesday, July 26, 1972

WASHINGTON (UPI) — The Senate voted Monday the withdrawal of all U.S. forces "on land, sea, or air" from Indochina in exchange for the release of American prisoners of war.

In two critical votes, the Senate approved cutting off funds to maintain U.S. forces in Indochina in four months if the POWs are freed.

It was the first time that the Senate approved legislation cutting off funds for the Vietnam war. But it has passed policy statements in favor of ending the war by a certain date.

The Senate first voted 50 to 45 for cutting off the money and then overcame a last-moment effort by administration Republicans to kill the far-reaching antiwar amendment. That vote was 49 to 46.

Among the small group of senators absent for the votes was Sen. George S. McGovern, the Democratic presidential nominee who has long been an antiwar leader.

Chairman John C. Stennis, D-Miss., warned "this amendment could scuttle the Paris peace talks. Sensitive, delicate,

(Continued on Back Page, Col. 1)

Nice Try, Sticky-Fingers

COLUMBUS, Ohio (AP)—A thief would have gotten away from the house he was robbing except for one big slip.

After getting the television set and some other items, the thief tried to remove a ring from the finger of t h e sleeping homeowner. He used soap to slip the ring off, but only got himself arrested by awakening its owner. The home-owner then—for the police—put the finger on the thief.

BULLETIN

WASHINGTON (UPI) — The Senate voted Monday night to kill a $1.8 billion foreign military assistance bill nullifying adoption of the strongest antiwar amendment yet voted.

Ice Goes Like Hotcakes in NYC

Residents of the borough of Queens in New York City surge forward in an attempt to purchase blocks of dry ice during a power failure affecting more than 215,000 persons in the metropolitan area. The few people that were able to get the ice had to pay $8 a block. The blackout was caused by a failure of feeder cables in a Brooklyn electrical substation. Story on page 5.   (AP)

HOUSE REJECTS MOVE FOR VIET PULLOUT OCT. 1

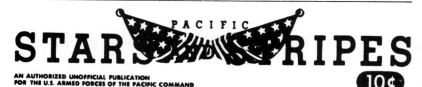

PACIFIC STARS AND STRIPES

AN AUTHORIZED UNOFFICIAL PUBLICATION
FOR THE U.S. ARMED FORCES OF THE PACIFIC COMMAND

10¢

Vol. 28, No. 224

Saturday, Aug. 12, 1972

Compiled From AP and UPI

WASHINGTON—In a victory for President Nixon, the House Thursday rejected a mandate to pull U.S. forces out of the Indochina war by Oct. 1 in return for release of American prisoners and a limited cease-fire.

By a vote of 228 to 178, the House maintained its position of never approving a measure setting a date for withdrawal of U.S. forces from Vietnam. By that vote, the House approved a move by Rep. Richard Bolling, D-Mo., to strike from a $2.1 billion military foreign aid bill an end-the-war provision added by the Foreign Affairs Committee, the first time that panel has done so.

The proviso would have ordered a halt to U.S. combat activity throughout Indochina and a total withdrawal of American forces by Oct. 1, subject only to a return of all prisoners, a verified accounting of missing in action, and a limited cease-fire to safeguard withdrawing Americans.

President Nixon's public negotiating offer to the Communists calls for a U.S. military withdrawal from South Vietnam four months after release of American prisoners and establishment of an internationally supervised cease-fire throughout Indochina.

Antiwar members suffered a tactical blow earlier in the day when they failed in their bill to change the amendment's deadline from Oct. 1 to Dec. 31 in an effort to attract additional support. Some of the House's most fervent opponents of the war joined with hawkish members to beat down the move, 304 to 109.

That defeat also apparently cost the amendment's supporters the backing of Speaker Carl Albert and Democratic Leader Hale Boggs, Louisiana, both of whom had voted for the date change.

Boggs told the House there was no chance the amendment could become law before Oct. 1 and "I'm not going to do a useless thing that could be misinterpreted around the world."

Albert never was heard from,
(Continued on Back Page, Col. 1)

Quang Tri Fight Rages On

SAIGON (AP) — South Vietnamese marines cleared the southern sector of Quang Tri City except for isolated snipers, field reports said Thursday, and South Vietnamese bomber pilots claimed they knocked out 14 enemy tanks six miles to the southwest.

But 400 North Vietnamese held firm in the northern half of Quang Tri City, including in the Citadel, according to the reports.

A communique issued at northern military headquarters in Hue said four supply trucks
(Continued on Back Page, Col. 1)

TV Extends In the Navy

By MARC HUET
S&S Washington Bureau

WASHINGTON — Television at sea, until now a luxury enjoyed only by men aboard the largest ships in the fleet, will be shared by the crews of another 135 warships under a new $9 million Navy program.

Starting in January the Navy will install closed circuit television systems aboard six ships a month to improve communications between admirals, ships captains and crewmen, as well as provide more news infor-
(Continued on Back Page, Col. 3)

What Big Ears You Have

They say that in the middle of an Iowa cornfield you can actually "hear" the corn growing. In St. George, Del., however, the Lester Farm owners could only hear the birds stripping the crop. So they hired live scarecrows—with guns— and stationed them on platforms throughout the fields. Another duty of the guards is to watch for passersby in cars who stop and help themselves to some big ears before they have a chance to get to the market. (AP)

BULLETIN

SAIGON (AP)—The U.S. command announced Friday that the lone remaining U.S. infantry unit in Vietnam is going home. The 3rd Bn., 21st Inf., will be leaving Da Nang Saturday.

Battle of Budget: Pentagon Fires at McGov

WASHINGTON (UPI) — The Pentagon accused Democratic presidential nominee George S. McGovern Thursday of flying in the face of reality with his suggestion that defense spending be cut by $30 billion.

In a 200-page counter-attack peppered with references to McGovern by name, the Defense Department said: "Those who suggest that we can solve our public spending problem by peeling some easy billions off the defense budget are arguing not only with the Pentagon but with reality, and reality is a formidable opponent."

McGovern has proposed to cut the defense budget —now an overall $82.3 billion —by $30 billion. He lost an initial test of the concept when the Senate last week refused to hold military spending for the new fiscal year to last year's level —a $4 billion cut.

The defense document, entitled "The Economics of Defense Spending: A Look at Realities," charged:

—It is a myth the defense budget keeps growing. In reality, it said, once inflation is discounted this year's defense budget is the lowest since 1951.

—It is a myth that more money is being poured into new weapons. In reality, it said, over the past nine years funds devoted to new weaponry rose only 4 per cent and, after discounting inflation, actually fell 24 per cent.

—It is a myth that McGovern's proposal to trim defense spending by $30 billion, or more than one-third, would convert the economy from a war to a peace base. Claiming the nation is on a war footing when defense takes up only 4 per cent of the economy is "torturing the English language," it said.

—It is a myth defense contractors soak the taxpayer for billions in unwarranted profits. In reality, the report said, a study by the Government Accounting Office showed profits on defense work were lower than the profits on commercial sales made by the same firms.

—It is a myth that cutting defense budget would vastly increase the funds available for social and economic programs.

In actuality, the document said, federal, state and local governments this year are already spending $275.6 billion on nondefense programs and this is expected to reach the $420-$480 billion range by 1978. "It is rather difficult to maintain," the report said, "that we could achieve wonders with, say, $500 billion to spend on social and economic programs —wonders which would somehow escape us if we had 'only' $480 billion to spend."

Kissinger and Rumors Are Flying

WASHINGTON (AP) — Presidential adviser Henry A. Kissinger and the North Vietnamese he has been meeting with secretly in Paris, Le Duc Tho, are heading for South and North Vietnam respectively.

The White House announced Tuesday that Kissinger is flying to Saigon for two days of talks with President Nguyen Van Thieu on the Vietnam war and negotiations for peace.

In Paris, a spokesman for the Viet Cong peace delegation confirmed that Le Duc Tho will leave Wednesday for Hanoi. He acts as special adviser to the North Vietnamese delegation in Paris.

The spokesman, Ly Van Sau, would make no further comment on Tho's trip but observers in Paris immediately connected it with Kissinger's mission and with the future of Thieu.

Press Secretary Ronald L. Ziegler said Kissinger will arrive in South Vietnam late Wednesday Saigon time, leave late Friday, and report back to President Nixon this weekend before the Republican National Convention opens in Miami Beach on Monday.

The much-traveled Kissinger has been in Switzerland visiting his parents after a secret session with North Vietnamese negotiators in Paris last Monday.

Ziegler said Kissinger is making his first trip to Saigon since July 1971, for "a general review of all aspects of the Vietnam problem, including the negotiations in Paris."

Kissinger is slated to confer with U.S. Ambassador Ellsworth Bunker and the U.S. commander in Vietnam, Gen.

(Continued on Back Page, Col. 3)

Strategy Puzzles Pentagon

Reds Send More Men South

PACIFIC

STARS AND STRIPES

10¢

AN AUTHORIZED UNOFFICIAL PUBLICATION
FOR THE U.S. ARMED FORCES OF THE PACIFIC COMMAND

Vol. 28, No. 229   Thursday, Aug. 17, 1972

WASHINGTON (UPI) — Pentagon officials say thousands of fresh North Vietnamese troops have crossed the Demilitarized Zone into South Vietnam during the past "week or so."

The new troop movements puzzled Defense Department analysts, who admit they don't quite know what to make of North Vietnam's strategy. They said the reinforcements barely offset the number of Communist troops killed in recent weeks.

"It looks like they're pouring good money after bad," said one expert. "You reinforce success. You don't reinforce failure, but it looks like that is what they are doing."

Defense Secretary Melvin R. Laird, while not referring directly to the report, said at a news conference in Miami Beach that the North Vietnamese "have the capacity for staging another spectacular." but he said he did not know when or where it would come.

However, he predicted the South Vietnamese, while they would suffer some defeats, would win a vast majority of their battles — "around 80 per cent."

(In a related subject, Laird said "extreme caution" was being used by U.S. pilots to (Continued on Back Page, Col. 1)

Fischer Ekes Out A Draw

REYKJAVIK (UPI) — Bobby Fischer and Boris Spassky traded blunders Tuesday night in the 14th game of their world chess championship then quickly agreed to a draw after the 40th move rather than adjourn the game.

Fischer, who had been denied advance money for the match and threatened with a million-dollar lawsuit, nearly lost the match on an error on the 20th move but laid a simple trap for the Russian world champion, who fell for it.

Fischer retained a full three-point lead in the $250,000 match, taking an 8½ to 5½ point advantage. The 15th game of the 24-game series is scheduled for Thursday.

Both players completed their 39th and 40th moves within seconds, then Spassky stretched out his hand and Fischer grabbed it. Scattered applause from a record 1,800 fans, including the Soviet ambassador and the mayor of Reykjavik, greeted them.

Fischer, who opened with his queen's bishop pawn and then made a protest to arbiter Lothar Schmid that the lighting was not bright enough, blundered on the 20th move by bringing his bishop (Continued on Back Page, Col. 1)

A South Vietnamese soldier warily surveys the ruins of Quang Tri City from the second floor of a shattered house. He was watching for enemy troops in other buildings. (AP)

Jane's Films Shot Down

BORGER, Tex. (UPI) — A drive-in theater manager has canceled plans to screen the movie "They Shoot Horses, Don't They?" starring actress Jane Fonda in protest of her recent trip to Hanoi.

C. M. Shearer, manager of the Buena Vista Drive-In, said Monday he would run a film about motorcycle gangs titled "Chrome and Hot Leather" in place of Miss Fonda's film.

"We kicked this picture around for about a year trying to decide what was the best thing to do," Shearer said. "We have now decided it is only fitting to discontinue showing Jane Fonda films."

Mobbed by Relatives in NYC

3 POWs Back in Full Uniform

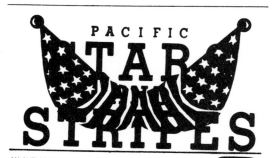

AN AUTHORIZED UNOFFICIAL PUBLICATION
FOR THE U.S. ARMED FORCES OF THE PACIFIC COMMAND

10¢

Vol. 28, No. 273   Saturday, Sept. 30, 1972

Panel May Call McCain

Pilot: Navy Flew Illegal Strikes

Compiled From AP and UPI

WASHINGTON — A former pilot implicated the Navy Thursday in unauthorized bombing attacks on North Vietnam, senators said.

"If this fellow's testimony was right," said Sen. Stuart Symington, D-Mo., "more than one service was involved in preplanned bombing raids regardless of reaction."

"I am greatly disturbed by what I heard," said Sen. Richard Schweiker, R-Pa., after listening to William Groepper, a former Navy lieutenant and A7 Corsair pilot, at the closed-door inquiry of the Senate Armed Services Committee.

Schweiker said the allegation should be traced up the chain of command.

"I think we should talk to McCain," he said, referring to Adm. John McCain, who at the time was the overall Pacific and Indochina air war commander.

The probe had focused on the firing of Air Force Lt. Gen. John D. Lavelle for unauthorized raids he ordered last November through March, before the White House ordered renewed heavy bombing of North Vietnam. The inquiry has also been into civilian control of the military.

Under the "protective reaction" rules of the air war, aircraft escorting reconnaissance planes could only attack air defense targets if there was
(Continued on Back Page, Col. 1)

Tanaka, Chou Seal Relations

PEKING (AP) — Prime Minister Chou En-lai announced Thursday night that China and Japan have decided to establish diplomatic relations and terminate the state of war between the two countries.

The 74-year-old premier said in a farewell toast at a glittering banquet in the Hall of the People given by Prime Minister

Related Story, Page 6

Kakuei Tanaka of Japan that this historic step will make a "positive contribution" to the relaxation of tension in Asia and to world peace.

Tanaka, 54, who arrived here Sunday on state visit, said normalization of relations is only
(Continued on Back Page, Col. 4)

Air Force Maj. Edward Elias is kissed by his wife, Georgia, upon his return to the U.S. Thursday night in New York. He was one of three freed POW's.   (AP)

That's David, Capital D-a-

HONOLULU (AP) — Kekoa Kaapu, a candidate for mayor here, might have problems getting voters to remember him if he used his full name.

His full name is Kekoalauli-ionapalihauliuliokekoolau David Kaapuawaokamehameha.

The first name means "The fine-leafed koa tree on the verdant cliffs of the Koolau Mountains," and the last name means "the awa-cup bearer of Kamehameha the great."

Compiled From AP and UPI

NEW YORK — Three Ar... ...in prisoners of war came home from Hano. in full uniform Thursday night, dramatically displaying the decorations they had won as combat pilots in North Vietnam.

They landed at Kennedy Airport at 6:54 p.m. and 30 minutes later voluntarily entered Defense Department cars to be driven away. By so doing, they submitted to a reunion with the government whose overtures they had spurned during the long trip from Hanoi.

Behind them they left a quartet of American antiwar activists, into whose hands the POWs were delivered 12 days ago in North Vietnam.

"We have just witnessed a recapture scene," said one of their former chaperones, Cora Weiss, "one incarceration replacing another."

Another, the Rev. William Sloane Coffin, said: "It's quite clear the Pentagon and State Department want men released only if they are in uniform and speaking their lines."

However, the three POWs were reported as having voted among themselves and agreed to don the uniforms while enroute from Copenhagen aboard a Scandinavian Airlines System transatlantic jetliner. The uniforms had been put aboard during a stop in Moscow. A military tailor reportedly was aboard to assure a good fit.
(Continued on Back Page, Col. 1)

Moving, American Style—It's a Drag

NEW HAVEN, Conn. (AP) — Psychiatrists say moving is far more stressful than generally believed and is a contributing factor in depression among American women.

"When you ask a bunch of depressed people about events that have occurred in their life recently, moving was about the third most frequent event," says Myrna M. Weissman, codirector of Yale University's Depression Research Unit.

"In no way should we say that depression is caused by moving," she says. "It could be a contributing factor; we feel it is substantial."

Dr. Weissman's studies, outlined in "Society" and the Yale Alumni Magazine, dealt with depressed women. Those women who had been through a move generally didn't connect their illness to the move, Dr. Weissman and coworker Eugene S. Paykel wrote.

The women attributed it, instead, to financial problems, loneliness, marital friction, career frustrations, etc., but "almost always, however, these problems were the result of poor adaptation to the stresses
(Continued on Back Page, Col. 5)

Thieu Calls Urgent Talks

Viet Cease-Fire Rumors Fly

PACIFIC
STARS STRIPES
10¢
AN AUTHORIZED UNOFFICIAL PUBLICATION
FOR THE U.S. ARMED FORCES OF THE PACIFIC COMMAND

Vol. 28, No. 288   Sunday, Oct. 15, 1972

WASHINGTON (AP) — President Nguyen Van Thieu has summoned the chief of South Vietnam's Paris peace talks delegation and the ambassador to Washington to Saigon for urgent consultations concerning negotiations aimed at a Vietnam settlement, official spokesmen in Saigon announced Saturday.

The South Vietnamese Foreign Ministry said that Ambassador Pham Dang Lam had been recalled from Paris and Ambassador Tran Kim Phuong from Washington. A spokesman said he had no specific details.

There also were reports that the South Vietnamese ambassador to London, Vuong Van Bac, also had been summoned back to Saigon, but the Foreign Ministry said it could not confirm this.

Rumors were circulating in Washington that an internationally supervised cease-fire has been agreed upon at the private talks in Paris. According to these rumors making the rounds, China, Russia and France would serve as the supervisors of the cease-fire.

"I have no information on this," said the South Vietnamese Foreign Ministry spokesman in Saigon. "Rumors are all over. The ambassadors are being called back to Saigon to clear up speculation and other problems."

The settlement also was reported to include a variation of a three-segment government which would include representatives of the Thieu regime, South Vietnam neutralists and members of the National Liberation Front, the political arm of the Viet Cong.

This coalition would prepare for a general election to be held in South Vietnam to determine its future form of government.

State Department officials warned against speculation that minimized the difficulties ahead in reaching any kind of settlement.

Le Duc Tho, it was noted, pointed out the difficulties still to be surmounted and U.S. Presidential Press Secretary Ronald L. Ziegler said he would not challenge Tho's assessment.

The slight crack in the official wall of secrecy surrounding the negotiations appeared after Kissinger and his top assistant, Gen. Alexander M. Haig Jr., reported to Nixon and Secretary of State William P. Rogers on their talks with North Vietnamese negotiators Xuan Thuy and Tho.

When Tho, a member of the North Vietnamese Politburo, left Paris Friday for Moscow and Hanoi he reportedly told Chinese and Russian officials at Orly Airport that there still are many difficult things to settle.

At the White House, Ziegler
(Continued on Back Page, Col. 1)

PRESIDENT NIXON AND HENRY KISSINGER CONFER AT BREAKFAST   UPI

33 Hurt in Racial Clash Aboard Carrier Kitty Hawk

HONOLULU (AP) — A fight involving black and white sailors aboard the attack aircraft carrier Kitty Hawk off Vietnam Thursday left 33 men injured, three seriously, the Pacific Fleet Command reported Friday.

Two of the injured were flown to shore-based hospitals for treatment and another was scheduled to be flown ashore, a Navy spokesman said. The remainder were treated for minor injuries aboard the ship and re-

turned to duty, he said.

The Navy said "order has been fully restored" aboard the carrier and that it is "continuing to perform its mission at Yankee Station" in the Tonkin Gulf.

The Kitty Hawk commanding officer, Capt. Marlin W. Townsend Jr. of Washington, D.C., and the executive officer, Cmdr.

Benjamin W. Cloud, of El Cajon, Calif., have talked to the crewmen about the incident in hopes of learning what caused it and to prevent a recurrence, the spokesman said.

Other Navy officials are also investigating.

Further details on the incident were not immediately available, the spokesman said.

Lot of Green for Green

LOS ANGELES (AP) — The city fathers of San Pedro, near Los Angeles, are uprooting imitation plants and shrubs and replacing them with natural vegetation. The plastic trees and plants were planted three years ago. The cost was $50,000. The imitation plants just didn't hold up. It is hoped that the natural plants will prove to be more durable.

Nixon Gets Defense Bill

WASHINGTON (AP) — The Senate passed by voice vote and sent to President Nixon Friday a compromise $74.3 billion defense appropriation bill.

Although one of the largest Pentagon money bills in history, it is $5.2 billion less than the amount requested by President Nixon.

In a related action Thursday, the Senate passed and sent to the White House a separate $2.3-
(Continued on Back Page, Col. 4)

350-Lb. Porker Wins Presidential Race

By The Associated Press

Voters, do you find the electioneering a bit dreary, the speechmaking too straight-faced in this campaign year? Don't despair — there's still a presidential pig race in Portland, Ore.

And a motorcycle-riding candidate whose mother writes speeches for him. And another who offered himself to voters as a Valentine. And another with a campaign worker accused of stealing slippers while canvassing.

As a rule, the 1972 campaign season hasn't exactly left them rolling in the aisles. But there have been some events to provoke a giggle, if not the outright guffaw.

The Portland presidential pig race featured two 350-pound hogs clad in red-white-and-blue blankets, one bearing a McGovern

sign, the other a Nixon sign. The Nixon pig waddled across the finish line first, but it was close.

Dakin Williams, brother of playwright Tennessee Williams, read speeches written by his mother and distributed photos of himself aboard a motorcycle "revving up" for his campaign. But a state court ruled that the American Party didn't qualify for the Illinois ballot and Williams is out of the race for U.S. Senate.

Democratic Rep. Ken Hechler, who manipulates a pink jeep around the hills and hollows of West Virginia in his search for votes, went on television seated on a cushion with a huge Valentine under his chin. "Voters in the 4th District, will you be my Valentine?" he asked. He won the primary.
(Continued on Back Page, Col. 2)

'PEACE AT HAND'

* * * * * * * * * * * * * * *

Matter of Weeks: Kissinger

PACIFIC

STAR ~~~ RIPES

AN AUTHORIZED UNOFFICIAL PUBLICATION
FOR THE U.S. ARMED FORCES OF THE PACIFIC COMMAND

10¢

Vol. 28, No. 301   Saturday, Oct. 28, 1972

Shipping Strike on W. Coast

SAN FRANCISCO (UPI)—Deck officers went on strike Wednesday in Pacific Coast ports, threatening "creeping paralysis" of the American maritime fleet on the West Coast and Hawaii.

The Federal Mediation Service summoned both sides to a meeting in Washington, D.C., Thursday in an effort to settle the strike by the 10,000-member Masters, Mates and Pilots Union.

Foreign flag vessels were not affected by the strike, which came less than nine months after settlement of a 135-day West Coast longshoremen's walkout.

Member companies of the Pacific Maritime Association and Grace Lines, Seatrain and Sea-Land were hit by the strike, called when 4 1-2 months of negotiations over a new labor contract broke down.

The major issue in the strike is an employer proposal to use money from the pension fund to train junior officers whose ranks are threatened by growing automation in the industry.

Pickets were posted at the vessel Japan Bear in San Francisco at dawn, and deck officers on American flag ships went on strike as their ships (Continued on Back Page, Col. 5)

Presidential adviser Henry Kissinger adjusts his glasses as he tells newsmen in Washington that "peace is at hand" in Vietnam.
(AP)

Compiled From AP and UPI

WASHINGTON – Presidential adviser Henry Kissinger said Thursday "peace is at hand" in Vietnam.

Kissinger announced that a settlement of the Vietnam war, the longest in U.S. history, could be signed "within a matter of weeks or less."

In Huntington, W. Va., President Nixon said Thursday night he is confident that differences blocking a final Vietnam peace settlement "can and will be worked out."

Speaking for the first time publicly about what he termed "a significant breakthrough" in the Vietnam negotiations, Nixon told an airport rally that, "I am confident we will succeed in achieving our objective—peace with honor and not peace with surrender in Vietnam."

Dismissing North Vietnamese charges of stalling, Kissinger said Hanoi had been asked to join in one final negotiating session to resolve all remaining differences in the way of a cease-fire.

The agreement already reached, disclosed by Hanoi and confirmed by Kissinger at a news briefing Thursday,

Related stories, Pages 3, 5 and 6

calls for a total U.S. troop withdrawal and prisoner release within 60 days after the accord is signed.

North Vietnam, in breakthrough concessions Oct. 8 in Paris, dropped its demand for the overthrow of the Thieu regime in Saigon in favor of a three-part coalition government.

A Hanoi Radio broadcast Thursday said the United States had agreed to sign a peace pact in Paris next Tuesday, but then backed off and asked for further negotiations, saying it was having difficulty getting Saigon to go along.

In the first Saigon reaction, the government's official radio said: "A separate agreement between North Vietnam and the United States does not concern us in any way. We in South Vietnam have the right to self-determination," the commentator said.

Kissinger told newsmen during an hour-long briefing that the United States and North Vietnam have agreed on most major provisions of a settlement.

But Kissinger said that one more negotiating session "lasting no more than three or four days" is necessary.

It could still be after the first of the year before all (Continued on Back Page, Col. 1)

Terms of Proposed Vietnam Peace Plan

HONG KONG (AP) — This is North Vietnam's summary of the peace terms it says it and the United States agreed to, and which Henry Kissinger has confirmed:

1. The United States will respect the independence, sovereignty, unification and territorial integrity of Vietnam.

2. The United States will stop all bombing of North Vietnam and all mining of North Vietnamese waters. Twenty-four hours after the peace agreement is signed, a cease-fire will take effect in all of South Vietnam. All American and allied troops will be withdrawn within 60 days.

3. After signing, steps will be taken for the immediate return of prisoners of war held by both sides.

4. At cease-fire, the two present administrations in South Vietnam (the South Vietnamese government and the Viet Cong) will negotiate with each other to set up elections for a national coalition government. The two administrations will also negotiate with each other on dis-

position and reduction of the troops of each side.

5. Unification of North and South Vietnam will be "realized gradually by peaceful means."

6. An international committee on military control and supervision will be formed and an international conference on Vietnam will be called within 30 days of the signing of the peace agreement.

7. The sovereignty and neutrality of Cambodia and Laos will be recognized by all parties in the Vietnam War. The

United States will end all military activities in Laos and Cambodia, withdraw all troops and not reintroduce troops or weapons into Laos and Cambodia.

8. Ending of the war will create conditions for establishment of relations between the United States and North Vietnam under which the United States will contribute to reconstruction in North Vietnam and throughout all Indochina.

9. The peace agreement will take effect immediately upon being signed by the U.S. and North Vietnam.

AT&T Wins Approval For $145 Mil. Rate Hike

WASHINGTON (UPI)—The Federal Communications Commission Wednesday authorized American Telephone & Telegraph Co. to raise annual long-distance telephone rates by $145 million for a total of $395 million in rate increases since January, 1971.

The seven-member commission gave AT&T 30 days to say how it plans to implement the higher rates. But it was not known when they actually would take effect.

The decision was announced at the conclusion of a late Thanksgiving eve commission meeting exactly two years and two days after AT&T first requested an increase of $546 million, which was de-
(Continued on Back Page, Col. 1)

PACIFIC STAR STRIPES

AN AUTHORIZED UNOFFICIAL PUBLICATION
FOR THE U.S. ARMED FORCES OF THE PACIFIC COMMAND

10¢

Vol. 28, No. 328   Friday, Nov. 24, 1972

Crew of 6 Rescued

FIRST B52 SHOT DOWN

Compiled From AP and UPI

SAIGON — The United States lost its first B52 bomber to enemy fire in the Vietnam war Wednesday and disclosed that another $15-million, F111 fighter-bomber had vanished, the fourth in less than two months, on a mission over North Vietnam.

While the U.S. command here declined to say what caused the B52 loss, military sources' here and in Washington said the big plane was hit by enemy fire during the heaviest B52 raids of the war over North Vietnam.

The eight-engine stratofortress crashed near Nakhon Phanom in eastern Thailand shortly before midnight while trying to make it back to its base at Utapao, 400 miles to the southwest. All six crewmen bailed out and were rescued, the command said.

Command spokesmen said the cause was not determined but other sources said the plane was believed to have been hit by a Soviet-built SAM missile during a bombing run near Vinh, a North Vietnamese coastal city. It was able to fly about 100 miles before the crew was forced to abandon the plane.

Sources said Wednesday's crash was being officially listed as a "combat loss," meaning that it was downed by hostile fire.

It was the first of the huge $8 million Strategic Air Command Stratofortresses lost to enemy fire in the seven years they have been flying missions in Indochina Several have been hit by ground fire and at least 10 have crashed from operational causes. There are about 150 B52s operating out of Guam and 55 out of Thailand.

An announcement by the U.S. command said, "A U. S. Air Force B52 crashed shortly be-
(Continued on back Page, Col. 1)

Sometimes, War's Swell

These Cambodian soldiers have plenty to smile about as a pretty female joins them aboard a truck headed out to an operation along Route 5, north of Phnom Penh. Cambodian women serve with the Khmer Army and usually perform such duties as cooks, medics and radio operators. (AP)

Nixon OKs Ships, Jets To China

THURMONT, Md. (AP) — President Nixon lifted a rigid government ban Wednesday on travel of U.S. aircraft and ships to Communist China.

The action, announced by a spokesman at Nixon's Camp David, Md., retreat, is a first step toward eventual establishment of scheduled air and sea service to the long-isolated Communist superpower.

The changes in government regulations do not automatically, however, clear the way for scheduled service. A complicated set of details still must be worked out before U.S. airlines can routinely land in such cities as Peking, said press secretary Ronald L. Ziegler.

Officials said Commerce Department approval still would be required before U.S. airlines could begin service to China. Also required would be approv-
(Continued on Back Page, Col. 2)

Value Added Taxes Motorist

NEW YORK (AP)—That was no quarter George Roth realized in panic, after he put a coin in a New York City parking meter last week. It was a two-cent piece—a rare U.S. coin minted in 1864 and valued at about $30.

Roth appealed to the parking meter people in the city finance department. The coin was located Wednesday, and Roth got it back after paying 25 cents for the meter and five cents for legal penalty and interest.

Army Sent Wrong Body Home—Mom

BUFFALO, N.Y. (AP) — The mother of a U.S. Army private supposedly killed in a traffic accident in Germany last week says the body sent here by the Army for burial was not the body of her son.

Mrs. Marcella Smith said Tuesday she received a telegram from the Army Nov. 13 informing her that her son, Pvt. Lott D. Smith, 21, had been killed in a traffic accident that day.

Smith was assigned to the 8th Inf. Div.

On Nov. 16, Mrs. Smith received another telegram, this one from the Army's Memorial Affairs Agency in Washington, D.C., informing her that her son's body had arrived in New York City and instructing her to make arrangements for burial.

The body arrived here the next day under military escort. When Mrs. Smith saw it, she said it was not her son.

Other members of the family viewed the body at a funeral home and said the same thing: the body was not that of Lott D. Smith.

Mrs. Smith has refused to sign a release stating that the body is that of her son.

Army officials said Smith was identified by his commanding officer in Germany and that it was
(Continued on Back Page, Col. 2)

NIXON HALTS BOMBS: HANOI TO NEGOTIATE

PACIFIC STARS & STRIPES

AN AUTHORIZED UNOFFICIAL PUBLICATION
FOR THE U.S. ARMED FORCES OF THE PACIFIC COMMAND

10¢

Vol. 29, No. 1   Monday, Jan. 1, 1973

WASHINGTON (AP) — President Nixon halted the massive bombing of North Vietnam's heartland Saturday after North Vietnam agreed to resume "serious negotiations" with Henry Kissinger on Jan. 8.

The White House announcement came against a backdrop of protests at home and abroad of the war's heaviest raids on the Hanoi - Haiphong complex. And it apparently followed a clear signal from Hanoi's leaders that they are ready

Related stories, Pages 4, 5, 6

to bargain earnestly with Kissinger, Nixon's assistant for national security affairs.

Deputy press secretary Gerald L. Warren announced that Kissinger's negotiations with North Vietnam's Le Duc Tho and Xuan Thuy would resume (Continued on Back Page, Col. 1)

Everglades Disaster

93 of 177 Survive Crash

Compiled From AP and UPI

MIAMI, Fla. — The watery terrain of the Everglades apparently cushioned the crash of a giant Eastern Air Lines Tristar jet and was responsible for the "almost incredible" survival of 93 of the 177 persons aboard, a federal official said Saturday.

Eighty-four were believed dead in the crash, the worst domestic air disaster of 1972.

John H. Reed, chairman of the National Transportation Safety Board, visited the wilderness area 20 miles west of Miami where the Lockheed L1011 jet went down Friday

Related stories, Page 3

night and said that the 93 apparently lived because of the "nature of the terrain, the water in the Everglades environment. This cushioned the impact."

Among the passengers aboard the New York-to-Miami flight were a number of babies, airline officials said.

The Coast Guard said the survivors were pulled from the wreck and surrounding water and muck by crews who toiled through the black night in mud that sometimes reached their waists.

The three-engine, $18 million plane, which can carry 226 passengers, had been cleared for landing at Miami International Airport when it disappeared from the radar screens at 11:42 p.m. EST Friday and smashed (Continued on Back Page, Col. 1)

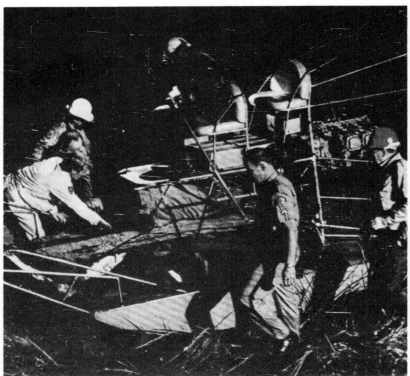

Rescue workers remove an injured victim (in blanket) from an air boat which brought him from the scene of the crash of an Eastern Air Lines TriStar in the Florida Everglades. Eighty-four of the 177 aboard the plane were believed dead in the Friday night crash. The plane was approaching Miami International Airport when it fell into the swampy terrain. (UPI)

Panel Rejects Pension Raise

WASHINGTON (UPI) —A House subcommittee Friday rejected a proposed increase in military pensions on grounds the estimated long-term $137 billion cost would endanger other Defense Department spending or else require an increase in taxes.

The subcommittee on retired-pay revisions reported that "after the most careful consideration," it recommended the parent Armed Services Committee drop the proposal.

The proposal would have allowed retired military people to base their retired pay on the (Continued on Back Page, Col. 4)

Stars & Stripes Takes a Holiday

Because of the Jan. 1 holiday, there will be no *Pacific Stars & Stripes* dated Jan. 2. This is the only day of the year on which the paper is not published.

Normal schedules will be resumed with editions dated Wednesday, Jan. 3.

Today's editions contain four pages of comics.

U.S. BARES BLUEPRINTS FOR 'PEACE THAT HEALS'

PACIFIC STARS STRIPES

10¢

AN AUTHORIZED UNOFFICIAL PUBLICATION
FOR THE U.S. ARMED FORCES OF THE PACIFIC COMMAND

Vol. 29, No. 25　　　　　　　Friday, Jan. 26, 1973

WASHINGTON (AP) — Washington a n d Hanoi unveiled Wednesday the terms of an intricate peace accord to end America's longest war, and negotiator Henry A. Kissinger expressed confidence a Saturday cease-fire in South Vietnam would later spread across all of Indochina.

But Kissinger, explaining that the U.S. seeks "a peace that heals," and his North Vietnamese negotiating counterpart said there were no secret peace terms.

The chief U.S. negotiator made these other major points in his 90-minute White House news conference:

—About 145,000 North Vietnamese troops remain in South Vietnam, but Kissinger said their numbers "should over a period of time be subject to considerable reduction" because they cannot be reinforced, resupplied or replaced.

—The release of American prisoners of war held in North Vietnam and Laos will begin by mid-February in Hanoi and will be completed at 15-day intervals during the 60-day period when U.S. troops are being withdrawn from the South.

—The political independence of South Vietnam is guaranteed and its future form, including the fate of President Nguyen

Related stories, Pages 2, 3, 4, 6; chronology of war, text of President Nixon's cease-fire address, Pages 12, 13.

Van Thieu's government, will be determined, without outside interference, by the South Vietnamese themselves.

—A National Council on National Reconciliation and Concord will be organized among the South Vietnamese themselves on a three-part basis solely to organize the elections and implementation of the agreement, not to act in any way as a coalition government.

—The demilitarized zone continues as a temporary military demarcation line which cannot be violated under any circumstances by military forces of either side, Kissinger said. Neither Cambodia or Laos can be used as infiltration routes or as bases for foreign troops, he said.

—The agreement in no way restricts U.S. military forces off Vietnam's shores or in Thailand, he said. "The deployment would be more geared to the war situation" than to anticipation of an established peace, Kissinger added.

—Discussion of U.S. economic aid to all of Indochina, including North Vietnam, will come "only after the signature of the agreement and after its implemention is well ad-
(Continued on Back Page, Col. 1)

Trade Set at Saturday Signing

U.S., Hanoi to Swap POW Lists

Compiled From AP and UPI

SAIGON — The United States will be given a list of American prisoners of war Saturday when a Vietnam peace treaty is signed in Paris, according to details of the agreement disclosed by Radio Hanoi Wednesday night.

"Lists of prisoners will be exchanged on the date the agreement is signed," Radio Hanoi said.

The agreement provides for a return of military and civilian prisoners to be completed within 60 days of the signing, or by March 27, Radio Hanoi said.

"Information regarding missing and dead will be sought with assistance from all sides," Radio Hanoi reported.

In Washington Henry Kissinger said Wednesday the first Americans freed from prison camps in Southeast Asia will fly out of Hanoi aboard a U.S. Air Force jet within 15 days after the cease-fire agreement is signed Saturday.

Defense Department sources said the initial family reunions probably will take place within 10 days of the first release.

Under terms of the cease-fire, the first returnees will include persons who are seriously ill, wounded or maimed, old persons and women. Most will be military personnel but some could be civilians.

Officials at the Defense and State Departments have identified 587 U.S. military personnel and about 40 American civilians as prisoners of war in Southeast Asia. An additional 1,335 servicemen and 11 civilians are listed as missing. Some of them may be captives.

The only two American women on the list are missionaries — Dr. Eleanor Vietti, a Houston, Tex., physician who was taken prisoner in 1962, and Betty Ann Olsen of Meadowbrook, Pa., who
(Continued on Back Page, Col. 2)

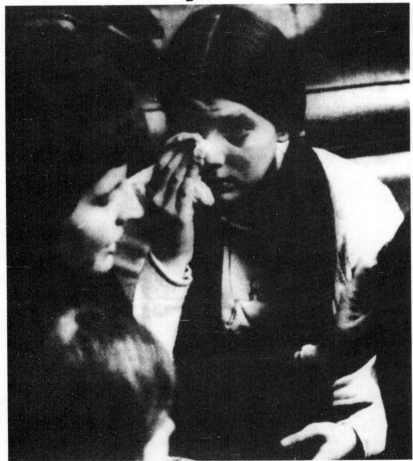

Debbie Christian, 13, daughter of Lt. Cmdr. and Mrs. Mike Christian of Virginia Beach, Va., wipes the tears from her eyes after hearing the news of a cease-fire in Vietnam. Debbie can't remember her father, a Navy flier, who has been a POW for more than six years. (AP)

Army Freezes Orders; No More GIs to Vietnam

WASHINGTON (UPI) — The Army Wednesday cancelled all orders for Vietnam "effective immediately" because of the cease-fire scheduled to be signed in Paris Saturday.

"No individual will be permitted to return or continue to RVN (the Republic of Vietnam) without prior Department of the Army clearance," the order said. An Army spokesman said he could think of no circumstances under which such clearance would be given.

The spokesman said the order would have an immediate effect on "about 2,000" officers and enlisted men who already had received orders to proceed to Vietnam.

He said some of these personnel were on leave and would have to be contacted either by their former home bases or receive the order via the news media.

"It's particularly important to reach those people who are in transit right now," the spokesman said.

Army personnel are granted 30 days of leave before their departure to Vietnam. In most cases, the spokesman said, the Army has on file a telephone number where men on leave can be reached. He said any men with Vietnam orders who
(Continued on Back Page, Col. 2)

PACIFIC STAR STRIPES

10¢

Vol. 29, No. 26   AN AUTHORIZED UNOFFICIAL PUBLICATION FOR THE U.S. ARMED FORCES OF THE PACIFIC COMMAND   Saturday, Jan. 27, 1973

Battles Before Cease-Fire

GI Killed as Reds Shell Base

Compiled From AP and UPI

SAIGON—An American Marine was killed and 21 other Americans were wounded early Friday morning when 22 Communist rockets hit Bien Hoa Air Base, 14 miles northeast of Saigon, with the planned cease-fire only two days away, military spokesmen said.

The unidentified American killed may be the last to die in the Vietnam war. A cease-fire is to become effective at 8 a.m. Sunday, Saigon time.

Spokesmen said initial reports showed only the number of casualties and rockets and that the attack happened "sometime since midnight." Two Vietnamese civilians were killed and six injured in homes outside the base.

The war surged on the ground and in the air Thursday.

American B52 strikes rattled windows in Saigon while fighter-bombers and helicopters continued their "war as usual" rou-

Related stories, Pages 2, 3, 4, and 6; text of peace settlement, Pages 12 and 13.

tines. The Communists invaded a village 50 miles from the capital, poured 4,000 shells onto South Vietnamese troops in Quang Tri Province and attacked an infantry unit in the Mekong Delta.

Ironically, a U.S. Army helicopter unit at Bien Hoa had begun the process of transforming its aircraft from a war-time role to a peacekeeping role in Vietnam in preparation for the cease-fire.

The helicopters and American crewmen are being assigned to support joint military commissions and an international commission in implementing the truce.

Helicopters, that once ripped through North Vietnamese and Viet Cong positions with rockets and bullets, were being altered to carry the Communist representatives who will join American and South Vietnamese on four-party joint military commissions.

Distinguished by vertical white stripes from nose to tail
(Continued on Back Page, Col. 3)

Earth's Heavy Artillery

Smoke and ashes rise above the Icelandic Westman Islands in this aerial photo of the island of Heymaey. The town of Vestmannaeyjar is at center, just below the smoke spiral. All 5,000 residents of the town have been evacuated to Reykjavik. Lava from the volcano has formed a new hill 328 feet above sea level. Fears grew that the town may be destroyed. **(AP)**

Others Will Help —Thieu

Compiled From AP and UPI

SAIGON — President Nguyen Van Thieu predicted Thursday that many nations will join South Vietnam in fighting the Communists if they violate the cease-fire and wage new war.

Thieu made the prediction when asked whether he felt confident that South Vietnam could successfully fight the Communists after the Americans leave, in the event of renewed hostilities.

"I think that if the Communists violate the cease-fire and if they wage new war, the war will re-begin with new conditions. Not only the Vietnamese people will fight, but I think the war will have the participation of many other ones," he said.

Asked specifically whether he had a promise of help from the United States if the war resumes, Thieu replied: "Let's see in a few days." He then added he could not disclose his understanding with the United States.

Thieu spoke to newsmen after an hour-and-a-half address to 500 information cadres who will fan out throughout the country to inform the Vietnamese people about the cease-fire.

Thieu's refusal to elaborate on what he meant when he said
(Continued on Back Page, Col. 3)

More Than War At Steak . . .

NEW YORK (UPI) — American Vegetarians Inc. Thursday asked for a "worldwide cease-fire on animals" to coincide with the Vietnam cease-fire.

"We can all stop today hunting, slaughtering, eating, wearing, and experimenting on billions of animals each year," a spokesman for the group, Robert Pinkus, said.

"We cannot remain at peace as long as we exploit animals for food, clothing, medical research and sport," he said.

It's What's Happening, POW, Baby...

WASHINGTON (AP) — "Hey, big daddy," says a Pentagon pamphlet for returning prisoners of war, "when your young son or daughter comes to you and says, 'Do you dig?' you can say, 'Lay it on me dude, and right on.'"

The pamphlet is a dictionary of slang expressions to help POWs—some of whom haven't been home in eight years—understand the language of today's youth.

The head of a household, advises the pamphlet, is "big daddy." Being high on either drugs or alcohol is "blasted," while to focus attention on something is to "tune in."

"This is a part of the language and the slang being used by the youth of today—your sons and daughters," says the pamphlet.

The POWs also can be expected to be unaware that Americans first landed on the moon July 20, 1969; that Richard Nixon was elected in 1968 and re-elected in 1972, or that "U.S. infantry troops entered the South Vietnamese village of Song My (My Lai) in March 1968 and murdered 450 civilians."

Summaries such as the latter are included in the pamphlet to bring the prisoners up to date on major events, sports highlights and deaths of prominent individuals since 1965.

The pamphlets will be handed
(Continued on Back Page, Col. 4)

IT'S ALL OVER

★ ★ ★ ★ ★ ★ ★ ★ ★ ★ ★ ★

Thieu Sends Thanks to America

PACIFIC STAR AND STRIPES

AN AUTHORIZED UNOFFICIAL PUBLICATION
FOR THE U.S. ARMED FORCES OF THE PACIFIC COMMAND

10¢

Vol. 29, No. 28   Monday, Jan. 29, 1973

Peace Brings End to Draft 5 Mos. Early

WASHINGTON (AP)—Secretary of Defense Melvin R. Laird announced Saturday that "use of the draft has ended."

His action, placing the nation's armed forces on an all-volunteer footing for the first time in nearly 25 years, came five months ahead of President Nixon's goal.

In a message to senior defense officials, Laird said:

"With the signing of the peace agreement in Paris today, and after receiving a report from the secretary of the Army that he foresees no need for further inductions, I wish to inform you that the armed forces henceforth will depend exclusively on volunteer soldiers, sailors, airmen and marines."

Laird's decision cancels plans to draft about 5,000 men before next June 30, when legal authority to induct young men into the armed forces will expire.

Pentagon manpower officials said that the flow of volunteers, spurred by a series of military pay raises and improved fringe benefits, has encouraged them

(Continued on Back Page, Col. 3)

GI, Civilian Hikes Thawed

By MARC HUET
S&S Washington Bureau

WASHINGTON — The Defense Department Saturday announced the end of the military and civilian promotion freeze effective Feb. 1. The Pentagon also said the ban on hiring civilian employes is also lifted.

Deputy Defense Secretary Kenneth Rush, in a memo to the Army, Navy and Air Force, said hiring and promotions are authorized in line with President Nixon's 1974 budget.

"The austerity of the funding levels in that budget will require your continued attention to insure that only those personnel (Continued on Back Page, Col. 2)

Groovin' With Mao

OMAHA (AP) — An Omaha teen-ager wrote Chinese Premier Chou En-lai that he thought China's national anthem was "groovy." Eighteen-year-old John Pirnot received a recording of the anthem from Peking — along with a bill for 40 cents. John says: "I was really surprised. I'm glad someone cared enough to help me."

Secretary of State William P. Rogers signs the peace agreement in Paris to end the Vietnam war. The U.S. delegation includes (from left) William Sullivan, deputy secretary of state for Southeast Asian affairs; Ambassador William Porter; Assistant Secretary of State Marshall Green (partially hidden); and acting chief of the U.S. delegation at the talks, Hayward Isham. (AP)

Compiled From AP and UPI

SAIGON — The Vietnam war ended Sunday. It came to a halt at 8 a.m. as a cease-fire agreement went into effect.

Church bells rang out and the Saigon government voiced its gratitude to the Americans who helped it survive.

The cease-fire was underwritten

Related stories Pages 2, 3, 4, 6

a dozen hours earlier by the signing of peace agreements in Paris. A night of deadly fighting in various parts of South Vietnam preceded the hour of truce, however.

This last-minute effort to grab land left details of positions to be straightened out in the spotted pattern of disputed holdings that already mark the map of South Vietnam.

The four-nation group that is supposed to supervise the peace and pave the way for final agreements was in only preliminary stages of organization, and that too posed uncertainties.

It is, in fact, uncertain whether the 1,160 observers from Canada, Indonesia, Hungary and Poland will be effective even after the com-

(Continued on Back Page, Col. 1)

Truce Hour Arrives, Attacks Raging

Compiled From AP, UPI, and
S&S Vietnam Bureau

SAIGON — Although a cease-fire came to Vietnam at 8 a.m. Sunday, rocket and mortar attacks continued right up to the deadline, and explosions continued in Saigon even after the cease-fire.

An American was killed Satur-

day night in the last hours of hostilities, probably the last American to die in the war. He was the fourth American killed since the cease-fire agreement was announced Wednesday.

Explosions could be heard in downtown Saigon after the cease-fire went into effect. The U.S. command, flooded with

calls, said it did not know the cause but recurring blasts sounded like an ammunition dump blowing up in the Saigon area.

Just before dawn, and less then two hours before the designated time of the start of the cease-fire, Communist forces slammed Soviet-built rockets

into Saigon's Tan Son Nhut AB and adjoining areas. Military spokesmen said first reports indicated one Vietnamese civilian was killed and 15 were wounded.

At 7:55 a.m., U.S. spokesmen could say only that approximately seven rounds hit near

(Continued on Back Page, Col. 2)

PACIFIC
STARS STRIPES

10¢

Vol. 29, No. 29   AN AUTHORIZED UNOFFICIAL PUBLICATION FOR THE U.S. ARMED FORCES OF THE PACIFIC COMMAND   Tuesday, Jan. 30, 1973

War Goes On Despite Pact

U.S. Begins Vietnam Pullout

SOUTH VIETNAMESE SOLDIERS RUN FOR COVER IN POST-TRUCE FIGHTING 30 MILES NORTHWEST OF SAIGON.

AP

Hanoi Names 555 POWs; No Word on 1,347 Missing

WASHINGTON (AP) — North Vietnam has told the United States that 555 American military men are alive in Communist prison camps in North and South Vietnam, the Pentagon said Sunday night.

Still in doubt was the fate of 1,347 other Americans missing in action, many of whom may eventually be presumed dead.

The North Vietnamese still had not released the names of Americans held prisoner in Laos, the Pentagon said. But a spokesman said such a list was expected.

Before the cease-fire Saturday, the Pentagon had said it knew of 591 prisoners in Communist camps in Vietnam but

expected that some were dead. In Laos, 317 were considered either captured or missing.

All American prisoners of war are to be released within the next 60 days. Hanoi gave the United States the POW list in

Related stories, Pages 2, 3 and 6. List of prisoners, Page 5.

connection with the signing of the cease-fire agreement Saturday.

The process of notifying next-of-kin began at 5:30 p.m. EST Saturday and continued around-the-clock through the weekend.

It brought joy and relief to those families whose men were acknowledged by North Vietnam to be alive and grief to the

relatives of men either listed as dead or whose names did not appear.

As the Pentagon sorted out the servicemen's names on the list received from Paris, word was flashed to casualty assistance officers around the country.

The officers, each responsible for the family of one of the 1,-925 missing and captured U.S. servicemen, personally notified each family's home with word that their man was alive, dead or still missing.

Among the prisoners listed as alive were Navy Lt. Everett Alvarez Jr., and Army Maj. Floyd J. Thompson, believed to be the longest held American

(Continued on Back Page, Col. 2)

Compiled From AP and UPI

SAIGON—The United States Sunday began the withdrawal of the remaining 23,000 American troops in Vietnam amidst a cease-fire shattered in its infancy by dawn to dusk fighting from the demilitarized zone to the Mekong Delta.

U.S. officials said they anticipated more hard fighting ahead.

The Saigon command reported more than 4,000 North and South Vietnamese casualties in the five days since the announcement of the cease-fire last Wednesday. The U.S. command reported four Americans dead and four missing during the same period.

The cease-fire did not officially begin until 8 a.m. Saigon time Sunday. A land grab preceded the truce and continued beyond the time designated for a halt in the fighting.

The United States stepped up its troop withdrawal schedule to about 800 men for the first two days of the cease-fire, compared to an average of 100 men a week for the last several weeks.

The peace agreement signed in Paris Saturday calls

(Continued on Back Page, Col. 1)

Aged in Rye— That's the Secret

LOS ANGELES (UPI) — Charlie Smith is about 130 years old, probably the oldest man in the nation, and he says the secret of his long, long life is an unusual concoction of rye whiskey, fruit and cola followed by a couple of aspirins.

Smith revealed his formula to a science class at E. Manfred Evans Adult School.

Nixon Budget: Cut Govt., No New Taxes

KEY BISCAYNE, Fla. (AP)—Declaring it is "time to get big government off your back and out of your pocket," President Nixon told the nation Sunday he is sending Congress a peacetime budget holding the line on taxes and slashing several popular federal programs.

A day after the formal end of

American fighting in Vietnam — the nation's longest war — the President said in a nationwide radio address that his $269-billion budget "will give us the chance. . . to make our new era of peace a new era of progress."

Nixon's budget goes to Congress at noon Monday, but he

set the stage for his battle of the budget with Congress by unveiling some of its key provisions in the radio address taped before he flew to Florida on Friday.

—He is proposing "some very sharp reductions in some very familiar programs . . . regarded as sacred cows in the

past." As examples he cited the Hill-Burton hospital construction program, urban renewal assistance and special aid for schools near federal installations.

—He has searched for waste in "every nook and cranny of the bureaucracy." His own ex-

(Continued on Back Page, Col. 2)

3 WORDS SAID IT ALL: 'GOD BLESS AMERICA'

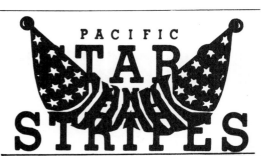

PACIFIC STAR AND STRIPES

AN AUTHORIZED UNOFFICIAL PUBLICATION
FOR THE U.S. ARMED FORCES OF THE PACIFIC COMMAND

10¢

Vol. 29, No. 44   Wednesday, Feb. 14, 1973

Col. Phones Nixon: The Men Say Thanks

SAN CLEMENTE, Calif. (AP) — President Nixon talked by telephone Monday with an Air Force colonel held captive by the North Vietnamese for nearly eight years and told him, "Your sacrifice has not been in vain."

"I want you to know how enormously proud we are of you and all the men," Nixon told Col. Robinson Risner, of Oklahoma City, Okla., who initiated the phone call from Clark Air Base in the Philippines.

In their four-minute conversation, Nixon told the officer, a prisoner of war for 7½ years, that the call was "one of the most moving moments" of his presidency.

Press secretary Ronald L. Ziegler, who relayed details of the conversation, said the 48-year-old pilot, a World War II veteran told Nixon, "All of the men would like to meet you personally and express gratitude for what you have done.

"My time is yours on that point," Nixon responded. Ziegler said the President added that a meeting could be arranged after the prisoners are reunited with their families and loved ones.

Because "you and the men have been through so much," the President said, "Nothing would mean more to me than to meet with you personally and express gratitude on behalf of myself and the American people for your sacrifices."

Ziegler said no specific time was set for a presidential meeting with the returning POWs.

The press secretary said the colonel thanked Nixon for "his personal efforts to get us out of (Continued on Back Page, Col. 2)

Lt. Cmdr. Everett Alvarez Jr. is greeted by Adm. Noel Gayler, commander-in-chief, Pacific (center), and Lt. Gen. William G. Moore, 13th Air Force commander, at Clark A.B., the Philippines. Alvarez had been held captive in North Vietnam since 1964. (UPI)

'It's Robbie, All Right'

Emotional Return of a Hero

CLARK AIR BASE, Philippines (AP)—"It's Robbie, all right," said the middle-aged U.S. Air Force colonel standing in the crowd as a trim figure poked his head from the open door of the C141 and then emerged on the arm of an escort.

A roar went up from the hundreds of American Air Force men assembled at planeside. The colonel joined in and began clapping. Tears were coursing down his face.

The object of their applause straightened up as his foot touched the tarmac. He smiled and walked unescorted to a microphone and began speaking. After 7½ years as a prisoner of war, Robbie Risner was back among his own kind, the U.S. Air Force professionals.

Col. Robinson Risner, 48, was one of the 116 American war prisoners released from North Vietnam Monday. And he was also one of the most famous.

The daring aviator from Oklahoma City, Okla., is a veteran flier, his experience dating to World War II and Korea.

Risner was a natural for the Vietnam war because he was serving as commander of the 67th Tactical Fighter Squadron at Kadena Air Force Base, Okinawa, when President Lyndon B. Johnson began the air war against North Vietnam early in 1965.

Risner took his squadron of F105 bombers to Korat, Thailand, and began launching daily missions against Hanoi supply lines and communications networks. He became so well known that he was a cover subject for Time magazine.

Then on Sept. 16, 1965, Risner's luck ran out. He was shot down and captured by the North Vietnamese.

The Air Force mourned the loss of one of its favorite sons.

"Just a few months before he went down I was in Washington to see him get presented with the Air Force Cross for his Vietnam flying, and that is the best medal the Air Force can give," said one colonel watching him deplane Monday.

As the years went by, many more fliers were shot down over Vietnam. But the name of Risner was still a magic one among Air Force professionals. While in prison he was promoted to the rank of full colonel.

Little was heard from the captured flier until August of 1968. Rennie Davis visited Hanoi then as the head of a pacifist mission to pick up three released U.S. prisoners of war, and reported meeting Risner and several others.

Davis reported the flier looked in excellent
(Continued on Back Page, Col. 5)

By HAL DRAKE and SPEC. 4 TOM LINCOLN
S&S Philippines Bureau

CLARK AB, R.P. — One hundred fifteen American pilots, released a few hours before from the darkness of a Hanoi prison, landed under an overcast sky at this base late Monday and walked into the sunlight of a vibrant, triumphal welcome — one in which the spirits of many returnees seemed to glow brighter than

Related stories, Pages 2, 6; pictures, Pages 12-13

those of the 2,000 persons who turned out to greet them with cheers, banners and chants.

Several hours later 26 other Americans, including a civilian who had been a Viet Cong prisoner for a month less than nine years, were brought from Saigon on a C9A medevac plane after an earlier release had been stalled by hours of tense negotiation. All but one man walked from the plane. The 19 servicemen and seven civilians, tired but happy, were greeted by the tireless crowd. One greeter waved an American flag at them.

Hospital authorities said initial examinations showed the men to be in good health. Their morale and discipline was very good, a statement said. They were allow-
(Continued on Back Page, Col. 1)

TORTURE!

POWs Reveal Horrible Suffering In Prisons; Say Some Murdered

Compiled From AP and UPI

Former U.S. prisoners of war told on Thursday of torture, beatings and starvation at the hands of North Vietnamese guards trying to force antiwar statements from the servicemen.

Giving the first detailed account of life in Communist prisons, the men said some of the prisoners were tortured to death, blinded and maimed. Others spent months and even years in solitary confinement. Several former POWs said they broke under the pain.

They spoke of being treated like animals, of screaming for hours, of humiliation and isolation, of constant beatings and lack of medical attention, of being denied food to t h e point where a grain of rice was treasured.

The men said the North Vietnamese paid no attention to the Geneva Convention provisions on the treatment of prisoners.

Navy Cmdr. Richard A. Stratton, captured in January 1967 and displayed at a North Vietnamese news conference where the Communists claimed he confessed to war crimes, demanded that his captors be brought to trial.

The picture of life in prison emerged at news conferences held by the former prisoners after the release of the last known POWs. The men previously refused to discuss their captivity, fearing for the lives of those still held

(Continued on Back Page, Col. 1)

PACIFIC STARS STRIPES

10¢

Vol. 29, No. 89   AN AUTHORIZED UNOFFICIAL PUBLICATION FOR THE U.S. ARMED FORCES OF THE PACIFIC COMMAND   Saturday, March 31, 1973

Nixon Imposes Controls

MEAT PRICES FROZEN

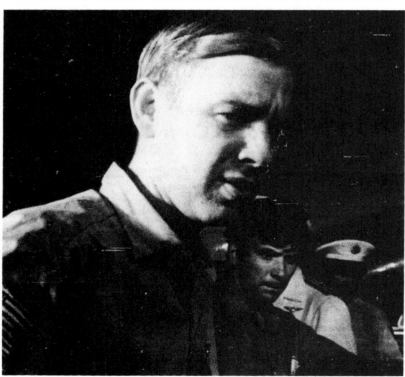

The last man on the list of prisoners of war released by Hanoi, Lt. Cmdr. Alfred H. Agnew of Albany, Ga., arrives at Clark AB in the Philippines.   (S&S Photo by Sgt. 1. C. Don Gunn)

WASHINGTON (AP) — President Nixon Thursday night clamped a ceiling on retail and wholesale prices of beef, pork and lamb—in effect freezing them near current levels—in a move to soothe consumer unhappiness over soaring food costs.

He announced the major economic move in a prime-time broadcast address to the nation declaring:

"The ceiling will remain in effect as long as is necessary to do the job. Meat prices must not go higher. With the help of the housewife and farmer, they can and should go down."

Under orders Nixon gave his Cost of Living Council, meat prices, for an indefinite period, cannot exceed an index based on prices for the past 30 days.

This means, economic experts said, that prices in effect are frozen at about their present level.

The President's order does not apply to prices at the farm level—only to meat processors, meat wholesalers and meat retailers. By avoiding controls at the farm level, officials said, they hope to spur increases in production to help bring down prices.

Nixon announced his action in an address which hailed also the end of America's involvement in the long and costly Vietnam war and sounded a call for unity in the search for world peace.

He also sought public support for his budget, contending that spending increases sought by Congress would mean a 15-per-
(Continued on Back Page, Col. 2)

GIs Say So Long, Vietnam

Compiled From UPI and AP

SAIGON — The United States shut down its direct military involvement in Vietnam Thursday and Gen. Frederick Weyand said that "peace with honor has been achieved."

The last United States troops, laughing and joking, left the country where almost 46,000 other Americans died.

Weyand, the 6-foot-6 commander of American forces in Vietnam, boarded his four-engine jet wearing a chest full of ribbons, a garland of Vietnamese flowers and an ear-to-ear grin.

The closest thing to regret among the officials was probably expressed by U.S. Ambassador Ellsworth Bunker, a close friend of President Nguyen Van Thieu.

The tall, white-haired Bunker stood next to Weyand on the hot, sun-drenched tarmac at Tan Son Nhut's VIP terminal. He looked sad and appeared to have tears in his eyes.

Although the 2,501 Americans
(Continued on Page 5)

Brown Cow---Wow!

ISLIP, N. Y. (AP) — A dozen teen-agers had a fancy slogan as they picketed against high meat prices outside a supermarket in Islip. They waved signs reading "Don't Eat Meat." and chanted. "How now brown cow. two-forty-nine a pound. wow!"

'Day of Joy, Pride' for Last Returnees

By SPEC. 5
LOU TRUCKENMILLER
S&S Philippines Bureau, and AP

CLARK AB, R.P.—North Vietnam freed its last 67 U.S. prisoners of war Thursday. Two giant C141 transports brought them to Clark Air Base for their first stop on the way home.

The release of the 67 cleared the Communist prisons in In-

dochina of the 587 Americans Hanoi had reported were captives at the signing of the c e a s e-fire agreement two

Related stories, Pages 2, 6, 7

months ago. But the Viet Cong turned up another man who will be freed this weekend.

The first C141 from Hanoi landed 40 men early Thursday night in a drizzle that failed to dampen the enthusiasm of a cheering crowd of 600 Americans.

The second C141 touched down 42 minutes later with the other 27.

"This is a day of joy and pride," the senior man on the first flight, Air Force Lt. Col. James W. O'Neill, 42, of Las

Vegas, Nev., told the exuberant crowd. "What could be more joyous than to be delivered from your enemies and return to your friends.

"The pride we have in our nation and our government could not be greater. And this day justifies our faith. POWs never have a nice day, but we
(Continued on Back Page, Col. 2)

IT'S OVER

Most Yanks Got Out

Compiled From AP and UPI

SAIGON—The United States pulled out of Vietnam Tuesday. All but a handful of Americans fled the country aboard Marine helicopters by early Wednesday and left it up to the Vietnamese to find peace.

The Americans were ordered out Tuesday by new President Duong Van Minh to meet one of the Communists' major conditions for peace talks — an end to the U.S. presence. Political sources said the Communists and the Saigon government had agreed in principle to call a cease-fire.

President Ford then ordered Marines to evacuate the last Americans assigned to the U.S Defense Attache's Office within 24 hours. Ford promised in his statement that force would be used only to protect lives.

Aboard the USS Blue Ridge, command ship for the evacuation, a correspondent said the Navy announced 4,582 persons, about 900 of them Americans, had been lifted out by the evacuation that began at mid-afternoon Tuesday. Forty ships of the U.S. 7th Fleet were gathered in the South China Sea for the task.

Former Vietnamese Premier, Vice Air Marshal Nguyen Cao Ky, natty in his khaki safari suit with maroon scarf around his neck, stepped aboard the command vessel. He said nothing to reporters.

Naval spokesmen said Mrs. Graham Martin, wife of the U.S. ambassador to South Vietnam, arrived before the first official wave of helicopters left three carriers off Vung Tau for the evacuation run.

The few Americans remaining in Saigon apparently were mostly newsmen.

The departure ended an era that cost the United States 14 years, $150 billion and more than 50,000 lives —the last of which in combat were two U.S. marines killed in a Communist attack on Saigon's airport early Tuesday that spurred the pullout.

The evacuation came 17 days

(Continued on Back Page, Col. 1)

PACIFIC STARS AND STRIPES

AN AUTHORIZED UNOFFICIAL PUBLICATION
FOR THE U.S. ARMED FORCES OF THE PACIFIC COMMAND

15¢

Vol. 31, No. 120   Thursday, May 1, 1975

A U.S. Marine points a rifle at South Vietnamese trying to climb over the wall at the U.S. Embassy Wednesday in desperate attempts to get aboard the evacuation flights. Marines guarding the embassy had a tough time keeping order as the Vietnamese panicked and tried to throw themselves over the walls and wire fences. (UPI)

SAIGON (AP) — The Saigon government surrendered unconditionally to the Viet Cong Wednesday, ending 30 years of bloodshed.

The surrender was announced by President Duong Van "Big" Minh in a five-minute radio address.

As he spoke, the city of Saigon fell quiet and shellfire subsided.

Minh said:

"The republic of Vietnam policy is the policy of peace and reconciliation, aimed at saving the blood of our people. I ask all servicemen to stop firing and stay where you are. I also demand that the soldiers of the Provisional Revolutionary Government (PRG) stop firing and stay in place.

"We are here waiting for the provisional revolutionary government to hand over the authority in order to stop useless bloodshed."

On the same Saigon radio broadcast, Gen. Nguyen Huu Hanh, deputy chief of staff, called on all South Vietnamese generals, officers and servicemen at all levels to carry out Minh's orders.

"All commanders," Hanh declared, "must be ready to enter into relations with commanders of the Provisional Revolutionary Government (Viet Cong) to carry out the cease-fire without bloodshed."

South Vietnamese officers said they had no other choice.

The surrender came within hours of the evacuation of all Americans except a handful of newsmen from Saigon

---

Reaching the decision to pull out, Page 3. Other coverage on Pages, 6, 7, 12-13.

---

and the closing of the U.S. Embassy which was later looted along with the residence of U.S. Ambassador Graham A. Martin.

South Vietnamese officers complained that the U.S. evacuation had panicked the army and that many top officers and most of the air force had pulled out, leaving the armed forces depleted and Saigon an open city, as Communist-led forces closed in.

(A few people appeared to brave the around-the-dock curfew minutes after the announcement, UPI said, but shellfire continued and there was sporadic small arms fire in the heart of the city after the president's brief address.

(Minh spoke as Communist forces fought toward the very center of the city, which by mid-morning had seemed to be in a state of panic and imminent collapse.

(Police were ordered to raise white flags over their stations.

(The U.S. Embassy was burned by looters.

(They carried away desks, chairs and typewriters from the building the Americans had evacuated.

(Vietnamese still waited in the Embassy compound for evacuation. Among them was an American with his Vietnamese wife and children, UPI said.)

Despite the U.S. evacuation, it was certain that the Saigon army would fall anyhow whether the Americans stayed or not.

More than a dozen North Vietnamese divisions were ringing Saigon while the capital was defended by less than a division of green troops.

The Viet Cong had rejected a cease-fire and negotiations proposed earlier by Minh and demanded in effect an unconditional surrender to include these terms:

—The withdrawal of Americans.

(Continued on Back Page, Col. 1)

EPILOGUE

It was a thin story on an inside page—the Vietnamese made a cautious promise to return the known remains of twenty-six Americans carried on Defense Department rolls as missing in action. At last, those waiting at home would know, and there would be private and dignified grief. Others would still wait. There are 2,477 Americans still missing and never accounted for in Indochina. Dead? For many, this must be accepted as a tragic probability. Alive? Until there is confirmed, yes-or-no proof, an accounting for every last name and life, this hopeful possibility can't be discounted. In *Pacific Stars and Stripes,* their story has never died.

On June 18, 1985, National POW–MIA Day was observed on American bases all over the Pacific. At Clark AB in the Philippines, there was a retreat ceremony and missing-man flyover—a formation with the right wingman gone.

Where, asked Lt. Col. Tony A. Marshall, was Capt. Steve Cuthbert, the pilot who burst from a cockpit with him so long before? Marshall later came out of a prison in Hanoi called the Zoo. He never saw Cuthbert after that flashing blur, the moment they ejected from a crippled fighter.

"The only thing that bothers me is that there can be people over there who are listed as missing in action," Marshall told Mike Van Hoecke of the *Pacific Stars and Stripes* Philippines Bureau. "My stay convinced me that the North Vietnamese may still be holding people for some kind of political advantage, or possibly because some prisoners have maltreatment stories that would reflect badly on the North Vietnamese.

"Steve could be one of those people."

To many other American newspapers, a dead war is a dead issue. How many would print Marshall's appeal for a missing friend? Our report quoted words spoken by President Reagan a year earlier:

"We write no last chapters. We close no books. We put away no final memories. An end to America's involvement in Vietnam cannot come before we've achieved the fullest possible accounting of those missing in action."

On *Pacific Stars and Stripes*, neither the Longest War nor the Longest Wait are over—not until that last life has been accounted for.